TRANSFORMATIONS

Women, Gender & Psychology

SECOND EDITION

Mary Crawford

University of Connecticut

Connect
Learn
Succeed™

TRANSFORMATIONS: WOMEN, GENDER & PSYCHOLOGY,
SECOND EDITION

6 7 8 9 10 11 QVS/QVS 19 18 17 16 15

ISBN 978-0-07-353215-8
MHID 0-07-353215-0

Vice President & Editor-in-Chief: *Michael Ryan*
Vice President & Director of Specialized Publishing: *Janice M. Roerig-Blong*
Editorial Director: *William Glass*
Senior Sponsoring Editor: *Gina Boedeker*
Director of Marketing & Sales: *Jennifer J. Lewis*
Managing Development Editor: *Meghan Campbell*
Senior Project Manager: *Jane Mohr*
Design Coordinator: *Margarite Reynolds*
Cover Designer: *Studio Montage, St. Louis, Missouri*
Cover Image: © *Carol Wolfe, photographer*
Buyer: *Susan K. Culbertson*
Media Project Manager: *Sridevi Palani*
Compositor: *Laserwords Private Limited*
Typeface: *10/12 Janson*
Printer: *Quad/Graphics*

Library of Congress Cataloging-in-Publication Data

Crawford, Mary (Mary E.)
    Transformations: women, gender, and psychology/Mary Crawford.—2nd ed.
        p. cm.
    ISBN 978-0-07-353215-8 (pbk.)
    1. Women—Psychology. 2. Gender identity. 3. Feminist psychology. 4. Sex role. 5. Sex
    differences (Psychology) 6. Social change. I. Title.
    HQ1206.C733 2011
    155.3'33—dc22

                                                                                    2011005341

www.mhhe.com

To Roger

About the Author

∾

MARY CRAWFORD is professor emerita of psychology and former director of the Women's Studies Program at the University of Connecticut. She has taught the psychology of women and gender for 35 years. As a faculty member at West Chester University of Pennsylvania, she earned the Trustees' Award for Lifetime Achievement for her research and teaching on women and gender. She has also held the Jane W. Irwin Chair in Women's Studies at Hamilton College, served as distinguished visiting teacher/scholar at the College of New Jersey, and directed the graduate program in women's studies at the University of South Carolina. Professor Crawford received her PhD in experimental psychology from the University of Delaware. She is a consulting editor for *Sex Roles*, an associate editor of *Feminism and Psychology*, and a Fellow of both the American Psychological Association and the American Psychological Society. Mary Crawford has spoken and written about women's issues for audiences as diverse as the British Psychological Society, the Swedish Research Council, and the Oprah Winfrey Show. Books she has authored or edited include *Gender and Thought: Psychological Perspectives* (1989); *Talking Difference: On Gender and Language* (1995); *Gender Differences in Human Cognition* (1997); *Coming into Her Own: Educational Success in Girls and Women* (1999); *Innovative Methods for Feminist Psychological Research* (1999); *Practicing Perfection: Memory and Piano Performance* (2002) and, with Rhoda Unger, a widely used text and reader, *Women and Gender: A Feminist Psychology* (4th ed., 2004) and *In Our Own Words* (2nd ed., 2006). Her most recent book, *Sex Trafficking in South Asia: Telling Maya's Story* (2010) is based on her research as a Fulbright Senior Scholar in Nepal.

Contents

∾

PART 3   *Gender and Development*

Chapter 5   Sex, Gender, and Bodies   126

PART 5   *Gender and Well-Being*

Chapter 12   Violence against Women   370

Chapter 13   Psychological Disorders, Therapy, and Women's Well-Being   405

Preface

〜

I wrote this book to share my excitement about the psychology of women and gender. I chose *Transformations* for the title because this book explores many kinds of transformations. As I complete the second edition, the concept of transformation remains central to my thinking about this branch of psychology.

First, this book reflects the developmental transformations of a woman's life. Each of us progresses in turn from gender-innocent infant to gender-socialized child; from girl to woman; and from young woman to old woman. The process of developing a gender identity and a sexual identity are transformative. Think too of the transformation from sexual inexperience to sexual maturity and agency, and the shift in identity that happens as a young person goes from being a student to a working adult or an older person retires from paid work. Motherhood is another profound transformation of self, roles, and behavior. And too often, girls and women victimized by gender-based violence are forced to transform themselves from victim to survivor. Being a woman is not a static condition, but rather a dynamic, ever-shifting social construction.

A second meaning of my title reflects the transformation that made this book, and others like it, possible. Only a few short years ago, women were routinely omitted from psychology textbooks, research on women was scarce, much of the existing research was negatively biased, and women themselves encountered resistance to becoming psychologists and engaging in research and practice. Today, the psychology of women and gender is a flourishing part of psychology. The perspectives of feminist psychology have changed research, practice, and theory in every area of psychology. Women now earn the majority of professional degrees in psychology, and the majority of psychology departments offer undergraduate courses in women and gender. These changes, which came about through feminist activism and struggle, have been astonishingly successful.

This book represents yet another kind of transformation: the change in my thinking about how best to integrate this now-huge field of study for instructors and make it accessible for students. I've been teaching the psychology of women and gender since 1975 and writing about it for students since 1992. This book offers a fresh approach and a new synthesis of the field. I'm gratified that the first edition was adopted by many instructors and became a student favorite. This second edition is the result of an ongoing dialogue with instructors and students who used the first edition. It reflects the most current research and theory, with more than 340 *new* references to research published since the first edition. It is designed to speak to today's students without talking down to them. After describing the book's distinguishing features and conceptual framework, I'll focus on what's new in this edition.

A Focus on Multiculturalism and Diversity

Throughout this book, women of color in the U.S. context and women around the world are presented as centrally important in feminist theory and research. This starts in Chapter 1, where Black feminist and global feminist perspectives are introduced and gender is compared to other systems of social classification such as race and ethnicity. It continues in Chapter 2 with extended discussion of how systems of oppression are linked and mutually reinforcing, and Chapter 3, with the inclusion of racial and ethnic stereotypes and global images of women. Chapter 4, The Meanings of Difference, focuses on the social dimensions that define difference and cause some groups to be evaluated as less worthy than others. Having set the theoretical framework for integrating diversity, each chapter for the remainder of the book incorporates the experiences of women of diverse sexualities, ethnicities, social classes, (dis)abilities, nationalities, and ages.

Fortunately, there is an increasing amount of research being done with lesbian, gay, transgender, and queer people; with women and men of color; with people who have disabilities; and with international populations. Integrating these dimensions of diversity throughout the book, I explore how they structure girls' and women's experiences including gender socialization, adult relationships, parenting, physical health, and psychological well-being.

Every chapter incorporates dimensions of diversity. Here are a few examples: research on lesbian couples (Chapter 8), ethnic diversity and sexual identities (Chapter 7), stereotypes of race and social class (Chapter 3), culture, ethnicity, and the expression of emotion (Chapter 4), the wage gap, workplace sex discrimination, and sexual harassment in relation to ethnicity and gender (Chapter 10), cross-cultural differences in aging (Chapter 11), sexual scripts across ethnic groups and cultures (Chapter 7), feminist therapy for diverse women (Chapter 13), disability and sexuality (Chapter 7), the diversity of women who mother, including ethnic minorities, teen mothers, and lesbian mothers (Chapter 9), and the effects of ethnicity and social class on gender socialization (Chapter 6).

Cross-cultural studies and multicultural perspectives are valuable for many reasons. First, they can help students learn that what seems natural, normal, and perhaps biologically ordained in their own culture is not universal. Second, they can foster critical thinking on women's status and rights as a global problem. Finally, incorporating diversity into psychology textbooks means that girls and women whose voices were formerly silenced and whose presence was invisible are now seen and heard. Textbooks like this can play a part in transforming psychology from its formerly White, middle-class North American focus into a psychology of all people. For all these reasons, I am passionate about making sure this book reflects women in all their diversity.

Gender: A Social System Linked to Status and Power

Transformations presents a broad, comprehensive theoretical framework for understanding how the lives of all people, but particularly the lives of girls and women, are shaped by gender. Rather than conceiving gender as a collection of individual traits or attributes, this book presents gender as a *social system* that is used to categorize people and is linked to power and status.

The gender system is analyzed throughout the book at three levels: sociocultural, interpersonal, and individual. Because conceptualizing gender as a social system is important from the start, the second chapter of the book is devoted to gender, status, and power. This chapter explains the gender system and how it works at each of the three levels and demonstrates how they are linked.

As Chapter 2 explains, at the sociocultural level men have more institutional and public power, and therefore political, religious, and normative power is concentrated largely in the hands of men. Of course, all men are not equally privileged, nor are all women equally disadvantaged. The gender system interacts with systems based on race/ethnicity, social class, heterosexuality, and other dimensions of difference. An understanding of the gender system at this level provides a context for the other levels and reduces the tendency to think of gender as mere sex differences.

At the second level of the gender system, gender is created, performed, and perpetuated in social interaction—what social constructionists call *doing gender*. I explore this topic not just as the social display of differences, but also as the social display of status and power. Gender-linked behaviors such as interrupting and smiling, for example, reflect and perpetuate women's subordinate status.

The gender system operates at the individual level as women internalize their subordinate social status. Well-documented psychological phenomena such as denial of personal discrimination, lack of entitlement, and gendered psychological disorders such as depression can be related to internalized subordination. In summary, by conceptualizing gender as a social system operating at three levels, my goal is to provide students with an analytical tool for understanding how gender affects all our lives in both public and private domains.

I have retained other conceptual and organizational features from the first edition of *Transformations*. These include its comprehensive coverage of women's physical health and psychological well-being. This book integrates health issues into every chapter. Moreover, a broad conception of health is used, including wellness, fitness, and optimal adjustment. Women's psychological health and well being is comprehensively addressed in Chapter 13, contributed by Britain Scott. Rejecting an approach that merely catalogs sex differences in psychological disorders, Britain provides a thought-provoking analysis of the social construction of female madness. After showing how women have been institutionalized, medicated, and placated by traditional therapy, Britain offers a positive alternative in discussing feminist therapy and its value to diverse women.

This edition also retains and updates the first edition's comprehensive and positive coverage of older women. In writing Chapter 11, The Second Half: Midlife and Aging, I drew on the most recent research on aging, and incorporated the latest data on health issues such as hormone replacement therapy and heart disease. I also explore the social role changes associated with aging, both positive and negative. A section of this chapter is devoted to life in an aging woman's body. For example, fitness and wellness are important in middle and later life for many women, yet rarely mentioned in textbooks. I discuss research showing the benefits of continued physical activity in middle and later life. Older women's sexuality, too, is rarely discussed; here, the stigmatization of older women's sexuality—and women's resistance to it—is a focus of attention. These are dimensions on which older women resist the cultural message that aging is only decay and decline. Although most student readers are far from midlife, I believe that they will find this chapter engaging and thought-provoking.

I have also retained and expanded the first edition's spotlight on the gendering of emotion and emotionality. Emotion is, of course, strongly gender-linked in many ways. Emotionality is a core aspect of feminine gender stereotypes; male and female children are socialized differently for emotional expressiveness; and social actors express emotion according to display rules that are defined by gender and culture. Chapter 4, The Meanings of Difference, critically explores the social construction of emotional expressiveness and the social construction of women as the (over)emotional sex. Building on this foundation, later chapters discuss emotionality as a critical part of gender role socialization and emotion in relationships throughout life.

One of the key features of this book is its positive message about social change. Studying the psychology of women and gender can be a rewarding experience for students. However, learning about sexism, oppression, and the difficulty of changing the gender system can also be overwhelming. I have found that, even though most social science research focuses on problems, it is crucial to offer students a focus on solutions as well. In other words, it is important that students learn not only what is wrong about the gender system, but also what is happening to change it. Therefore, this book does more than focus on injustice and inequality. Every chapter ends with a section titled Making a Difference that focuses on the social changes that have been achieved and are continuing. In keeping with the organizing theoretical framework of the book, social changes at the societal/cultural, interpersonal, and individual levels are presented and evaluated. Transforming psychology, and transforming the world, toward being more woman-friendly and less oppressive is an ongoing process. A central message of this book, and one that closes each chapter, is that every student can be a part of this transformation.

New in This Edition

This edition retains and expands many successful innovations from the first edition. In addition, it has innovations of its own.

A New Chapter on Violence against Girls and Women

The choice to add this chapter was based on feedback from reviewers and instructors about the first edition. They consistently requested that this important topic should be the focus of a dedicated chapter rather than integrated into other chapters.

I agreed, and, with coauthor Annie Fox, have written an all-new chapter for this edition. Beginning with a global perspective on gender-based violence, including honor killings and sex trafficking, Chapter 12 moves to a discussion of violence in the media and the prevalence and effects of pornography. The chapter then explores the predictors, prevalence, social contexts, and consequences of gender-linked violence across the lifespan, including child sexual abuse, dating violence, acquaintance rape, spousal abuse, and elder abuse. Each type is placed in its immediate social context *and* connected to a larger analysis. For each type of violence, we focus on how researchers, policy makers, and activists are working to end it.

A Focus on Research Methods

From the start, this book has been based on scientific knowledge about women and gender. In this edition, the research *process* gets more attention. I believe it is important to show students how scientific knowledge is acquired, to help them see the methods and processes by which researchers reach their conclusions. Therefore, I've added some new features toward that goal. In Chapter 1, a new section explains that psychological researchers use a variety of quantitative and qualitative methods, and defines several of the most commonly used, briefly discussing their strengths and limitations. This background prepares students for the more sophisticated discussions that follow in Chapters 1 and 4 about sources of sex bias in psychological research, the meaning of statistical significance (including what it does *not* mean), the role of values in psychological research, and feminist values in research.

The methodological emphasis is reinforced by another new feature of this edition: Research Focus boxes throughout the text zero in on a specific study showing its method, results, and importance. These boxes feature diverse methods including surveys, experiments, and case studies. In addition to these spotlighted studies, I have increased the number of graphs and tables throughout the text that summarize the results of other studies. Also, when describing individual studies verbally, I report the methods and results of both classic and recent research in enough detail that students can see *how* the researcher reached her conclusions. In all these ways, my intention is to help students understand how claims about women, men, and gender difference should be based on evidence and reasoning, and to learn to think critically about the production of knowledge.

Areas of Current Research Are Highlighted

Since the publication of the first edition, several areas within this field have burgeoned, yielding new insights and research directions. This edition comprehensively updates and features new research and theory on embodiment, objectification theory, stereotype threat, and intersex and transgender identities, to name just a few.

Increasingly, feminist theorists and researchers are focusing on women's experience in their bodies as a determinant of their psychological experiences and identities. New work on women's bodily objectification addresses not only the social consequences of inhabiting an objectified body, but also the affective, cognitive, and behavioral consequences to women of their own objectification: shame, anxiety, sexual dysfunction, and so on. In contrast to the first edition, which featured a chapter on embodiment, this edition integrates recent theoretical and empirical developments on embodiment and objectification throughout, in sections on objectification theory, the impact of gender stereotypes, and stereotypes of female athletes (Chapter 3), bodily configuration and gender identity (Chapters 5 and 6), the bodily changes of puberty (Chapter 6), attractiveness, disability and sexuality (Chapter 7), others' reactions to pregnant women (Chapter 9), and living in an aging body (Chapter 11). I am indebted to Britain Scott for contributing her expertise in this area and for coauthoring Chapter 3, Images of Women.

Stereotype threat is another active research area, with many new studies on gender stereotypes and math performance, as well as on the interactions between gender and ethnic/racial stereotypes in creating stereotype threat. This new research is covered in Chapters 3 and 4. Finally, Chapter 5, Sex, Gender, and Bodies, on the biology and cultural meaning of sexual differentiation, has been extensively reorganized and updated to focus on psychological questions of identity in intersex and transgender people, and on how the cultural construction of these categories reveals underlying assumptions about sex and gender. I believe that this chapter offers the most comprehensive and engaging theoretical and empirical treatment of these topics available to student readers. When I teach the course, it always generates intense interest and involvement from students.

A Student-Friendly Text

As a teacher, I care very much about engaging students' interest and holding their attention. *Transformations* is readable, lively, and easy to follow. The student-friendliness of this text is achieved in several ways. First, I adopt a selective focus on research. I make no attempt to emulate the style of a *Psychological Review* article that sequentially describes every study ever done on a topic! Rather, I make selective use of *classic* studies that first demonstrated an important phenomenon, as well as the most *current* results and theories. I explain meta-analysis early in the text in a student-friendly way, and wherever meta-analyses are available to organize large research literatures I cite and discuss them.

In my own classroom teaching, I often use a light touch to diffuse tension, encourage dialogue on sensitive topics, and counter resistance to feminist knowledge. In this book, I incorporate that lighter touch with a generous sprinkling of cartoons, boxed features, visual aids, and photographs that enliven the pages. Finally, each chapter ends with Exploring Further, which offers research resources, Web sites, and information for activism.

In my own teaching, I also use *In Our Own Words: Writings from Women's Lives*, (Crawford & Unger, 2006), a reader I developed specifically to connect the psychological research and theory in textbooks with the voices and experiences of diverse girls and women. *In Our Own Words* is a collection of short (2–20 pages) essays, each with a distinctive personal voice. Some are humorous (Gloria Steinem's "If Men Could Menstruate"), some are poignant (Judith Ortiz Cofer's "The Story of My Body"), and all are memorable.

In Our Own Words is organized into five sections: Making Our Voices Heard; The Making of a Woman: Bodies, Power, and Society; Making Meaning; Making a Living: Women, Work, and Achievement; and Making a Difference. A section of five to seven readings and their associated two-page introduction can be read along with a textbook chapter. Another way to use the reader is to ask students to write brief reaction papers on selections of their choice, connecting them to research and theory in the textbook. *In Our Own Words* provides a stimulus for student interest and class discussion and an experiential counterpoint to research.

The forthcoming *Transformations* 2/e Instructor's Manual is a comprehensive resource containing test items (multiple choice, short-answer, and essay), video listings, classroom demonstrations and other techniques for stimulating active involvement, suggestions for using Worldwide Web resources, and much more. Contact your McGraw-Hill representative for further information about supplements that accompany this text.

Acknowledgments

Writing a textbook is a daunting task. I could not have done it without the support of a host of family, friends, and colleagues.

I am grateful to Britain Scott for contributing her excellent Chapter 13, Psychological Disorders, Therapy, and Women's Well-Being, as well as coauthoring Chapter 3. Britain's expertise adds a great deal to this book. Working with Britain, I appreciated not only her expertise but also her attention to lively writing, her passion for the issues, and her ability to meet deadlines.

Annie B. Fox, M.A., an advanced graduate student in social psychology at the University of Connecticut, coauthored this edition's new chapter on violence against girls and women. Annie also contributed hundreds of hours of reference checking and preparation of tables, figures, and text boxes for the new edition. Annie, I thank you for your expertise and writing. Working with these strong and capable younger women gives me renewed hope that the feminist transformation of society will continue.

I am grateful for the wider network of support that makes my work possible— a collegial faculty and administration here at the University of Connecticut, and friends and family who put up with the absent-mindedness and crankiness of a writer in the throes of a big project. Special thanks go to my developmental editor at McGraw-Hill, Meghan Campbell; and senior project manager, Jane Mohr. I thank, too, the instructors and students who wrote me after using the first edition and the pre-publication reviewers for this edition who generously provided me with feedback on all or parts of the manuscript: Joyce Carbonell, Florida State University; Zoe Peterson, University of Missouri-St. Louis; Nancy Schwartz, University of North Florida; Silvia Sara Canetto, Colorado State University; Erin Richman, University of North Florida; Meara M. Habashi, University of Alabama; Dionne Stephens, Florida International University; Julie B. Hanauer, Suffolk County Community College; Christina Van Puymbroeck, Estrella Mountain Community College; and Judy Wilson, Palomar College.

Finally, I wish to acknowledge, as I do in every book I write, my partner of 37 years, Roger Chaffin. Roger, a professor of cognitive psychology at the University of Connecticut, has his own full schedule of teaching, mentoring, and research, yet he always manages to be there when I need support, wise counsel, and encouragement. Thank you, Roger.

Mary Crawford
November 2010

PART 1

Introduction

CHAPTER 1

Paving the Way

$\mathcal{T}$his book is called *Transformations*. I hope you find this title intriguing. I chose it because we are living in an era when opportunities for girls and women have changed dramatically, and psychology has played a part in those changes. Still, gender equality is a transformation that is not yet complete. Consider the current situation:

- After more than 230 years of U.S. democracy, only 17 percent of the U.S. Congress and 12 percent of state governors are women.
- In the United States, women earn about 77 cents for every dollar earned by men. Worldwide, the difference is even greater—women earn only about 66 percent of what men earn.
- The United Nations estimates that 100 million women are missing from the global population—dead because, as females, they were unwanted.
- Women are heads of state in 29 countries around the world, yet in others they lack basic human rights such as going to school.

Although some things have changed for the better, a worldwide wage gap, under-representation of women in positions of status and power, and significant problems of violence against girls and women persist. Gender, sexuality, and power are at the core of social controversies around the world.

Beginnings

We are living in an era in which nothing about women, sexuality, and gender seems certain. Entering this arena of change, psychology has developed research and theory about women and gender. This branch of psychology is usually called *feminist psychology*, the *psychology of women*, or the *psychology of gender* (Russo & Dumont, 1997). Those who use the term feminist psychology tend to emphasize theoretical connections to women's studies and social activism. Those who use psychology of women tend to focus on women's lives and experiences as the topics of study. Those who use psychology of gender tend to focus on the social and biological processes that create differences between women and men. This book includes all these perspectives and uses all three terms. There is a lot to learn about this exciting field.

How Did the Psychology of Women Get Started?

As the women's movement of the late 1960s made women and gender a central social concern, the field of psychology began to examine the bias that had characterized its knowledge about women. The more closely psychologists looked at the ways psychology had thought about women, the more problems they saw. They began to realize that women had been left out of many studies. Even worse, theories were constructed from a male-as-norm viewpoint, and women's behavior was explained as a deviation from the male standard. Often, stereotypes of women went unchallenged. Good psychological adjustment for women was defined in terms of fitting into traditional feminine norms—marrying, having babies, and *not* being too independent or ambitious. When women behaved differently from men, the differences were likely to be attributed to their female biology instead of social influences (Marecek et al., 2002).

These problems were widespread. Psychologists began to realize that most psychological knowledge about women and gender was **androcentric,** or male-centered. They began to rethink psychological concepts and methods and to produce new research with women as the focus of study. Moreover, they began to study topics of importance to women and to develop ways of analyzing social relations between women and men. As a result, psychology developed new ways of thinking about women, expanded its research methods, and developed new approaches to therapy and counseling.

Women within psychology were an important force for change. Starting in the late 1960s, they published many books and articles showing how psychology was misrepresenting women and how it needed to change. One of the first was Naomi Weisstein (1968), who declared that the psychology of that era had nothing to say about what women are really like, what they need, and what they want because psychology did not know very much at all about women. Another was Phyllis Chesler, whose book *Women and Madness* (1972) claimed that psychology and psychiatry were used to control women.

The new feminist psychologists began to do research on topics that were previously ignored. In 1974, there was not a single journal article on achievement in women; in 1993, there were 161. Similar growth has occurred in the number of articles on many other topics, including rape and sexual assault, women's work lives, body image, sexual harassment, and feminist therapy (Worell, 1996). In fact, the new field soon developed its own professional research journals focusing on the psychology of women or gender: for example, *Sex Roles*, which began publishing in 1975; *Psychology of Women Quarterly* (1977); *Women and Therapy* (1982); and *Feminism & Psychology* (1991).

Teaching students about the psychology of women has been an important contribution of feminist psychology from the start. Before 1968, there were virtually no college courses in the psychology of women or gender; today, over half of psychology departments offer these courses. The psychology of women and gender is being integrated into courses in introductory psychology, too. The androcentric psychology of the past has been replaced by a more encompassing perspective that includes the female half of the population and acknowledges all kinds of human diversity (Morris, 2010).

The psychology of women and gender is rich in theoretical perspectives and research evidence. Virtually every area of psychology has been affected by its theories and research (Marecek et al., 2002). This book is an invitation to explore the knowledge and participate in the ongoing debates of feminist psychology.

Psychology and the Women's Movement

The emergence of interest in women and gender took place in a social context marked by changing roles for women and the growth of a feminist social movement in the 1960s. Questioning psychology's representation of women was part of the general questioning of women's place that was led by women's liberation activists.

The First and Second Waves

The women's movement of the 1960s was not the first. A previous women's rights movement had reached its peak more than a hundred years earlier with the Seneca Falls Declaration of 1848, which rejected the doctrine of female inferiority then taught by academics and clergy (Harris, 1984). However, this *first wave* of the women's movement lost momentum in the 1920s, after women had won the vote, because women believed that voting would lead to political, social, and economic equality. Psychology's interest in sex differences and gender waned.

With the rebirth of the women's movement in the 1960s, researchers again became interested in the study of women and gender. Women psychologists and men who supported their goals also began to work toward improved status for women within the field of psychology. Feminist activism made a big difference for women of this era, who had been openly discriminated against. Psychologist Carolyn Sherif remembered it this way:

> To me, the atmosphere created by the women's movement was like breathing fresh air after years of gasping for breath. . . . I did not become a significantly better social psychologist between 1969 and 1972, but I surely was treated as a better social psychologist. (Sherif, 1983, p. 280)

Activists—mostly graduate students and newcomers to psychology—formed the Association for Women in Psychology (AWP) in 1969. At about the same time, others—mostly older, more established psychologists—lobbied the American Psychological Association (APA) to form a Division of the Psychology of Women. This Division 35 was officially approved in 1973. Divisions on ethnic minority psychology (Division 45), gay/lesbian issues (Division 44), and the study of men and masculinity (Division 51) were established later, with the support of Division 35. Progress in incorporating women also occurred among Canadian psychologists (Parlee, 1985) and the British Psychological Society, where there is now a Psychology of Women Section (Wilkinson, 1997a).

These organizational changes acknowledged the presence of diverse women in psychology and helped enhance their professional identity (Scarborough & Furumoto, 1987). And none too soon—women now earn more than 70 percent of PhDs awarded in psychology, and ethnic minorities earn 24 percent (American Psychological Association, 2010; Morris, 2010).

The Third Wave

AWP continues to thrive, holding annual conferences that welcome students. Division 35, now named the Society for the Psychology of Women, is one of the larger and more active divisions of APA. Feminist theory and activism continue to develop as younger women tackle some of the unfinished business of the first two waves, such as ensuring reproductive freedom, ending violence against girls and women, and integrating women into leadership positions, through groups such as the Third Wave Foundation.

Third-wave feminism developed in the 1990s as young women responded not only to the gains of second-wave feminism but also to its limitations. It is less connected to the psychological establishment than earlier feminist movements were. Some third-wave groups, such as the Riot grrrls, came out of the antiestablishment punk movement. Riot grrrl bands and zines of the 1990s often proclaimed the joys of women's sexuality, self-reliance, and empowerment. Third-wave groups emphasize social activism—women working collectively for social justice—just as their second-wave counterparts did before them. Though the issues and the voices have changed, third-wave feminism is clearly connected to its foremothers' visions (Baumgardner & Richards, 2000, 2005).

Voices from the Margins: A History

Until recently, the power to define and pursue knowledge has been largely in the hands of men. Men controlled the institutions of knowledge, and even when women acquired expertise, they did not always get the respect or status they deserved. History is full of stories about learned women whose work was attributed to their fathers, their brothers, their teachers, or "anonymous."

One illustration of how a woman could have outstanding expertise and yet be denied legitimacy is the story of Mary Calkins (1863–1930), who attended Harvard University during the latter part of the 19th century. Because Harvard was an all-male university, she was permitted to take courses only if she sat behind a curtain or got private tutoring. Despite completing an impressive PhD dissertation, she was denied a PhD from Harvard because she was a woman. Nevertheless, Calkins taught for many years at Wellesley College, established an experimental laboratory there, and made important contributions to psychology. She was the first woman president of both the American Psychological Association and the American Philosophical Association. In 1927, toward the end of her life, a group of distinguished male psychologists and philosophers, all Harvard degree holders, wrote to the president of Harvard requesting that Calkins be awarded the degree that she had earned. Their request was refused (Scarborough & Furumoto, 1987).

Although Mary Calkins triumphed personally, her life illustrates the way even outstanding women may be marginalized. For example, she taught for her entire career at a small women's college where she did not have doctoral students. Under these conditions, her theories and research projects did not receive the recognition and follow-up they deserved. Similar stories have been uncovered about other early feminist psychologists (Scarborough & Furumoto, 1987). If a woman scientist does not have the power to have her research and theories taken seriously and passed on to the next generation, she is being denied true equality.

By the early 1900s, women had begun to gain access to higher education in the United States and Europe. Some of the first scientifically trained women devoted their research efforts to challenging accepted wisdom about the extent and nature of sex differences. Helen Thompson Wooley conducted the first experimental laboratory study of sex differences in mental traits. In interpreting her results, she stressed the overall similarity of women's and men's performance. She also was openly critical of the antiwoman prejudices held by some male scientists, remarking daringly in a 1910 *Psychological Bulletin* article: "There is perhaps no field aspiring to be scientific where flagrant personal bias, logic martyred in the cause of supporting a prejudice, unfounded assertions, and even sentimental rot and drivel, have run riot to such an extent as here" (Wooley, 1910, p. 340).

The work of these pioneering women psychologists opened the way for research to replace unexamined assumptions about women's so-called natural limitations (Rosenberg, 1982). Determined to demonstrate women's capacity to contribute to modern science on an equal basis with men, they chose their research projects to challenge beliefs about women's limitations. In a sense, their research projects were dictated by other people's questions. Faced with the necessity of proving their very right to do research, these women labored to refute hypotheses that they did not find credible. Moreover, they worked in a social context that denied them opportunities because of their sex and forced them to make cruel choices between work and family relationships (Scarborough & Furumoto, 1987). Their story is one,

> in many ways, of failure—of women restricted by simple prejudice to the periphery of academe, who never had access to the professional chairs of the major universities, who never commanded the funds to direct large-scale research, who never trained the graduate students who might have spread their influence, and who, by the 1920s, no longer had the galvanizing support of a woman's movement to give political effect to their ideas (Rosenberg, 1982, p. xxi).

The efforts of women and minorities remained voices from the margins until relatively recently (see Box 1.1). The existence of AWP, Division 35, women's studies programs, and dozens of feminist journals guarantee that research on the psychology of women and gender will not fade away again as it did in the 1920s. Because the psychology of women developed in a social context of feminism, it is important to look closely at the relationship between the two.

Box 1.1   Women and APA

In its 115-year history, the American Psychological Association has elected 11 women to its presidency.

APA's women presidents are

1905 Mary Whiton Calkins, AM	1987 Bonnie R. Strickland, PhD
1921 Margaret Floy Washburn, PhD	1996 Dorothy W. Cantor, PsyD
1972 Anne Anastasi, PhD	2001 Norine G. Johnson, PhD
1973 Leona Tyler, PhD	2004 Diane Halpern, PhD
1980 Florence Denmark, PhD	2007 Sharon Stephens Brehm, PhD
1984 Janet Taylor Spence, PhD	

What Is Feminism?

The writer Rebecca West noted in 1913: "I myself have never been able to find out precisely what feminism is: I only know that people call me a feminist whenever I express sentiments that differentiate me from a doormat" (quoted in Kramarae & Treichler, 1985, p. 160). Nearly a hundred years later, it seems that feminism and the women's movement are still controversial and difficult to define (See Figure 1.1). Exactly what is feminism and what does it mean to call oneself a feminist?

FIGURE 1.1   Sisterhood is complicated.

Source: Copyright © Lynda Barry. First printed in *Newsweek*, 1994. Courtesy Darhansoff, Verrill, Feldman Literary Agents.

Feminism Has Many Meanings

Contemporary feminist theory has many variants. Each can be thought of as a different lens through which to view the experiences of women, and, like different lenses, each is useful for focusing on particular phenomena.

What are the most influential feminist theoretical perspectives? In the United States, they include liberal, radical, womanist (woman of color), and cultural feminism. Belief in these different branches of feminism has been defined, reliably measured, and shown to predict people's behavior (Henley et al., 1998). As feminism expands worldwide, there is a new emphasis on global feminism as well. Let's look briefly at each perspective.

Liberal feminism is familiar to most people because it relies on deeply held American beliefs about equality—an orientation that connects it to political liberalism. From this perspective, a feminist is a person who believes that women are entitled to full legal and social equality with men and who favors changes in laws, customs, and values to achieve the goal of equality. The liberal feminist perspective has fostered research on such topics as how people react to others when they violate gender norms (Chapter 2), how children are socialized to accept gender roles (Chapters 4 and 6), and sex discrimination in employment (Chapter 10). It emphasizes the similarities between males and females, maintaining that given equal environments and opportunities, males and females will behave similarly.

Radical feminism emphasizes male control and domination of women throughout history. This perspective views the control of women by men as the first and most fundamental form of oppression: women as a group are oppressed by men as a group. According to radical feminists, oppression on the basis of being a woman is one thing all women have in common. Radical feminist theory has fostered much research on violence against women (see Chapter 12). Some radical feminists have endorsed *separatism,* the idea that women can escape patriarchy only by creating their own woman-only communities. For example, the Michigan Womyn's Music Festival, an annual event for over 35 years, is grounded in the radical tradition; only women (and children of both sexes) are welcomed, because the organizers intend to create a safe and empowering environment for women.

Woman-of-color feminism, or *womanism,* began with criticism of the White women's movement for excluding women of color; the word womanism was coined by African American writer Alice Walker. This type of feminism focuses on issues of importance to minority communities: poverty, racism, jobs, health care, and access to education. In general, womanists do not see men of color as their oppressors but as brothers who suffer the effects of racism just as women of color do; therefore, womanism is particularly inclusive of men and rejects the notion of separatism. People who adopt this feminist perspective emphasize the effects of racial stereotyping (Chapter 3) and prejudice (Chapters 2 and 10). They also point out the strengths and positive values of minority communities, such as the multigenerational support and closeness of African American families (Chapter 9).

Cultural feminism emphasizes differences between women and men. This perspective stresses that qualities characteristic of women have been devalued and should be honored and respected in society. It views some gender differences in values and social behaviors as either an essential part of womanhood or so deeply socialized that they are virtually universal and unlikely to change—for example, the tendency for women to be more nurturing and caring than men. Cultural feminism has been useful in understanding the importance of unpaid work contributed by women, such as caring for the young, the ill, and the elderly (Chapters 9–11).

Feminism is a worldwide social movement. *Global feminism* focuses on how prejudice and discrimination against women are related across cultures, and how they are connected to neocolonialism and global capitalism. Issues of special concern to global feminists include sweatshop labor, unequal access to health care and education, sex trafficking, and violence against girls and women in developing countries (Chapter 12). An important part of global feminism is the recognition that Western feminists do not have all the answers for women from other cultures. For example, in some societies women are strongly pressured to undergo genital cutting (Chapter 7) or required to veil their faces and bodies in public. Though Western women may criticize these practices, it is important to remember that Western society also restricts women's bodily freedom and integrity through practices like sexual harassment in public places and pressure to seek the perfect body through dieting and cosmetic surgery (Chapters 2, 3, and 11). Strategies for change work best if they come from within each culture, rather than being imposed from outside (hooks, 2000).

The diversity of frameworks and values in feminist thought may seem confusing, but it is also healthy and productive. Different feminist perspectives can be used to develop and compare diverse viewpoints on women's experiences. This book draws on a variety of feminist perspectives, using each as a lens to help clarify particular topics, and sometimes comparing several feminist perspectives on an issue. However, within psychology, liberal feminism and cultural feminism have generated more debate and research than any other views. Therefore, Chapter 4 is devoted to contrasting liberal and cultural feminist perspectives on the question, "Just how different are women and men?"

Is There a Simple Definition?

Feminist perspectives share two important themes. First, feminism values women as important and worthwhile human beings. Second, feminism recognizes the need for social change if women are to lead secure and satisfying lives. Perhaps the simplest definition of a *feminist* is an individual who holds these basic beliefs: that women are valuable and that social change to benefit women is needed. The core social change that feminists advocate is an end to all forms of domination, those of men over women and those among women (Kimball, 1995). Therefore, perhaps the simplest definition of *feminism* is one proposed by Black feminist theorist bell hooks (1984): it is a movement to end sexism and sexist oppression. (The definition and implications of sexism are explored more fully in Chapter 2.) Broad definitions allow feminists to work for political and social change together, while recognizing that ideas about how to reach their goals may differ.

Can men be feminists? Certainly! Men can hold the values I've described as feminist: they can value women as worthwhile human beings and work for social change to reduce sexism and sex discrimination. Some men who share these values call themselves feminists. Others prefer the label *profeminist,* believing that this term acknowledges women's leadership of the feminist movement and expresses their understanding that women and men have different experiences of gender.

Feminist perspectives in general can be contrasted to *conservatism* (Henley et al., 1998). Social conservatives seek to keep gender arrangements as they have been in much of the past, with men holding more public power and status and women being more or less defined by their sexuality and their roles as wives and mothers. Conservatives often urge a return to what they consider the good old days when there were (apparently) no lesbian, gay, or transgendered people, good young women all got married and produced babies, abortion and divorce were out of the question, and the world of work and achievement was a man's world.

The conservative view has usually been justified on the grounds of biology or religion. The biological justification states that gender-related behaviors are determined by innate and unchangeable biological differences far more than by social conditions. Therefore, women should not try to do things that go against their nature. For example, if women are biologically destined to be more nurturing due to the fact that they are the sex that gives birth, it is unnatural and wrong for women to limit their childbearing or take on jobs that may interfere with their nurturing roles. The religious justification (often combined with the biological justification) is that a supreme being ordains female submission and subordination. For example, some religions teach that women must be obedient to their husbands; others forbid contraception, or grant only men the right to divorce. Some forbid women to be in positions of authority or spiritual power. As I was writing this chapter, the Roman Catholic Church announced that ordaining women as priests is a sin on a par with child sexual abuse (Vatican Angers Many, 2010). Just a few years earlier, the Southern Baptist Church urged a return to female submission as a solution to social problems such as child abuse and violence against women.

Over the past 40 years, attitudes toward women have grown less conservative and more liberal in the United States, but social conservatism is still a powerful political force, and more subtle forms of prejudice against women have emerged (see Chapter 2). The history of women in psychology teaches us that psychologists are not immune to such prejudice. The attitudes that permeate a culture also seep into scientific research. One important goal of feminist psychology is to challenge hidden biases in research and thus to foster better research on women and gender.

Methods and Values in Psychological Research

Psychology's Methods

Psychologists use a variety of research methods to answer their questions. The diversity of methods allows psychologists to tailor a method that is right for the question they seek to answer.

Most psychologists use *quantitative methods:* those that involve measuring behavior, averaging it over a group of people, and comparing groups with statistical tests. Ideally, quantitative methods allow for the use of random samples, so that the results can be *generalized,* or applied to more people than just the few who were studied.

Some quantitative methods, such as *surveys,* are largely descriptive: they report the beliefs, attitudes, or opinions of groups of people. A good example is the public opinion poll, where attitudes toward gay marriage or affirmative action are assessed. In the interests of efficiency, all participants are asked the same questions. Therefore, it is extremely important that the survey is designed to ask the right questions, and to provide meaningful answer options.

Correlational studies can determine whether two or more variables are related to each other, but they cannot determine whether that relationship is causal. For example, correlational research has demonstrated that, as more American women began to work outside the home over the past 40 years, the divorce rate rose. But it cannot answer the question of why women's work and the divorce rate rose together. Is it because working women are not good wives? Or because women who can support themselves are less likely to stay in bad marriages? Or perhaps it's because there has been a widespread shift away from traditional attitudes during the last 40 years, so that both divorce and women's working are more socially acceptable? Other kinds of research are needed to answer questions of causality on this topic—research that I'll describe in Chapters 8 and 10.

If a researcher is interested in change over time within the same individuals, she might use a *longitudinal design,* measuring variables at two or more points in time. An example would be to ask couples about their marital satisfaction both before and after the birth of their first child. Statistical techniques allow the researcher to see which variables at Time 1 predict behavior at Time 2. Another approach is to do *archival research,* where the researcher looks for relationships among variables in a preexisting set of data such as national test scores.

Many psychologists rely on *experiments,* in which one or more variables are systematically manipulated to determine whether there is a causal relationship among them. Experiments are often considered the gold standard of methods, because finding out whether a change in Variable A *causes* a change in Variable B is important to scientific understanding and theory building. Moreover, most experiments are done under carefully controlled laboratory conditions, which increases psychologists' confidence that they are measuring variables accurately.

Other psychological research methods are *qualitative:* they explore a topic in an open-ended way, without trying to systematically count or manipulate behaviors. *Interviews* (usually individual) and *focus groups* (usually groups of 3–12) are the qualitative methods most often used by psychologists. Often, researchers summarize qualitative data by grouping participants' comments by theme; they may also quote the participants directly. Sometimes, participants' talk is analyzed as to how it represents a societal discourse or reveals underlying attitudes. Other examples of qualitative research are the *case study* (an in-depth study of a single individual) and the *ethnography,* in which the researcher works within a community and tries to learn its customs and beliefs. Qualitative methods provide an intimate look at participants' thoughts and feelings. However, because they generally use small, nonrandom samples and non-numerical measures, qualitative studies are not easily generalized to larger populations.

I've used most of these quantitative and qualitative methods myself, as I've studied women and gender over the course of my career. What I've learned by doing research is that each method has its strengths and weaknesses. As I describe research (my own and others') for you throughout this book, I will tell you what method was used, and I will remind you from time to time that the results of scientific research are always limited and subject to interpretation.

Scientific research is often represented to students as a purely objective process in which a neutral, disinterested scientist investigates and reveals the secrets of nature. However, psychology has sometimes been anything but neutral in explaining the behavior of women. Feminist psychologists have identified specific methodological flaws in traditional research on women.

Toward Gender-Fair Research

Let's look briefly at the research process. The researcher starts by generating a question to be answered by gathering information systematically. The question may originate in a theory, a personal experience, or an observation, or it may be raised by previous research. The next step is to develop a systematic strategy for answering the question—often called *designing the research*. In the design stage, a method is selected, such as experiment, survey, or case study. Research participants are chosen, materials such as questionnaires or laboratory setups are devised, and ways to measure the behaviors in question are decided on.

Next, the data are collected and analyzed so that patterns of results become clear. Because most psychologists rely on quantitative methods, statistical techniques are usually used for this task. The researcher then interprets the meaning of his or her results and draws conclusions from them. If reviewers and journal editors judge the research to be well conducted and important, the results are published in a scientific journal where they can influence future research and theory. Some research makes its way from journals into textbooks, influencing teachers and students as well as other researchers. Some even gets reported in the mass media, opening the possibility that it may influence millions of readers' and viewers' beliefs.

Biases can enter into the research process at any stage. In describing a few common types of bias at each stage, I will focus on gender-related examples. However, the principles of gender-fair research also apply to eliminating biases related to such characteristics as race/ethnicity, social class, or sexual orientation (Denmark et al., 1988).

Question Formulation

The process of creating research questions is perhaps the most neglected and understudied part of the scientific enterprise. Textbooks and research courses say very little about where hypotheses come from or how to decide if a question is worth studying (Wallston & Grady, 1985). It is not surprising, then, that unexamined personal biases and androcentric theories often lead to biased research questions. Gender stereotypes related to the topic can bias the question and therefore the outcome of the study.

For example, in the past, many studies of leadership defined it in terms of dominance, aggression, and other stereotypically male attributes. It is only recently that psychologists have developed more inclusive definitions of leadership that include the ability to negotiate, to be considerate of others, and to help others resolve conflicts without confrontation—the "people skills" that make leaders more effective. Another example of bias in question formulation is found in the large amount of research on mothers who work outside the home. Much of it focuses on the question of whether the mothers' work endangers their children's psychological welfare. There is much less research on whether fathers' work endangers their children's welfare or on whether mothers' employment might benefit mothers or children.

Designing Research

In the design phase of research, one important aspect is deciding how to measure the behaviors under study. If the measures are biased, the results will be, too. An extreme example of a biased measure comes from a survey study of women's sexuality. Participants were asked to describe their roles in sexual intercourse by choosing one of the following responses: passive, responsive, resistant, aggressive, deviant, or other. The outcome of this research might have been very different if women had also been allowed to choose from alternatives such as active, initiating, playful, and joyous (Bart, 1971; Wallston & Grady, 1985).

Another aspect of the design phase is the choice of a comparison group. The results and conclusions of a study can be very different depending on which groups are chosen for comparison with each other. For example, one group of researchers was involved in a longitudinal study of aging among a selected group of college-educated professional men. When they decided to add a sample of women, the biomedical scientists on the research team suggested that they should add the sisters of the men already in the study. Because they had the same parents, these two groups would be similar in physiological characteristics. The social scientists on the research team, however, suggested that the appropriate sample would be college-educated professional women who would be similar in social status. Although one choice is not necessarily right and the other wrong, the choice is conceptually important. The conclusions reached about gender differences in aging might be very different depending on which group of women was chosen, and the group chosen depends on assumptions about what kind of explanations (physiological or social) are most important (Parlee, 1981).

Choice of research participants is subject to many possible biases. Since the 1940s psychology has come to rely more and more on college student samples, creating biases of age, social class, and developmental stage (Sears, 1986). And the college students who participate in psychological research are not even representative of all American college students, because they are likely to be drawn mostly from introductory psychology courses, and because research is done mainly at universities and elite colleges, not at community colleges and less selective ones. The psych department subject pool may be a handy way for researchers to fill their quota, but it is far from representative of humanity!

Another important bias in choosing participants is that, for most of psychology's history, males were more likely to be studied than females, and male-only studies were considered representative of people in general. In contrast, when researchers used an all-female sample, they were more likely to state it in the article's title, to discuss their reasons for studying women, and to point out that their results could not be generalized to men (Ader & Johnson, 1994). It seems that psychologists felt it was important to indicate the limitations of an all-female sample, but they saw nothing remarkable about an all-male sample—males were the norm. Fortunately, psychology became more aware of sampling biases over time, and the proportion of male-only studies has been decreasing since the 1970s (Gannon et al., 1992).

Other types of sampling bias still persist. Research on ethnic minority people of both sexes is scarce except when they are seen as creating social problems (Reid & Kelly, 1994). There is abundant research on teen pregnancy among African American women, for example, but little research on their leadership, creativity, or coping skills for dealing with racism. Poor and working-class women, too, have been virtually ignored (Bing & Reid, 1996; Reid, 1993). And women who happen not to be heterosexual will have trouble finding people like themselves in psychological research. Reviews of all psychological studies published from 1975 to 2009 have shown that nonheterosexual people were included in less than 1 percent of research, and lesbians and bisexual women were significantly less likely to be studied than gay and bisexual men (Lee & Crawford, 2007, in press).

Many well-known psychologists, both female and male, have pointed out that psychology, supposedly the science of human behavior, is more accurately described as the science of the behavior of college sophomores, and straight White male college sophomores at that. Feminist psychology, with its valuing of women as worthy subjects of research and its recognition of all kinds of human diversity, provides an important corrective to this type of bias.

Analyzing Data: A Focus on Differences

Psychologists have come to rely on quantitative methods, and therefore they almost always use statistical tests in data analysis. Over the past 35 years, both the number of articles using statistics and the number of statistical tests per article have increased. Statistics can be a useful tool, but they also can lead to conceptual difficulties in research on sex and gender.

Statistical models lead to a focus on differences rather than similarities. The logic of statistical analysis involves comparing two groups to see if the average difference between them is statistically significant. Unfortunately, it is not easy to make meaningful statements about similarities using statistical reasoning.

It is also unfortunate that statisticians chose the term *significant* to describe the outcome of a set of mathematical operations. As used by most people the word means important, but as used by statisticians it means only that the obtained difference between two groups is unlikely to be due to mere chance. A statistically significant difference does not necessarily have any practical or social significance (Favreau, 1997). The meaning and interpretation of difference will be discussed in more detail in Chapter 4.

Interpreting and Publishing Research Results

Psychology's focus on group differences affects the ways that results are interpreted and conveyed to others. One type of interpretation bias—termed *overgeneralization*—occurs when gender differences in performing a specific task are interpreted as evidence of a more general difference, perhaps even one that is considered permanent and unchangeable. For example, because samples of highly gifted junior-high boys score higher on SAT math tests than similar samples of girls, some psychologists have argued that males in general have a biological superiority in math ability.

Another kind of interpretation bias occurs when the performance style more typical of girls or women is given a negative label. For example, girls get better grades in school in virtually every subject, but this is not usually interpreted as evidence that they are superior in intelligence. Instead, girls' academic achievement may be discounted; they are sometimes said to get good grades by being nice or compliant.

Overgeneralizing and other interpretation biases encourage us to think of men and women as two totally separate categories. But it is simply not true that "men are from Mars, women from Venus." On many traits and behaviors, men and women are far more alike than different. Even when a statistically significant difference is found, there is always considerable overlap between the two groups (see Chapter 4).

Problems of interpretation are compounded by publication biases. Because of reliance on the logic of statistical analysis, studies that report differences between women and men are more likely to be published than those that report similarities. Moreover, the editorial boards of most journals still are predominately made up of White men, who may perhaps see topics relevant to women and ethnic minorities as less important than topics relevant to people more like themselves (Denmark et al., 1988). Until feminist psychology was formed, there was very little psychological research on pregnancy and mothering, women's leadership, violence against women, or gender issues in therapy.

Bias continues after publication. The media notice some findings, but others are overlooked. Television and the popular press often actively publicize the latest discoveries about gender differences. Of course, some of these differences may not be very important, and others may not hold up in future research, but the public is less likely to hear about that, because gender similarities are not news.

In summary, research is a human activity, and the biases held by those who do research can affect any stage of the process. As more diverse people become psychologists, they are bringing new values, beliefs, and research questions. They also may question and challenge the biases in others' research. Feminist psychologists have led the way by demonstrating that gender bias exists in psychological research and showing how it can be reduced.

Gender-fair research is not value-free; that is, gender-fair research practices do not eliminate value judgments from the research process. Androcentric research is based on the value judgment that men and their concerns are more important and worthy of study than women and their concerns. In contrast, gender-fair research is based on the value judgment that women and men and their concerns are of equal worth and importance (Eichler, 1988).

Feminist Values in Research

Although feminist psychologists have been critical of psychology, they remain committed to it, expressing feminist values in their work (Grossman et al., 1997). What are some of these values?

Empirical Research Is a Worthwhile Activity

Although feminist psychologists recognize that science is far from perfect, they value its methods. Scientific methods are the most systematic way yet devised to answer questions about the natural and social world. Rather than abandon those methods or endlessly debate whether there is one perfect feminist way to do research, they go about their work using a rich variety of methods, theories, and approaches. Good research on women and gender is necessary and important (Peplau & Conrad, 1989; Kimmel & Crawford, 2000).

Research Methods Must Be Critically Examined

Feminist theorists have pointed out that methods are not neutral tools; the choice of method always shapes and constrains what can be found (Kimmel & Crawford, 2000). For example, which is the better way to study female sexuality—by measuring physiological changes during arousal and orgasm or by interviewing women about their subjective experiences of arousal and orgasm? The two methods might produce very different discoveries about female sexuality (Tiefer, 1989).

Traditionally, experimentation has been the most respected psychological method. However, experimental methods have been criticized for at least two reasons. First, in an experiment, the researcher creates an artificial environment and manipulates the experience of the participants. Because of this artificiality, behavior in the laboratory may not be representative of behavior in other situations (Sherif, 1979). Second, experiments are inherently hierarchical, with "the powerful, all-knowing researchers instructing, observing, recording, and sometimes deceiving the subjects" (Peplau & Conrad, 1989). The inequality of the experimental situation may be particularly acute when the researcher is male and the person being studied is female (McHugh et al., 1986).

On the other hand, many important advances in understanding women and gender have come about because of experimental results. For example, experimental research has helped us understand gender stereotypes and their impact (see Chapter 3). Just as any research method can be used in biased ways, any method can be used toward the goal of understanding women and gender. When a variety of methods are used, results based on different approaches can be compared with each other, and a richer and more complete picture of women's lives will emerge.

Both Women and Men Can Conduct Feminist Research

Most feminist researchers in psychology are women. The membership of APA's Division 35 is more than 90 percent female, and women have been leaders in developing new theories and conducting new research about women and gender ever since the first women earned their PhDs in psychology. However, it is important not to equate female with feminist and male with nonfeminist. Women who are psychologists work in every area from physiological to clinical psychology. Women psychologists may or may not personally identify as feminists, and even when they do, they may not bring a feminist perspective to their research. Also, male psychologists can identify as feminist. Men can and do conduct research on women and gender, and many conduct research on masculinity, men's lives, and male gender roles. Of course, all psychologists—male and female, feminist and nonfeminist—should, at a minimum, try to conduct their research in gender-fair ways and work to eliminate gender bias from their professional practices and behaviors.

Science Can Never Be Fully Objective or Value-Neutral

Science is done by human beings, all of whom bring their own perspectives to their work, based on their personal backgrounds. Because the perspectives of dominant groups in a society are normative, they are not always recognized as being infused with dominant group values. When others—women and minorities, for example—question the assumptions of the dominant group, the underlying values are made more visible.

One of the most important insights of feminism is that research and the creation of knowledge do not occur in a social vacuum. Rather, each research project or theory is situated in a particular period in history and a particular social context. The psychology of women and gender is not unique in being affected by social currents such as feminism, conservatism, and liberalism. All of psychology is affected. Moreover, psychology in turn affects social issues and social policy through providing ways to interpret human behavior. Because psychology is a cultural institution, doing psychological research is inevitably a political act (Crawford & Marecek, 1989).

Although the effects of values on the scientific process are inevitable, they need not be negative for women. Like many other feminist psychologists, I believe that psychology should admit its values and acknowledge that they are part of the research process (Crawford & Marecek, 1989). Opening our values to scrutiny can only strengthen our research. An awareness of the politics of science can help feminist psychologists use science to foster social change and improve women's lives (Peplau & Conrad, 1989).

Social, Historical, and Political Forces Shape Human Behavior

Because feminists believe that gender equality is possible, although it has not yet been achieved, they are sensitive to the ways that social contexts and forces shape people's behavior and limit human potential. Feminist psychologists try to understand not only the effects of gender, but also the effects of other systems of social classification such as race, social class, and sexual orientation. They try to clarify the ways that sociocultural forces, as well as biological and psychological ones, affect behavior.

Feminist psychologists respect the diversity of women and recognize that it is important to study varied groups. For example, White U.S. women generally have lower self-esteem than men, but this is not true of African American women. Such differences can show how women's psychology is affected by their social and cultural backgrounds, not just their biology.

About This Book

This book draws on the work of hundreds of psychologists, both women and men, who have contributed to the ongoing process of transforming psychology. It also draws on the work of feminist theorists and researchers in other disciplines, including philosophy, history, anthropology, sociology, political science, and cultural studies. This book, then, provides both a critique of androcentric knowledge about women and an introduction to the groundbreaking research that has emerged from feminist psychology.

As you read the chapters that follow, you will see that certain threads run through them. Three of these threads in particular are important to highlight at the start. First, *women have not yet achieved full equality with men*. There are persistent differences in power and social standing that shape women's lives. In many cultures and time periods, women have been treated as second-class citizens. Some of the inequalities are glaring—such as denying women the right to vote, own property, use public spaces, or make decisions about our own bodies. Other inequalities are more subtle—such as being subjected to everyday sexist hassles or being paid less at work. Everywhere, power differences are implicated in the shocking worldwide prevalence of violence against girls and women. Gender, power, and social status are so important that they are the focus of Chapter 2. The causes and effects of various kinds of violence against girls and women are highlighted in Chapter 12.

A second thread that runs throughout this book concerns *differences and similarities*. Women and men are not complete opposites of each other. Rather, there is a great deal of overlap in the psychology of women and men. Gender differences are important, but we should also think about gender similarities. When gender differences do occur, we should ask where they come from and how they connect to differences in power and social position.

Another kind of difference is differences among women. Women are not all alike, and we should not assume that all women necessarily have much in common with each other simply because they are women. A woman who is wealthy and privileged may, for example, have more in common with wealthy and privileged men than she has with poor women. African American and Latina women share with the men of their ethnic groups—and not with White women—the experiences of racism. Lesbians share the experience of being in a sexual minority with bisexuals and gay men, not with heterosexual women. Women of color and White women may both encounter sexism, but in very different ways. Dimensions such as age and (dis)ability are relevant, too. The viewpoints and concerns of older women and women with disabilities are not necessarily the same as those of young, able-bodied women. Studies of different groups of women can help us to understand how biological, social, and cultural factors interact to influence behavior and, equally important, help us understand the diversity of women.

In writing this book, I have tried to respect and express the diversity of women's (and men's) experiences. Over the years, I have noticed that feminist psychologists often use metaphors of gender as a lens or prism through which to view the social structure. Viewing psychological and social phenomena through the lens of gender allows us to see aspects of social reality that are otherwise obscured. However, like any lens, gender can reveal only some features of the social landscape. Lenses such as race, class, and age reveal other, equally important features. Throughout your study of this book, I invite you to consider what women have in common as women, how their experiences may or may not differ from those of men, and also how women differ from each other.

A third thread that runs throughout this book is that *psychology can contribute to social change*. Traditionally, psychologists have focused on changing individuals. They have developed techniques to change attitudes, increase insight and self-understanding, teach new behavioral skills, and reduce or eliminate self-defeating thinking and behaviors. They have applied these techniques in a variety of educational and therapeutic settings. In this book there are many examples of how feminist psychology has adapted and used these techniques.

However, research on women and gender indicates that there are limits to the power of individual change. Many of the problems that confront women are the result of social structures and practices that put women at a disadvantage and interfere with their living happy, productive lives. Social-structural problems cannot be solved solely through individual changes in attitudes and behavior; rather, the social institutions that permit the devaluation and victimization of women must also be changed. Therefore, throughout this book I discuss the implications of psychological research for changing institutions such as traditional marriage, language use, child rearing, the workplace, and the media. Every chapter ends with a section called *Making a Difference*, which showcases how individuals and groups are changing society toward a more feminist ideal.

A Personal Reflection

Because I believe that personal values shape how a researcher approaches his or her topic, I would like to share with you a little about myself and the experiences and values that shaped the writing of this book.

I started out as a psychologist in the field of learning theory. I was taught that to be a good scientist I must separate my personal or social concerns from my scientific problem solving. My dissertation was an analysis of species-specific reactions in rats and their effects on classical and operant conditioning. I enjoyed doing research. It was exciting to learn how to design a good study, do statistical tests, and write an article for publication. Learning theory is one of the oldest branches of psychology; methods and theories were highly developed, and I could learn how to do it all from well-established experts. My mentor and dissertation advisor was a good scientist and a kind man who treated me with respect. He understood that as a single mom with two young children I was juggling a lot of competing demands, and he encouraged me to become the best researcher I could.

However, soon after I completed my PhD research, my feelings about being a psychologist began to change. More and more, my research seemed like a series of intellectual puzzles that had no connection to the rest of my life. In the lab, I studied abstract theories of conditioning, accepting the assumption that the principles were similar for rats and humans. In the "real world," I became involved in feminist activism and began to see things I had never noticed before. I saw sex discrimination in my university and knew women who struggled to hold their families together in poverty. Trying to build a new egalitarian marriage and bring up my children in nonsexist ways made me much more aware of social pressures to conform to traditional gender roles. I began to ask myself why I was doing a kind of psychology that had so little to say about the world as I knew it. I turned to the study of women and gender in order to make my personal and intellectual life congruent and to begin using my skills as a psychologist on behalf of social change.

Today, I still value my early research for teaching me how to go about scientific inquiry systematically and responsibly, but I have changed my views about what the important questions in psychology are and which theoretical frameworks have the most potential. I chose to develop a new specialization, the study of women and gender, and I have been doing research in this area ever since. I write this book in the hope that it will contribute in some small way to the creation of a transformed psychology, by introducing the psychology of women to the next generation of students (and future psychologists).

I have taught the psychology of women to graduate and undergraduate students for nearly 35 years. My students have differed in their racial and ethnic backgrounds, age, life experience, and sexual orientation. Their personal beliefs and values about feminism, women, and gender varied a great deal. In short, my students have been a diverse group of people. I have welcomed that diversity, and in this book I try to reflect what I have learned from it. Whatever your own background, I welcome you, my newest student, to the study of women and gender. I hope that it will make a difference for you.

I anticipate that you, like many of my students before you, will experience growth in at least some of the following areas as a result of your studies:

- *Critical thinking skills.* By studying the psychology of women, you can learn to evaluate psychological research critically and become a more astute, perceptive observer of human behavior.
- *Knowledge and understanding about social inequities.* The focus is on the gender system, sexism, and sex discrimination. However, gender always interacts with other systems of domination such as racism and heterosexism.
- *Empathy for women.* You may come to appreciate the experiences and viewpoints of your mother, your sisters, and your women friends better. In addition, women students may experience a heightened sense of connection with women as a group.

- *A commitment to work toward social change.* Psychological research and knowledge only matters when it is used.
- *The ability to see the larger context of women's lives.* The psychology of women is linked to their place in society and culture.
- *The understanding that "women" is a complex category.* Women are a diverse group and must be studied in the context of their lives.

Many of my past students have told me that their first course in women and gender raised as many questions as it answered, and was at times challenging, even upsetting. From these students I learned that I cannot promise my future students any easy answers. Acquiring knowledge is an ongoing process, for professional researchers as well as for college students. I invite you to join me in that journey.

Exploring Further

Marecek, J., Kimmel, E. B., Crawford, M., & Hare-Mustin, R. T. (2002). Psychology of women and gender. In I. B. Weiner (Series Ed.) & D. K. Freedheim (Vol Ed.), *Comprehensive Handbook of Psychology: Vol. 1. The History of Psychology* (pp. 249–268). New York: Wiley and Sons.
An overview of the development of feminist psychology and its effects on psychology as a science and a profession dedicated to helping people. The volume includes a chapter on the contributions of ethnic minorities to psychology and chapters on the history of other fields such as developmental psychology.

Rojas, Maythee (2009). *Women of color and feminism.* Berkeley: Seal Press.
Rojas addresses the challenges faced by women of color, from sexist and racist stereotyping to inadequate health care and education. In describing how women of color triumph over adversity and injustice, this important book integrates the theoretical, practical, and activist sides of feminism.

Feminist Voices in Psychology. http://www.feministvoices.com
A new multimedia Internet archive featuring the women of psychology's past and the diverse voices of contemporary feminist psychologists. In interviews available on the site, feminist pioneers talk about their challenge to mainstream psychology and experts in feminist psychology talk about ongoing challenges and future directions for women and feminism in psychology.

A Feminist Theory Dictionary. http://afeministtheorydictionary.wordpress.com
A weblog that is fun to browse and learn from. It provides definitions of concepts about feminism, women, sexuality, and gender, along with lively ongoing commentary and debate about feminist issues.

The Feministing Community. http://feministing.com
Feministing is an online community for feminists and their allies. The site fosters community building through blogging and social networking (a Facebook site, a YouTube page, and more). The Feministing community encourages activism by providing a forum for a variety of feminist voices and organizations.

PART 2

Gender in Social Context

CHAPTER 2

Gender, Status, and Power

❧

- **What Is Gender?**
- **Gender Shapes Societies and Cultures**
    Gender and Power
    Justifying Gender Inequality
- **Gender Shapes Social Interactions**
    The Cognitive Impact of Gender
    Gender as a Presentation of Self
    "Doing Gender"
    Constructing Gender through Female Bodies
    Constructing Gender in Interaction
- **Gender Shapes Individuals**
    Identity, Power, and Gender Differences
    Sexist Attitudes
- **Linking the Levels of Gender: A Summary**
- **Making a Difference**
    Transforming Ourselves
    Transforming Interpersonal Relations
    Transforming the Structures of Inequality
- **Exploring Further**

Women are simply not endowed by nature with the same measures of single-minded ambition and the will to succeed in the fiercely competitive world of Western capitalism. . . . The momma bird builds the nest. So it was, so it ever shall be.

—Political commentator Patrick Buchanan

If combat means living in a ditch, females have biological problems staying in a ditch for 30 days because they get infections and they don't have upper body strength. . . . On the other hand, men are basically little piglets. You drop them in the ditch, they roll around in it.

—Former Speaker of the U.S. House of Representatives,
Newt Gingrich, on women in the military

I think everyone has to work at being a man or a woman. Transgendered people are probably more aware of doing the work, that's all.

—Transgender activist Kate Bornstein

As far as I'm concerned, being any gender at all is a drag.

—Rock musician Patti Smith

*T*hese speakers have very clear opinions about men, women, and gender. Yet their words reflect contradictory notions about the meanings of these concepts. Gingrich believes that women have biological limitations that make them unfit for military duty, although men's "piglet" qualities do not seem to be a problem. Buchanan relegates women to being mama birds. In contrast, Patti Smith and Kate Bornstein view sex and gender almost as a choice, like a costume that one can choose to wear—or not.

Sorting out the multiple and conflicting meanings of biological sex, femininity, masculinity, and the social roles related to them has not been an easy task for psychologists. In this chapter we separate sex from gender and look at how gender is related to status and power.

What Is Gender?

Researchers who study the psychology of women distinguish between the concepts of sex and gender, a distinction that was first made in the late 1970s (Unger, 1979b). *Sex* was defined as biological differences in genetic composition and reproductive anatomy and function. Human infants are labeled as one sex or the other, female or male, at birth, based on the appearance of their genitals. It sounds like a simple and straightforward matter, though in fact it can be surprisingly complex (see Chapter 5).

Gender, in contrast to sex, was originally defined as "those characteristics and traits socioculturally considered appropriate to males and females," the traits that make up masculinity and femininity (Unger, 1979b, p. 1085). All known societies recognize biological differentiation and use it as the basis for social distinctions. In our own society, the process of creating gendered human beings starts at birth. When a baby is born, the presence of a vagina or penis represents sex—but the pink or blue blanket that soon enfolds the baby represents gender. The blanket serves as a cue that this infant is to be treated as a boy or girl, not as a generic human being, from the start.

According to these definitions, sex is to gender as nature is to nurture. That is, sex pertains to what is biological or natural, while gender pertains to what is learned or cultural. The sex/gender distinction was important because it enabled psychologists to separate conceptually the social aspects of gender from the biology of sex, and opened the ways to scientific study of such topics as how children are socialized to conform to their society's gender expectations. Distinguishing sex from gender was an important step in recognizing that biology is not destiny—that many of the apparent differences between women and men might be societally imposed rather than natural or inevitable.

However, the sex/gender distinction made at that time was soon seen to be limited. First, it sets up sex and gender as a nature/nurture dichotomy. Most psychologists now acknowledge that nature and nurture are so intertwined in human psychology that it is often impossible to determine the exact contribution of each. Another problem is that viewing gender as a set of stable, socialized traits does not capture the dynamic, interactive ways that people act out their own gender roles and respond to others according to their gender (Deaux & Major, 1987; Crawford, 1995). The trait view of gender also fails to recognize that gender is a culturally shared system through which societies organize relations between males and females (Bem, 1993), or that it marks social power and status (Henley, 1977; Crawford, 1995). A broader concept of gender was needed.

In this book, I take a dynamic approach, defining **gender** as *a classification system that influences access to power and resources and shapes the relations among women and men*. All known human societies make social distinctions based on gender.

Gender distinctions occur at many levels in society. Their influence is so pervasive that, like fish in water, we may be unaware that they surround us. Gender-related processes influence behavior, thoughts, and feelings in individuals; they affect interactions among individuals; and they help determine the structure of social institutions. The processes by which differences are created and power is allocated can be understood by considering how gender is played out at three levels: societal, interpersonal, and individual. In this chapter I describe how gender distinctions are created and maintained at these three levels, and how the levels are linked. Throughout the book, I will return to these levels of analysis to help illuminate how gender works.

Gender Shapes Societies and Cultures

Most societies are *hierarchical*—they have one or more dominant groups and other subordinate groups. The dominant group has more of whatever that society values, whether it be cattle, land, the opportunity to get a good education, or high-paying jobs. In other words, the dominant group has more *power*—defined as the ability to control the outcomes of others by providing or withholding resources—and higher *status*—defined as social standing that elicits respect (Keltner et al., 2003). Societies organize hierarchies on the basis of a variety of arbitrary distinctions—tribe, caste, skin color, religion—and these vary from one society to another. Gender, however, is used universally. To a greater or lesser degree, most modern societies are *patriarchal,* a word that literally means "ruled by the fathers." Patriarchal social systems allocate more power and higher status to men.

Gender and Power

The power conferred by gender is pervasive and multidimensional. For example:

- By and large, men make the laws that everyone must obey. According to the United Nations, in the year 2008 women accounted for only about 18 percent of members of national parliaments and congresses worldwide.
- Organized religion is a powerful influence in maintaining patriarchy. The Jewish, Islamic, and Christian traditions all view the deity as masculine, prescribe subservient roles for women, and limit women's participation and influence within the religious establishment (Galliano, 2003). Cross-culturally, greater religiosity is linked with hostility toward women and opposition to gender equality (Harville & Rienzi, 2000).
- Men have more control over public discourse. For example, although 60 percent of journalism students are female, very few women are in positions of power in the media (Cai Chunying, 2009). On television and radio, women are relatively invisible as voices of authority. Cross-culturally, stereotypical and demeaning images of women are prevalent in the mass media (see Chapter 3).
- According to the United Nations, men have more wealth and more leisure time in virtually every society. Much of the work women do is unpaid (child care, subsistence farming, and housework). When they work for pay, women earn less than men for similar or equivalent tasks (see Chapter 10). Therefore, women have less wealth despite working longer hours than men.
- Women have less access to education than men do. In developing countries, more boys are sent to school, while girls are kept at home to care for younger siblings and do housework. Worldwide, literacy rates are lower for women (Callister, 2007). In developed countries, where girls and women have access to education, studies show that boys get more attention from teachers and are more often allowed to dominate class time (Beaman et al., 2006).
- Men have more political and military power in most societies. In the United States, 88 percent of police officers and 85 percent of the military (including 98 percent of the highest-ranking officers) are men. There is no modern society in which women, as a group, control the political practices or the means of warfare (Sidanius & Pratto, 1999).

Justifying Gender Inequality

Not only do dominant groups have more power, they use a variety of tactics to hold on to their power and maintain inequity among groups (Sidanius & Pratto, 1999). *Legitimizing myths* are attitudes, values, and beliefs that serve to justify hierarchical social practices. Many of the legitimizing myths of patriarchy emphasize that women are fundamentally different from men. They may be seen as evil and treacherous (in need of control), or incompetent (in need of restriction for their own good). They may be regarded as helpless, overemotional and fragile (in need of protection), or pure and self-sacrificing (to be put on a pedestal). Such myths are deeply embedded in culture. For example, the archetype of women as evil and treacherous recurs in religion (witch hunts, Eve), fairy tales (wicked stepmothers), personality stereotypes (women are seen as gossipy, catty), and myths about rape (the belief that women frequently make false accusations in order to trap men). Legitimizing myths are often so widely accepted that they seem to be undeniably true.

Prejudice is a negative attitude or feeling toward a person because of his or her membership in a particular social group. The negative attitudes and feelings could include disdain, hatred, or simply feeling uncomfortable around members of the devalued group. Prejudice often includes the belief that it is acceptable or right to treat others unequally. Prejudice on the basis of sex or gender is termed *sexism*. For example, the belief that it is more important to give boys than girls a good education is sexist. However, sexism is often more subtle and complicated than in this example; we return to sexist prejudice later in this chapter. A related prejudice is *heterosexism,* or negative attitudes and beliefs about lesbian, gay, transgendered, and bisexual people.

Discrimination involves treating people unfairly because of their membership in a particular group. A teacher who pays more attention to the boys in class or a committee that preferentially awards scholarships to male students is engaging in *sex discrimination*. Many studies have found that sex discrimination is common, for example, in hiring and promotion on the job (Crosby et al., 2003).

A widespread and systematic pattern of prejudice and discrimination is sometimes termed *oppression*. For example, from 1996 to 2002, the Taliban government oppressed women and girls in Afghanistan by denying them basic human rights such as health care, education, freedom of movement, and a voice in public affairs (Brodsky, 2003). Today, the Taliban are still burning girls' schools and throwing acid in the faces of women who dare to walk about unveiled. In many parts of the world, women and girls are still denied basic human rights.

In addition to gender, other ranking systems, such as race, class, age, and sexuality, also influence social power and can be the basis of prejudice, discrimination, and oppression. Like White women, people of color often face discrimination in employment (Crosby et al., 2003). Feminist research and theory emphasize that these systems are connected—they operate simultaneously in social institutions and everyday interactions, often outside awareness (Weber, 1998). Being White, male, middle or upper class, and heterosexual confers advantages that often are not even noticed by those who have them (Rosenblum & Travis, 1996).

Gender Shapes Social Interactions

Gender affects interactions among people in everyday life. Here we look at how people notice gender and how status and power are conveyed through gender cues.

The Cognitive Impact of Gender

Think of the last time you bought coffee or a snack. Quickly, try to describe the person who waited on you by listing that person's most important characteristics. Try to give the best "eyewitness testimony" you can.

What characteristics did you list first? People were asked to do a similar task—describe the person who had just sold them a subway token—in a study meant to show that gender is an important category in interpersonal interaction (Grady, 1977). Gender was indeed important. Participants *always* mentioned that the token seller was a woman; in fact, it was the first or second characteristic listed by every single participant. In this case, the token seller happened to be not only female but also African American. Statistically, mentioning ethnicity first would provide more information—"female" rules out only half the U.S. population, while "African American" rules out about 85 percent. But people do not categorize along statistical lines. Some categories are more salient or noticeable than others—and gender is one of the most salient of all. Many other studies have shown that people overrely on gender as a cognitive category. For example, when research participants watch a video of a discussion group, and later mistakenly mix people up in trying to remember who said or did what, they are more likely to confuse two people of the same gender than two of the same age, ethnic group, or even the same name (Fiske et al., 1991).

Gender is so important that when gender cues are ambiguous, people engage in cognitive puzzle solving to figure out the "correct" gender. Try reading the following story (adapted from John & Sussman, 1989, p. 264). After each segment, state whether you think each of the two characters is female or male:

> The scene is a singles bar where some people are dancing, and others are sitting around socializing or drinking at the bar. Chris walks purposefully toward Pat and begins a conversation. After a few minutes, Chris asks Pat to dance. Pat agrees . . .
>
> Chris's sex?
>
> Pat's sex?
>
> As they start to dance, Pat says to Chris, *"You're a good dancer. I don't come across many people who dance this well."*
>
> *"Thank you,"* says Chris with a slightly embarrassed smile. *"I think you dance well too."*
>
> *"What do you do for a living?"* asks Pat.
>
> *"I'm a high school teacher,"* answers Chris. *"And you?"*
>
> *"I'm a research technician,"* says Pat, *"but I'm thinking of getting into computers."*
>
> As the music ends, Pat says, *"You are a very interesting person. I'd like us to talk some more . . . why don't we sit over here?"*
>
> Chris's sex?
>
> Pat's sex?
>
> Chris orders more drinks, and they continue to talk. *"I'd like to get to know you better."*
>
> Pat replies, *"I find you exciting too, but I'm not sure I'm able to handle too much familiarity now. I'm really interested in my career. . . ."*

Chris's sex?

Pat's sex?

"I understand," says Chris, *"but I'd really like to see more of you."*

"I'm going to think about it," says Pat. *"Why don't we stop off at my place for coffee and . . ."*

Chris's sex?

Pat's sex?

When research participants tried this task, they changed the sex of the two characters from one scenario to the next, as the gender cues shifted (John & Sussman, 1989). They tried to make sense of the interaction by deciding who was male and who was female according to gender-typed behavior—even though this meant they had to "resex" Chris and Pat as they went along! Did you do the same? Apparently, it is cognitively easier to change Pat and Chris's sex than to recognize that they might engage in gender-inconsistent behaviors. Interestingly, not one participant thought that both characters might be men, or both women.

By creating experimental situations in which gender cues are ambiguous, psychologists have demonstrated how much we ordinarily rely on such cues. In real life, the cues are usually clear; when they're not, it makes us uneasy (see Figure 2.1). The cognitive salience of gender leads to treating women and men as members of a group rather than as individuals.

People tend to perceive their own social group more positively than other groups, a tendency termed the ***intergroup bias effect.*** They also tend to character-ize outgroup members as being all alike and having similar qualities, the ***outgroup***

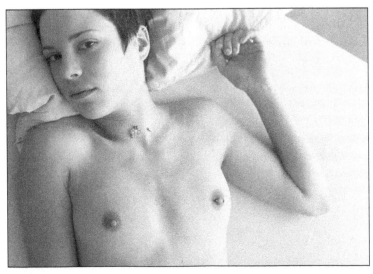

FIGURE 2.1
Female or male? We usually take gender cues for granted (hairstyle, body shape, clothing, ornaments) but the cues can be ambiguous and unsettling.

homogeneity effect. We can see these tendencies in action in a study where women and men talked about each other.

In this study, college students in same-sex pairs were asked to discuss "American men" and "American women" for 5 minutes each (Harasty, 1997). In these open-ended discussions, participants generalized more when talking about the gender outgroup than when talking about their own gender group. In other words, male pairs made more comments of the "women are all like that" variety, and female pairs made more "men are all alike" comments. When talking about people of their own sex, they were more specific and less likely to generalize about the entire group. The most general comments tended to be negative, suggesting that outgroup members are not only viewed as all alike but not quite as good as the ingroup.

When people evaluate outgroups, they treat high-status and low-status outgroups differently. When college students were asked to rate 17 social groups on various traits, their responses tended to cluster into two types of outgroups: those who were competent but not likable and those who were incompetent but likable. Low-status groups such as Latinos, housewives, and people with mental retardation or physical disability were judged likable but incompetent. High-status groups, which included rich people, feminists, and businesswomen, were judged as competent but dislikable. These results suggest that people are threatened by high-status outgroups and defend themselves by believing that members of such groups are unfriendly, uncaring, and not likable (Fiske et al., 1999).

Because they are perceived as outgroup members, women who are public figures often get a double whammy of prejudice directed at them. Let's take the 2008 nomination of Sonia Sotomayor to the Supreme Court as an example. As a Latina and a woman, she was a member of two low-status outgroups in the realm of politics. Predictably, she was criticized as incompetent and not smart enough for the job. As a distinguished female judge, she was a member of a high-status outgroup, and was criticized as competent but unlikable—a domineering "bully on the bench" (Collins, 2010).

Intergroup biases can lead to characterizing an entire group by the actions of one member. For example, a person may say, "I worked for a woman once and she was impossible. Never again." Using gender as a cue to status, and casting female employers as the outgroup, this individual is treating them as completely homogeneous; if one woman is a difficult boss, they all are! Male employers are the higher-status ingroup, so a difficult male employer is likely to be seen as an individual. Even after more than one experience with a male boss who acts like a bully or tyrant in the office, it is rare to hear people say they would never again work for a man.

Gender as a Presentation of Self

Not only do we respond to others on the basis of gender, we strive to present ourselves as gendered beings. We turn now to exploring how people perform the gender that is assigned to them.

Imagine that you are deciding what to wear for a job interview. You want the job and expect that the interviewer will be an important man. Now imagine that you find out that the interviewer has very traditional—even sexist—attitudes toward women. When college women were put in this situation as research participants, they changed their style according to their expectations about the interviewer. When they expected to meet a sexist man, they wore more makeup and accessories than when they expected to meet a nonsexist man. Although the interviewer knew nothing about their expectations and behaved similarly to all, the women made less eye contact with the "sexist" man and gave more conventional responses to his questions about their plans for marriage and children (von Baeyer et al., 1981). This is an example of **self-presentation,** or acting out a self in response to the expectations of others.

Both women and men tailor their self-presentation to the audience. In a classic study, female college students were given a description of a male student who was either desirable or undesirable as a potential date and who was characterized as having traditional or more modern values. When the women thought they would have the opportunity to meet the man, they changed their descriptions of themselves to fit the man's traditional or modern values—but only if he was attractive (Zanna & Pack, 1975). A later study showed that male students do exactly the same thing when they think they will have a chance to meet an attractive woman (Morier & Seroy, 1994).

Self-presentation is a strategic choice. For example, women may not label themselves as feminists or express feminist opinions in public or in mixed-sex groups because of its undesirable connotations. Men, in contrast, may express liberal views in public or in mixed-gender groups, but more sexist views around other men. In one study, the men followed just this pattern, endorsing more positive and "politically correct" attitudes about feminism when they thought their attitudes would be more public (Rosell & Hartman, 2001). In another study, in which real-life conversation among friends was recorded, a woman talked about gender stereotypes in subtly different ways when with her female peers than when in a mixed-sex group. With women she directly referred to the disadvantages stereotyping causes for women; with men, she talked about the disadvantages of stereotypes for society in general (Stapleton, 2001). Which behaviors reflect the real attitudes of the people in these studies? Perhaps the reality is constructed by—and changes with—the situation.

Self-presentation strategies make sense because they may have a positive influence on others. Clearly, people's behavior influences how others respond to them. People's actions may even produce the very behaviors they expect from others. This is illustrated by a classic study that involved deceiving people about their interaction partner. Pairs of college women and men had telephone conversations. Unbeknownst to the women, the men had been provided with photographs of random women, some attractive and some unattractive. Thus, each man thought he was conversing with either an attractive or an unattractive woman, but the actual person he talked to was not the one in the photo he saw. Next, independent judges listened to the women's part of the conversation and rated each woman on her personality. Women who had been labeled as attractive were rated as friendlier, more sociable, and more likable than those who had been labeled as unattractive. What was happening here? Apparently, the men treated the women differently in subtle ways, so that the conversation brought out the best in those who were treated like attractive women (Snyder et al., 1977). This kind of influence is most likely to occur when people are relying on minimal information about another person—such as initial encounters (Valentine et al., 2001).

These studies show that gender can become a *self-fulfilling prophecy*. In other words, expectations can make the expected events come true. The earliest studies on self-fulfilling prophecies showed that they can have powerful and lasting effects. When a teacher was led to believe that a particular child was gifted, the child's IQ score went up, even though that child had been randomly selected (Rosenthal & Jacobson, 1968). Apparently, the teachers' beliefs led them to unwittingly treat the "gifted" children in ways that fostered their intellectual growth.

"Doing Gender"

With these dynamic processes in mind, gender can be viewed as a social performance: like actors in a play, people enact "man" or "woman." With themselves and others as the audience, they actively create and construct their gender. From this perspective, gender is not something people *have,* like brown eyes or curly hair, but something that people *do* (West & Zimmerman, 1987). In this ongoing performance, "being a woman" is created by social consensus:

> There is no such thing as "being a woman" outside the various practices that define womanhood for my culture—practices ranging from the sort of work I do to my sexual preferences to the clothes I wear to the way I use language (Cameron, 1996, p. 46).

The performance of gender is sometimes deliberate. Have you ever seen the TV and print ads for 900 lines that promise conversations with "Hot babes!" and "Sexy, horny women!"? One researcher interviewed a group of phone sex workers employed on these lines (Hall, 1995). The sex workers reported that they consciously strove to create themselves as the fantasy women that their clients desired. Because phone sex does not provide visual cues, the sex workers created the sexy "babes" of porn fantasy entirely through their language. As sellers of a commodity, the workers were aware of what kind of women's language is marketable as sexy: feminine or flowery words, suggestive comments, and a dynamic intonation pattern (breathy, excited, varied in pitch, lilting).

This study illustrates that people cooperate in producing gender (Marecek et al., 2004). To the male callers, the fantasy woman constructed entirely through language was presumably satisfying. Callers paid well for the service, and many requested the same worker on repeat calls. The sex workers reported that they liked their jobs because they earned good money and had low overhead (they did not need expensive clothing and they could work from home). One even said that she often washed the dishes while talking to a caller. Strikingly, one of the most successful phone sex workers was a man who impersonated a woman. Clearly, this man was adept at performing femininity.

Of course, gender performances are not limited to femininity. Indeed, femininity has meaning only in contrast to masculinity. The gender system requires that men "do" being a man as much as women "do" being a woman. In a study of male college students' conversation while watching a basketball game on TV, the students bragged about their sexual exploits with women and gossiped about other men, especially those they did not like, whom they denigrated as "gay," "artsy-fartsy fags," and "homos." In their talk, these young men displayed their heterosexuality and distanced themselves from other men who were supposedly less masculine. This kind of talk "is not only *about* masculinity, it is a sustained performance *of* masculinity" (Cameron, 1997, p. 59).

Constructing Gender through Female Bodies

Gender is socially constructed through our actions, our roles, our verbal and non-verbal language, and our cognitive processes. Gender is also socially constructed through physical appearance. That is, femininity and masculinity are expressed through clothing, hairstyle, body exposure, and so on. But the burden of gender construction is not equally borne by male and female bodies. By far, the majority of gender construction in contemporary industrialized cultures takes place through women's appearance.

Consider a hypothetical scenario: Suppose a group of women and men were banished to the wilderness for several months with no mirrors, razors, grooming products, or labor-saving devices (and no reality-television crew lurking in the trees). Would the group come back to our civilization looking more "feminine" or more "masculine"? Well, let's see, they'd be hairier, dirtier, stronger smelling, more muscular . . . doesn't sound much like our culture's idea of femininity. To us, more physically natural means more masculine; more groomed, scented, modified, and adorned means more feminine. In her book, *Beauty Bound*, clinical psychologist Rita Freedman (1986) put it this way:

> Not only is a woman socialized to act differently than a normal adult, but to look different as well—more like a female than a person. Her lips must be redder, lashes longer, waist smaller, skin smoother . . . props and paint accentuate gender differences, creating some that have no basis in nature (blue eyelids) and exaggerating others that are minimal (hairless legs). Shape of brows, contour of feet, style of hair become potent substitutes for natural sex differences (pp. 30, 53).

Clothing and accessories also communicate femininity. Jeans are gender-neutral, but if they are supertight they are feminine. Plain tie shoes are gender-neutral, but add a high heel and they are feminine. T-shirts are gender-neutral, but with a deeply scooped neck and cap sleeves, they are feminine. Skirts and dresses are feminine. Anything with bows or lace is feminine. Hair ornaments are strictly for the girls. In contrast, our culture no longer designates any clothing or accessories as clear signals of masculinity, except, perhaps, the jock strap.

Both femininity and masculinity are performances to some extent, but a feminine appearance is more of a put-on than a masculine appearance (see Figure 2.2). In the process of assuming a feminine persona, a woman's body becomes more than her means of interaction with the material world; it becomes a visible marker serving to maintain socially constructed gender differences and gender roles. Of course, males and females naturally look different; being able to distinguish between the sexes is important to heterosexual reproduction, and secondary sex characteristics

FIGURE 2.2

Gender as a performance. The same woman, Susan McNamara, is shown in both photographs. On the right, Ms. McNamara is dressed for her job as a Las Vegas dancer. On the left, she is less concerned with "doing gender."

like breasts and beards help us to do so. But a natural need to make distinctions does not necessitate that the bulk of differentiation must take place through female appearance. That *women's* bodies primarily serve as the canvas on which we paint gender may have to do with power.

Doing gender is not just a matter of creating and displaying differences. When women and men are doing gender they are also "doing status" and women in particular are "doing subordination." In other words, the gender category male is socially and cognitively linked with greater prestige, prominence, and value than the gender category female (Cohen et al., 1972; Ridgeway, 1992). Therefore, doing gender disadvantages females (Rashotte & Webster, 2005).

Constructing Gender in Interaction

It is important to remember that, outside the realm of appearance, doing gender usually takes place without reflection or conscious awareness. Unlike phone sex workers or Vegas dancers, most people are not *consciously* striving to produce a gendered persona when they interact with others. Instead, like the women who shaped their own behavior to meet what they thought were the expectations of an interviewer, or the men who disparaged "fags" in the studies described earlier, most people do gender without thinking consciously about the process. And they do it even though, if asked, they would say they believe in gender equality (Rashotte & Webster, 2005). Women's second-class status is created and maintained as people do gender in everyday social interaction. Let's look at how this can happen.

Talking Down, Ordering Around, and Silencing

Members of subordinate groups may be treated disrespectfully in everyday conversation. Dominant group members may use particular ways of talking or kinds of talk to assert and maintain their status, especially when the person they are talking to wants to be seen as an equal (Ruscher, 2001).

The most basic kind of conversational disrespect is not allowing the other person to be heard at all by interrupting, controlling the topic, and taking up most of the talk time. A great deal of research shows that men use these tactics in conversation with women more than they do with other men and more than women do with each other. For example, a classic study in which researchers listened in on same- and mixed-sex conversations in public places showed that 96 percent of interruptions in male-female conversations were by male speakers. In same-sex pairs, interruptions were about equally divided between the two speakers (Zimmerman & West, 1975). Of course, not all interruptions are hostile. Sometimes, a listener jumps in and interrupts out of interest and enthusiasm. These sorts of interruptions are relatively gender-neutral. However, men do more *intrusive interruptions*—the kind that are active attempts to end the other speaker's turn and take over the conversation. Moreover, men make a larger proportion of intrusive interruptions in unstructured and naturalistic settings than in the lab—settings that more closely resemble everyday interaction (Anderson & Leaper, 1998).

If a woman does interrupt another speaker, she risks social disapproval—especially if she interrupts a man. When college students heard audiotapes of (carefully matched) same- and mixed-sex interactions, they gave the lowest ratings to a woman who interrupted a man. Both male and female participants saw her as more rude and disrespectful than interrupters in the other pairs. Their judgments reflect the view that men *should* have higher status in conversation. When a woman interrupts a man, she is doing more than just breaking a politeness rule; she is violating the social order that gives more respect to men (LaFrance, 1992; Youngquist, 2008).

Despite widespread beliefs that women are more talkative, men have been shown to take more than a fair share of talk time in a variety of settings including classrooms, business meetings, and informal conversations (Crawford, 1995). In one review of 63 studies done over a 40-year period, 34 studies showed men talking more than women overall, and only 2 showed women talking more than men (the others showed no differences or had mixed results) (James & Drakich, 1993). The differences were most apparent in relatively formal, task-oriented situations, such as committee meetings, classrooms, and problem-solving groups; in these settings, men talked more in about three-quarters of all studies. However, even in ordinary social conversation, over 37 percent of studies showed men talking more than women, and only 6 percent (one study) showed women talking more than men. These results suggest that context does make a difference: men dominate talk more in contexts where there is more at stake in terms of asserting one's status and getting one's own way.

Conversational dominance can be more subtle than just taking up most of the talk time. For example, imagine that you are teaching someone how to do the wash. Would you be more likely to use direct commands ("Put the whites in one pile") or suggestions ("It's probably best to separate the whites and the colors")? The use of imperative (command) verbs can be a way of talking down, which implies that the learner is not very competent. In an interesting study of gender, status, and language, college students learned how to do the Heimlich maneuver by watching a slide show (Duval & Ruscher, 1994). This task was chosen because it was gender neutral and unfamiliar to most students. After watching the slide show, participants were asked to explain the Heimlich maneuver to either a male or female participant who had not seen the slides. The researchers predicted that men would use more direct orders in explaining the technique to women than to other men, because they would presume that women held lower status and less knowledge than themselves. As predicted, men used more imperative verbs when teaching a woman than were used in any of the other teacher-learner pairs. Being ordered around as though incompetent may create a self-fulfilling prophecy in which the learner comes to think of herself as less capable.

Conversational dominance is an important aspect of doing gender because it so clearly involves women "doing subordination." But is this invariant across race, ethnicity, and cultures? Very little research has been done on this question. However, one study compared African American and European American adolescents in mixed-sex discussion groups. Overall, the African American groups showed more gender equality in conversational style than the European American groups (Filardo, 1996). More research is needed on diversity and communication style.

Nonverbal Messages

Tara and Tom are assistant managers at separate branches of a local business. They meet for lunch to talk about ideas for increasing profits. When Tom talks, Tara keeps her eyes on his face and smiles a lot. When Tara talks, Tom gazes out the window. When he wants to jot something down, he borrows Tara's pen without asking. While they talk, Tom leans away from Tara and pulls the papers on the table between them closer to him. When they get up to leave, Tara looks closely at Tom's face to assess whether he has found the meeting useful. Tom touches Tara lightly on the shoulder.

As this example shows, not all communication relies on words. Here we consider how gendered patterns of nonverbal communication convey status and power in North American society. Although Tara and Tom are ostensibly meeting as equal colleagues, their nonverbal communication patterns convey a clear message about who is more powerful and important.

High-status people have more nonverbal privileges and fewer nonverbal obligations. They can take up more space, invade the space of others, and touch them and their possessions. They are less obligated to show their interest and involvement in others' talk. Pioneering research by psychologist Nancy Henley led her to propose the theory that when women and men interact, the nonverbal behavior of men is like that of high-status, dominant individuals, and the nonverbal behavior of women is like that of lower-status, submissive individuals (Henley, 1973, 1977). (See Figure 2.3.) This nonverbal dominance not only reflects status differentials, it performs—and thus perpetuates—them. With Henley's theory in mind, let's look at each of the differences shown by Tom and Tara.

Many studies have found that women smile much more than men do in interaction (Hall, 2006; LaFrance et al., 2003). Smiling is a socially positive activity that conveys emotional expressiveness and shows interest and involvement, but are all those smiles genuine? High- and low-status people may give (and get) different kinds of smiles. When people are interacting with equal- or lower-status others, their smiles are likely to be consistent with the emotions they report. However, when they are interacting with higher-status others, their smiles are less related to their actual positive emotions (Hecht & LaFrance, 1998). In other words, when high-status people smile at others, it is because they are feeling good; when low-status people smile it may be because they feel a need to please their interaction partner. High-status people probably should not assume that their subordinates are overjoyed or even interested just because they are smiling. Women, like low-status people, seem to feel an obligation to smile (LaFrance, 2001). If a woman violates that obligation, she may be admonished to "Cheer up" or asked "What's the matter with you?"

The patterns of looking and speaking used by Tom and Tara also reflect status differences. Looking at conversational partners when they are speaking communicates respect and interest. The more power and status a person has, the less they need to offer this kind of respect. High-status people look at their subordinates while speaking to them, but tend to look away when it's the subordinate's turn to

FIGURE 2.3
Cues to status in interaction include patterns of smiling, posture, gesture, eye contact, talking, and listening.

talk—a pattern termed *visual dominance.* In a study of interaction in mixed-sex pairs, visual dominance was about equal in women and men who had more expertise on the topic than their conversational partners. However, when their expertise was the same as their partner's, men showed more visual dominance than women. In other words, when participants lacked any other cues to status, they relied on gender, and enacted the men's dominance in eye contact (Dovidio et al., 1988).

When Tom leaned away from Tara and pulled the papers closer to himself, he was echoing a gendered pattern of distancing behavior documented in research. In one study, college students in same- and mixed-gender pairs were given 10 minutes to build a domino tower (Lott, 1987). When working with a woman, men more often turned their faces or bodies away and put the dominoes closer to themselves than when they worked with another man. (Women treated men and other women alike.) This kind of microdiscrimination reflects and reinforces men's higher status.

Probably the most ambiguous nonverbal behavior between Tom and Tara was Tom's parting touch. Did it communicate friendship? Sexual interest? Or "Don't forget that I'm in charge here"? Like many other nonverbal behaviors, touch can communicate either intimacy or dominance. Whether A is "caressing" or "pawing" B, being affectionate or invasive, can be hard to determine (Ruscher, 2001). (See Figure 2.4.) Henley suggests that intimacy behaviors can be distinguished from dominance behaviors by whether the recipient welcomes the touch and whether she can comfortably reciprocate it. Men, because of their higher status, are allowed to initiate more touch with women. This gender privilege is most evident in public settings among people who are not intimately connected (Major et al., 1990).

In a creative field study, college student researchers were trained to unobtrusively observe professors interacting at professional conventions (Hall, 1996). The researchers did not just determine whether men touched women more than vice versa. They coded the kinds of touch that were used: brief "spot" touches or more personal pats and hugs; what body parts were touched (hand, arm, shoulder); and the apparent function (greeting, affection, control). Also, they independently assessed each professor's status based on number of publications, the prestige of the professor's university, and related measures. There was strong evidence that lower- and higher-status people initiated different kinds of touch. Lower-status people initiated more handshakes, but higher-status people more often touched others' arm or shoulder. It seemed that high-status people were *displaying* status through using more intrusive arm-and-shoulder touch, while lower-status people were trying to *gain* status by politely offering to shake hands. Gender was important, too. When the male and female professor in a pair had equal status, men initiated more touching. In other words, gender itself served as a cue to status when all else was equal, and women were treated like lower-status others.

FIGURE 2.4

Touch can be an ambiguous cue in social interaction. Is this a friendly gesture of support after a long day at the office—or is it sexual harassment?

Cues to dominance don't always work the same way for women and men. If women try to assert dominance through touch, their behavior may be misinterpreted as a sexual move. Or it may evoke negative reactions. In one experiment, participants interacted with low-status and high-status interviewers (undergraduate students wearing jeans and sneakers versus graduate students in business clothes) and then rated the interviewers. Low-status women who initiated touch were liked least of all. Status had no effect on liking for men who initiated touch (Storrs & Kleinke, 1990).

Gender differences in nonverbal behavior are not due entirely to power and status. Nonverbal behavior has many functions and varies considerably according to age, ethnicity, and culture. Nonverbal behavior may also be related to physical size differences. Clearly, though, one function of nonverbal cues is to signal the unequal status of women and men.

Hassles and Stressors

If women are indeed treated as a subordinate group, we would expect that they would often experience "hassles" that are related to second-class status. Research confirms that these hassles are a part of life for women. When college women and men were asked to keep diaries of sexist incidents and their impact in a series of studies, the women reported an average of one to two such incidents each week, while men reported only about one every two weeks (Swim et al., 2001). Here are a few examples of the experiences reported by women:

Gender role stereotyping: "You're a woman, so fold my laundry."

Demeaning remarks: "I was hanging out with some friends when one guy in the apartment said, "Yo bitch, get me some beer!"

Sexual objectification: Walking home from a party, a woman encountered three men. One complimented her on the belt she was wearing, and another said, "Forget the belt, look at her rack."

Although both women and men experienced demeaning remarks, the tone of the remarks differed. Comments aimed at men were usually about men in general. For example, one man reported hearing someone say that "men are jerks." Women were far more likely to experience personal, sexually degrading and objectifying remarks (Swim et al., p. 36–37, 42).

Living with everyday sexism has a negative effect on the well-being of both women and men. In these studies, participants who experienced more sexist hassles reported higher anger, anxiety, and depression, along with lower self-esteem and reduced comfort in social situations. Because women experience significantly more sexist hassles overall than men, the impact on them is greater.

Studies using more diverse samples show similar results. When researchers used a detailed survey to measure women's experiences of sexism within the past year and also over a lifetime, they found that such experiences are almost universal—99 percent of the women had experienced a sexist event at least once, and 97 percent within the past year (Klonoff & Landrine, 1995). The most common experiences included being subjected to sexist jokes (94 percent), being treated with a lack of respect (83 percent), being called sexist names, and being sexually harassed (82 percent for each). A majority of the women surveyed (56 percent) said that they had been hit, pushed, or physically threatened because of being a woman. (See Table 2.1.)

The sample of more than 600 women in this study was ethnically and economically diverse. Women of color and White women reported experiencing similar kinds of sexist events; however, women of color reported more sexist experiences

TABLE 2.1   Women's Experiences of Sexism

Item	Percent Who Experienced It within Lifetime*	Percent Who Experienced It within Past Year*
Treated unfairly by teachers/professors	53	25
your employer, boss, or supervisors	60	32
your coworkers, fellow students, or colleagues	58	37
people in service jobs (store clerks, servers, bartenders, bank tellers, mechanics)	77	62
strangers	73	59
people in helping jobs (doctors, nurses, psychiatrists, case workers, dentists, school counselors, therapists, pediatricians, school principals, gynecologists)	59	40
your boyfriend, husband, or other important man in your life	75	50
Denied a raise, promotion, tenure, good assignment, job, or other such thing at work that you deserved	40	18
People have made inappropriate or unwanted sexual advances to you	82	55
People failed to show you respect	83	62
Been really angry about something sexist that was done to you	76	52
Forced to take drastic steps (filing a grievance/lawsuit, quitting your job, moving away) to deal with a sexist incident	19	9
Been called a sexist name like bitch, cunt, chick, or other names	82	54
Gotten into an argument or a fight about something sexist that was done or said to you or somebody else	66	44
Been made fun of, picked on, pushed, shoved, hit, or threatened with harm	56	29
Heard people making sexist jokes or degrading sexual jokes	94	84

Source: From Klonoff, E. A., & Landrine, H. (1995). The schedule of sexist events: A measure of lifetime and recent sexist discrimination in women's lives. *Psychology of Women Quarterly, 19,* 439–472. Copyright © 1995 by John Wiley & Sons. Reprinted by permission. Percentages have been rounded to the nearest whole number.

*Percentages are those women who said they had experienced each type of incident *because of being a woman.*

overall. Like the college students in the diary studies, these women also experienced psychological costs. The number of sexist experiences reported was related to the overall number of psychological and physical symptoms reported and to specific problems such as depression, premenstrual symptoms, and obsessive-compulsive behaviors. In fact, sexism statistically predicted psychological and physical problems better than other measures of stressful life events alone (Landrine et al., 1995). The impact of sexist hassles is also clear in a study of military personnel (Murdoch et al., 2007). More women than men (80 percent versus 45 percent) reported having experienced such stressors as sexual harassment or challenges about their sexual identity. Both male and female personnel who reported more stressor experiences had poorer social and work functioning, more physical problems, and more symptoms of posttraumatic stress disorder, depression, and anxiety.

Recent research has shown that heterosexist hassles have negative effects on lesbian, gay, and bisexual (LGB) individuals. When asked to keep daily diaries, a sample of LGB people reported that experiencing heterosexist hassles led to increased anger and anxiety. Moreover, these experiences caused the LGB participants to lower their own acceptance of themselves as LGBs, and negatively influenced their perceptions of other lesbians, gays, and bisexuals (Swim et al., 2009).

Clearly, being treated like a second-class citizen in everyday interactions is a major source of stress for members of subordinate groups, whether they are people of color, LGBs, or women. (For more on societal sources of women's psychological distress, see Chapter 13.) Sexist, racist, and heterosexist events have a greater negative impact than do other life events on psychological and physical health because they are " inherently demeaning, degrading, and highly personal; they are attacks upon and negative responses to something essential about the self that cannot be changed" (Klonoff & Landrine, 1995, p. 442).

Double Binds

Why do women (and members of other subordinated groups) put up with unequal treatment? Why don't they just start acting like members of the dominant group? Surely, women can tell sexist jokes, order men around, interrupt them, and call them names (see Figure 2.5). Aside from the fact that this kind of equality would create a pretty unpleasant society to live in, there are other reasons.

An important aspect of being part of a subordinated group is that subordinate status creates *double binds,* or "damned if you do, damned if you don't" situations. If the subordinate group member acts like a member of the dominant group, she is criticized for stepping out of her place and not being a model member of her subordinate group. If she acts like a model subordinate group member, she is criticized for not being as competent as dominant group members. Double binds create no-win situations.

Studies of everyday social situations have shown that women often face double binds. This occurs partly because dominant behaviors are strongly associated with men. In one study, college students and other young adults were shown a list of dominant and submissive social behaviors and asked to rate how often a typical man or woman would behave that way. The participants reported that dominant acts (setting goals for a group, refusing to back down in an argument) were more likely

FIGURE 2.5

Perhaps not the best kind of equality . . .

Source: © Tom Cheney/The New Yorker Collection/www.cartoonbank.com

to be done by a man, and submissive acts (accepting verbal abuse, not complaining when overcharged at the store) were more likely to be done by a woman (McCreary & Rhodes, 2001). Because dominant behaviors are linked in people's belief systems with men, they may be less effective when used by women.

Let's take the example of communication style. In American society, speaking up for oneself, expressing opinions, and being assertive about one's rights are valued—so much so that assertiveness training workshops are a popular type of psychological self-improvement. Many of these workshops are aimed specifically at women. However, when women adopt this new assertive style, they may be judged differently than men who speak the same way. In one study, college students and older adults were asked to read scenarios in which a male or female speaker behaved assertively but respectfully (for example, politely asking a supervisor not to call him/her "kiddo" in front of clients). Participants, especially those who were older and male, judged assertive women as equally competent but less likable than assertive men (Crawford, 1988). The double bind is obvious: women, but not men, have to choose between being unassertive (and letting others dominate them) and being assertive (and risking being disliked).

Other studies also show that so-called masculine speech is less effective for women than for men. Male raters viewed women who spoke in a competent, assertive style as less likable, less influential, and more threatening than men who used the same style—unless they went out of their way to appear warm and friendly (Carli, 2001). It's not surprising that women adjust their speech style to appear more (or less) assertive, depending on whether the topic is gender-linked and whether they are talking to a male or a female—even when it's on e-mail (Palomares, 2009).

It's not only speech style that creates double binds; even a woman's appearance can do so. Studies from the early days of research on beauty stereotypes found that attractive women who were targeted for evaluation were not perceived in a purely positive light. In one, attractive female targets were rated as more likely to be vain, snobbish, and poor marriage partners than less attractive female targets (Dermer & Thiel, 1975). In another, male and female targets were evaluated for managerial and nonmanagerial positions. Attractiveness was a consistent advantage for male candidates, but was an advantage for female candidates only when they were applying for a nonmanagerial position. The researchers hypothesized that more attractive women were perceived as more feminine, and thus better suited for gender-stereotypical jobs such as secretary (Heilman & Saruwatari, 1979). A different research team reported a similar pattern in perceptions of political candidates: attractiveness was consistently advantageous for men, but more attractive women candidates were seen as more feminine, and thus less qualified for the stereotypically masculine role of elected official (Sigelman et al., 1986). Although much of the research on attractiveness as a double bind for women was done in the 1970s and 1980s, its message is still relevant. Media attention to Hillary Clinton's pantsuits, Sarah Palin's hairstyle, and the shape of Michelle Obama's upper arms illustrate that women are still judged largely by their appearance.

The double bind of beauty creates practical dilemmas for women as they try to negotiate how much they should focus on looking sexy and attractive. There are no simple answers to these dilemmas. In one recent experiment, evaluations of sexily dressed women were different depending on whether they had high-status or low-status jobs. Participants evaluated a videotaped female target whose physical attractiveness was held constant, but who was dressed in sexy or businesslike attire and allegedly either a manager or a receptionist. Participants were more negative toward the sexily attired manager and rated her as less competent than the neutrally attired manager. In contrast, the dress style of the receptionist had no effect on their judgments of her likeability or competence. These findings suggest that a sexy self-presentation harms women in high-, but not low-, status jobs (Glick et al., 2005).

The Gender Management Game

Gender is an asset for men because masculinity is linked with perceptions of dominance, competence, and normative behavior. Gender is a liability for women because these dominant and masterful characteristics are still not equally valued in women, and the characteristics that *are* valued—a tentative, soft speech style, feminine attractiveness—are not always associated with competence. The ever-present possibility of being devalued, disliked, or discounted for behaving in ways that are acceptable for men means that women must adopt ***gender management strategies:*** ways of behaving that are aimed at softening a woman's impact, reassuring others that she is not threatening, and displaying niceness as well as (not too much) competence. It isn't easy; behaviors that make a woman appear more competent (like speaking up about her own ability) also may make her appear less likable (Rudman & Glick, 1999).

What happens to women who do not play the gender management game? An example is the case of Ann Hopkins, who was denied a partnership in a major corporation despite the fact that she had contributed more billable hours and brought in more earnings than any of the 87 male employees proposed for partner—$25 million in revenue (Fiske et al., 1991). The reason? Hopkins was told that she lacked interpersonal skills, ought to go to "charm school," wear makeup and jewelry, have her hair styled, and dress in more feminine clothes. Hopkins sued, and a group of eminent psychologists served as expert witnesses on her behalf when the case (*Hopkins v. Price Waterhouse*) went to the U.S. Supreme Court. Fortunately, the Court was not fooled by the excuses given for denying Hopkins her promotion. Ruling in her favor, they specifically pointed out the double bind she had been placed in:

> An employer who objects to aggressiveness in women but whose positions require this trait places women in an intolerable Catch-22: out of a job if they behave aggressively and out of a job if they don't (as cited in Fiske et al., 1991).

Gender Shapes Individuals

To a greater or lesser extent, women and men come to accept gender distinctions visible at the social structural level and enacted at the interpersonal level as part of the self-concept. This process is called ***gender typing.*** As individuals become ***gender-typed,*** they ascribe to themselves the traits, behaviors, and roles normative for people of their sex in their culture. Gender typing is an important part of identity for most people, and the topic has generated a great deal of psychological research. In Chapter 6, we will look in detail at the gender-typing process during childhood and adolescence. Here, in keeping with the theme of power and status, I focus on how women's subordinate status becomes internalized.

People accept much more than the traits designated as masculine or feminine in their culture. They also internalize the ideologies that support the gender system. These ideologies become consensual—they are shared by members of dominant and subordinate groups alike (Sidanius & Pratto, 1999). In other words, members of both the dominant and subordinate groups come to believe the legitimizing myths of the dominant group, and develop attitudes that serve to justify its dominance. When members of subordinate groups accept the myths that justify their inequality, the dominant group usually does not need to control them through force or other harsh methods. Instead, subordinates usually control themselves (Foucault, 1972; Marecek et al., 2004).

Identity, Power, and Gender Differences

Do women internalize their devaluation and subordination? Do they accept the legitimizing myths that keep them in their place? Jean Baker Miller (1986) has looked closely at the relationship between power and feminine personality. She proposed that because women are a subordinate group in society, they develop personality characteristics that reflect their subordination and enable them to cope with it.

Dominant groups define acceptable roles for subordinates, which usually involve services that the dominant group members do not want to perform for themselves. Thus, women, minorities, and poor people are more likely to be in low-status, low-paying jobs that often involve cleaning up the waste products of the dominant group or providing them with personal services. Roles and activities that are preferred are closed to subordinates. Subordinates are said to be unable to fill those roles, and the reasons given by the dominants usually involve subordinates' deficiencies of mind or body. In our society, the status and pay accorded nurses, teachers, homemakers, and child-care workers versus physicians, attorneys, carpenters, and auto mechanics reflect devaluation of "women's work," and it is easy to find people who believe that women are unsuited for certain prestigious or demanding jobs.

Being a subordinate has psychological consequences, too, according to Miller. Subordinates are encouraged to develop psychological characteristics that are useful and pleasing to the dominant group, and the ideal subordinate is described in terms of these characteristics, which

> form a certain familiar cluster: submissiveness, passivity, docility, dependency, lack of initiative, inability to act, to decide, to think, and the like . . . qualities more characteristic of children than adults—immaturity, weakness, and helplessness. If subordinates adopt these characteristics they are considered well-adjusted (1986, p. 7).

According to Miller, there are a great many women who believe, consciously or not, that they are less important than men. People in subordinate social groups may be the last to recognize their own predicament and may even participate in perpetuating it. Strange as it may seem, "oppression is very much a cooperative game" (Sidanius & Pratto, 1999, p. 43).

Denial of Personal Discrimination

The American legal system is based on the idea of fairness: If you believe you have been wronged or discriminated against, you have the right to seek justice.

Unfortunately, a large research literature in social psychology shows that victims of injustice often do not recognize that they are being treated unfairly.

It's not that people are blind to discrimination at the group level. If you ask Latino/as about racial discrimination in the United States, or ask women about sex discrimination, or ask gay and lesbian people about heterosexist discrimination, they are very likely to acknowledge that such discrimination does happen. However, when asked if they have ever *personally* been discriminated against, they are much less likely to acknowledge that it has happened to them. This discrepancy is termed ***denial of personal discrimination*** (Crosby et al., 2003).

Denial of personal discrimination is pervasive. It has been documented in women, ethnic and linguistic minorities in Canada, as well as women, gay and lesbian people, and African Americans in the United States (Crosby et al., 2003). In the first, now-classic, study (Crosby, 1982), a large sample of employed women and men in the northeastern United States were asked in detail about their perceptions of the position of working women and about their satisfaction with their own working position. The researcher was surprised to find that, although the employed women were, by objective measures, victims of salary discrimination, they weren't any less happy about their treatment at work than the men were. They did acknowledge the disadvantages faced by working women in general, but, "It seemed as if each woman saw herself as the one lucky exception to the general rule of sex discrimination" (Crosby et al., 2003, p. 104). Of course it is logically impossible for a group to be subject to discrimination and for every individual in that group to be exempt from it!

Denial of personal discrimination is probably related to the need to believe in a just world, where each person gets what he or she deserves (Crosby et al., 2003). It may also be related to shifting standards of evaluation—people may evaluate a salary of X dollars a week as merely adequate for a man but very good for a woman, instead of comparing them equally (Biernat & Kobrynowicz, 1999). And denial of personal discrimination is related to belief in the legitimizing myths of the dominant group. In other words, the more one accepts ideologies that justify the status quo of power and status, the less one perceives discrimination. This was tested in a study comparing high-status groups (European Americans and men) with low-status groups (African Americans, Latino/a Americans, and women). The more that members of low-status groups accepted the belief that America is an open society where anyone can get ahead if they just work hard enough, the less likely they were to report that they had experienced discrimination. Next, the researchers rigged a laboratory situation in which women experienced rejection by a man (not being offered a desirable job in the experiment) or men experienced the same rejection from a woman. The more a woman believed in the myth of the open society, the less likely she was to believe that her rejection was due to discrimination. In contrast, the more a man believed in the myth, the more likely he was to believe he'd been discriminated against. Thus, believing in upward mobility—the ideology of the dominant group—affects how people interpret whether they have experienced discrimination (Major et al., 2002).

Denial of personal discrimination has important social consequences. When members of subordinated groups do not have a sense of personal injustice, they may be slow to take action against their own disadvantaged situation. "Protests are not likely if the wronged party has little awareness of being wronged. It is hard to correct a problem if the problem goes unrecognized" (Crosby et al., 2003, p. 103).

How Much Is Your Work Worth? Gender and Entitlement

You are an employee in an assisted living facility for older adults. Your supervisor is considering offering the residents help with shopping and asks you to generate some ideas on whether it would be a good idea to encourage online shopping. Because it's an extra project, the supervisor asks you to suggest how much you think you should be paid for the task of writing down your thoughts on this issue.

In an experiment where the situation was similar to our example (Jost, 1997), the women who participated paid themselves 18 percent less and rated their ideas as less original than did the men, despite the fact that independent judges (who did not know the gender of the authors) rated the men's and women's work as equally good. Research studies have repeatedly shown that when women and men are asked to specify an appropriate pay rate for their work, women say their work is worth less than men do (Steil et al., 2001). They seem not to feel entitled to equality.

Women often justify the lower pay they give themselves by believing that their work is not as good as others' work, but even when they recognize that the quality of their work is equal, they still may pay themselves less (Major, 1994). Like denial of personal discrimination, this is a pervasive phenomenon that deters women from taking action or protesting against their subordinate status. Like denial, it may reflect internalization of the values of the dominant group.

Women's relative lack of entitlement is partly based on actual experience of lower pay. In one study, college students were asked about their expectations of earnings in the future. The women tended to believe that they deserved less than did the men. However, this gender difference in entitlement was accounted for by differences in the actual earnings from the students' most recent summer jobs, where the women had earned less than the men on average (Desmarais & Curtis, 1997). Gender differences in entitlement also reflect other kinds of status inequalities. When researchers experimentally raised women's status (by telling participants that women were particularly good at the task), the gender difference disappeared—high-status women paid themselves as much as men did (Hogue & Yoder, 2003).

Whatever the underlying reasons for denial of personal discrimination and gender differences in entitlement (and there may be several), these lines of research suggest that, as Miller's theory predicts, those who are treated like second-class citizens learn to accept inequality as the norm. When this happens, members of the dominant group may not even have to exercise prejudice and discrimination very often. They can count on members of the subordinate group to do it to themselves.

In later chapters we look at other gender-related differences that may reflect internalized subordination. Girls may lose self-esteem and confidence in their academic ability, especially in mathematics and science, as they progress through the educational system (Chapter 4) and are more likely to suffer from disturbances of body image, eating disorders, and depression (Chapters 3 and 13). These differences are not natural. They are shaped by differential opportunities and maintained in social interaction. They are the product of the gender system.

Sexist Attitudes

Sexist prejudice is not just a matter of men disliking women. Sexist attitudes are more complicated than that. Both women and men agree that women are generally nicer and more pleasant than men (Eagly & Mladinic, 1993). Moreover, attitudes toward women have changed in a positive direction over past decades. However, sexism persists. Today's sexism is likely to be more subtle and conflicted than the sexism of the past.

Contemporary sexism aimed at women is likely to be *ambivalent:* it involves both hostility and benevolence toward women (Glick & Fiske, 1996). *Hostile sexism* involves the beliefs that women are inferior and that they are threatening to take over men's rightful (dominant) place. People who score high on hostile sexism agree with statements like these:

- Women seek to gain power by getting control over men.
- Most women interpret innocent remarks or acts as being sexist.

Benevolent sexism emphasizes that women are special beings to be cherished and protected, as measured by items such as these:

- A good woman should be set on a pedestal by her man.
- Many women have a quality of purity that few men possess.

If benevolent sexism reflects a positive view that women should be cherished and protected by men, why is it a problem? Although benevolent sexism seems less harmful than hostile sexism, it has several insidious dangers. It exaggerates the differences between women and men (see Chapter 4). It may lead women to accept rules and regulations about where they can go and what they can do because "it's for your own good" (Moya et al., 2007). It may impair women's performance on cognitive tasks by causing them to doubt their ability (Dardenne et al., 2007). Moreover, people who are pure, innocent, fragile, and worthy of protection are not likely to be thought of as capable leaders. Being put on a pedestal may offer some compensation for the patriarchal status quo. However, life on a pedestal can be quite confining.

Men who endorse both kinds of sexism—termed *ambivalent sexists*—have polarized images of women. For example, they acknowledge that "career women" are intelligent and hardworking, but they also believe that they are aggressive, selfish, and cold. The women they feel the most positive about are those in roles that serve men's needs, such as homemakers and "sexy babes" (Glick et al., 1997). Ambivalent sexism is hard to change because benevolence is often not recognized as a form of prejudice by either women or men (Baretto & Ellmers, 2005). Thus, a sexist man can easily deny his prejudice. ("But I *love* women; I think they're wonderful and deserve to be treasured!") This paternalism may hinder him and others from recognizing the more hostile aspect of his sexism (". . . as long as they stay in their place").

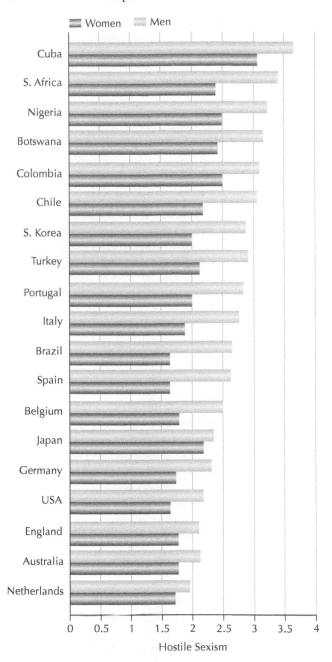

FIGURE 2.6 Hostile sexism across countries.

Source: From Glick, P., et al. (2000). Beyond prejudice as simple antipathy: Hostile and benevolent sexism across cultures. *Journal of Personality and Social Psychology, 79*, 770. Copyright © 2000 by the American Psychological Association, Inc. Reprinted with permission.

Ambivalent sexism has been measured in more than 15,000 people in 19 nations (though the samples were heavily weighted toward college students) (Glick et al., 2000). Both hostile and benevolent sexism were found to be quite common. In every country studied, men endorsed hostile sexism more than women did, although the gender differences were much larger in some countries (South Africa, Italy) than in others (England, the Netherlands). (See Figure 2.6.) Surprisingly, though, women endorsed benevolent sexism as much as men did in about half the countries studied—and in four countries, women scored higher than men did (see Figure 2.7). Patterns of correlations showed that the more sexist a nation's men were, the more women of that nation endorsed benevolent sexism.

Moreover, the differences among countries in this study were systematically related to women's status and power within each society. Using measures of gender inequality developed by the United Nations that assessed such factors as women's proportion of seats in parliament, earned income, literacy rates, and life expectancy, the research team found that the more that men in a given country endorsed sexist beliefs, the lower the status of women in that country.

Benevolent sexism is correlated with hostile sexism, and the two sustain patriarchy in complementary ways. Benevolent sexism rewards those women who accept conventional gender norms and power relations. Thus, women tend to endorse benevolent sexist beliefs when they think that the men around them do (Sibley et al., 2009). Hostile sexism punishes women who challenge the status quo. For example, when a sample of English college men read a scenario about an acquaintance rape, those who scored higher in hostile sexism were more likely to think that the victim's resistance was not sincere, and to say they might behave the same way as the rapist in the same situation (Masser et al., 2006). In societies where a great many men are hostile sexists, women may cope by believing that if they behave according to the societal rules for good women, they will be protected. "The irony is that women are forced to seek protection from the very group that threatens them, and the greater the threat, the stronger the incentive to accept benevolent sexism's protective ideology" (Glick & Fiske, 2001, p. 113).

Sexist attitudes such as these portray women as *either* competent and autonomous *or* likable and worthy, and they are one source of many double binds like those described earlier. Both hostile and benevolent sexism help perpetuate the higher status and social power of men.

Sexism is related to prejudice against other lower-status groups. *Social dominance orientation (SDO)* is a general measure of how much an individual supports the domination of supposedly inferior groups by superior groups (Sidanius & Pratto, 1999). SDO is relevant to many dimensions of discrimination, including race, religion, sexuality, gender, and nationality. People who are high in SDO tend to agree with statements like these:

- This country would be better off if inferior groups stayed in their place.
- To get ahead in life, it is sometimes necessary to step on other groups of people.

People who are high in SDO tend to show racial and ethnic prejudice, sexism, heterosexism, acceptance of rape myths, and political conservatism (Christopher & Mull, 2006). They tend to support social policies that favor

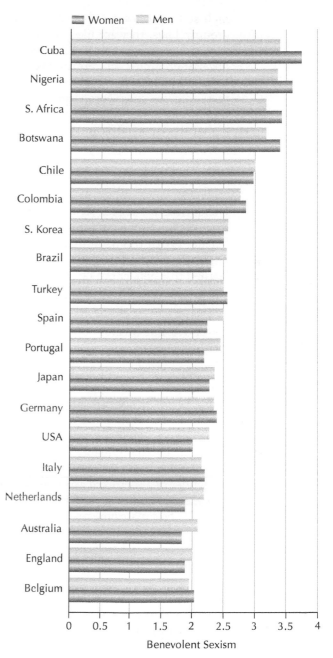

FIGURE 2.7 Benevolent sexism across countries.

Source: From Glick, P., et al. (2000). Beyond prejudice as simple antipathy: Hostile and benevolent sexism across cultures. *Journal of Personality and Social Psychology, 79,* 770. Copyright © 2000 by the American Psychological Association, Inc. Reprinted with permission.

high-status groups and oppose policies that would give more power to lower-status groups. Thus, they are likely to support more spending on prisons and the military, and oppose women's rights, gay and lesbian rights, universal health care, anti-poverty programs, and affirmative action. Men and women have been measured on SDO in 45 samples totaling over 19,000 participants in 10 countries. In 39 of these samples, men scored significantly higher on SDO than did women, and in 6, they scored about the same; there was not a single sample in which women scored higher than men (Sidanius & Pratto, 1999).

Linking the Levels of Gender: A Summary

Gender has a complex structure of meanings. Feminists initially distinguished it from sex by defining it as the traits and roles considered appropriate for males and females. With this definition, they emphasized that gender is a socialized part of self and identity. Today, the understanding of gender is much broader. We have learned that gender can be conceptualized as:

- A universal system of social classification that accords greater power and status to men
- A dynamic process of performing what it means to be female or male
- An aspect of individual identity and attitudes

When focusing on gender as a social system, we emphasized societal power structures that support patriarchy. When focusing on gender as a self-presentation and a performance, we emphasized the many small, almost invisible ways that people present themselves as gendered beings and conform to others' gender-based expectations, emphasizing that for women, doing gender also means doing subordination. The performance of gender is usually not a conscious, self-aware choice; rather it is a more or less automatic response to social pressures. When focusing on gender as a socialized aspect of individuals, we saw that both males and females become gender-typed—they become more or less acceptable examples of what it means to be a masculine man or a feminine woman in their particular culture. Gender becomes part of the self and identity. The three levels of the gender system are linked, reinforcing each other.

There is one important aspect of gender that characterizes all these levels: power. Patriarchy is a system that accords more power and higher social status to men. Gender is expressed differently in different societies, and the degree of women's subordination varies across time and place, but there are no known cultures where women have more social and political advantages than men.

Making a Difference

Women's movements around the world and across time have been made up of women and men working to secure equal human rights for all. The first wave of feminist activists included the suffragists who achieved the vote for women in the early 1900s. The second wave, whose activism began in the 1960s, worked on reproductive rights, workplace equality, sexism in the media, and an end to violence against women. Many younger women identify as third-wave feminists who are defining their own goals for the next round of social change.

Transforming Ourselves

Most women have internalized at least some of the sexist messages of our culture. As documented in this chapter, some doubt their abilities or do not feel entitled to equal treatment. The chapters that follow document that many women feel shame about their bodies, their sexuality, or the normal changes of aging; feel guilt about not being perfect mothers; or blame themselves for having been subjected to rape, incest, or sexual harassment. This self-hatred is fostered by exposure to media images (Chapter 3), gender socialization in childhood and adolescence (Chapter 6), and the experience of having lower status and power in everyday interactions and relationships.

What can women do to change these beliefs and attitudes? In the 1970s, second-wave feminists developed *consciousness-raising (C-R) groups,* in which women met informally to talk about their lives as women. Women who took part in these groups began to see that their problems were not just individual deficiencies but were related to society's devaluation of women. Consciousness-raising groups encouraged social action, leading to such activities as opening shelters for battered women and protesting against sexist advertising. However, as women made some social progress in the 1970s and 1980s, many of these groups became more individually focused and then disappeared altogether (Kahn & Yoder, 1989). Nevertheless, many organizations working for social change have incorporated the values and norms of C-R groups into their process.

C-R groups often led to positive changes for the women in them, including an altered worldview, greater awareness of sexism, positive changes in self-image, increased self-acceptance, and increased awareness of anger (Kravetz, 1980). Consciousness-raising became a model for feminist therapy because it offered women an opportunity to share experiences without being treated as patients and because C-R groups assumed that the social environment plays a major role in women's problems and difficulties (Brodsky, 1973). Today, although C-R groups are no longer a popular resource, feminist counseling and therapy empower women who want to make changes in their lives (see Chapter 13).

Although relatively few women take part in feminist therapy, many develop political and personal values compatible with feminism in other ways. Some women develop feminist values after having personal experiences with sexism. These negative experiences can lead to transformative moments in which a woman suddenly realizes that she lives in a sexist society and wants to change it, not just for herself but also for other women (Cole et al., 2001).

Still another route to feminist consciousness and activism is education. When people learn to think critically about the gender system, they may become motivated to work for social justice. The growth of women's studies programs and courses focusing on women and gender may be filling some of the gap left by the disappearance of C-R groups (Cole et al., 2001; Davis et al., 1999). Women's studies classes often provide powerful consciousness raising (James, 1999). In one study, taking a single women's studies course led to a decrease in the passive acceptance of sexism, an increase in commitment to feminism, and plans for social activism (Bargad & Hyde, 1991).

Do women's studies courses change men's attitudes? In one study, the attitudes of male students changed in a profeminist direction, but not as much as the attitudes of female students (Steiger, 1981). However, most women's studies classes do not include enough male students to provide an adequate research sample. There is a need for more and better research on how to change men's attitudes toward women, both inside and outside the classroom.

Transforming Interpersonal Relations

As this chapter has shown, gender inequity is reproduced in everyday interactions with others, often outside our awareness. Even the most well-meaning people can respond to others in sexist ways, and sexist patterns of interaction lead to self-fulfilling prophecies. These social processes are largely invisible and taken for granted.

Doing gender can be disrupted when people become more aware of how the gender system operates. One important strategy for change is to pay attention to how we often respond to others as members of a category (see Chapter 3). Knowing how power and attractiveness create double binds for women can help change the categorization processes that create sex discrimination. Psychological research on power and stereotyping was influential in the Supreme Court decision in the Price-Waterhouse v. Ann Hopkins case, in which Hopkins won the partnership she had earned (Fiske et al., 1991).

When awareness of sexism is raised, small acts of resistance can follow. Writer Gloria Steinem called this kind of resistance "outrageous acts and everyday rebellions" (Steinem, 1983). For example, everyday ways of doing gender are disrupted when people refuse to be cooperative or silent in the face of sexism. It isn't easy to speak up when you hear a sexist remark. However, research has shown that it can be effective. Confronting prejudice is most likely to change attitudes when the confrontation is nonthreatening in tone and when it comes from someone who is not a member of the target group (Monteith & Czopp, 2003). In other words, White people who speak out against racism, men who speak out against sexism, and straight people who speak out against heterosexism may be particularly likely to be heard—especially if they do it with respect and tact.

As another kind of "everyday rebellion," you might try disrupting gender norms. (What happens when a woman holds the door open for a man, or pays the bar tab for both?) One feminist proposed a "smile boycott": for an entire day, try smiling only when you are genuinely pleased, and keep a journal about your own and others' reactions. Do you think the results would be different for males and females who decline to smile?

People can also rely on the power of collective action—working together for social justice. For example, although not everyone can run for the Senate, each of us can donate time or money to political candidates who share our values. We can unite with others who may be devalued for their differences, working to end racism and heterosexism. Both women and men can support others who work for change; in particular, women can choose to support and mentor each other. The motto of one feminist organization that provides leadership seminars for women is "Lift as you climb."

Transforming the Structures of Inequality

Transforming gender at the social structural level is linked with the individual and interactional transformations just described. When people are empowered as individuals, they can speak out against injustice, and they can begin to change the institutions, laws, customs, and norms that harm girls and women. The effect is reciprocal, as speaking out leads to increased feelings of self-efficacy and empowerment.

However, social change is not easy; attempts to change power relations almost always provoke backlash. Certainly, there has been a strong backlash against each wave of feminist activism throughout history. Today, the backlash ranges from repeated media claims that "feminism is dead" to the murder of doctors connected with women's health clinics. Moreover, change does not always result in progress. Feminist activists worked for no-fault divorce laws, only to find that they worsened the economic consequences of divorce for women (see Chapter 8). When Title IX legislated equality in sports opportunity in schools and colleges, the number of coaching positions for women's sports rose—but men took 75 percent of the new jobs. Attempts to change society must be reevaluated periodically to judge whether they have had their intended effects and also whether they have had unanticipated negative effects. Fortunately, social science research can help find the answers.

As feminism becomes a more global movement, the status of women in other nations become more visible (Kristoff & WuDunn, 2009). Many societies deny women basic human rights such as freedom of movement, education, and a voice in government. Feminist activist groups have intervened in such human rights violations as the sexual slavery trade that takes Asian girls as young as nine to brothels in India, Thailand, and other countries. They have founded organizations to rescue these girls and provide them with education and medical care. Moreover, they speak up about the pervasive devaluing of females that underlies the slave trade in girls. Other activists are working on issues such as sweatshop labor in Asian countries, female genital surgery in African countries, and rape as a tactic of war around the world. Yet global feminism may bring troubling questions of who is entitled to define a problem and whose viewpoint should determine what constitutes a solution. For example, Western feminists may be appalled by compulsory female genital surgery, but the women who perpetuate it may see themselves as protecting their daughters from social rejection (Chapter 7). Whose viewpoint should prevail?

New women's issues, reflecting the differences in women's positions in diverse cultures, continue to emerge. The Internet is a powerful tool for connecting activists around the world and creating dialogue among diverse groups of women. For example, organizations such as Women Leaders Online/Women Organizing for Change draw attention to human rights abuses and provide information on how women can make their voices heard in protest.

Many societies now guarantee women equal rights under the law. Some have recognized the need to remedy existing imbalances in political power by mandating women's participation in government. For example, in Norway, a fixed proportion of political candidates from major parties *must* be women. The United States has a much less activist approach to integrating women into positions of political and social power. However, the Supreme Court has ruled in support of affirmative action plans that seek to monitor fairness in access to education and employment (Crosby, 2004).

An end to patriarchal inequality is still a vision for the future, and not yet a reality. The global feminist vision is one of a just and caring society "that will give not only to men but also to women, bread and roses, poetry and power" (Alindogan-Medina, 2006, p. 57). Nobel Peace Prize Laureate and leader of Burma's democracy movement, Aung San Suu Kyi, put it this way: "The education and empowerment of women throughout the world cannot fail to result in a more caring, tolerant, just and peaceful life for all."

Exploring Further

∽

Brodsky, A. (2003). *With all our strength: The revolutionary association of the women of Afghanistan.* New York: Routledge.
This book documents the courage and fortitude of Afghani women under the Taliban, as they risked their lives to support other women during an extremely oppressive regime.

Paludi, M. (2010). (Ed.) *Feminism and women's rights worldwide.* Santa Barbara: Praeger.
This comprehensive three-volume set is an excellent collection of chapters by some of the best researchers in the field. It provides an in-depth look at what has been accomplished by feminist activism and what still needs to be done.

Society for the Psychological Study of Social Issues, http://www.spssi.org
APA's Division 9, SPSSI is an international group of psychologists and other social scientists who share a common concern with research on psychological aspects of important social issues facing social groups, communities, our nation, and the world. SPSSI publishes the *Journal of Social Issues* and welcomes student members.

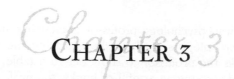

CHAPTER 3

Images of Women

Mary Crawford and Britain Scott

- **Words Can Never Hurt Me?**
  Language about Women and Men
- **Worth a Thousand Words: Media Images**
  Representing Women and Men
  Face-ism
  Sexual Objectification
  Invisible Women
- **Stereotypes about Women and Men**
  The Content of Gender Stereotypes
  Sexuality Stereotypes
  Race and Social Class Stereotypes
  Are Stereotypes Accurate?
  Stereotypes Are Hard to Change
- **The Impact of Stereotypes**
  Stereotypes, the Self, and Stereotype Threat
  Stereotypes, Status, and Power
  Stereotypes and Sexist Behavior
  How *Not* to Stereotype
- **Making a Difference**
  Transforming Language
  Challenging Objectification
- **Exploring Further**

- An African American psychology professor is enjoying attending a national convention for psychologists until, as she is leaving the hotel restaurant, a White woman asks the professor to show her to a table. Although she was wearing a suit and carrying an armful of books, the professor had been mistaken for a waitress (West, 2008).
- In the film *Legally Blonde*, Elle (Reese Witherspoon) has to work harder than all the other students at Harvard Law. She's smart enough, but she's also blonde and pretty. Stereotyped as a "dumb blonde," she gets little respect.
- Charlene, who loves sports cars, is ready to buy one. When she goes into the auto showroom, one salesperson asks if the car is for her boyfriend, and another asks if she knows how to drive a stick shift.

*T*hese examples illustrate the power of cultural beliefs about women. Whether we like it or not, we are affected by societally prevalent views of women (and men). This chapter describes how verbal, visual, and mental representations of women in our culture affect how women feel about themselves and how we all think about, and behave toward, women.

Words Can Never Hurt Me?

When people use language to communicate with others, they make choices that are not only practical but also political. The term ***linguistic sexism*** refers to inequitable treatment of women and men that is built into the language. Feminists have worked to draw attention to sexist language and to change it (Crawford, 2001).

Language about Women and Men

In the 1970s, research on linguistic sexism identified several varieties. Researchers found that language patterns sometimes trivialized women, with gender-marked terms such as *steward* and *stewardess*. Other terms sexualized and devalued women. There were far more negative sexual terms in English for women than for men, and words referring to women tended to acquire more negative meanings over time (Schultz, 1975). (See Box 3.1.) Linguistic sexism also marked both women and men who deviated from expected occupations and roles with terms such as "career woman" and "male nurse."

Some of these practices have changed, but the transition to nonsexist language is not complete. For example, *stewardess* has been replaced by the gender-neutral *flight attendant*, but women's sports teams are still the "Bronco-ettes" or the "Lady Lions." One college has "Lady Rams," which doesn't even make anatomical sense! Let's look at other varieties of linguistic sexism.

Mrs. Man

Language traditionally marked women as the possessions of men. Until recently, a woman's marital status was designated by the use of *Mrs.* or *Miss*; *Mr.*, the corresponding title for men, was neutral with respect to marital status. When feminists proposed *Ms.* as a parallel term to *Mr.*, they were accused of being dangerous radicals bent on mutilating the English language (Crawford et al., 1998). Women who used *Ms.* were seen as more masculine and less likable than women who stuck to the traditional titles (Dion, 1987). Although *Ms.* has become much more accepted, a recent study found that women who used it were still seen as more masculine and less feminine than those who used *Mrs.* or *Miss* (Malcolmson & Sinclair, 2007).

The practice of a woman taking her husband's name upon marriage is a heritage of patriarchy. The majority of women still follow this custom, and choosing to keep one's own name is controversial because of its symbolic meaning. Because of this, some married women change their name depending on the situation. For example, a woman may hyphenate her name in some situations but not others, or use her husband's name in family contexts and her birth name in professional contexts. In a study of 600 married women, about 12 percent engaged in name shifting (Scheuble & Johnson, 2005). This shifting may reflect women's ambiguity about their identity as wives versus individuals, or their concern that others might disapprove of their naming choices.

For same-sex couples, changing names does not carry patriarchal baggage, and there is no social pressure to do so. In a study of 30 lesbian and gay couples in committed relationships, only one woman had changed her name, and most had no plans to do so, although some participants said they would consider hyphenating their names. The main reasons they gave for choosing to keep their own names were maintaining personal and professional identities, avoiding hassles, and resisting heterosexual norms (Clarke et al., 2008).

He/Man Language

In many languages, the word for *man* is used to refer to humans in general—in Spanish, it's *hombre*, in French, *homme*, in Italian, *uomo*. In English, this generic use of *man* was long commonplace in academic as well as everyday language—as in "a history of man," "the rights of man," and "the man in the street." Because English does not have a gender-neutral singular pronoun, speakers must choose either *he* or *she* (contrary to popular usage, "they" is not singular); traditionally, *he* was chosen to refer to both males and females.

Unfortunately, these "generic" masculine terms are not really generic at all. A great deal of research over the past 35 years has shown that when people read *he, his,* and *man,* they think of men, not people in general (Henley, 1989; Gygax et al., 2008). Moreover, this interpretation affects their behavior. When male and female college students read an essay titled "The Psychologist and His Work," which used *he* throughout, the women later remembered the facts in the essay more poorly than when they had read the same essay in a gender-inclusive (*he or she*) version—despite the fact that they could not remember which form they'd read. The differential language had no effects on memory among the men (Crawford & English, 1984).

There may be a cognitive bias that goes beyond language. Even when they hear gender-neutral terms, people may still assume a male is the subject. This **people = male bias** has been demonstrated in multiple languages, including English, French, German, and Norwegian (Gygax et al., 2008; Merritt & Kok, 1995; Silveira, 1980; Gabriel & Gygax, 2008). For example, when participants read a set of gender-neutral instructions and were then asked to describe a (sex-unspecified) character, they produced three times as many spontaneous descriptions of males as females (Hamilton, 1991).

There is even an **animal = male bias.** When children in three age groups and adults were shown stuffed toys (a dog, a deer, a mouse, and so on) and asked to tell stories about them, both children and adults showed an overwhelming bias toward using masculine pronouns. For example, 100 percent of 3- to 10-year-old children and 100 percent of adults used *he* to refer to a teddy bear. Preschool-age children used *he* to refer to a dog (100 percent), a mouse (95 percent), a deer (87 percent), a snail (94 percent), and a butterfly (88 percent). Only cats were seen as (sometimes) female, mostly by girls. Even when the experimenters tried to disrupt the bias by using feminine pronouns to introduce the animals ("Here is a panda bear. She's eating bamboo now, but she had fish for breakfast"), 100 percent of the children still used masculine pronouns in their own stories (Lambdin et al., 2003).

Babes, Chicks, Ho's and Bitches

Slang referring to women is much more likely to have sexual meaning than is slang referring to men (Crawford & Popp, 2003). Some sexualized terms refer to women as body parts, from the relatively mild *skirt* and *tail* to *piece of ass* and *cunt.* When students were asked to list slang terms for both sexes, 50 percent of the terms for women had sexual connotations, compared to 23 percent of the terms for men (Grossman & Tucker, 1997). The most common terms for women were *chick, bitch, babe,* and *slut;* for men, they were *guy, dude, boy,* and *stud.* As these examples show, the terms for women are not only more sexual, but more negative.

Terms that belittle women, like *babe* and *doll,* communicate women's lower social status relative to men. Other terms dehumanize women or their body parts by referring to them as animals: think of *chick*, *bitch*, *cow*, *pussy*, and *beaver*. Terms that describe women as food, such as *honey* in the United States and *tart* in the United Kingdom, imply that women are to be consumed by men. All the linguistic biases described so far add up to real, though sometimes subtle, forms of discrimination. Let's look at a specific arena in which language treats men as the norm and women as deviants: media coverage of athletes.

Venus and Mr. Federer: Describing Female and Male Athletes

Media descriptions of female athletes differ from descriptions of male athletes in several ways. Female athletes and their sports are asymmetrically **gender marked** when reporters use terms such as "basketball" and "women's basketball" to refer to men's and women's sports, respectively; the underlying message is that men's basketball is the norm while women's is the variation (Messner et al., 1993). A 2010 *Sports Illustrated* cover headlined Linsdsey Vonn as "America's Best Woman Skier," though few men could compete with her. The relative social power of women and men is subtly communicated when commentators refer to female athletes as girls, but do not call male athletes boys, or when they use the women's first names (Ana, Serena, Svetlana) but the men's last names and title (Federer or Mr. Federer) (Koivula, 1999).

The achievements and losses of women athletes are often described in gender-typical and trivializing ways (Messner et al., 1993). When figure skater Sarah Hughes triumphed at the 2002 Olympics, the *Boston Globe* described her gold medal as a "highly prized bauble," a term generally reserved for costume jewelry. In Spanish coverage of the 2004 Olympics, many defeated sportswomen were described as "crying" or "in tears" while their tearful male counterparts were labeled "exhausted" and "distraught" (Crolley & Teso, 2007). And, in the 2010 Olympics, an announcer referred to Lindsey Vonn and Julia Mancuso as "ski divas." Apparently, barreling down a mountain on two sticks at 70 miles an hour means you are a drama queen, not an athlete.

Often, media commentary focuses on women athletes' physical appearance and sex appeal more than on their performance (Kane, 1996; Messner et al., 2003). When high school basketball player Candace Parker became the first girl to win the McDonalds All-American slam dunk contest in 2004, one judge commented that now he expected a "bevy of lovely ladies" would follow in her footsteps (Block, 2004). Chinese diver Guo Jingjing, winner of two 2004 gold medals, was described by the *Chinese Sports Daily* as "Beautiful Goddess on the Springboard" (Wu, 2009). Moreover, like other female public figures, female athletes are more likely than male athletes to be identified as parents or spouses in media reports (Koivula, 1999). In the 2010 Olympics, a male announcer described a six-time world champion skier as "the 33-year-old mother of a 10-year-old." The implicit message is that these women may violate traditional gender roles by being athletic, but they still have traditional heterosexual appeal, so their athleticism is tolerable.

Are we affected by language about female athletes? A recent study at four-year colleges and universities in the southern United States found a negative correlation between the use of sexist team names, such as those described earlier, and athletic opportunities for women students (Pelak, 2008). The lack of opportunities cannot be attributed to the team names, but both reinforce a cultural bias against women's sports participation. Two studies on the impact of descriptions of female athletes found that when a woman athlete was described in terms of her attractiveness, both male and female readers perceived her as more attractive but as less talented and aggressive; women athletes described as heterosexual were considered more ideal, more physically attractive, and more respectable than those whose sexual orientation was left unspecified (Knight and Giuliano, 2001; 2003).

Worth a Thousand Words: Media Images

Every day, each of us is exposed to hundreds of images of women and men, most of them from the mass media: television, newspapers, magazines, movies, comics, video games, billboards, and the Internet. Most of the time, we pay little attention to these images; however, media images of women and men create a distorted reality that does affect us. Let's look more closely at media images of women compared to those of men.

Representing Women and Men

In general, women are underrepresented in the media. About 51 percent of the population is female, yet females appear in media less often than males. For example, a survey of prime-time TV characters from 1993–2004 showed an average of 39 percent female over this time span, an improvement over the 35 percent average found between 1966–1992, but still far from representative (Greenberg & Worrell, 2007). And it's not just the shows; women are underrepresented in commercials for all types of goods except health and beauty products, and this gap has not changed since first measured in the 1980s (Ganahl et al., 2003). Similar patterns of underrepresentation have been shown in other countries, including Great Britain and Saudi Arabia (Nassif & Gunter, 2008), Kenya (Mwangi, 1996), Portugal (Neto & Pinto, 1998), and Japan, where the ratio of males to females on TV is 2:1 (Suzuki, 1995). No form of media is immune to the underrepresentation bias. (See Figure 3.1a and b.) Women and girls are even underrepresented in the comics (LaRossa et al., 2001), in children's picture books (Hamilton et al., 2006), and on cereal boxes (Black et al., 2009).

Sheer numbers may be the least of the problems in media depictions of women. Media images portray women and men quite differently in personality attributes. When researchers analyzed the portrayal of women and men in 1,600 commercials shown on popular TV shows, both the White and African American male characters were more aggressive, active, and gave more orders than female characters did. The White female characters, but not the African American ones, were more passive and emotional than the male characters (Coltrane & Messineo, 2000).

The media also show women and men in different settings and occupations. For example, one study examined nearly 8,000 illustrations of men in magazines aimed at women, men, and general readers. In male-oriented magazines, men were almost always shown in work and occupational roles, almost never as husbands

FIGURE 3.1a
This photo of Ivan Pavlov and his colleagues in his lab appeared in an introductory psychology textbook used by thousands of psychology students.

or fathers. Images of men with their families or taking care of children showed up only in women's magazines (Vigorito & Curry, 1998). Women's work, in contrast, is downplayed. TV ads are less likely to show women than men at their jobs (Coltrane & Adams, 1997) and more likely to show women than men at home (Coltrane & Messineo, 2000). The most recent studies available reconfirm this bias. Using a sample of 124 prime-time TV programs from 2005 and 2006, researchers found that female characters are still mainly shown as involved with romance, family, and friends, while male characters are mainly shown in work roles (Lauzen et al., 2008).

These differential gender portrayals occur cross-culturally. In India, for example, TV ads portray women almost exclusively in contexts of choosing products to make them better housekeepers and mothers (Roy, 1998). In Japan, just as in the United States, most women work outside the home, but a study of Japanese TV ads showed that depictions of workers were predominantly male (Arima, 2003).

FIGURE 3.1b
Unfortunately, some of Pavlov's colleagues were erased from the historical record. This is the original, complete photo. How might the selective elimination of women in the history of psychology affect students' attitudes and beliefs about women scientists?

In a comparison of TV ads in Great Britain and Saudi Arabia, women appeared more often in domestic settings, and less often at work or leisure, than men, and were much more likely to promote products for body care and household cleaning (Nassif & Gunter, 2008).

Face-ism

Some differences in how the media represent men and women are less obvious than others. Although most people do not notice, the composition of images of men and women is quite different. This phenomenon has been termed *face-ism* (Archer et al., 1983). Face-ism is measured as the proportion of the overall image devoted to the face.

As Figure 3.2 illustrates, the facial prominence in published images is usually higher for men. In a study of more than 1,700 photos from magazines and newspapers, the average index for men was .65, and for women only .45. In other words, two-thirds of a typical photo image of a man featured his face, while less than half of a typical image of a woman featured hers (Archer et al., 1983).

How prevalent is face-ism? A look at photos published in 11 different countries found similar results—more facial prominence for men. The researchers also examined paintings in art museums, finding that face-ism has occurred from the

FIGURE 3.2   Face-ism in images of women and men.

17th century onward and increased over time (Archer et al., 1983). In a study of news magazines, the face-ism index favored not only men over women but also European American over African American people; Black women had the lowest face-ism index of all (Zuckerman & Kieffer, 1994). Face-ism favoring men even occurs in women's magazines (Nigro et al., 1988).

Research on face-ism has been done since the 1980s. Today, it is still very easy to find examples of face-ism everywhere from advertising to politics. In one recent study, titled "Do male politicians have big heads?" researchers analyzed online head shots of political figures (governors, senators, members of Parliament, and so on) in Canada, Australia, and Norway. In all countries, male politicians had greater facial prominence than female politicians, even when actual differences in body size and proportion were controlled (Konrath & Schwarz, 2007). Another researcher analyzed nearly 800 photos from news articles in *Time*, *Newsweek*, *People*, and other popular U.S. magazines (Matthews, 2007). When the occupation depicted in the photo was intellectually focused (politician, scientist), men's faces were more prominent than women's, and when it was physically focused (sports figure), men's bodies were more prominent than women's. These results show that even when women and men are in similar occupations, they are depicted differently.

Furthermore, men are shown as having more of the crucial attribute for each kind of occupation—whether it was intelligence or physical competence.

Why should we care about face-ism? It can have real effects on how individuals are evaluated by others. We tend to associate a person's individuality, personality, and intelligence with his or her face. When students were asked to rate the same people shown in different photos, they rated an individual higher on dominance, ambition, and intelligence when the photo had a higher face-ism index (Archer et al., 1983; Zuckerman & Kieffer, 1994). In other words, seeing more face and less body in an image leads us to think of the person as more outstanding in character and ability. The widespread tendency to show more of men's faces and women's bodies may function without our awareness to focus attention on men's character and women's physical characteristics.

Sexual Objectification

Women's bodies are not just pictured more than men's, they are also *sexualized* more than men's. Overall, one of every four White women and one in 10 Black women in U.S. television commercials is dressed or posed in a sexually provocative way, compared with one in 14 men (Coltrane & Messineo, 2000). In ads, women are often shown partially undressed or completely nude, even when revealing the body has nothing to do with using the product. Content analyses of international television and magazine advertising suggest that although levels of female nudity vary across cultures, more female than male nudity is cross-culturally universal (Nelson & Paek, 2005; 2008).

When women's bodies are sexualized in media, the women themselves are often reduced to those bodies—or even just parts of them (see Figure 3.3). This is what is meant by *sexual objectification*. Popular films and television shows sexually objectify women more than men, and entire shows dedicated to women's bodies as entertainment are commonplace. Today, in addition to traditional beauty pageants (Miss America), we have fitness competitions, swimsuit specials, and the *Victoria's Secret Fashion Show*. Popular men's lifestyle magazines such as *FHM*, *Maxim*, and *Stuff* typically feature a scantily clad, sexually posed woman on the cover—and more inside (Krassas et al., 2003). Sources like Spike TV, iPhone applications like "Bikini Blast" and "iStrip," and countless Internet sites offer an endless supply of sexually objectified women.

Portraying women as sex objects may be increasingly widespread, but it is not new; something that *is* relatively new is the objectification of *virtual* women. Since the early days of animation, artists have drawn caricatures of women and female creatures (e.g., Minnie Mouse), but only few of these early renderings were intended to be sex objects (e.g., Betty Boop). Over time, however, the sexualization of female cartoon characters has become commonplace. Compare Disney's *Snow White* (1937) with *The Little Mermaid* (1989) and the contrast is stark: Snow White's dress modestly covers her child-like figure while the hourglass-shaped mermaid is all but busting out of her shell-bra. These days, with computer software or Internet sites like myvirtualbabes.com, even amateur artists can create virtual sex objects according to their own specifications.

FIGURE 3.3   Objectified women.
(left) A fashion model's body is used as canvas for paint and glued-on beads. But at least she has a head—unlike the woman on the right.

Every day we gaze upon myriad objectified images of women. These images not only reduce women to their bodies, they represent women unrealistically—in idealized and distorted ways.

Idealization and Distortion

Media have long been saturated with idealized images of feminine beauty (Banner, 2006). Consider the corseted Gibson Girl of the 1890s, the boyish flapper of the 1920s, the full-figured pin-up of the 1950s, Twiggy in the 1960s, and the ultraslim yet busty models of today. Ideals have changed with the fashions, but what hasn't changed is the fact that all have required substantial modification of women's natural appearance.

Importantly, the idealized standards that surround us today are unattainable by live women. For decades, the beauty and fashion industries have employed heavy makeup, deceptive clothing, artful lighting, careful posing, and photo retouching to create ideal images. In recent years, however, digital technology has taken this to a new level, allowing radical alteration and complete fabrication of images of women without viewers realizing how artificial the images are. In real life, even actresses and models don't look like the images we see. In the publicity shots for the film King Arthur, for example, before-and-after photos published online showed that actress Keira Knightley was gifted by the photo retoucher with not only flawless skin but also with bigger breasts, thinner arms, and a smaller waist (Borland, 2008).

The contemporary ideal is characterized by extreme thinness, but this has not always been the case. Published body measurements of Playboy centerfold models and Miss America contestants have shrunk over the past 40 years. Many current models meet the weight criteria for anorexia. At the same time, the actual body size of adult Americans has gotten heavier (Garner et al., 1980; Owen & Laurel-Seller, 2000; Spitzer et al., 1999). The latest version of the ideal woman is not only extremely thin but also large-breasted—a size 4 in the hips, 2 in the waist, and 10 in the bust (Harrison, 2003). Of course, this figure rarely occurs in nature—it must be created through surgical intervention. In a sample of college students, both men and women who had more exposure to ideal images on television showed higher levels of approval for women's use of cosmetic surgeries such as liposuction and breast augmentation (Harrison, 2003). It seems that the more TV you watch, the more you believe that real women's bodies are just not good enough.

We are so accustomed to unrealistic images of women that we may not take notice when a representation of a woman's body has been so drastically altered it no longer resembles a human being. When women see Steve Madden ads that feature models proportioned like Bratz dolls, they buy shoes instead of cringing in horror! Sometimes representations of women's bodies are turned into actual objects. A couple of recent innovations include mousepads picturing attractive models with 3-D squishy breasts or buttocks on which the user can rest his wrist and a remote control in the shape of a buxom bikini-clad woman's torso. Women's body parts turned into actual objects are the epitome of objectification.

How does it impact women to be surrounded by idealized, sexualized, and dehumanized versions of themselves? How are women's perceptions of their bodies shaped by being treated as objects? How does the objectification of women's bodies affect their social interactions? We will address these questions by exploring research on women's objectification.

Body Image

The term *body image* refers both to the mental picture one has of one's appearance and the associated feelings about the size, shape, and attractiveness of one's body (Dorian & Garfinkel, 2002). Many researchers have studied the link between body image and overall self-esteem and most have found that women are more strongly invested in their physical appearance and are more dissatisfied with their bodies than men are. These concerns begin in childhood and extend across the lifespan (e.g., Murnen et al., 2003). And they occur in every ethnic group. A review of nearly 100 studies of body dissatisfaction showed that White, Asian American and Hispanic women had similar levels of body dissatisfaction. African American women were only slightly less dissatisfied with their bodies (Grabe & Hyde, 2006).

Many theorists attribute the gender discrepancy in body image, at least in part, to the impact of idealized beauty images on women. Men do sometimes express dissatisfaction with aspects of their bodies, such as muscularity and body size (e.g., Vartanian et al., 2001)—the very aspects that are becoming increasingly emphasized in idealized media images of men (Daniel & Bridges, 2010; Leit et al., 2002).

Numerous experiments that have exposed women to images of attractive models and then measured their self-esteem, perceptions of their own attractiveness, and mood have found significant negative effects (Grabe et al., 2008; Groesz et al., 2002). Most researchers theorize that these negative effects are the result of the *social comparison* process (Want, 2009). That is, idealized beauty images make women feel bad because their own appearance suffers by comparison. But, there may be more going on than social comparison. In their original context, beauty images are often accompanied by messages that relentlessly remind women that attractiveness is central to femininity, that it matters in every situation, that it is what matters most in women, and that you cannot be beautiful unless you alter the natural body. Perhaps ideal images presented in the laboratory negatively impact women not merely because they set a high standard of comparison, but also because they remind women of these more general messages and of their objectified status.

Some studies on women's responses to idealized images have found no effects or *positive* effects. Why these inconsistencies? One factor that seems to matter is a woman's level of body dissatisfaction at the outset. Women who are more dissatisfied with their bodies respond more negatively to ideal images in experiments and in real life. Another factor is the instructions given to participants. Negative effects are more likely when the participant is *not* thinking about the images in terms of appearance (Want, 2009). This may be counterintuitive, but it seems that the social comparison process is automatic. Actually thinking about that gorgeous model in the image may help women consciously override the tendency to compare themselves with her.

Most of the research on the impact of media images has been done with White college students. But women of color are affected, too. African American teens are larger consumers of mass media than comparable White teens, and highly likely to be exposed to images of highly sexually objectified Black women. In a survey of African American high school girls, their concerns about appearance were predicted by how much they identified with their favorite Black TV character and female music artist (Gordon, 2008). For example, those with greater Black media identification were more likely to agree with statements such as, "Using her looks is the best way for a girl to attract a guy."

As Western media images of women spread across the globe, we may see a worldwide increase in women's body dissatisfaction. Fashion magazines sold in Tibet these days have White European models on the cover (Etcoff, 1999). In China, there is a massive marketing of cosmetics to help women create a Westernized appearance (Johansson, 2001). Although makeup was banned after the Iranian Islamic revolution in 1979, Iran now ranks as the second largest cosmetics market in the middle east (AFP, 2010). Even in the small Himalayan country of Nepal, women are participating in beauty contests where they are judged by Western norms, and are beginning to report body dissatisfaction and disordered eating (Crawford et al., 2008; 2009).

Self-Objectification

Psychologists Barbara Frederickson and Tomi-Ann Roberts's (1997) **objectification theory** explains that in a sexually objectifying culture, girls and women learn to "internalize an observer's perspective as a primary view of their physical selves" (p. 1): they engage in **self-objectification**. This idea is not original to Frederickson and Roberts—many writers and researchers before them have described how women perceive themselves as objects that exist to be evaluated by others (e.g., Beauvoir, 1953; Berger, 1972; McKinley & Hyde, 1996)—but objectification theory is important because it delineates the psychological and behavioral consequences of self-objectification.

Self-objectification involves habitual and chronic preoccupation with self-surveillance that disrupts a woman's connection to her subjective experiences and divides her attention. Continual body monitoring not only creates a sort of splitting of self—between the subjective self and the self as object—it also claims cognitive resources and interrupts thinking with feelings about appearance concern. Here are a few examples of U.S. women describing their habitual self-surveillance and body shame:

> If there is a mirror, I will most likely do a quick glance to make sure that my looks are in order (i.e., hair in place, no lipstick on the teeth or smudged makeup) . . . it boosts my confidence to periodically look at myself and reassure myself that I look good. (A 26-year-old.)

> I look and compare myself to other women constantly. (A 24-year-old.)

> I find my weight to be an obsession. I think of it at least 20 times per day. This makes me think that there is something wrong with me psychologically. (A 45-year-old.) (Crawford et al., 2009)

These theorists suggest that self-objectification divides attention between self-surveillance and other mental tasks. We know from cognitive psychology that our mental resources are limited. We can only think about so many things at once. As long as women are devoting some of their mental resources to the emotional and cognitive processing associated with self-objectification, fewer resources will be available for other applications. See Box 3.2 for research confirmation of the link between self-objectification and cognitive performance.

Objectification theory has led to a great deal of important research that has confirmed links between self-surveillance, body shame, and negative psychological consequences for girls and women (Moradi & Huang, 2008). For example, research has shown that self-objectification is related to eating disorders in adolescent girls and female college students (Tylka & Hill, 2004), and that self-surveillance is linked to anxiety and depression in female (but not male) college students (Muehlenkamp & Saris-Baglama, 2002; Tiggemann & Kuring, 2004). The desire to be and look like one's favorite media icon predicts body image concerns, self-surveillance, and body shame in female college students (Greenwood, 2009). Thus, as objectification theory predicts, the cultural images that surround us become internalized, with harmful psychological results.

Even women who do not suffer from obvious psychological distress related to their appearance are affected by self-objectification in troubling ways. Women in the United States spend tens of billions of dollars annually on makeup, hair care, skin care, and cosmetic surgery, in an attempt to improve or remedy aspects of their bodies that they perceive as flawed. Self-objectification can explain the antagonistic relationship that many women have with their own bodies. Women's language about their bodies is frequently hostile and combative in tone. Women talk about "watching" their weight and "fighting" their fat. They "tame" their hair and "control" their tummies. We do not flinch when a woman says she "hates" her

Box 3.2 ∞ Do I Look Fat in That? The Swimsuit-Sweater Study

In a creative experiment, Barbara Frederickson and her colleagues measured women's and men's performance on math problems after trying on a sweater or a swimsuit. Participants were told they were participating in an experiment related to "emotions and consumer behavior." Men and women were randomly assigned to try on either a swimsuit or sweater in a room with a full-length mirror and told they were to evaluate the item of clothing. While acclimating to the item of clothing (they were asked to wear it for 15 minutes), participants were asked to complete a set of math problems, ostensibly for another experiment being conducted in the education department (there was no other experiment—the math problems were actually part of the experiment they were participating in).

The research team found that men's math performance was unaffected by the experimental manipulation whereas women's math performance suffered in the swimsuit condition, which temporarily heightened their self-objectification. Wearing the swimsuit produced body shame for women, but not for men. Although men reported feeling

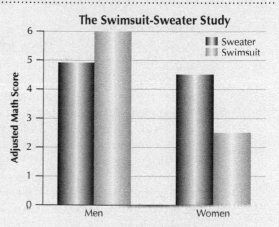

more "silly, awkward, and foolish" than women, women reported feeling more "disgust, distaste, and revulsion" than men.

Source: Frederickson, B. L., et al. (1998). That swimsuit becomes you: Sex differences in self-objectification, restrained eating, and math performance. *Journal of Personality and Social Psychology,* 75, 269–284, Figure 3 (p. 279). Copyright © 1998 by the American Psychological Association, Inc. Reprinted with permission. Contributed by Annie B. Fox.

butt, thighs, tummy, wrinkles, and so on. When was the last time you heard a man say he "hated" any part of his body?

Women's self-loathing paves the way for beauty maintenance behaviors that are actually self-destructive. Though lung cancer is a serious risk, women smoke to curb their appetites. Heedless of the risk of melanoma, women visit tanning salons. Around the world, dangerous skin-lightening products are widely used among women of color because of beauty ideals that equate higher social status with whiter skin (Browne, 2004). Some of the treatments to which women subject their own bodies would seem like torture if they were inflicted by another person. For example, women limit their food intake, depriving themselves of required nutrients. They take dangerous supplements to alter their natural appetite and metabolism. They use carcinogenic chemicals to color their hair (Zheng, 2004) and inject neurotoxins to paralyze their facial muscles so that wrinkles will not show. They force their feet into high-heeled shoes that cause back and foot problems and make ordinary walking a painful experience. Encouraged by TV shows such as *Extreme Makeover, How Do I Look?* and *Ten Years Younger,* they go under the scalpel to add, remove, or modify body parts.

Invisible Women

Who is left out of media representations of women? A short answer might be, "Any woman who is not White, young, thin, rich, feminine, and sexually available!" Let's look at some of the women who remain underrepresented or invisible.

Women of Color

Every year, the magazine *Vanity Fair* releases a "New Hollywood" issue on the latest and hottest celebrities. When the March 2010 issue hit the newsstands, critics immediately noticed that every woman on the cover was "extremely thin and very very white" ("Vanity Fair's Hollywood Issue," 2010). Kristen Stewart and Evan Rachel Wood made the cover—but not Gabourey Sidibe (*Precious*), Zoe Saldana (*Avatar*), and Freida Pinto (*Slumdog Millionaire*), all of whom had starred in recent megahits.

Unfortunately, *Vanity Fair* is not an exception. In a content analysis of articles in major women's magazines, White women were overrepresented, and Latina and Black women were underrepresented. (The good news: the bias decreased over the time period studied, 1999–2004, and women of color were more likely to be shown in professional roles over time) (Covert & Dixon, 2008). People of color, and particularly women of color, are underrepresented in other media, too. In a study of nearly 2,500 characters in TV ads, for example, only about 10 percent were African American, 2 percent were Asian American, and 1 percent were Latino/as (Coltrane & Messineo, 2000). The percentage of main characters on prime-time TV who are African American has ranged from 6 percent in the 1960s to 18 percent in the period between 1993 and 2004—an indication of progress in this area. However, Hispanics, Asian Americans, and Native Americans combined still make up less than 1 percent of the characters, and their visibility has not increased over time (Greenberg & Worrell, 2007). Latino/as, who are about 12 percent of the U.S. population, are virtually invisible in TV programming. In the movies, Latina women are usually in supporting, even demeaning, roles as maids and housekeepers (Lewis, 2002). Good movie roles for women of color are hard to find. After her brilliant turn as the monstrous mom in *Precious*, the actress Mo'Nique was asked by an interviewer whether she'd gotten a lot of job offers. Her reply? "Ain't a damn soul called me." (Carter, 2010).

Older Women

If a Martian observer were to estimate the U.S. population demographics from TV, he or she might think that some mysterious virus had killed off all the human females over the age of 40. Older women are among the least visible groups in the mass media. TV newscasters can have gray hair and wrinkled brows only if they are male. Studies from the 1970s to the present show that the majority of female characters in commercials are under the age of 35. One study compared the actual proportion of people over the age of 51 in the U.S. population with the representation of characters in a large sample of prime time commercials. Although people over the age of 51 are 27 percent of the population, they accounted for only 18 percent of the characters in the commercials. And despite the fact that there are increasingly more women than men the older people get (because women live longer on average), two-thirds of the older characters were men (Ganahl et al., 2003).

The U.S. media are not alone in the bias against older people. A study of prime-time TV characters in Germany showed that only 8 percent appeared to be over the age of 60 (compared to 22 percent of the actual population), and two-thirds of those were male. Older women were depicted much more negatively than older men (Kessler et al., 2004).

Bigger Women

Most women in the media are thin. When a token overweight woman is portrayed, she is rarely allowed to be like other women. Her weight defines her, making her unlovable. A 2009 reality show, *More to Love*, featured an overweight man selecting a wife from among a group of overweight women, underscoring the idea that fat people belong with each other. The character of Ellenor Frutt on *The Practice* was so needy and vulnerable that she dated a psychopath who attacked her with a butcher knife. As an overweight woman, she was portrayed as unappealing to normal men (Mintz, 2003). On *Friends*, the character Monica had repeated flashbacks about being overweight and rejected in high school. In an analysis of sitcoms, male characters directed more positive comments toward thinner female characters, and more negative ones to heavier characters (Fouts & Burggraf, 2000). Most of the negative comments to heavier women were followed by laughter, showing that it is socially acceptable to ridicule overweight women. Food ads often portray thinness as a woman's major goal in life and depict women's appetites and eating behaviors in moralistic terms. Women are told that it is bad or sinful to have an appetite unless it is for diet foods (Kilbourne, 2002).

A recent study of images that accompanied online news stories about obesity found that 72 percent of the images depicting an overweight person were negative and stigmatizing (Heuer et al., in press). Compared to images of normal-weight people, images of overweight people were significantly more likely to exclude their heads or show only their abdomens, and overweight people were less likely to be shown fully clothed, professionally dressed, or exercising. In another study, participants were assigned to read a news story about obesity that was accompanied by either a typical photo of an obese woman (eating junk food or emphasizing body size) or an atypical photo (nicely dressed or exercising). Participants who viewed the typical photos expressed more negative attitudes toward obese people than those who viewed the atypical photos (McClure et al., in press).

Studies suggest that overweight women suffer socially and economically as a result of antifat attitudes fostered by the media. For example, being large is a liability for women in the workplace, where obesity may lead to bias in hiring (Pingitore et al., 1994) and is associated with self-reports of employment discrimination (Rothblum et al., 1990), and lower pay (Maranto & Stenoien, 2000).

Poor women

Another group unlikely to appear on your TV is poor women. Almost all characters on prime time TV are middle class or wealthy. On afternoon talk shows, working-class women are shown as out of control, belligerent, and victims of dysfunctional families. In the print media, newspapers and magazines feature poor women (particularly women of color) in stories about welfare reform, but not in stories about other issues. Few women are called upon to comment on issues of poverty, although the majority of poor people in the United States are women and children. In one analysis of media coverage of welfare reform, 77 percent of the experts used as sources were male (Flanders, 1997). Most poor and low-income women, who struggle to work and care for families under difficult conditions, are not considered worthy of air time (Bullock et al., 2001).

Athletic Women

Studies conducted over the last three decades have consistently found that women's sports are underrepresented relative to rates of participation in both print and broadcast journalism. Women's sports are afforded significantly fewer photographs, fewer column inches, and less air time than men's sports. Various studies have confirmed that women's sports receive less than 10 percent of total television and newspaper coverage (Hall, 2008). An analysis conducted by the Women's Sports Foundation revealed that only 29 of 416 *Sports Illustrated* covers from 1997–2005 were of women (and eight of these were swimsuit issues; Hall, 2008). Women who participate in sports considered sex-appropriate (e.g., figure skating, gymnastics, tennis) receive more coverage than women engaged in other sports, but they are still underrepresented (Kane & Parks, 1990; Koivula, 1999).

Like language used about women athletes, discussed earlier, images of women athletes often deemphasize their abilities while highlighting their femininity and heterosexual appeal (Duncan, 1990; Fink & Kensicki, 2002). Women athletes are frequently pictured *not* engaged in their sports, wearing jewelry, makeup, and revealing clothing. They are sexually objectified in pictorials reminiscent of the *Sports Illustrated* swimsuit issue. Many female athletes willingly participate because they believe it will boost their careers and draw attention to women's sports. But, does this attention bolster support for women's athletics—or does it reduce women's athletics to just another form of women's bodies as sexual entertainment? When a woman curler from the small European country of Andorra decided to raise money for her sport by creating a calendar of nude women curlers from around the world, she did indeed attract the attention of National Public Radio's *Only a Game* show, but the interview did little to advance the sport of curling when the male host asked skeptically, "Are there enough attractive female curlers to fill 12 months' worth of calendar?" (National Public Radio, 2005).

A few women athletes are now getting the lucrative product endorsement contracts usually offered to men; however, endorsements are gender biased too. An analysis of 169 endorsements found 91.7 percent included male athletes only 12.4 percent included female athletes, and 17 of the 21 that featured women were sexually suggestive or contained partial nudity (Garu et al., 2007). Consider the example of race-car driver Danica Patrick: before her rookie debut in 2005, women drivers were generally pictured in the few endorsements they made as strong and athletic; Patrick's intentional promotion of her feminine sex appeal (such as in the Go Daddy commercial that aired during the 2010 Superbowl) gained her substantially more endorsement opportunities than her predecessors, but her strategy changed the image of women race-car drivers and has left her trying to modify her public image by equally emphasizing her competence (Ross et al., 2009).

Voices of Authority

Women are relatively invisible in the media as responsible citizens and experts. The news media focus on the actions, opinions, and expertise of men much more than women. For example, studies of Sunday morning talk shows found that 77 percent of the 2,150 guests who appeared in 2005–2006 were men (Garofoli, 2007) and more than half of the episodes in 2004–2005 did not include a single woman (The White House Project, 2005). Studies in many countries—the United States, Australia, Denmark, France, and Portugal—show that 70 to 90 percent of the authoritative voiceovers in TV commercials are male (Bartsch et al., 2000; Furnham & Mak, 1999; Neto & Pinto, 1998).

No matter the context, women are likely to be presented in a way that focuses on their appearance, family roles, and bodies rather than their words and ideas—a practice that has been documented since the 1970s (Foreit et al., 1980). This kind of bias makes it more difficult for women to be taken seriously. For example, in an article about a presidential campaign appearance by Hillary Clinton (Keller, 2003), women who attended were described in trivializing terms: "a fortysomething from Newton with suspiciously jet black hair who's risking perspiration stains on her cashmere sweater," "a well-tailored woman in her fifties," "a middle-aged woman wearing expensive glasses," "a fortyish black woman." In contrast, men were described by their names and occupations ("healthcare worker Andy Johnson"). Their age, race, and fashion preferences were not considered relevant. Collectively, Clinton's supporters were referred to as "the chevre and Chardonnay sisterhood," and one was quoted as saying that Clinton has "beautiful skin, and let me tell you, that's important to women." In other words, Clinton's supporters were portrayed as ditzy middle-aged women, not politically informed voters.

Even when women have the authority to be heard, their appearance is paramount. News reporter Katie Couric, the first female solo anchor in network news history, posed for *Harper's Bazaar* (March 2010) in a "tough-and-sexy photoshoot featuring smoky, kohl-rimmed eyes, a one-shouldered Calvin Klein sheath, and a pair of Gucci platform shoes," to accompany an article in which she talked about her current romance and her use of Botox to hide wrinkles (von Pfetten, 2010). We can hardly imagine Brian Williams or Anderson Cooper being asked to pose for a fashion spread like this.

It should be clear by now that the language we use about women and the images of women that we see can affect us. A review of experimental studies confirmed that presenting participants with biased media images increases their acceptance of gender-biased beliefs (Herrett-Skjellum & Allen, 1996). Now we will turn to a discussion of those gender-biased beliefs and how they affect our perceptions of, and behavior toward, the real women in our lives.

Stereotypes about Women and Men

Stereotypes can be thought of as theories that people carry around in their heads about how members of a particular group think, look, and behave, and how these attributes are linked. An individual may be unaware that he or she holds stereotypical beliefs or behaves in accordance with them. Still, the network of associations around a group forms a *schema,* or mental framework, that guides people as they experience the world around them (von Hippel et al., 1995). For a particular schema to be considered a stereotype, the content of the schema must be similar to others' schemas for the same group. For example, Charlotte may believe that short people are grumpy, but this belief is idiosyncratic, not stereotypical. On the other hand, if Charlotte believes that women are more likely than men to become emotional in a crisis, her belief, which is shared by many others, is a stereotypical belief. *Gender stereotypes* are networks of related beliefs that reflect the "common wisdom" about women and men.

Stereotyping is not an all-or-none matter; four limitations are especially noteworthy. First, people do not say (unless forced to choose) that women and men are complete opposites; instead, they think that women and men differ *on average,* and they allow for overlap (Deaux & Lewis, 1984). Second, although most people know the stereotypes, not everyone believes them. Third, stereotypes tend to have the biggest influence when you are registering a first impression of a stranger or thinking generally about a category of people (Deaux & Lewis, 1984). Fourth, the activation of stereotypes in our minds tends to be an automatic process that is not under our conscious control, and it happens even if we don't believe the stereotypes. However, we do have some control over whether we use stereotypes or not (Devine & Sharp, 2009).

Most of the students at Alpha University, for example, know that the stereotypical female cheerleader is an airhead and the stereotypical male football player is a dumb jock, but not everyone believes that this is true. And even among those who believe the stereotype, there may be differences in how important it is to their judgments about a particular cheerleader or football player. Those who actually know football players and cheerleaders are more likely to judge them as individuals. On the whole, though, people operate as though stereotypes are valid and use them in communicating with others (Ruscher, 2001). As a result, a quip about a ditzy cheerleader or a slow-witted jock is easily understood at Alpha U—it is part of the "common wisdom" of stereotypical thinking. But some people may stop and reflect about such a remark—they are trying not to stereotype.

The Content of Gender Stereotypes

In general, people associate gender with a variety of attributes including physical characteristics, personality, behaviors, and roles.

Physical Characteristics

Physical appearance is particularly important because it is the first thing we perceive when we meet someone. In fact, this information is conveyed within one-tenth of a second (Locher et al., 1993). More than any other stereotype component, it activates other components.

The special role of appearance was shown in a classic study in which participants read about a hypothetical woman or man. The target person was described using one component of gender stereotypes: either personality traits, gender-role behavior, occupation, or physical characteristics. Then the participants were asked to judge the probability that the target would have other stereotypical characteristics. When targets were described as having stereotypically feminine physical characteristics, such as being dainty, soft, and graceful, participants were very certain that they would also have feminine personalities, occupations, and gender-typed behaviors. Parallel judgments were made about men: when they were described as tall, strong, and sturdy, participants were very sure they would also have stereotypically masculine personalities, gender-role behaviors, and jobs. If the initial descriptions focused on traits, occupations or behaviors, participants were not nearly as certain that they could tell what the target would be like on the other dimensions (Deaux & Lewis, 1984).

Personality Traits

When people are asked to respond to lists of traits by choosing whether each trait is more characteristic of a woman or a man, or by rating the typicality of each for women and men, they attribute such traits as independent, competitive, decisive, active, self-confident, dominant, competent, unemotional, adventurous, and ambitious more to men. In contrast, they attribute traits such as warm, gentle, understanding, nurturing, helpful, aware of others' feelings, expressive, emotional, submissive, and sensitive more to women. The traits considered characteristic of men are *instrumental* and *agentic:* they describe a person who is an active agent and an effective "doer." The traits considered characteristic of women are *affective* and *communal:* they describe a person who is concerned with feelings and other people. The instrumental/affective (or agentic/communal) dimension of gender stereotypes was first found 40 years ago (Broverman et al., 1972) and is still found today (Spence & Buckner, 2000).

Several cross-cultural studies have shown that agentic/instrumental traits were associated with men and communal/affective traits were associated with women in virtually every nation studied (Best, 2001; Williams & Best, 1990). This suggests that gender stereotypes of agency and communality are universal. However, there are other explanations. First, cross-cultural studies typically rely on college student samples, which may be exposed to Western cultural influences and which do not represent their countries' population as a whole. Second, most cross-cultural studies have measured only trait stereotypes. Perhaps there is more variability in other components of gender stereotypes—physical attributes, social roles, and so on. Until there is more cross-cultural research, the universality of gender stereotypes is an open question.

Role Stereotypes

Many behaviors and social roles are stereotyped as more typical of women or men. This aspect of stereotyping becomes evident when people are asked to think of particular *types* of women and men. In the first study of gender subtypes (Deaux et al., 1985), participants found it easy to think of subcategories for women and men. For women, the types included the housewife/mother, who was believed to be self-sacrificing, focused on her family, and nurturing. The housewife/mother subtype is closest to the more general stereotype of women, suggesting that a *real* woman is a wife and mother. Another type, the sexy woman, was described less in terms of personality and more in terms of physical characteristics: having a good body, long hair, nail polish, and so on. (The lack of overlap between these two also suggests that moms are never sexy, and sexy women are never moms—a point we'll take up in Chapter 9.) Another type was the athletic woman, described in terms of physical characteristics (muscular, strong) as well as traits (aggressive, masculine). Finally, participants nominated a career woman type, seen as smart, hardworking, organized, and not very feminine.

Corresponding categories for men included blue-collar, athletic, macho, and businessman. Although the characteristics attributed to each type differed, all of the male types were seen as masculine—blue-collar men were described as hardworking, macho men as hairy-chested—and none were seen as having any feminine traits or behaviors. In contrast, some of the female types were seen as more feminine than others (e.g., housewives versus career women). Beliefs about these subtypes of women and men were as strongly held as beliefs about women and men in general.

To a large extent, people still differentiate between the housewife/mother and career woman subtypes, and the housewife subtype remains closest in attributes to the generic female or supposedly typical woman (Eckes, 1994; Irmen, 2006). However, there is some evidence that because of changes in the social roles of women, the generic woman stereotype is starting to include attributes previously assigned only to masculine female subtypes such as the career woman (Diekman & Eagly, 2000).

Occupational Stereotypes

Are there specific occupational gender stereotypes? This question, first asked in a 1975 study, was assessed again more than 20 years later (Beggs & Doolittle, 1993). When women and men were asked to classify each of 129 occupations as masculine, neutral, or feminine, 124 of them were classified the same way as they had been in 1975. Most jobs were perceived as gender-typed, not gender-neutral. Manicurist had the most feminine rating, and miner the most masculine one. Probably because women's workforce participation increased during this period, the majority of jobs were rated less masculine in the 1990s than in 1975. Still, only one (sales manager) went from masculine to neutral.

A recent series of experiments investigated the extent to which the use of occupational gender stereotypes is automatic versus under our conscious control (Oakhill et al., 2005). Participants were asked to decide whether pairs of occupation labels and kinship labels could refer to the same person. Some pairs were gender stereotype–congruent (e.g., sister-secretary, father-plumber), some were incongruent but possible (brother-nurse), and some were impossible (uncle-landlady). The accuracy and speed of participants' decision making was worse for stereotype-incongruent possible terms than for stereotype-congruent possible terms, suggesting that gender stereotypes are automatically activated as soon as an occupation name is read and we cannot necessarily suppress them even when it makes sense to do so.

Sexuality Stereotypes

Gender and sexuality are closely linked in most people's cognitive schemas. Gay, lesbian, bisexual, and transgendered people pose a problem for gender stereotypes because these stereotypes are implicitly heterosexual. Traditionally, people solved this cognitive problem by putting lesbians into the male/masculine schema and gay men into the female/feminine one. This was even true for physical characteristics, which are key to overall stereotyping. For example, early sexuality researchers claimed to find "long clitorises, narrow hips, small breasts, and deep voices" in lesbians (Kitzinger, 2001). Even today, lesbians are stereotyped as "butch" or "mannish" and gay men are stereotyped as effeminate (Blashill & Powlishta, 2009).

Women who are particularly strong, either in personality or physical skills, are likely to be stereotyped as lesbians, a cognitive trick that helps maintain two stereotypes: heterosexual women as the weaker sex and lesbians as mannish. For example, two longstanding and still prevalent myths about women in sports are "Sports make girls masculine" and "Only lesbians play sports" (Hall, 2008). Of course, some athletes are lesbians—and so are some teachers, attorneys, and flight attendants. Most women in all these occupations are heterosexual. "Clearly, any correlation made between athleticism and sexual orientation is misleading" (Hall, 2008, p. 107). One study confronted participants with a challenge to the "woman athlete = lesbian" idea by measuring their perceptions of heterosexual hypermuscular female bodybuilders (Forbes et al., 2004). Participants assumed that these women were less feminine, less popular, less attractive, and worse mothers than average women (and that their male partners were extramasculine).

Both in and outside the realm of athletics, sexuality stereotypes may be a means of keeping women subordinated. As long as the label "lesbian" carries a social stigma, it can be used as a weapon against any woman.

Race and Social Class Stereotypes

Most psychological studies of gender stereotypes have asked participants about "typical" women and men. A big problem with this approach is that participants (who are most often college students) may equate "typical" with White and middle-class. This only becomes apparent when researchers specifically ask about race or class. For example, when researchers asked college students to list traits for "American women" and "Black women," there was no overlap in the top-ranked traits. Typical American women were seen as intelligent, materialistic, and sensitive (similar to stereotypes of White women), whereas typical Black women were seen as loud, talkative, and aggressive (Weitz & Gordon, 1993). When students were asked to describe societal stereotypes of White, Black, middle-class, and lower-class women, they described White women as more dependent, emotional, and passive than Black women. Again, White women resembled the "typical" women of earlier studies that did not ask about race. Also, lower-class women, compared to middle-class women, were stereotyped as more dirty, hostile, inconsiderate, and irresponsible (Landrine, 1985).

Stereotypes about race and gender interact for African American women. In one recent study, White college students rated fictional characters' speech and also generated sample dialogue for the characters. This method allowed an indirect assessment of stereotypes about the characters' race and sex. Black target characters (both female and male) were rated as more direct and emotional, and less socially appropriate, than White ones were. Female characters (both Black and White) were rated as less direct and more emotional than men were. The dialogues that students created were less grammatical and more profane for Black speakers than White speakers (Popp et al., 2003). Thus, race and gender stereotypes held contradictions for African American women. As African Americans, they were perceived as loud, talkative, aggressive, and socially inappropriate. As women, they were perceived as sensitive, emotional, and indirect.

Three stereotypical subtypes of Black women are Mammy, Jezebel, and Sapphire (West, 2008). The prototype of the Mammy goes back to *Gone with the Wind*, in which Mammy was a happy slave whose huge breasts and perpetual smile symbolized her role as nurturer, while her dark complexion, bandana-covered hair, broad features, and fat body marked her as asexual. Aunt Jemima, a Mammy symbol for over a century, finally lost her bandana in the 1990s. Originally, Aunt Jemima spoke in a caricature of slave dialect: "Honey, . . . Yo know how de men folks and de young folks all loves my tasty pancakes" (West, 2008, p. 289). Today's Pine-Sol Lady may not wear a slave's bandana but she is still smiling, overweight, motherly, and calling people "Honey" (see Figure 3.4).

The Jezebel is a stereotype of a highly sexed Black woman. During slavery, owners and traders brutalized African women by raping them, forcing them to bear children who would be sold away from them, and forbidding them to marry African men. There was a conscious attempt to destroy Black families. The victims were blamed, and the oppression justified, by portraying Black women as immoral, seductive, and promiscuous. Today, the Jezebel stereotype is represented in music videos, hip-hop music, advertising, and pornography as the hoochie or the "ho."

The Sapphire icon is domineering, aggressive, strong, and unfeminine. This stereotype, too, probably originated in slavery, when Black women were forced to do heavy labor alongside Black men, and it served both to justify their oppression and to separate them from the passive, frail, and domestic role occupied by White Southern women. Sapphire is a hostile, tongue-lashing nag who drives men away and bullies everyone else (West, 2008). She is the Black woman with attitude and anger who gets into seemingly every reality TV show, the gangsta girl of hip-hop legend, and the Madea grandmother who can tell off anyone and follow up with a fistfight. Like the Mammy and the Jezebel, the Sapphire stereotype may be a distortion and exaggeration of coping strategies that enabled Black women to survive centuries of oppression.

So far we have talked only about research that has used Black or White targets. Are gender stereotypes linked to race/ethnicity stereotypes in other groups? The evidence is limited, because few studies have been done, but the answer seems to be that gender and ethnicity do interact in stereotypical beliefs. When a multiethnic group of college students were asked to list adjectives that described men

FIGURE 3.4   Comedian Diane Amos is best known as the Pine-Sol lady.

and women of different ethnic groups, they agreed on the characteristics shown in Table 3.1. You can see from the table that the characteristics they came up with are a combination of traits, physical characteristics, and role behaviors. Some gender stereotypes were represented in all groups. For example, women, whether Mexican, Asian, African, or Anglo in origin, were all believed to be pleasant and friendly. Although the men in various groups did not share specific traits, all were seen as having some instrumental or agentic characteristics such as being achievement oriented or hardworking. Equally interesting, however, are the perceived differences across ethnic and gender groupings. Overall, stereotypes of African Americans and Mexican Americans were more negative than stereotypes of Asian and Anglo Americans. Although participants were not asked about social class stereotypes in this study, they spontaneously associated Mexican Americans with lower-class people (Niemann et al., 1994).

Are Stereotypes Accurate?

Stereotypes, to some extent, reflect the social world, and some hold a kernel of truth (Jussim et al., 2009). If your stereotypical image of a secretary is female, and a computer scientist, male, you are more accurate than not, because the proportions of women and men in these occupations are in fact different. We saw earlier that occupational stereotypes had changed somewhat as women's actual

TABLE 3.1   Gender and Ethnic Stereotypes

Participants in this study were asked to list the first 10 adjectives that came to mind when they thought of members of each group. Here are the traits they listed most often.

Anglo-American Males	*Anglo-American Females*
Intelligent	Attractive
Egotistical	Intelligent
Upper class	Egotistical
Pleasant/friendly	Pleasant/friendly
Racist	Blond/light hair
Achievement oriented	Sociable/socially active

African American Males	*African American Females*
Athletic	Speak loudly
Antagonistic	Dark skin
Dark skin	Antagonistic
Muscular appearance	Athletic
Criminal activities	Pleasant/friendly
Speak loudly	Unmannerly
	Sociable/socially active

Asian American Males	*Asian American Females*
Intelligent	Intelligent
Short	Speak softly
Achievement oriented	Pleasant/friendly
Speak softly	Short
Hard workers	

Mexican American Males	*Mexican American Females*
Lower class	Black/brown/dark hair
Hard workers	Attractive
Antagonistic	Pleasant/friendly
Dark skin	Dark skin
Noncollege education	Lower class
Pleasant/friendly	Overweight
Black/brown/dark hair	Baby makers
Ambitionless	Family oriented

Source: Niemann, Y. F., Jennings, L., Rozelle, R. M., Baxter, J. C., & Sullivan, E. (1994). Use of free responses and cluster analysis to determine stereotypes of eight groups. *Personality and Social Psychology Bulletin, 20,* 379–390, from Table 2 (p. 383). Copyright © 1994 by the Society for Personality and Social Psychology, Inc. Reprinted by permission of SAGE Publications.

distribution in the workforce changed. In order for stereotypes to function as effective cognitive shortcuts, they need to be at least somewhat anchored in reality (Ottati & Lee, 1995).

However, it is not always clear what counts as reality. What criteria should be used to defend or refute stereotypical judgments is always open to debate, and often the debater's position depends on his or her social and political agenda. More important than arguing over whether stereotypes are accurate is to recognize that even when they are somewhat accurate as an overall group judgment, they may be very inaccurate when making judgments about individuals. Relying on stereotypes can cause harm:

> It *matters* when stereotypes are misused. It matters when an employer hires a man rather than a woman for a given job because he believes that men are inherently more suited for it. It matters when girls are told that they should take English rather than mathematics in high school. It matters when a Black family is excluded from the possibility of owning a house in a nice neighborhood because a real estate agent believes that they will have too many children and not take care of the property. In this sense, the critical issues of stereotyping go beyond the question of whether the perceiver, on average, is accurate in his or her perceptions, to the potential negative outcomes . . . (Stangor, 1995).

Even when stereotypes contain a kernel of truth, they are *never* true of every group member. Unfortunately, despite their limitations as cognitive aids and their harmful social potential, stereotypes are not easily dislodged.

Stereotypes Are Hard to Change

Gender stereotypes have been studied for over 50 years. During that time, there have been enormous changes in gender-related attitudes and behaviors. Attitudes toward women's rights have become more liberal and many women have entered professions once reserved for men (Spence & Buckner, 2000). However, gender stereotypes have changed remarkably little. Various studies measured gender stereotypes as early as the 1950s, and later studies compared these to stereotypes in the 1970s and 1990s (Lueptow et al., 1995; Werner & LaRussa, 1985). In these studies, the majority of traits believed to characterize women and men in the 1950s were still thought to apply decades later. However, some negative stereotypes about women had dropped out. Women had supposedly become nicer, but not more competent.

In a relatively recent study, a sample of U.S. college students was asked to rate the typical male and female student on instrumental and expressive traits that were first measured in the early 1970s (Spence & Buckner, 2000). The results were quite clear: on virtually every instrumental trait, both male and female students agreed that the typical male is higher, and on virtually every expressive trait, they agreed that the typical female is higher. At least on these trait measures, gender stereotypes had changed very little since the early 1970s.

If social reality is changing, why are stereotypes relatively static? People tend to hang on to their stereotypical beliefs even when they are challenged by new or incongruent information, for several reasons (von Hippel et al., 1995). We may cling to stereotypes because they help us feel good about ourselves. Jokes and stories about dumb blondes or effeminate gay men may serve to make others feel superior. And since "everybody" knows that blondes or gay men are "all like that," stereotypes serve to make the ingroup members feel more cohesive and in tune with each other. When someone makes a remark about fags, JAPs, or welfare queens, the ingroup gets to feel superior to the outgroup (Ruscher, 2001).

Stereotypes also persist because they are useful cognitive shortcuts, helping us to allocate cognitive processing time efficiently and get through the day with a minimum of mental effort. Stereotypical thinking helps keep us from getting bogged down as we navigate a complex social world. There is a lot of evidence consistent with this view of stereotyping. For example, people rely on stereotypes more when they are least alert—"morning people" stereotype more at night, and "night people" do it more in the morning. And most people rely on stereotypes more when they are under time pressure or overloaded with incoming information (von Hippel et al., 1995).

Another reason stereotypes survive is that they influence the amount and kind of information that the individual takes in. When you have a well-developed schema, you tend to encode information that is congruent with the schema, then stop encoding. You do not perceive the incongruent information that is all around you. As an example, imagine a group of four women and four men working together on a committee. One of the women is more talkative than average. If other group members hold the stereotypical belief that women talk or gossip a lot, they may pick up on her talkativeness and notice it. But perhaps the other three women say very little, and on balance more of the talking is done by the four men (a normative pattern discussed in Chapter 2). Because the silent women are stereotype-incongruent, their behavior is less likely to be encoded into memory and used to form judgments.

Stereotypes about gay, bisexual, and lesbian people may be even more resistant to change than gender stereotypes because people may interact with gays and lesbians quite often without realizing it. Thus, gay or lesbian people who do not match the stereotypes (the lesbian who wears dresses or does flower arranging, the gay man who drives an SUV or plays football) may not be recognized as such (Garnets, 2008).

Another cognitive mechanism that helps stereotypes persist in the face of incongruent information is the formation of subtypes. If Trisha, who believes that women love children, meets a woman who is focused on her career and has little interest in children, she may protect her stereotype by putting the woman into a "career woman" subtype. Career women are unfeminine, Trisha may decide, but real women still love children.

The Impact of Stereotypes

Stereotypes matter! Here we look at three ways in which stereotypes have very real effects: they become part of the self-schema and may cause stereotype threat and create harmful self-fulfilling prophecies; they reinforce differences in status and power; and they prime sexist behavior and lead to discrimination.

Stereotypes, the Self, and Stereotype Threat

Because gender is such an important dimension in perceiving and evaluating others, the gender schema becomes part of the self-schema. In other words, people may come to believe that the attributes of their gender stereotypes are true expressions of their identity.

Research offers both good news and not-so-good news about today's self-schemas. The good news is that, compared to earlier generations, today's college women see themselves as more instrumental. They endorse traits such as "acts like a leader," "self-reliant," and "assertive" just as much as college men do. However, men still rate themselves higher on about 40 percent of instrumental traits. Thus, the gender gap in instrumentality is narrowing, but not yet closed. The not-so-good news is that women and men still see themselves as very different in expressiveness. Virtually every expressive trait—kind, emotional, understanding, warm, gentle, tender, and so on—still is endorsed significantly more by women than by men (Spence & Buckner, 2000). Thus, gender stereotypes are still being internalized as part of the self. Although the stereotypes are internalized somewhat differently than in the past, the change is not equal for women and men. Women are seeing themselves as more instrumental, but men are not seeing themselves as more expressive.

When people know that there is a negative stereotype about their group's abilities, the pressure caused by their fear of confirming the stereotype can interfere with their performance—a phenomenon called *stereotype threat*. For example, Aisha may perform below par on a math test because she is preoccupied with concern about confirming the stereotype that women are inferior in mathematics. (For research on stereotype threat, see Chapter 4.)

In addition, stereotypes may generate *self-fulfilling prophecies* because they often depict not only a consensus about the way things are but also the way they should be. In other words, they are not just descriptive, but *prescriptive:* they prescribe how the ideal woman or man *should* think, look, and behave. For example, a woman who does not want to have children not only violates the stereotype that women are nurturing but may be judged an inadequate woman; a man who is not ambitious or strong may be seen as not a real man. Prescriptive stereotypes create strong pressure for women to act feminine and men to act masculine—to play by the rules of gender.

Stereotypes, Status, and Power

In general, people with more power engage in stereotyping of people with less power (Keltner et al., 2003). Powerful people pay more attention than less powerful people to stereotype-consistent information, and less attention to information that might contradict their stereotypes. Although both these tendencies contribute to maintaining imbalances, they make sense cognitively and socially. Powerful people may seek to confirm beliefs that work for them. And they do not need to pay much attention to the individual differences among the powerless, because their well-being does not depend on it. For example, a worker must pay more attention to the moods and demands of the boss than the boss must pay to the worker's, because the boss controls important outcomes for the worker.

Group-based power differences also increase the tendency to stereotype. Recall that people who are higher in social power (men compared to women, European American compared to African American) tend to be higher in social dominance orientation, or SDO (see Chapter 2). In turn, SDO predicts the tendency to stereotype others—with higher SDO scores linked to more stereotyping. Importantly, research on *behavioral confirmation* suggests that when higher-power people (such as men) interact with lower-power people about whom they hold stereotypes (such as women), they may—intentionally or unintentionally—treat those people in ways that actually elicit stereotype-consistent behaviors, even when the stereotype is inaccurate (Chen & Bargh, 1997; Snyder & Klein, 2005). Their stereotypes are then confirmed—the self-fulfilling prophecy described in Chapter 2.

Stereotypes and Sexist Behavior

Another harmful effect of stereotypes is that they can prime sexist behavior. Consider the example of an award-winning study grounded in real-world sex discrimination.

In the early 1990s, women workers at the Stroh's brewery in Minnesota sued the company over sexual harassment in the workplace. The attorney representing the women introduced Stroh's infamous "Swedish Bikini Team" beer commercials as evidence that Stroh's tolerated a hostile workplace. Her argument was that any company that produces such sexist and objectifying commercials is sending a clear message to its employees about how to regard women. (These commercials can still be found on YouTube—check one out at http://www.youtube.com/watch?v=LtnMtrEB1-I.) The case settled out of court, but graduate student Laurie Rudman was inspired to investigate how commercials that portray women as sex objects affect male viewers. Using a computer-timed word-recognition task, Rudman and her colleague Eugene Borgida found that men who had watched sex-object commercials were quicker to recognize words associated with the sex-object female stereotype (e.g., bimbo) than were men who had viewed commercials that did not portray women as sex objects. Moreover, when they were asked to interview a female job applicant, these men rated her as less competent, and remembered less about her résumé and more about her appearance. In other words, activation of the stereotype distorted men's perceptions of the female applicant and affected their behavior toward her (Rudman & Borgida, 1995).

How Not to Stereotype

Are stereotyping and its negative consequences inevitable? No. Admittedly, it isn't easy to change or eliminate stereotypes. Because they are part of the cognitive process of categorization, they are relatively automatic, and they are activated without awareness. But people can make conscious decisions to pay attention to their automatic stereotyping and to combat their natural tendency to judge others stereotypically.

Although more than 100 studies since the late 1980s have demonstrated automatic activation of stereotypes, researchers have identified several types of interventions that disrupt this process and allow people to exercise some control over their stereotyping (Blair, 2002; Lenton et al., 2009). One factor that can make a big difference is the motivation of the perceiver (Blair, 2002).

For example, people rely less on stereotypes when they are trying to be accurate in their judgments of others. In one study, participants were provided with both stereotypical and nonstereotypical information about another individual and instructed to convey their impression to another person. Participants conveyed more balanced (less stereotypical) information when they were in situations that stressed the importance of accuracy (Ruscher & Duval, 1998). Instead of disregarding nonstereotypical information that was provided to them, they included it in their accounts. This study suggests that a conscious effort to be accurate will reduce stereotyping.

There is also evidence that nonprejudiced people can suppress or override their stereotypes (von Hippel et al., 1995). In other words, virtually everyone is aware of stereotypes such as the mammy, bimbo, hottie, and housewife; the words and images of our culture routinely activate these stereotypes. Prejudiced people—those who score high on the measures of sexism and racism described in Chapter 2—are likely to rely on such stereotypes when they are automatically activated; the stereotypes affect their judgments and behavior. Less prejudiced people stop and think about the stereotypes, and replace them with more accurate information, so they are less likely to respond to others as stereotypes and more likely to respond to them as individuals. *Not* stereotyping requires being open minded, paying attention, and making a conscious choice, but it can be done.

Making a Difference

Sexist representations are everywhere in our culture, and they can be powerful agents in fostering biased attitudes and discriminatory behavior. Feminists view these representations as an important opportunity for education and work toward societal change. Here we look at some of their efforts.

Transforming Language

Feminists from many cultures and societies have taken action to change linguistic sexism through *feminist language reform:* efforts to eliminate gender bias in the structure, content, and usage of language and to provide nonsexist alternatives (Pauwels, 1998). Feminist language reform has modified old language and also created new language (Crawford, 2001).

One of the biggest successes in feminist language reform has been the adoption of nonsexist language guidelines. By the mid-1970s, major educational publishers and professional organizations (such as APA and National Council of Teachers of English) had adopted such guidelines. In 1975, the U.S. Department of Labor eliminated gender bias in occupational titles. Government agencies adopted nonsexist language in Germany, Italy, France, Spain, and other countries at around the same time (Pauwels, 1998).

Guidelines for nonsexist language led to noticeable and important changes. Occupational titles and terms are now almost always gender-neutral—letter carrier has replaced mailman, and chairperson is an everyday word. There has been a dramatic drop in the use of pseudo-generic masculine terms in magazines and newspapers in all the countries studied (Pauwels, 1998). Politicians are usually very careful to refer to citizens as "he or she" and troops as "our men and women in uniform."

However, nonsexist language guidelines did not address more subtle aspects of linguistic sexism such as the people = male bias. Nor did they address the blatant sexism of referring to women in terms of animals, appearance, and sexuality. In 2003, a cover story in *New York* magazine on successful women executives still asked whether men would want to go to bed with these "chicks." And during the 2008 presidential campaign, Fox News referred to Michelle Obama (a graduate of Princeton and Harvard Law) as "Obama's baby mama," repeatedly displaying this offensive description onscreen.

Feminists have provided new words for new times by adding many terms to the English language. Some, such as *herstory*, were aimed at making people think twice about hidden sexism. Others named aspects of women's experience that had been invisible. The writer Gloria Steinem expressed the importance of naming and the influence of 1970s feminist activism on language when she said, "We have terms like 'sexual harassment' and 'battered women.' A few years ago, they were just called 'life.'" (Steinem, 1983, p. 149.)

Lesbian, gay, bisexual, and transgender activists, too, have taken over the power to name. Gay activists coined *heterosexism*, *homophobia*, and *biphobia*. Rejecting the psychiatric label *homosexual*, they adopted *gay*, and made *LGBTQ* a convenient shorthand term for diverse sexualities. Formerly derogatory epithets such as *queer* and *dyke* are being reclaimed as positive badges of identity (Marecek et al, 2004).

Despite resistance and backlash (such as the term *feminazi*), efforts to change language are ongoing. They are important because "Language is more than just talk. In using language, we create our social reality. By changing language, we can contribute to changing that reality" (Crawford, 2001, p. 244).

Challenging Objectification

Women's objectification is a profitable commercial enterprise. We are unlikely to see significant change in the behaviors of profit-driven organizations until they receive the message that women's objectification is going to cost them.

As consumers, we have tremendous power to influence popular culture. People dismiss women's objectification with the convenient phrase, "sex sells." This is not unlike dismissing sexual harassment or sexual violence against women with "boys will be boys." Just because something happens doesn't mean it has to be accepted. And women's objectification is not sex; it is dehumanization of half the population, a process that strips women of their personhood. Ours is a society that is shaped by economic forces. If anything is going to change with regard to women's objectification in our commercially driven culture, well-informed consumers are going to have to use their voices—*and dollars*—to educate the people producing the images, the products, and the services that rely far too much on objectification of women. Consider this example:

In the fall of 2009, consumers were offered an iPhone application as part of a promotion for Amp energy drink. The application, called "AMP UP Before You Score" offered men tips to help them "get lucky" with two dozen different "types" of women (illustrated by cartoon drawings), such as the "Rebound Girl" who's got mascara tear tracks and clutches a carton of ice cream, the "Aspiring Actress" who's dressed like a waitress, the "Artist" who's pictured chewing on a paintbrush, and 21 more, including "Married," "Twins," "Women's Studies Major," "Cougar," and "Foreign Exchange Student." (http://www.huffingtonpost.com/2009/10/12/amp-up-before-you-score-p_n_317716.html.)

The app provided links to online Wikipedia entries and other information that would help men dupe women into believing that they share their specific interests. As the iTunes description put it, "know what makes her tick before you open your mouth, so she'll like what she hears when you do." For example, men who wanted to pick up a "treehugger" could immediately obtain a phony carbon footprint score. The app also allowed users to create "Brag Lists" of their successes to share with their buddies on e-mail, Facebook, or Twitter.

As soon as the app was released, there was an outpouring of outrage in the blogosphere, in response to which an apology appeared on Twitter:

> Our app tried 2 show the humorous lengths guys go 2 pick up women. We apologize if it's in bad taste & appreciate your feedback. #pepsifail

Note that the apology did not say anything about discontinuing the app. Importantly, though, it was tagged with "pepsifail," thus identifying PepsiCo, the producer of the Amp drink, as the corporation behind the controversial marketing campaign. The online furor increased and zeroed in on Pepsi until, after a week of firestorm, the company responded to consumers and pulled the application.

Many feminist activists and everyday citizens have worked to raise awareness of the harm done by sexist and stereotyped words, images, and beliefs, and to provide positive alternatives. Those who wish to get involved in education and activism against sexism in the media can find information through groups such as the ones listed at the end of this chapter. One good example of ongoing activism is educator Jean Kilbourne, who has become a familiar presence on college campuses through her videos documenting sexism in advertising (see Box 3.3). Despite a long history of feminist activism on cultural representations of women, the need for change is as great as ever.

BOX 3.3 ⟳ Jean Kilbourne: Media Activist

"No one in the world has done more to improve the image of women in the media than Jean Kilbourne."[1] Kilbourne is an award-winning educator and an activist through her work on women's depiction in the media. In 1969, she began by lecturing to college students on how advertisers misuse images of women to sell products by showing them as sexual objects and setting unrealistic beauty standards. From her powerful lectures came one of the most popular educational films of all time, *Killing Us Softly: Advertising's Images of Women*. The film and its sequels, *Still Killing Us Softly*, *Killing Us Softly 3*, and most recently, *Killing Us Softly 4*, along with Kilbourne's writings, *Can't Buy My Love: How Advertising Changes the Way We Think and Feel*, have raised awareness of media sexism in generations of students. Because of the depth of her research and the relevance of her work, Kilbourne has served as an advisor to two former surgeon generals and is on the board for the Women's Action Alliance and the Media Education Foundation. In 2008, Kilbourne was honored by the organization *Reclaim the Media* as one of 21 "media heroes" for her groundbreaking and influential work. Kilbourne's activism is especially exemplary because its message is spread through various media including books, newspapers, films, and television. The *New York Times Magazine* named her one of the most popular speakers on college campuses across the United States. Her work spans audiences from government officials to college students. Her research has transcended the scholarly or purely academic realm and has become a form of educational activism. By recognizing the damage that advertising has done to women, Kilbourne is working to remedy it not only by speaking out, but also by trying to make society take responsibility for its attitudes toward women that are reflected in advertisements.

[1] Elaine LeGaro, Chair of the Women's Committee of the American Federation of Television and Radio Artists.

Source: http://www.jeankilbourne.com/. Contributed by Meghan Deveau and Annie B. Fox.

Exploring Further

∾

About Face (www.about-face.org). About Face's mission is "to equip women and girls with tools to understand and resist harmful media messages that affect self-esteem and body image." Its lively Web site has a gallery of winners and another of offenders. And catch its "Covert Dressing Room Action" video on YouTube.

Ellen Cole and Jessica Henderson Daniels (Eds.). (2005). *Featuring females: Feminist analyses of media*. Washington, DC: APA.
Psychologists report their original research analyzing the portrayals of women in reality television shows, films, news programming, magazines, video games, and advertising. This book addresses how aging, race/ethnicity, body image, gender roles, sexual orientation and relationships, and violence are treated in the media. The authors maintain that it is important for consumers to become media literate and critical of stereotypical representations of women and gender.

The Feminist Majority Foundation (http://feminist.org) has created a list of alternative feminist magazines on its Web site (http://feminist.org/research/zines.html). Feminist 'zines such as Bust (www.bust.com) are smart and funny alternatives to the mainstream media, and there are options for younger girls, too, like New Moon Girls (http://www.newmoon.com/magazine/).

Media Watch (www.mediawatch.com) was founded in 1984 to challenge abusive stereotypes and other biased images commonly found in the media through education and activism. Its videos are available on YouTube and it has a Facebook group.

CHAPTER 4

The Meanings of Difference

$\mathcal{M}$ost people believe that women and men differ in many important ways. As one pop-psych best-seller put it, "Men are from Mars, women are from Venus." On the other hand, I once saw a T-shirt that proclaimed, "Men are from Earth. Women are from Earth. Deal with it!"

Certainly, the images and stereotypes discussed in Chapter 3 present women and men in dramatically different ways. But what are the *real* differences between boys and girls or women and men in traits, abilities, and behaviors? Often, students of psychology want "the facts and just the facts," and they expect the science of psychology to be able to provide those facts. Psychology does have powerful research methods. However, the study of group differences is not just a matter of establishing facts, because differences that show up in psychological research are open to debate about their origins, meaning, and importance.

The Politics of Difference and Similarity

Some differences between groups do not matter very much in Western society. Almost no one divides the social world into people with freckles and those without, or people who can wiggle their ears and those who cannot. Other differences, like the ones in Figure 4.1, matter very much. These differences have social and political consequences; they represent dimensions of privilege versus disadvantage (Morgan, 1996). In feminist theory and political movements, there have long been two ways of thinking about gender-related differences (Kimball, 1995), grounded in liberal and cultural feminism respectively (see Chapter 1). The *similarities tradition* claims that women and men are very much alike in intelligence, personality, abilities, and goals. This tradition stems from liberal feminism and is used to argue for equality of the sexes. After all, if men and women are far more alike than different, shouldn't they be treated equally?

The *differences tradition* claims that there are fundamental differences between women and men that should be recognized and honored. This tradition, stemming from cultural feminism, is used to argue that society should give more recognition to the activities, traits, and values of women. After all, if taking care of other people and relationships (traditionally viewed as feminine characteristics) were rewarded as much as dominance and personal ambition (traditionally viewed as masculine characteristics), wouldn't the world be a better place?

Both these ways of thinking have been used to generate research and to form political strategies. Debates about which approach is better have gone on for a long time. In this book I explore both traditions, looking at important research from each. The goal is not to decide which tradition is better. Rather, I hope you will decide that there is value in both—that "double visions are theoretically and politically richer and more flexible than visions based on a single tradition" (Kimball, 1995, p. 2).

Because claims about group differences may be politically and socially controversial, there has been a lack of agreement in *defining* difference, problems in

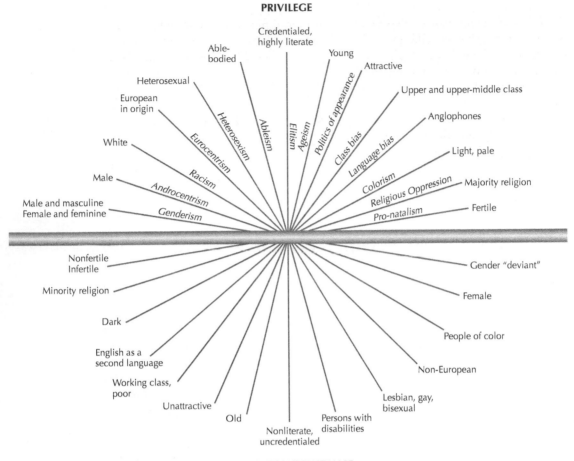

FIGURE 4.1

Intersecting dimensions of privilege and oppression. An individual may be socially evaluated on any of these dimensions. For each dimension, there is clearly a good and bad end. Some of us are multiply privileged by occupying the favored end of most dimensions; others are multiply oppressed.

Source: Ann Diller, Barbara Houston, Kathryn Pauly Morgan, and Maryann Ayim, *The Gender Question in Education: Theory, Pedagogy, and Politics,* Figure 8.1 (p. 107). Copyright © 1996 by Westview Press, Inc. Reprinted by permission of Westview Press, Inc., a member of the Perseus Books Group.

measuring difference, and issues of *values and interpretation* in understanding results. Let's examine these controversies in more detail.

Defining Difference and Similarity

Determining the facts about gender differences sounds relatively easy: a psychologist measures a group of women and a group of men for a trait or ability and computes the average difference between the groups. There is a long

FIGURE 4.2   Calvin learns how men and women are different.

Source: CALVIN AND HOBBES © 1990 Watterson. Reprinted with permission of Universal Uclick. All rights reserved.

tradition of this kind of research. When I did a quick *PsychInfo* search for studies referencing sex differences or gender differences from 1967 to 2010, I found 79,146 articles!

You might think that with all these studies, some definitive answers would emerge. However, the meaning of *difference* can be very ambiguous. Suppose you heard someone explain why there are more men than women judges in the United States by saying, "Let's face it, women just don't reason like men. When it comes to reasoning ability, they just don't have what it takes." Your first reaction might be that this is just an outdated stereotype (see Figure 4.2). Your second reaction might be to ask yourself what evidence could be brought to bear on this claim.

The speaker has asserted that there is a gender-related difference in reasoning, a cognitive ability. Before we examine the evidence, let's consider what he or she might have meant. One interpretation is that all men and no women have the ability to reason—in other words, that reasoning ability is dichotomous by sex. If the entire population of men and women could be measured on a perfectly valid and reliable test of reasoning ability, the two sexes would form two nonoverlapping distributions, with the distribution for women being lower. *But despite a hundred years of research on gender-related differences, no one has ever discovered a psychological trait or cognitive ability on which men and women are completely different.*

Because it would be ridiculous to argue that women are categorically inferior as shown in Figure 4.3a, the speaker probably means something else when talking about difference. Perhaps he means that there is a ***mean difference*** (i.e., an average difference), such that the mean for women is slightly lower (Figure 4.3b) or very much lower (Figure 4.3c) than the mean for men. However, an average difference doesn't tell us very much by itself. Sets of distributions can have the same differences in means but large differences in ***variability,*** defined as the range or spread of scores.

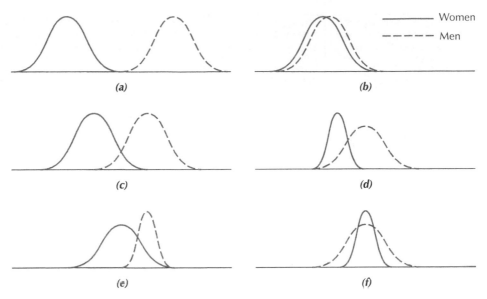

FIGURE 4.3   Some possible distributions of reasoning ability in females and males.

Figure 4.3d shows males more variable than females and 4.3e shows females more variable than males. Looking at the areas in which males' and females' distributions do not overlap in each set shows that the meaning of difference is different for each. That is, the proportion of women who score below the lowest-scoring men and the proportion of men who score above the highest-scoring women differ greatly from one set of hypothetical distributions to the next.

Moreover, these are not the only possible population distributions. Women and men could be equal on average, but one sex could be more variable, as shown in Figure 4.3f; here, the area where females and males overlap is larger than those where they do not.

Most research on gender-related differences reports a mean difference between a sample of women and a sample of men, with statistical tests to determine whether the difference is ***statistically significant*** (unlikely to have occurred by chance). As noted in Chapter 1, the concept of statistical significance is not the same as the ordinary meaning of "significant." A difference may be statistically significant yet be so small that it is useless in predicting differential behavior in other situations. In other words, statistical significance is not the same as importance.

How large does a statistically significant difference have to be before we are justified in labeling men and women more different than similar? Should the importance of a sex difference be judged in terms of average scores, in terms of the variability for each group, or in how much the distributions for women and men overlap? And how do we compare the results of several studies of the same trait or ability when the results vary? How many studies are sufficient to settle a question? How consistent must the results be? Is it important to measure the trait or ability in people of different age groups, social classes, ethnic groups, and cultures—or is it safe to assume that what is true for North American college students is true for all people? The answers to these questions involve value judgments about the meaning of difference.

Measuring Differences

Suppose a psychologist wanted to test the claim that there is a gender difference in reasoning ability. She might compare a sample of women and a sample of men on a standard test of reasoning, matching the two groups on any other factors that might affect reasoning ability, such as years of education. She would compare the average scores of her two groups with an appropriate statistical test to determine whether the difference she obtained was likely to have occurred by chance.

The logic of experimental design and hypothesis testing leads psychologists to put more weight on findings of difference than on findings of similarity. Statistical tests allow psychologists to be fairly confident that when a difference is judged to exist, the conclusion is an accurate one. But when a difference is *not* found, psychologists cannot know for certain that there is no difference in the population; the result could be just a failure of this experiment to detect the difference. They may conclude that they should try again, not that the hypothesis about a difference was wrong. Relying on similar logic, as discussed in Chapter 1, professional journals are less likely to publish articles that report similarities between women and men than they are to publish reports of differences. The possibility of overemphasizing differences is a built-in limitation of hypothesis testing.

Sources of Bias in Gender Research

Even when a study is done methodically and ethically (and the great majority of published psychological research is), it may reflect unintended gender bias. As discussed in Chapter 1, bias can occur in deciding what topics are important and how to study them (question formulation and research design), during data analysis, and when interpreting and publishing research results.

One of the most persistent sources of bias in gender-difference research is the difficulty of separating gender from all the other factors it is related to in our society. The interaction of gender with other factors leads to **confounding**, in which the effects of two or more variables are mixed, and it becomes impossible to decide which variable is causing experimental effects.

For example, suppose we were matching participants for our imaginary experiment on reasoning ability. We would certainly not choose to compare a male sample with college degrees to a female sample of high-school graduates, because this would confound gender and educational level. Obviously, the different backgrounds and experience of the two groups could account for differences in reasoning ability. But even when a researcher attempts to measure comparable men and women, it is often hard to decide what characteristics should be matched. Suppose researchers compared female and male college students. Although male and female college students are matched on level of formal education, the women and men may have very different backgrounds in mathematics, science, and the liberal arts and may be concentrated in different majors. These differences may be irrelevant to some research questions but crucial to others.

Meta-Analysis: A Useful Tool

A technique called *meta-analysis* can resolve some of the issues of definition and measurement in research on gender differences. Basically, meta-analysis uses quantitative methods to summarize the results of research done by different people at different times (Hedges & Becker, 1986). It allows researchers to integrate the results of many studies on a topic and to assess the magnitude and consistency of difference effects statistically (Hyde & Linn, 1986).

In doing a meta-analysis, the investigator first identifies all relevant studies on a topic. The next step is to summarize the results of each study in a common unit of measurement. There are different degrees of statistical significance, and the results of some studies may be stronger than others. In meta-analysis, studies can be classified in terms of the magnitude of the gender-related difference. Finally, meta-analysis allows researchers to group studies by subcategory and thereby assess the influence of variables other than gender. For example, if a researcher did a meta-analysis of studies on gender and reasoning ability, she might categorize the studies according to the type of task used or whether there was time pressure in the situation. Perhaps the gender difference only occurs when the task is male-oriented or when there is time pressure. A variable that interacts with another variable to change its effect is called a *moderator variable*.

Meta-analysis helps researchers interpret data from large numbers of studies and allows them to estimate the size of a gender-related difference. It simplifies the study of other variables that interact with gender—which is important because there almost always are other factors involved—and helps unravel possible confounding variables. Throughout this book, I report the results of meta-analyses on many gender-difference topics.

But meta-analysis cannot wholly compensate for the biases in the original studies or ensure objective interpretation. Reviewers must still decide which studies are relevant and whether several measures of the same construct (such as different tests of reasoning ability) are measuring the same thing. Moreover, there could be an overlooked source of bias common to all the studies in a meta-analysis, which could lead to an overall conclusion that is biased (Hedges & Becker, 1986). If most of the tests of reasoning ability used in research happened to use problems and examples more familiar to men, for example, a false gender difference might show up in a meta-analysis.

No statistical technique can resolve all problems of interpreting differences. Meta-analysis can show which variables moderate the occurrence of gender differences, but it does not allow conclusions about the *causes* of the differences. Moreover, there is still room for disagreement about how big a difference must be to count as an important one. The meaning of differences is still at issue, because it is human beings who make meaning out of numbers.

Interpreting Results: Values and Ideology in Research

It is not always easy to see the values and assumptions underlying interpretations of data about gender. Students learn that science is value-free and that scientists are objective, impartial seekers of truth. But values and beliefs related to gender have affected research throughout the history of science (Gould, 1981; Harding, 1986). A brief history of the scientific study of some gender issues will help clarify the connections between values and practice.

Throughout most of Western history, the intellectual and moral inferiority of women was seen as self-evident. The first systematic empirical research on women conducted by scientists of the late nineteenth century took women's inferiority as a given and was aimed at uncovering its biological determinants (Gould, 1980; Hyde & Linn, 1986; Russett, 1989; Shields, 1975). In other words, most scientists at that time were convinced that women were not as intelligent as men and they focused on finding biological differences between women and men to explain what they were sure was true. One way to understand their focus is to think about it in its political context. In an era of agitation over women's rights, members of the dominant social group needed to document the inferiority of other groups in order to defend the status quo. "You are women and hence different," was the message conveyed. "Your differences disqualify you for the worldly roles you seem, most unwisely, to wish to assume" (Russett, 1989, p. 23). Sometimes the scientists' antifeminist bias was expressed directly; one British anthropologist presented an allegedly scientific paper denouncing the "superficial, flat-chested, thin-voiced Amazons, who are pouring forth sickening prate about the tyranny of men and the slavery of women" (cited in Russett, 1989, p. 27).

The Female Brain: Different and Inferior

Historically, sexism, racism, and class bias were often intertwined and the brain often was the battle site (Bleier, 1986; Winston, 2003). First, researchers asserted that the inferiority of women and people of color was due to their smaller brains. One prominent scientist asserted that many women's brains were closer in size to those of gorillas than to the brains of men (cited in Gould, 1981). Similarly, scientists measured cranial size in skulls representing various "races" and concluded that the races could be ranked on a scale of cranial capacity (and hence intelligence) with darker people such as Africans at the bottom, Asians intermediate, and White European men at the top. The brain-size hypothesis foundered when it occurred to scientists that, by this criterion, elephants and hippos should be much more intelligent than people. They then turned to the ratio of brain size to body weight as a measure of intellectual capacity. Little more was heard of this measure when it was discovered that it actually favored women.

Giving up on gross differences such as brain size, scientists turned to examining supposed differences in specific regions of the brain. When it was believed that the frontal lobe was the repository of the highest mental powers, the male frontal lobe was seen as larger and better developed. However, when the parietal lobe came to be seen as more important, a bit of historical revisionism occurred. Women were now seen as having similar frontal lobes but smaller parietal lobes than men (Shields, 1975).

When size differences in brain regions proved impossible to document, the debate shifted to the *variability hypothesis*. It was asserted that men, as a group, are more variable—in other words, although men and women may be similar on average, there are more men at the extremes of human behavior. Variability was viewed as an advantageous characteristic that enabled species to evolve adaptively. The variability hypothesis was used to explain why there were so many more highly intelligent men than women. Only men could achieve the heights of genius.

The Female Mind: Different and Deficient

The history is similar for another type of research, the measurement of human abilities, which began in the nineteenth century with Sir Francis Galton's studies of physical variation and motor skills. Galton measured height, grip strength, and reaction time because he thought they reflected mental ability. When physical abilities failed to correlate with intellectual functioning, the mental testing movement was born. When tests of mental ability failed to demonstrate male intellectual superiority, scientists returned to the variability hypothesis to explain how apparent similarity reflected underlying difference, claiming that men and women might be equal on average, but only men appeared at the upper end of the distribution of mental ability (Hyde & Linn, 1986; Shields, 1982).

Some of the first generation of women who became psychologists worked to dispute these claims. For example, Leta Hollingworth and Helen Montague examined the hospital records of 2,000 newborn infants to test the variability hypothesis. Others examined gender-related differences in emotionality and intelligence (Wooley, 1910). Few differences were found. However, widespread beliefs about innate gender differences in mental abilities persisted. Today, the search for biological differences underlying intellectual functioning continues.

The Lessons of History

The history of attempts to find biologically based sex differences illustrates some important points about the study of gender-related differences. Much of this history shows haphazard testing for a wide variety of differences. Of course, the number of possible differences is infinite, and demonstrating the existence of one or many gives no information about their causes. Perhaps most important, this history illustrates that scientific knowledge is historically and contextually limited. In hindsight, it is easy to see how the racist and sexist prejudices of past eras led researchers to search for justifications of the inferiority of women and people of color. It is less easy to see how personal values affect the work of contemporary scientists, but such influences surely exist. Even today, the traits attributed to women and minorities are less socially desirable than the traits attributed to men. Because White men remain the norm by which others are judged, and because this dominant group is mostly in charge of designing, producing, and interpreting scientific research, science may sometimes be enlisted in support of the social status quo.

How can we begin to make sense of the differences between women and men? One approach is to analyze these differences in terms of the gender system—to consider how they are produced and maintained at the sociocultural, interactional, and individual levels. To make this task easier, I will focus on two areas where differences have been shown to be socially (as well as statistically) significant: mathematics performance and emotionality.

Gendering Cognition: "Girls Can't Do Math"

Women and men are much more similar than different in cognitive ability and skills (Halpern, 1992; Maccoby & Jacklin, 1974). However, math ability and achievement is one of a very few areas where research shows consistent gender differences. Let's look at these differences in mathematics performance.

There are two widely used ways to measure math ability and achievement: school achievement and performance on standardized tests such as the SAT-M. On standardized tests, boys come out ahead. In school achievement, girls come out ahead. From elementary school through college, girls and young women of all ethnic groups get better grades than boys and young men, even in areas in which the boys score higher in ability tests. Girls are less likely to repeat a grade, get assigned to special education classes, or get in trouble over their behavior or schoolwork, and they are more likely to take honors and AP classes, make the honor roll, and be elected to a class office (Coley, 2001; Hill et al., 2010; Hyde & Kling, 2001). Their higher academic achievement is rarely interpreted to mean that girls are more intelligent. Rather, it is claimed that girls get their higher grades by being quiet and neat, following directions, and trying hard to please their teachers. This may be an example of devaluing the characteristics of a subordinated group. In actuality, girls' higher grades are linked not only to their ability to refrain from disruptive behavior in class but also to their drive for mastery (Kenney-Benson et al., 2006).

Girls' performance on standardized math tests is better than boys' in the elementary school years; in high school they perform equally or slightly less well than boys (Hyde & Kling, 2001; Muzzatti & Agnoli, 2007). A generation or two ago, in the 1940s to 1960s, the differences in favor of boys were much larger. Then girls started to take more math classes; today college-bound high school girls are just as likely as college-bound boys to take four years of math (Hill et al., 2010). Now, the similarities outweigh the differences, and there is a lot of overlap between the distributions of males' and females' scores. This historical change is often interpreted in terms of the gender similarities tradition: given equal opportunity, girls will perform as well as boys.

There is, however, a well-documented difference favoring males in *advanced* mathematics performance. For the past 30 years, boys have scored consistently higher on the math portion of the SAT than girls. For example, the 2009 gender gap was 35 points, two points greater than the previous year (2009 College Bound Seniors, 2010). In national math talent searches using the SAT and similar tests, far more boys than girls are identified as gifted, and the gifted boys score higher than the gifted girls (Hill et al., 2010). The gender gap in math scores occurs within every ethnic group tested (White, Black, Hispanic, and Asian American), and it also occurs on the GRE test, which is used for admissions to graduate school.

What a puzzle for psychological research to unravel! Girls do better than boys on standardized tests in math and get better grades. Yet, by the time they are in high school, they score lower on advanced math. And they are far less likely than boys *with the same test scores* to major in math or pursue a math-related career (Ben-Zeev et al., 2005; Hill et al., 2010).

What Factors Influence Mathematics Performance?

As you might expect, many factors influence the development of gender differences in math performance. Some researchers emphasize the possibility of biologically based differences in ability. Others emphasize social factors such as gender stereotypes, gender-linked differences in math self-confidence and attitudes, and stereotype threat.

Biological Perspectives

Gender differences, especially in advanced mathematical reasoning, may be in part influenced by gender-linked genetic contributions, hormonal influences, or differences in brain structure (Hill et al., 2010). So far, however, no one has been able to specify exactly what the relevant biological differences are or how they might work to produce performance differences. The existence of a sex-linked gene for math ability was ruled out a long time ago (Sherman & Fennema, 1978). There are some physical differences in female and male brains, but whether these are related to cognitive differences is not yet understood. Some gender-linked differences do not occur cross-culturally (Ben-Zeev et al., 2005), and others have been getting smaller over time (Hill et al., 2010). For example, 30 years ago there were 13 boys for every girl who scored over 700 on the SAT math exam at age 13; today there are just 3 boys for every girl. It's still a big difference, but the fact that it's shrunk so much suggests that environmental influences must be important. In a recent review of more than 400 articles on why women are underrepresented in math and science, the researchers concluded that the evidence for biological factors was weaker than the evidence for social factors (Ceci et al., 2009). But possible connections between gender-linked biological influences and intellectual performance continue to be explored.

Math as a Male Domain

Close your eyes and visualize a mathematician. Chances are your image is of a cerebral-looking man with glasses and an intense but absent-minded air—an Einstein, perhaps. Early research showed strong stereotypes that math was for men, and nerdy men at that. When elementary and senior high school students were asked about their perceptions of people in math-related careers such as science, engineering, and physics, they described white-coated loners, isolated in laboratories, with no time for family or friends. Not surprisingly, female mathematicians were stereotyped as unattractive, masculine, cold, socially awkward, and overly intellectual (Boswell, 1979; 1985). Related to the stereotype of math as a male domain is the stereotype that boys and men are better at math. At the center of these math stereotypes is the instrumental/affective dimension described in Chapter 3. Because gender stereotypes ascribe autonomy and rational thought to men, it is difficult to imagine women enjoying (and being good at) a career that calls for these attributes. Because emotion and connection to others are ascribed to women, a woman who is in a male-stereotyped occupational field such as math or science may be seen as atypical and unfeminine.

In the past, it was thought that the belief that math is for the guys was held largely by girls and women, and that it deterred them from choosing math courses and math-related activities. However, a meta-analysis of math attitudes has shown that males hold this belief much more strongly than females do (Hyde et al., 1990). This finding suggests that gender-related influences on math choices work at the interactional and social structural levels at least as much as at the individual level. In other words, we can no longer conclude that women's underrepresentation in math and science is entirely due to their own choice that math is not for them. Rather, it may be at least partly due to others' beliefs that math is not for women. Such beliefs can create self-fulfilling prophecies (Chapter 2), as others' behavior may put subtle pressure on girls and women to conform to stereotypical expectations.

Learning the Lesson: "I'm Just Not Good at Math."

Even when they take the same courses, boys and girls may experience different worlds in the classroom. Research on classroom interaction confirms that boys and girls are not always treated similarly. At all grade levels, a few males often dominate classroom interaction while other students are silent and ignored (Eccles, 1989). Gender interacts with race: White males get the most attention from teachers, followed by minority males and White females; minority females get the least attention of any group. And this discrimination takes a toll: girls of all ethnic backgrounds, but particularly African American girls, become less active, assertive, and visible in class as they move through the elementary grades (Sadker & Sadker, 1994).

Sexism in the classroom may be benevolent (Hyde & Kling, 2001). Teachers may be trying to protect the feelings of girls by not calling on them for difficult questions or by praising their appearance, not their performance. As we learned in Chapter 2, however, benevolent sexism has its costs. Girls may do their best when they are challenged, not protected, in school. Classroom sexism can also be hostile. For example, girls experience sexual harassment from their peers and teachers more often than boys (American Association of University Women Educational Foundation, 2001).

By the time they are 8 or 9 years old, girls are losing their confidence that they can do math as well as or better than boys, and their change in attitude is independent of their actual performance. When they have trouble with a math problem, they tend to attribute it to their lack of ability, and they are more influenced by what they believe their teacher thinks about them than by their own actual performance (Dickhauser & Meyer, 2006). Fifth-grade girls report less enjoyment and pride in their math achievement than fifth-grade boys do, and more anxiety, hopelessness, and shame (Frenzel et al., 2007). In middle school, although their grades remain better than boys' grades, girls rate themselves lower in math ability, consider their math courses harder, and are less sure that they will succeed in future math courses. A meta-analysis has shown that girls' lower confidence about their math abilities is a consistent finding, although the gender difference is not large (Hyde et al., 1990). It may start as early as the third grade: In one study of 476 students in second through fifth grade classes in Italy, the second-graders did not differ in their math self-confidence—but by third grade, the boys' self-confidence was higher. By fifth grade, both girls and boys agreed that boys are better at math (Muzzatti & Agnoli, 2007).

As math self-confidence declines, and the stereotype that boys are better at math is internalized, girls begin to differ from boys in their more general attitudes about math. Compared to boys, they are more likely to say that they don't like math very much and don't consider it very important to their future. They also report that they put in lower levels of effort in math class (Muzzatti & Agnoli, 2007). In other words, they disengage from math, despite performing just as well as boys do, and look elsewhere for sources of self-esteem. Over time, boys' math self-confidence and the value they ascribe to math declines too, but not as much as it does for girls. For adolescent girls, self-esteem is linked more to confidence in their physical attractiveness to boys than it is to confidence in their academic ability (Eccles et al., 2000).

Parents of girls probably play a part in these attitude changes. Parents tend to attribute a daughter's success in math to hard work and effort, and a son's success to talent. They view math as more difficult for daughters and more important for sons. Parents' stereotypical beliefs about gender differences predict children's later beliefs about their math abilities (Tiedemann, 2000). Parents' beliefs may be expressed subtly (just a little more praise for Johnny's math grade than Susan's) or more overtly (only Dad helps with math homework; Mom says it's beyond her) but they may add up to convey the message to boys that they have natural math aptitude. Girls, on the other hand, may learn that hard work cannot entirely make up for their lack of ability.

Stereotype Threat

One important way that beliefs about gender and math ability may affect performance is through stereotype threat. As discussed in Chapter 3, when people know that there is a negative stereotype about their group's abilities, the pressure caused by their fear of confirming the stereotype can interfere with their performance.

Typically, stereotype threat is studied in laboratory experiments. In one such study, college students were given a tough math test after being told that men and women usually do equally well on it. The women and men achieved similar scores. Another group of students took the same test after being told that significant gender differences were expected. In this group, the men outperformed the women.

A third group was given the test with no mention of gender similarities or differences (similar to an SAT testing situation). In this group, the men also outperformed the women (Spencer et al., 1999). These results suggest that the gender gap in math performance is at least partly due to stereotype-influenced beliefs and expectations. When women believe that men will do better than they will on a math test (either because they're led to by the experimenter or because they have learned this belief elsewhere), they tend to produce the expected results. However, when the stereotype of female inferiority is explicitly challenged, women perform as well as men.

Hundreds of studies of stereotype threat have been conducted in the past decade, both in the United States and other countries. They have demonstrated effects of stereotype threat on female and ethnic and racial minority students, from elementary school children through high school, college, and graduate students. Together, they provide a great deal of information about what activates stereotype threat, the factors that influence it, who may be affected by it, and how it can be prevented or alleviated. A meta-analysis of 151 experiments has shown that the damaging effects of stereotype threat are consistent for both women and minorities (Nguyen & Ryan, 2008). Here, we will focus on stereotype threat related to gender and math performance.

Stereotype threat is likely to be activated whenever the negative stereotype of the group (in this case, that girls aren't good at math) is salient or explicit in the situation. For example, just taking a test in the presence of men may activate stereotype threat for women. In one study, students were tested on difficult math problems in small groups composed of all men, all women, or different male/female combinations. When tested with other women, women got 70 percent of the items correct. When the group was one-third male, their scores dropped to 64 percent. And when women were outnumbered by men, they got only 58 percent correct. Group composition had no effect on the men's performance (Inzlicht & Ben-Zeev, 2000). It seems that being in the minority hinders women's performance by increasing anxiety and stereotype threat. For another example of how stereotype threat directly affects women's math performance, see Box 4.1

Stereotype threat can be activated just by making gender identity salient. In a classroom study of 7- to 8-year-old French girls and boys, the children were primed to think about gender by being given a picture to color. For boys, the picture was of a boy holding a ball; for girls, it was a girl holding a doll. A control group colored a landscape picture. Following this priming for gender identity, the children worked on math problems from a standardized test. Gender priming disrupted the girls' ability to solve the more difficult problems, but had no effect on the boys' problem solving (Neuville & Croizet, 2007).

Exactly how does stereotype threat disrupt performance? When activated, it arouses stress-related physiological responses; it causes the person to focus too much on how she is doing at the task; and it requires her to try to suppress negative thoughts and emotions (Schmader et al., 2008). All these effects combine to disrupt working memory and interfere with the ability to generate good problem-solving strategies (Quinn & Spencer, 2001).

Stereotype threat may occur quite often for women in male-dominated areas of study. For example, female college students in math, science, and engineering

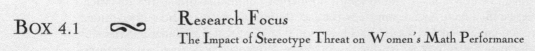

Box 4.1   Research Focus
The Impact of Stereotype Threat on Women's Math Performance

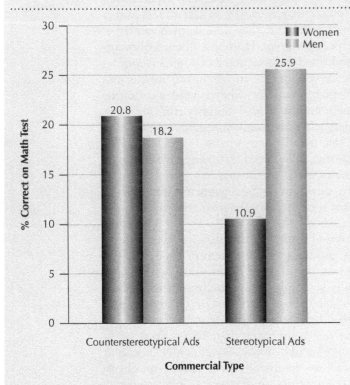

In this study, female and male college students were selected on the basis of having good math attitudes and achievement. The students then saw television commercials. Some of these commercials were gender-stereotypical (a woman bouncing on her bed with joy over a skin product, or drooling with pleasure over a brownie mix); others were counter-stereotypical (a woman speaking knowledgeably about health care issues). All students then took a difficult math test. Although none of the ads had anything to do with math, viewing the stereotypical commercials caused the women's subsequent math performance to drop quite noticeably because women became anxious about fulfilling the stereotype. Men's performance was not affected, probably because sexist stereotypes of women were not personally relevant to them.

Source: Adapted from Davies et al., 2002.

report higher levels of stereotype threat than those in the arts, education, and social science (Steele et al., 2002). Women who pursue math and science careers are in the minority for most of their working lives, and stereotype threat may be an ongoing problem for them. In one intriguing study, female engineers who interacted with men who behaved in sexist ways later performed worse on an engineering test (but not on an English test) than those who interacted with nonsexist men (Logel et al., 2009).

Stereotype threat can affect just about anyone who is a member of a group that is negatively stereotyped. What happens when gender and ethnicity both foster negative stereotypes? In a study of 120 Latino/a and White college students, ethnicity-based stereotype threat reduced math performance for Latinos and Latinas, and gender-based stereotype threat reduced performance for Latinas and White women. In other words, Latinas were disadvantaged by both gender-based and ethnic-based stereotype threat (Gonzales et al., 2002).

Ethnic and gender stereotypes sometimes contradict each other. Asian American women, for example, may be stereotyped as not good at math (because they are female) or good at math (because math ability is stereotypically attributed to Asians). To see how these contradictory stereotypes affected math performance among Asian American women, researchers manipulated the salience of gender or ethnic identity by having one group fill out a questionnaire about gender and another a questionnaire about ethnicity before taking a math test. A control group filled out a general questionnaire that did not reference ethnicity or gender. As predicted, women in the ethnicity-primed group did best on the math test; those in the control group did next best; and those in the gender-primed group did worst (Shih et al., 1999). Both male and female Asian Americans who are highly identified with their ethnic group may experience a "stereotype boost"—improved performance when the ethnic stereotype is activated (Armenta, 2010).

Stereotype threat can even disrupt the performance of White men. When researchers tested a group of White male students by evoking the stereotype that Asians are better at math than White Americans, their performance on a difficult math test dropped in comparison to a neutral control group—even though these students were all highly competent at math (Aronson et al., 1999).

Research on stereotype threat has shown that several factors influence how likely it is to happen and how severely it impacts performance. For example, women's math performance is more affected by subtle, rather than blatant, priming of stereotypes. A girl or woman is more vulnerable if she identifies with math as a somewhat important domain for her. Task difficulty is important, too—negative effects usually show up only on difficult tasks, not easy ones (Keller, 2007; Nguyen & Ryan, 2008).

Can stereotype threat be prevented? The answer is yes—several strategies have been shown to be effective in preventing its activation. One strategy is simply to teach women about the possibility of stereotype threat—being informed seems to prevent or lessen its effects (Johns et al., 2005). Another strategy is to counter the negative stereotype with a positive stereotype that is relevant to the individual. For example, activating the belief that "college students are good at math" or "students at elite colleges like mine usually don't experience stereotype threat" prevents female college students from being affected by the women-and-math stereotype. Stronger and more direct countermessages work better than subtle ones (McGlone & Aronson, 2007; Nguyen & Ryan, 2008; Rydell et al., 2009). A third strategy is to remind women of other aspects of their identity—in effect, to convey that "you are not only a female, but a writer, a friend, a student," and so on. In one study, students who were asked to draw detailed self-concept maps later performed better on a difficult math test than students asked to draw simple self-concept maps, probably because the task evoked their multiple identities (Gresky et al., 2005). In another study, students who wrote about their most valued personal characteristic were later immune to stereotype threat (Martens et al., 2006). In general, anything that makes gender identity or gender stereotypes less salient in a math testing situation, and other identities more salient, reduces the likelihood that stereotype threat will disrupt girls' and women's performance.

Social Implications of Gendered Cognition

Girls and boys still grow up in a gendered world (see Chapter 6): dolls and princess attire for girls; microscopes, building sets, and computers for boys. One implication of the gender gap in math performance in the United States is that our society needs to pay more attention to the intellectual development of girls. One way to help young girls develop their cognitive abilities is to provide them with computers and so-called boys' toys. Psychologist Diane Halpern, an expert on cognitive sex differences, has said, "We may be shortchanging the intellectual development of girls by providing them with only traditional sex stereotyped toys" (Halpern, 1992, p. 215). Another strategy is to offer educational environments that optimize chances for girls and young women to do well in math and science. (See Box 4.2.)

A second implication of the math gap is that our society's emphasis on test scores may be misplaced. At least 1.5 million high school students take the SAT each year, and another 1 million take the ACT. The purpose of these standardized tests is to predict college grades. But although women score lower on such tests, they get better grades than men in college. In fact, females who score 33 points lower on the math SAT earn the same grades as males in the same college math courses. The tests thus underpredict women's performance (Gender Bias in College Admissions Tests, 2007). This *female underprediction effect* compromises women's right to equal education. Testing activists have charged that a test that underpredicts the performance of more than half the people who take it is so unfair that it should be considered consumer fraud.

The consequences of the underprediction effect are serious (Hyde & Kling, 2001). Nearly all four-year colleges and universities use test scores in admissions decisions. Because women's college grades are higher than their test scores predict, some women are rejected in favor of male applicants who will do less well in college. Moreover, women lose out on millions of dollars in financial aid. For example, the majority of National Merit Scholarships go to upper-income White and Asian American males (National Merit Scholarship Corp., 2010). Girls also lose out on opportunities to participate in special programs for the gifted when SAT and PSAT scores are used to determine eligibility. Finally, an individual's test scores affect her self-confidence and her future academic goals (Hill et al., 2010).

At least one testing specialist maintains that standardized tests are deeply androcentric:

> Excluded are whole areas of human achievement that contribute to success in school and work. . . . Such characteristics and skills as intuition, motivation, self-understanding, conscientiousness, creativity, cooperativeness, supportiveness of others, sensitivity, nurturance, ability to create a pleasant environment, and ability to communicate verbally and nonverbally are excluded from standardized tests. Content that is not tested is judged less valuable than that included on tests (Teitelbaum, 1989, p. 330).

Although standardized tests are supposed to be objective, they are written by subjective human beings who reflect the values of their society. Furthermore,

BOX 4.2 ∽ Your Daughter (or Niece or Little Sister) the Rocket Scientist

How to Encourage Girls in Math and Science

Although girls are told from a very young age that they can be whatever they want—a doctor, lawyer, scientist—a recent report from the American Association of University Women found that girls aren't following this advice, particularly when it comes to pursuing careers in fields such as science, technology, engineering, and math. So how do we get (and keep) girls interested in becoming rocket scientists? Here are some of the main suggestions from the AAUW report:

1. Teach her that intelligence grows. Students who have a "growth mindset"—that is, they believe that intelligence can be increased through effort and hard work—are more likely to persevere through academic challenges and succeed in all fields (including math and science) compared to individuals who have a "fixed mindset"—those who believe that their intelligence is innate and unchangeable. Research has shown that there is no gender difference in math and science performance for students with growth mindsets.

2. Talk about stereotype threat. From a young age, children are aware of the stereotype that boys are better at math and science than girls. Unfortunately, research on stereotype threat shows that when people know about a stereotype related to their group, their performance on a task related to the stereotype can be impaired. The negative effects of stereotype threat can be overcome by talking to girls about it.

3. Remind her that Bs and Cs are okay. Girls are often harder on themselves in courses where they think that boys are more innately skilled (namely, math and science). If she doesn't receive an A, she might think she is confirming the stereotype that boys are better than girls in math. Encourage girls to think that tests are fair assessments of their understanding of the material, not their gender. It may also be beneficial to ask your daughter's teachers to set clear standards for assessments.

4. Encourage her spatial skills. One domain where boys consistently outperform girls is in spatial

skills, such as the ability to mentally rotate objects. However, it is possible for girls to easily improve their spatial reasoning, and not just through playing with Legos! Activities such as sewing, painting, and video games can all develop and enhance girls' spatial skills, particularly their ability to perform mental rotation.

5. Expose her to women working in science. The low visibility of women in science fields likely contributes to the maintenance of math and science stereotypes for girls. Expose girls to role models and mentors in these fields— even pointing out female television characters who are scientists can be beneficial. Involve her in afterschool programs and camps that emphasize women in science and technology careers—such experiences offer excellent role models.

To read the full AAUW report, go to http://www.aauw.org/learn/research/whysofew.cfm. Then read the full KiwiMagazine blog series from which this list is adapted; go to http://kiwimagonline.com/kiwilog/education/your-daughter-rocket-scientist. Contributed by Annie B. Fox.

test takers bring to the test different feelings about themselves and the test, and thus interpret items differently. There is no such thing as a value-free test (Teitelbaum, 1989). Because many important decisions are made on the basis of testing in our society, more research is needed on the tests themselves and how they produce similarities and differences among groups. And other criteria besides test scores should be taken into account for college admissions and scholarships.

Finally, beliefs about women's alleged inability to do mathematical and scientific thinking foster the continued exclusion of women and ethnic minorities from many careers. Science, math, computer science, and engineering are still among the most male-dominated fields. (See Figure 4.4.) The higher the level, the fewer women there are. For example, the most recent data show that only 17 percent of people with doctorates in computer and information technology are women (Hill et al., 2010). The underrepresentation of women in science, math, and technology is a serious problem. These jobs are interesting, prestigious, and will continue to be in high demand over the next decades. Plus, they pay well! Women are losing out on good career opportunities when they forgo these fields. Even more important than individual success is the fact that science, math, and technology are crucial to the future of our country, as we try to solve problems with the environment, resource use, food production, and health care. Ignoring half the population means that we are not getting the full pool of talent needed to meet the challenges of the twenty-first century (Hill et al., 2010).

Researchers in the similarities tradition have tried to demonstrate that, given the same opportunities, women can do math and science as well as men. By questioning the size of cognitive differences and examining how they are socially produced, feminist researchers have made a contribution toward equality. Yet, equality has not been achieved, although women, particularly White women, have made

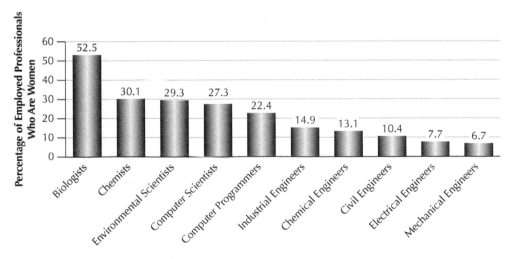

FIGURE 4.4 Women in selected science and technology occupations, 2008.

some very real gains. The belief persists that math and science are male domains; women of color continue to be extremely underrepresented in science; and discrimination against women persists.

Social change requires collective action. One success story started when women scientists at the Massachusetts Institute of Technology (MIT) decided to work together to end gender discrimination at their institution. At MIT's School of Science, there were 197 tenured men and only 15 tenured women. The 15 women, all of whom suspected that discrimination was taking place, demanded an investigation, which showed that they had been given less lab space and lower salaries than their male colleagues and had been excluded from positions of power. In response, MIT raised the women's salaries an average of 20 percent, equalized retirement benefits, and pledged a 40 percent increase in female faculty (Zernike, 1999). The success of the MIT women scientists shows that discrimination can be confronted and successfully challenged through persistence, courage, and collective action.

Gendering Emotion: "Boys Don't Cry"

Who are more emotional—women or men? Chances are the answer that pops into your mind is "Women!" When most of us think of emotion, gendered images come to mind—a woman who cries over the slightest upset, or blushes with embarrassment. Let's look more closely at gender and the experience and expression of emotion.

Emotion Stereotypes

The belief that women are more emotional than men are has been documented for as long as stereotypes have been measured (Broverman et al., 1972; Plant et al., 2000; Shields, 2002). It is widely held not only in the United States, but many other countries (Williams & Best, 1990). Not only are women stereotyped as the emotional sex, but particular emotions are attributed to women. Table 4.1 shows the emotion stereotypes of a sample of U.S. college students and working adults. Notice that a far greater number of emotions, both positive and negative, are attributed to women. Only three emotions—anger, contempt, and pride—are thought to be more characteristic of men. Emotion stereotypes are so cognitively ingrained that, in lab experiments, people are actually faster at perceiving angry expressions on men and happy expressions on women than vice versa (Becker et al., 2007).

Are emotion stereotypes applied equally to all women? In one study, when participants were asked about the communication style of African American and European American women and men, they viewed women's speech as more emotional, and African American's speech as more offensive, impolite, and socially inappropriate (Popp et al., 2003). These racially linked stereotypes suggest that African American women may be viewed differently depending on whether their race or gender is salient in a particular situation. If their gender is salient, their talk may be perceived as overemotional; if their race is salient, the same way of talking may be perceived as aggressive and rude.

TABLE 4.1   Emotion Stereotypes for American Males and Females

Male Emotions	Female Emotions	Gender-Neutral Emotions
Anger	Awe	Amusement
Contempt	Disgust	Interest
Pride	Distress	Jealousy
	Embarrassment	
	Fear	
	Guilt	
	Happiness	
	Love	
	Sadness	
	Shame	
	Shyness	
	Surprise	
	Sympathy	

Source: Adapted from Plant, A. E., Hyde, J. S., Keltner, D., & Devine, P. G. (2000). The gender stereotyping of emotions. *Psychology of Women Quarterly, 24,* 81–92.

A closer look at the stereotype of women as the emotional sex reveals that it depends on a peculiar definition of emotion. Emotional displays by men are often not labeled as emotionality. In fact, it is easy to think of examples of men expressing strong emotions: a tennis star throwing a tantrum on the court, a football team hugging each other ecstatically after a touchdown, an angry man yelling at another driver at a stoplight. But when people think of women as the emotional sex, it seems they are thinking of those emotions which women are allowed to express more than men are, such as sadness, love, surprise, and fear. The stereotype of women as the emotional sex is maintained in part by excluding anger from the everyday definition of emotion (Shields, 2002). A woman who cries when the dog dies may be seen as emotional, but a man who kicks the dog may not be.

Are there gender differences in emotionality that support the stereotype that women are more emotional than men? In studies done in the United States, women and men show consistent differences in expressing their own emotions and recognizing the emotions expressed by others. In talking and writing, women use more emotion words than men do (Brody & Hall, 2000). When asked about their emotional experiences, women report more intense emotions (both happy and sad) than men do—and the more they believe in emotion stereotypes, the more they report intense emotions for themselves (Grossman & Wood, 1993). They are more aware of their own and others' emotional states than men are (Barrett et al., 2000). Women are also somewhat more skilled at recognizing emotions expressed by others—termed ***decoding ability*** (Hall et al., 2000), and they tend to score higher on tests of emotional intelligence—a hazy concept that is often used in applied psychology to predict job performance (Joseph & Newman, 2010). But not every study finds these patterns, and some find contrary results. For example, when adolescent boys and girls talked with their parents about interpersonal dilemmas, the girls used more emotion words than the boys, a result that is stereotype-consistent. However, there was no gender difference in the use of words about anger, and boys used more words expressing sadness when talking with fathers than girls did, findings that are counter-stereotypical (Aldrich & Tenenbaum, 2006).

Like other gender-related differences, there is more overlap and similarity than difference between the emotionality of women and men as a group. To understand the similarities and the differences, let's look at ways in which emotionality and its meaning are socially constructed at the sociocultural, interpersonal, and individual levels.

Culture, Ethnicity, and Emotionality

Expressing Emotion

Ever since Darwin (1872), scientists have studied how emotions are expressed. Cross-cultural studies can help us understand similarities and differences in emotional expression. Early studies showed that people from different cultures could usually identify the emotions depicted in a set of posed photographs, leading psychologists to theorize that emotional expression is a biological universal with an evolutionary basis. However, a recent meta-analysis shows that people are somewhat better at recognizing emotions when they are expressed by a member of their own culture than when they are expressed by a member of a different cultural group (Elfenbein & Ambady, 2003).

Although the expression of emotions may be a biological universal, different cultures teach different techniques for channeling emotional expression. Every culture has **display rules** that govern which emotions may be expressed, under what circumstances, and how (Safdar et al., 2009). For example, in some cultures people are expected to shriek, wail, and cry loudly at funerals. If there are not enough family members to provide a suitably loud chorus, professional mourners may be hired to do the job. In other cultures, people are expected to show respect for the dead by quiet, emotionally subdued expressions of grief.

A society's display rules often incorporate gender stereotypes. In the United States, where women are expected to smile more than men are, more women than men undergo medical procedures such as collagen injections in the lips and teeth bleaching to increase the display value of their smiles. In Japan, however, a wide, teeth-baring smile is considered impolite for a woman, and a woman may hide her smile behind her hand (see Figure 4.5). In a cross-cultural study comparing display rules in Japan, Canada, and the United States, Japanese were less emotionally expressive overall than the other groups. However, gender-related display rules were similar in all three cultures: men expressed powerful emotions more than women, whereas women expressed the emotions of powerlessness (fear, sadness) as well as the positive emotion of happiness, more than men did (Sadfar et al., 2009).

FIGURE 4.5   Cross-cultural differences in smiling.

Do emotion display rules vary for different ethnic groups within our own society? One way to find out is to ask people of different ethnicities about how men and women are expected to experience various emotions. When members of four American ethnic groups (African Americans, Asian Americans, European Americans, and Hispanics) were asked this question, many differences emerged (Durik et al., 2006). Recall that among White European American participants, anger and pride are stereotyped as more suitable for men. Among African Americans, both these emotions were stereotyped as equally suitable for women and men. When asked about the positive emotion of love, European Americans and African Americans were similar to each other: both thought that women express love much more than men do. Asian Americans, however, differentiated less between women and men, and overall reported less expression of love. Among all ethnic groups, respondents expected women to express more guilt and embarrassment than they expected from men. These patterns of differences and similarities across ethnic groups show that the rules for expressing emotions are learned within specific cultural contexts.

Experiencing Emotion

Cultural differences affect the experience of emotion, not just its display. For example, college students in Japan reported feeling generally happier when they were experiencing emotions tied to interconnections, such as friendly feelings toward another. American college students, on the other hand, were happier when experiencing emotions tied to separateness, such as pride in an achievement (Kitayama et al., 2000).

These findings have been linked to broader differences between two types of cultures: some cultures encourage the development of an ***independent self*** whereas others foster an ***interdependent self*** (Markus & Kitayama, 1991). The United States and Western Europe hold up the independent ideal: each individual is seen as unique, and the task of each individual is to fulfill his or her potential and become an autonomous person. Much of the rest of the world has a very different ideal: individuals are seen as connected in a web of relationships, and their task is to maintain those connections by fitting in, staying in their proper place, and building reciprocal relationships with others. Cultural differences in the sense of self are illustrated in contrasting proverbs from the United States and Japan:

The squeaky wheel gets the grease. (United States)
The nail that sticks up gets hammered down. (Japan)

Most of the research on gender and emotions has been conducted in Western countries that place a premium on independence. Interestingly, gender differences in feeling as well as in expressing emotion are much smaller in collectivist countries than individualistic ones. In collectivist cultures, both women and men are allowed to feel and express emotion; in individualistic ones, females are assigned the task of compensating for the emotional deficits of the other half of the population (Fischer & Manstead, 2000).

Emotionality and Social Interaction

Learning the Emotion Rules

Children learn their culture's rules for displaying emotion at an early age. In our own society, one important influence is "emotion talk" from parents. Many studies have shown that parents are more likely to talk about people and emotions with their daughters than with their sons. Moreover, they talk to daughters and sons about different emotions. In one study of children between the ages of 2 1/2 and 3, 21 percent of mothers discussed anger with a son during a half-hour conversation, whereas not a single mother discussed anger with a daughter. Mothers also used more positive emotion words (e.g., happy) with girls (Fivush, 1989). Other studies show that both mothers and fathers are much more likely to discuss fear and sadness with a daughter than with a son (Fivush et al., 2000; Fivush & Buckner, 2000). This differential attention to girls' and boys' emotions soon has its effects: By the time they are 3- to 4-years-old, girls are more likely than boys to bring emotion talk into a conversation—especially talk about sad experiences (Fivush & Buckner, 2000).

As children begin to think about emotion in gendered ways, the social environment shapes different consequences for girls and boys. In a study of preschoolers, girls who expressed anger (but not those who expressed sadness or distress) were likely to be rejected by their peers, while boys who expressed anger tended to be popular with their peers (Walter & LaFreniere, 2000). And girls learn early to hide their negative feelings, because their emotional expressions are supposed to be "nice." For example, think about how you would act if someone gave you a gift you didn't like. Most adults have learned the social norm that, in this situation, you should pretend to be happy. When researchers presented first- and third-grade children with disappointing gifts, the girls showed more positive and less negative emotion than the boys, indicating that they had already internalized this rule and were better than the boys at masking their true feelings (Davis, 1995).

Children learn not only the display rules but also *feeling rules* (Shields, 2002). That is, they learn what it means to experience an emotion, what others expect them to feel, and how they are supposed to recognize emotions in others. All these lessons are deeply gendered. "Emotion education includes not only 'because you are a boy, feel/show X," but also "feel/show X in order to become a boy'" (Shields, 2002, p. 91). For example, a study of White suburban teenage boys showed that they valued teasing and bullying because their identity was connected to suppressing emotional reactions. Hostile interactions with others gave them practice in "sucking it up" and "taking it like a man" (Oransky & Marecek, 2002). For both boys and girls, doing emotions appropriately becomes an important part of doing gender, of performing one's identity as a boy or girl.

Through a Gender Lens

Beliefs about the different emotionality of males and females may influence perceptions of others' emotions. Classic studies have shown that observers who are asked to judge the emotions of babies and young children from video clips rely on gender as a cue. When told that the neutrally dressed child they are viewing is a boy, they perceive more anger than when told they are viewing a girl (Shields, 2002).

The influence of gender on perceptions of emotions occurs for adults, too. In one study, participants viewed photos of women's and men's faces displaying specific emotions (Plant et al., 2000). Some photos clearly portrayed anger, others clearly portrayed sadness, and still others showed a more ambiguous blend of anger and sadness. When people looked at the slides, what they saw depended on whether a woman or a man was displaying the emotion. Even though the actors in the photos had identical expressions, participants saw men's blended expressions as angrier than women's, and women's blended expressions as sadder than men's. Moreover, participants used the same gender lens even when the expressions quite clearly represented a single emotion. They rated women's anger as less angry than men's anger, and saw sadness where there was none in women's angry expressions. In another study, participants saw photos from a standardized set that portrayed clear, intense emotions. Again, participants perceived the angry male as showing more anger than the angry female; the angry female, but not the male, was seen as fearful (Algoe et al., 2000).

These studies show that gender stereotypes of emotion are powerful enough to lead people to misperceive others' feelings, even when they are quite clearly expressed. They also imply that, for women, anger is truly the forbidden emotion. An angry woman is so disturbing and unacceptable that people refuse to see anger in a woman's clearly angry expression, and instead choose to see sadness or fear. Furthermore, this research shows that people make gender-biased judgments about the reasons for emotional behavior in order to hold on to their stereotypes.

Do gender expectations about emotion lead to self-fulfilling prophecies? In one intriguing study, researchers manipulated the gender expectations to find out (Grossman & Wood, 1993). Male and female participants viewed slides designed to elicit negative emotions. Half the participants were given no special information about emotions, whereas the other half were told that research has shown a positive link between emotional responsiveness and mental health. In the first condition, where gender expectations were presumably operating as usual, women gave more intense emotional responses than men did. However, in the second condition, where participants were, in a sense, given permission to express emotion (because it's "mentally healthy"), men's responses were as emotional as women's were. This study suggests that gendered emotional displays are part of the performance of masculinity and femininity—of doing gender.

Gendering Emotion: A Summary

The social construction of females as the emotional sex occurs in many ways. Cultures differ in their rules for displaying and feeling emotion, but most societies have rules that are gender-linked. Emotionality is one of the core characteristics of feminine stereotypes cross-culturally. In our own society, this stereotype is maintained in part by defining emotionality more in terms of the emotions attributed to women than the emotions attributed to men. Stereotypes influence perceptions, so that identical behavior by a woman or a man may be seen as expressing different emotions. Moreover, stereotypes open the way for self-fulfilling prophecies. People expect women to be more emotional; therefore they may treat them in ways that encourage emotion displays.

Social Implications of Gendered Emotionality

Gender differences in emotionality are not socially neutral. Instead, they are linked to power and status, and they affect the roles, occupations, and opportunities considered appropriate for women and men.

Emotion, Status, and Power

Expressing emotion is linked to status and power as well as to gender. Emotionality may be taken as a sign of weakness if the emotions expressed are sadness, grief, or fear. However, other emotions are reserved for the powerful. People recognize this social fact, and expect different emotions from high- and low-status people in the same situations. For example, when college students read scenarios about employees receiving positive performance evaluations, they believed that a low-status employee should feel more appreciation, whereas a high-status employee should feel more pride. When the scenario described a negative evaluation, participants expected that the low-status employee should feel sad or guilty, whereas the high-status employee should feel angry (Tiedens et al., 2000). Notice that the emotions expected of high-status people—anger and pride—are identical to the ones expected of European American men (Plant et al., 2000). The right to get angry and show it is one kind of social power.

Another link between emotionality, status, and power is related to the roles and occupations considered to fit women and men. A person who shows fear and sadness is unlikely to be thought of as a potential leader in government, business, or the military. A person who shows anger, contempt, and pride is unlikely to be thought of as a potential full-time parent, teacher, or nurse.

In all the studies I have described, there is much more overlap than difference in women's and men's emotionality—just as there is in other gender-linked differences. Unfortunately, emotionality remains a core part of feminine stereotypes. As other gender categories (like intelligence and math ability) are challenged and changed, emotion may become more and more important in differentiating men from women. "In an era where neither 'masculine' work nor 'masculine' clothing unambiguously define gender as difference, emotion is one of the few remaining contested areas . . . in which drawing a line between masculine/manly and feminine still works" (Shields, 2002, p. 136).

There is no reason to think that a person cannot be emotionally expressive and also rational, yet the traits seem polarized in the minds of perceivers, with rational man and emotional woman on opposite sides of the divide. Historically, women's presumed emotionality was used to justify their exclusion from education and career opportunities. Earlier in this chapter, I described how nineteenth century scientists considered women's reasoning ability to be lesser than men's. They also considered women's emotions to be more delicate, sensitive, and unstable. Therefore, they reasoned, women had better be confined to the home, where their out-of-control emotions could be contained. If women were allowed to take part in public life, their weaker reasoning capacities might be "swamped by the power of emotion" (Shields, 2002, p. 72). Some of the founders of American psychology shared this view. As late as 1936, Lewis Terman claimed that, compared to men, women were more tender, sympathetic, and loving, but also more timid, fearful, jealous, and suspicious. Luckily, women's submissiveness, docility, and lack of adventurousness tended to keep them out of trouble, according to Terman (cited in Shields, 2002).

Echoes of this age-old prejudice still pop up from time to time. In the 1990s, women attempted to gain admission to two all-male colleges, the Virginia Military Institute and South Carolina's Citadel. These universities serve as openings to the social networks that control political and economic power in the South. Both offer military-type education. Although they were funded by taxpayer money, they continued to deny admission to women long after female cadets had been integrated into the U.S. Military Academies. When their discriminatory admissions policies were challenged, VMI and the Citadel claimed that women were unsuited for the military life because of their feminine natures. In testimony to the U.S. Supreme Court, attorneys for VMI claimed psychological research had proved that

> Women are physically weaker; that they are more emotional and cannot take stress as well as men; that they are less motivated by aggressiveness and suffer from fear of failure; and that more than a hundred physiological differences contribute to a "natural hierarchy" in which women cannot compete with men (United States of America v. Commonwealth of Virginia, 1994, p. 4).

In response, a large group of feminist psychologists (a group I was part of) testified in a friend of the court brief that the VMI witnesses had misrepresented and misused the psychological research on gender differences. In ruling against VMI's discriminatory policy, the Court stated that generalizations about women's natures, even if they may apply to some women, do not justify denying equal opportunity to all.

Emotions and Relationship Conflict

Because women are perceived to be the experts at emotion, they may be expected to be in charge of others' feelings as well as their own (see Figure 4.6). Stereotypes about the emotionally inexpressive male suggest that men need to be coaxed into recognizing and expressing their feelings, and that it is women's job to do so. Moreover, women are expected to be responsible for keeping a relationship smooth and free of conflict. Because of these expectations, romantic relationships can become destructive traps for women who put their commitment to the partner and the relationship ahead of their own needs (White et al., 2001). Married women may be expected to take on the role of emotion manager not only for their spouses but also for their children, and to mediate among spouse, children, and

FIGURE 4.6   **When men are emotionally inexpressive, others are left to guess their feelings.**

Source: © Tom Cheney/The New Yorker Collection/www.cartoonbank.com

other family members. Being responsible for everyone else's feelings can be a full-time job and a major source of stress. (Women's relational work is discussed more fully in Chapter 10.)

Men in our culture are likely to learn that expressing anger is an acceptable and effective means of controlling others. Societal acceptance of men's anger and aggression puts heterosexual women at risk of violence from their relationship partners. Men who are violent in dating and marital relationships often hold the belief that violence between intimates is acceptable (White et al., 2001). (For more on relationship violence, see Chapter 12.) At the same time, emotional inexpressiveness when it comes to positive feelings may serve to preserve status and power differentials that benefit men. Refusing to recognize the feelings of a partner or a child may be a means of control and a privilege of the more powerful. And as long as women are primarily responsible for maintaining emotional connection, their opportunities in work, achievement, and public life will be curtailed, and they will continue to be at risk for destructive and violent relationships.

Curtailing emotional expressiveness has costs for men, too. Men who score high on a measure of stoicism tend to show little emotional involvement with others, dislike the expression of feelings, and have little tolerance for emotion. These men report a lower quality of life overall than less emotionally restricted men and women do. A particular concern is that they are unlikely to seek psychological help when they have adjustment problems, which has implications for their long-term mental health (Murray et al., 2008).

Making a Difference

Claims about sex differences have often been used to justify keeping women in their place. Even today, hypotheses about female inferiority and claims of new gender-linked psychological differences keep turning up. Gender differences are the socially constructed product of a system that creates categories of difference and dominance. Because gender is a system of social classification that operates at the sociocultural, interactional, and individual levels, changing the social consequences of gender difference can take place at all those levels.

The Individual Level: Thinking Critically about Differences and Similarities

In this chapter, I've focused on two areas where gender-linked differences have been demonstrated: math performance and emotionality. However, it is important to remember that there are many more areas of thinking, reasoning, personality, and behavior that consistently show *no* gender-linked differences. Thus, one important part of thinking critically about gender and difference is to recognize that differences occur against a background of overall similarity, and there are far more areas of similarity than areas of difference.

Moreover, there is much more variability *within* each sex than *between* the sexes on cognitive skills, abilities, and personality traits. Therefore, it is impossible to predict much about a person's behavior by gender alone, even in an area where overall gender-linked differences exist. For example, recall the VMI admissions decision. It may be true that, on average, more men than women are interested in military-style education and prepared to undergo it. However, it is much harder to predict the performance of an individual woman or man. Will Taisha do better than Howard at VMI? That depends not only on their gender, but their fitness, intelligence, and determination. Just knowing Howard or Taisha's gender does not tell us much, because average group differences are not very good predictors of individual behavior.

At the individual level, each of us can try to think about gender-linked differences in all their complexity, resisting the urge to treat women and men as opposites. Even though it is tempting to think that "men are from Mars, women are from Venus," women and men are much more similar than different. Thinking critically and responsibly about alleged gender differences can help foster social change on behalf of equality.

The Interactional Level: Difference and Discrimination

We have seen that gender-linked differences are important to the social definition of masculinity and femininity. Therefore, even when women and men behave in similar ways, they may be seen as different. For example, recall the women scientists at MIT who were treated as though they were not as capable or valuable as their male colleagues, although their scientific work was similar. Emotional displays, too, may be judged differently depending on whether the emotion is coming from a woman or a man. Gender-biased perceptions of behavior create ample opportunities for self-fulfilling prophecies. Being aware of this possibility, and guarding against it, helps ensure gender fairness in evaluations of others.

Even if a gender-linked difference can be reliably demonstrated, it does not justify group discrimination. Suppose you are a parent who is told that your daughter should probably not apply for an AP math class because in the past, girls in this class have had a higher failure rate than boys. You probably would insist that your daughter be evaluated as an individual, not as a gender category. If her grades, motivation, and skills qualify her for AP math, her gender is unimportant. One solution to gender discrimination, then, is to assess people as individuals. However, this is sometimes impossible. If 2,000 people are applying to an elite college that can take only 300, admissions officers feel they must rely on test scores. For this reason, it is very important to ensure that the measures are fair.

Activist organizations are keeping watch on the testing industry. For example, after the group FairTest filed a complaint with the Office of Civil Rights over gender bias in the National Merit Scholarship competition, the test was changed, and the proportion of semifinalists who were female increased significantly.

The Sociocultural Level: Creating Opportunities for Equality

When gender differences in cognitive abilities and personality traits emerge, they are almost always preceded by differences in social environments and experiences. Comparisons of different ethnic and social groups within and across cultures suggest that diversity in cognitive skills and personality is strongly related to sociocultural factors. The similarities tradition argues that these differences would diminish or disappear with equal opportunity and gender-fair environments. Thus, psychologists and educators have created programs to equalize opportunity for girls and women in math and science.

One example is "Calculating the Possibilities," a summer program for high school juniors and seniors funded by the National Science Foundation (Pierce & Kite, 1999). Girls were selected for this program on the basis of grades, interest in science, and previous course work. For four weeks, the girls lived on a college campus. During this time, they visited corporations where they interacted with female scientists in pharmaceutics, engineering, medicine, and other areas. They met with career counselors who helped them explore their interests and goals. Moreover, each girl worked with a mentor on research projects in chemistry, biology, and other fields. Other activities included guest speakers and e-mail mentoring from women scientists. Asked what they liked about the program, the young women were very positive:

> Everything! This was the best learning experience! I learned about researching science and that it is fun and interesting. I learned women have a place in this world and a right to work for it.

> The visits have shown me that women still have a long way to go to be equal. I liked working with the mentors. Their experiences and stories have been very helpful in ways that are impossible to describe. It shows scientists can be real people (Pierce & Kite, 1999, p. 190).

Very few high school or college students receive the personalized science teaching and mentoring of a program like this. But sometimes even very simple efforts can help. In one recent study, middle school girls saw a 20-minute video about the lives of female engineers and the benefits of engineering careers. The video emphasized how engineers can help people and society, and encouraged students to think of themselves as capable of being an engineer. The result? An increase in the girls' interest in engineering careers (Plant et al., 2009). A society that cares about equal opportunity needs to make programs like these more available to girls.

The similarities tradition, grounded in liberal feminism, has provided the impetus for special programs in math and science for girls. It is hard to imagine the federal government sponsoring programs to equalize emotional expressiveness, relational orientation, and empathy. According to the differences tradition, these are so-called feminine characteristics that are less valued by society. Researchers in the differences tradition argue that women and their characteristic activities should be reappraised (Jordan et al., 1991). Women have been assigned the tasks of fostering others' development and taking care of others, tasks that require empathy and communality. Yet neither they nor society as a whole have been encouraged to value these interactions and activities, which may be underpaid on the job (see Chapter 10) and taken for granted at home (see Chapter 9).

Psychology and its theories have failed women by devaluing their strengths, according to researchers in the differences tradition. Many psychological theories of human development focus on *autonomy* as the end point. That is, the ideal adult is seen as one whose sense of self is entirely separate from others, and who is independent and self-reliant. If you are thinking that this sounds like the overall stereotype of men, you are right. But very few people are truly autonomous, and when individuals appear to be so, it is usually because many other people are quietly helping them. The idea that psychological development is a process of separating from others may be an illusion fostered by dominant men. Perhaps instead of the John Wayne/Clint Eastwood ideal of the autonomous man, theories of human development should stress human connection and caring. From this perspective, the criteria for human development should include the ability to engage in relationships that empower others and oneself; empathy, not autonomy, becomes the ideal (Jordan et al., 1991).

Can Similarities and Differences Be Reconciled?

Researchers in both the similarities and the differences traditions have recognized that sociocultural aspects of gender govern access to resources; for example, social forces work to keep women out of careers in math and science, and to overvalue the attributes of dominant groups in society. Both traditions also recognize that gender can become internalized—as when women come to think of themselves as bad at math and good at understanding others' feelings. The similarities tradition encourages a focus on equity for girls and women in family, work, and educational settings. The differences tradition suggests that women's characteristics, such as greater emotional connectedness with others, are strengths, not weaknesses.

Individual feminists may feel an affinity for either the differences or the similarities tradition (Hare-Mustin & Marecek, 1990). And a particular kind of research may be useful for a specific political goal. However, both traditions have an important place in feminist theory. Whether we are making comparisons by gender, culture, or some other category, similarities *and* differences can be shown, and they both have strengths and limitations (Kimball, 2001). Becoming familiar with both traditions can help address a very important question: How is the gender system made invisible so that socially produced gender seems inevitable, natural, and freely chosen?

Exploring Further

～

AAUW (www.aauw.org).

> The American Association of University Women is a nationwide network of more than 100,000 members that advances equity for women and girls through advocacy, education, and philanthropy. One of its most important contributions is to sponsor and

report research on women in math, science, and technology. Its Web site features many new initiatives in this area.

FairTest. (www.fairtest.org)

An activist organization that works to curtail the misuse of standardized testing and foster testing that is fair to women, ethnic minorities, and economically disadvantaged people.

Shields, Stephanie (2002). *Speaking from the heart: Gender and the social meaning of emotion.* Cambridge, UK: Cambridge University Press.

This important book explores how emotion is played out in the movies, on the sports page and the athletic field, and in our public and private lives. It offers new ways to think about how emotion is represented and experienced.

PART 3

Gender and Development

CHAPTER 5

Sex, Gender, and Bodies

"*It*'s a girl!" or "It's a boy!" At birth, a child's sex is announced to the world. It is the first label attached to this new person by parents and society, and it will have profound importance throughout the child's life. Why? What does it mean to be male or female?

In our society, three assumptions about sex are so fundamental that most people have never thought about them (Kessler & McKenna, 1978). The key assumptions are these:

- There are two, and only two, sexes.
- Sex exists as a biological fact independently of anyone's beliefs about it.
- Sex and gender naturally go together.

According to the first two assumptions, bodies always fall into two clear, natural categories, based on biological facts. The third assumption is that gender follows naturally from sex. In other words, once a child's sex is recognized, either at birth or by imaging during pregnancy, the process of becoming gendered will follow a normal and natural course. A female baby should come to know that she is a girl, accept her female sex as a core part of her identity, act like a girl, and grow into a heterosexual woman. Likewise, a male baby should grow up unambiguously masculine in his identity, interests, roles, and sexuality. These assumptions are the basis of the gender system (Chapter 2), which prescribes different roles for the two sexes and awards more power and status to men.

Are these three assumptions valid? Biological sex and its relationship to psychological gender turn out to be surprisingly complex and unpredictable—not at all a neat binary system in which sex and gender are always congruent. This chapter explores sex and its complex relationships with gender and sexual orientation, beginning with the question of how sex develops.

How Does Sex Develop?

Sex is usually defined as two reproductive forms within a species. The female and the male of the species have specialized structures, organs, and hormones that result in different roles in reproduction. Thus, sex involves much more than just being born with a penis and scrotum or a clitoris and vagina. No one characteristic defines sex. Sex involves a cluster of biological attributes—including genetic, hormonal, and anatomical components—that develop gradually before birth. Let's look at how sex is formed during prenatal development—a process called *sexual differentiation.*

Sexual Differentiation during Fetal Development

Each human being has a set of 46 chromosomes in each cell of the body. Each of us inherits these 23 chromosome pairs, one of each pair from the mother and the other from the father. Of these, 22 pairs are *autosomes,* and one pair is composed of the *sex chromosomes,* called the X and Y chromosomes. The X chromosome is similar in size to the autosomes, but the Y chromosome is much smaller; it contains fewer than 50 genes, compared with 1,000 to 2,000 on the X chromosome (Wizemann & Pardue, 2001).

Genetically, a female is defined as a person who has two X chromosomes, and a male is defined as one who has an X and a Y chromosome. The newly conceived embryo inherits one X chromosome from the mother and either an X chromosome or a Y chromosome from the father. Therefore, genetic sex is determined at the moment of conception.

During the first month or so after conception, there is no visible indication of the fetus's sex. The fetus has no internal or external sex organs, only embryonic structures from which these will later develop. For example, the fetus has a structure that will become *either* a clitoris or a penis, depending on whether it follows a male or female developmental pathway (Fausto-Sterling, 2000). However, the fetus does not remain in this unisex state for long. Genes on the sex chromosomes, particularly on the Y chromosome, soon initiate sexual differentiation.

I'll first describe sexual differentiation in males, because it is better understood than in females. Starting at about the sixth week of pregnancy, a gene called the *sex-differentiation region of the Y chromosome* (**SRY**) causes the embryonic sex glands, or *gonads,* to grow and develop into *testes,* the pair of male sex glands that much later (starting at puberty) will produce sperm (Sinclair et al., 1990). Of course, only genetically male fetuses develop testes, because only they have a Y chromosome.

Once the testes are formed, they produce several steroid hormones collectively known as *androgens.* In turn, these androgens shape the development of a typical male body. The androgen *testosterone* causes the internal structures of male sexual anatomy to develop, such as the tubes that will later transport sperm from the testes. *Dihydrotestosterone* causes the penis to grow and the testicles to form. *Mullerian duct inhibiting hormone* (**MIH**) prevents the internal embryonic structures from developing into female organs such as a uterus.

When all these hormones are activated at the right times and in the right sequence during prenatal development, the fetus develops male sexual and reproductive anatomy. By the twelfth to fourteenth week of the mother's pregnancy, the process is complete. The fetus is male—genetically, hormonally, and anatomically.

How does sex develop in female fetuses? Much less is known about this process, probably because in the past many reproductive biologists were more concerned with male development and considered females to be the default pathway. In other words, when there is no Y chromosome to stimulate androgen production, the fetus develops as a female. This approach represents females as the product of an absence or lack—as the sex that just happens when there is no Y chromosome. Because of this androcentric view, there has been little research on the processes underlying female development until quite recently (Vilain, 2006).

There may be parallel or similar processes taking place in male and female development. The X chromosome probably contains several genes that cause sexual differentiation (Fausto-Sterling, 2000). In the female fetus, the gonads develop into *ovaries,* the pair of female sex glands that contain eggs. At puberty, the ovaries produce steroid hormones called **estrogens**. However, estrogens do not function in the fetal development of females exactly the same way that androgens do in male fetal development. The female structures of vagina, labia, and clitoris develop largely before the ovaries are formed, so their development cannot be due to estrogens. Instead, estrogens may be important later in fetal development—but the processes are not yet fully understood (Fitch & Denenberg, 1998).

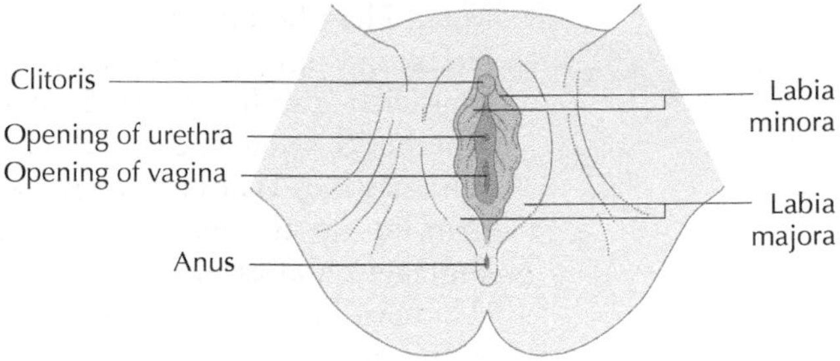

Just as in males, the process of sexual differentiation in females is complete by the twelfth to fourteenth week

FIGURE 5.1   Female external sexual anatomy at birth.
Source: Adapted from González, J. L., Prentice, L. G., & Ponder, S. W. (2005). *Newborn Screening Case Management. Congenital Adrenal Hyperplasia: A Handbook for Parents.* Texas Department of State Health Services. http://www.dshs.state.tx.us/newborn/hand_cah.shtm, Figure 5.

of the mother's pregnancy. The genetically female fetus now has the internal structures (uterus, ovaries, and Fallopian tubes) and external anatomy (vagina, clitoris, labia) of a female. (See Figure 5.1.)

As you can see, sexual differentiation involves coordinated processes influenced by both genetic and hormonal factors. Once the internal structures and external anatomy of sex are established, the sex hormones (androgens and estrogens) are not produced in quantity again until puberty. At that time, the ovaries or testes, along with other glands, produce the hormonal surges that lead to the development of a sexually mature adult body. Females and males both produce androgen and estrogen, but in greatly different amounts, throughout much of the adult lifespan.

Variations in Fetal Development: Intersexuality

In the great majority of cases, all the components of biological sex are congruent with each other. An XY fetus develops testes, produces androgens, and develops a penis and testicles. An XX fetus develops a vagina and clitoris, ovaries and a uterus. Based on the appearance of its genitals at birth, the infant is given the sex label female or male (its **assigned sex**) and raised as either a girl or a boy.

However, about 1.7 percent of babies vary in some way from the biological norm of two distinct sexes (Fausto-Sterling, 2000). In other words, the components of biological sex are not entirely congruent for these individuals. To put this percentage of the population in perspective, sexual variations occur twice as often as albinism, about as often as cystic fibrosis, and about half as often as Down's syndrome (Kessler, 2002). **Intersexuality** is a collective term for a number of specific variations on the theme of biological sex; people with any of these variations are usually referred to as **intersexed**.

Intersexuality has been recorded in many cultures and historical eras. People who did not fit either sex category often became sources of social controversy, and their cases have come down to us through historical records:

- In 1843, a Connecticut resident, Levi S., was not allowed to vote because town officials said he was "more female than male," and only men had the right to vote. They brought in a physician who examined S. Seeing a penis and testicles, the physician declared S. male; S. was allowed to vote. However, the physician later found that S. menstruated and had a vagina. It is not recorded whether S.'s vote was cancelled.

- Thomas(ine) Hall joined the Colonial army as a male at the age of 22, after growing up as a female. After military service s/he took up women's clothing again and earned a living sewing lace. Virginia court records show that Thomas/Thomasine went to court claiming to be both a woman and a man, with both a small penis and an underdeveloped vagina. After some indecision and confusion, the Court ruled that Thomas(ine) was indeed both a woman and a man, and must wear men's clothing plus an apron.
- In Italy, in 1601, after a blacksmith and soldier named Daniel Burghammer gave birth to a baby, he "confessed" to being "half male and half female." The Church called the child a miracle, but granted his wife a divorce because Burghammer did not fit the definition of a husband.

Biologist Ann Fausto-Sterling (2000), who provided these historical examples, points out that making a clear distinction between male and female has been central to law, religion, and politics in many cultures. Those who didn't fit in sometimes were forced to choose male or female and stick with the choice; if they could not or would not, they were punished or shunned.

Some intersex variations are visible—the person's genitals or other aspects of appearance are anomalous. Others, such as chromosome irregularities, may not result in any overtly noticeable bodily differences. What variations on the theme of biological sex occur, and do they affect behavior?

XYY Males: Born Criminals?

Some people have a genetic composition of XYY, or even XYYY. Because the Y chromosome and associated hormone production lead to male sexual differentiation, these people look pretty much like other men, except that they are taller than average (usually over six feet in height). Unless they had a specific reason for having a genetic test done, most men with this condition would be unaware of it.

Does an extra Y chromosome affect behavior? Early studies showed that XYY men were overrepresented in prison populations. Based on this evidence, many people began to believe that the biology of XYY men determined their criminality. The belief was reinforced when the media (falsely) claimed that one notorious mass murderer was an XYY male and therefore "born to kill."

The evidence about XYY males and violent behavior turned out to be quite different from the media hype. A large, well-controlled study was conducted comparing XYY men to genetically typical men and to men with another chromosomal irregularity—XXY, or *Klinefelter's syndrome.* Klinefelter's syndrome causes men to have a less masculine physique and appearance (small penis and testicles, enlarged breasts, and sparse body hair), along with increased risk of learning disabilities (Diamond & Watson, 2004). The researchers predicted that, compared to the XY men, the undermasculine XXY men would have an exceptionally low rate of criminality, whereas the overmasculine XYY men would have an exceptionally high rate, particularly for violent crimes (Witkin et al., 1976).

The results were a surprise. Contrary to prediction, a man's chromosomal composition was not directly related to his criminal record. What did predict criminality? Lower intelligence and educational level were associated with crime, and both XXY and XYY men were disadvantaged on these factors compared to XY men. As for violence, there was no relationship with chromosomal status. Less-intelligent people, including some of the men with chromosomal irregularities, were most often in prison for nonviolent crimes like burglary. In other words, the notion that an extra Y chromosome causes men to be violent criminals was *not* supported. Rather, some chromosomal irregularities may affect intelligence, which in turn may be linked to lowered educational attainment and greater likelihood of imprisonment.

The furor over "killer chromosomes" illustrates the dangers of simplistic thinking about biological determinism. For example, because of the alleged link between the extra Y chromosome and violence, it was proposed that newborn males be subjected to mass testing for extra chromosomes. At least one TV crime drama ran a plot line about an angelic-looking but monstrously evil XYY little boy. Mass testing for chromosomal status could have stigmatized all those found to have chromosomal irregularities. In turn, stigma could lead to the kind of differential treatment that creates behavioral confirmation and self-fulfilling prophecies. How might a boy's life be shaped by others' beliefs that he was born to kill?

Androgen Insensitivity

Maria Patiño, Spain's top female hurdler, was on her way to the Olympic Stadium in 1988 to start her first race when she was barred from competition for failing the sex test. Patiño looked like a woman, and believed she was a woman "in the eyes of medicine, God, and most of all in my own eyes." However, the test (mandatory only for female athletes) had shown that Patiño's cells contained Y chromosomes, and examinations revealed that she had no uterus or ovaries, but did have testes. Patiño was publicly humiliated by the press. After devoting her life to her sport, she was stripped of all her titles and medals, deprived of her athletic scholarship, and forbidden to compete in the future. Her boyfriend left her (Fausto-Sterling, 2000, pp. 1–2).

Maria Patiño had discovered, in an exceptionally cruel and public way, that she had an anomaly termed ***complete androgen insensitivity syndrome*** (CAIS) (Diamond & Watson, 2004). Her genetic composition was XY, but her body was completely unable to process androgens. Therefore, the androgens that had been produced by her testes during fetal differentiation did not prompt the development of male reproductive structures. Externally, she looked like any other woman; her testes were hidden in the folds of her labia. When she reached puberty, her testes and other glands had produced enough estrogens that she developed the breasts and body curves of a typical woman.

Maria Patiño challenged the International Olympic Committee's policy of sex testing. Eventually, she was allowed to rejoin the Spanish Olympic Team

(Fausto-Sterling, 2000). However, other Olympic athletes have not had such happy endings to their sex disputes with the IOC. At the 1996 Atlanta Olympics, 3,387 women were tested, and 8 were found to have androgen insensitivity or other intersex conditions. They were barred from competition and instructed to feign injury so that no one would know the real reason for their leaving the Games. It was not until the 2000 Summer games in Sydney, Australia, that the IOC discontinued sex testing for women ("Gender verification suspended," 2000). Runner Caster Semenya is the most recent victim of sex testing (see Box 5.1).

The Missing X

About once in every 3,000 births an individual is born with an XO chromosomal composition—instead of a second X or a Y, there is a missing sex chromosome, an anomaly called *Turner syndrome* **(TS)** (Fausto-Sterling, 2000). The fetus with this

---

Box 5.1 ∾ Caster Semenya

In August 2009, Caster Semenya, an 18-year-old South African track and field athlete, dusted her competition in the 800-meter race at the World Championships, winning a gold medal and running the fastest time in the 800 meters that year. Unfortunately, her remarkable win was not without controversy. Citing concerns over improvements in her race times in 2009 (which are often associated with performance-enhancing drugs), the International Association of Athletic Federations (IAAF) ordered Semenya to undergo what they term "gender verification testing," although its purpose is to determine the sex of an athlete. Semenya was banned from competition until testing was complete. Although never named as official reasons for pursuing gender testing, Semenya's muscular build, deep voice, and masculine facial features likely played a role. Competitors and spectators alike all questioned whether she was female, and at competitions, Semenya often had to go to the bathroom with a member of the competition so they could visually verify her sex.

Gender verification testing requires a physical examination, as well as the involvement of a gynecologist, an endocrinologist, a psychologist, an internal medicine specialist, and a gender expert. After extensive testing and examinations, the

condition lacks androgens and estrogens (other than those produced by the mother's body) during development. As a result, the fetus does not develop complete internal reproductive structures. Externally, however, people with Turner syndrome look like normal females, with a vagina, clitoris, and labia (recall that female genitals develop in the absence of androgens). Girls with Turner syndrome are short in stature, and they may have cognitive deficits in some math and spatial visualization tasks, such as map reading and mental rotation of objects (Mazzocco, 2009). These deficits are not directly related to the sex chromosomes or hormones, and their exact cause is still unclear (Collaer & Hines, 1995).

In the strictly genetic definition of sex, people with Turner syndrome are neither male (XY) nor female (XX). However, because their external genitals are female, they are labeled females and raised as girls. When they reach the age of puberty, girls with Turner syndrome are given estrogens to stimulate the development of breasts and an adult woman's body shape. Like CAIS women, those with Turner syndrome may be given vague half-explanations for their infertility and their need for supplemental hormones.

BOX 5.1 ～ Caster Semenya (Concluded)

experts convened and made their determination as to whether Caster Semenya was male or female—but this decision is not as straightforward as some might think. At what point is a female athlete (or anyone else for that matter) considered a woman? Is it the presence of a vagina? Or ovaries? Even the standards used by the IAAF are unclear. Could that be because gender is not necessarily the binary category that most assume? Before the IAAF decision was released, a reporter asked Semenya's former coach what he thought the outcome would be. His response—"Caster will remain Caster."

In November 2009, Semenya and the IAAF decided that she could keep her world championship medal and the accompanying prize money. Although some news outlets reported that Semenya had higher than normal testosterone and both male and female genitalia, the IAAF stated that results of the gender testing would remain private. In July 2010, Semenya was once again allowed to compete as a female athlete, and won her first race following a nearly one-year layoff.

The need to classify people as either male or female is so embedded in society that individuals who fail to conform are subjected to questioning, ridicule, and are often dehumanized. Although Semenya had the support of her family, friends, coaches, and country, and identifies as a female, she still had to verify her "true" sex to be allowed to compete as a female. However, important questions remain—when an individual is intersexed, should they be allowed to compete as male or female? Is there another way of classifying people unrelated to gender that would allow for fair athletic competition? What do you think?

Sources: Levy, A. (2009, November 30). Either/Or: Sports, sex, and the case of Caster Semenya. *The New Yorker*, pp. 45–59.

Longman, J. (2009, November 19). South African runner's sex verification results won't be public. Retrieved July 25, 2010, from http://www.nytimes.com/2009/11/20/sports/20runner.html?_r=1&adxnnl=1&adxnnlx=1280257218-0VRIqrDal6eneGsmaAQdQQ

Smith, D. (2009). Caster Semenya Row: Who are white people to question the makeup of an African girl? It is racism. Retrieved July 25, 2010, from http://www.guardian.co.uk/sport/2009/aug/23/caster-semenya-athletics-gender

Contributed by Annie B. Fox

Ambiguous Bodies

Because people with CAIS and Turner syndrome look like females, they are treated like females and raised accordingly. In contrast, some intersex conditions result in bodies that are visibly ambiguous: the external genitals may be some combination of penis-like and vagina-like structures and the internal glands and organs may be intersexed as well. Historically, people with sexually ambiguous bodies were called *hermaphrodites,* after the Greek deities Hermes and Aphrodite, who according to myth produced a child with all the attributes of both its father and mother (Fausto-Sterling, 2000).

Sexually ambiguous bodies may result from a number of genetic, hormonal, and environmental influences. For example, people with *partial androgen insensitivity* **(PAIS)** may have an external sex organ that could be classified as either a large clitoris or a small penis. Internally, they have male testes, but instead of being located in a scrotal sac, the testes may be located in the abdomen or in the labia (Diamond & Watson, 2004).

One of the most common conditions producing a sexually ambiguous body is *congenital adrenal hyperplasia* (CAH), a genetically inherited malfunction of one or more of the enzymes needed to make the steroid hormone cortisol (Fausto-Sterling, 2000; Hines, 2004). This hormone deficiency causes the mother's body to overproduce other hormones, which act as androgens on the developing fetus. When the condition is discovered at birth, the androgen overproduction is stopped (with cortisone). Similar conditions have occurred when pregnant women were prescribed hormones to prevent miscarriage, which had androgenic effects on the fetus.

As we have learned, androgens are responsible for the formation of male reproductive structures and anatomy. Female (XX) fetuses with CAH and related disorders develop female internal structures—the uterus, ovaries, and fallopian tubes. However, at birth their external genitals may look like those of infant males, or may be ambiguous. The clitoris may be enlarged and capable of erection. The labia may fuse (grow together) so that the vagina is hidden and the infant appears to have a male scrotum (see Figure 5.2).

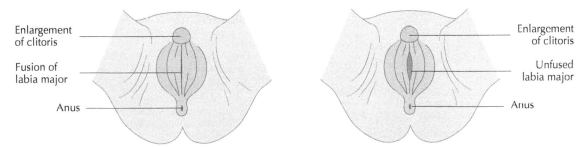

FIGURE 5.2   Ambiguous genitalia of female infants due to CAH.

Source: Adapted from González, J. L., Prentice, L. G., & Ponder, S. W. (2005). *Newborn Screening Case Management. Congenital Adrenal Hyperplasia: A Handbook for Parents.* Texas Department of State Health Services. http://www.dshs.state .tx.us/newborn/hand_cah.shtm, Figure 5.

Occasionally, genetic females with CAH are labeled male at birth, and raised as boys. In one study, for example, this had occurred in about 6 percent of cases (Zucker, 2001). Others have been reassigned at their request (see Box 5.2). Today, the condition is usually recognized at birth, at least in developed countries, and CAH infants are assigned as females. As infants or toddlers, their unusual genitals are surgically changed to a more typical female appearance.

The occurrence of intersex conditions demonstrates that two of the three key assumptions about sex are not universally true. The great majority of human beings do have one of two distinct bodily forms, female or male, along with a corresponding genetic composition and hormonal history. However, some do not. We turn now to the third assumption: that sex and gender naturally go together.

Research Focus

BOX 5.2   ∽   Juan and Ana and Juan: A Case Study of Gender Reassignment

The American Academy of Pediatrics recommends that XX intersex individuals with CAH be assigned to the female sex. However, a recent case study in the *Journal of Sexual Medicine* suggests that this practice may cause harm to individuals with CAH who identify as male. Juan Carlos Jorge and colleagues examined the case of Juan/Ana (pseudonyms), an XX intersex individual with CAH. Juan was born in the 1960's and initially assigned to the male sex. When Juan was a baby, his mother noticed he was having trouble urinating, and after a series of tests and a physical examination, doctors determined that Juan was a genetic female with CAH. Doctors requested changes to his birth certificate to indicate that he was a female, and she was given the name Ana.

During childhood, Juan/Ana was treated with hormones and at age 11, underwent genital surgery to complete the physical transformation to the female sex. Juan/Ana's mother consented to these treatments, believing it was medically necessary for the CAH condition as described to her by doctors. Despite treatment, Juan/Ana continued to identify as male, and psychiatric evaluations confirmed his male gender identity (although this information was absent in his medical file). He reported, "I'm a boy because I like girls. . . . I'm a boy because I have something down there that girls do not have."

By early adulthood, Juan/Ana decided to change his appearance to be male. He underwent surgery to remove the uterus, ovaries, and vaginal canal, but decided not to undergo surgery to construct a penis. When interviewed by Jorge and colleagues, Juan consistently told stories of his childhood and early sexual experiences that were consistent with male gender identity. As an adult, Juan entered a long-term relationship with a heterosexual woman, and served a father-figure to her children and grandchildren. Despite attempting to regain legal status as male for 10 years, Juan has been unable to do so.

Juan/Ana's case illustrates how, in the past, treatment of intersex individuals often took place without their informed consent. It also illustrates the need for the medical establishment to develop better guidelines for sex assignment of intersex individuals. We know very little about why genetic sex and gender identity may not always go together, and a cookie cutter system of sex assignment may do harm to individuals whose self-identified gender is inconsistent with their sex and does not fit guidelines from the medical community.

Source: Jorge, J. C., Echeverri, C., Medina, Y., & Acevedo, P. (2008). Male gender identity in an XX individual with Congenital Adrenal Hyperplasia. *Journal of Sexual Medicine, 5,* 122–131.

Contributed by Annie B. Fox

Sex, Gender Identity, and Gender Typing

For most people, the genetic, hormonal, and anatomical aspects of sex are congruent. At birth, their assigned sex fits these components. As they emerge from infancy, they develop a *core gender identity,* a fundamental sense of belonging to one sex or the other. Almost always, a child develops a core gender identity that corresponds to his or her biological sex. For most children, the core identity is learned by the age of three. Once formed it is usually permanent (Zucker, 2001). The child then becomes gender-typed, adhering to the rules of the gender system of his or her culture. For example, girls are expected to engage in whatever behaviors their culture defines as appropriate for girls and to refrain from those defined as out of bounds for girls. Each individual also develops an erotic and affectional attraction to others, most often heterosexual.

The underlying assumption is that all the components of sex and gender should fit together. A genetic female should have a core gender identity as a female. She should also become a girly girl, preferring feminine toys, clothing, and pastimes, and later she should become a heterosexual woman. Echoing the gender stereotypes discussed in Chapter 3, the assumption is that physical attributes, traits, and behaviors are all tightly linked. If they are not, the person is not developing normally. Whether a man or woman is gender-typed and heterosexual is taken as evidence for his or her essential maleness or femaleness (Fausto-Sterling, 2000; Kessler, 2002).

Intersexuality and Identity

Is gender identity predicted by an individual's chromosomal makeup, prenatal hormones, external genitals, assigned sex, or some combination of these and other factors? Researchers have addressed this question by studying gender in intersexed people. The medical literature often refers to these people as experiments of nature that allow scientists to examine the effects of biological irregularities that they could not ethically induce. (Of course, it would be unethical to do experimental studies of factors influencing human sexual differentiation.) But it is important to recognize that intersexed people are *people* first and foremost. Like other people, they have personal identities, friends and families, sexual desire and intimate relationships, achievement goals, and dreams for their future. Although they do not fit the gender categories allowed by society, they have to live in a gender-divided world.

When an individual's biological sex is a variant, what happens to his or her gender? There is a great deal of research attempting to determine which (if any) aspects of biological sex are responsible for one's core gender identity and gender typing.

Growing Up with Turner Syndrome

It is clear that one does not need two X chromosomes to develop a core gender identity as female. Despite their chromosomal differences from the norm, individuals with Turner syndrome are assigned as females, and develop a core gender identity as female. Girls with Turner syndrome are similar to other girls in their interests and activities.

Although Turner syndrome does not cause problems with gender identity and gender typing, it may cause other developmental problems. For example, the very short stature of girls with this syndrome, and their lack of the hormones that induce puberty, may lead to problems of social adjustment. They and their families may have to make decisions about taking growth hormones in childhood as well as estrogens to stimulate puberty. There is a need for health care practitioners to be sensitive to the psychosocial development of girls who have Turner syndrome (see Box 5.3).

Box 5.3   ∽   As a Woman with Turner Syndrome

As a woman with Turner Syndrome, I have faced some interesting and unique challenges. Turner Syndrome (TS) is a genetic disorder that affects the sex chromosome pair. There is a wide range of functioning within the TS population, characterized by a variety of physical, neuropsychological, and psychosocial difficulties. As someone living with the disorder, I have had to struggle with some important questions that have helped me to grow both personally and professionally.

The specific challenges I have faced have changed and developed as I have matured. Having the short stature commonly associated with TS, I remember being 12-years-old and wanting so badly to reach five feet. After three years on growth hormone, my interest in height waned and I began asking doctors how I could look more like my girlfriends who were developing breasts, curves, and a "grownup" look. Now that I am entering the

professional world, I find myself aware of presenting myself in an age-appropriate manner despite my younger appearance. As an adult woman searching for a partner to share my life with, I wondered how and when it was appropriate to share the details regarding my infertility with a significant other: what does it mean to me? What might it mean to my partner? Will I find someone who will understand? I have been lucky enough to find a wonderful man who *does* understand. We are happily married and plan to adopt children in the future.

The questions and experiences I have struggled with have made me a better person. As I train to be a child psychologist, I know that my personal experience makes me more insightful and compassionate when working with families. I am also very proud to be a woman with TS who can provide support and resources to others living with the disorder. As I frequently tell others with TS: although we do not have control over the fact that we have a disorder, we do have control over our attitude and the lessons we learn from our experiences. In this way, I view TS as a great opportunity to grow and help others in the process. That perspective has made all the difference!

Please contact the Turner Syndrome Society of the United States at 1-800-365-9944 or www .turnersyndrome.org for more information.

Contributed by Jessica Lord.

Androgen Insensitivity and Identity

Complete androgen insensitivity is a rare condition, occurring in fewer than 1 in every 100,000 births. Because of their female genital appearance, most infants with CAIS have been classified as female and raised as girls. These girls establish a core gender identity as female. In a review of 156 CAIS cases, long-term follow-ups showed that 100 percent had established and maintained a female gender identity and, as adults, none were dissatisfied with their gender or had attempted to change sex (Mazur, 2005). Because the child looks and acts like a normal girl, she is treated like a girl, and her gender identity is congruent with her assigned sex.

Neither the girl with CAIS nor her family may be aware of her condition during her childhood. However, when she reaches the age of puberty, her family may seek medical attention because she does not begin to menstruate. At that point, she may be given vague explanations that do not reveal her XY status. Even her parents may not know the truth (Diamond & Watson, 2004). Like Olympic athlete Maria Patiño, most individuals with CAIS grow up certain of their female sex. They may never learn of their intersex condition because they are given selective information by their physicians and family. Problems, if any, occur when the intersex condition and the core gender identity are brought into conflict.

The Impact of CAH

A great deal of research has focused on girls with CAH because researchers believed that they could provide evidence about the effect of androgens on core gender identity and gender typing. Certainly, the exposure to androgens during fetal development influenced these girls' bodies. Do the androgens also affect their identity, interests, and abilities?

Girls affected by CAH almost invariably develop a core gender identity as females. In other words, neither the exposure to androgens nor the families' reactions to their ambiguous genitals at birth disrupt gender identity: CAH girls think of themselves as females and are comfortable with their female identity (Fausto-Sterling, 2000; Dessens et al., 2005; Gooren, 2006; Zucker, 2001). In the rare cases where CAH girls have been raised as boys, the majority developed a male gender identity because their assigned sex fit their genitals and they were socialized as boys (Zucker, 2001). However, they may be more likely to develop problems with gender identity than CAH girls raised as girls (Dessens et al., 2005).

Do girls with CAH act more like boys in their play patterns and other aspects of gender-typing? Dozens of studies have been done in this area. Usually, CAH-affected girls are compared with their non-CAH sisters or other female family members; sometimes they are compared with boys. Typically, CAH-affected girls are somewhat more active and more likely to be tomboys, and they play with boys' toys more than other girls do (Zucker, 2001). Some studies report that they are more aggressive than other girls are (Matthews et al., 2009). They are stronger than other girls and perform more like boys on tasks such as throwing balls or darts at a target (Collaer et al., 2009). In summary, it seems that their gender-related behaviors are more masculine than other girls' behaviors (Gooren, 2006).

This area of research is controversial. Critics point out that factors other than prenatal hormonal exposure could be responsible for the behavioral differences between girls with CAH and other girls (or boys). First, it is quite likely that parents and other adults may react differently to a daughter who is born with a penis than to her more typical sister or brother. Second, the high activity level of CAH girls could be a side effect of medications such as cortisone (Zucker, 2001), and this in turn could affect toy preferences and play patterns. (Boys' toys usually encourage more active play than girls' toys.) As we learned in Chapter 4, defining and measuring gender differences is complex; searching for the *causes* of observed differences adds another layer of complexity. In this area, different experts have reviewed the same studies and reached opposite conclusions. Either "the results provide little support for a role for prenatal hormones in the production of gender differences" (Fausto-Sterling, 2000, p. 75) or prenatal exposure to androgens "sculpts the brain" (Hines, 2009, p. 438) and "masculinizes" behavior (Zucker, 2001, p. 110).

In summary, gender identity in intersexed children seems to be largely (but not entirely) dependent on social factors. Being assigned as a female and brought up as a female usually outweigh biological inconsistencies in the components of sex, particularly when the external appearance is clearly female. However, this does not mean that gender identity and gender typing are unrelated to biological sex. Some girls with CAH develop in less gender-typed ways than unaffected girls; whether this is due to prenatal hormones, physical appearance differences, social factors, or some combination of these and other factors is still unknown. Some intersexed people may have problems with gender identity that have not yet been documented by psychological researchers because of the secrecy and stigma surrounding these conditions. What the research does tell us is that there is not a simple, direct relationship between physical sex and psychological gender (see Box 5.4). Instead, the relationships are complex, multidetermined, and still somewhat mysterious.

BOX 5.4 ∾ Research Focus
David Reimer: The Boy Who Was Raised as a Girl

In 1965, Janet and Ron Reimer gave birth to healthy twin boys, who were named Bruce and Brian. Nine months later, during what should have been a routine circumcision, Bruce's penis was destroyed in a surgical accident. Desperate to find a way for their son to live a normal life, the Reimers were referred to Dr. John Money, an expert in gender identity at Johns Hopkins University.

Dr. Money believed that at birth, children were gender neutral. It was nurture—not nature—that determined gender identity. The Reimer case presented a once-in-a-lifetime opportunity for him to demonstrate his nurture theory because Bruce

had an identical twin brother who would be raised as a boy—a perfect matched control case. He suggested that Bruce undergo gender reassignment surgery and be raised as a girl. Bruce's parents, teenagers at the time, believed there was no other option that would allow their child a "normal" sexual life, and agreed to raise Bruce as a girl, renaming him Brenda. Brenda underwent surgery to remove her testicles, as well as procedures to construct a vagina. Later, she was given estrogen therapy to promote female pubertal development (i.e., breasts). Brenda wore dresses and was encouraged to play with dolls, to reinforce her female gender identity.

Continued on next page

Box 5.4 ∾ Research Focus
David Reimer: The Boy Who Was Raised as a Girl (Concluded)

During Brenda's childhood, the Reimer family made trips to Johns Hopkins to meet with Dr. Money who attempted to reinforce Brenda's female gender identity and heterosexual orientation using questionable techniques such as showing her pornographic images of heterosexual sex. He also involved Brenda's brother in these treatments, having Brenda and Brian simulate sexual positions. Throughout the 1970s, Dr. Money proclaimed the success of the "John/Joan case" (the pseudonym he used to refer to Bruce/Brenda) in medical journals, books, and in speeches all over the country. Although Brenda was not born intersexed, Dr. Money used the case to support his theories about the treatment of intersexed individuals, arguing that they could adapt to a gender identity consistent with the outward appearance of their genitalia, but inconsistent with their genetic sex.

Despite Dr. Money's claims that Brenda had successfully adopted a female gender identity, Bruce's transition to Brenda was hardly successful. Brenda played with her brother's toys, refused to wear dresses, and was constantly teased and harassed at school for her lack of femininity. Although the Reimers reported Brenda's behavior to Dr. Money, he dismissed it as a phase or a lack of compliance on their part. At the advice of a psychiatrist and against the orders of Dr. Money, the Reimers decided to tell Brenda the truth about her past when she was 14. Unfortunately, the damage had already been done.

Brenda decided to revert back to her biological sex. He began testosterone injections, underwent surgery to remove breasts and reconstruct a penis and testicles, and gave himself the name David. Although he eventually married and adopted his wife's children, he never fully recovered from his traumatic childhood, suffering from severe depression and anger. David's family was also deeply impacted by what had occurred in David's childhood. His mother suffered from depression and attempted suicide, his father became an alcoholic, and his brother, who suffered from depression and drug use, died of a drug overdose in 2002.

When David was 30, he met Dr. Milton Diamond, a longtime critic of Dr. Money who had been interested in the John/Joan case in the 1970s. Dr. Money had stopped publishing reports on the case in the late 1970s and Dr. Diamond wondered what had become of John/Joan. When David found out that Dr. Money had touted his gender reassignment as a success and that the case was used to promote gender reassignment surgery for intersex people and those with genital injury, he decided he wanted to go public about what really happened to him. Dr. Diamond published a report in a medical journal in 1997 and David decided to work with journalist John Colapinto on a book about his life and childhood, *As Nature Made Him: The Boy Who Was Raised a Girl*, published in 2000. David's case was also featured in a BBC documentary, and received a great deal of media attention. As the details of the case became widely known, Dr. Money's research ethics were criticized by many. Although David's story ends tragically—he committed suicide in 2004—going public about his case brought attention to the need for revised guidelines for the ethical and clinical treatment of intersexed individuals. David's tortured life also shows that science does not yet fully understand how physical sex and psychological gender are related in the human psyche.

Contributed by Annie B. Fox.

Transsexualism

James Morris had a full and adventurous life. After serving in the British military as a war correspondent, he became a successful journalist, married happily, and fathered five children.

Although Morris had an enviable life, he felt that something was very wrong. From earliest childhood he believed that he was meant to be a woman, not a man. After much introspection and conflict, Morris began a 10-year process of transitioning to being a woman. Following years of hormone treatments, he underwent sex change surgery: his penis and testicles were removed, and an artificial vagina was constructed. Morris and his/her wife were divorced, but remained emotionally close, bonded by friendship and their mutual love for their children. Jan Morris continued her career as a writer, and now has more than 30 books to her credit.

Morris's book *Conundrum* (1974) articulates one person's struggle with having been "born in the wrong body." After changing sex, this formerly athletic and adventurous man described his pleasure in the ordinary rituals of femininity: wearing makeup and soft clothes, engaging in small talk with neighbor women, being helped with tasks like parallel parking or opening a bottle of wine. Becoming a woman made Morris acutely aware of disadvantages women may face: "addressed every day of my life as an inferior, involuntarily, month by month, I accepted the condition" (p. 149). However, she felt that the benefits—being helped, flattered, and treated more kindly—outweighed the costs.

Jan Morris is certain that she found her true self as a woman. Even the ordeals of hormonal and surgical treatments seemed a small price to pay for having her sex congruent with her gender: "I would have gone through the whole cycle ten times over, if the alternative had been a return to ambiguity or disguise" (p. 145). She describes her transsexual journey as "thirty-five years as a male . . . ten in between, and the rest of my life as me" (p. 146).

Gender Identity Disorder

Morris's account reflects the view that a person whose biological sex does not fit his or her core gender identity has a psychological disorder. *Gender identity disorder* (GID) is an official psychiatric category for those individuals who experience a disjunction between their assigned sex and their core gender identity. The APA defines GID as a strong and persistent desire to be the other sex or belief that one is really the other sex (American Psychiatric Association, 1994; 2000). In children, GID is diagnosed by asking the child and his/her parents not only whether the child behaves like or wants to be the other sex, but also by asking about toy preferences, dress-up and fantasy play, and peer relationships. Although twice as many girls as boys report cross-gender behavior, boys are far more likely to be diagnosed as having GID (Zucker, 2008).

About 1 in 30,000 adult men and 1 in 100,000 women apply for sex change surgery; however, the number of people who fit the criteria for GID may be considerably higher, since not all those who meet the diagnostic criteria choose to have surgery. Like James/Jan Morris, many transsexuals report feeling trapped in the wrong body. Many say that they were aware of their sex/gender conflict from early childhood, but took a long time to articulate it and act on it.

Individuals with GID are not physically intersexed. Although psychological researchers have sought differences in brain structure or hormone processing in transsexuals, their results so far have been preliminary, inconclusive, or negative (Einstein, 2007; Swaab, 2009; Ujike et al., 2009). Almost always, the genetic sex, hormonal history, and reproductive anatomy of transsexual individuals form an unambiguous biological sex as female or male (Gooren, 2006). Their childhoods are typically unremarkable except for their growing sense that they are different from other children and that their assigned sex is a mistake. This awareness, and their resistance to being gender-typed in accordance with their sex, often causes conflicts with parents (Morgan & Stevens, 2008). Eventually, the contradictions may become impossible to live with, and they may elect to change their appearance and behavior to what they believe is their true sex.

Changing Sex

The transition from one sex to the other usually takes place over a long period of time. A woman may change her sex appearance by binding her breasts and getting a man's haircut. A man may wear makeup and women's clothes and strap his penis between his legs. Some transsexuals use hormonal supplements: estrogens to grow feminine breasts and reduce body hair on a male, or androgens to build muscle bulk and deepen the voice of a female (Wassersug et al., 2007). Others undergo sex-reassignment surgery. Female-to-male transsexuals may have surgeries to remove the breasts, uterus, and ovaries, but not all opt for constructing a penis, because the surgery is complicated and the results often disappointing (Morgan & Stevens, 2008).

The transsexual person must adjust to a changing body, learn new ways of behaving, and accommodate to others' reactions to the new body and behavior (Bolin, 1996). As we learned in Chapter 2, innumerable small differences in verbal and nonverbal behavior mark gender in social interaction. A man who becomes a woman must not only dress like a woman; he should also walk, sit, talk, flirt, sip coffee, and throw a ball like a woman. To pass as a woman, s/he should have feminine interests and activities. And s/he must learn how to respond when treated like a woman. One male-to-female transsexual reported that in addition to hormone treatment, "I spent almost a year going out in public and getting comfortable with myself as a woman, working on my presentation, my voice, my mannerisms, makeup and dress . . . laying the groundwork as best I could for the person I wanted to become" (Wassersug et al., 2007, p. 107).

Not all transsexuals go as far as having sex-change surgery. It is quite possible to pass as the other sex without surgery, because in daily interactions we rely on social cues, not genitals, to judge someone's sex (Kessler & McKenna, 1978). Passing is much more a matter of fulfilling others' social expectations for a man or a woman than of having male or female genitals. Some researchers estimate that two-thirds of those who are living as the other sex on a full-time basis have not had sex-change surgery.

Clinical records of sex-change surgeries show that there are more male to female (MTF) than female-to-male (FTM) transsexuals. (See Figure 5.3.) However, these records may underestimate the number of FTM transsexuals. Because it is relatively simple for a woman to don men's clothes and change her body contours with testosterone injections, and relatively difficult to construct a passable penis, FTMs may be more likely than MTFs to pass without undergoing surgery (Devor, 1997). Another possible reason for the apparently greater number of MTFs is that the rules for masculinity are more restrictive than the rules for femininity. A woman

FIGURE 5.3

Female-to-male transsexual Matt Kailley, shown here before and after his transition, hosts a blog and Web site for transsexual people and those who want to learn more about transsexualism: http://tranisfesto.com/.

who wears pants, cuts her hair short, and plays rugby is hardly controversial, but a man who wears dresses, uses makeup, and asks for help carrying a bag of groceries would likely experience severe social sanctions. Therefore, gender-role atypical men may be quicker than atypical women to turn to surgery.

With modern surgical techniques, health outcomes of sex reassignment are usually good. In a study of 55 MTF and FTM transsexuals in a Dutch clinic, the great majority reported improvement in their sexual functioning (De Cuypere et al., 2005). However, another study of 50 postsurgery MTF individuals at a Belgian clinic showed that they were satisfied with their appearance and self-image, but not entirely satisfied with their sexual functioning (Weyers, 2009). Does sex-change surgery relieve the psychological distress of transsexual individuals? Surprisingly, the research does not strongly support this outcome. For example, a pre- and post-surgery study of 40 MTF transsexuals at a clinic in England showed that there were no significant differences in their psychological functioning following surgery (Udeze et al., 2008). There is a need for more research on long-term outcomes of sex reassignment surgery.

Many cases of sex-change surgery have made headlines in the media. When the prominent economist Donald McCloskey became Deirdre McCloskey, her story was recounted in the *Chronicle of Higher Education* (Wilson, 1996) and in an interview on National Public Radio. McCloskey mourned the loss of her marriage and the alienation from her children, but nevertheless felt that she had made the right choice, indeed the only choice, for her psychological well being. Concert pianist David Buechner's sex change and subsequent stage debut as Sara Buechner were covered by *the New York Times* (Jacobs, 1998). Stories like these engage our sympathy. It must be very difficult to live one's life feeling trapped in the wrong body, and even more difficult to undergo the process of sex change.

Sex and Sexual Orientation

It may seem obvious, but one of the biggest differences between women and men is that the great majority of men are attracted to women, and the great majority of women are attracted to men. *Sexual orientation* is a multidimensional concept involving erotic attraction, affectional relationships, sexual behavior, erotic fantasies, and emotional attachments. The gender of one's sex partners is only one component, and not always the most important one. Often, the various components are inconsistent within the same person (Hoburg et al., 2004; Rothblum, 2000). Moreover, a person's sexual orientation may change over time. And some researchers have suggested that women's sexual orientation is more fluid and changeable than men's (Bailey, 2009)—a topic we will further explore in Chapter 7. Despite the complexity of defining it, researchers have looked for genetic and hormonal influences on sexual orientation.

Is There a Gay Gene?

Several studies have shown that same-sex sexual orientation runs in families. In other words, lesbian, gay, and bisexual (LGB) people tend to have a higher-than-average number of LGB people among their relatives. These studies suggest that either particular family environments or genetic factors could increase the likelihood of LGB orientations, but cannot distinguish between the two kinds of factors. Recently, some researchers have turned to *twin studies* to help separate the influences of genetics and environment. These studies compare *monozygotic* (MZ) or identical twins with *dizygotic* (DZ) or fraternal twins. MZ twins are genetically identical, whereas DZ twins are only as genetically alike as any other siblings are. If MZ twins share the same sexual orientation more often than DZ twins do, it suggests that there is some genetic contribution to sexual orientation (Hines, 2004).

Studies of male twins provide evidence consistent with a genetic influence. For example, in one study, 66 percent of the MZ co-twins of gay men were also gay, compared with 30 percent of the DZ co-twins (Whitam et al., 1993). This study also found one set of MZ triplets who all were gay. Of course, MZ twins may be treated more similarly than DZ twins, because they look exactly alike and may have very similar temperaments. A better way to separate heredity from environment requires studying twins who were reared apart (for example, by being adopted at birth into different families). As you might expect, gay men with a twin adopted into a different family are rather rare, and only a few cases have been studied. These cases, too, suggest that male MZ twins are more likely than male DZ twins to share a gay sexual orientation (Hines, 2004).

For females, however, the story is different. Some twin studies show the same pattern as the studies with men—female MZ twins are more similar in sexual orientation than female DZ twins are. However, others show little or no relationship between genetic similarity and lesbian or bisexual orientation. In the rare cases of female MZ twins reared apart, none of the pairs studied have shared a lesbian or bisexual orientation (Hines, 2004).

There is still much to be learned about genetic contributions to sexual orientation. Certainly, there is no single "gay gene" that determines whether a person becomes gay, straight, or bisexual. If there is a genetic predisposition, it appears to be stronger in men than in women. Little is known about how such a genetic predisposition might work. Is there a group of genes that codes directly for a particular sexual orientation? Do genes influence sexual orientation indirectly, perhaps by predisposing to personality traits or interests that influence sexual orientation? Or do genes influence prenatal hormones in some way that relates to sexual orientation?

In summary, the evidence for a genetic component to sexual orientation is preliminary. Even for males, where the evidence is strongest, there is also strong evidence for nongenetic factors: across all studies, more than half of the co-twins of gay men are not gay (Hines, 2004). For females, the picture is even less clear, and whether there is a genetic component to the sexual orientation of females is still an open question.

Hormones and Sexual Orientation

Recall that XX and XY fetuses experience different exposure to gonadal hormones during fetal development. Male fetuses are exposed to androgens, whereas female fetuses are not. Do fetal androgens play a role in the later development of sexual attraction to women? One way to study the effects of fetal hormonal exposure on later sexual orientation is to assess the sexual orientation of people whose intrauterine hormonal exposure was atypical.

Individuals with partial androgen insensitivity syndrome (PAIS) are XY males who effectively receive little androgen during fetal development and therefore develop ambiguous genitalia. Depending on the appearance of the genitals at birth, the individual may be assigned as either a male or a female, and the genitals are surgically altered to fit the assigned sex. Regardless of which sex they are brought up as, individuals with PAIS usually develop a heterosexual orientation—those brought up as girls become attracted to men, and those brought up as boys become attracted to women. In these cases, it is clear that a normal dose of fetal androgens was not necessary for the individual to develop a sexual orientation toward the other sex. Despite their similar hormonal histories, the individuals raised as boys and those raised as girls developed different sexual orientations, illustrating that there is a lot of flexibility in human psychosexual development (Hines, 2004).

Other researchers have asked whether an excess of androgens during fetal development could predispose a female to become attracted to women. To answer this question, they have looked at the sexual orientation of women with a history of CAH, which causes exposure to fetal androgens. (Recall that CAH also causes intersexed male-appearing genitals that are surgically altered in infancy.)

The majority of CAH women identify as heterosexual. However, when they are compared to their non-CAH sisters or other female family members, CAH-affected women are more likely to report having lesbian or bisexual experiences (Meyer-Bahlburg et al., 2008). Some studies suggest that they are more likely than other girls to want to change their sex (Swaab, 2009). Taken together, studies suggest that CAH women are more likely to have lesbian orientation, fantasies, or experience—and less likely to have heterosexual orientation, fantasies, or experience—than unaffected comparison groups.

Critics point out that these studies lacked a common definition of sexual orientation. Some studies assessed fantasies, others assessed same-sex experiences, and still others asked about long-term relationships. As discussed earlier, sexual orientation is a multidimensional concept. When studies do not agree on its definition and measurement, it is difficult to combine and compare them. Moreover, many CAH-affected women have had genital surgery, which may affect their ability to experience sexual pleasure and their comfort in intimate situations with men. What is clear is that prenatal hormones do not fully determine sexual orientation, because the great majority of women with prenatal exposure to androgens identify as heterosexual.

Sex as a Social Construction

The presence of intersex bodies challenges the fundamental assumption that everyone is either male or female and that this is an "irreducible fact" (Kessler & McKenna, 1978, p. vii). The presence of naturally occurring variations in biological sex also challenges the assumption that gender follows naturally from sex. If sex is not a distinct binary system, why does gender have to follow a binary pattern of masculinity/femininity?

According to some feminist theorists, sex is a *social construction,* which means that the assumptions underlying our commonsense beliefs about it are the products of a specific culture, not universal or fixed truths about nature (Marecek et al., 2004). In other words, sex is a belief system rather than a fact (Crawford, 2000). However, in every culture, the belief system about sex seems perfectly natural to members of that culture. In our own society, most people firmly believe that sex is a biological dichotomy. It is hard to recognize that what is taken as fact might be the product of social negotiation and cultural consensus.

Even the label "It's a girl!" or "It's a boy" is a social construction. As we have seen, this classification is usually based on the appearance of the external genitals—but genitalia are only one aspect of biological sex. Relying on genital appearance, and not other determinants of sex, is the product of a social consensus. And sex classification is the crucial first step in creating gender. "It is *because* we have already classified someone as male or female that all the other gender attributions we might use—masculine, feminine, lesbian, gay, transsexual—make sense" (Crawford, 2000, p. 8). The concepts of core gender identity and sexual orientation, for example, presume that each infant *is* male or female *before* these psychological processes begin.

Questions of how we become gendered are interesting and important, of course. But even more important is the question of how the social reality of two, and only two, sexes is constructed in the first place (Golden, 2008). Here we look at the process of making social decisions that *create* two sexes by exploring the medical treatment of people who are intersexed or transsexual. These treatments spark heated debate because they involve tailoring unruly bodies to fit the only two sex categories that are permissible in our society.

Constructing Two Sexes

For many years, the standard treatment for intersex conditions began with assigning a child the label of male or female as soon as possible after birth. This was followed by medical and surgical interventions designed to alter the genitals to look more "normal." These surgeries were done before the child was old enough to consent to them. Often, parents were not given the exact diagnosis. As intersexed children grew older, they were rarely told the truth about their condition. Instead, their medical records were sealed. Here, we consider the social implications of each step in this process.

When physicians recognize that an intersexed child has been born, they attempt to decide what they term the *optimal gender* for the child. By this they mean, "Which sex will the child fit best?" The criteria for best fit are flexible. Physicians consider whether such children have reproductive potential as a male or female, whether they will be able to function sexually as a male or female, and whether they can be made to look like a typical male or female. If the child is old enough to have formed a core gender identity before the condition is diagnosed, this also must be taken into account.

As you can imagine, deciding a child's optimal gender is a complex matter involving both medical criteria and social norms. Some critics have suggested that the criteria may be applied in sexist ways: for those children who are assigned as males, sexual function is primary, whereas for those assigned as females, reproductive capability is given more weight (Fausto-Sterling, 2000; Kessler, 1998, 2002). In other words, for males, the ability to have an erection and engage in heterosexual sex is the primary criterion, but for females it is the potential for motherhood, not sexual functioning or pleasure.

Although medical professionals use the concept of optimal gender among themselves, they consider the indeterminacy of the child's actual sex too unsettling a concept for parents. Critics claim that in treating intersex children and counseling their families, the medical profession uses a gender doublespeak whereby they deliberately hide the intersex status. Instead of saying that the infant is a mixture of female and male and that they are deciding on an optimal gender, they tell the family that they know the "true" sex and will "correct" the "incomplete development" (Fausto-Sterling, 2000; Kessler, 1998). Even when physicians perform major surgery on intersex children (for example, removing the testes from CAIS girls) they consider it best not to be too candid. As one group of medical researchers wrote:

> An intersex child assigned to become a girl . . . should understand any surgery she has undergone not as an operation that changed her into a girl, but as a procedure that removed parts that didn't belong to her as a girl . . . (although the gland removed is a functioning testis) in the patient's own formulation it is best regarded as an imperfect organ . . . not suited to life as a female, and hence removed. (Cited in Fausto-Sterling, 2000, p. 65).

Why do physicians conceal the truth about intersex from patients and their families? Traditionally, they have believed that the child's core gender identity might be compromised, and that this would lead to psychological conflict and poor adjustment. This reflects the assumptions that there must be only two sexes and that gender identity and gender typing must follow biological sex. Although physicians know that some infants do not fit the pattern, they have felt obigated to pretend that the sex/gender binary is universal.

The social construction of two sexes has resulted in withholding personal medical information from intersex people. In one case, an androgen-insensitive child had surgery to remove sex glands when she was too young to consent or understand the procedure. After puberty, doctors explained her need for estrogen pills and her infertility by telling her that her ovaries had not been normal and her uterus had not developed. Of course, this child, a genetic male, never had either a uterus or ovaries (Kessler, 1990). What would happen to this person's trust in her physicans and her family, and to her gender identity, if she found out the truth? Today, the policy of concealment is being challenged, partly because follow-up studies show that many intersexed people felt deceived and coerced into treatment and were not happy with the results (Brinkman, 2007; MacKenzie et al., 2009).

In constructing unambigous genitals for intersexed infants, the medical profession enforces a standard that allows no overlap between male and female genitals. For an intersexed child to be considered a functional girl, she must have a clitoris that is smaller than the smallest permissible penis for a boy. If her clitoris is "too big," it will be surgically "downsized" (Fausto-Sterling, 2000, p. 60). In the past, surgeons often removed the clitoris of intersexed girls entirely. Today, clitoral reduction surgery is performed. Despite considerable natural variability in clitoral size at birth, physicians often rely on their personal impressions or opinions about the appropriate size and appearance of this organ. Psychologist Suzanne Kessler (1998; 2002) compiled a list of the adjectives used in the medical literature to describe clitorises that were perceived as needing surgical reduction. The list includes *defective, deformed, obtrusive, offending, troublesome,* and *disfiguring.* Clearly, these are value judgments. It is the physician, and not necessarily the child, her parents, or her future sex partners, who is troubled by a clitoris that is "too big."

Some intersexed individuals have genital surgery several times during the first few years of life, followed by more surgery after puberty (Fausto-Sterling, 2000). Female-assigned children may face repeated surgeries to construct a vagina. Following surgery, instruments must be inserted into the vagina daily by the parents in order to keep the new structure open. A male-assigned child may have genital surgery in order to repair or construct an acceptable penis. The medical literature reports hundreds of techniques for this task, along with techniques to repair the unsatisfactory results of previous surgeries. The costs of genital surgery include visible scarring, loss of sexual sensation, and loss of the ability to reach orgasm. Interviews with adult intersexed people, as well as medical data on the results of genital surgery, have shown that poor overall appearance and dissatisfaction with the results are common (Kessler, 2002; Hines, 2004).

The medical interventions aimed at intersexed children also have other costs. Because they may not have access to their medical records, the affected individuals may not know about medical conditions that could compromise their health. Moreover, due to repeated experiences of surgery, and the suspicion that they are being deceived, some intersexed people distrust the medical profession to the extent that they fail to get help for other conditions, causing overall health to degenerate (Kessler, 2002).

Physicians and other professionals who treat intersexed patients are faced with difficult decisions involving not only medical criteria, but also ethical and social dilemmas. Their problems of diagnosis and treatment are increased because there is very little information available on the outcome of previous decisions in similar cases. Most patients are not followed up over long periods to see how their sex assignment has worked out for them. Also, it is impossible to know how a person with the same condition might have fared if assigned to the other sex. Unfortunately, life-altering decisions may be made with little evidence about whether they have proved to be good decisions for others in past cases (Kessler, 2002).

There are encouraging signs that the medical management of intersexuality is changing. In 2006, a group of 50 international experts on intersex published a consensus statement: parents should not be encouraged to pursue surgery for intersex infants because there is no good medical evidence that cosmetic genital surgery improves quality of life for intersex people (Golden, 2008).

The changing norms in medical management of intersex conditions show that sex is not just a biological given. Its meaning is negotiated through social decision making. In social negotiations, members of dominant groups have more power to define reality. In this case, the medical profession has had more power to define the sex of intersex individuals than the intersex people themselves, or their families, have had. The consequences for intersex people have sometimes been tragic, because they have been subjected to life-altering medical treatments without informed consent. Only recently is treatment being revised in a more humane direction. A different but equally complex set of issues comes up when fully informed and consenting adults choose to change their sex.

Rethinking Transsexualism

Transsexual people have engaged in a long struggle to have their condition recognized by the medical profession. Their demands for legal recognition and medical care have forced society to recognize and name their problem, and to help them change sex both physically and socially. However, not everyone believes that labeling cross-sex gender identity as a psychiatric disorder is entirely a positive change. Some argue that the diagnostic category of gender identity disorder contributes to stigmatizing people of diverse sexual identities and labels some ordinary behaviors as mental illness based solely on the sex of the person doing them (Winters, 2006). Other critics point out that the there is no evidence that cross-gender identity or behaviors in themselves create psychological problems or distress. In some cultures, they are quite normal (Lev, 2006; Vasey & Bartlett, 2007). Rather, it is the stress of being stigmatized that creates such problems (Sanchez & Vilain, 2009). A third criticism is that the GID diagnostic category has had the paradoxical consequence of reinforcing the idea that there are and can be two and only two sexes and that gender must conform to one or the other. "By requesting surgery to make their bodies match their gender, transsexuals enacted the logical extreme of the medical profession's philosophy that within an individual's body, sex and gender must conform" (Fausto-Sterling, 2000, p. 107). Their dilemmas of identity may be a result of our binary system of sex and gender. Indeed, the criteria for a diagnosis of GID are entirely based on the binary model (Golden, 2008). If you do not feel like a man, then you *must* be a woman—there is no other choice available.

But, given the social construction of sex as a binary system, what other options have transsexuals had? If they wanted to obtain surgery, it was necessary to present themselves within the binary framework (Johnson, 2007). Their only alternative was to adopt as closely as possible the physiology, appearance, and roles of the so-called opposite sex. For example, the more stereotypically feminine a man acted, the more likely it was that he would be ruled eligible for surgery. In order to convince the medical authorities of his "true" sex, he had to be the best, most stereotypical example of a woman that he could manage. Thus, transsexuals have participated in the social construction of sex and gender by changing their bodies to be a better fit to the system that allows only two categories and insists that gender must conform to sex.

Jan Morris, who felt that her transsexualism was both biological and spiritual, wondered whether transsexualism would still occur in a society that did not enforce gender differences. "Would my conflict have been so bitter if I had been born now, when the gender line is so much less rigid? If society had allowed me to live in the gender I preferred, would I have bothered to change sex?" (p. 172).

In summary, the medical treatment of intersex and transsexualism provides evidence that sex is a process of social consensus and social enforcement, not a natural biological dichotomy. Constructing two and only two sexes through surgical intervention may be done with the best of intentions, but it also may reinforce the belief that these two categories are the only natural and acceptable ones (Golden, 2008). However, there are other ways to categorize the human body and psyche.

Beyond the Binary

For those of us brought up within a binary system of sex and gender, it may be difficult to think outside the boxes. However, in some cultures, the idea that people come in more than two sexes is commonplace. In other words, these cultures have women, men, and others (Williams, 1987). In our own culture, as well, some people are beginning to challenge the idea that one must choose between only two sex or gender categories. We turn now to these steps beyond the binary.

More Than Two Sexes

Societies that have a third-sex category are found in many parts of the world. These categories contrast with our own society's binary categories of female/male, masculine/feminine, and gay/straight. They are neither, both, and all of the above. The social roles and social positions of third-sex people vary across cultures. Let's look at a few examples.

Third Sexes across Cultures

In India about half a million people identify as *hijras* (Reddy, 2005) or *Aravanis* (Mahalingam, 2003). Hijras and Aravanis represent a third-sex category and have an ambiguous social position, being sometimes revered and sometimes persecuted.

Hijras take female names and wear women's clothes, but they set themselves apart from women by being much more sexually overt in their behavior. Unlike proper Indian women, they wear heavy makeup, joke about sex, and wear their hair loose. One's genitals do not determine being a hijra. Some hijras have male genitalia, some were born biologically male but chose to be castrated, and still others were born with intersexed genitals. Within their society, hijras are not considered to be women, because they cannot bear children; they are not considered to be men, because they do not function sexually as men. Hijras form a northern Indian sect that is considered to incorporate the divine powers of the goddess; they sing and dance at weddings and birth celebrations, and traditionally are asked to bless newborn babies (Nanda, 1990).

In southern India, hijras are known as Aravanis. Like their counterparts in north Indian society, they dress as women, and may use hormones or surgery to affect a sex change. However, they are not merely trying to mimic true women; rather, "gender-bending is central to their identity," and they "pride themselves on being 'superwomen,'" a third gender that both enacts femininity and flouts it (Mahalingam, 2003, p. 491).

In Thailand, there are third-sex people called *kathoeys* (Herdt, 1997). Kathoeys have male genitalia but wear women's clothes. Like hijras, they do not try to pass as proper women; instead, they "behave and dress in dramatic, loud, brash ways that violate the norms of femininity in Thai culture" (Marecek et al., 2004, p. 207). They are sometimes called "ladyboys" or "halfmen," and, in interviews, they describe being both admired and rejected (Totman, 2003).

In the South Pacific, Samoans call the third sex *fa'afafine,* which translates as "in the way of a woman." Typically, fa'afafine are biological males who dress as women and take up women's tasks such as caregiving and teaching. They are highly valued as dancers and entertainers, and usually treated with respect and acceptance (Vasey & Bartlett, 2007). However, although they are treated like women in social interactions, they are clearly differentiated from biological women and men (Vasey

& VanderLaan, 2009). A popular nickname for the fa'afafine is "50/50s," because they can be both masculine and feminine. Like men, they are allowed to tell bawdy jokes, engage in dirty dancing, and play baseball; like women, they are allowed to be artistic, concerned with fashion and appearance, and willing to babysit for small children (Fraser, 2002; Vasey & VanderLaan, 2009).

Anthropologists and historians studying North American Indian cultures have found that more than 150 of these societies have (or had in the past) a third-sex category that the anthropologists term the *berdache* and Native Americans themselves sometimes term *two-spirit people* (Wilson, 1996). The characteristics of berdaches have varied widely across different Native American cultures and across time (Fausto-Sterling, 2000). Most often, berdaches were biological males who wore women's clothes and took up some of the roles and tasks of women. However, they could also adopt men's customs and clothing, switch back and forth, or combine the two (Roscoe, 1996). Thus, their gender was changeable and not always congruent with their sexual anatomy. Berdaches were often seen as particularly creative and artistic.

A category known as *pledged virgin* is unusual because it is a third-sex category for women. This category exists in areas of the Balkans (the former Yugoslavia) (Gremaux, 1996). A pledged virgin takes over a man's roles when there is no man available—for example, when all the male children in a family die before adulthood. A pledged virgin is no longer thought of as a woman. S/he wears men's clothes, does heavy work, and even serves as a man in the military. Unlike other third-sex categories, pledged virgins do not engage in sexual activity.

Third-Sex Categories and the Gender System

In their respective cultures, third-sex people are not considered to be gay. Berdaches are expected to have sex with supposedly heterosexual men, not with women or with each other. Fa'afafine, too, have sex with supposedly heterosexual men, often initiating young men and giving them practice at having sex before they become sexually active with women. Most straight men in Samoa report having had sex with a fa'afafine at some time in their lives; this is not considered to be gay sex (Vasey & VanderLaan, 2009). In other words, sex is defined as a social role rather than as a particular anatomy. Third-sex people may be accepted in cultures where homosexuality is strongly tabooed, such as India and Samoa. As one Samoan explained, the preacher might preach that being gay is un-Godly at the same time there is a fa'afafine singing in the church choir every Sunday (Fraser, 2002, p.74).

Across cultures, there are more opportunities for biological males than for biological females to opt for a third category. As we have seen, hijras, Aravanis, katheoys, and fa'afafine all are biological males (or, more rarely, intersexed). The pledged virgin category is unusual; few societies allow women a third-sex role. Some Native American societies permitted biological females to become berdaches by taking up some of the clothing and tasks of men, but these societies were rare (Roscoe, 1996).

Why are third-sex categories more often available to males than to females? Beliefs about sex and gender may hold the answer. One unique study asked

100 Aravanis about their beliefs regarding the possibility of sex change (Mahalingam, 2003). The Aravanis thought that gender role transgressions were equally acceptable for girls and boys. For example, they saw nothing wrong with a boy who wanted to wear flowers in his hair or a girl who wanted to do carpentry. However, when asked whether a girl could *become* a boy, or vice versa, they were virtually unanimous in agreeing that only a boy could change sex, by dressing like the other sex, having surgery, or performing a religious ceremony. In other words, they saw *male* sex as changeable and fluid, but *female* sex as unchangeable and fixed. The only way they thought a girl might become a boy was through reincarnation.

Of course, all the Aravanis were themselves biological males who had changed sex. They were also Hindus, whose religion emphasizes goddess worship and represents female identity as primordial, strong, and powerful. Thus, the irreducible facts of sex and gender for the Aravanis were influenced by their culture, religion, and social position, and are quite different from our own irreducible facts.

In summary, the various third-sex categories around the world challenge more than the assumption that sex is a binary category. Societies that include a third sex may view sex and sexual orientation as changeable depending on the social situation (Roscoe, 1996). These views contrast with our own society's belief that sex and sexual orientation are biologically fixed and permanent. They also challenge diagnostic categories such as gender identity disorder. For example, Samoan fa'afafine were unquestionably gender-deviant as children, but most report that their deviance was a source of joy and fulfillment, not psychological distress (Vasey & Bartlett, 2007).

The Transgender Movement

Transsexuals in our own society have challenged the permanence of sex. However, transsexuals could be viewed as buttressing the idea that sex must be binary, that people are either male or female. When transsexual adults like Jan Morris and Deirdre McCloskey describe their identities as opposite to their biological sex and change their bodies to fit the opposite sex category, they may reinforce the idea that there are only two possibilities. Many transsexuals think of themselves as suffering from gender identity disorder because their body and their gender are in conflict—they are trapped in the wrong body (Golden, 2008; Tiefer, 2000). However, others whose core gender identity does not fit their physical body have begun to analyze their situation differently.

The **transgender movement** is a social movement for the acceptance of more than two sex categories (Marecek et al., 2004). *Trans* means beyond or across, and transgender activists see themselves as crossing the boundaries of gender (Golden, 2008). Within the transgender movement, some people permanently adopt a transgender identity that is neither female nor male. They do not see themselves as in transition from one sex to another. Instead, they see themselves and others like them as a third-sex category. For example, transgender activist Kate Bornstein describes herself as a gender outlaw and has said, "I am not a man—about that much I am very clear, and I've come to the conclusion that

I'm probably not a woman either" (Bornstein, 1994). Or they may view sex and gender as continuous, like sliding scales on which a person can place him/herself at any point. Some transgender people take up life as the other sex while keeping their biologically given bodies intact—they are men with vaginas and women with penises. Others have sex change surgery but keep their prior sexual orientation—so a heterosexual man who becomes a woman also becomes a lesbian (Bolin, 1996; Fausto-Sterling, 2000). For transgender activists, transgender is not only a personal identity but a political umbrella covering a social movement (Davidson, 2007).

As we learned in Chapter 3, changing language can be a way of raising consciousness and drawing attention to a social or political issue. Transgender activists have adopted new pronouns; Leslie Feinberg (1996), for example, identifies as a "he-she." Some have appropriated older terms or proposed new terms for alternative sex categories, including androgyny, butch, femme, hermaphrodite, drag king, she-male, genderqueer, boy-dyke, girlfag, and many others (Stryker, 1998, p. 148). They also use the term "transpeople," sometimes shortened to "trannies" (Golden, 2008).

Some transgender activists claim that their lives reveal the social construction of sex, and thus their perspectives are crucial to feminist social change. Rather than try to pass as the other sex or become the other sex, they wish to "make their crossing visible, to pose it as a counter to the dominant account that there are only two sexes" (Marecek et al., 2004, p. 207). The transgender movement is sometimes heralded as a "radical re-visioning of sex and gender" (Fausto-Sterling, 2000, p. 107) or "guerilla warfare against dominant constructions of sex, gender and sexuality" (Marecek et al., 2004, p. 207). But not everyone agrees that sex and gender should be deconstructed. Other transsexuals still want to live as their chosen sex, to fit into the binary system of sex as an ordinary woman or man. They do not want the burden of being revolutionaries (Elliot, 2009).

What would happen to the gender system if the "irreducible fact" of sex were discarded? Would the acceptance of transgender imply that our current concepts of sex and gender would disappear entirely? Anne Fausto-Sterling (2000) suggests that it would not erase these categories, but would allow us to focus more on variability and less on conformity. If our society were to develop more inclusive definitions of sex and gender, it would become more like the other societies I've discussed that have allowed some people to be neither male nor female, but "other." It would also open up alternatives to the surgical "correction" of intersexed people. If the stigma of having an ambiguously sexed body were diminished, some people with unusual bodies might choose to keep them and enjoy them as they are.

But merely recognizing variability or allowing a third-sex category does not guarantee that the gender system will change. As we learned in Chapter 2, the gender system is not just a matter of individual beliefs; it is a system of social classification that governs access to power. If sexual variability were recognized and accepted, laws and customs that regulate marriage and sexual behavior would have to change too.

Making a Difference

Transforming Society: Equality for Sexual Minorities

The medical treatment of intersexed people is increasingly being questioned. Some intersexed individuals and their advocates characterize the standard medical management of intersex as a form of child abuse. One activist made these comparisons:

> Like other incest survivors, intersex children are physically and sexually violated by those we trust the most, those same people who claim to have our best interest at heart. Like other incest survivors, intersex children are told not to ask questions or tell anyone else about our experiences. Like other incest survivors, intersex children learn that there is something wrong with who we are, and made to feel ashamed and guilty. And, like other incest survivors, many intersex people are starting to break the silence (Koyama, 2002).

Cheryl Chase is one activist who has broken the silence. Chase's history was not unusual for an intersexed person in our society. Born with ambiguous sex glands but the internal organs of a female, she was assigned as a boy at birth because she had a large clitoris, and raised as a boy for the first 1½ years of her life. However, she was then reassigned as a girl. Her clitoris was surgically removed. Her parents took their physician's advice and eliminated all evidence of her past as a boy. Her name was changed, her clothes were replaced, and her baby pictures destroyed (Fausto-Sterling, 2000).

Chase's intersex history was kept secret from her. When she had to have further surgery as a teen, she was told that it was a hernia operation. It was not until much later in life that she entered therapy for severe depression and began to piece together the facts. Cheryl Chase realized that many of the difficulties she had experienced in growing up and her lack of sexual fulfillment were due to her treatment and the stigma attached to her intersex condition by the medical profession and therefore by her family. In 1993, Cheryl Chase founded the Intersex Society of North America, a nonprofit organization "dedicated to ending shame, secrecy and unwanted genital surgeries on people born with an anatomy that someone decided is not standard for male or female" (isna.org). In 2007, ISNA formed a new group, Accord Alliance, which today is a leader in improving health care and outcomes for intersex people and their families.

Transgender and intersex activists believe that the most important issue is not genitals, it is stigma and discrimination. People whose genitals do not match their gender may suffer grave consequences from a society that cannot tolerate them. In one court case, a jury awarded a mother nearly $3 million in damages after the death of her son following a traffic accident. Paramedics had stopped treating the son, who was cross-dressed, when they discovered his male genitals (Taylor, 2007). The 1999 film *Boys Don't Cry* dramatizes the true story of Teena Brandon, whose male gender identity did not match her female body. (See Figure 5.4.) Teena succeeded in passing as a male, Brandon Teena, for a time, but when her gender-crossing was discovered, she was brutally raped and murdered.

FIGURE 5.4
Hilary Swank as Brandon Teena in the 1999 film *Boys Don't Cry*.

At a more mundane level, virtually every form of identification (drivers' licenses, passports, medical records) requires that the person check "M" or "F." Which box applies to those who have the genitals of one sex and the appearance, mannerisms, and gender identity of the other—or who feel that neither applies? Transgender and intersex people may experience legal difficulties if their apparent sex does not match their official sex. In several cases, their marriages have been annulled. At present, 43 states allow amendments to a birth certificate after gender-reassignment surgery, but others have refused and one (Tennessee) specifically forbids changing the official birth certificate. Marriage laws and health insurance benefits are confusing and contradictory from one state to the next; transgendered and transsexual people routinely face employment discrimination and are not uniformly covered by hate-crimes legislation (Taylor, 2007).

Activists say that, due to the risk of discrimination and violence, transgender and intersex people need legal protections, such as the International Bill of Gender Rights proposed by transgender activists. (See Box 5.5.) Some transgender activists also propose changes in how we use sex categories in everyday life. For example, Leslie Feinberg suggests that sex labels should be removed not only from passports and drivers' licenses, but also from birth certificates, allowing each individual to define her or his own sex when ready (Feinberg, 1996). Although a sex label may *seem* necessary for identification purposes, there are many other attributes that are more visible (height, eye color) and more definitive (DNA, fingerprints) (Fausto-Sterling, 2000).

Transforming Ourselves: Accepting Biological and Social Diversity

The contents of this chapter make many students very uncomfortable. The most disturbing idea of all may be the idea that sex is a social construction. Suzanne Kessler and Wendy McKenna (1978), authors of a pioneering book on the social construction of sex, called the belief in two biological sexes an "incorrigible

BOX 5.5   &   An International Bill of Gender Rights

The International Bill of Gender Rights (IBGR) was first drafted and adopted at the International Conference on Transgender Law and Employment Policy (ICTLEP) in August 1993. Below are some of the rights included in the document.

The Right to Define Gender Identity

All human beings have the right to define their own gender identity regardless of chromosomal sex, genitalia, assigned birth sex, or initial gender role; and further, no individual shall be denied Human or Civil Rights by virtue of a self-defined gender identity which is not in accord with chromosomal sex, genitalia, assigned birth sex, or initial gender role.

The Right to Free Expression of Gender Identity

All human beings have the right to free expression of their self-defined gender identity; and further, no individual shall be denied Human or Civil Rights by virtue of the expression of a self-defined gender identity.

The Right to Control and Change One's Own Body

Individuals shall not be denied the right to change their bodies as a means of expressing a self-defined gender identity; and further, individuals shall not be denied Human or Civil Rights on the basis that they have changed their bodies cosmetically, chemically, or surgically, or desire to do so as a means of expressing a self-defined gender identity.

The Right to Sexual Expression

No individual's Human or Civil Rights shall be denied on the basis of sexual orientation; and further, no individual shall be denied Human or Civil Rights for expression of a self-defined gender identity through sexual acts between consenting adults.

The Right to Form Committed, Loving Relationships and Enter into Marital Contracts

Individuals shall not be denied the right to form committed, loving relationships with one another or to enter into marital contracts by virtue of their own or their partner's chromosomal sex, genitalia, assigned birth sex, or initial gender role, or on the basis of their expression of a self-defined gender identity.

The Right to Conceive, Bear, or Adopt Children;
The Right to Nurture and Have Custody of Children and to Exercise Parental Capacity

Individuals shall not be denied the right to conceive, bear, or adopt children, nor to nurture and have custody of children, nor to exercise parental capacity with respect to children, natural or adopted, on the basis of their own, their partner's, or their children's chromosomal sex, genitalia, assigned birth sex, or initial gender role, or by virtue of a self-defined gender identity or the expression thereof.

Source: Adapted from Feinberg, L. (1996), pp. 171–175.

proposition"—in other words, a belief that is deeply held and stubbornly resistant to change. However, they maintain that as long as "female" and "male" are seen as "external, objective, dichotomous, physical facts," sex and gender will be a basis for discrimination and oppression. "Unless and until gender, in all of its manifestations *including the physical*, is seen as a social construction, action that will radically change our incorrigible propositions cannot occur" (1978, p. 164). Kessler and McKenna urged that "People must be confronted with the reality of other possibilities, as well as the possibility of other realities." In this chapter, I have attempted to explore both realities and possibilities, encouraging you to begin to think of sex as not just female and male, but neither, both, and all of the above.

Exploring Further

❧

Boys Don't Cry (1999).

Hilary Swank won critics' praise in this film for her portrayal of Teena Brandon, who was raped and murdered for gender transgression. Enforcing sex and gender conformity in spite of individual difference and diversity can have tragic consequences.

Crawford, M. (Ed.). (2000). *A reappraisal of gender: An ethnomethodological approach. Feminism & Psychology,* 10, 7–72.

Twenty-five years after Kessler and McKenna wrote their landmark book on sex as a social construction, it was still controversial. In this special journal feature, commentators (including a feminist sexologist, sex/gender researchers, and transgender activists) discuss its impact and implications for the future, and Kessler and McKenna offer their response.

Fausto-Sterling, Anne (2000). *Sexing the body: Gender politics and the construction of sexuality.* New York: Basic Books.

Very few people can claim expertise in reproductive biology, feminist theory, *and* the history of science. Fausto-Sterling is an exception. In this richly detailed book, she shows how cultural assumptions create biological realities.

Reis, E. (2009). *Bodies in doubt: An american history of intersex.* Baltimore: Johns Hopkins University Press.

An expert historian offers a cultural, social, and medical history of how intersexuality has been regarded in America from early to modern times, showing that the meaning of ambiguous bodies is culturally determined.

Third Wave Foundation (www.thirdwavefoundation.org)

A feminist activist group that works nationally to support young women and transgender youth ages 15 to 30. The foundation is led by a board of young women, men, and transgender activists and its goal is to work toward gender, racial, economic, and social justice by supporting young feminists and developing their leadership skills.

CHAPTER 6

Gendered Identities:
Childhood and Adolescence

- **Theories of Gender Development**
    Social Learning Theory
    Cognitive Theories
- **Gender in the Child's Daily Life**
    Parental Influences
    Peer Influences
    Gendered Environments
    Media Influences
    Ethnicity, Social Class, and Gender Typing
    Children and Poverty
- **Leaving Childhood Behind: Puberty and Adolescence**
    Changing Bodies
    Gender Intensification
- **Vulnerabilities of Adolescence**
    Self-Silencing and Self-Esteem
    Peer Culture and Harassment
- **Making a Difference**
    Transforming Social Interactions: Enlarging the Options for Girls
    Transforming Ourselves: Resisting Gender Typing
- **Exploring Further**

"*A*s the twig is bent, so the tree will grow." This proverb reflects the belief that what children learn in their early years shapes them for their entire lives. One of the most important tasks of children in all cultures is to learn how to be a woman or a man in their society.

Becoming gendered is a process whereby people learn to fit in to the gender system. It takes place in a context of greater male power and status—the sociocultural level of the gender system. It is conveyed in everyday interactions in families, schools, and playgrounds—the interactional level of the system. Finally, gender becomes a part of the self for both boys and girls—the individual level of the gender system. As childhood progresses into adolescence, gendered identities and behaviors take on new importance, initiating a lifelong presentation of oneself as a man or a woman.

Theories of Gender Development

Some psychological approaches to gender development stress how the environment shapes children's learning and behavior. Others stress cognitive factors within the child. The differences between these theories are relative, not absolute. Most developmental psychologists recognize that becoming gendered is a result of biological, cognitive, and social factors interacting with each other.

Social Learning Theory

Almost everyone can remember childhood events that taught what a good girl or boy should—or shouldn't—do. Perhaps we were expected to do gender-specific household chores—boys may take out the trash, while girls set the table for dinner. We may have been encouraged to follow a same-gender example, "Susan doesn't talk back to *her* mother. . . ." When asked to explain how and why adult men and women seem so different from each other, students frequently remember events like these and express the idea that "we've all been conditioned by society." This way of thinking about gender is consistent with *social learning theory,* an approach that emphasizes how children learn gendered behavior from their environment (Mischel, 1966, 1970; Bussey & Bandura, 2004).

Learning through Reinforcement

Social learning theory draws its principles from experimental research on learning (Bandura & Walters, 1963). According to the theory, people learn their characteristic behavior patterns mainly through the process of *reinforcement.* Behavior that is followed by desirable consequences is reinforced, and is more likely to occur in the future. If a behavior is never reinforced, it will eventually stop.

Reinforcement of gender-linked behaviors is not always obvious. Parents do not usually follow their little girl around feeding her candy when she picks up a doll and frowning at her when she picks up a toy bulldozer! But behavior shaping can be effective without being noticeable. If Dad merely glances up from his computer with

FIGURE 6.1
The gender-differentiated environments of children's rooms, with more action toys for boys, foster gender-typed activities.

a warm smile when little Debbie is coloring quietly in her coloring book but stays absorbed in his work when she builds a block tower, she will, according to social learning theory, be more likely to color than to build towers in the future. The newly learned behavior may generalize to other situations—Debbie may begin to prefer coloring books to blocks at preschool as well as at home. The lesson may also be quite broad—Debbie may learn that, in general, quiet play is nicer than active play.

Learning gender-typed behavior is made easier when parents set up the environment in such a way that some activities are more likely to occur (and thus be reinforced) than others. And research from the 1970s to the present shows that most kids' physical environments are very gender-stereotyped, so much so that untrained observers can instantly tell whether they are seeing a photo of a boy's room or a girl's room (Sutfin et al., 2008). If a boy's room is filled with sports equipment and furnished in sturdy furniture that can "take a beating," he is probably more likely to engage in rough-and-tumble play than is his sister, whose room is done in pink-and-white ruffles and furnished with a dressing table. (See Figure 6.1.) Parents may then notice and reinforce the difference with approving comments about how "boys will be boys" and "she's a real little princess."

According to social learning theory, the effects of reinforcement occur whether or not the adult is deliberately attempting to influence behavior. An adult need not *intend* to teach a lesson about gender for her or his behavior to serve as a reinforcer for a child. Parents, teachers, grandparents, and other adults may sincerely believe that they treat boys and girls similarly while they actually are reinforcing very different behaviors.

Learning through Imitation and Observation

Social learning theory proposes that people also learn by observing others and imitating their behavior. *Imitation*—copying someone else's behavior—seems to be spontaneous in young children (see Figure 6.2). Children imitate language, as many a parent has found to their dismay when a swear word used in an unguarded

FIGURE 6.2   Children learn by imitating adults.

moment is repeated by their toddler. And they imitate all sorts of other behaviors. A young boy shaves with a toy razor while his father does the real thing; a young girl plays with her dolls as her mother feeds the baby. Imitation is often expressed in play, as children play house or play school.

Observational learning occurs through watching others' behavior. Even though it may not always be imitated right away, the lesson is stored for later use. A boy might observe that his father spends a lot of time watching sports on TV and later develop the same interests. A small girl may observe her mother shopping for clothes, planning new outfits, applying makeup, doing her hair, and dieting to lose weight. She learns through these observations that attractiveness is a very important dimension for women, although she might not express that knowledge very much until she is older.

A classic study by Albert Bandura (1965) illustrates the operation of both reinforcement and imitation in learning to be aggressive. In Bandura's study, children were shown one of three films. In all the films, an adult behaved aggressively by hitting and kicking a large toy clown. In the first film, the adult was rewarded; in the second, the adult was punished; and in the third, no specific consequences followed the aggression. The children were then given the opportunity to play with the toy clown. Just as social learning theory would predict, the children imitated the aggressive behavior most when it had been reinforced; that is, children who had seen the first film were more aggressive than those who had seen either of the other films. Overall, boys were more aggressive than girls.

In the next part of the experiment, the children were offered small treats for performing as many of the adult model's aggressive behaviors as they could remember. Here all the children were more aggressive and overall the girls were nearly as aggressive as the boys. Bandura's experiment shows that children imitate adult models even when they are not directly reinforced for doing so. In particular, they imitate models who are rewarded. Furthermore, children may learn a particular behavior through observation but show no evidence of learning the behavior until it is reinforced—like the girls in the second part of the experiment.

Learning Gender

Social learning theory explains gender identity and gender typing as the result of moment-to-moment, day-to-day interactions between the developing child and the immediate social environment—mother, father, and other caretakers; the media; school; and playmates. It assumes that what a child learns about femininity and masculinity will vary according to his or her social class, ethnic group, and family composition—including any and all social and environmental factors.

When gender-typed behavior is particularly visible, it is readily learned. Most preschool children see their mothers in largely gender-typed roles simply because mothers are more likely to be responsible for housework and childcare, activities that a child can observe often and directly. If only women are seen cleaning house and changing diapers, both boys and girls may learn that these are women's work. When mothers and fathers go to their jobs outside the home, the child does not observe their work directly. Even if the home environment is relatively gender-neutral, kids usually have plenty of opportunities to see gender-stereotypical behavior in the media.

Although social learning theory emphasizes environmental influences on gender typing, cognitive factors also play a role (Bussey & Bandura, 2004). Once children know that there are two gender categories and have developed a core gender identity, they pay more attention to same-gender models than to other-gender models. The likelihood that a child will imitate the behavior of same-gender adults depends on what proportion of same-gender adults display the behavior. In other words, a preschool-age girl who sees one TV show about a woman who races sports cars may or may not play with toy cars. However, if she sees dozens of TV shows and commercials featuring women who take care of babies and children, she is very likely to play with dolls and imitate the child care behaviors that she has seen on TV. The more gender typical a behavior is, the more likely a child will imitate it.

Social learning theory implies that we can reduce gender typing in children. Parents, schools, and the media could choose to reinforce and model more adventurous, instrumental behavior for girls and more nurturing, cooperative behavior for boys. Implicit in the theory is the idea that gender typing can be lessened or even eliminated if we as a society and as individuals choose to do so.

Cognitive Theories

- Neil, age 6, has liked to draw ever since he could pick up a crayon. His drawings have earned him lots of attention and praise from his preschool teachers, and the refrigerator at home is covered with them. His parents are proud of his talent, and even took him to meet a real artist in his studio. They are amazed when Neil suddenly loses interest in drawing, saying that "art is for girls."
- Rosa, age 3½, goes to a female pediatrician for her regular checkups and has an aunt who is a physician. Therefore, her parents are astounded to hear her announce to a playmate, "Girls can't be doctors! Girls are nurses and doctors are boys!"

These behaviors are hard to explain using social learning theory. How did Neil and Rosa learn their gender typed beliefs when *non*stereotypical beliefs and attitudes were being reinforced and modeled for them? One answer to this question is offered by cognitive developmental and gender schema theories of gender development. These two cognitive theories offer the intriguing idea that children willingly socialize themselves to be masculine or feminine (Martin & Ruble, 2004).

Cognitive Developmental Theory

This approach to gender development began by building on the research of Jean Piaget, who observed that young children think in ways that are qualitatively different from older children and adults (Kohlberg, 1966). Piaget believed that children move through a fixed series of stages in their cognitive development and there are concepts they cannot grasp until they have reached the appropriate cognitive stage. Children's predictable errors in thinking indicate that they have different, less mature ways of thinking than adults—less sophisticated modes of cognitive organization. Regardless of what stage they have reached; however, children actively strive to interpret and make sense of the world around them. According to the cognitive developmental approach, gender identity and gender typing are the outcome of children's active cognitive structuring of their physical and social world.

Children understand some things about the concepts of sex and gender long before others. A 2- or 3-year-old child can answer correctly when asked if he or she is a boy or a girl, and are able to classify others too (Zosuls et al., 2009). However, the child may believe that people can change sex by changing their hairstyles or clothing. (At age 2½, one of my children maintained stubbornly that the *real* difference between boys and girls was that only girls wear barrettes.) The child may believe that boys can grow up to be mommies, as the following conversation between two young boys shows:

> Johnny (age 4½): *I'm going to be an airplane builder when I grow up.*
>
> Jimmy (age 4): *When I grow up, I'll be a mommy.*
>
> Johnny: *No, you can't be a mommy. You have to be a daddy.*
>
> Jimmy: *No, I'm going to be a mommy.*
>
> Johnny: *No, you're not a girl, you can't be a mommy.*
>
> Jimmy: *Yes, I can.*
>
> (Kohlberg, 1966, p. 95)

This conversation illustrates that children's understanding of gender is concrete and limited. Johnny, who is slightly older, understands **gender constancy**—he knows that gender is permanent—while Jimmy does not. By the age of 6 or 7, almost all children understand gender constancy. According to cognitive developmental theory, this is a result of cognitive maturation.

Once children know that they are, and always will be, one sex or the other, they turn to the task of matching the societal expectations for people of their sex. Almost immediately after they learn to label themselves and others by sex, children start to engage in gender typed play (Zosuls et al., 2009). They start to value behaviors, objects, and attitudes that are consistent with their sex label. Girls want to do girly things like wear dresses. Boys, too, behave as though they are thinking, "I am a boy: therefore I want to do boy things; therefore the opportunity to do boy things (and to gain approval for doing them) is rewarding" (Kohlberg, 1966, p. 89). Children may exaggerate gender roles: boys proclaim anything remotely associated with girls as yucky and girls have been known to avoid boys' activities like the plague. (One little girl I know gave up soccer because the uniforms were not pretty.) This exaggeration may be due to children's need to keep gender categories cognitively distinct (Maccoby, 1980).

External rewards and punishments for gender-typed behavior are relatively unimportant, according to this theory. Rather than being passively influenced by whatever reinforcers the social environment sends their way, children actively try to fit their beliefs, values, and behaviors to their sex (see Figure 6.3). In their search to become the best possible girl or boy, children rely on reinforcers mainly as a guide to how well they are doing.

As girls become aware of the categories of masculinity and femininity, they may also recognize the status advantages of men. How do girls then come to value their devalued role enough to want to follow it? In fact, some do not—many girls are tomboys throughout middle childhood (Hyde et al., 1977). Most girls eventually do adopt feminine ways. They may find some aspect of femininity (such as nurturance) more appealing than some aspect of masculinity (such as aggression). Moreover, adult women have more power than young girls and that may provide a reason for the young girls to identify with them. However, the cognitive developmental approach does not provide a complete answer to the question of how

FIGURE 6.3

As predicted by cognitive developmental theory, girls often seek out feminine activities and roles.

girls come to adopt an orientation that is associated with low power and status.

Like social learning theory, cognitive developmental theory has generated a great deal of research. This research supports the idea that children's understanding of gender is related to their cognitive maturity. Research does not support the theory's claim that children become gender typed only after they acquire an understanding of gender constancy. On the contrary, children show a preference for gender-typed objects and activities by the age of 3 (Maccoby, 1998), even though, typically, they do not fully understand gender constancy until several years later.

Gender Schema Theory

A more recent cognitive approach downplays developmental stages in favor of a focus on the cognitive structures that comprise a child's knowledge about gender.

As discussed in Chapter 3, a schema is a network of mental associations. According to schema theory, it is difficult or impossible to understand information when you cannot connect it to a schema or when you unintentionally connect it to the wrong schema. However, when incoming information fits a pre-existing schema it is readily noticed, stored, and remembered. (See Box 6.1 and try it for yourself before looking at the answers in Box 6.2.)

Gender schema theory uses this cognitive approach to explain gender typing. Like other schemas, the gender schema is used by the individual as an aid to thinking and understanding (Bem, 1981). According to gender schema theory, the gender schema is learned very early, and it guides the individual in becoming gender typed. As children learn the contents of their society's gender schema, they learn which attributes are linked to their own sex, and hence to themselves. Gender schema theory conceives of gender typing as a readiness to organize the world in terms of gender and to process information in terms of gender associations. This is more than just learning how boys and girls are ranked on each dimension—that boys are supposed to be stronger than girls, for example—but also that the dimension of strength is more important in evaluating boys (Bem, 1981).

In other words, a difference between people who are highly gender typed and those who are not is that gender typed people have a well-developed gender schema

---

BOX 6.1 ∽ Schematic Processing: A Do-It-Yourself Demonstration and a Riddle

1. Read the following paragraph and then, without looking back at it, try to recall as much of it as possible. Write down every idea you remember from the paragraph.

The procedure is actually quite simple. First, you arrange things into different groups. Of course, one pile may be sufficient, depending on how much there is to do. If you have to go somewhere else due to lack of facilities, that is the next step; otherwise you are pretty well set. It is important not to overdo things. That is, it is better to do too few things at once than too many. In the short run this may not seem important but complications can easily arise. A mistake can be expensive as well. At first the whole procedure will seem complicated. Soon, however, it will become just another facet of life. It is difficult to foresee any end to the necessity for this task in the immediate future, but then one never can tell. After the procedure is completed, one arranges the materials into different groups again. Then they can be put into their appropriate places. Eventually they will be used once more and the whole cycle will then have to be repeated. However, that is part of life.

Many students find that understanding and remembering this paragraph is very difficult. For an explanation, see Box 6.2.

2. Try to solve this riddle—and ask a few friends.

A big Indian and a little Indian are sitting on a log. The big Indian points to the little Indian and says, "That Indian is my son." The little Indian points to the big Indian and says, "That Indian is not my father." Both are telling the truth. How is this possible?

For the answer, see Box 6.2.

Source: A Do-It-Yourself Demonstration, reprinted from *Journal of Verbal Learning and Verbal Behavior*, vol. 11, no. 6, J. D. Bransford & M. K. Johnson, "Contextual Prerequisites for Understanding: Some Investigations of Comprehension and Recall," p. 722, Copyright 1972, with permission from Elsevier.

and rely on it spontaneously in making sense of the world—they are ***gender-schematic.*** Less gender typed people have less developed gender schemas and rely more on other schemas—they are ***gender-aschematic.*** The difference is a matter of degree because everyone in our society has developed some sort of schema for gender.

Gender schemas lead to selective attention and selective memory. In one experiment, 5- and 6-year old children saw pictures of boys and girls doing stereotype-consistent activities (such as a boy playing with a truck) and stereotype-inconsistent ones (such as a girl using a hammer). A week later, when the children's memory for the pictures was tested, they tended to misremember the stereotype-inconsistent pictures—for example, they thought they had seen a boy using a hammer (Martin & Halverson, 1983). This study suggests that as early as the age of five, children have gender schemas and use them to filter information as they categorize the world around them. By this age, they already believe that certain occupations are for men and others are for women. When asked what they would like to be when they grow up, they are likely to choose an occupation that is stereotyped for their gender (Helwig, 1998).

Gender schema theory suggests that children *can* be brought up in ways that minimize the development of a gender schema, and thus bypass gender-stereotyped

BOX 6.2 ∾ Schematic Processing: Answers and Explanations

1. Why is it so difficult to make sense of the paragraph in Box 6.1? The words are ordinary and the sentence structure is simple. Yet most people find it frustrating to read and difficult to remember the ideas in the paragraph for even a short time. The reason is that comprehension and memory depend on the activation of a schema. This paragraph does not activate any particular schema for most people, and that makes it vague, ambiguous, and difficult to understand.

   The title for the paragraph is "Washing Clothes." If you now look back at it, you will find that you read it with a new understanding and your memory for the ideas will be much better. The clothes-washing schema provides the structure that interrelates and explains all of the previously obscure details. Without the schema, the individual sentences are straightforward but their relationship cannot be grasped.

2. The answer to the riddle is that the big Indian is the little Indian's mother.

Why is this riddle difficult for many people to solve? Even the most ordinary sentences require the reader to go beyond the information given and use their own stores of information about the world—their personal schemas. For most North Americans, the schema for "Indian" is based on stereotypes from movies and stories about the Wild West. Therefore we automatically think "male" when we think "Indian." Because the schema activated by "Indian" assumes "male," the schema is not much help in solving the riddle.

Puzzles like this can help us understand aspects of our schemas that we are normally unaware of in everyday comprehension. If you had been asked directly "Can the word *Indian* refer to a female?" you would no doubt answer yes. Yet if you found this riddle difficult, it is because your mental representation of "Indian" is primarily male. (Incidentally, does this riddle help you see why Native American people prefer not to be called Indians?)

thinking and behavior. If others around them paid less attention to gender, children would not automatically categorize by it, any more than they automatically categorize in terms of eye color. If they were taught to use the concept of sex to refer to anatomical differences, they would not assimilate irrelevant dimensions to the gender schema. They would differentiate male and female in sexuality and reproduction, but other aspects of behavior would remain gender-neutral (Bem, 1983).

In summary, social learning and cognitive theories emphasize different influences on children's gender development. Social learning theory maintains that children are shaped by the people and environments they encounter in everyday life. Cognitive theories emphasize that the child's mind is actively trying to comprehend and categorize gender information. Cognitive developmental theory proposes that this occurs in distinct stages, whereas gender schema theory emphasizes the gradual development of a complex mental network about gender and its assimilation to the self. No single theory has all the answers, but virtually all psychologists agree that social forces interact with biological and cognitive factors in gender development (Powlishta et al., 2001). In what follows, we will look in detail at gender influences in children's lives, showing how these factors interact to produce adults who fit in to the gender system.

Gender in the Child's Daily Life

Starting almost immediately after birth, an infant is viewed differently and treated differently depending on its sex. The effect of this treatment is to mold children into the gender norms of their culture. At first, parents and family are the strongest influence on gender. As the child grows, peers become more important. Meanwhile, toys, books, movies, and TV provide highly gendered messages. The child's own concept of gender interacts with all these influences, as he or she forms cognitive schemas and progresses to more cognitively mature ways of thinking about gender. These influences—from adults, other children, the media, the physical environment, and the child's own cognitive development—construct gender at the interactional level. They are all important in shaping adults who fit into their society's gender system and we will look at each in more detail.

Parental Influences

As soon as a woman announces that she is pregnant, others ask—boy or girl? Today, parents in developed countries usually know the sex of their child before its birth via ultrasound imaging. But this is a recent development. Throughout history, there were many superstitious methods of guessing the future baby's sex. If the mother "carries high," it is a boy; if she "carries low," it's a girl. If the fetus is active, moving and kicking a lot, it must be a boy. If the mother is sick during pregnancy, it's a girl. In much of this folk wisdom, the symbolically more negative characteristic of a pair (low/high, sick/healthy) was used to predict a girl. And there are many folk methods for insuring the birth of a son, such as taking herbs, eating particular foods, and even wishful thinking (see Figure 6.4).

The birth of a girl is a disappointment in many traditional cultures, as these proverbs show:

To be born a girl is to have an ill fate. (Nepal)

One daughter is more than enough; three sons are still too few. (South Korea)

Boys: The Preferred Sex

In some societies, the preference to have a son is so extreme that it reduces the survival rate of baby girls. Throughout history, some societies have practiced *female infanticide*. In ancient Greece, infant girls were sometimes left on a mountainside to die of exposure or be eaten by wild animals (Rouselle, 2001). Sex-based infanticide has been documented in about 9 percent of cultures and girls are the sex targeted most often

FIGURE 6.4

Posters like this can be found adorning the walls of many village homes in rural China. The reason is a folk belief that if a married woman looks at images of boy babies, she is more likely to conceive sons.

(Hrdy, 1988). Although no society today officially approves of female infanticide, there are persistent reports that it still takes place in areas where girls are particularly devalued. For example, in rural China, there are far more births of boys than girls recorded. In the southern Indian state of Tamil Nadu, the death rate for female infants—when there is no obvious medical cause—is 5 to 17 times higher than for male infants (Mahalingam et al., 2007). Women describe methods such as poisoning infants over a period of several days by mixing milk with a toxic tree sap (Diamond-Smith et al., 2008). The high rate of female infanticide in this region prompted the government to offer bonuses to parents whose daughters survived childhood (Miller, 2001).

Selecting boys for survival occurs in other ways, too. There is strong evidence that *female-selective abortion*—aborting healthy fetuses only because they are female—is widely practiced in East and South Asian countries including South Korea, China, India, Taiwan, and Pakistan. For example, almost immediately after fetal sex-determination techniques became available in Indian cities, social workers reported huge imbalances in the gender ratio of aborted fetuses; one study of 8,000 abortions showed that 7,997 were female fetuses (Hrdy, 1988). Some Asian immigrant groups in the United States and Canada may practice female-selective abortion in those countries as well (Miller, 2001).

Experts estimate that in the past two decades, millions of healthy female fetuses have been aborted in Asian countries alone (Miller, 2001). The problem is most acute in societies where there is increasing prosperity (allowing couples to pay for fetal sex tests and medical abortions) along with strong traditional ideas about the greater worth of sons (Dugger, 2001; "India's Religious leaders", 2001). Methods of sex-selective abortion, female infanticide, and neglect of baby girls are common knowledge in these societies (Diamond-Smith et al., 2008).

Female infanticide, female-selective abortion, and neglect and starvation of girls in early infancy have severely affected the sex ratio in many countries. In China, officials predict a shortage of some 40 to 60 million women by 2014 and say that the skewed gender ratio is already causing violent competition for wives among men (Baculinao, 2004). Only in South Korea is there a trend toward a more normal sex ratio, probably because modernization is weakening traditional attitudes that foster an extreme preference for sons (Chun & Das Gupta, 2009).

The reasons for son preference are related to patriarchy. The more patriarchal a society is, the more males control economic, political and social power, and the more the ideology of gender supports their continued dominance. In some traditional Asian societies, females tend to be economically dependent on fathers and husbands, have lower social status, and are considered impure or polluting. Tradition holds that only a son can provide for his parents in their old age. All of these factors combine to influence both women and men to prefer having sons and avoid having daughters. Moreover, because of dowry systems that require a bride's family to provide large sums of money and costly possessions to the groom's family, the birth of a daughter is an economic disaster. In southern India, although sex-selective abortion is illegal, mobile ultrasound/abortion clinics cruise rural villages advertising, "Pay 50 rupees now to save 50,000 rupees later" (Diamond-Smith et al., 2008; Miller, 2001).

An underlying reason for son preference and the patriarchal violence that ensues from it is that the characteristics attributed to females are biologically fixed and unchangeable. This belief, termed *essentialism,* is prevalent in societies with high rates of female infanticide and other forms of violence against girls and women. It is *men's* belief in essentialism, not women's, that is related to acceptance of gender-linked violence. It seems that when men believe that women are all the same and can never change, it becomes acceptable to control their numbers and their freedom through violence (Mahalingam et al., 2007).

Are boys the preferred sex in Western society? In our society, people often say that they just want a healthy baby, and they would like to have both boys and girls to complete their family. However, there are indicators that boys are still valued more than girls, especially by men. For example, in Gallup Polls (which measure the attitudes of large representative samples of U.S. adults), the overall preference for a boy has remained virtually unchanged over 60 years of polling (Leonhardt, 2003). Men in particular prefer boys by a large margin (45 percent versus 19 percent; the remainder express no preference).

Further evidence suggesting a preference for boys comes from divorce statistics showing that spouses with sons are less likely to get divorced than those with daughters. Families with both boys and girls are intermediate in divorce rate. Based on the huge samples provided by U.S. Census data, researchers have shown that the higher divorce rate for families with daughters has existed at least since the 1940s. Overall, the more girls a family has, the more likely the parents will divorce (Leonhardt, 2003). This pattern is found in every region of the country, regardless of family size, racial/ethnic group, and educational level. While it is quite small in magnitude, its persistence over time and the fact that it occurs in diverse ethnic and social class groups suggest that it reflects something important about the relative value of girls and boys. The statistical data is open to many interpretations (remember that correlations don't reveal why two variables are linked). Some social scientists have suggested that fathers may be less satisfied and less involved in family life when they have only daughters, and that men's preference for sons "almost certainly plays a role in creating the divorce gap" (Leonhardt, 2003, p. 4).

Parents: Not Gender-Neutral

From the first minutes of a baby's life, its parents are forming impressions of this new little person. Do parents perceive their babies in gender-stereotyped ways? In one study, mothers and fathers were asked to rate their newborns on a list of attributes provided by the experimenters. Parents of sons rated their babies as stronger, as well as less delicate, feminine and fine-featured than did parents of daughters. However, when asked to provide their own descriptions of the baby, the parents used language that did not differ according to the baby's sex (Karraker et al., 1995). This study suggests that gender stereotyping of infants can be primed—in this case, by providing a list of gender-stereotyped attributes. Of course, our society provides many ways to prime gender stereotypes about infants (see Box 6.3).

BOX 6.3   ∾   Research Focus
Gender Stereotyping Starts Early

....

"It's a boy!"
"It's a girl!"

A study conducted by Judith Bridges (1993) of the visual images and verbal messages in birth congratulations cards sampled 61 cards announcing the birth of a girl and 61 cards announcing the birth of a boy from 18 stores and 4 different municipalities in Hartford, Connecticut. Content analysis of the cards revealed stereotypical differences between the boy and girl cards. Visual images on boy cards included more physical activity, such as action toys and active babies, than that of girl cards. Girl cards included more verbal messages of expressiveness, including sweetness and sharing. Surprisingly, boy cards presented a message of happiness for the parents or the baby, more than girl cards.

Even though this study was conducted more than 15 years ago, birth congratulations cards still tend to portray gender stereotyping. When

I checked out the greeting card section of a local convenience store in 2010, I found that most of the cards portrayed girl and boy babies very differently. In fact, there were only two gender neutral cards in the whole section! In addition to the obvious pink versus blue distinction, three of the boy cards featured messages that referred to the baby as the new "little man" or "little guy" of the house. On the front of one girl card was the phrase "Viva la Diva!" written in glitter. Inside the card, there was a congratulatory message to the new parents on the arrival of their new "fashionista." What activities and traits do these cards imply that parents can expect from their children? How might these expectations create self-fulfilling prophecies?

Source: Contributed by Annie B. Fox and Michelle Kaufman.

When they were asked the same questions a week later, mothers in this study no longer stereotyped their infants, but fathers still did (Karraker et al., 1995). The mothers may have decreased their tendency to stereotype because they got to know their babies as individuals, whereas the fathers, who had less contact with the infants, did not. Many other studies of infants and young children show that fathers view their children in gender-stereotyped ways more than mothers do. Although fathers may stereotype more, they have less opportunity to convey their gender schemas to their offspring because they spend much less time overall with infants and young children (Tenenbaum & Leaper, 2002).

Differences in parental behavior may provide important models for children to observe and imitate. Everything a father or mother does when the children are present provides an example of expected female and male behavior. Take nurturance, for example. In most societies, young children see that mothers are the ones who take care of their bodily needs, soothe and comfort them, and play gently with them (Bronstein, 2006).

One of the most important ways parents socialize babies and young children is by talking to them. As we learned in Chapter 4, girls and boys get different kinds and amounts of talk about emotion, contributing to gender differences in emotionality (Chapter 4). Overall, mothers talk more to children than fathers do, and their talk is more supportive and emotion-focused, while fathers' talk is more directive and informative (Leaper et al., 1998). These differences in parental behavior are congruent with gender stereotypes of expressiveness for females and instrumentality for males. Mothers also talk more and use more supportive speech to their daughters in particular. This pattern is consistent with socializing girls toward connectedness and communality.

Parents also play with their sons and daughters differently during the preschool years. They do more pretend and fantasy play with girls, and fathers in particular do more rough and tumble, physical, and pretend-aggression play with boys (Lindsey et al., 1997; Lindsey & Mize, 2001). In a meta-analysis of over 150 North American studies, fathers were more likely than mothers to encourage their children toward gender-typed play and activities (Lytton & Romney, 1991).

It is clear that children pick up the messages their parents send. In one study of 4-year-olds, almost half of the boys said that they could not play with girls' toys because their fathers would think they were bad (Raag & Rackliff, 1998). In a meta-analysis, parents' attitudes about their own masculinity/femininity as well as their gender-stereotyped attitudes about others significantly predicted their children's gender-related beliefs and attitudes. The more traditional the parent's gender ideology, the more gender typed their children were. Interestingly, the effect was stronger for mothers (Tenenbaum & Leaper, 2002). Thus, the gender schemas of children, which are applied both to themselves and to others, are formed partly through exposure to their parents' gender schemas.

Before you conclude that parents are entirely responsible for turning out gender typed girls and boys, it is important to remember two points. First, meta-analyses show that the areas where parents treat their sons and daughters similarly are more numerous than the areas where they treat them differently (Lytton & Romney, 1991). Second, parental treatment of children may be influenced by the children's own characteristics. Parents may talk more to girls because girls on average are more responsive to talk. They may play more rough and scary games with boys because boys enjoy them more. The child's characteristics probably interact with the parent's beliefs about gender to influence parents' differential treatment of sons and daughters. Finally, there are plenty of other influences over which parents have little control.

Peer Influences

From an early age, children choose to play with same-gender friends—a pattern called *gender segregation.* This preference emerges around the age of two, when girls start to orient more toward playing with other girls; boys' preference for other boys develops about a year later (Powlishta et al., 2001). Gender segregation increases steadily during the preschool years. By age 4½, about 90 percent of a child's social playtime is with same-gender others (Martin & Fabes, 2001). This spontaneous gender-sorting occurs not only in our own society but also in others (Maccoby, 1998).

Adults do not usually initiate or encourage gender segregation. Why then do children self-segregate by gender? One explanation, based on cognitive developmental theory, is that they want to fit into their prescribed gender roles, and it's easier in same-sex play groups. Another theory is that children choose others with compatible play styles. According to this explanation, boys on average have a higher activity level than girls (a difference that may have a biological basis), and may prefer to play with others who are as active as they are. Girls may be more verbally and socially advanced, and prefer to play with others who are as good at sharing and communicating as they are (Moller & Serbin, 1996). In other words, boys think girls' games are slow and boring, and girls would rather play with other girls because they think boys are pushy and always get their way (Shields, 2002).

When children are observed playing alone, the play style of boys is similar to the play style of girls (Maccoby, 1998). When they play in groups, however, their play styles diverge and become increasingly gender typed (Martin & Fabes, 2001). Boys' play in gender-segregated groups involves more competition, confrontation, and risk-taking; girls' play in their groups involves more negotiation, cooperation, talking about oneself, and contact with adults (Maccoby, 1998). The more territorial and physical a game is, the more likely it is that elementary school children will segregate while playing it (Kelle, 2000). In other words, gender differences in play are shaped by the peer context.

Gendered play in turn affects friendship styles. By the time they are in fourth or fifth grade, girls' friendships are organized around confiding in each other and talking about others, whereas boys' friendships are more often organized around sports and other activities. These different friendship styles continue into adulthood. The playgroups of childhood are an important step in creating each new generation of gender-typed adults (Maccoby, 1998).

Gender-segregated play is not just a matter of difference. It is also a matter of status. Boys in particular create in-group solidarity and derogate the out-group (girls). For example, boys taunt other boys who do not conform to group norms by calling them faggot (Thorne & Luria, 1986) or sissy (Edwards et al., 2001). They also reinforce gender segregation by teasing and making jokes about romantic attraction. If Tory is a low-status, unpopular girl, boys may tease another boy by accusing him of liking her and saying that he will get "cooties" from her. Girls rarely tease other girls for being tomboys or accuse boys of having cooties. When a girl picks a fight, she may be called mean, but she is not accused of being like a boy (Shields, 2002). Usually it is boys who patrol the boundaries between groups by encouraging opposition between boys and girls, defining cross-gender contact in terms of sex and pollution, and scapegoating some girls as "untouchables" (Thorne & Luria, 1986). For unpopular girls like Tory, hostile teasing from high-status boys may make playtime into a nightmare (Keltner et al., 2001).

Boys learn competitive, dominance-oriented play styles, and girls learn more cooperative styles, girls are at a disadvantage in mixed groups. The tactics they use to gain power and influence with other girls (persuasion and negotiation) simply do not work with boys. In one early study, children were allowed to play with a movie-viewing toy in groups of four (two boys and two girls). Only one child at a time could see the movie. In this situation, boys ended up with three times as much viewing time as girls (Charlesworth & LaFreniere, 1983). Similar patterns may occur when children have to share computers in a classroom or compete for a teacher's attention (see Chapter 4). The tactics boys learn in all-boy play groups help them achieve dominance in many different kinds of interactions.

We should not conclude that girls are not competitive or not interested in status. The difference seems to be that girls' play style teaches them interpersonal skills, which they prefer to use over overt physical aggression, whether they are competing or cooperating. When girls want to be aggressive and dominant, they may engage in **relational aggression**—hostile acts that attempt to damage another's close relationships or social standing (Crick & Rose, 2000). In other words, a girl may spread a rumor about another girl, give her the silent treatment, or say "I won't be your friend if you don't do it my way!" Relational aggression can be just as harmful as physical aggression.

Traditionally, psychologists have claimed that there is a consistent gender difference in aggression, with boys being more aggressive than girls from early childhood (Maccoby & Jacklin, 1974). This supposed gender difference may have been the result of an androcentric definition of aggression, a kind of research bias discussed in Chapters 1 and 4. It largely disappears when relational aggression is taken into account (Crick & Rose, 2000). For example, when fifth graders were asked who bullied other children the most, they nominated boys who were physically aggressive and girls who were verbally or relationally aggressive, so that, overall, girls and boys were seen as equally likely to bully (Lee, 2009).

Gender segregation and the resulting differences in interaction style are not absolute or inevitable. In an observational study of elementary school children on their playgrounds, there was a great deal of variety in play. Unsegregated and nonstereotypical play actually occurred quite often. The strictest segregation was among the most popular and socially visible students; others quietly went their own way, often violating the rules of gender segregation (Thorne, 1993). Cross-gender friendships do occur, though they may be kept out of sight. I remember a middle-school friendship with a boy who, like me, was obsessed with chemistry experiments. We never talked at school, but on Saturdays we happily burned holes in our parents' carpets as we tried to mix potions that could eat through any substance. Our friendship was underground but it was important to both of us.

Gendered Environments

Girls and boys grow up together, but their environments foster different activities, values, and beliefs. Here we look at just one of many aspects of the environment: the toys children play with.

When I was eight I really wanted a chemistry set. I asked for it for my birthday, but got a Cinderella watch instead. I liked the watch but I still wanted a chemistry set. I put it on my Christmas list but Santa failed me. Finally, on my ninth birthday, my wish was granted and my career in chemical catastrophes began. I was not surprised, years later, to come across a study showing that children were more likely to get an item on their Christmas list if it was gender-stereotypical than if it was not (Etaugh & Liss, 1992). My parents weren't being mean; they just relied on their gender schemas when providing me with toys. And they weren't alone. Studies conducted from the 1970s onward, in several countries, show that boys and girls as young as 5-months-old are provided with different toys, such as more vehicles for boys and more dolls for girls (Nelson, 2005; Pomerleau et al., 1990; Rheingold & Cook, 1975). Gender typing in toys is not due only to parents' influence. From an early age, children themselves express strong preferences for gender-typed toys. By the time they are 1½ years old, boys typically prefer trucks to dolls and girls typically prefer the opposite.

Gendered toy preferences increase during the preschool and elementary school years (Powlishta et al., 2001). Both boys and girls continue to play with gender-neutral toys. It is only the supposedly opposite-gender toys that they avoid—and boys do this more than girls do. Children develop activity preferences, too, based on their toys. In general, girls' toys are associated with attractiveness, nurturing, and housework skills, whereas boys' toys are associated with violence, competition, and danger (Blakemore & Centers, 2005).

These gender-typed patterns are blatantly reinforced by stereotypical marketing that is directly aimed at children. Large retailers like Toys "R" Us clearly distinguish boys' aisles, with brightly colored action figures, tanks, trucks, and guns, from girls' aisles, with pastel-colored crafts, dolls, toy appliances, and makeup kits (Bannon, 2000). Children are steered away from gender neutrality by the way the store is structured. It seems that no toy or activity is exempt from having gender imposed on it. (See Box 6.4.) Even with an undeniably gender-neutral toy, such as a bicycle, manufacturers create two versions—a pink, flower-trimmed bike with a wicker basket for girls, and a black, heavy-duty BMX version for boys. When the Disney movie Tangled came out in 2011, a girls-only bike was marketed complete with a Tangled hair-care kit. Distinctions like these may foster the development of extended gender schemas in young children. It's as though the adults in their lives are telling them, "Gender is the most important category in the world—even your bike has to have one!"

BOX 6.4   ∾   Dracula and the Princess

Halloween is a time for fantasy, when children can dress up and pretend to be just about anything or anybody. However, even the fantasy play of Halloween is gender stereotyped. In a study by Nelson (2000), the researcher analyzed 469 costumes and sewing patterns for Halloween. Less than 10 percent of children's costumes were gender neutral. Girls' costumes tended to depict princesses, beauty queens, and other examples of traditional femininity, such as a Colonial Belle, Blushing Bride, or Pretty Mermaid. Boys' costumes were also stereotypical, depicting characters who battle opponents, such as Bronco Rider, Dick Tracy, or Hercules. Boys' costumes were more likely to portray famous villains, such as Captain Hook, Wolfman, or Frankenstein.

In costumes depicting death, there was an especially large difference in gender stereotypes. Boy's costumes included Dracula, a devil, and the Grim Reaper, accessorized with blood, body parts, or weapons. The few villainous costumes for girls emphasized their erotic nature—Sexy Devil or Bewitched—or their harmless charm—Little Skull Girl or Pretty Little Witch.

Although Halloween costumes may seem like harmless fun, they are another example of the way in which gender stereotypes are transmitted to children and gender roles are acted out in play.

Media Influences

The books children read, the TV shows they watch, and the video games they play are all powerful sources of gender socialization. Starting in the 1970s, feminists drew attention to gender stereotyping in children's readers and storybooks. Several studies from the 1970s to the early 1990s showed that boys and men more often were represented as independent, active, competent, and aggressive, whereas girls and women more often were shown as passive, helpless, nurturing, or dependent. Overall, males appeared much more often than females as the main character.

Gender stereotyping declined but did not disappear in the 1990s. A study of 83 children's books published from 1995 to 1999 showed that about half of the main characters were female, a big improvement from the past. But most of the women still were shown as mothers or grandmothers, with the occasional washerwoman or witch thrown in (Gooden & Gooden, 2001). Men were shown in a much greater variety of roles and occupations than women, but they were rarely shown taking care of children, and no man was ever shown doing household chores. A content analysis of school readers during the same time period showed that male characters were more argumentative, aggressive, and competitive, whereas female characters were more affectionate, emotionally expressive, passive, and tender (Evans & Davies, 2000).

Have things changed in the twenty-first century? Not so much. A study of 200 top-selling and award-winning children's books that were published after 2001 showed that there were nearly twice as many male as female main characters—a throwback to the 1970s. Females were far more likely to be shown nurturing others, and both males and females were shown almost exclusively in stereotypical occupations. The good news: Females were no longer more passive or more likely to be rescued (Hamilton et al., 2006).

With help like this, it's not surprising that children learn gender at an early age—even when they cuddle up with Mom or Dad for a bedtime story. As psychologist Mykol Hamilton put it, children's books provide "nightly reinforcement of the idea that boys and men are more interesting and important than are girls and women" (Hamilton et al., 2006, p. 764).

Most children spend a lot more time watching TV and playing video games than they spend with their reader or library book. The typical child watches TV approximately 38 hours each week. Even young children (ages 2–7) get in about 25 viewing hours each week (Rideout et al., 1999). In fact, children spend more time with entertainment media than they do with any other activity except school and sleeping, and many children watch TV for more hours each week than they spend in school (Anderson et al., 2003). A meta-analysis showed that the more a child watches TV, the more likely he or she is to have gender-stereotyped beliefs (Herrett-Skjellum & Allen, 1996). This is not surprising—we learned in Chapter 3 that television programs and commercials present extremely stereotyped images of women and men.

Video games may surpass all other media both in popularity and in sexism. Gaming is the leading online activity for children over the age of 6—about 84 percent reported that they played a video game in the past month and 20 percent played every day. Gamers also spend time reading gaming magazines, participating in gaming blogs, and talking with friends about games (Dill & Thill, 2007). Boys aged 11 to 14 are the biggest gamers of all.

What are kids learning from video games? One research team summarized the gender messages like this: "a sexist, patriarchal view that men are aggressive and powerful and that women are not healthy, whole persons but sex objects, eye candy, and generally second-class citizens" (Dill & Thill, 2007). Females are consistently underrepresented in video games. However, it may be better when women are absent, since when they do appear it is usually as sex objects, helpless victims, or targets of aggression. Male characters are shown with far more abilities and powers (Miller & Summers, 2007). And male characters are much more aggressive than female characters. (For more on violence in the media and its effects, see Chapter 12.)

Video games are more popular with boys, but Barbie dolls and all the media products connected with them are more popular with girls (see Figure 6.5). Among U.S. girls aged 3 to 10, 99 percent own at least one Barbie doll, and the average number owned is eight. Girls also have Barbie videos, games, and other accessories. Many girls report going through a phase where they identified intensely with Barbie, thought she was perfect, and wanted to be just like her (Dittmar et al., 2006). But Barbie's proportions give girls an everyday model of extremely unrealistic body shape. If Barbie were a full-size woman, she would have a 42-inch bust, 18-inch waist, and 33-inch hips, and her body weight would be so low that she could not menstruate (Dittmar et al., 2006; Gray & Phillips, 1998). The odds of a real woman having the same proportions as Barbie are 1 in 100,000. Ken is considerably more realistic—the odds of a man having his proportions are about 1 in 50 (Norton et al., 1996).

Should we be concerned about children's exposure to media stereotypes? According to cognitive developmental and gender schema theories, children are actively seeking the meaning of being a boy or a girl. The lessons they learn from the media get attached to their own gender schemas and to their sense of self. According to social learning theory, the more often children see models of gendered behavior, the more likely they are to imitate it and store it up for later use. All these theories suggest that children who are bombarded with gender stereotypes in their toys,

FIGURE 6.5
Barbie is everywhere. These little girls are playing outside their house in Kathmandu, Nepal.

TV shows, and games are likely to make these messages part of their own identity and to expect that this is how women and men should look and behave in real life. Very little research has measured the effect of exposing children to gender-stereotyped media images, but there seems to be cause for concern. In one study, 5- to 8-year-old girls saw images of Barbie dolls, Emme dolls (a larger weight woman based on the full-figure model of the same name), or no dolls, and then completed measures of body image. Younger girls exposed to the Barbie images reported a lower satisfaction with their bodies and a greater desire to be thinner than girls in the other conditions (Dittmar et al., 2006). Body dissatisfaction can lead to unhealthy eating, excessive dieting, and ultimately to eating disorders. Perhaps Barbie is not just a harmless fashion toy.

Fashion marketing is also at the forefront of a disturbing trend to sexualize girls at younger and younger ages (American Psychological Association, 2007). Bratz dolls, dressed in sexy togs such as miniskirts and fishnet stockings, are popular with girls as young as four. One corporation was poised to release a line of dolls aimed at girls 6 and up based on the Pussycat Dolls, a rock group that features suggestive lyrics, bad girl demeanor, and sexually revealing clothing. This not-so-good idea was dropped only after a grassroots campaign from parents and media activists. Sexy clothing, cosmetics, perfumes, and spa manicures are being marketed to very young girls, not just by messages about smelling good and looking pretty, but through hints about being sexually attractive.

Ethnicity, Social Class, and Gender Typing

A child's socialization is affected not only by gender but also by other factors such as ethnicity and social class, and these may be intertwined. Parents' attitudes about gender are often based on their ethnic group's cultural heritage. For example, Asian American families may retain the tradition that women should be nurturing and home-oriented and that men should be strong and stoic, but also family-oriented, and these ideals are still passed on to Asian American children (Bronstein, 2006).

When a sample of Latinas aged 20 to 45 were asked in in-depth interviews what their parents taught them about how girls and boys should behave, the majority recalled traditional role expectations. Their brothers were granted more freedom, while the girls were expected to help with housework, learn to cook, and behave properly. A second, larger sample of Latino/a college students supported these findings and showed that gender socialization messages were usually conveyed by the same-gender parent: fathers taught boys what was expected of them and mothers taught girls (Raffaeli & Ontai, 2004).

In African American families, extended-family relatives and neighbors are often very involved in children's lives, forming an extended community of discipline and guidance. In general, studies suggest that African American children are less likely to rely on gender-stereotypical thinking than European American children are (Leaper, 2000). For example, by age 6, most White boys have learned that only girls like babies, and they show little interest when invited to play with an infant. However, at age 10, African American boys are still equally as responsive as girls are to the infant (Reid & Trotter, 1993).

Just over half of all African American children are raised by a single-parent mother who works outside the home. Therefore, African American children see women as both providers and caretakers, which may be particularly important for girls. Several studies show that African American girls and women do less gender-stereotyping and hold less stereotypical attitudes than their European American counterparts, and less than African American boys and men. When African Americans are compared with European Americans from single-mother homes, the differences are smaller. Thus, these ethnic group differences may be due to growing up in different kinds of family structures (Leaper, 2000).

Social class differences in African American households may also create different gender socialization patterns. In a recent interview study of a class-diverse group of African American parents, there was generally strong support for gender equality. Most parents stressed that they had high educational goals for both boys and girls, and they expected both their sons and daughters to learn independence and equality of roles. As one mother said,

> I will definitely teach my son that men and women are equal; he is not the head of anybody. His wife will always have input and say-so in whatever is going on in their lives. And he needs to know that . . . when we were growing up, boys washed dishes, boys cooked; girls washed dishes, girls cooked. My mother taught us pretty equally to do everything, just in case you were on your own you wouldn't have to depend on somebody (Hill, 2002, p. 497).

However, some of the families studied were newly arrived in the middle class—they had come from poor families or were less educated than others in the sample. These parents gave more mixed messages to their children. For example, one mother said that she wanted her daughter to be a warrior for racial justice, and also that she wanted her to be respectable, sit properly, avoid being loud, and act like a lady. Fathers in this group were more likely to be worried that their sons would become homosexual if they were not taught traditional masculinity. This study suggests that African American parents' support for gender equality depends on how secure they feel in their middle-class status; more secure families were more able to take the risk of raising gender-flexible children (Hill, 2002).

Children and Poverty

The United States is a wealthy nation and the poverty that exists in the midst of this wealth is often invisible. More than 35 million Americans live below the poverty line, including over 14 million children (Arnold & Doctoroff, 2003). Poor children face many obstacles to healthy development, both in their social environments and in their physical environments.

Children from low-income families are exposed to more violence at home, in their neighborhood, and at school than those from middle-income families. They are more likely to experience parents' divorce, family breakup, and foster care (Evans, 2004). Poverty makes it difficult or impossible for parents to provide for their children's needs. Poor parents are more likely than middle-class parents to be working two or more jobs and working later hours. For the parents' this means having less time to read to children, help with homework, take them to the library, or supervise their play. They often lack basic resources like a reliable car, health insurance, and decent childcare. Moreover, poverty is strongly linked to depression in parents, leading to less consistent and effective parenting (Belle, 2008). From infancy onward, poor children are exposed to more punishment and less positive parental interaction than are middle-income children.

Poverty has a "devastating negative effect on academic achievement" for both girls and boys (Arnold & Doctoroff, 2003, p. 518). Poor children receive less cognitive stimulation and enrichment than wealthier children do. They are less likely to have a computer or Internet access at home. Their schools cannot fill the gap because they are likely to have less qualified teachers, outdated facilities, and few educational materials (Evans, 2004).

The physical environment of poverty includes higher exposure to toxins such as lead poisoning and air pollution, along with crowded and inadequate housing. For example, poor children are over four times as likely to have high levels of lead in their blood, 3.6 times more likely to live in houses infested with rodents, and 2.7 times more likely to have not enough heat in the winter, compared with other children. Multiple stressors in the social and physical environment have a cumulative effect on poor children (Evans, 2004).

I have focused on poor children in our own nation but childhood poverty is a worldwide problem. In poor and developing countries, many children lack safe drinking water and basic sanitation. Their housing is particularly inadequate and may be located in flood zones, toxic waste areas, or other undesirable locations (Evans, 2004). They may not be able to go to school or even have a school to go to.

Childhood poverty affects both boys and girls, but it is not gender-equal in its effects. In the United States, because boys are more likely to act out and cause trouble for others, their problems may receive more attention, and more programs are available to help them. The problems that are more likely to afflict girls, such as underachievement, depression, and poor mental health, are less often noticed and treated (Arnold & Doctoroff, 2003). In developing countries, girls are often kept at home to do household work, denying them the education that could help lift them out of poverty. In most parts of the developing world, there is a gender gap in literacy, with fewer girls than boys learning to read (UNESCO, 2000).

Leaving Childhood Behind: Puberty and Adolescence

When does a child become an adult? *Puberty* is a series of physiological events that changes a child into a person capable of reproducing. However, there is much more to being an adult than the capability to reproduce. The period after puberty and before adulthood, termed *adolescence,* is the time that a society allocates for young people to mature and grow into their adult roles. The adolescent must negotiate sexuality, independence, and personal identity, while being not yet an adult.

The biological changes of puberty and the social meanings of adolescence are closely intertwined, because the biological changes take place in a cultural context that defines their meaning. For adolescent boys, the maturing body signifies an increase in status and power. As boys grow taller and more muscular, they are given more freedom. For girls, the maturing body signifies a more mixed status. It is wonderful to become a woman, and some girls eagerly await their first period and first bra. On the other hand, girls may not be granted more freedom—in fact, their independence may be curtailed. In this section, I discuss the physical changes of puberty and their social meaning.

Changing Bodies

Puberty begins with a rise in hormonal production that gradually causes the body to mature. For girls, the first external sign may be a ***growth spurt*** or the development of ***secondary sex characteristics***—breasts and body hair. The growth spurt is not just a gain in height, but also a gain in body fat. This increase is necessary and normal. In order for a girl to begin menstruating, she must reach a critical level of body fat (Frisch, 1983). Healthy adult women have up to twice as much body fat as healthy adult men (Warren, 1983). However, developing womanly curves conflicts with societal norms for extreme thinness at the same time as it makes girls' sexuality visible to all. Many girls are uncomfortable about their changing bodies:

> I was developing very early as a 6ᵗʰ grader and I didn't like my body at all . . . my boobs were just so big that, I mean, I am still busty and I mean, they are huge and I was a small person and they got in my way . . . and I really hated them . . . I just remember feeling that I was going to grow up and the only thing that I would be good for was something like a Playboy bunny (Lee, 2003, p. 89).

Although gaining weight and adding body fat are a normal part of becoming sexually mature for females, girls may interpret this process as becoming fat. During adolescence, there is a dramatic increase in girls' concern about their weight (Smolak & Striegel-Moore, 2001). In a study of factors that predict body dissatisfaction, the most important factors were not only actually being overweight but also the perceived pressure from others to be thin, a belief in a "thin-is-better" ideal, and lack of social support (Stice & Whitenton, 2002).

White girls in particular tend to tie their self-esteem to their weight, whereas African American girls tend to be more satisfied with their bodies. For example, 40 percent of a large sample of African American girls, and only 9 percent of White girls, said that they felt attractive (Phillips, 1998). Although body dissatisfaction was higher among the White girls, it was present in both ethnic groups. The preoccupation with weight can have serious health consequences. For example, girls may start smoking and using diet pills in attempts to eliminate body fat (Phillips, 1998). Some girls develop eating disorders—a topic that will be discussed in Chapter 13.

The onset of menstruation—termed ***menarche***—is the most visible and dramatic sign of puberty. Menarche occurs at about 12½ years of age on average. European American girls reach menarche several months later than African American and Latina girls, and earlier than Asian American girls; these ethnic differences may be related to average body weight. However, there is a great deal of variability in its timing. Some girls reach menarche as early as age 8 (O'Sullivan et al., 2001).

Virtually every woman remembers the day she got her first period:

So I was 10 years old and didn't understand any of it. In fact I misunderstood most of it. What I remember about it from the book was that somehow the menstrual blood came out on the outside of your lower abdomen somehow like it seeped through your skin! . . . So I told my mother and it was like "oh," she did seem rather pleased but it wasn't like the kind of pleased where if I got a really good grade or . . . the solo in the school play . . . She pulls out the Kotex kit and that is when I begin to connect, this is what it is, it doesn't come out of your stomach! (Lee, 2003, p. 93).

When it came, I was a high school exchange student in Europe, staying with the family of a friend. I felt like I was out of control, that something was happening to me that I couldn't stop. I bled terribly all over the sheets and was horribly embarrassed telling my friend's aunt (especially since I didn't know the right words, menstruation is hardly one of the common vocabulary words you have to learn). . . . I felt like it was all happening to someone else, not me, like I was watching myself in a movie and now was this sexual being (Lee, 2003, p. 87).

I saw blood on my underwear and it was like I just sat on the toilet . . . and I am like "mom." She comes in and she was like, "What? Well honey, congratulations, you are a little lady now." I am like, "Say what?!!"(Lee, 2003, p. 93).

Girls receive both positive and negative messages about this aspect of becoming a woman (see Figure 6.6). Although some studies have shown that women feel positive about menstruation as a sign of good health and an affirmation of womanhood, menstruation is more often associated with disgust, shame, annoyance, secrecy, and a list of "do's and don'ts" in our society as well as in many others (Johnston Robledo et al., 2006; Marvan et al., 2006; Reame, 2001). (See Box 6.5.) In one study of U.S. college students, about two-thirds said that they knew nothing about their own mothers' menstrual experiences, and their mothers had reacted negatively when told about the girls' first period (Costos et al., 2002). Menstruating women are still stigmatized. In one creative study, college students saw a woman "accidentally" drop either a hair clip or a tampon in front of them. Students were

FIGURE 6.6
Source: STONE SOUP © 2002 Jan Eliot. Reprinted with permission of Universal Uclick. All rights reserved.

BOX 6.5 ∾ **Call It Anything but Don't Call It Menstruation**

Societies generate euphemisms to disguise or soften the meaning of taboo topics. Menstruation has generated many euphemisms. Which of these have you heard and which are new to you?

Bunny time (Australia)

Monthlies (Australia)

Mary is visiting (Belgium)

I have my moon (Canada)

Blowjob time (England)

Blobbing (England)

Lingonberry days (Finland)

Japanese week (Germany)

Monthly tax (Germany)

Cranberry woman (Germany)

Casual leave (India)

Out of doors (India)

Aunty Mary (Ireland)

Jam Rag (Ireland)

Cookies (Mexico)

Little Miss Strawberry (Japan)

Ketchup (Japan)

The tomato soup overcooked (Netherlands)

Mrs. Noodles (New Zealand)

Doing time (Nigeria)

I have the red label in the old typewriter (Portugal)

Aunt Bertha (Scotland)

My aunt parked her red Porsche outside (South Africa)

Granny came in a red Ferrarri (South Africa)

Wearing the red beret (Vietnam)

The curse (United States)

The plague (United States)

Aunt Flow (United States)

Riding the cotton pony (United States)

On the red (United States)

Shark week (United States)

Source: Museum of Menstruation & Women's Health (www.mum.org). Contributed by Michelle Kaufman and Annie B. Fox.

---

then asked about their attitudes toward the woman, although they did not know that their responses had anything to do with the incident. When the woman had dropped the tampon, participants (both male and female) rated her as less likable and competent, and sat further away from her, than when she had dropped the hair clip (Roberts et al., 2002).

The media contribute to stigmatizing menstruation. For many years menstrual products were banned from TV and radio, and magazine ads were so vague that it was hard to tell what was being advertised. Even today, most ads stress that menstruation must be kept secret (Merskin, 1999; Simes & Berg, 2001). For a sign that times are changing, see Box 6.6. In 2003, the FDA approved a continuous oral contraceptive, *Seasonale*, designed to suppress menstruation. Medically, menstrual suppression is controversial, and there are *no* long-term studies of its effects. But a study of 22 articles in the popular press just before the debut of Seasonale showed that very few mentioned the lack of long-term research, and most characterized menstruation as messy, annoying, unhealthy, inconvenient, and unnecessary. Advocates of menstrual suppression were quoted twice as often as those who opposed it, and suppression was endorsed not only for women with severe menstrual problems

BOX 6.6   ∾   Tampon Ads for a New Age

Did you know that words and phrases such as *vagina* and *down there* are off-limits for advertisers on television . . . even in advertising for feminine hygiene products? Commercials and print advertisements for products like pads and tampons have historically been cheesy, using gimmicks like blue liquid poured from a beaker, or women in yoga poses, dressed all in white. The Kimberly Clark corporation, maker of Kotex, has long been one of the offending companies. In 2010 the company launched a new campaign, U by Kotex, in which they make fun of themselves and other feminine hygiene companies for their ridiculously inaccurate portrayals of menstruating women and feminine care products. Perhaps you have seen the commercial from Kotex, "Obnoxious" which features a young "racially ambiguous" woman, dressed in white, speaking about how you'll buy whatever feminine care product she tells you to because you want to be like her. The commercial ends with the statement, "Why are tampon ads so obnoxious?" and then flashes to the new Kotex-U brand tampon. In print ads, the campaign spoofs the notion that women need to hide their tampons from men and conceal the fact that they have periods. While Kotex may be turning the tables on feminine care advertisers, they have already encountered resistance from networks who still view menstruation as taboo. It seems that the Kotex campaign has the power to begin to destigmatize menstruation—however, the success of the campaign remains to be seen and will ultimately be determined by consumers. What do you think about how advertisers portray menstruation and menstrual products? Is the Kotex-U campaign a better alternative?

but for just about anyone (Johnston-Robledo et al., 2006). This biased reporting is worrying in light of research showing that women's primary source of information about the risks and benefits of menstrual suppression is . . . you guessed it, the media (Rose et al., 2008). The mixed messages of "You're a young woman now," "You will be disgraced and humiliated if anyone discovers that you are having your period," and "Menstruation is something that any woman would get rid of if she could" may leave girls wondering what is so wonderful about becoming a woman.

Gender Intensification

Many young girls are tomboys: they like boys' toys, sports, and active games. In a three-generational study of college students, their mothers, and their grandmothers, a two-thirds majority said they had been tomboys during childhood. They also said that they stopped being tomboys at some point, and the average age reported was 12.6 years, almost exactly the age the average girl reaches puberty. However, it was not the physical changes of puberty that caused these girls to give up their tomboy ways. Although they still liked active, adventurous play, they reported that they quit doing these things because of social pressure to be feminine (Morgan, 1998).

The shift from tomboy to young lady illustrates the process of **gender intensification**—or increased pressure to conform to gender roles beginning in early adolescence (Signorella & Frieze, 2008). By the time they are 11 or 12 years of age, girls start to get more messages from parents, other adults, and peers to act feminine, stake their self-esteem on being attractive, and conform to social norms for females. It's not that girls necessarily believe they are really more feminine now, and boys that they are more masculine, but rather that their roles and behaviors change. For example, they become more gender-typed in their household chores, and spend more time with their same-sex parent (Priess et al., 2009).

As you might expect, the timing of puberty affects the timing of these messages. The earlier a girl matures, the earlier she is subject to gender intensification. On the one hand, early maturity may make a girl more popular with boys. Early-maturing girls date more than late-maturing girls and are more likely to get involved with boyfriends in middle school and junior high (Brooks-Gunn, 1988). On the other hand, early-maturing girls experience a more stressful adolescence. For example, they get lower grades and score lower on achievement tests than late-maturing girls. They engage in more risky behaviors such as smoking, drinking, and early sexual intercourse, and they have higher rates of depression and eating disorders than late-maturing girls. Altogether, early maturation is associated with a host of developmental problems for girls (Ge & Natsuaki, 2009).

These timing effects may occur because early-maturing girls tend to become part of an older, more experienced peer group involved in activities that they imitate. Pressures can come from adults, too, who expect a physically mature girl to behave like an adult woman—as discussed in Chapter 3, physical characteristics are particularly important in triggering gender stereotypes. However, a 12-year-old girl with the body of a woman is still a 12-year-old girl emotionally, cognitively, and in her life experience.

Another change that comes with adolescence—and may be an aspect of gender intensification—is girls' participation in sports. Girls' sports participation tends to dwindle as they grow older, probably because most sports are still considered masculine. In a 2006 Internet survey of college-age women and men, participants classified football, weightlifting, rugby, basketball, motocross, skateboarding, snowboarding, wakeboarding, surfing, and soccer on the masculine side, and only swimming, tennis, volleyball, and gymnastics as neutral or feminine (Hardin & Greer, 2009). Highly feminine gender-typed girls are more likely to drop out of masculine sports than less feminine girls are (Guillet et al., 2000). This may be because they are concerned about appearing unfeminine.

We are exposed to the message that girls, as a group, lack athletic skills whenever we hear the common insult leveled at boys (and girls) that they "throw [or run, or play, or hit . . .] like a girl." Surrounded by discouraging messages like these, and lack of support for the development of their physical potential, many girls come to believe that they are the weaker sex. A meta-analysis of research on sex-related differences in physical self-confidence found an overall moderate effect size favoring males, particularly on masculine tasks (Lirgg, 1991). Girls learn that raw physicality is incompatible with the performance of femininity. It is unfeminine to have muscles, to be strong, fast, tough, or better than boys (Koivula, 2001).

Vulnerabilities of Adolescence

The transition from childhood to adulthood has traditionally been thought of as a time of increasing self-confidence and competence. However, for some girls adolescence is a time of *decreasing* self-confidence and self-esteem as they learn that speaking out and being themselves leads to trouble (Brown, 1998).

Self-Silencing and Self-Esteem

Interviews with adolescent girls during the middle-school and junior-high years showed that many stifled their own feelings and thoughts in an effort to fit in and be seen as a nice girl—a phenomenon termed *self-silencing* (Brown & Gilligan, 1992). The girls in this study were from privileged backgrounds and attended a private school. However, they are not the only ones to experience self-silencing. In another study, girls from diverse racial and ethnic backgrounds were asked to complete the sentence, "What gets me into trouble is _____." More than half the girls answered "my mouth" or "my big mouth." (Taylor et al., 1995). In a Canadian study of 149 teen girls who had eating disorders, self-silencing was strongly correlated with their symptoms; the more anxious they were about social acceptance, the more they were dissatisfied with their bodies, and the more they strove to be thin (Buchholz et al., 2007).

Self-silencing can be contrasted with ***relational authenticity***—the congruence between what a girl thinks and feels and what she does in relationship situations—in other words, how much a girl is able to be herself (Impett et al., 2008). Authenticity can promote psychological health and well-being. Self-silencing and a loss of authenticity may occur among adolescent girls because they come up against a "wall of 'shoulds' in which approval is associated with their silence" (Brown, 1998). The pressure to be a perfect girl—not just pretty and smart but always nice and polite, never angry or oppositional—leads a girl to doubt the truth of her own knowledge and feelings.

Self-esteem refers to a person's overall level of positive self-regard and self-respect. It is measured by asking people to agree or disagree with statements such as "I feel good about myself and who I am." Do adolescent girls suffer from low self-esteem? Meta-analyses of hundreds of studies of self-esteem in children and adults of all ages showed that boys and men scored higher than girls and women, though the difference on average is small. This difference first emerges at adolescence (Kling et al., 1999; Major et al., 1999). When different ethnic samples were examined separately, the gender self-esteem gap occurred only among European Americans. Self-esteem was also related to social class, with the gender gap largest in economically disadvantaged groups. In other words, a girl's self-esteem is dependent not only on her gender, but also on other factors that influence her place in society.

Low self-esteem is a cause for concern because it is linked to problems with psychological adjustment, physical health, and life satisfaction. One reason that an adolescent may develop self-esteem issues is that appearance becomes much more important socially. Of course, this is true for boys as well as girls. In a Canadian study of seventh to eleventh graders, over one-third of both girls and boys said that their overall self-esteem was *determined* by their appearance (Seidah & Bouffard, 2007). But girls, more than boys, find their flesh figuratively and literally squeezed into an unrealistic beauty ideal (Pipher, 1994). The body that was once an ally in exploring the world now becomes an adversary that must be forced into submission to an artificial appearance standard. Girls' self-surveillance, body dissatisfaction, and body shame all increase at puberty (Lindberg et al., 2007). Girls who reach puberty later than average and girls who are more satisfied with their bodies show less of a drop in self-esteem during high school; for most girls though, body satisfaction, authenticity, and self-esteem all are at their lowest points in early adolescence (Impett et al., 2008). In a 5 year longitudinal study of over 180 girls as they went from Grades 8 to 12, the good news was that, on average, both authenticity and self-esteem increased steadily over the high school years. However, those who were higher in authenticity in eighth grade grew more in self-esteem over the course of the study, suggesting that it is important to help girls hold on to their own thoughts and feelings (Impett et al., 2008).

Peer Culture and Harassment

A school principal in Maine described an incident in which the girls said that the boys were scaring them by saying,

> "You're my girlfriend. And I'm gonna marry you and . . . we're gonna have sex." . . . it got pretty aggressive and real loud and pretty soon there were lots of things coming out from all the boys: "Yeah, we're gonna have sex with you," and "Yeah, we're gonna rape you; we're gonna kill you." And "Yeah, 'cause you're our girlfriend." And then one boy said, "I'm gonna put an engagement ring on you 'cause that's what you do when you love someone, but I'm gonna NAIL it on 'til the blood comes out! (Brown, 1998, p. 104).

These children were six and seven years old. Too young to fully understand the meaning of words like sex and rape, they nevertheless acted out a scenario of masculine dominance: "The boys felt powerful using hostile language they knew would strongly affect the girls; the girls . . . felt uncomfortable, frightened, and angry" (Brown, 1998, p. 105).

Research shows that gender-related harassment by peers is prevalent in schools and that it intensifies as children reach adolescence (Petersen & Hyde, 2009). When the American Association of University Women (AAUW) conducted a national survey of students in Grades 8 through 11, they found that 83 percent of girls and 79 percent of boys had experienced harassment. This included behaviors such as spreading sexual rumors, making remarks about one's body or sexuality, forced kissing, and unwanted touching (AAUW, 2001). White girls reported the most sexual harassment, followed by African American, and Latina girls. Although the overall rates were nearly gender-equal, the consequences were not. In this study as well as others, boys tended to view sexualized attention as flattering; they reported that it makes them feel proud of themselves. Girls were much more likely to report that it makes them feel frightened, self-conscious, and embarrassed. Recent research has shown that peer sexual harassment increases girls' self-surveillance and body shame (Lindberg et al., 2007). As discussed in Chapter 3, these aspects of self-objectification are associated with many negative psychological and physical health consequences.

Some studies show that boys get even more harassment than girls do because they are targeted by other boys. For example, in one research study of ninth graders, 45 percent of the boys and only 19 percent of the girls reported having been harassed by a same-gender classmate. However, more girls reported being harassed by boys (58 percent) than vice versa (48 percent) (Petersen & Hyde, 2009). In other studies, girls are more often the targets. In a large study of 14- and 15-year-old students in the Netherlands, girls were more than twice as likely as boys to report incidents of unwanted sexual attention at school (Timmerman, 2003). For boys, the most common forms were verbal taunts such as "gay" or "homo." For girls, there was more physical harassment. As one girl reported, "I was pawed and blocked. I was very frightened and helpless. It was a group of boys" (p. 239). In an interview study of Australian high school students and teachers, both boys and girls reported that boys taunted girls with names (like whore, bitch, slut, and skank), as well as comments on body shape (whale), and specific body parts (flat chested, watermelons, nice arse). Some boys reported that "guys just go up to a girl and grab her . . . grab her tits" (Shute et al., 2008, p. 481).

Although sexual harassment can happen to anyone, girls or boys who violate gender norms are most often targets for peer aggression. Those who are believed to be gay or lesbian are targeted with names like *fag* and *queer* (Boxer et al., 1999; Hunter & Mallon, 2000). The term *slut* is freely applied to girls for even the most minor gender transgression, as shown in this incident at a summer camp, when Molly (age 9) walked into the boys' locker room by mistake:

> Many of the boys laughed at her and ridiculed Molly for her mistake. Brian (age 11) said, "She just wanted to look at our private stuff," and Thomas (age 12) called her a "slut." Molly started to cry (McGuffey & Rich, 1999, p. 622).

In the middle-school years, the gender boundaries are policed by a few "alpha boys," who keep potential transgressors in line by name-calling, exclusion, and physical aggression (McGuffey & Rich, 1999). The dominant boys exert influence over both girls and other boys. As girls enter adolescence and become more concerned about their appeal to boys, these tactics take on even more power to control and limit their behavior.

A striking feature of peer gender harassment among children and teens is that it often takes place in full view of adults, who may do little to stop it. Often, teachers stand by and watch without comment as sexual teasing and harassment take place, which provides a powerful message to both boys and girls (Shute et al., 2007). Girls may report harassment only to be told, "Boys will be boys." In a particularly hor-rifying incident, gang rapes of female students were reported at a major Japanese university. In response, a member of Parliament said in a public forum, "Boys who commit group rape are in good shape. I think they are rather normal. Whoops, I shouldn't have said that" (French, 2003, p. A4).

Girls may be encouraged to interpret their experiences of gender-related harassment and hostility in terms of heterosexual romance. For example, after the "We're gonna rape you" incident described earlier, 7-year-old Melissa struggled to understand how boys who she thought were her friends could be so hostile. She was comforted when she remembered that her grandfather had told her "If boys chase you then that means that they love you" (Brown, 1998, p. 105). Although Melissa's grandfather probably meant well, I doubt whether this is a good lesson for Melissa to learn. For more on the ideology of heterosexual romance and its relationship to violence against girls and women, see Chapters 7 and 12.

Unfortunately, teachers may also be perpetrators of sexual harassment. Stu-dents of all ages are legally protected from all sexual contact with teachers (Watts, 1996). However, teacher–student sexual harassment is amply documented. A sur-vey of high school students in the Netherlands found that 27 percent of reported unwanted sexual behavior at school was done by a teacher, principal, or other adult authority. The perpetrators were overwhelmingly male, the victims mostly female. Teacher harassment was more severe and led to more negative psychological con-sequences than peer harassment (Timmerman, 2003).

The power imbalance between teachers and students leads to under-reporting of this kind of violence because students are afraid of the consequences. When a 13-year-old Japanese girl brought charges against her 51-year-old teacher for fon-dling her in a school office, more than 40 teachers signed a petition asking that he should be treated leniently. The girl was rejected by her classmates, and her best friend told her that she had ruined the teacher's life. The girl replied that it had been the other way around (French, 2003).

Making a Difference

Feminists have maintained that raising children to be highly gender-typed is harm-ful to boys and girls because it closes off possibilities for both. As long as kids are raised to believe that there are certain things they cannot or should not do because of their gender, society is losing potentially unique contributions and individuals are losing potential sources of fulfillment.

Transforming Social Interactions: Enlarging the Options for Girls

Many feminist researchers and parents have explored alternative approaches to bringing up children (Katz, 1996). First, what examples should parents offer? Chil-dren who grow up in families where parents share child care and household work are less gender typed in the preschool years than those who grow up in more tra-ditional families (Fagot & Leinbach, 1995). Similarly, those whose mothers work in gender-neutral or male-dominated occupations have less gender-typed interests and beliefs (Barak et al., 1991). Parents can start by becoming more flexible in their expectations for their children, rather than pushing them into gender-stereotyped activities. (Bem, 1998).

For girls in the vulnerable teen years, the main issues are keeping a healthy identity and self-esteem, becoming comfortable with a woman's body, and expressing sexuality in relationships. We discuss the latter topic in the chapters that follow. For now, let's look at the factors that help prevent self-silencing and foster healthy self-esteem in adolescent girls.

In one study of a diverse sample, girls were asked what made them feel good about themselves. Athletics topped the list (Erkut et al., 1997). (See Figure 6.7.) Girls who participate in sports do better academically and are less likely to drop out of school, and they have lower rates of stress and depression and higher self-esteem. Improved self-esteem among girls who participate in sports stems from feelings of physical competence, improved body image, and feeling less constrained by a feminine gender role (Richman & Shaffer, 2000). It is not only physically beneficial for girls and women to be active. It is psychologically beneficial to experience the body as instrumental instead of just decorative.

FIGURE 6.7

Involvement in sports and outdoor recreation may help protect girls against self-objectification.

Sports are not the only venue in which girls and young women can challenge the limitations of femininity by actively inhabiting their bodies. Outdoor recreation is becoming increasingly popular for women (Henderson & Roberts, 1998) and may offer different benefits than sports. Like sports, outdoor recreation is consistent with traditional masculinity but not with traditional femininity. The idealized feminine form does not have mass or muscles. It does not assume unbecoming postures, such as those required in rock climbing. For girls and young women whose relationship with their bodies is focused on appearance concerns, trading media and mirrors for trees and trails can be a liberating experience. Outdoor educator S. Copeland Arnold (1994) explains,

> My experiences in Outward Bound as a young woman deeply affected my sense of self-acceptance, self-esteem, and body image. I gained an appreciation for my strength and agility. . . Rather than an object to be adorned and perfected, my body became an ally (pp. 43–44).

Another important influence that girls say helps them feel good about themselves is creative self-expression—music, art, or theater (Erkut et al., 1997). In an ethnically and geographically diverse sample, these activities provided opportunities to meet a challenge (a reason especially important to more affluent girls, European American and Asian American girls, and those in urban areas), and also just because they were enjoyable or involved being with friends (most important to girls from rural areas).

Providing creative activities may be one route to supporting girls. For example, the ACT NOW! Program sponsors MOVIExperience, a program that provides 11- to 14-year-old girls with the tools to make 20-minute movies about their lives. Each girl selects a site, creates a story, and improvises the action for the camera. During the process, girls work collaboratively to express themselves, drawing on their own experiences, dreams, and imagination. According to its Web site, the program builds self-esteem, helps girls speak out, and fosters cooperation. As one 12-year-old girl said, "I didn't really know who I was. The movie let me express myself. It showed me that a lot of people like me for who I am." More about programs to empower adolescent girls can be found at www.actnow-online.org and www.empoweragirl.org

Service to others is another experience that helps girls feel good about themselves (Erkut et al., 1997). When more privileged girls help those who are disadvantaged, both groups benefit. In one successful program, students from a women's college served as mentors to inner-city high school students who were mostly from poor Hispanic and immigrant families (Moayedi, 1999). The high school girls visited the college campus, participating in leadership and career workshops. Both the college students and the high school girls learned from this experience. As one college mentor said, "My friend Elisabeth has nobody to count on. She came here with nothing in her pockets to start a new life from the bottom. That is why I have learned more from her" (pp. 237–238). As for the high school girls, they reported that before the mentoring program they had never been on a college campus, knew few White people, and had never thought about going to college. As a result of the program, their goals were enlarged and their options expanded.

Children from disadvantaged backgrounds particularly need mentoring to help them overcome the deficits induced by poverty. *Big Brothers/Big Sisters* program is a nationwide attempt to foster healthy development in disadvantaged children through mentoring. Involvement in Big Brothers/Big Sisters has been shown to improve children's grades, academic skills, and relationships with parents and peers (Grossman & Tierney, 1998).

Transforming Ourselves: Resisting Gender Typing

Many educational programs have been designed to reduce gender stereotyping or change gender-related attitudes in children. In these programs, girls are introduced to counter-stereotypical examples (a woman scientist) or read about nurturing boys and achieving girls. Unfortunately, they are usually not very effective (Bigler, 1999). Changes in children's attitudes following the programs are few and short-lived. Their messages may simply be outweighed by the many stereotypical messages children receive about gender at home and from the media. Gender stereotyping is very resistant to change in adults (Chapter 3), and the same is true for children.

On the other hand, girls and boys are not just passive victims of gender socialization. On the contrary, many girls actively resist gender pressures and develop identities in opposition to the norms of femininity. In a study conducted in Israel, girls who continued being tomboys into their adolescent years were less gender-typed as adults (Safir et al., 2003).

Understanding how girls resist becoming gender typed may require close study of their own accounts of their experience. In an ethnographic study of girls in a small town in Maine, psychologist Lyn Mikel Brown (1998) reported that working-class girls, in particular, tend to "fight verbally, and physically when necessary, to speak the unspeakable, to be nurturing and also tough and self-protecting," disrupting the boundaries of femininity. They are not the good girls their teachers want but they may be holding on to their identities in a system that does not understand or value them.

Understanding and supporting girls is a crucial area for feminist research and activism, because girls have the potential to contribute to a post-patriarchal society. Lyn Mikel Brown has suggested that we need to help girls to accept themselves

> as complete and whole beings, with a range of feelings and thoughts connected to their experiences. Teaching girls how to pinpoint what is causing them anger or pain and how to act on their feelings constructively provides a kind of warrior training for social justice (Brown, 1998, p. 224).

Exploring Further
~

Bem, S. L. (1998). *An unconventional family*. New Haven, CT: Yale University Press.
A personal memoir by a prominent feminist psychologist about how she and her husband tried to bring up ungendered children. The now-grown children, Emily and Jeremy, have their say too. This book is controversial—see the review in the journal *Feminism and Psychology*.

Hardy Girls Healthy Women. (http://hghw.org)
Founded by feminist psychologist Lyn Mikel Brown, this nonprofit organization is dedicated to providing girls and young women with opportunities, programs, and services that empower them. Hardy Girls programming, resources, and services are grounded in psychological research in girls' development and focus on social structural changes.

New Moon Girls. (www.newmoon.com)
New Moon Girls is an online community and magazine that is international and multicultural. At New Moon, girls create and share poetry, artwork, videos, and more; chat together; and learn. It provides a safe Internet community for girls 8 to 14 and a print magazine designed to build self-esteem and positive body image.

Plan International: Because I Am a Girl
Plan's campaign is to fight gender inequality, promote girls' rights and lift girls out of poverty. Across the world, girls face the double discrimination of their gender and age. They are denied access to health care and education, and face violence, abuse, and harassment. You can see Plan's most recent report on the status of girls around the world, and get involved in helping, at their Web site, http://plan-international.org.

PART 4

Gendered Life Paths

CHAPTER 7

Sex, Love, and Romance

$\mathcal{S}$ex, love, and romance seem like natural events—instinctive, unlearned, and universal. For example, think about a kiss. Perfectly natural, right? In Western societies, kissing is seen as an instinctive way to express love and increase arousal. Yet in many cultures, kissing is unknown. When people from these cultures hear about our kissing customs, they agree that these practices are dangerous, unhealthy, or just plain disgusting. When members of one African community first saw Europeans kissing, they laughed and said, "Look at them—they eat each other's saliva and dirt" (Tiefer, 1995, pp. 77–78).

Strange as it may seem, sex, like kissing, is not a natural act. In other words, sexuality is not something that can be understood in purely biological terms. Instead, it is a social construct.

How Is Sexuality Shaped by Culture?

Individuals develop their own sense of sexual identity and desire in the context of their particular time in history, their social class, ethnic group, religion, and gender roles. Every culture throughout the world controls human sexuality (Kimmel, 2007). Because men have more social and political power, this control usually works to their benefit. For women, cultural constructions of sexuality lead to an ongoing tension between pleasure and danger (Vance, 1984).

What Are Sexual Scripts?

Each individual has a biological capacity for sexual arousal, but people learn rules that tell them how to have sex, with whom they may have it, what activities will be pleasurable, and when the individual is—and is not—allowed to take advantage of the biological potential for sexual enjoyment (Gagnon & Simon, 1973). Together, the repertoire of sexual acts that is recognized by a particular social group, the rules or guidelines for expected behavior, and the expected punishments for violating the rules form the basis of *sexual scripts* (Kimmel, 2007).

Sexual scripts can be thought of as schemas for sexual concepts and events. They are used in guiding one's own behavior and in interpreting others' behavior. For example, when college students back in the 1980s were asked to list what people would typically do on a first date, they agreed on things like worry about appearance, get dressed, go out, get to know each other by joking and talking, try to impress date, kiss goodnight, and go home. This first-date script featured men asking for the date and initiating physical contact (Rose & Frieze, 1989). Do you think that dating scripts have changed since then? In recent studies, much of the old date script is gone, but it is still more likely to be the guy who initiates the interaction and makes the first advances (Krahé et al., 2007; Seal et al., 2008).

Sexual scripts operate at societal, interactional, and individual levels. They are part of cultural institutions (e.g., sexual behaviors are regulated by law and religion), they provide norms for interpersonal behavior (e.g., the first-date script), and they are internalized by individuals (some behaviors come to be seen as exciting and others as disgusting).

The Content of Sexual Scripts

Throughout this chapter, we consider women's sexuality and intimate relationships in terms of both biological potentials and the influences of society's sexual scripts. We start by looking at the content of contemporary sexual scripts.

Romantic Ideology: A Core Element of Sexual Scripts

Romantic ideology includes the belief that love is all you need; true love lasts forever; true lovers become one; love is pure and good; and anything done in the name of love cannot be wrong (Ben Ze'ev & Goussinsky, 2008). The ideology of love is positive, but it is sometimes used to justify horrible acts such as stalking, sexual assault, and even murder (see Chapter 12).

In our society, the ideology of romantic love is everywhere (see Figure 7.1). From earliest childhood, girls are encouraged to identify with heroines who are rescued by a handsome prince (Cinderella), who are awakened from the coma of virginity by the love of a good man (Sleeping Beauty, Snow White), or who transform an extremely unpromising prospect into a good catch through their unselfish devotion (Beauty and the Beast).

One pervasive source of romantic ideology is the romance novels displayed in supermarkets and shopping malls. Each of their covers features a woman (almost always young, White, beautiful) gazing rapturously up into the eyes of a tall, strong, and handsome man. Their titles and their plots tell women that "love is everything." According to publishers' surveys, romance novels account for 56 percent of mass-market paperback sales in the United States. Romance novels aimed specifically at adolescents are sold through school book clubs, gaining in popularity every year. Although most romance novels are published in the United States, England, and Canada, their readership is global (Puri, 1997).

No one would claim that these novels are great literature. They follow a predictable script: love overcomes all obstacles. The heroine attracts the hero without planning or plotting on her part. In fact, she often fights her attraction, which she experiences as overwhelming, both physically and emotionally—her knees go weak, her head spins, her heart pounds, and her pulse quickens. The hero is often cold, insensitive, and rejecting, but by the end of the novel the reader

FIGURE 7.1
Romantic ideology and imagery are all around us.

learns that his coldness has merely been a cover for his love. The heroine is swept away and finally gives in to the power of love and desire. Her life is made meaningful only by her love for a man.

Why do so many women enjoy these fantasies? For adolescent girls, romance novels provide a way to make sense of their emerging sexuality (Christian-Smith, 1994). For hardworking wives and mothers, reading romances is an escape from humdrum reality into a reassuring fable of women transforming men. Although the hero is initially cold, patronizing, sometimes even brutal, he actually loves the heroine, and the power of her love transforms him into a sensitive and caring partner. In reading the romance, women may learn to interpret a male partner's insensitivity or controlling behavior as evidence that underneath the gruff exterior is a manly heart of gold (Radway, 1984). Not surprisingly, this is an appealing fantasy. It also may be a dangerous one (see Chapter 12).

TV provides another major source of romantic scripts. According to a Harris poll, nearly half of U.S. teens say that it is their major source of information about love and romance (Ben Ze'ev & Goussinsky, 2008). What lessons are they learning? In a content analysis of the 25 prime-time TV shows most watched by teens, the predominant script was of heterosexual, male-dominant relationships that sustained gender inequity. Males were portrayed as sexually active and aggressive, whereas females were portrayed as willingly objectifying themselves (Kim et al., 2007). In a study of reality TV dating shows, college students who were more involved in watching such shows were more likely to think of relationships as adversarial (males and females are in a contest with different goals). They were more likely to believe that men are driven by sex, that appearance is very important in relationships, and that dating is a game (Zurbriggen & Morgan, 2006). These results are correlational and cannot determine if the dating shows *caused* such attitudes, but nevertheless it is interesting that male students, more than female ones, said they watched reality dating shows to learn about real relationships.

In summary, romantic ideology encompasses positive aspects of love, such as mutual devotion and intimacy, but also conveys more dubious or even harmful messages: A woman is nothing without a man, and men should be aggressive initiators of love and sex, whereas women should be coy, receptive gatekeepers (Krahé et al., 2007). A man's controlling behavior is acceptable and even exciting if it is done in the name of love (Ben Ze'ev & Goussinsky, 2008). A woman should objectify herself if that's what it takes to be loved. In contrast, taking care of yourself and your partner by practicing safe sex is rarely part of the script (Alvarez & Garcia-Marques, 2009). And it almost goes without saying that all the scripts are heterosexual.

Are Sexual Scripts Changing?

Sexual scripts have changed over time and continue to do so in both positive and negative ways. On the one hand, today's sexual scripts are more egalitarian than in the past—they portray both women and men as interested in sexual pleasure and active in pursuing it (Dworkin & O'Sullivan, 2007). On the other hand, today's scripts often treat sex as just a game. One group of researchers analyzed all the articles on how to have better sex from 70 issues of various widely read magazines for women (Cosmo, Glamour) and men (Maxim, Men's Health). They found that most of the advice was about technique (try new positions, learn new tricks) and variety (try rough sex, porn, props, etc). Advice that focused on good sex as part of a relationship (intimacy, communication) was far down on the list. Men were depicted as wild, aggressive, and animalistic in their sexuality, whereas women were advised to be coy, indirect, and focused on the man's pleasure (Ménard & Kleinplatz, 2008).

How Do Sexual Scripts Differ across Ethnic Groups and Cultures?

Scripts about sex, love, and romance are influenced by race and class as well as by gender (Mahay et al., 2001). Table 7.1, based on a national sample, shows some aspects of scripts that differ among ethnic groups in the United States. Scripts about sex, love, and relationships are even more variable from one society to another (Goodwin & Pillay, 2006). For example, people in the United States believe that love is necessary for marriage. But in most of the world, marriages are arranged by family members, not by the bride and groom. Romantic love may be viewed as irrelevant or even destructive. In a study of college students in 11 cultures (India, Pakistan, Thailand, Mexico, Brazil, Japan, Hong Kong, the Philippines, Australia, England, and the United States), participants were asked whether they would marry someone they were not in love with, if the person had all the other qualities they desired. In India and Pakistan, about half said yes. In Thailand, the Philippines, and Mexico, about 10 to 20 percent agreed. However, in the other countries, including the United States, only a tiny minority of people said they would marry without love (Levine et al., 1995). Within each country, male and female respondents were similar in their beliefs.

In a culture like ours, where romantic love is strongly endorsed, not being in a relationship can be pretty lonely. One study compared college students in the United States and Korea, a culture where romantic love is not as important as family obligations (Seepersad et al., 2008). The U.S. students felt lonelier than the Korean students when not in a relationship, and happier when they were in one. Apparently, U.S. culture amplified both the positive and negative feelings around romantic love.

Cultural beliefs about sex and romance affect more than feelings; they lead to ethnic group differences in sexual behavior. For example, compared with American college students, Chinese students start dating at a later age, date less often, and are less likely to have sex with their dates (Tang & Zuo, 2000). A comparison of Asian and non-Asian students in a Canadian university showed that the Asian students were more conservative in their behavior (for example, they were less likely to have had sexual intercourse or to masturbate, and they had fewer partners if sexually active) (Meston et al., 1996). In another study, ethnically diverse girls in Grades 6 to 8 in the United States were asked what is the best age to have sex for the first time. Asian American girls gave the highest average age (21.7 years) and the African American girls the lowest (19.2 years). However, for all groups, the

TABLE 7.1   **Societal Scripts about Sexuality Differ in American Ethnic/Racial Groups, Even When Social Class Is Accounted for**

| | Ethnic/Racial Group | | | | | |
| | African American | | Mexican American | | White | |
Sexual Script	**Male**	**Female**	**Male**	**Female**	**Male**	**Female**
There's been a lot of discussion about the way morals and attitudes about sex are changing in this country. If a man and a woman have sex relations before marriage, do you think it is always wrong, almost always wrong, wrong only sometimes, or not wrong at all? (% Wrong)	25.5	38.3	27.7	41.8	21.6	30.3
What if they are in their teens, say 14 to 16 years old? In that case, do you think sex relations before marriage are always wrong, almost always wrong, wrong only sometimes, or not wrong at all? (% Wrong)	67.6	83.2	75.9	92.4	73.5	84.6
My religious beliefs have shaped and guided my sexual behavior. (% Agree)	49.5	69.2	51.8	60.9	44.4	56.6
I would not have sex with someone unless I was in love with them. (% Agree)	43.3	77.0	56.6	78.3	53.1	76.4

Source: Mahay et al. (2000). Race, gender, and class in sexual scripts. In E. O. Laumann & R. T. Michael (Eds.), *Sex, love and health: Private choices and public policies* (pp. 197–238). Chicago: University of Chicago Press.

more a girl believed she could succeed in school and work, the less likely she was to predict early sexual activity for herself (East, 1998). Clearly, sexual scripts are part of larger life scripts, both of which are shaped by a person's social group and perceived opportunities.

The Western ideal of romantic love is spreading as the rest of the world adopts U.S. and European media. However, it gets interpreted in terms of local norms. In India, for example, dating is usually unacceptable and women are expected to be virgins when they marry. Romantic love has little or nothing to do with choosing a life partner; most marriages are arranged by the couple's families. Yet India, where many middle-class women read English, may be the world's largest sales outlet for romance novels. A study of more than 100 young, single, middle-class Indian women suggested that reading romance novels is a form of cultural resistance. In them, women explored alternative kinds of relationships with men. They admired the spunky, feminine-but-strong heroines. And they gained information about sexuality. As one woman said, she had learned about the biology of sex at school, but it was from romance novels that she learned there is nothing wrong with sex—indeed, that it is pleasurable (Puri, 1997). For better and for worse, romance novels, reality TV, and lifestyle magazines are part of the globalization of Western culture.

Adolescent Sexuality

How Does Sexuality Emerge in the Teen Years?

With puberty comes a surge in sexual interest and behavior. During the last 40 years, there have been large changes in patterns of sexual activity in the teen years, both in the United States and around the world:

- More teens are having sexual intercourse outside of marriage.
- The increase has been greater for girls.
- First intercourse is occurring at an earlier age, on average.

In the 1940s, only about 33 percent of U.S. females (and 71 percent of males) had intercourse outside marriage by the age of 25 (Kinsey et al., 1948, 1953). Sexual scripts of the time emphasized virginity before marriage for girls; for boys, not so much. In the most recent national study 70 percent of females and 78 percent of males reported having intercourse prior to marriage (Laumann et al., 1994). The gender gap in sexual experience has almost disappeared. However, boys still have first sex at an earlier age than girls despite reaching puberty at a later age.

Comparisons of countries around the world show that the average age of first intercourse is similar (between 16–18 years in most countries). However, the percentage of unmarried women who have intercourse is lower in Latin American countries than in the United States or Africa, due to the influence of Catholicism. Increasingly, North American values are contributing to changing sexual norms, so that intercourse outside marriage is becoming more globally widespread (Hyde & DeLamater, 2011).

What Factors Influence the Decision to Have Sex?

The initiation of sexual behavior depends very much on social factors. For both boys and girls, one of the strongest predictors of sexual activity is the *perceived* level of sexual activity of their best friends (Miller et al., 1997). In other words, teens start having sex partly because they think their friends are doing it. In the words of one teen girl, "I just felt like everyone else was doing it and they were all talking about it and I didn't have anything to talk about so I was like, yeah I might as well" (Skinner et al., 2008, p. 596).

This raises troubling questions of free choice versus peer pressure (Aarons & Jenkins, 2002). In a study of sexually active girls aged 14 to 19 in urban Australia, the girls participated in in-depth interviews about their first experience of inter-course. Some said that they had been ready for the event—comfortable with the timing and with their first partner, "I waited with my boyfriend for ages just until I felt ready, until I trusted him and that took a long time." Others reported that their first intercourse had been unwanted. Often, they had been intoxicated at the time, "I was 15, I was stupid, young, I shouldn't have done it. It just sort of happened at a party. I was drunk. He was drunk. It was bad." Some said they had given in to pres-sure despite being unready. "I just did it to keep him happy" (Skinner ct al., 2008, pp. 596–597). In a major national study in the United States, women of all racial and ethnic groups were significantly more likely than men to report that their first sex was unwanted (Laumann & Michael, 2000).

Parents have some influence on their teens' sexual behavior (Miller et al., 1997). In a study of urban African American teens, girls' delaying their first inter-course experience was related to the amount of time spent with their mother and boys' was related to the amount of time with their father (Ramirez-Valles et al., 2002). Both African American and White girls who feel close to their parents and talk to them about sex engage in less sexual behavior than girls who do not (Murry-McBride, 1996). These studies show that it is important for parents to express support, love, and care for their teens while allowing them growing independence. One recent study followed a large sample of teens longitudinally for a year. At the start of the year, none of the teens had yet been sexually active. The biggest factor in these teens delaying sexual initiation over the study's time period was paren-tal caring; parental efforts to control their behavior were less effective (Longmore et al., 2009).

Although adults are quick to attribute teens' behavior to raging hormones, the relationship between hormones and sexual activity is complex. Hormonal levels have a strong effect on the level of a girl's sexual interests but only weak effects on her sexual behaviors (Udry et al., 1986). An earlier age of menarche has been asso-ciated with earlier sexual activity among both Black and White adolescents (Smith, 1989; Zelnick et al., 1981), probably due to both hormonal changes and social pres-sures. As discussed in Chapter 6, early puberty leads to early gender intensification, which has many consequences for girls. Girls who have sex at an early age are less likely to use contraception reliably and are more at risk of unwanted pregnancies than those who wait until they are older (Manlove et al., 2009).

Are Teens Having Safer Sex?

We've noted that young people often base their sexual decision making on what they think others are doing. This is true for risky behavior as well as sexual initia-tion. A large-scale study of U.S. college students showed that the students believed that their peers engaged in more risky behavior than the peers actually reported—and they based their own risk-taking on their perceptions of what others were doing (Lewis et al., 2007). This study and others like it suggest that one way to reduce risky sexual behavior is to provide young people with accurate information about norms for their peer group.

Traditional sexual scripts focus on men's needs and condone male power and control in relationships. As a result, women often may be unable to assert a claim to safety during sexual activity (Chrisler, 2001; Gomez & Vanoss-Marin, 1996). The consequence is an increased risk of unwanted pregnancy and sexually transmitted diseases (STDs). These include bacterial infections (such as chlamydia and gonorrhea), viral infections (such as herpes and genital warts), and HIV (which causes AIDS). All these STDs are transmitted by genital, anal, or oral sexual contact, and all can have serious long-term health consequences (Amaro et al., 2001; Chrisler, 2001). Although STDs are a risk for sexually active people in any age group, teens are particularly vulnerable because they tend to have more partners and because they are inconsistent in using protection. Of the 19 million new cases of STDs reported each year in the United States, nearly half occur in young people aged 15 to 24 (Hyde & DeLamater, 2011).

The AIDS epidemic continues. The World Health Organization estimates that over 60 million people worldwide are infected, almost half of whom are women. In the United States, women now account for 26 percent of AIDS cases. The great majority (80 percent) of U.S. women living with HIV/AIDS became infected through heterosexual contact; injection drug use accounts for most other cases. HIV/AIDS is now the *leading* cause of death for African American women aged 25 to 34, and the fifth for all women in the same age group (Hyde & DeLamater, 2011).

Condoms are the most effective means of preventing HIV infection during heterosexual contact. But media depictions of romance almost never include the use of condoms in sexual encounters. This may be one reason why many people do not use condoms consistently even when they know about their effectiveness. In a study of female college students, those who read the most romance novels had the most negative attitudes and intentions about condom use (Diekman et al., 2000). This study also showed that including safe sex scripts in romance stories led to more positive attitudes towards condoms.

Sexually active singles underestimate their AIDS risk because they use inaccurate decision rules (Malloy et al., 1997). Many believe that it is OK to have unprotected sex with someone they know well and like (Williams et al., 1992). For example, interviews with 187 18- to 35-year-old Puerto Rican women in New York revealed that 64 percent engaged in unprotected sex with their primary partners (Dixon et al., 2001). Singles may judge their risk of AIDS based on their partners' appearance ("He doesn't look sick" or "She is too good-looking to have AIDS"). While they may use condoms for first-time sex with a new partner, they believe that when they are in a relationship, they do not have to worry about protection from STDs (Hammer et al., 1996; Misovich et al., 1997).

Of course, these beliefs and behaviors are dangerous. People tend to have a number of different partners during their single years; even if they are monogamous while in each relationship, their partners may have engaged in risky behavior in the past. In relationships, people are in effect having sex with every other person their partner has had sex with. Even if they do not have intercourse, other activities such as oral sex can transmit STDs. Because people value relationships, and want to trust their current partner, they may refuse to recognize the risks (Joffe, 1997; Misovich et al., 1997).

Experiencing Sexuality

First Intercourse: Less Than Bliss?

Sociologists and psychologists have studied the factors that influence the decision to have sex for the first time. But what about the *experience* of first sex? There has been much less research. In our society, it's called losing your virginity, and the script is romantic. Here's one example, taken from a Harlequin romance novel:

> For a long timeless moment Roddy gazed down at the sleeping figure, watching the soft play of moonlight on her features. . . . Gently he pulled back the blankets and lay down beside the motionless girl. She turned in her sleep, one hand flung out towards him. Tenderly he stroked a dark strand of hair from her face, then pulled her into his arms. . . . Still half drugged from brandy and sleep, she found herself stroking his hair. "Such a perfect dream," she murmured, her eyes already beginning to close again.
>
> "No dream, my lady," and Roddy's mouth found hers, silencing her words. Tenderly he slipped the ribbon straps of her nightdress over her shoulders, and her body arched up towards him as his fingers traced a burning path across her breast. A groan vibrated deep in her throat as he threw her nightdress to the floor. Then his body was pressed along hers and she gasped at the feeling of skin on naked skin. . . .
>
> Driven now only by pure instinct, she moved against him, raining kisses down on his hair-roughened skin, tracing her fingers down the hard strength of his muscled chest. His breathing became ever more ragged, his hands slipping under her to pull her closer still, and she gave a tiny cry of surrender as he finally claimed her body, her fingers digging his shoulders as they moved together in frenzied rhythm. A vast well seemed to surge up within her, and as the room exploded into fragmented light she heard a voice crying "I love you" . . . (Elliot, 1989, pp. 116–118).

There may be a gap between the romantic ideal and reality. In a study of 1,600 American college students, women reported more guilt and less pleasure than men did when remembering their first sexual intercourse. When asked to rate the pleasure of their first intercourse on a 1 to 7 scale, the women gave it an average score of 2.95 (Sprecher et al., 1995). This account is from a sexual autobiography written by a college sophomore, reproduced here exactly as she wrote it:

> I don't think I will ever forget the night that I did lose my virginity. It was this past September (September 7th to be exact). My boyfriend and I had been going out for six months. I met him at a party late that night, but, by the time I had gotten there, he was extremely drunk. We came back to my room because my roommate was not going to be there. . . . Well, my boyfriend was very drunk and very amorous to say the least. Once we got into bed, I knew exactly what he had in mind, he was all hands and lips. I figured that we might as well have sex. . . . So, I made the decision to let him do whatever he wanted. For the actual act of sex itself, I hated it the first time. Not only was it painful but, it made a mess on my comforter. I hated my boyfriend at that time. I actually kicked him out of my room and sent him home. I was upset for a lot of reasons: My boyfriend was too drunk to remember the night so, I had made the wrong decision in letting him do whatever he wanted; there had been no feelings involved; I hadn't enjoyed it in the slightest; I had lost my virginity and betrayed my parents. I was upset for just a couple of days.
>
> After that first night, the sex between my boyfriend and myself has been great (Moffat, 1989, pp. 191–192).

Losing one's virginity has many meanings. Researcher Laura Carpenter (2005) explored those meanings by interviewing a diverse sample of 61 young people—straight, gay, lesbian, of varying religions, socioeconomic backgrounds, and ethnicities. Three ways of thinking about sexual initiation stood out in the interviews. The first, mentioned by about half the respondents, was that virginity is a gift given by one partner to the other. Not surprisingly, the gift metaphor, which may be influenced by abstinence-only sex ed programs in schools, was used more by heterosexual women. The second view, endorsed by more than one-third of respondents, was that virginity is a stigma to be gotten rid of. The stigma metaphor was used more by heterosexual men, but some women used it, too, in rejecting traditional notions of femininity. The third view was that virginity loss is a step in a process—for heterosexuals, a process of becoming an adult—for LGBTs, a process of coming out. The qualitative research method used in this study does not permit us to make conclusions about the general population, but it does provide a rich picture of how the people in the sample made meaning of their own experiences. As Britney Spears could attest, virginity means different things to different people.

How Do Women Experience Orgasm?

Women who have not had a lot of sexual experience are sometimes unsure about whether they have had an orgasm because they do not know how it is supposed to feel. One way to get an idea of the subjective experience of orgasm is to ask women to describe their own behaviors and sensations. Shere Hite (1976) collected detailed surveys from more than 3,000 women, but this represented responses from only about 3 percent of the questionnaires she distributed. There is no way to know how accurately the women who chose to respond represent all women. The major strength of Hite's work is that she used open-ended questions, and many of her respondents wrote lengthy detailed answers. A few sample descriptions of orgasm are given in Box 7.1.

Is the experience of orgasm different for women and men? Research suggests that the experiences are similar. In a study in which college students were asked to write descriptions of their orgasms, judges (psychologists and physicians) could not reliably distinguish women's and men's descriptions (Vance & Wagner, 1976). In another study, students chose adjectives from a list to describe their experiences of orgasm (Wiest, 1977). Again, there were no significant differences in responses by women and men.

Evils of Masturbation or Joys of Self-Pleasure?

Stimulating one's own genitals is a very common sexual practice. Traditionally, this practice was given the clinical term *masturbation*, which made it seem like a disorder. Indeed, masturbation was thought to cause everything from dark circles under the eyes to insanity. However, the majority of people today believe that it is neither harmful nor wrong (Oliver & Hyde, 1993). More positive terms for masturbation include *self-pleasuring* and *self-gratification*.

Women usually masturbate by stimulating the clitoris, either by hand or with a vibrator. Other methods include pressing the clitoral area against a pillow or

BOX 7.1 ∾ Women's Accounts of Orgasms

- Before, I feel a tremendous surge of tension and a kind of delicious feeling I can't describe. Then orgasm is like the excitement and stimulation I have been feeling, increased, for an *instant*, a hundredfold.
- It starts down deep, somewhere in the "core," gets bigger, stronger, better, and more beautiful, until I'm just four square inches of ecstatic crotch area!
- There is an almost frantic itch-pain-pleasure in my vagina and clitoral area that seems almost insatiable, it is also extremely hot and I lose control of everything, then there is an explosion of unbelievable warmth and relief to the itch-pain-pleasure! It is really indescribable and what I've just written doesn't explain it at all!!!
- The only way I can describe it is to say it is like riding a "Tilt-a-Whirl."

Source: Shere Hite, *The Hite Report: A Nationwide Study of Female Sexuality* (New York: Seven Stories Press, 2004), p. 122. Copyright © 1976, 1981 by Shere Hite. Reprinted by permission of the publisher.

using a stream of water while in the bath or shower. Most women who masturbate engage in sexual fantasies while doing so. Hite's survey respondents described both their techniques and their fantasies (see Box 7.2).

There is a persistent gender difference in masturbation experience. Curiously, women do not report more negative attitudes toward masturbation than men do, but they are definitely less likely to say they do it (Das, 2007; Oliver & Hyde, 1993). Only about 42 percent of women in a national study reported that they had ever masturbated, compared to virtually all the men (Laumann et al., 1994). Women's greater body dissatisfaction may be a factor. In a study of women at

BOX 7.2 ∾ Women's Accounts of Masturbation

- I lie down and begin to fantasize in my mind my favorite fantasy, which is a party where everyone is nude and engaging in group sex, lovely, lovely sex, all positions, kissing, caressing, cunnilingus, and intercourse. After about five minutes of this I am ready, very lubricated. I lift one knee slightly and move my leg to one side, put my middle finger on or around the clitoris and gently massage in a circular motion. Then I dream of being invited to this party and all those delicious things are happening to me. I try to hold out as long as possible, but in just a minute or two I have an orgasm. . . . After several orgasms in this manner I start thinking of what's for dinner and the party is over.
- I don't masturbate like anybody else I ever heard of. I make a clump in the bedding about the size of a fist (I used to use the head of my poor teddy bear, but since I became too old to sleep with a teddy bear, a wad of the sheets has to suffice) and then lie on my stomach on top of it so that it exerts pressure on my clitoris. I then move my hips in a circular motion until I climax—very simple.

Source: Shere Hite, *The Hite Report: A Nationwide Study of Female Sexuality* (New York: Seven Stories Press, 2004), pp. 74, 92–93. Copyright © 1976, 1981 by Shere Hite. Reprinted by permission of the publisher.

a family planning clinic, the White women who reported a higher frequency of self-pleasuring had higher body satisfaction. However, there was no relationship between body satisfaction and self-gratification for Black women (Shulman & Horne, 2003).

Both women and men may use self-pleasuring to complement a satisfactory sex life with a partner or to compensate for lack of a partner (Das, 2007). Experience in self-pleasuring has positive effects on women's sexual satisfaction with a partner. For example, in a study of married women aged 18 to 30, those who had experienced orgasm through self-gratification had more orgasms with their partners, greater sexual desire, more rapid arousal, higher self-esteem, and greater marital satisfaction than those who had not (Hurlbert & Whittaker, 1991). Self-pleasuring can be an important way for a woman to learn about her pattern of sexual arousal and satisfaction. Through practice, she can learn what fantasies are most arousing, what kinds and amounts of stimulation are most enjoyable, and what to expect from her body. For these reasons, sex therapists frequently use education in self-pleasuring for women who are unable to experience orgasm with a partner (LoPiccolo & Stock, 1986). Feminist writers have encouraged women to use self-gratification as a route to erotic skill and sexual independence (Dodson, 1987). The woman who can enjoy solo orgasms is not dependent on a partner for sexual pleasure and can enjoy sexual satisfaction without risk of pregnancy or STDs.

Lesbian and Bisexual Women

So far, the discussion in this chapter has been about heterosexuality, because it is the dominant, socially approved form of sexual expression and the one that has clear, pervasive scripts. Let's turn now to other sexual identities and experiences. First, I will discuss sexual orientation in historical and social context, and then describe the process of developing a personal identity as a lesbian or bisexual woman.

A Social History of Lesbianism

Throughout the nineteenth century, many women in North American society had intense friendships, in which they spent weeks at each others' homes, slept in the same beds, and wrote passionate and tender letters to each other describing the joys of perfect loving harmony and the agonies of parting. These relationships sometimes were part of a lifelong commitment. No one labeled these women homosexuals or lesbians (Faderman, 1981; Smith-Rosenberg, 1975). Of course, we have no way of knowing how many of these relationships involved sex. They certainly involved romance, attachment, and intimacy. But homosexuality was not yet a concept in popular use.

By the early twentieth century, lesbianism came to be seen as a serious form of pathology. Lesbians were "sick" and the "disease" was serious. The change in attitude may have come about because women were beginning to demand political and social equality with men. First-wave feminists were campaigning for women's education and the vote, and more women were entering the workforce. When women's attachments to other women had the possibility of leading to alternatives to heterosexual marriage and dependence on men, they were stigmatized and controlled. Feminists in particular were likely to be diagnosed as suffering from the newly invented disease of lesbianism (Kitzinger, 1987).

The medical and psychiatric establishment continued to evaluate lesbianism as a pathological disorder until the second wave of feminism in the late 1960s. Responding to pressure from women's and gay liberation activists, the American Psychiatric Association conceded that there is no evidence that homosexuality in itself is a disorder and removed this "sexual deviation" from its official manual of psychiatric diagnoses in 1973. Overnight, millions of people who had had a psychiatric disorder became normal, a compelling example of the power of social institutions to construct—and reconstruct—reality.

Research has tended to echo society's model of lesbianism. When lesbianism was labeled a form of pathology, research by physicians, psychiatrists, sexologists, and psychologists focused on theories of causes (note that there is little research on the causes of heterosexuality), on juicy details of the deviant behaviors, and on how to "cure" it (Kitzinger, 1987). Bisexuals were usually lumped with gay men and lesbians or ignored altogether (Rust, 2000). The results of the first sex surveys in the 1950s were controversial and shocking: 28 percent of the women had engaged in some sort of lesbian sexual activity; 13 percent had had at least one sexual experience with another woman leading to orgasm (Kinsey et al., 1953). This is quite a lot of "pathological" women.

Later laboratory research showed that the pattern of physiological change in the sexual response cycle is the same regardless of whether one's partner is a woman or a man (Masters & Johnson, 1979). By the 1980s, some sex researchers were suggesting that women are better at making love to women than men are, and that lesbians have more satisfying relationships. We have seen lesbianism transformed from an official psychiatric disorder to a lifestyle choice in a few decades. The effects on LGBT individuals of these rapid changes in the social construction of lesbianism can only be guessed at.

Although societal attitudes about gays, bisexuals, and lesbians are changing in a positive direction, they are still largely negative. One example: In national surveys in the 1970s, 81 percent of respondents said that sexual relations between two same-sex adults are always or almost always wrong; today, 60 percent still agree with that judgment (Hyde & DeLamater, 2011). Studies in several countries—including the United States, Norway, and Turkey—show that men's attitudes are more negative than women's (Anderssen, 2002; Herek, 2002; Sakalli, 2002). In 85 countries around the world, sexual acts between consenting same-sex adults are illegal, and may be punished by imprisonment, beatings, or execution (Clarke et al., 2010). In the United States, anti-gay hate crimes and harassment are common, which discourages lesbians and gay men from becoming socially visible.

Defining Sexual Orientation

Definitions of lesbianism reflect the political and social complexities of the category and have changed over time. In the 1960s, second wave radical feminists focused on lesbianism as a refusal to accept male dominance:

> Lesbian is a label invented by the Man to throw at any woman who dares to be his equal . . . who dares to assert the primacy of her own needs (Radicalesbians, 1969, cited in Kitzinger, 1987, p. 43).

Other definitions have focused on intimacy and attachment:

> . . . a woman who loves women, who chooses women to nurture and support and to create a living environment in which to work creatively and independently, whether or not her relations with these women are sexual (Cook, quoted in Golden, 1987, p. 20).

Still others emphasize the individual's self-definition, as well as her behavior:

> . . . a woman who has sexual and erotic-emotional ties primarily with women or who sees herself as centrally involved with a community of self-identified lesbians . . . and who is herself a self-identified lesbian (Ferguson, quoted in Golden, 1987, p. 21).

Definitions of bisexuality are equally complex. A bisexual woman is capable of emotional and sexual attachment to both women and men. However, traditionally some researchers and clinicians have maintained that there is no such thing as a true bisexual, implying that they are just confused or indecisive and will eventually decide to be either gay or straight (Rust, 2000). Bisexuals may feel that they fit in with neither gay nor straight culture. They may be accused by the gay community of wanting to avoid the stigma of the homosexual label and using cross-sex relationships to hide from their own homosexuality (Ault, 1996; Rust, 1993; 2000).

Some feminists argue that bisexuality is a revolutionary concept because it challenges the "little boxes" of sexual orientation and pushes society beyond dualistic thinking about sexuality (Firestein, 1998). Indeed, some people adopt bisexual identities to reflect their gender politics—they are attracted to *people*, not gender categories of males and females—or as a challenge to the belief that everyone can be neatly labeled (Rust, 2000). Nevertheless, individuals identifying as "bi" face difficult choices about how to present themselves in everyday life (Ault, 1996).

It is clear that women do not always mean the same things when they say "I am a lesbian" (or bisexual). A pioneering study done in England by psychologist Celia Kitzinger (1987) compared the explanations or stories about the experience of lesbianism given by 41 self-identified lesbians ranging in age from 17 to 58. Five viewpoints emerged from a close comparison of the accounts.

The first viewpoint was the idea of lesbianism as personal fulfillment. Women who viewed themselves primarily in this way were sure of being lesbians, were unashamed of their orientation, and thought of themselves as happy, healthy individuals:

> I have never stopped feeling relief and happiness about discovering myself and, you know, accepting about myself and finding all these other women, and it means that I'm happy almost every day of my life. . . . I've never regretted being a lesbian . . . (Kitzinger, 1987, p. 99).

A second viewpoint defined sexual preferences in terms of love: Lesbianism was seen as the result of falling in love with a particular person, who just happened to be a woman. Though defining themselves as lesbian, these women felt that they could or would have a heterosexual relationship if they fell in love with a man. A third viewpoint had to do with the feeling of being "born that way," yet resisting sexual labeling:

> I'm me. I'm . . . a social worker; I'm a mother. I've been married. I like Tschaikowsky; I like Bach; I like Beethoven; I like ballet. I enjoy doing a thousand and one things, and oh yes, in amongst all that, I happen to be a lesbian; I love a woman very deeply. But that's just a *part* of me (Kitzinger, 1987, p. 110).

The fourth view identified women who came to lesbianism through radical feminism:

> It was only through feminism, through learning about the oppression of women by men and the part that the enforcement of heterosexuality, the conditioning of girls into heterosexuality plays in that oppression, it was through that I decided that whatever happens I will never go back to being fucked by men . . . that decision was made because I'm a feminist, not because I'm a lesbian. I take the label "lesbian" as part of the strategy of the feminist struggle (Kitzinger, 1987, p. 113).

A final view identified women who saw their sexual orientation as a sin or weakness—a "cross to bear." These women were sometimes ashamed of being lesbians, said they would not have chosen it, and would be happier if they were heterosexual.

This classic study explored the multiple meanings women give to their sexuality and its relationship to the rest of their lives. Each of the ways these women subjectively experienced their sexuality had both costs and benefits for the individual.

Psychologists have not yet agreed on the best way to define sexual orientation, but most would say that it encompasses not only sexual behavior, but also sexual attraction, love, intimacy, fantasies, and most important, the individual's subjective sense of his or her sexual identity.

Developing a Lesbian or Bisexual Identity

Gay, bisexual, and lesbian adolescents do not have an easy time. They are at higher risk for low self-esteem, emotional isolation, poor school performance, dropping out, and a variety of other problems. Being rejected by their families is strongly related to mental health problems in LGB youth. In one study of White and Latino/a young people, those who reported higher levels of family rejection during adolescence were 8 times more likely to report having attempted suicide, 6 times more likely to report high levels of depression, and 3 times more likely to use illegal drugs or engage in unprotected sexual intercourse compared with peers from families that did not reject them (Ryan et al., 2009).

As you might expect, LGB teens may find it difficult to accept their sexual orientation. Let's look at this process among women. The process of *coming out,* or accepting lesbianism as a part of one's identity, may be slow and erratic. However, being out is related to greater social support, improved relationships, and lower psychological distress in lesbians of all ages (Jordan & Deluty, 2000; Morris et al., 2001). (See Figure 7.2.)

FIGURE 7.2
For women who love women, coming out is associated with better
psychological adjustment.

A woman can come out as a lesbian at a young age, or not until much later
in her life. When it occurs at midlife, coming out has been likened to a second
adolescence. One woman, who came out as a 56-year-old grandmother, explained:
"I simply did not know there was any other way to live than heterosexual. I knew
I was pretty miserable, but I just accepted that as part of the way things had to be"
(Lewis, 1979, p. 19).

Women may first come into contact with lesbians or the idea of lesbianism in
many ways. Linda Garnets, a feminist psychologist and professor of LGBT studies,
described her own moment of truth:

> I remember the first time I met a lesbian couple. I was beginning to think that I might
> really be a lesbian, so I wanted to meet some other people who were gay. I knew very
> few gay people, and I had numerous fantasies about how they were going to look and
> act. I vividly remember standing by my front door waiting for them to arrive and having
> every possible stereotype about them. I thought they were going to ride up on motor-
> cycles and have greasy hair and tattoos. I was shaking. But when I opened the front
> door, there stood two of the most ordinary-looking women. I thought they must be at
> the wrong apartment (Garnets, 2008, p. 233).

So far, I've been describing sexual identity as though it is fixed and unchangeable: Once a woman recognizes the essential truth that she is gay, straight, or bi,
she's set for life. However, women's sexual identity seems to be, at least potentially,
more fluid and changeable than that (Bohan, 1996; Golden, 1987; Rust, 1993,
2000). Some women identify first as heterosexual, then as lesbian, later as bisexual.
Others go through these changes in reverse.

In a study of lesbians and bisexual women aged 14 to 21 years, self-identification had changed over time for many of the young women; more than half who identified as lesbian had identified as bisexual at some time in the past, and the majority had had sexual activity with both other women and with men (Rosario et al., 1996). In the first longitudinal study of lesbian and bisexual women, participants were first interviewed when they were between 16 and 23-years-old and again two years later. Half had changed their sexual orientation more than once, and one-third had changed between the two interviews—more evidence for the fluidity of women's sexual identities and behaviors (Diamond, 2000).

Ethnic Diversity and Sexual Identity

Almost all the research on lesbian and bisexual women has relied on all-White or predominantly White samples. Does identity development differ for women of different ethnic and racial backgrounds? Focusing on Latina lesbians, one researcher noted:

> Because as a Latino she is an ethnic minority person, she must be bicultural in American society. Because she is a lesbian, she has to be polycultural among her own people. The dilemma for Latina lesbians is how to integrate who they are culturally, racially, and religiously with their identity as lesbians and women (Espin, 1987a, p. 35).

Latina lesbians are perhaps more likely to remain in the closet, keeping their orientation secret from family and friends, than White lesbians because most members of their ethnic group strongly disapprove of lesbians. However, families who become aware of a daughter's lesbianism are unlikely to openly reject or disown her. They will remain silent, accepting the situation tacitly but not openly (Castañeda, 2008).

In a questionnaire study of 16 Latina lesbians, the respondents, like White participants in previous research, showed a wide range of subjective understandings of their lesbianism. They also wrote eloquently about the difficulty of integrating their ethnic and sexual identities. This woman had earlier said that being a Cuban and being a lesbian were equally important to her:

> I guess that if the choice were absolute, I would choose living among lesbians . . . but I want to point out that I would be extremely unhappy if all my Latin culture were taken out of my lesbian life. . . . I feel that I am both, and I don't want to have to choose (Espin, 1987, p. 47).

African American lesbians also have described issues of integrating multiple identities and group memberships: as lesbians, as members of the Black community, and as part of the larger culture with its racism, sexism, and heterosexism, as this case study shows:

> Diane (hesitated) to discuss her lesbian feelings while in college. The college she attended was predominantly White, and Diane relied a great deal on the Black community there for support. She considered that coming out to these individuals might jeopardize her acceptance in this group. Although Diane continued to explore her lesbian

feelings internally, she also continued to date men. Several years later, as she did begin to come out to others, she feared that identification as a lesbian might pull her away from what she considered her primary reference group—Black Americans (Loiacano, 1993, pp. 369–370).

African American families typically support each other in their struggles with racism, but may not have the same perspective about heterosexism. Also, African American religious groups have often been silent on issues of sexual orientation (Greene, 2000). The small samples used in research to date make it difficult to generalize about African American lesbians and underscore the need for more research within the Black community (Hatton, 1994). However, it is clear that, like other women of color, Black lesbians "face the challenge of integrating more than one salient identity in an environment that devalues them on all levels" (Greene, 2000).

Asian American lesbians, too, face issues of multiple identities. Within Asian cultures, any public or open expression of sexuality is unacceptable. However, the private expression of sexuality may actually be quite flexible. Parents often put strong pressure on girls not to be sexually active in any way, to restrain their desires and impulses for the sake of the family. This may be restricting to young women, but, on the other hand, it creates no gulf between lesbian and straight sexual activity. Because *all* sexual behavior is regarded as a private matter, lesbian and bisexual behavior may not be stigmatized as much as in the majority culture (Chan, 2008).

In a cross-cultural study of identity development, women aged 18 to 35 in Brazil, Peru, the Philippines, and the United States were asked "At what age did you realize that you would be heterosexual (or homosexual)?" In all four countries, lesbians reached this point of identity development at a later age than heterosexuals (Whitam et al., 1998). Little is known about factors that contribute to developing a healthy lesbian identity. One study asked over 60 lesbian activists about factors that contributed to their successful coming-out process. These women mentioned being part of a gay community, using self-help and counseling, and acceptance by their families as important (Bringaze & White, 2001).

More research is needed on how women integrate sexual identity with other aspects of their sense of self. One model for integrating identities comes from Native American cultures, where there is a tradition of accepting different sexes and sexualities, as Chapter 5 discussed. Some gay, lesbian, and bisexual Native Americans describe themselves as *two-spirit people*. By taking this traditional name, they feel that they are returning to their Native American communities (Wilson, 1996).

Romantic Love and Sexual Pleasure

The Experience of Romantic Love

Given that the ideology of romance is directed largely at women, it might be expected that women are more romantic in their beliefs about relationships than men. The opposite seems to be true. Studies show that, at least among the young, predominantly White college students studied by most researchers, men are more likely to believe that true love comes only once, lasts forever, and overcomes obstacles such as religious differences. They are more likely to believe in love at first sight and to be game players, enjoying flirtation and pursuit. Consistent with their beliefs, men report falling in love earlier in a new relationship. They also feel more depressed, lonely, and unhappy after a breakup and are less likely to initiate the breakup than their female partners. Women are more likely to report feeling joy or relief after breaking up (Choo et al., 1997; Peplau & Gordon, 1985).

Women, on the other hand, report more emotional symptoms of falling in love—feeling giddy and carefree, floating on a cloud, and being unable to concentrate. Once a relationship has moved beyond its first stages, they may become more emotionally involved in it than their male partners.

The reasons for these differences in the experience of romantic love are unclear (Peplau & Gordon, 1985). Men may fall in love more readily because they rely more on physical attractiveness to decide whom to love—a characteristic that is easy to see at the start of a relationship. They may also react more quickly because the cultural script says that men should initiate a relationship. Women traditionally may have been more pragmatic because, in choosing a mate, they were choosing a provider as well as a romantic partner. Yet they may appear more emotional because cultural norms allow them to admit to having feelings.

Gender-related differences in the experience of romantic love are not large, and there is a great deal of overlap in the beliefs and self-reported behaviors of women and men. But the differences are interesting because they do not always fit stereotypical expectations. Perhaps future researchers will examine them in more detail.

Do Romantic Scripts Affect Women's Sexual Experiences?

Young women, especially those of the dominant White culture, are exposed to many messages that tell them love is everything to a woman. At the same time, they learn that finding fulfillment and self in the love of a man is outside their control. In the traditional romantic script, it is the man who actively initiates and pursues; the woman may resist for a while but finally gives in to his desire.

These beliefs inform the sexual scripts of teens and young adults. Research on dating couples and marital partners shows that men are more likely than women to initiate sex. People are emotionally vulnerable in sexual encounters; the woman who wants to initiate sex and the man who wants to say no may fear being rejected and labeled as deviants. It feels more comfortable and secure to follow familiar patterns, as expressed by this British 16-year-old girl being interviewed by a researcher:

INTERVIEWER: Do you think boys always take the lead?
RESPONDENT: Yeh.
I: Yeh? And do you want them to or—
R: Yeh! Definitely! It's tradition (laughs).
I: Yeh? Why? Does it feel better or does it—
R: I don't know? I just think they should.
I: Yeh.
R: 'Cause I wouldn't, so I would expect them to, really.
I: So why wouldn't you?
R: I don't know? 'Cause I am the girl? (both laugh) (Sieg, 2000, p. 501)

Boys seem to agree and research shows that this aspect of sexual scripts is slow to change. In a recent study of male college students in ongoing relationships, more than half said that they initiated sex either all or most of the time. The reasons they gave included "I'm the man," "She's a girl," "It's not in her nature," and "I'm more aggressive/more of a top/more dominant." Interestingly, most of the men who were in charge of sexual initiation in their relationship said they would like it to be more equal, although they were not actively trying to make this change happen (Dworkin & O'Sullivan, 2007).

When a woman wants to respond positively to a man's sexual initiative, she may still feel that she ought to offer *token resistance*—in other words, to say no when she actually intends to have sex. Both women and men engage in token resistance for a variety of reasons: they want to test their partner's response, add interest to a boring relationship, or prevent being taken for granted (Muehlenhard & Rodgers, 1998). However, saying no when they really mean yes may have serious negative consequences for women. It discourages honest communication and perpetuates restrictive gender stereotypes. Most important, it may teach men to disregard women's refusals. If men learn from experience that "no" is often only a prelude to "yes," they may become more aggressive with dates (Muehlenhard & Hollabough, 1988). Romantic scripts also encourage people to think of lovemaking as something that "just happens." Although sex may seem perfectly natural, mutual pleasure does not just happen every time. Women who take responsibility for their own pleasure and who take an active role in sex are more likely to experience pleasure than those who are passive. Satisfying sex depends on communication, learning, and initiative on the part of both partners. In a study of a community sample of 104 couples in long-term relationships, the (unsurprising) results showed that sexual self-disclosure helps the partners understand each others' needs and contributes to overall relationship satisfaction as well as sexual satisfaction. These results held for both women and men. Being able to talk about sexual likes and dislikes helps couples establish and maintain mutually pleasurable sexual scripts (MacNeil & Byers, 2009).

Do Romantic Scripts Lead to Sexual Dysfunction?

Because our society does not give women the same permission to be fully sexual that it gives men, women may experience less sexual joy. A meta-analysis showed that women express somewhat more anxiety, fear, and guilt about sex than men (Oliver & Hyde, 1993). However, the women and men did not report any overall difference in sexual satisfaction. Most of the participants in these studies were college-age students. Other research suggests that adult women in heterosexual relationships experience less pleasure in sexual activity than their partners. In national samples, women were much more likely than men to report lack of interest or pleasure in sex (Laumann et al., 1999), and men reported more emotional and physical satisfaction in their relationships (Waite & Joyner, 2001).

Acceptance of traditional sexual scripts is implicated in women's sexual dysfunction and suppression of desire. Sexual pleasure and orgasm require an awareness of one's own needs plus a feeling that one is entitled to express those needs and have them met. Women's recognition of themselves as sexual beings is blocked in many ways by cultural influences. Women are more likely to feel ashamed of their bodies because of objectification, as discussed in Chapter 3. In one study of college women, about one-third reported being preoccupied with thoughts about their bodily appearance during sexual intimacy (Wiederman, 2002). Women may also feel guilty or selfish about having needs and fear their partners' disapproval if they express their needs. In a study of over 600 dating couples, the women on average reported that they felt less confident about their ability to talk about sexual health, pleasure, and sexual limits than their male partners reported. Those with less traditional attitudes about sexuality were better at communicating about sexual issues and more comfortable with initiating or refusing sex (Greene & Faulkner, 2005).

One effect of sexual scripts concerning male aggressiveness and female passivity is that sexual behaviors may proceed on his, not her, timetable, and the woman's pleasure may be reduced. When both partners believe that it is natural for the man to initiate a sexual encounter and take the lead throughout, it is he who decides what activities the couple will (and will not) try, the duration of intercourse, and the sequence of events. With such little control, it is unlikely that the woman will have her needs met. If the man prefers only brief foreplay, the couple may proceed to penile penetration before the woman is aroused, making intercourse painful, and unpleasant for her. (The term *foreplay* itself implies that penis-in-vagina is the main event, with hugging, kissing, talking, genital touching, and all other sexual activities merely a prologue.) Women typically need more stimulation to have an orgasm than men do. If intercourse seems to be over almost before it has begun, the woman who has accepted a passive role may be reluctant to ask for more stimulation. Repeatedly engaging in sex when one is not aroused and not satisfied may lead to clinical sexual problems (Tevlin & Leiblum, 1983).

One way to see that passivity is a learned script rather than a natural mode for women is to compare the behavior of the same women with both female and male partners. When bisexual women were with a female partner, they were much more active and initiating than when they were with a male partner (Masters & Johnson, 1979). Women who take an active, autonomous, and assertive part in sexual expression are more likely to be orgasmic (and multiorgasmic) (Radlove, 1983).

Another aspect of sexual scripts is the idea that the man's pleasure is the only real goal. One researcher analyzed the content of scientific presentations at a world sexology conference: of more than 400 presentations, only 8 were focused on women's pleasure (Segal, 2005, cited in Tiefer, 2007). Along with the relentless media emphasis on "how to please your man," it's not surprising that women sometimes come to believe that they should focus entirely on their partner's pleasure. Some sex manuals instruct women to fake orgasm, act like prostitutes, or perform strip routines for their partners. To feminists, advice like this raises troubling questions of where consent ends and coercion starts. Faking arousal, pleasure, and orgasm may become so ingrained that the woman may not be able to distinguish between her own sexual desire and her desire to please. Her sex life may come to feel like a part she is acting or a service she performs on demand.

Social Contexts of Sexual Expression

Sexuality, including beliefs, values, and behavior is always expressed in cultural context. It is social, emergent, and dynamic (White et al., 2000).

Cultural Variations in the United States

Religion and social class separate ethnic and cultural groups within the United States. Like their White peers, African American girls learn different lessons about sex and love, depending on their social class and religion. They may be brought up in strict homes, receiving explicit warnings from their mothers about men and sex, or in more relaxed ones where sexual activity is regarded as good and pleasurable (Joseph & Lewis, 1981). In several studies, African American teenage girls have reported strong conflicts between their sexuality and their plans for an education (Tolman & Brown, 2001). Behaviorally, African American women are more conservative in some ways than White women—less likely to masturbate or to engage in oral sex (Hyde & DeLamater, 2011). Attitudes may differ, too; some writers have suggested that Black women may be less likely than their White counterparts to believe in romantic love and more likely to maintain strong feelings of independence (Williams, 1997).

Like Black women, Latinas in the United States are a diverse group with respect to social class. In addition, their families come from many different countries, including Cuba, Puerto Rico, Guatemala, and Mexico. Despite this diversity, there are some commonalities affecting romantic and sexual attitudes and behaviors. Because of historical influences and the Catholic religion, virginity is an important concept. In Hispanic cultures, the honor of a family depends on the sexual purity of its women. The Virgin Mary is presented as an important model for young women, and abstaining from sex before marriage is stressed (Castañeda, 2008; Espin, 1986).

The traditional Hispanic ideal for men is one of ***machismo***—men are expected to show their manhood by being strong, demonstrating sexual prowess, and asserting their authority and control over women. Women's complementary role of ***marianismo*** (named after the Virgin Mary) is to be sexually pure and controlled, submissive, and subservient. Their main sources of power and influence are in their roles as mothers. These traditional roles vary widely with social class, urban versus rural locations, and generational differences (Castañeda, 2008). Nevertheless, the cultural imperatives of virginity, martyrdom, and subordination continue to exert influence over the experience of love for Hispanic women. This socialization pattern can create difficulties in sexual expression and increase vulnerability to partner violence and HIV infection (Espin, 1986; Raffaelli & Ontai, 2001; Salgado de Snyder et al., 2000).

In Asian cultures the public expression of sexuality is suppressed and sexual matters are rarely discussed. Yet sexuality is viewed as a healthy and normal part of life. The Confucian and Buddhist roots of Asian cultures stress women's roles as wives, mothers, and daughters and place strong importance on maintaining family harmony. Influenced by these traditions, Asian Americans tend to be more sexually conservative than people of other ethnic groups; for example, Asian American college students are less likely to be sexually active than their White peers (Chan, 2008).

Cross-cultural and ethnic group differences in attitudes toward sexuality and sexual practices remind us that there is no "right" way to think about sexuality.

Attractiveness and Sexual Desirability

Physical attractiveness is an important factor in romantic relationships (Sprecher & Regan, 2000). Good looks are especially important to men choosing a prospective sexual partner or mate, as shown by research in many cultures. Typically when asked to list the qualities they want in a romantic partner, men emphasize physical attractiveness and women emphasize earning ability and/or personal qualities (Eastwick & Finkel, 2008). (See Figure 7.3.) This attractiveness bias may seem a bit depressing for ordinary-looking women with great personalities, but there are other aspects to consider. First, it may apply only to hookups, not steady relationships. When college students in the United States (Nevid, 1984) and in India (Basu & Ray, 2001) were asked to rate physical, personal, and background characteristics they consider important in a sexual relationship, the predictable results were that males favored physical characteristics; whereas, females favored personal qualities. However, when rating characteristics they considered important in a long-term, meaningful relationship, both men and women emphasized personal qualities more than looks. And in both studies there was considerable overlap between the traits desired by women and men.

Another limit to the importance of attractiveness is that what people *say* they want may not be the same as what they actually choose. To illustrate this, I'll describe a study that used speed dating followed by questionnaires to assess partner preferences (Eastwick & Finkel, 2008). College students were recruited to participate in rounds of 4-minute speed dating, in which they kept notes about

FIGURE 7.3

FOR BETTER OR FOR WORSE © 1999 Lynn Johnston Productions. Reprinted with permission of Universal Uclick. All rights reserved.

the interaction and recorded their interest in seeing the speed-date partners again. After the event, they were repeatedly asked whether they'd be interested in seeing each of their partners again, by means of questionnaires over a one-month period. Unexpectedly, both women and men valued looks, earning power, and personality equally. The most curious result was that there was no relationship between what they said and the choices they made, either on the questionnaires or in real life. For example, participants who said that physical attractiveness was very important in a dating partner were no more likely than others to like, be attracted to, or feel "chemistry" with partners they found physically attractive. It seems that when it comes to romance, people may not know what they really want.

Preferences for romantic partners' qualities are related to sexist attitudes about gender. Women who score high in benevolent sexism (beliefs that women should be put on a pedestal and protected by men) are more concerned about a potential partner's earning power and resources than are women who score low on this measure. Men who score high on hostile sexism (opposition to women outside of traditional roles) are more concerned about a potential partner's attractiveness than men who score low on this measure (Travaglia et al., 2009). This study shows that people with more sexist beliefs about gender role ideologies prefer partners who have traditional masculine/feminine qualities—earning power for men and looks for women.

Disability and Sexuality

Disabled girls and women, like nondisabled women, are judged by their attractiveness. Additionally, they are judged against an ideal of the physically perfect person who is free from weakness, pain, and physical limitations. In a study of attitudes about the sexuality of disabled and nondisabled women, Australian college students expressed much more negative attitudes about the disabled women's sexuality, and men were more negative than women (Chandani et al., 1989). Interviews with women who had cerebral palsy showed that one of the psychological tasks they faced was reconciling their bodies and experiences with society's norms for women (Tighe, 2001).

Parental attitudes and expectations for their daughter with a disability can have an important effect on the daughter's sexual development. In a study of 43 women with physical and sensory disabilities (including cerebral palsy and spinal cord injury), many of the parents had low expectations of heterosexual involvement for their daughters because they saw them as unable to fulfill the typical role of wife and mother. Some of these daughters became sexually active partly out of rebellion and a desire to prove their parents wrong, while others remained sexually and socially isolated. In contrast, other parents saw their daughters as normal young women, with the disability being only one of their many unique characteristics. These young women became socially and sexually active as a matter of normal growing up. One interviewee reported:

> In childhood, I was led to believe that the same social performance was expected of me as of my cousins who had no disabilities. I was a social success in part because my mother expected me to succeed (Rousso, 1988, p. 156).

Women with disabilities confront stereotypes that sexual activity is inappropriate for them; that people with disabilities need caretakers, not lovers; that they cannot cope with sexual relationships; that they are all heterosexual; that they should feel grateful if they find any man who wants them; and that they are too fragile to have a sex life. When people express these stereotypical beliefs, it is difficult for a woman with disabilities to see herself as a potential sexual and romantic partner. These beliefs can interfere with a disabled woman's sexual expression and her chances for having relationships. In a national survey that compared women aged 18 to 83 with and without disabilities, the disabled women were less satisfied with the frequency of dating and perceived personal and societal barriers to dating relationships (Rintala et al., 1997). Indeed, disabled women are less likely to be married than disabled men, and more likely to be abandoned by their partners when a disability like multiple sclerosis is diagnosed (Chrisler, 2001; Fine & Asch, 1988). Critics have charged that psychology has contributed to the marginalization of people with disabilities because there has been little psychological research on healthy functioning, sexual identity, and sexual relationships within this group, and almost none that includes people of color (Greenwell & Hough, 2008).

Is Sex Talk Sexist?

A negative evaluation of female sexuality is deeply embedded in language, as Chapter 3 discussed. Linguists agree that languages develop an abundance of terms for concepts that are of particular interest or importance to a society. English has many terms describing women and their genitals in specifically sexual ways, and most of these are negative—*whore* (*ho*), *bitch, cunt,* and *gush* are a few examples. Absences in language are also revealing. For men, *virile* and *potent* connote positive masculine sexuality, as do other, more colloquial terms such as *stud, macho man,* and *hunk.* However, there is no English word for a sexually active woman that is not negative in connotation.

Slang words for sexual intercourse (*ramming, banging,* and *nailing*) suggest that it is something violent and mechanical done to women rather than a mutual pleasure. The same verb can even be used to describe harm and sex—as in "she got screwed." One anthropologist who studied college students in their natural habitat (the dorm), reported that about one-third of the young men talked of women, among themselves, as "chicks, broads, and sluts." Their "locker-room style" was characterized by "its focus on the starkest physicalities of sex itself, stripped of any stereotypically feminine sensibilities such as romance, and by its objectifying, often predatory attitudes toward women" (Moffat, 1989, p. 183).

In another study, New Zealand psychology students were the researchers. They observed how their friends talked about sex in their daily life settings for a week and then analyzed the metaphors used. The four most common kinds of metaphor were food and eating (*munching rug, tasty, fresh muffin,* and *meat market*), sport and games (*muff diving, getting to first base, chasing,* and *scoring*), animals (*pussy, spanking the monkey,* and *hung like a horse*), and war and violence (*whacking it in, sticking, pussy whipped,* and *launching his missile*). Males were two and a half times more likely to be the active agent ("He scored her sister") than females ("She turns my crank") or both partners ("They've been bonking away"), reflecting the tendency to objectify women (Weatherall & Walton, 1999).

U.S. college students, too, have been studied, by asking them to report the sexual language they used. Male students, especially those who were members of fraternities, were more likely than female students to use degrading terms to refer to female genitals and aggressive terms to refer to sex acts. These same students next listened to a conversation in which one speaker told another about having sex with someone they had recently met. When the sex partner was talked about using the more degrading terms, he or she was viewed as less intelligent and lower in morality (Murnen, 2000).

It is easy to see how women might become ambivalent about sexual pleasure when the very language of sex suggests that the female role is synonymous with being exploited or degraded. Negative language about women and sexual acts probably encourages both women and men to view women and their sexuality negatively. By making it hard to imagine alternatives, sexist language also inhibits social change. However, feminists have added new terms to the language, naming women's experiences (date rape, sexual harassment, and girl power). Gay activists, too, have added to the language of sexuality (gay, straight, bi, and coming out). Language change is an ongoing process (Crawford, 2001).

Studs and Sluts: Is There Still a Double Standard?

Traditionally a *sexual double standard* was an important component of sexual scripts. Women were severely sanctioned for any sexual activity outside of hetero-sexual marriage, while for men such activity was expected and tolerated. Boys had to "sow their wild oats," while girls were warned that a future husband "won't buy the cow if he can get milk for free." Because of the double standard, fewer young women than young men were sexually active (Laumann & Michael, 2000).

For women the double standard was often connected with a Madonna/whore dichotomy. Women were either "the pure, virginal, 'good' woman on her pedestal, unspoiled by sex or sin" or "her counterpart, the whore . . . consumed by desires of the flesh . . . dangerous and inherently bad" (Ussher, 1989, p. 14). A woman could not belong to both categories and women who enjoyed sex were relegated to the "bad." Oliva Espin (1986) describes this dichotomy in Latin culture:

> To enjoy sexual pleasure, even in marriage, may indicate lack of virtue. To shun sexual pleasure and to regard sexual behavior exclusively as an unwelcome obligation toward her husband and a necessary evil in order to have children may be seen as a manifesta-tion of virtue. In fact, some women even express pride at their own lack of sexual plea-sure or desire (p. 279).

By the 1970s, the double standard had decreased. Access to contraception, the sexual revolution, and women's liberation were said to have made women and men equally free to express themselves sexually outside of heterosexual marriage. Evi-dence that the double standard is gone comes mainly from laboratory experiments in which college students are asked to judge the sexual behavior of a hypothetical woman/man. In recent studies, the results usually (but not always) show women and men being judged equally for sexual behavior (Crawford & Popp, 2003; Fugere et al., 2008; Marks & Fraley, 2005).

However, we should not be too quick to believe that women and men are now equally free to be sexual. First, several recent studies of hypothetical situations have shown that there is still a double standard for behavior that is unusual or out of bounds. Women who get a sexually transmitted infection or engage in threesomes are still judged more negatively than men who do (Jonason & Marks, 2009; Smith et al., 2008). Second, although people may deny the double standard when asked about it hypothetically on a questionnaire, they do not always behave that way in their daily lives. Researchers who have done their studies by interviewing their participants, meeting with them in small groups, or just hanging out with them find that the double standard is still used to control girls and women's sexual autonomy (Crawford & Popp, 2003). For example, a study of African American mothers and their teens showed that the mothers used a double standard in educating their offspring about sexuality. Only girls were talked about as clean or dirty, slutty or not. Boys were just told to be careful and take precautions (Fasula et al., 2007).

There is evidence that a teen's social status is differentially affected by sexual activity, depending on whether that teen is male or female. In a study that used data from a national longitudinal study of adolescent health, boys who had more sexual partners were more accepted by their peers, but for girls the correlation was in the other direction: more sexual partners led to less peer acceptance (Kregear & Staff, 2009). Sexual labels are still used to control and harass girls in public situations. For example, when middle-school students (age 11–14) were observed in their daily interactions, the researchers reported that girls were often labeled whores, bitches, and sluts.

> Joe and Hank walked over to a girl sitting at a table and repeatedly called her "slut-face" and "whore." They asked if her rates had gone down, or if they were still a quarter. They also told her they knew she'd "fuck any guy in the school" . . . She finally said, "Fuck you," at which point Hank and Joe backed off and left her alone (Eder et al., 1995, p. 130).

Silencing Girls' Sexuality and Women's Desire

Because attitudes toward girls' sexuality are mixed, their normal bodily desires may be denied, and girls may learn that their sexuality is pretty much a taboo topic.

What role do parents play in educating girls about their sexuality? Unfortunately, many parents are uncomfortable discussing sexuality with their adolescents. Parents may mislabel sexual parts of the body or simply give them no names at all—especially for girls. Mothers are more reluctant to name the sexual parts of their daughters' anatomy than their sons' and do it at a later age. Few girls know they have a clitoris or that it is a separate organ from the vagina; many confuse the urinary opening with the vagina. Boys learn to personify their penises with names like *johnson* or *dick*, to ascribe power and strength with names like *cock* and *tool*, or to make everyday comparisons (testicles are *nuts* or *balls*). Girls learn to talk about their genitals, if at all, with terms such as *down there*, *privates*, *between your legs*, *nasty*, or *bottom*. It is not surprising that after years of objectification of their bodies and shamed silence about their sexual embodiment, many young women are far more prepared to look sexy than to be sexual.

Can schools fill the education gap? In many U.S. schools sex education has been shaped by pressures from conservative parents and religious groups who believe that knowledge about sexuality encourages sexual activity. There is a "behind-the-scenes war" being waged between conservatives and liberals (Hyde & Jafee, 2000, p. 292), and adolescents are in the line of fire. (See Box 7.3.) Many schools have adopted federally funded programs like *Sex Respect*, which teach that abstinence is the only safe and moral approach to sexuality. Middle-school children are taught to chant slogans such as "Don't be a louse, wait for your spouse," and take chastity pledges in class (Hyde & Jafee, 2000).

These programs present heterosexual marriage as the sole place for sexual expression. They encode gender stereotypes of boys as sexually insatiable aggressors and girls as defenders of virginity (Hyde & Jafee, 2000). At best, girls are taught that they should avoid being victims of teen pregnancy and STDs. They also learn that "good girls just say no" to sex. But nowhere do they hear the suggestion that

---

Box 7.3 ∾ Is Sex Education a Crime?

In March 2010, the Healthy Youth Act took effect in Wisconsin. The law requires schools with sex education courses to provide age-appropriate, unbiased, accurate information regarding the prevention of sexually transmitted diseases and the use of birth control. Sounds sensible, right? However, one district attorney sent a letter to the five school districts in his county instructing them to drop their sex education courses or teachers could face criminal charges.

In his letter, District Attorney Scott Southworth said that the new law promotes the sexual assault of children because they will be taught how to use contraception. Furthermore, teachers who follow the new law—for example, by providing students information on how to use and obtain contraceptives—could be charged with contributing to the delinquency of a minor, and could face up to six years in prison. Southworth claimed that teachers could be charged because a "natural and probable consequence" of the information they provide is that it may lead teens to have sex. He also objected to the fact that the law may require teachers to discuss homosexuality and transsexual and transgendered people. He stated that, "In effect, the new law injects an intense amount of politics into our human growth and development classrooms, and places our teachers and children into a position of discussing extremely controversial issues that will likely conflict with the religious beliefs and values of most Juneau County families."

The school districts and teachers were put in a double bind: follow the law, provide students with accurate information about their own bodies and how to stay safe, and face potential criminal charges—or deny children and teenagers access to important information that scientific research has shown could prevent risky behavior, teen pregnancy, and sexually transmitted diseases.

Sources: Holewa, L. (2010). Wisconsin DA threatens arrest for local sex-ed teachers. *AOL News Online.* Retrieved August 2, 2010, from http://www.aolnews.com/nation/article/wis-da-threatens-arrest-for-local-sex-ed-teachers/19430578

Southworth, S. (2010, March 24). 2009 Wisconsin Act 134—Sex Education Mandates. [Letter from Scott Southworth to School Board Members and District Administrators, Juneau County]. Contributed by Annie B. Fox.

girls and women might like, want, need, seek out, or enjoy sexual activity (outside of heterosexual marriage). Even in the more enlightened programs, girls see educational videos only about menstruation while boys are seeing films about wet dreams, erections, and penis size. And LGBT students' need for information may be ignored altogether.

This kind of sex education does not allow young women to come to terms with their own feelings of sexuality. It "allows girls one primary decision—to say yes or no—to a question not necessarily their own" (Fine, 1988, p. 34). By emphasizing to girls how easily they can be victimized, it may also convey the idea that women are weak and vulnerable, and men are predatory. Black feminist theorist bell hooks (1989) poignantly described how as a teenager, she began to think of men as enemies of her virginity. "They had the power to transform women's reality—to turn her from a good woman into a bad woman, to make her a whore, a slut" (p. 149).

Because society constructs sexuality in terms of the presumably dangerous and uncontrollable urges of boys and men, girls and women are assigned the role of keeping everything under control by wanting only romance, never sex (Tolman & Brown, 2001). Young women get little opportunity to learn how to say no at whatever stage of sexual activity suits them, and no chance to learn when they would rather say yes—or be the one who asks. By assuming that girls and women are not active agents in their own sexuality, sex education contributes to muting women's desires:

> The naming of desire, pleasure, or sexual entitlement, particularly for females, barely exists in the formal agenda of public schooling on sexuality. When spoken, it is tagged with reminders of "consequences"—emotional, physical, moral, reproductive, and/or financial. . . . A genuine discourse of desire would invite adolescents to explore what feels good and bad, desirable and undesirable, grounded in experiences, needs, and limits (Fine, 1988, p. 33).

Women's sexual agency and desire also have been relatively invisible in sex education materials for adults. Up to the 1950s, sex manuals described women as slow to become aroused and capable of being sexually awakened only by the skill of their husbands in the security of marriage. Musical metaphors abounded, women were characterized as harps or violins that only the male master musician could cause it to give forth beautiful melodies. The sex manuals of the 1960s and 1970s urged women to be sexually free, but it was still on others' terms. After analyzing the manuals' contents, one feminist researcher asked, "Clearly, the new liberated woman is 'sensuous' and sexy—but is she sexual, on her own behalf?" (Altman, 1984, p. 123). Today, conservative marriage manuals such as *The Surrendered Wife* advise that no woman should refuse to have sex with her partner just because she doesn't feel like it.

Even in feminist theorizing it is hard to find positive accounts of erotic experiences. A large proportion of feminist writing about sexuality has come from a radical perspective that views men and heterosexuality as oppressive. These writers explore sexual domination but leave the question of how to represent women's experiences of heterosexual desire, power, and pleasure still open for debate.

Controlling Women's Sexuality

Radical feminist perspectives suggest that male dominance is fundamentally sexual. In other words, the power that men have over women is expressed and acted out in male control of female sexuality. Male dominance can define and shape the very meaning of a woman's sexuality (MacKinnon, 1994). One place where cultural control is particularly overt and harmful to women is the practice of genital cutting in order to insure that women are properly subordinated.

Female genital mutilation (also termed *female circumcision,* although it involves much more drastic procedures than male circumcision) is a common practice in at least 28 African countries as well as parts of Asia and the Middle East. It is usually done to girls between the ages of 4 and 12. It may involve removal of part or all of the clitoris (*clitoridectomy*), cutting away the clitoris plus part or all of the inner lips of the vulva (*excision*), or in addition to excision, sewing the outer lips of the vulva together to cover the urinary and vaginal entrances, leaving only a small opening for the passage of urine and menstrual blood (*infibulation*). A woman who has undergone infibulation must be cut open for childbirth (Abusharaf, 1998).

Genital surgery is usually performed by a midwife who has no medical training. The surgery often takes place under unsanitary conditions; therefore, complications such as infection and hemorrhaging are common. The presence of open wounds makes women extremely vulnerable to HIV infection. Other long-term health consequences, especially for infibulated women, include chronic pelvic and urinary tract infections, childbirth complications, and depression. Because the clitoris is damaged or removed, circumcised women feel little or no sexual pleasure and do not have orgasms. "Circumcision is intended to dull women's sexual enjoyment, and to that end it is chillingly effective" (Abusharaf, 1998, p. 25).

According to Amnesty International, which has investigated genital mutilation as a human rights issue, 135 million women living today have been subjected to the process. The World Health Organization estimates that each year another 3 million girls are cut (Odeku et al., 2009). Genital mutilation is spreading to countries where there are large numbers of refugees from Africa, Asia, and the Middle East. Great Britain outlawed it in 1985 when three girls bled to death after the procedure but no one has ever been prosecuted under the law (Laurance, 2001).

Why does this custom persist? It is believed to purify women and control their sexual desire, making them more docile and obedient. Women who remain uncut are disrespected and become social outcasts. Those who have been cut are marriageable. The practice of genital surgery has been very resistant to change. However, studies show that the more educated women are, the less willing they are to allow their daughters to be cut. As women in developing countries make gains toward social equality, becoming less dependent on marriage for survival, their attitudes may change. Meanwhile, the genital cutting of girls reflects the social and economic powerlessness of girls and women (Odeku et al., 2009).

The custom of genital mutilation is the result of a cultural construction of sexuality that may seem barbaric to outsiders. However, it was actually a common practice in England and the United States only a century ago, when clitoridectomies were done by physicians to cure upper-class women of having too much interest in sex. One health expert advised parents of girls who masturbated to apply pure carbolic acid to the clitoris (Michael et al., 1994). And some current Western practices seem barbaric to outsiders, too. What counts as normal depends on one's cultural standpoint:

> Today, some girls and women in the West starve themselves obsessively. Others undergo painful and potentially dangerous medical procedures—face lifts, liposuction, breast implants, and the like—to conform to cultural standards of beauty and femininity . . . people in the industrialized world must recognize that they too are influenced, often destructively, by traditional gender roles and demands (Abusharaf, 1998, p. 24).

Making a Difference

Sexual norms are changing rapidly in Western societies and these changes have global impact (see Box 7.4). The increasing acceptance of same-sex and extramarital sexual behavior have been liberating in some ways, but a sexual double standard remains, and women's sexuality is still suppressed, both overtly (genital mutilation) and covertly (the double standard). Here I will focus on efforts to empower women to protect themselves and to make sexual choices without coercion or shame—to be in charge of both the dangers and the pleasures of their sexuality.

Safer Sex

What can be done to reduce risky sexual behavior? Psychologists have developed strategies that work for a wide variety of groups including urban minority teenagers and college students (Fisher & Fisher, 2000; Fisher et al., 1996; 1999). Successful strategies depend on giving people *information* about how STDs are transmitted, increasing their *motivation* to reduce their own risk, and teaching them *specific skills and behaviors*. These skills and behaviors might include practice in talking about condoms with a partner, avoiding drinking or drug use before sex, or learning how to buy and use condoms.

Community-based efforts are important, partly because school-based programs are often inadequate, and partly because many students are not invested in school learning. One example is *Esperanza*, a peer-education program serving urban teens of diverse race, class, and sexual orientation (Ashcraft, 2008). Esperanza's peer educators offer programs to schools and youth organizations about STDs, pregnancy prevention, sexual decision making, and healthy relationships. The information is beneficial to recipients and to the peer educators, who themselves are low-income urban teens, both gay and straight. One peer educator said, "You can't always believe what you hear . . . and that's why they (friends) come to me now for all this sex stuff, because it's like, '*She* has the information . . . *She's* got the lowdown on it'" (Ashcraft, 2008, p. 645).

Another example is the program developed by psychologist Michelle Kaufman for the Big Sisters/Little Sisters organization (Kaufman, 2010). This program provides accurate information on sexuality and how to talk about it to big sisters whose

BOX 7.4 ∾ A New View of Women's Sexuality

Throughout the 1980s and 1990s, academic and popular thinking increasingly emphasized the medical, biological, and genetic bases of behavior and behavioral problems. It suddenly seemed like hormones and the brain featured in every news story and research study about learning, memory, gender, sexuality, children's behavior problems, mental health, moods, emotions, drinking problems, criminal offenses, and on and on. The trend was valiantly resisted by feminists and social scientists who called it "medicalization" and insisted it was a bias that underestimated the importance of culture, learning, personality and other psychosocial, and political influences. Medicalization wasn't entirely a recent trend but it escalated due to publicity about new genetics and neuroscience research.

Leonore Tiefer, PhD

In 1998, medicalization in sex research and sex therapy made a huge leap forward with the appearance of Viagra, the first "sexuopharmaceutical." During the 1980s and 1990s I was employed in men's sexual health clinics in NYC hospitals. These clinics, based in urology departments, were replacing the sex therapy clinics in departments of psychiatry. It seemed to me that the turning sex therapy over to urologists, surgeons primarily concerned with medical conditions of the urogenital organs, was resulting in fewer patients learning about sexual psychology and technique, fewer couples receiving counseling, and most patients receiving medical treatments and prescriptions.

I wrote critically about the "medicalization of sex" I was observing—about how sex was becoming more like digestion than dancing! I was concerned that this would produce some negative effects: more pressure to be sexually "normal," standardized sexual performance goals, sexual self-consciousness, and insecurity. I believed that

people would have less understanding of how culture, emotions, and individuality get expressed in sexuality.

In 1998 the publicity surrounding Viagra was immense and journalists began to ask, "Where is the Viagra for women?" I thought the growth of a medicalized women's sexuality could be a harmful trend and eclipse twenty years of research on the social context of women's sexualities (e.g., gendered double standards, prevalence of violence against women, and pervasive media objectification).

As a result of this, in 1999 I used the feminist organizing skills I had learned in the 1970s to start "The New View Campaign (NVC)," a grassroots initiative to challenge the over-medicalization of sex and emphasize the aspects of sexuality that celebrate sexual culture, diversity and variety rather than medical norms and treatments. Our activities have included:

- A Web site (newviewcampaign.org) with coverage of our activities and many resources about women's sexuality

---

BOX 7.4 ∾ A New View of Women's Sexuality *(Concluded)*

- A manifesto that criticized "female sexual dysfunction" and offered an alternative view of women's sexual problems
- Producing a book
- Three conferences (San Francisco in 2002, Montreal in 2005, Las Vegas in 2010)
- A manual for classroom and workshop use
- An online listserv
- Online courses for health professionals
- Testifying at the U.S. Food and Drug Administration's advisory hearings in 2004 and 2010 when drugs for "female sexual dysfunction" came up for approval
- A street demonstration to protest female genital cosmetic surgery

- An art gallery event to celebrate genital diversity
- Expanding into Facebook and Twitter social networking
- YouTube videos
- Interviews, op-eds, and blogs in the media

Our membership is intergenerational and interdisciplinary, and we focus equally on academic scholarship and political activism. We hope our lasting legacy will be to contribute to several movements: feminism, critical health studies, anti-corporate public health, and humanistic sexology. Check out our Web site and join us!

Source: Contributed by L. Tiefer, PhD.

---

little sisters are approaching adolescence. The girls in this program come from difficult family situations and are at high risk for early sexual initiation, teen pregnancy, and STDs. Helping them to understand and claim their sexuality, through talking with the big sister they trust, is an important initiative.

In educating about sexuality, what works depends on the norms of the group. For example, messages that stress risk to the individual may work better in more individualistic cultures, whereas messages that stress harm to one's family may work better in more collectivist cultures (Murray Johnson et al., 2001). Generic appeals like "just say no" or "practice safer sex" are unlikely to change behavior. Most important, researchers need to develop feminist approaches that recognize the diverse realities of women's lives: male control of sexual decision making, coercion by male partners, economic dependence on men, and substance abuse are all factors in women's risky sexual behavior. Even those who are not disadvantaged by these factors are shaped by sexual scripts that tell them that love is all and a woman should do anything to please her man. Empowering women to control their own bodies is key to their sexual health (Amaro et al., 2001).

Better Sex

- Lily, a 17-year-old Latina interviewed in a study of girls' sexual desire, was asked what makes her feel sexy. Her reply referred to her boyfriend: "When he says that I look sexy, that's one of my sexy days." Though the interviewer repeatedly asked her how she herself felt, she continued to describe what her boyfriend thought (Tolman & Brown, 2001, p. 143).

- Debra and her husband have four small children. They used to have inter-course four or five times a week, but now it's more like once or twice. Debra seeks therapy because her husband is not satisfied with how often they have sex. She undergoes medical and therapeutic testing. Although the tests reveal no hormonal or physiological abnormalities, the sex therapist prescribes tes-tosterone to increase her sexual desire (cited in Tyler, 2009).

Do you see any problems here? Both Lily and Debra are defining their sexuality in terms of someone else. Lily, still a teen, has probably not thought much about her own bodily responses and desires; she views herself through the eyes of another. Debra, although older and more experienced, is pressured by her husband and the therapeutic establishment to define normal sexuality in terms of his desires. Rather than ask about the context of their relationship (What is it about a house full of young kids that dampens sexual desire? How are they protecting against another pregnancy? Do they talk together about what helps them get in the mood for sex?), the therapist reinforces the husband's perspective and prescribes a powerful hor-mone to a woman who is physiologically normal.

There are alternatives to androcentric thinking about sexuality. Feminists are actively creating and supporting theories of sexuality that celebrate diversity and integrate the social context of sexual expression.

Feminist theorists have developed the concept of *sexual subjectivity* to encom-pass aspects of sexuality from a feminist perspective. Sexual subjectivity includes three key components:

- Awareness of one's own sexual desires and responses
- A belief that one is entitled to sexual pleasure
- The ability to stand up for one's sexual safety and sexual pleasure (Schick et al., 2008)

In other words, it "consists of knowing what one wants and how to get it as well as knowing what one does not want and how to stop it" (Schick et al., 2008, p. 226). Of course, for women, achieving healthy sexual subjectivity is easier said than done because it conflicts with norms about gender-appropriate behavior.

Sexual attraction and erotic arousal are not merely programmed into us by the culture. Often, they may even contradict cultural dictates, as shown when some women develop healthy lesbian and bisexual identities or use feminist thinking to claim their sexuality. Research has demonstrated links between being a feminist and developing a healthy sexual subjectivity. In a study of 342 college women, three groups were compared: those who endorsed feminist values and self-identified as feminists; those who endorsed feminist values such as equal pay but did not label themselves feminists (termed egalitarians); and nonfeminists, who rejected every-thing about feminism. Feminists had the most positive attitudes about sexuality. Egalitarians had ambivalent attitudes. On the one hand, they were confident that they could be sexually assertive; on the other hand, like nonfeminists, they endorsed the sexual double standard. Egalitarians seem to think that sexual freedom is fine for themselves, but not for other women, whereas feminists were more aware of cultural constraints on all women and still positive about sexuality (Bay-Cheng &

Zucker, 2007). Other studies also have found that feminist beliefs and rejection of traditional gender roles are linked to greater sexual subjectivity and greater sexual satisfaction in women (Schick et al., 2008) and in men, too (Sanchez et al., 2005).

In spite of the social control placed on women's sexuality, most women desire and enjoy sexual pleasure with men and/or with other women. It is well to remember that in spite of social pressures from all sides, some women, some of the time, do manage to love their bodies, define sexual pleasure in their own terms, and have good sex!

Exploring Further

∾

Boston Women's Health Book Collective and Judy Norsigian (2005). *Our bodies, ourselves: A new edition for a new era*. New York: Touchstone.

This is the latest edition of the book that started a feminist revolution in women's health by establishing women as the experts on women's bodies. The diversity of women's sexual identities and expression is respected in this indispensible reference book for women of every age and life stage.

Hyde, Janet S., & DeLamater, John (2011). *Understanding human sexuality* (11th ed.). New York: McGraw-Hill.

A matter-of-fact, nonsexist college text on human sexuality. This book, written with wisdom and humor, provides a great deal of factual information.

Kaschak, Ellyn, & Tiefer, Leonore (Eds.). (2001). *A new view of women's sexual problems*. Binghampton, NY: Hawthorne.

These innovative feminist theorists demonstrate that standard views of sexuality are male-centered, neglect the relational context of sexual expression, and ignore differences among women. They set out a new approach that balances psychological, social, and cultural factors with medical and biological factors. A brilliant contribution to understanding women's sexual selves.

The Vagina Monologues. (DVD). (2002). An HBO Production.

Created and performed by Eve Ensler, this dramatic performance captures Ensler's unique performance of her controversial work. She performs interviews she conducted with other women about their vaginas, sex, orgasms, and menstruation.

CHAPTER 8

Commitments:
Women and Close Relationships

*H*appy endings like the ones in romance novels and TV reality shows about dating and marriage appeal to women's hopes of finding the real thing and settling down to a lifetime of happiness. Romantic relationships lead—at least sometimes—to a desire to make a commitment to one partner. In our society that commitment often leads to marriage and when people marry they almost always hope it will last a lifetime. Not all enduring commitments to a partner take the form of marriage. Lesbian couples have not had the right to marriage, and more and more heterosexual couples live together without getting married.

In this chapter we explore the kinds of commitments couples make to each other and the consequences of these commitments for women.

Marriage

As a very old joke puts it, "Marriage is an institution—but who wants to live in an institution?" This joke recognizes that marriage is a way that societies regulate private relationships between couples. Laws and statutes stipulate who may marry whom—for example, same-sex couples have been prohibited from marrying and, in the past, interracial marriages were forbidden. Laws also regulate the minimum age for marriage, the division of property when a marriage dissolves (indeed, whether they are permitted to dissolve), and the responsibilities of each partner within the marriage (what behaviors constitute grounds for divorce). Religious codes and social norms also regulate marriage and divorce.

Although people in Western societies are aware that marriage is a legal contract subject to regulation by the state, they rarely think of it that way in relation to themselves. Rather, they are influenced by the ideology of love and romance, choosing their partners as individuals and expecting to live out their married lives according to their own needs and wishes. (See Figure 8.1.) Nevertheless, the rights and responsibilities imposed by the state may have consequences for both partners, especially when the marriage ends.

As an institution, marriage has a strong patriarchal heritage (Grana, 2002). Historically, wealth and titles were passed on only through male heirs. In many countries married women are still regarded as the property of their husbands. In the United States most women still give up their own name and take their husband's name upon marriage. The institutional aspects of marriage shape behaviors and attitudes through cultural scripts:

> An institution is a way of life that is very resistant to change. People know about it; they can describe it; and they have spent a lifetime learning how to react to it. The idea of marriage is larger than any individual marriage. The role of husband or wife is greater than any individual who takes on that role (Blumstein & Schwartz, 1983, p. 318).

Marriage then, is both a personal relationship and a scripted social institution.

FIGURE 8.1   Most people look forward to marrying.

Who Marries and When?

More than 90 percent of people in Western societies marry at some time in their lives. Marital patterns are divergent across ethnic groups. For example, African American women are the least likely of any group to be married. However, there has been very little research on marriage using African American, Hispanic, Asian American, or other ethnic group samples, and little on working-class people (Orbuch & Brown, 2006). Most research on American marriage has been done with White, middle-class samples, and it's helpful to keep this bias in mind while exploring this topic.

In general, women marry at younger ages than men do. Women in developing areas of the world marry very young. In many parts of Africa and Asia, the average young woman is married before she reaches the age of 18 (United Nations, 1995). In contrast, the typical first-time bride in the United States now is about 25-years-old; just one generation ago, she was 20. For first-time grooms, it is 26.8-years-old, up from 22.8 (Teachman et al., 2006). A similar trend is occurring in other industrialized countries.

Why are American women marrying later? They are more likely than women of previous generations to invest in higher education. Also, advances in contraception have made premarital sex and living-together arrangements less risky. For Black women, there is a shortage of marriageable men, due to a number of socioeconomic forces (Orbuch & Brown, 2006). (See Chapter 9 for more on African American family patterns.) Economic factors may play a part too, when young people find it difficult to become financially independent (Teachman et al., 2006).

Whatever the causes, the tendency to marry later has important implications for women. The increased time between high school and marriage offers opportunities to broaden their experiences. A woman who enters her first marriage at an older age is likely to have had some experience of independent living; has probably held jobs and supported herself; and has had time to get more education, which exposes her to a variety of viewpoints and experiences and also increases her employment opportunities. All in all, she is more likely than a younger woman to enter marriage with a well-developed sense of self and broad horizons for her life.

Who Marries Whom?

In a cross-cultural study, more than 9,000 people from 37 nations representing every part of the world were asked to assess the importance of 31 characteristics in a potential mate (Buss et al., 1990). The characteristics included good health, chastity, dependability, intelligence, social status, religious background, neatness, ambition, and sociability. The participants were young (their average age was 23) and typically urban, well educated, and prosperous—in other words, they are not representative samples from their countries. Nevertheless, their answers give an interesting picture of what women and men from diverse cultures look for in a potential marriage partner.

No two samples ordered the characteristics in exactly the same way. The biggest difference across cultures was in a cluster of characteristics reflecting traditional values such as premarital virginity, being a good cook and housekeeper, and desire for a home and children. For example, samples from China, Indonesia, India, and Iran placed great importance on virginity; whereas, those from Scandinavia considered it irrelevant.

Overall, cultural differences were much more important than gender differences. Men and women from the same culture were more similar in their mate preferences than were men from different cultures or women from different cultures. In fact, men's and women's rankings were virtually identical overall, with a correlation of +.95. This gender similarity suggests that each culture—whether Bulgarian, Irish, Japanese, Zambian, Venezuelan, or whatever—socializes men and women to know and accept its particular script for marriage. When all 37 cultures were considered, an overall picture of an ideal mate emerged. Both women and men rated mutual attraction and love, dependable character, emotional stability, and pleasing disposition as the four most important characteristics in a potential marriage partner.

There were some gender differences; however, across cultures women were somewhat more likely to emphasize a partner's earning capacity and ambition, whereas, men were more likely to emphasize good looks and physical attractiveness. A later study found that women's preferences for men with material resources was greatest in countries where the women had the least ability to gain resources on their own. In other words, in countries where women were denied equal access to education and jobs, they were more likely to look for men who could support them (Eagly & Wood, 1999).

Many other studies have focused on spouse choices in the United States. In general, these studies, like the cross-cultural one just described, show that the desires of men and women are more similar than different. However, men remain somewhat more traditional in their thinking about marital scripts and roles. Overall, women desire more flexible marital patterns than men do (Amato et al., 2007).

"Marrying Up" and "Marrying Down": The Marriage Gradient

Individual couples usually end up being closely matched on social class and ethnicity as well as on characteristics such as height, SAT scores, attractiveness, and age. Couples are also similar in values: Religious people tend to marry other religious people, conservatives marry other conservatives, and feminists marry other feminists (Michael et al, 1994). Cross-culturally, when there are differences within a couple, it is usually the man who is older, is better educated, and has a more prestigious occupation (United Nations, 1995).

The tendency for women to "marry up" and men to "marry down" by sorting themselves into couples in which the man has the higher prestige and income potential is called the *marriage gradient.* The marriage gradient probably came about because women had little access to education and high-status occupations and could achieve economic security only through marriage. In the United States, women's tendency to marry up has decreased as they have caught up to men in earning power and educational opportunity.

Will the marriage gradient continue to exist, even though women have more equality today? Recent studies of U.S. college students suggest that both women and men value such attributes as intelligence, desire for children, and a pleasing personality when choosing a mate—but that wealth and status are still important attributes that women look for in men (Regan et al., 2000; Stewart et al., 2000). When playing a game in which they "designed" an ideal long-term mate by "purchasing" desirable characteristics, female students were willing to pay the most for status and resources when designing a man, and male students were willing to pay the most for physical attractiveness when designing a woman (Li et al., 2002). Even when young women are relatively empowered on their own, it seems that many still prefer a man with status and wealth—and men care less about their partner's money than her looks.

Varieties of Marriage

In the United States, many marriage patterns coexist. I will classify marriages into three types (traditional, modern, and egalitarian) based on three important characteristics: the division of authority, how spousal roles are defined, and the amount of companionship and shared activities they provide (Peplau & Gordon, 1985; Schwartz, 1994).

Traditional Marriage

In a *traditional marriage,* both the husband and wife agree that the husband should have greater authority; he is the head of the family, or the boss. Even in areas in which the wife has some decision-making responsibility (such as household shopping), he retains veto power over her decisions. The wife is a full-time homemaker who does not work for pay. Clear distinctions are made between the husband's and wife's responsibilities. She is responsible for home and child care, and he is the breadwinner. Couples in these marriages may not expect to be best friends; rather, the wife finds companionship with other women—neighbors, sisters and other kin, or members of her church. The husband's friendship networks are with male kin and coworkers, and his leisure activities take place apart from his wife.

Attitudes toward traditional marriage have changed a great deal in the past few decades. These changes do not mean that marriages based on traditional beliefs and values are entirely a thing of the past. Certain religious groups still strongly endorse traditional marriage. For example, Orthodox Jews, Latter-Day Saints (Mormons), some evangelical Christian sects, the Promise Keepers, and Nation of Islam insist that distinct gender roles and submission by the wife to her husband are necessary for marital and societal stability (Hewlett & West, 1998; Mathews, 1996). Women may also find their marriages becoming more traditional than they initially expected, if they leave paid employment after the couple has children. About 38 percent of women with children under the age of 6, and 25 percent of those with children under 18, are not employed (Gilbert & Kearney, 2006).

Modern Marriage

In *modern marriage,* the spouses have a "senior partner–junior partner" or "near-peer" relationship. Modern wives work outside the home, but, by mutual agreement, the wife's job is less important than the husband's. He is the bread-winner and she is just working to help out. Moreover, it is expected that her paid employment will not interfere with her responsibilities for housework and child care. Within modern marriage, the husband and wife may spend an equal amount of time on paid work, but that work has different meanings because of the belief that the man is the real provider (Steil, 2001). Modern couples emphasize companionship and expect to share leisure activities. They value togetherness and may discuss husband/wife roles rather than taking them for granted as more traditional couples do.

Modern marriage may seem to be a relationship of equality when compared with traditional marriage, but the equality is relative. Traditional gender relations are a legacy that still have more financial responsibility and wives have more responsibility for the home and the children (see Figure 8.2). Modern wives do a *second shift* every day—they put in a day's work for pay and another day's work when they get home (Amato et al., 2007; Hochschild, 1989). Men are considerably more satisfied than women with this arrangement (Baker et al., 1996). Women may accept it because they want to be close to their children or they may put up with it because they do not know how to change it.

Egalitarian Marriage

Egalitarian marriage, once relatively rare, is becoming more common (Knudson-Martin & Mahoney, 2005; Schwartz, 1994). In *egalitarian marriages,* the partners have equal power and authority. They also share responsibilities equally without

FIGURE 8.2   Let's make a deal . . .

Source: Sylvia by Nicole Hollander. Reprinted by permission of Sourcebooks, Inc. and Nicole Hollander.

respect to gender roles. For example, one partner's paid job is not allowed to take precedence over the other's. In practical terms, this means that either partner might relocate to accommodate the other's promotion, or either would agree to miss work to care for a sick child. The ever-present tasks of running a household—cleaning, cooking, bill paying, errands—are allocated by interest and ability, not because certain jobs are supposed to be women's work and others men's work. One wife in an egalitarian relationship described her commitment to nonsexist task allocation like this:

> I believe that people should be flexible. A woman, if she can fix (the) light, she should fix the light . . . I don't believe in taking care of husbands . . . when I'm still showering, he irons my clothes for me . . . even cooking is not fixed, although I love to cook (Quek & Knudson-Martin, 2006, p. 64).

Such marriages are *post gender relationships;* the partners have moved beyond using gender to define their marital roles. More than any other type of marriage, an egalitarian relationship provides the couple with intimacy, companionship, and mutual respect. This husband, whose wife's educational and job status are equal to his own (both have master's degrees and their job rank is similar), says that he has no need to feel superior to her:

> I need (the relationship) to be equal. If I am in a more dominant kind of position, this will not make me feel right. I would only feel as if I'm not able to engage with the most important person in my life at the level I would like to engage in (Quek & Knudson-Martin, 2006, p. 61).

Because egalitarian couples share a great deal, they are likely to understand each other, communicate well, and choose to spend a lot of time together (see Figure 8.3). Often, each partner says that the other is his or her best friend, precious and irreplaceable, and that their relationship is unique (Risman & Johnson-Sumerford, 1998; Schwartz, 1994).

FIGURE 8.3   Egalitarian couples enjoy doing activities together.

Power in Marriage

Different marriage types reflect different beliefs about what the duties of husband and wife should be and how they should relate to each other. Completely egalitarian marriages are still relatively rare. Although Americans like to think of marriage as an equal partnership, men may still end up having more power. Why is it that the result of a stroll down the aisle and the words "I do" is often a long-term state of inequality?

One definition of power is the ability to get one's way or influence decisions (Blumstein & Schwartz, 1983). Researchers have sometimes studied marital power by giving husbands and/or wives lists of decisions they might have to make and asking them, "Who is usually the person that makes the final decision on this in your family?" In an important early study (Blood & Wolfe, 1960), more than 900 wives were asked who had the final say on whether the husband should change jobs (90 percent said their husbands always did) and on how much to spend on food (41 percent reported that the wives always did). Only 39 percent of the wives had decision-making power over whether or not they themselves should hold a paying job. Note that the decision with the most far reaching consequences, the husband's job, is one on which husbands had virtually uncontested power. In another early study of Canadian households, 76 percent of wives said that the husband was the boss and only 13 percent said that they both had equal power (Turk & Bell, 1972).

More recent research confirms that marital equality is still not the norm. Research studies suggest that less than one-third of heterosexual dual-career couples share marital roles in egalitarian ways (Amato et al., 2007; Gilbert & Kearney, 2006). For the majority, although roles and responsibilities are more balanced than in traditional marriages, there may still be a consistent pattern of inequality that is accepted by both partners. For example, even though women and men agree that women do far more housework and child care in most marriages, most don't see it as a problem. In a major survey first conducted in 1980 and replicated in 2000, the majority of respondents in both time periods said that this imbalance was fair (Amato et al., 2007). Couples may construct a ***myth of equality,*** refusing to acknowledge how gender socialization and social forces have steered them toward traditional roles (Knudson-Martin & Mahoney, 1996; 2005).

How Do Couples Justify Marital Inequality?

Power in marriage is both structural and ideological—it is related to societal structures that give men greater status and earning power and also to beliefs about who is better at nurturing or more suited to doing housework (Dallos & Dallos, 1997). How is marital power exerted and justified? How do couples create myths of equality and explain away inequalities in their own marriages?

When a sample of highly educated dual-career couples was asked about other couples' relationships, they defined equality in terms of task sharing. However, when asked about their own relationships, they talked less about who did the cooking and cleaning than about abstract concepts like mutual respect (Rosenbluth, et al., 1998). In fact, most of the couples had not achieved their ideal of equality: the women did more household work and their careers were secondary to that of their husbands' careers. They did not focus on adding up who did what around the house, perhaps because it would make the inequality painfully apparent. Redefining the situation is a common way to avoid perceiving injustice of all kinds (Steil, 2001).

In an in-depth study of 17 British couples, the wives and husbands were first interviewed together and then, 18 months later, they were interviewed separately (Dryden, 1999). The researcher was aware that, in general, married couples might not openly acknowledge inequality. Ideologically, most couples believe that marriage is supposed to be about love, sharing, and mutual respect. Wives might be particularly unable to challenge inequalities in their marriages because of being dependent on a husband's income or having young children to take care of. Openly admitting their dissatisfactions might be emotionally almost "too hard to bear" (p. 58). For husbands, admitting inequality might lead to a loss of power and privilege. Therefore, the researcher analyzed the interview data for subtle ways that the women and men justified the status quo.

The women used distancing, talking about behavior and roles in vague, hypothetical terms rather than challenging their husbands openly ("*Some* men sit around watching the telly all day . . ."). They minimized conflict or blamed themselves when it happened ("It's only silly little things we fight about and maybe I take them too seriously"). They also made positive comparisons between their husband and other people's husbands ("Some women have it really bad, their husbands don't do a thing to help, so I'm in a fairly equal situation"). These strategies helped the women create a vision of relative marital fairness for themselves and the interviewer.

Although the women's challenges were indirect and hedged with self-blame, the men often tried to deflect them, without actually mentioning inequality. Their strategies included describing their wives as inadequate ("If she were better organized, she could get all her work done with time left over") and themselves as "hard done by" (having to work long hours and needing more time out with the boys). The researcher noted that the husbands reflected back to their wives a negative identity that the wives had already created through self-blame—a "subtle undermining process that had the power to exacerbate in women a sense of lack of confidence, low self-esteem, and in some cases, depression" (p. 86). Clearly, these couples were doing gender in ways that preserved and perpetuated inequality in their marriages.

What Are the Sources of Men's Greater Power?

Many factors are associated with husband dominance in marriage (Steil, 1997). Social class and ethnicity make a difference: Black and working-class couples have less of a power differential than White middle- and upper-class couples. Wives who are employed have more power than those who work only at home. White middle-class women in traditional marriages may have less marital power than any other group of women.

One reason the power balance in marriage is weighted in favor of men is the influence of traditional gender ideology. If either or both spouses believe that the man *should* be in charge, he is likely to have more decision-making power. Traditional gender ideology is strongest in collectivist cultures, which stress responsibility to one's family and society above individual needs. Women in collectivist cultures are not allowed to prioritize their careers, to say no to serving men and children, or to place their own needs first. In a study of newly married couples in Singapore (a highly developed and economically successful Asian republic), some were working toward egalitarian relationships while others were still voicing traditional values about gender. One wife stated, "The man must always be the man of the house. He will make the major decisions." Another couple, asked about power and authority in their marriage, agreed with each other:

> She: *I have to be supportive. I still believe that behind every successful man is a wife, a loving wife.*

> He: *I would have more authority because our mindset is of the older generation* (Quek & Knudson-Martin, 2006, p. 60).

This traditional gender ideology is not limited to collectivist cultures. In the United States, it is often related to faith-based attitudes (God intended women and men to play different roles) or beliefs about human nature (gender differences are natural and built in to the species). For example, James (a school counselor) and Kwan (an accountant) have one child and another on the way. It is Kwan who insists that James is rightfully in charge, "I want the father to be the head of the house and I want him to lead or make important decisions." She describes her husband as "a big thinker" and "stronger" than she is, and describes herself as emotional. He says it's "not natural" for him to notice housework that needs doing, and that is why Kwan usually does it (Knudson-Martin & Mahoney, 2005).

Another explanation for greater male power in marriage comes from ***social exchange theory*** (Thibault & Kelley, 1959). This theory proposes that the partner who brings greater outside resources to the relationship will have the greater influence in it. The partner who has less to offer, be it status, money, or knowledge, will likely take a back seat. In American marriages, husbands usually bring more of three very important resources: money, education, and prestige. Husbands usually earn more than wives, even when both are employed full time. (This is true for a variety of reasons that I will discuss in Chapter 10.) As already noted, wives who have no income or employment of their own have the least power of any group of married women. Moreover, because of the marriage gradient, the husband in most marriages has a higher level of education than the wife. In American society, educational attainment brings status and prestige in itself and is also associated with higher income.

When the husband earns more, many couples agree that he automatically has the right to make financial decisions for the family. But the money he brings in also may give the husband the right to make other decisions that have nothing to do with money. In a British study, one wife described how things changed when she began to earn money on her own:

> Before, I had five children and was very vulnerable, I avoided raising some issues because I was worried that he would stop giving me any money . . . he threatened it a couple of times and that was enough . . . now I'm earning things have changed, I'm not so quiet about things I don't like now (Dallos & Dallos, 1997, p. 58).

Because of its practical and symbolic importance, it's not surprising that fights about money plague many marriages. In a study where 200 husbands and wives kept diaries about the conflicts they had with each other, money was not the topic they fought about about most often—children and chores topped the list. However, the fights about money were more severe, more problematic, and more likely to recur, even though couples (particularly the wives) kept trying to resolve them (Papp et al., 2009).

Social exchange theory implies that if the husband and wife have equal external resources, marital interaction will also be equal. But even in dual-career families, where the resources are fairly well matched, husbands' opinions still have more weight. Dual-career marriages also often fall short of being truly egalitarian in the relative importance attached to each partner's career. Which spouse, husband or wife, is more likely to relocate because the partner has a job offer in a different place? For the majority of couples, the wife is the one who adapts.

Social exchange theory is limited; it has focused on economic exchange while ignoring the symbolic value of gender roles. The breadwinner or provider role, still more important for men than women, means that men's capacity to earn money is more highly valued than their capacity to nurture children. For women, on the other hand, providing nurturance to husband and children is more valued than the ability to earn money. Even if a wife brings in as much money as her husband, she may not have equal power because her success is seen as undermining his provider role and interfering with her nurturing role. In other words, the same resource (in this case, earned income) may function differently for husband and wife.

Just how central is earning power to marital equality? Does its influence work the same way for husbands and wives? To answer these questions it is necessary to study couples in which the wives earn as much or more than their husbands.

Couples like these used to be rare but today about 30 percent of wives earn more than their husbands (Commuri & Gentry, 2005).

In one study, 30 couples in which the wife earned at least one-third more than the husband were compared with an equal number of couples in which the husbands earned at least one-third more than the wives (Steil & Weltman, 1991). Respondents were asked questions about the relative importance of careers ("Whose career is more important in the relationship?") and decision-making power ("Who has more say about household/financial issues?"). Consistent with social exchange theory, spouses who earned more saw their careers as more important and also had more say at home than spouses who earned less. Nevertheless, wives overall had less say in financial decisions, had more responsibility for children and housework, and felt that their husbands' careers were more important than their own.

In a more recent study, couples were interviewed repeatedly over a 2-year period. In each couple, the wife earned at least $10,000 more than her husband, and in some couples the gap was as much as $120,000. These couples struggled with how to honor the man's provider role even though he was not bringing home most of the bacon. One strategy they used was to pool their money into a shared account, making the gendered earning difference less obvious (Commuri & Gentry, 2005). A comparison group of couples in which the men earned more did not use this money management strategy nearly as much. Instead, each spouse paid expenses in proportion to his/her income.

The meaning of earning more money differs between White and racial/ethnic group samples. For African American women, who traditionally have had vital roles as wage earners for their families, a recent study has shown that earning more than their husbands affected their marital happiness negatively only if they also were highly religious and traditional in gender beliefs (Furdyna et al., 2008).

To sum it up, equal access to money can be an equalizer of power in marriage—but even when wives earn more money than their husbands, beliefs about the appropriate roles of women and men may still influence the balance of power in favor of men. This implies that in order to change power imbalances in marriage, both women's economic power and couples' gender ideology will have to change. Because women's earning power seems to be changing faster than gender ideology, couples where the woman out-earns the man use strategies like pooling their incomes to cope with the embarrassment of being gender-deviant. Shifts in gender ideology are occurring, too, and not only in the United States. A national study in Taiwan showed that Taiwanese wives' bargaining power in marriage has increased as their economic opportunities rise and traditional gender ideology falls (Xu & Lai, 2002).

Happily Ever After? Marital Satisfaction and Psychological Adjustment

"Happily ever after" is our society's romantic ideal of marriage. Does marriage bring happiness and fulfillment? We can examine the issue by looking at research on whether people are generally satisfied with the marriages they make and whether marriage has any relationship to psychological adjustment.

Does Marital Happiness Change Over Time?

The happiness and satisfaction of married couples varies greatly across the course of a marriage. Almost all studies of marital satisfaction over time show an initial "honeymoon period" followed by a substantial decline in happiness with the birth of the first child. Wives are more likely than husbands to become dissatisfied with the marriage over time. Satisfaction often hits its lowest point when the children are school-aged or adolescents. Some studies have shown that the happiness of the early years is regained or even surpassed in later life, when the children have grown and left home. In other studies, the happiness trend has been all downhill (Amato et al., 2007).

What accounts for the changes in marital happiness after the birth of children? When more than 700 women were studied during pregnancy and three months after the birth of their first child, they reported doing much more of the housework and child care than they had expected. Their negative feelings about their marriages were related to the violation of their expectancies of equal sharing. In other words, it was not the added domestic chores that made these new mothers less happy than they had been, but their feeling that the new division of labor was unfair. The more they had expected equality, the more dissatisfied they were (Ruble et al., 1988). Other studies have documented higher levels of depression in women whose hopes for shared child care were not achieved. Following up on this early research, 119 expectant couples in an ethnically diverse sample (White, African American, Asian American, and Hispanic) completed questionnaires about actual and expected household responsibilities before and after the birth of their baby, and were also observed interacting with the baby (Khazan et al., 2008). The study found that the more the women's wishes were unfulfilled, the more their marital satisfaction declined. In addition, when women's expectancies for (equal) help regarding infant care had been violated, parents' interactions regarding their infant showed subtle signs of conflict and poor coordination between the parents. To put it bluntly, when new dads refused to change diapers or get up at night, parenting interactions became a lot less friendly and cooperative, and parenting was less effective.

You might expect that happiness would decline less among women who feel respected and appreciated by their husbands, and this is just what was found in a study that followed couples for 6 years. Women whose marital satisfaction stayed the same or increased after giving birth were those who said that their husbands expressed love and were "tuned in" to their wives and their relationships. Those women whose marital satisfaction declined were those who perceived their husbands as negative or their lives as out of control and chaotic (Shapiro et al., 2000).

When children leave home, couples have fewer demands on their money and time. Many couples experience this stage of their marriage as a time of greater freedom and flexibility, and therefore their marital happiness increases. In a study of 300 middle-aged and older married couples, partners were observed as they discussed a current conflict and also as they collaborated on a task (planning errands). The older couples had higher marital satisfaction overall. When collaborating, they were both warm and assertive. Even when they disagreed they were less upset about it than the younger couples (Smith et al., 2009).

Is Marriage Linked to Psychological Well-Being?

Marriage seems to be good for both women and men. People who are married or living together in a sexually exclusive relationship report greater emotional satisfaction and physical pleasure from sex than single or cohabiting people do (Waite & Joyner, 2001). Marriage is also associated with better psychological adjustment in both women and men. However, the benefits are unequally distributed: Men are more satisfied than women with their marriages and receive greater mental health benefits from being married. Compared to single men, married men have fewer alcohol abuse problems, are less likely to commit crimes, and are less likely to have psychological disorders such as depression. They have greater career success, earn more money, are healthier, and live longer than never-married, widowed, or divorced men (Steil & Hoffman, 2006).

The psychological benefits of marriage are related to the balance of power. Both husbands and wives are most satisfied with their marriages when decision-making is relatively equal (Amato et al., 2007). Compared to relationships in which either partner dominates, more egalitarian relationships have more constructive communication, more affection and intimacy, greater sexual satisfaction, and more overall happiness with the marriage (Steil & Hoffman, 2006). Women in traditional marriages have the poorest psychological adjustment (Steil, 1997; Steil & Turetsky, 1987b).

A study of more than 800 dual-career professional couples tested the hypothesis that marital power is related to psychological well-being (Steil and Turetsky, 1987a). The researchers gathered information on each woman's earned income, her influence and responsibilities within the marriage, and her symptoms of psychological disorders. They also compared childless women and mothers.

For childless women, the more equal a woman's marital relationship, the more satisfied she was with her marriage—and marital satisfaction was an important factor in overall psychological well-being. The mothers experienced their marriages as significantly less equal than the childless women did, and the perceived inequality was directly related to psychological symptoms. Although the couples in this sample are not representative of all married couples, this study suggests that relative power and equality play an important role in married women's well-being.

Another cause of men's better outcomes in marriage is that wives may provide more emotional support for husbands than they receive in return (Steil & Hoffman, 2006). We will look at women's emotion work more closely in Chapters 9 and 10. Briefly, it includes things like confiding one's inner thoughts and feelings, asking about their partner's thoughts and opinions, offering encouragement, listening, and respecting the partner's point of view. Studies from the 1980s onward suggest that husbands usually depend on wives for emotional support; but too often, they do not offer equal support in return. Lacking the return of emotional support, women are less happy than their partners. In one study of more than 4,000 married persons—aged 55 and over—husbands said they were most likely to confide in their wives, while wives were less likely to confide in their husbands and more likely to turn to a friend, sister, or daughter. Both men and women who confided in their spouses had markedly higher marital satisfaction and overall psychological well-being than those who did not (Lee, 1988). The work of caring and emotional support that married women do may partly account for their husbands' better psychological adjustment.

Lesbian Couples

In the past, lesbian and gay couples were an invisible minority; today, they are at the center of an international debate about same-sex marriage (Peplau & Fingerhut, 2007). Here we will look at research on lesbian couples and their relationships.

In surveys of lesbians conducted over the last several decades, the majority of respondents were in a steady relationship (Peplau & Spalding, 2000). But it is difficult to know how many lesbian couples there are. It was not until the year 2000 that the U.S. Census added a category for unmarried partners. This census showed some 600,000 same-sex couples, with lesbian and gay men about equal in numbers. About 14 percent of these couples included at least one African American partner, and 16 percent included at least one Hispanic partner (Peplau & Fingerhut, 2007).

Lesbian and Heterosexual Couples Compared

When two women make a commitment to live together as lovers and friends, their relationship has some similarities to conventional marriage—but without the institutional aspects or the label. To date, there has been no research on legally married gay couples, because they are few and newly married.

The great majority of lesbian and gay couples still do not have access to conventional marriage. Some lesbian couples write their own wedding ceremonies, and some ask a minister or rabbi to perform a ceremony of union to bless their relationship, or enter into a civil union. One partner may legally adopt the other's children. Many include each other in their wills and insurance policies, buy homes together, or draw up contracts delineating rights and responsibilities to each other. All these are ways of giving the relationship some legal and institutional status (Blumstein & Schwartz, 1983; Cabaj & Purcell, 1998). Like heterosexual people, most LGBTQ people believe in marriage. In an Internet survey of more than 1,500 LGBTQ people in 27 countries, 95 percent agreed that same-sex couples should be allowed to marry just like different-sex couples are (Harding & Peel, 2006).

For many years, researchers and the public alike assumed that lesbian couples mimic traditional heterosexual roles, with one partner being the "husband" ("butch") and the other the "wife" ("femme"). This belief applies a heterosexual script to lesbian relationships. Most research shows there is no clear preference for masculine/feminine roles among lesbians (Peplau & Spalding, 2000). Instead, they tend to be more like friendships between peers. When lesbian partners describe their relationships, they use terms such as mutual respect, compatibility, shared decision-making, equal rights, and equal value for both partners (Garnets, 2008).

When lesbians do endorse butch/femme roles, it may be with different meanings than heterosexuals might assume. When a researcher asked a sample of 235 self-identified lesbians to define and apply these concepts to themselves, 40 percent of the sample said they were neither. The higher a woman's education and income, the more likely she was to have an independent (not butch/femme) identity (Weber, 1996). Only about 26 percent identified themselves as butch and 34 percent as femme. However, these women did not use butch/femme to represent husband/wife roles. To them, butch signified that they did not enjoy girly things such as makeup, dresses, and hair styling. Femme signified the freedom to enjoy a feminine personal style, while still being committed to loving women. They stressed that butch did not mean they were dominant, acted like men, or disliked being a woman, and femme had nothing to do with being submissive. In summary, the butch/femme dimension has been important to some lesbians, and it is linked to social class, but it is not about relationship dominance.

What Are the Characteristics of Lesbian Relationships?

Lesbian relationships can be described on the same dimensions as heterosexual marriages: companionship, communication, roles and the division of labor, power, and satisfaction.

Most lesbians reject gender roles (Peplau & Spalding, 2000). When looking for a long-term partner, they prefer characteristics such as intelligence and interpersonal sensitivity (Regan et al., 2001). They are more likely than gay men to live with their partner, to desire sexual fidelity and a steady monogamous relationship. They value emotional closeness and intimacy (Garnets, 2008).

Same-sex couples cannot assign the breadwinner role on the basis of gender, and they tend to value independence. Therefore, the importance of the work interests of each partner is more likely to be fairly equal than in heterosexual marriages. The great majority of lesbian and gay couples are in dual-earner or dual-career relationships. Just as they balance work roles, lesbians are highly likely to share household duties (Peplau & Fingerhut, 2007). They assign housekeeping chores on the basis of preference, skills, and ability, rather than roles. Unlike gay male couples, who tend to specialize (Tom always cooks and Larry always cleans), lesbian couples tend to do all the tasks equally often (Kurdek, 2007). However they divide the chores, the basic principle is fairness. For example, one couple (I'll call them Sue and Tonya) described to researchers how Sue managed the money and retirement funds for both, and in return, Tonya put in extra time caring for Sue's elderly mother (Bailey & Jackson, 2005). Each partner got to do what she did best, and each was grateful to the other for the mutually agreed-on division of labor.

Same-sex couples tend to share more leisure activities than heterosexual couples. They are more likely to socialize with friends together, belong to the same clubs, and share hobbies and sports interests. Perhaps, due to socialization, two women are more likely to have interests in common than a woman and a man; or perhaps most people need same-sex best friends, and lesbians can find a same-sex friend and a spouse in the same person. These ties may be one reason that when a relationship ends many former lesbian partners remain good friends (Clarke et al., 2010).

Power and Satisfaction in Lesbian Relationships

Most lesbians desire egalitarian relationships. Power differences in a lesbian relationship are usually due to the same factors that influence power in heterosexual relationships, such as one partner having greater resources (more money, status, or education), or one partner being more committed than the other. However, the egalitarian ideal may be more important than status and money in determining power relations among lesbians. Unlike heterosexual couples, many of whom believe that the man should be the head of the family, lesbian couples are more likely to start out with a belief in total equality. Therefore, money and other resources do not automatically equate to power. Pam (an office manager) and Linda (a writer) have been a couple for 15 years. Pam describes the "give and take" in their relationship:

> A couple of times I have been out of work and Linda has been really supportive. Also, she's been out of work, and I've had to support us. So, it's flip-flopped. And it's never any of that "I'm sick of supporting you" . . . Never. That would never happen in our relationship (Bailey & Jackson, 2005, p. 61).

The equality in lesbian relationships compared to heterosexual relationships has led some researchers to suggest that heterosexual couples may be able to learn from lesbians about how to negotiate egalitarian relationships (Clarke et al., 2010). Comparing the two kinds of relationships can also help researchers learn more about factors in the partners and in the social structure around them that fosters more egalitarian patterns of living.

In studies that have compared the self-reported satisfaction and happiness of lesbian and heterosexual couples, the results show few differences between the two. Like heterosexual women, lesbians are more likely than men to have a relational orientation toward sexuality, enjoying sex in committed relationships more than transient ones (Garnets, 2008). Satisfaction in lesbian relationships is higher when the two partners are equally committed to the relationship, when they have similar attitudes and values, and when they perceive their relationship as fair and equitable. Lesbian relationships tend to decline in satisfaction over time at about the same rate as those of heterosexual married people (Clarke et al., 2010; Kurdek, 2007; Peplau & Fingerhut, 2007). In one recent study of 75 lesbian couples in the United States and Canada, both partners in each couple took part in an Internet survey that measured personality factors, perceptions of equality, and relationship satisfaction (Horne & Biss, 2009). When partners perceived their relationship to be unequal, their anxiety about it, particularly among those whose attachment was insecure, led to lower relationship satisfaction. These results reinforce a conclusion drawn from earlier research: Equality is very important to lesbian partners.

External pressures affect relationships, too. Women who love women have to cope with prejudice and discrimination. Parents and other family members may reject or disown a lesbian daughter, remove her from a will, refuse to acknowledge the partner or the relationship, exclude the couple from family gatherings, or encourage them to break up. One important factor in relationship satisfaction for lesbians is having a good social support network. Receiving social support from friends and family is related to individual psychological adjustment as well as happiness in the relationship for both lesbian and gay couples (Berger, 1990; Kurdek, 1988). This suggests that gay activists are right in encouraging lesbians to come out to friends and family despite the risk of rejection. However, the evidence is mixed. Although some studies show that women who are out to significant others in their lives (family, friends, and employers) report more satisfaction with their partners, others find that relationship satisfaction is unrelated to disclosure about being a lesbian (Jordan & Deluty, 2000; Beals & Peplau, 2001).

Cohabiting Couples

Today many heterosexual couples choose to live together without being legally married. Sociologists give this arrangement the unromantic name *cohabitation.* Couples who do it usually call it living together—not a very precise term since roommates or parents and children can be said to live together, too. The absence of a suitable everyday term is one clue that cohabitation, though widespread, is not yet an institution in society. Another clue is that no national statistics are kept on cohabitation, whereas marriage and divorce statistics are part of public records (Teachman et al., 2006).

Who Cohabits and Why?

The rise in cohabitation is one of the most striking social changes of the past fifty years. Today, about half of all first marriages in the United States are preceded by living together. Although people are marrying later, they are not waiting for marriage to create a household. Increasingly, cohabitors are having children together as well (Teachman et al., 2006). Cohabitation is becoming not just a prelude to marriage but a substitute for it.

People choose to cohabit for a variety of reasons (Noller, 2006). For some, it is a trial period or a prelude to marriage, "Let's see if we're compatible." Others cohabit more as a matter of convenience than deep commitment; it's easier for two to pay the rent and cover the bills. A longitudinal study of nearly 200 married couples assessed the commitment and quality of their relationships first when they were dating, then yearly until they'd been married for an average of 7 years. The results showed that, overall, the women were more committed to the marriage than the men were. And there were interesting differences among the men: When the couple had cohabitated before becoming engaged, the man was less committed and dedicated to his wife than those who had cohabited only after getting engaged or not at all (Rhoades et al., 2006). In this study, commitment was measured in terms of working as a team, desire for a long-term future together, giving the partner high priority, and willingness to make sacrifices for the partner and the relationship. This study suggests that when a couple lives together before being engaged, a discrepancy between his and her commitment exists, and this discrepancy may persist even after years of marriage.

People who choose cohabitation have less education and lower incomes than comparable non-cohabitors (Teachman et al., 2006). They tend to be liberal in attitudes about gender roles. They are more sexually experienced and sexually active than non-cohabiters, and their relationships are less likely than married relationships to be monogamous. In a national sample of more than 1,200 women aged 20 to 37, the cohabiters were 5 times more likely than the married women to have sex with someone other than their partner—about 1 in 5 had sex with someone else while cohabiting. This was true for all ethnic groups studied (Forste & Tanfer, 1996).

As with married couples, issues of money, power, and the division of labor inside and outside the home can be sources of conflict. Cohabiting couples usually have a division of labor similar to modern marriage. They almost always expect that both partners will work outside the home. However, as with most married couples, women do more housework than men. In general, cohabiting relationships are lower in quality than marital ones, with more disagreements, fights and violence, and less perceived fairness and happiness. More than half of all cohabiting relationships break up within 2 years, and 9 out of 10 end within 5 years (Noller, 2006).

Does Living Together Affect Later Marriage?

Cohabiting couples may experience an unplanned pregnancy, which brings up the question of whether to get married (Sassler et al., 2009). Cohabitation is associated with premarital pregnancy among all ethnic groups and the likelihood of pregnancy during cohabitation is greater for Latina than White or African American women. Does pregnancy push cohabiters toward marriage? This, too, depends on the couple's ethnic group and on the quality of their relationship. One study showed that White women who got pregnant while cohabiting were likely to marry; there was no effect for African American women; and for Puerto Rican women, pregnancy lowered the odds of marrying before the birth of the child (Manning & Landale, 1996). A study that relied on in-depth interviews with 30 couples reported that those who believed they had a future together said they would be upset and dismayed over a pregnancy but would bear the child. A smaller group of couples said they would terminate the pregnancy. Other couples could not agree on what they would do (Sassler et al., 2009). In an interview study, cohabitors with children often said that they stayed together because it is a practical way to co-parent and share expenses, but becoming parents did not increase their commitment to each other or the relationship (Reed, 2006).

Is cohabitation related to later marital satisfaction? It would seem that if people use living together as a trial marriage, those who do go on to marry should be better adjusted and less likely to divorce. However, many studies have shown that former cohabitants are *more* likely to divorce (Noller, 2006; Teachman et al., 2006). There are ethnic and racial differences, too. Living together before marriage predicted later divorce in a U.S. national survey sample, but only for White women, not for African American or Mexican American women. (Phillips & Sweeney, 2005). Of course, a higher divorce rate for people who had previously cohabited is not necessarily an indication that cohabitation is a mistake. Because women who cohabit (and their partners) are more unconventional, independent, and autonomous than those who do not, they may be less likely to make a commitment and more likely to leave a marriage that does not meet their expectations (Rhoades et al., 2006; Teachman et al., 2006).

Ending the Commitment: Separation and Divorce

The United States has the highest divorce rate of any industrialized nation, a rate that has only recently leveled off after rising more or less steadily for over a century. Between 40 percent and 50 percent of American marriages end within 15 years (see Figure 8.4). The U.S. Census Bureau predicts that the U.S. divorce rate will continue to be among the world's highest. Using past trends to predict the future, statisticians estimate that today's new marriages will have a 44 percent chance of ending in divorce. Black women are considerably more likely than White women to end a marriage through divorce or prolonged separation, and Hispanic women less likely. Other countries have experienced similar increases in divorce rate, though none as extreme as the United States (McKelvey & McKenry, 2000; Orbuch & Brown, 2006; Teachman et al., 2006).

There is a large amount of research on divorce. In contrast, few studies have examined the process or consequences when a relationship ends without a formal divorce (Teachman et al., 2006). This can happen in several ways. Some spouses simply desert or abandon their families, leaving them without a division of assets or child support. Little is known about how these families fare. In others, marital partners separate permanently but do not get a divorce (McKelvey & McKenry, 2000). When relationships between cohabiting men and women or lesbian couples end, breakups occur without legal divorce. In one of the few studies that compared gay, lesbian, and heterosexual individuals who had broken up with a partner, the respondents from each group gave similar reasons and reported similar levels of distress (Kurdek, 1997). There is a need for more research on how non-marital relationships end. But for now, I will focus on heterosexual married couples that agree to divorce.

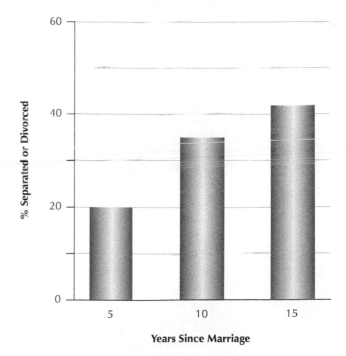

FIGURE 8.4   In the United States a large proportion of first marriages end in divorce within 15 years.

Source: First marriage dissolution, divorce, and remarriage: United States. (2001). National Center for Health Statistics.

What Are the Causes and Consequences of Divorce?

At the societal level, several factors have been correlated with the rising divorce rates. Divorce rates rise along with women's participation in the paid workforce, both in the United States and in many other countries. Wives' paid employment is not usually a direct cause of divorce. Rather, it seems that when women don't need a husband's income to survive, they are less likely to stay in unsatisfactory marriages (Teachman et al., 2006). Age at first marriage is also highly correlated with divorce: The younger the man and woman are when they marry, the more likely they are to divorce (Bramlet & Mosher, 2001). Other factors related to the rising divorce rate are changes in laws and attitudes; divorce is no longer the disgrace it once was and no-fault laws make it easier.

At the personal level, women and men tend to give somewhat different reasons for the break up of their marriages. In a study based on a national random sample of divorced people, women were more likely than men to mention their partner's infidelity, substance abuse, and mental or physical abuse as reasons for their divorce. Men were more likely to mention poor communication or say that they did not know the cause of the divorce. Other causes, such as incompatibility, were cited equally often by women and men (Amato & Previti, 2003). (See Table 8.1.)

Events and feelings early in a marriage may predict later divorce. In one recent study, those who were disillusioned within the first 2 years (as reflected in decreased love and affection and increased ambivalence) were more likely to end up divorced several years later (Huston et al., 2001). Substance abuse by either partner is an

TABLE 8.1　Perceived Causes of Divorce: Women's and Men's Accounts

Cause	Women (%)	Men (%)
Infidelity	25	16
Incompatible	19	20
Drinking or drug use	14	5
Grew apart	10	9
Personality problems	8	10
Lack of communication	6	13
Physical or mental abuse	9	0
Loss of love	3	7
Not meeting family obligations	5	1
Employment problems	4	3
Don't know	0	9
Unhappy in marriage	3	3

Source: Amato, P. R., & Previti, D. (2003). People's reasons for divorcing: Gender, social class, the life course, and adjustment. *Journal of Family Issues, 24*, 602–626, from Table 3 (p. 615). Copyright © 2003 by SAGE Publications, Inc. Reprinted by permission of SAGE Publications. Percentages have been rounded to nearest whole number.

important predictor of divorce in people who marry young (Collins et al., 2006), as shown in a longitudinal study of more than 450 people who were married by the age of 23. Those who used alcohol or marijuana to excess were more likely to be divorced by the age of 29.

Whatever the reasons for divorce, it has serious and long-lasting consequences for women. I will consider three types of consequences, each intertwined with the others in its effects: psychological adjustment, economic effects, and responsibility for children.

How Do People Psychologically Adjust to Divorce?

A considerable number of divorcing women (from 17 percent to 33 percent in different samples) describe their divorces as causing little or no psychological disturbance or pain. These women view their divorces as the end of a stressful or unbearable situation and the beginning of increased freedom. In a study of remarried couples who were asked to describe the effects of their earlier divorce, one woman reported that it was "a total weight lifted off my shoulders. . . . no tears were shed" and another said, "I breathed a sigh of relief because it had been so bad for so long" (Brimhall et al., 2008). For most women, however, adjustment to divorce includes feelings of anger, helplessness, and ambivalence, especially if the woman did not initiate the divorce; in an interview study, these women felt abandoned and vulnerable (Sakraida, 2005). Stress during divorce is related to a variety of physical health problems. (As with all correlational research, it is not possible to determine cause and effect in these studies.) Compared with married people, divorced people of both sexes have higher rates of illness, death, alcoholism, and serious accidents.

In general, the adjustment to divorce seems to be more difficult for men than women. Although both divorced men and women are more likely to commit suicide than their married counterparts, divorced men are 50 percent more likely to do so than divorced women. They are also more likely to show serious psychological disturbances (Price & McKenry, 1988). Women appear to be better at building and maintaining networks of close friends and family during and following divorce (Gerstel, 1988), and men may miss their partner's caretaking more (see Figure 8.5). However, women and men are similar in their responses to divorce in many other ways (Gove & Shin, 1989).

Adjustment to divorce depends on social support. A meta-analysis of 21 studies confirmed that having good friends and being part of a supportive network, such as a church or community group, help both women and men adjust to divorce (Krumrei et al., 2007). Post-divorce coping varies for different groups of women. In a study using a national sample of divorced or separated women with at least one child, Black women felt more positive about their personal ability to master their lives and their economic situation (McKelvey & McKenry, 2000). Three factors have been shown to help African American women adjust to divorce better than White women: they are more likely to live in multigenerational households, to have strong ties to their parents, and to have support from their church and their friends (Orbuch & Brown, 2006).

"This is goodbye—there are one thousand, eight hundred, and twenty-five meals for you in the freezer."

FIGURE 8.5

Source: © Barbara Smaller/The New Yorker Collection/www.cartoonbank.com

Divorce is usually discussed as a personal and social tragedy. But divorce may be an important way that women counter marital inequality, a way out of an oppressive situation (Rice, 1994). In a study of successful egalitarian marriages, almost half were not first marriages and most of the women said they had left their first marriage because of inequitable treatment (Schwartz, 1994). Research on remarried people shows that they interact with their partners in more egalitarian ways; for example, wives have more control over finances and share decision-making more with their husbands than in their first marriages (Ganong et al, 2006). Most research on divorce has assessed negative consequences. Few researchers have asked about positive ones, but when they do, many people report that their self-esteem increased, their enjoyment of life grew, their careers benefited, and they enjoyed the freedom and independence that followed the end of a troubled relationship (Tashiro et al., 2006). Divorce is a painful family transformation but also a potential opportunity for growth and change (Stewart et al., 1997).

What Are the Economic Effects of Divorce?

Divorce in the United States is an economic disaster for women. Research from the 1960s to the present has conclusively shown that the economic status of men improves upon divorce, while the economic status of women deteriorates (Sayer, 2006). The decline is greater for Black women than for White women. And no-fault divorce laws, designed to ensure equitable division of assets, have actually made the situation worse. As one divorce expert noted, the popular discourse is that relationships are based on romantic love and commitment, not "base financial motives." But marriage and divorce are also "economic arrangements with economic consequences" (Sayer, 2006, p. 385).

Why do women lose out financially with divorce? There are several reasons but structural factors are probably more important than individual ones (Sayer, 2006). The majority of state property laws assume that property belongs to the spouse who earned it. Since husbands usually have had greater earning power during the marriage, these laws result in men being awarded more of the couple's assets. The economic value of the wife's unpaid labor may not be considered. In other states, attempts to make divorce fairer for women have led to laws that order equal division of property. However, most divorcing couples (especially younger ones) have very little in the way of valuable property—perhaps a car (complete with loan payments), household furnishings, and a modest bank account, offset by credit card debt. Fewer than half have equity in a house. The biggest asset for the large majority of couples is the husband's earning power, at the time of the divorce and in the future.

As discussed earlier, the husband's career usually takes priority in both single-earner and dual-earner marriages. Couples invest their time, money, and energy in his advancement; frequently the wife will postpone her education or career plans in order to put him through school, and she will do the unpaid work at home that allows him to concentrate on his paid job. Courts have been slow to recognize that the benefits husbands gain from traditional and modern marriage patterns translate into economic advantages upon divorce. Only about 15 percent of all divorced women in the United States are awarded spousal support. Most awards are for a period of about 2 years; and in the past, less than half of the men ordered to provide such support have actually complied (Faludi, 1991; Price & McKenry, 1988).

Who Is Responsible for the Children?

Two-thirds of divorces involve children. More than half of all children in the United States will experience their parents' divorce before the age of 18, and they will then spend an average of about 5 years in a single-parent home, the great majority with their mothers (Arendell, 1997). The presence of children is an important factor in women's adjustment to divorce. The benefit of awarding custody to women is that most divorced women stay connected with their children and receive the emotional rewards of parenting more than most divorced men do. However, current custody arrangements also have costs for women. Being a single parent is not easy. The single mother may feel overwhelmed with responsibility, guilty at having separated the children from their father, and under pressure to be a supermom.

The lack of a husband's income is a big handicap for divorced women and their children. About 60 percent of divorced mothers with custody of their children are awarded child support. However, the average amount is only about $5,600 a year. Child support payments clearly do not cover the actual costs of bringing up a child. And few fathers provide extra help voluntarily. In recent studies, the majority of fathers no longer living with their families provided *no* monetary help with children's clothes, vacations, or uninsured medical expenses, and only one-third included their children on their health care coverage (Sayer, 2006).

Moreover, the majority of women entitled to child support do not receive it. Several national studies from the 1970s to the 1990s showed that only 25 percent to 50 percent of men ordered to pay child support did so, whether voluntarily or through having their wages garnished by the courts. Many who complied paid less than the designated amount; and one-fourth to one-third of fathers never made a single payment despite court orders. The most recently published studies show that this pattern continues. For example, in 2007, 47 percent of all mothers who were awarded child support received it; another 30 percent received some but not all of the funds awarded; and 23 percent received nothing at all. Black women are half as likely as White women to receive support, and the poorest, least educated women are the least likely of all (Grall, 2009). If the parents have been cohabiting but have not been formally married, the mother's chances of getting a child support award and actually getting any of the funds are even lower (Sayer, 2006).

Divorced women and their children must adjust to a lower standard of living. A single mother-household's per capita income declines from 20 percent to 44 percent, and its standard of living declines by about 30 percent to 40 percent on average (Sayer, 2006). Divorced women and their children often drop to a lower socioeconomic class, and this is particularly true for African American women (Orbuch & Brown, 2006). More than 25 percent of divorced women fall into poverty for some time within 5 years of divorce. For many women with children, the financial hardship that comes with divorce becomes the central focus of their lives, dictating where they can live, determining whether they and their children can afford health care or a college education, and affecting their psychological well-being (Sayer, 2006).

Remarriage

Most people who get divorced marry again—in the United States, about 85 percent do. The median time between a first divorce and remarriage is about 3 years (Ganong et al., 2006). Men are more likely to remarry than women, and White women more likely than Black or Hispanic women. In the United States, about half of all marriages involve at least one partner who was previously divorced (Ganong & Coleman, 2000). A cynic might say that remarriages represent a triumph of belief over experience; most people do not question the institution of marriage after they have been divorced. Rather, they believe that they chose the wrong partner last time and now know how to choose the right one. The rate of third (and fourth, and fifth . . .) marriages continues to increase, and these now make up more than

10 percent of the U.S. total. Apparently, people are determined to keep trying until they get it right (Ganong et al., 2006).

Are second marriages more successful? In general, the level of satisfaction in second marriages is about the same as in first marriages; as in first marriages, husbands are more satisfied than their wives (Ihinger-Tallman & Pasley, 1987). Decision making may be more equal than in first marriages, but remarried women still do more housework than their partners, and more child care, too, regardless of whether they are the mother or the stepmother of the children in the family (Ganong & Coleman, 2000; Ganong et al., 2006). Second marriages are even more likely to end in divorce than first marriages (Ganong & Coleman, 2000). Well over half of women who enter a second marriage later experience a second divorce.

The complex family structures and dynamics of second marriages ("his," "her," and "their" children, stepparents, ex-spouses, in-laws, and ex-in-laws) may be a source of stress. (See Figure 8.6.) Financial problems may be increased by lack of support payments from former husbands and many families have conflicts over how to allocate money to various household members (Ganong et al., 2006). (Who should pay Tiffany's college tuition—mother, father, or stepparent?) Second marriages may also be less stable because, once having violated the ideal of lifelong marriage, people are even less inclined to stay in unsatisfying relationships.

Many blended families develop strength and resilience, but there is little research on how they do it. In a recent small-scale study conducted among White South Africans, a parent and teenage child from each of 38 blended families were surveyed and asked an open-ended question about what had helped the family through stressful times (Greeff & Du Toit, 2009). Among the factors that correlated with good family adjustment were positive family relationships, communication,

FIGURE 8.6   Blended families may lead complicated lives.

mutual support among family members, a reliance on spirituality and religion, and activities that helped the family spend time together. This study cannot separate cause and effect; there is much more to learn about what makes blended families healthy for parents and children.

Making a Difference

To close this chapter, I consider two important areas where equality has not yet been achieved for relationship partners. First, same-sex relationships are not yet accorded the same respect and rights as heterosexual relationships. Resistance to same-sex marriages is upheld by heterosexist social structures as well as individual attitudes. Second, women in relationships with men often have less power than their partners, even when both partners believe in equality. Equality in heterosexual marriages is an individual-level and interactional-level problem as well as a sociostructural one.

The Right to Marry: Equality for Lesbian and Gay Couples

Marriage is both a personal commitment by two individuals and a legal institution that affects many aspects of life. LGBTQ activists have worked to raise awareness of the inequities that occur when LGBTQ couples are denied access to the rights that heterosexual couples have through marriage. (See Figure 8.7.) These rights are not trivial. The General Accounting Office, a U.S. government agency, estimates that marriage affects 1,138 federal rights including such basics as taxes and Social Security benefits.

FIGURE 8.7 Activists demonstrate for the right to gay and lesbian marriage.

Most LGBTQ individuals want the right to marry. In the United States, 74 percent of lesbians and gay men in a national survey said that they would like to legally marry someday if they could (Peplau & Fingerhut, 2007). And 95 percent of LGBTQ people in a poll conducted in 27 countries supported the right to marry (Harding & Peel, 2006). When surveyed about their reasons for wanting marriage rights, LGBTQ people emphasize basic fairness: The right to marry would mean that LGBTQs were no longer being treated like second-class citizens. They also point out that marriage has many positive aspects: It creates a structure that makes it easier to stay together during hard times, it provides practical benefits, and it helps couples feel closer and more committed to each other. Many believe that legalizing marriage would reduce prejudice against LGBTQ people in the long run (Peplau & Fingerhut, 2007).

However, LGBTQ individuals are not unanimously agreed that same-sex marriage is the best goal for LGBTQ activism. Some have argued that marriage is a deeply flawed patriarchal institution, and that LGBTQ people can create better alternatives within their own communities. Others reject the right of the government to legalize any relationships. These are minority views within the LGBTQ community, but they reflect the diversity of opinion on the issue. To learn more about the diversity of feminist views on both gay and heterosexual marriage, see the resources at the end of this chapter.

Among the heterosexual majority, societal views about LGBTQ relationships are changing fast, toward more acceptance. Some major religious groups now perform same-sex weddings. More and more employers are providing benefits such as health insurance coverage to same-sex partners (Peplau & Fingerhut, 2007). Gay, lesbian, and transgender people, once invisible, are now regularly featured in the media, and in increasingly positive ways. Efforts to equalize access to marriage still are strongly opposed and resisted, and the American public is divided on the issue. In one recent poll, a small majority (about 53 percent) was opposed to same-sex marriage, 36 percent were in favor, and 11 percent were undecided. However, the opposition is largely made up of older citizens; younger ones have more liberal views on this issue. And, although they may resist applying the symbolic and value-laden concept of marriage to LGBTQ couples, this does not mean that the American public is opposed to lesbian and gay relationships. A majority of Americans polled are in favor of civil unions that would give LGBTQ couples most of the same rights as heterosexual married couples (Peplau & Fingerhut, 2007).

In 1996, President Bill Clinton signed a bill termed the Defense of Marriage Act (though it is not clear why marriage needed defending, since LGBTQ people wanted to join the club, not attack it). This act defined marriage for the first time as a legal union between one man and one woman for all purposes of the federal government, thus denying LGBTQ individuals access to equality under federal law. Since then, several state governments have passed similar laws, with the result that rights governed by state law are also being denied to more LGBTQ people. As I write this book, only five U.S. states (Massachusetts, Iowa, New Hampshire, Vermont, and Connecticut, plus Washington DC) permit same-sex couples to marry. Belgium, Canada, The Netherlands, Norway, South Africa, Spain, and Sweden recognize same-sex marriages, and many more countries allow civil unions and other forms of officially recognized domestic partnerships (Clarke et al., 2010). By the time you read this book, the situation will probably have changed, perhaps in more than one direction. One U.S. state, California, legalized same-sex marriage in June of 2008, banned it again in November 2008, and is now engaged in a U.S. District Court case about whether the ban is unconstitutional. This case may reach the U.S. Supreme Court, with as yet unknown consequences.

A basic principle of feminist theory is that discrimination and oppression of all kinds are linked and should be resisted. The prejudice underlying opposition to same-sex marriage, as well as other forms of prejudice and discrimination against LGBTQ people, can be challenged. It is important that such challenges come from within the LGBTQ community and also from people who do not identify as LGBTQ but who care about equal rights for all. For more on how you can support LGBTQ couples' right to marry, see the Web sites and resources at the end of this chapter.

True Partnership: Equality in Heterosexual Marriage

Egalitarian marriage may be emerging as a life pattern of the future. But equality in marriage or long-term cohabitation is unlikely to happen just by wanting it. How many times have you heard people express the belief that "If two people love each other enough, their marriage will work"? This belief is part of a romantic ideology and a variation of "love conquers all." A related belief is that if the husband does not *intend* to oppress or dominate the wife, oppression and domination will not occur. Happy marriage, then, should be mainly (or entirely) a matter of picking the right person. One major conclusion that can be drawn from the research reviewed in this chapter is that power differentials between husbands and wives are *not* solely the result of individual differences. Rather, the *institution* of marriage has been organized around gender inequality. Even couples who try very hard to change their own behavior have problems achieving gender balance in marriage.

To have an egalitarian marriage, both wife and husband must be willing to integrate their work and family responsibilities despite social pressures to conform to more traditional roles. Women who value their work outside the home and set limits on the sacrifices they make for husbands and children may be perceived as cold, unfeminine, and selfish; men who do housework and child care and set limits on their career involvement may be perceived as weak and unmasculine. (One of my children once *begged* my husband not to wear an apron in front of the child's friends!) Fortunately attitudes toward the work and family roles of women and men have changed a great deal in the past 30 years and continue to become more flexible (Amato et al., 2007).

Women may have to lead the way to more egalitarian relationships because men are unlikely to fight a status quo that gives them many benefits. However, only when women perceive gender roles in relationships as unequal and unjust can they begin to change them. To recognize their position as unjust, women must be aware that other possibilities exist, must want such possibilities for themselves, must believe they are entitled to them, and must not feel personally to blame for not having them.

Women who are assertive in asking for equal sharing of housework and child care are more likely to get what they want. In a study of 81 married women with children, participants provided information about their and their husbands' work hours, incomes, and division of labor in the home. Also, they were interviewed twice over a 2-month period and asked to tell the story of the last time they'd discussed whether the husband should help more with housework or child care (Mannino & Deutsch, 2007). As predicted, power in marriage was related to the usual factors: the couple's gender ideology, their relative earnings, and so forth. But the woman's attempts to instigate change were important, too. At the second interview, the women who had tried to negotiate a fairer marriage had achieved change by assertively discussing their feelings and wishes with their husbands. The researchers concluded that change is most likely to happen when women are aware of inequality and willing to persist in discussing it with their husbands. In other studies with male participants, husbands often report that they had to first become aware of their gender entitlement before they could see the inequality and try to change: "When we first got married I thought I could make the decisions on money. But, I quickly learned we need to talk things over," one said, and another reported that he now reminds himself to do a fair share because "This is my house, these are my dishes, this is my baby just as much as hers" (Knudson-Martin & Mahoney, 2005, p. 243).

What social factors give women more negotiating power in relationships with men? If society allows more flexible commitments to paid work by both women and men, there will be less likelihood that the man's job or career will take precedence. (The interaction of work and family life will be discussed further in Chapter 10.) Economic power is a key factor. The single biggest obstacle to egalitarian marriage and cohabiting relationships is men's greater earning power, which steers couples into investing in his career and leaving the work at home to her. If our society invested resources in guaranteeing gender-equal pay, marriage and other committed relationships would quickly change in the direction of equality.

As the number of couples who are consciously trying to build egalitarian relationships increases, it should be easier for them to find each other and build supportive networks. Nontraditional arrangements are coming to be seen as legitimate, normal, and even routine (Knudson-Martin & Mahoney, 2005). Similar needs can be met for lesbian and gay couples by being part of a LGBTQ community, and perhaps in the future, by seeing their unions legitimized and accepted.

The movement toward egalitarian relationships will bring benefits for both women and men. Relieved of some of the economic burdens of traditional marriage, men will be freer to become involved with their children's growth and development. Women will experience better psychological adjustment. For both men and women, equality is linked to more satisfying relationships and greater intimacy. Equality in committed long-term relationships offers both women and men a chance to become more fully human.

Exploring Further

Change (www.change.org) is designed to provide information about a broad range of social movements, including women's rights, gay rights, and the environment. Online petitions at the Web site are a quick and easy way to get involved in activism for equal rights.

Feminism & Psychology: Special Issues on Marriage.

This noted journal asked feminist women and men to write about their views on LGBTQ and heterosexual marriage. The result is a superb collection of research articles, personal observations, and critical commentaries that spans three issues of the journal:

Volume 13, 4, November 2003.

Volume 14, 1, February, 2004.

Volume 14, 2, May, 2004.

Lambda Legal (www.lambdalegal.org) is a national organization committed to achieving full recognition of the civil rights of lesbians, gay men, bisexuals, transgender people, and those with HIV through education, public policy work, and challenges to discriminatory laws.

CHAPTER 9

Mothering

❧

The day my husband and I took our newborn son home from the hospital I sat on my bed with him in my arms. All of a sudden, I realized I was in love. It is an indescribable love, comparable to nothing else in life. I never would have believed it before becoming a parent (Deutsch, 1999, p. 228).

*M*otherhood is one of the most transforming events of a woman's life. It may seem the most natural thing in the world, a biological privilege accorded only to women. However, those aspects of society that seem most natural often are the ones most in need of critical examination. Like marriage, motherhood is an institution. Its meaning goes beyond the biological process of reproduction, encompassing many customs, beliefs, attitudes, norms, and laws. Like other institutions, it also has a powerful symbolic component. Yet women who become mothers are individuals. "Mother is a role; women are human beings" (Bernard, 1974, p. 7).

Motherhood raises troubling questions for feminist analysis. Liberal feminists have stressed that the institution of motherhood has been used to exclude women from public life, and they have shown how the myths and mystique of motherhood keep women in their place. Some radical and cultural feminists, on the other hand, have pointed out that motherhood is a woman-centered model of how people can be connected and caring (McMahon, 1995).

In this chapter, I will use a variety of feminist perspectives to address questions about mothering. What are the images and scripts that define mothers and motherhood? How do women go about choosing whether to have children, and to what extent are they allowed to choose? How does the transition to motherhood change women? What are women's experiences of birth and mothering? Finally, should motherhood be redefined?

Images of Mothers and Motherhood

Western society has strong beliefs about motherhood. The ideology of motherhood has been termed the ***motherhood mystique.*** It includes the following myths:

1. Motherhood is the ultimate fulfillment of a woman. It is a natural and necessary experience for all women. Those who do not want to mother are psychologically disturbed and those who want to but cannot are fundamentally deprived.
2. Women are instinctively good at caregiving and should be responsible for infants, children, elderly parents, home, and their husband. Good mothers enjoy this kind of work; a woman who doesn't is maladjusted or poorly organized.
3. A mother has infinite patience and the willingness to sacrifice herself to her children. If she does not put her own needs last, she is an inadequate mother.
4. A woman's intense, full-time devotion to mothering is best for her children. Women who work are inferior mothers (Hequembourg, 2007; Hoffnung, 1989; Johnston-Robledo, 2000).

Although these beliefs may seem outdated, the motherhood mystique lives on. It persists because it has important functions for the patriarchal status quo. Women are encouraged to sacrifice other parts of their lives for motherhood, which creates economic dependence on men and is used to justify women's lower status and pay at work. "The social order that elevates men over women is legitimated by women's devotion to child care, since it takes them out of the running for top-level jobs and political positions and defuses their consciousness of oppression" (Lorber, 1993, p. 170). The mystique may persist also because it is the one area in which Western society values connectedness and caring over individual achievement. Groups that have the most power economically and politically benefit by glorifying motherhood and defining it in ways that constrict and burden women.

The Decision to Have a Child

Having a child profoundly changes a woman's life. The emotional and economic costs of bringing up children are high. Yet the great majority of women have children.

Why Do Women Choose to Have Children?

There are practical reasons for having children, particularly in traditional societies. Children are necessary as workers (both at home and at jobs), as a path for passing on property and a customary way of life, and sometimes as a form of personal immortality. In postcolonial and underdeveloped societies, many children are lost to disease and malnutrition. Five or more children may have to be conceived for two to live to adulthood; these children may provide the only economic support for their parents' old age.

In industrialized societies, children have little economic value—in fact, they are a big economic liability—and psychological reasons for having children are given more weight. One traditional explanation for childbearing is the existence of a "maternal instinct." If wanting children is instinctive for women, why are so many powerful socialization forces directed at instilling this "instinct" in girls at a young age? (For example, recall the girl-toys discussed in Chapter 6.) Why have abortion and infanticide been features of so many human societies throughout history? Science historian Maria Vicedo-Castello (2005) examined a century of scientific theories and research about the maternal instinct and concluded that the search for it has largely been an attempt to justify traditional gender roles. These pseudo-scientific theories asserted that women's reproductive functions justify limiting their opportunities and roles. If scientists could prove that women are all alike— "born to love" rather than socialized to care for children—it would seem normal and natural to confine women to hearth and home. However, scientists have never been able to provide convincing evidence for a maternal instinct.

Rather than being instinctive, mothering is learned. Virtually all studies of single fathers show that when men are in charge of child care, they develop skills very much like those of women. In addition, they come to see themselves as nurturing, compassionate, and sensitive to the needs of others, all stereotypically feminine traits (Risman, 1998). Biological theories assume that women are programmed to care for children; socialization theories assume that women are more nurturing because of early learning. However, it is just as likely that a nurturing personality is created by being put into a nurturing role as an adult. The *process* of mothering is a kind of doing gender that produces—not surprisingly—people who can nurture others.

There is considerable social pressure on women to have children, pressure that has been called the **motherhood mandate** (Russo, 1979) (see Figure 9.1). In surveys and other kinds of research, Americans have long shown a strong bias against childlessness and one-child families (Baruch et al., 1983; Park, 2005). Deliberately choosing not to have children has been viewed as a sign of maladjustment in women, who were judged less mature, less socially desirable, and more selfish and materialistic than those who chose motherhood. And one child is not enough. Stereotypes have portrayed

"*So, have you two been doing anything reproductive?*"

FIGURE 9.1

Source: © Marisa Acocella Marchetto/The New Yorker Collection/www.cartoonbank.com

the only child as socially inadequate, self-centered, unhappy, and unlikable. (There is no evidence that only children actually are maladjusted.) Even in the 1990s, college students judged that women who were childless by choice were less fulfilled and more likely to be unhappy in later life (Mueller & Yoder, 1997).

Has the motherhood mandate decreased because of feminism? A recent study of college students' attitudes showed little negative bias toward hypothetical couples who were childless due to choice or to infertility, although couples who were temporarily childless were rated more positively than those who were permanently so (Koropeckyj-Cox et al., 2007). This suggests that, at least among college students, attitudes toward parenthood have become more flexible. When I ask my students, "Why have children?", they provide a long list of reasons: the desire to experience pregnancy and birth, to participate in the growth of another human being, to please a husband, to strengthen a relationship, to become an adult, to be needed and loved, and to pass on a family name or one's genes or one's values. Few people mention that the decision to have a child may still be influenced by the motherhood mandate. However, in American society as a whole, parenthood is still expected of women and, to a lesser extent, for men, and childlessness still is deviant (McQuillan et al., 2008). Procreation within marriage is endorsed by all major religions and has been characterized as a developmental stage of adulthood by psychologists, showing that it is still the normative choice.

Childless by Choice or Circumstance?

Fewer than 7 percent of American women remain childless voluntarily. Compared to women with children, these women are more likely to be highly educated, employed in high status occupations, less conventional, and less conservative in gender ideology (Park, 2005). Throughout history, the childless woman has been regarded as a failed woman (Phoenix et al., 1991; Rich, 1976). Given this negative image, why do some women choose not to have children? Reasons include financial considerations, a desire to pursue their education or career, the dangers of childbirth, the possibility of bearing a child with disabilities, concerns about overpopulation, and a belief that they are not personally suited to nurturing and caring for children (Landa, 1990).

In a qualitative study of women and men who chose childlessness, some women reported that their decision had been based on the models of parenting they'd seen. For example, Rose, an Italian American woman in her early 30s, said:

> My mother worked in the home all of her life . . . Not only did she take care of my sisters and I, but she took care of her mother and a sister with Down's syndrome. So her whole life was this caretaking. I guess I looked at that and saw her life and said I don't think I want that for myself . . . She doesn't have a life. Her children are her life . . . It's just . . . I don't know . . . I guess I want something *different* for my life (Park, 2005, pp. 387–388).

Other people talked about need for work and leisure time. Some women said they lacked a "maternal instinct" or just were not interested in children. As one put it, she did not dislike children but did not have the personality for taking care of them. "They're fine if they belong to somebody else and I can leave." Men were more likely to cite the expense and personal sacrifices required to raise children (Park, 2005).

In this study, it was clear that women sometimes agonized over their decision, even questioning whether they were normal:

> I do wonder what is not quite right with me that I have *no desire whatsoever* to have a child. Somehow that doesn't seem quite right. Because, you know, the persistence of the species *demands* that we procreate, to want children. And I have *nothing* there (p. 394).

Regardless of when the decision is made, it is common for women to have moments of doubt about it throughout their fertile years. The path of the childless woman has no clear map, and "each woman seems to be traveling alone . . . unaware that others are on the same road ahead and behind her" (Morell, 2000, p. 321).

Of course, childlessness is not always a matter of choice. In the United States, about one woman in six experiences fertility problems, and only about half who seek medical treatment are able to conceive. Women who want to but cannot bear children may be stigmatized, leading to feelings of guilt and failure:

His parents wouldn't leave me alone. They felt I wasn't trying. I was just feeling a failure—failure as a woman because you know this is what you are here for and I actually felt as though I had failed my husband because I wasn't giving him an heir to the throne (Ulrich & Weatherall, 2000, p. 332).

Accepting childlessness is a gradual process. In a study of women who had given up trying to conceive a child after years of treatment, the participants reported coming to a point where they realized that further efforts were futile. Exhausted and worn out, they felt profound grief and emptiness. At the same time, however, they felt relief at being out of the "medical machinery" and recognized an opportunity to take back their lives, moving on to other goals (Daniluk, 1996).

Does not having children (by choice or by chance) lead to unhappiness? As discussed in Chapter 8, marital satisfaction drops with the birth of the first child and may not return to its original level until children leave home. In a classic study of American women at midlife, there was no relationship between whether a woman had children and her psychological well-being (Baruch et al., 1983). The women in this study grew up in an era when the motherhood mandate was in full force, yet their well-being at midlife did not suffer because of childlessness. More recent studies of elderly people in several countries show that those who never had children had fewer social ties in old age than those who were parents, and were more likely to live alone or in an institution, but they were no less satisfied with their lives (Koropeckyj-Cox & Call, 2007; Park, 2005). These results contradict the belief that having children is necessary for a woman's happiness and fulfillment. Unless motherhood *and* refusal of motherhood are equally respected choices, women are not yet liberated (Morell, 2000).

How Does Society Restrict Women's Choices?

Women's choices about child rearing do not take place in a social vacuum. Most societies regulate women's rights to have—or not have—children. Moreover, practical and economic factors restrict options, especially for poor and minority women. For example, a poor woman may have to choose a birth control method based on its cost rather than its effectiveness.

Feminists advocate **reproductive freedom** for all women, an ideal that has not yet been achieved. This concept includes a range of issues, such as the right to comprehensive and unbiased sex education, access to safe and reliable contraception, an end to forced sterilization and forced birth control for poor and minority women, and access to safe and legal abortion (Baber & Allen, 1992; Bishop, 1989).

At the heart of the concept of reproductive freedom is the idea that all choices about reproduction should be made by the woman herself: It is her body and her right to choose. For this reason, feminist perspectives on reproductive freedom are often termed **pro-choice**. Because reproductive freedom affects every aspect of a woman's life, it has been a goal of every feminist movement throughout history. "Without the ability to determine their reproductive destinies, women will never achieve an equal role in social, economic, and political life and will continue to be politically subordinate to and economically dependent on men" (Roberts, 1998).

Contraception

Accidental pregnancies can be the result of a number of factors: contraceptive failure, lack of contraceptive knowledge or skill, lack of access to contraceptives, failure to use contraception, and unplanned or coerced sexual activity. Moreover, although women are expected to take most of the responsibility for safer sex, psychological factors, lack of power within heterosexual relationships, and sexual scripts make it difficult for many women to take control in this area.

Every form of contraception has drawbacks. Some methods are messy, inconvenient, and interfere with spontaneity (foam, condoms, and diaphragms). Some may cause weight gain, require daily remembering (the pill), or have the potential for long-term side effects. Some offer no protection against STDs. Some are expensive and not covered by insurance.

Problems with using contraceptives effectively are compounded for poor women and women in developing countries. For example, some methods cannot be used by women who are breastfeeding; but in countries without clean water supplies, breastfeeding is the only safe way to nourish an infant. Other contraceptive methods require supervision by medical professionals, which is prohibitive for the majority of the world's women (Owen & Caudill, 1996).

Family Health International's field studies have found that controlling one's fertility is often a mixed blessing in developing countries (Waszak et al., 2001). For example, in Egypt, family planning services are easily accessible and public acceptance is high. However, if a wife does not conceive a child soon after marriage, her husband's family may start looking for a replacement wife, and encourage her husband to divorce her. In Nepal, India, and other Asian countries, women who do not promptly produce sons after marriage are at risk of physical and psychological abuse and neglect. Family planning empowers women but it may also increase their anxiety and psychological distress when they live in contexts of extreme gender inequality. For contraception services to be effective, women's psychological needs and cultural contexts must be taken into account.

Abortion

Of the world's estimated 210 million pregnancies annually, about 40 percent are unplanned. Each year, about 46 million abortions occur worldwide and about 20 million of them are illegal. In the United States, about 1.2 million abortions take place each year, representing about 22 percent of pregnancies. Eighty-eight percent of these abortions take place within the first 12 weeks of pregnancy. Women choosing abortion tend to be young and poor—69 percent live below or near the federal poverty line. Black and Hispanic women are more likely to experience an unintended pregnancy than White women are. Of all abortions, 36 percent are for White women, 25 percent for Hispanic women, 30 percent for Black women, and 9 percent for other ethnic groups (Guttmacher Institute, 2010a).

Abortion has been legal in the United States since 1973, when the Supreme Court, ruling in *Roe v. Wade,* affirmed that women have a right to decide whether to terminate their pregnancies on the basis of the constitutional right to privacy. Abortion, the Court ruled, is a matter to be decided between a woman and her physician. Although the principle of choice was affirmed by this ruling, in practice there are many limitations and legal restrictions on women's choices.

How is abortion restricted? The ***Hyde Amendment,*** in effect since 1976, prohibits the use of federal Medicaid money for abortions except in cases of incest, rape, and when the mother's life is (medically) endangered. Because Medicaid provides health care for low-income families, poor women are the ones affected by this restriction, which forces them to choose between paying for an abortion out of their own inadequate incomes or carrying an unwanted fetus to term. Today, 99 percent of the public money spent on abortions for poor women must come from state (rather than federal) funds. But states may do little to provide for poor women, even those who are victims of incest or rape. Some refuse public funding for poor women and many have enacted restrictive laws directed at all women seeking abortions. These laws may require the consent of a husband or partner, mandatory waiting periods, and "educational" sessions that are designed to discourage women from the abortion option (Solinger, 2005). As of 2010, 37 states require prior notification or consent of parents for minors seeking abortion (Guttmacher Institute, 2010b). Starting in 2014, the new federal health-care program will allow federally subsidized health insurance plans to cover abortions, but only if policyholders pay for coverage separately. Meanwhile, the same old funding restrictions apply and states continue to enforce them ("Abortion Foes Win," 2010). The combination of legal restrictions and lack of public funding are designed to influence women not to get an abortion. Unfortunately for women's right to choose, they are very effective (Adamczyk, 2008).

A nonsurgical abortion procedure, developed in Europe in the 1980s, is ***mifepristone*** (Mifeprex), formerly known as RU-486. This drug, taken as a pill, safely induces abortion early in pregnancy by causing the uterine lining to slough off. Antiabortion groups prevented legalization of RU-486 in the United States for over a decade because they believed that it would make abortions more private and easy to obtain (the patient can go to her doctor's office for the pill, instead of an abortion clinic) and therefore less vulnerable to political pressure (Hyde & DeLamater, 2011). After a long campaign by women's health advocates, Mifeprex was finally, in 2000, made available to American women. But efforts to restrict access to nonsurgical abortion continue. A Federal agency has since refused approval for Plan B, a type of morning-after pill, for use without a prescription on the grounds that it might encourage young women to have unprotected sex (Harris, 2004). Despite political pressure, nonsurgical methods now account for 13 percent of all abortions in the United States (Guttmacher Institute, 2010a).

A different kind of restriction comes from harassment and violence at abortion clinics. The number of doctors who perform abortions has been dropping significantly for the past 3 decades, partly because of stalking, death threats, Internet hit lists, and murders of physicians and clinic staff (Cozzarelli & Major, 1998; Solinger, 2005; Vobejda, 1994). The most recent counts show that 87 percent of all counties in the United States do not have a medical practitioner who provides abortion (Jones et al., 2008). Picketing, bomb threats, and demonstrations affect clients, too. Studies of women who faced antiabortion protesters as they went to a clinic show that the encounters made women feel angry, intruded on, and guilty. However, they had no effect on the women's decision to have an abortion (Cozzarelli & Major, 1998).

In many developing countries in Africa and Asia, safe abortion is unavailable because medical facilities are scarce and laws are restrictive. Under these conditions, wealthy women can still obtain abortions, but poor women may resort to attempting self-induced abortion by taking caustic drugs or inserting objects into the vagina. In these countries, abortion mortality rates are hundreds of times higher than in the United States (Alan Guttmacher Institute, 2002; Cohen, 2007).

Feminists and conservatives agree that preventing unwanted pregnancies is a better option than terminating them through abortion. However, they disagree on how to reach this goal, with conservatives emphasizing abstinence and legal restrictions, and feminists emphasizing sex education, access to safe and legal abortion, and contraceptive options. The good news about abortion rates is that they are dropping steadily, both in the United States and worldwide. The decrease is bigger in developed countries, and particularly in those countries where abortion is legal and readily available. These are the same countries where use of contraception has been increasing. It may seem paradoxical, but restricting women's right to abortion does not reduce it as much as more liberal approaches do. The research suggests that the best way to reduce abortion is to provide women with other options that are in addition to it (Cohen, 2007).

Science, Censorship, and the Information Wars

One argument used in efforts to restrict abortion is that it has harmful physical and/or psychological consequences. In their zeal to abolish abortion, opponents have misrepresented the scientific evidence showing that it is generally safe for women. One example of misinformation is the claim that abortion causes breast cancer, a claim that has no scientific basis. Another example is the claim that women who have an abortion typically suffer guilt, shame, and lasting psychological damage—a *post abortion syndrome* (Major et al., 2009; Russo, 2008). This pseudo-fact has been widely disseminated on the Web by abortion opponents. Although psychology cannot resolve moral differences of opinion about abortion, empirical research can answer questions of the relationship between abortion and psychological well-being. Let's look at the evidence for and against "post abortion syndrome."

To determine the effects of abortion on women's mental health, the American Psychological Association sponsored and published several studies of the scientific research. These research reviews established that the legal termination of an unwanted pregnancy does *not* have negative effects on most women, and is no riskier to mental health than carrying an unwanted pregnancy to term (Major et al., 2009). Measurements of psychological distress usually drop immediately following the abortion and remain low in follow-up assessments. When a woman freely chooses a legal abortion, the typical emotion that follows is relief. In fact, abortion may be a milestone for a woman in taking control over her own life (Travis & Compton, 2001). The majority of women remain satisfied with the decision they made even years later (Major et al., 2009).

This does not mean that women are always perfectly well-adjusted after an abortion. In different studies, between 0.5 percent and 15 percent of abortion clients have experienced psychological problems that lasted from 1 week to 10 years following the abortion. The most important factor in a woman's adjustment after abortion is her adjustment prior to the abortion (Major et al., 2009; Russo, 2008). A history of mental health problems prior to the unwanted pregnancy greatly increases the chances that a woman will have mental health problems after an abortion (or, for that matter, after giving birth). Women obtaining abortions have a much higher average rate of past physical, sexual, and emotional abuse than other women, a factor that strongly affects their pre-abortion well-being and makes them more vulnerable to the effects of any life stress (Russo, 2008). Therefore, post abortion psychological problems may not be *caused* by the abortion, but co-occur with it.

Most women contemplating an abortion have mixed feelings about it. Even a woman who has no prior history of psychological problems may experience distress following an abortion if she was committed to the pregnancy, is aware of stigma surrounding abortion, feels the need to keep it a secret, has received little support from her family or friends, or believed in advance that she would have problems in coping (Major et al., 2009).

Women who experience severe distress following abortion may want to obtain psychological counseling. However, women should not have to deny their conflicts for fear of being labeled emotionally disturbed:

> Abortion, like other moral dilemmas, does cause suffering in the individuals whose lives are impacted. That suffering does not make the choice wrong or harmful to the individual who must make the choice, nor should the individual be pathologized for having feelings of distress. In fact, the shouldering of such suffering and of responsibility for moral choices contributes to psychological growth. (Elkind, 1991, p. 3)

Technology and Choice

Controversies about contraception and abortion show that the development of new reproductive technology does not always increase choices for women. The reality is that reproductive technology has introduced troublesome questions of ethics, morality, power, and choice. Indeed, the body may be the major battleground of women's rights for decades to come.

In Vitro Fertilization

Some couples who are unable to conceive a child use technologies such as *in vitro fertilization,* or *IVF,* commonly known as the test-tube baby procedure. A woman's ovaries are stimulated with strong fertility drugs so that they produce multiple eggs, which are then surgically removed. Her partner's sperm, obtained by masturbation, is combined with the eggs in a glass dish. If fertilization occurs, the embryos are inserted into the woman's uterus to develop (Williams, 1992).

Although IVF has been around since 1978, there has been almost no research on the psychological aspects of using this technology. The strong desire to become a biological mother is usually seen as natural. Women who are undergoing IVF and other medical interventions for fertility offer a variety of reasons why it is very important to them to have a child. Some reasons are related to personal identity (feeling useless or incomplete without a child); others to the marital relationship (to please the spouse, to improve a marriage); and others echo social expectations (it's part of a woman's role, all women should experience pregnancy and childbirth, pressure from family and friends) (Cassidy & Sintrovani, 2008).

The media are upbeat about the new reproductive technologies. They frequently feature heart-rending stories of a woman's quest for a child but rarely do these stories analyze how the need to have children is socially constructed. In an analysis of 133 news articles on IVF, 64 explicitly endorsed the belief that bearing children is the single most important accomplishment of adult life, and only two articles countered that belief (Condit, 1996). This suggests that our society creates a market for IVF by making fertility seem so central to a woman's identity that infertility becomes an intolerable problem to be fought at any cost (Williams, 1992).

IVF carries many risks. The fertility drugs and surgeries can lead to side effects and complications. The emotional costs are high and the success rate is low. A pregnancy through IVF leads to higher levels of psychological distress than a natural pregnancy, and the majority of couples have to cope with repeated failure as IVF does not work for them. On the other hand, those who succeed in having a child through IVF or other medically assisted methods generally report more positive relationships between mother, father, and child than comparison mothers who conceived naturally, and IVF children are as well-adjusted as others (Hahn, 2001).

Other Methods of Conception

IVF is only one of the reproductive technologies being used to allow couples to have children. Some methods are decidedly low-tech, with the kitchen turkey-baster the favored means of insemination and the couples themselves in control of the technology. In one case, a lesbian couple had a child with sperm donated by one partner's father to the other partner. Both genetic and social ties of grandparent to grandchild were thus created.

Some couples use reproductive technologies in order to pay others to breed children for them. Many feminists believe that this practice exploits women (Baber & Allen, 1992; Raymond, 1993). Others argue that contract pregnancy can have substantial benefits to all parties if it is stringently regulated (Purdy, 1992). As currently practiced, contract pregnancy raises seemingly insoluble ethical dilemmas. These are descriptions of actual cases:

> Robert M. contracts for a baby with Elvira J. without telling her that he is considering divorcing his wife Cynthia M. On learning of the pending divorce, Elvira refuses to give up the baby for adoption, although she allows the Ms to take the baby home with them on the condition that they seek marriage counseling. Six months later, Robert M. files for divorce, triggering a three-way custody battle between biological father, biological mother, and caretaker mother. Who is being exploited here? Does the fact that Elvira is a Latina with only a seventh-grade education make a difference? (Nelson, 1992)

> Mark C. and Cristina C. hire Anna J. to gestate an embryo grown from their sperm and egg. Finding herself attached to the child, Anna seeks visitation rights. A judge rules that Anna is not the child's mother (although it is she who has given birth), but merely a temporary foster mother, and denies her request. Anna is a Black single mother; the Cs' are White and Asian-American, respectively (Purdy, 1992).

Many feminists argue that women are at risk for exploitation by technologies that separate the genetic and physiological aspects of pregnancy. It is women's bodies that are manipulated and experimented on with these techniques. It is poor women, more often than wealthier ones, who are recruited as wombs for hire. More than ever, women may be viewed solely as egg providers and incubators, and motherhood defined to suit those with the most social power (Raymond, 1993; Ulrich & Weatherall, 2000).

The Transition to Motherhood

Becoming a mother changes a woman's life perhaps more than any other single life transition. Pregnancy, birth, and the transition to motherhood include both biological and social events. These events interact to produce changes in life circumstances, lifestyle, and work, as well as changes in relationships with partners, parents, and others. Once a woman becomes a mother, the role is hers for life, and she will be defined largely through that role, much more than men are defined through their roles as fathers. It is not surprising that motherhood profoundly affects a woman's sense of self. Let's look more closely at some of the changes that occur with pregnancy and motherhood and their effects on women's identities.

How Does Motherhood Change Work and Marital Roles?

More than 20 longitudinal studies have shown that the birth of a child can negatively affect family relationships, reducing psychological well-being and marital satisfaction (Walzer, 1998). Studies using large national samples show that parenthood results in bigger changes in women's lives than in men's, as they take on more child care and housework (Sanchez & Thomson, 1997). This gender-linked change was expressed in an interview by one new mother in a British study of adjustment to parenthood:

> I felt that once he'd gone out through that door then he didn't have to think about it until he came back through the door . . . When he went off in the morning his life hadn't changed. . . . It was the same as the day before we had her. But everything for me had just gone completely, you know, up in the air. Everything was different (Choi et al., 2005, p. 174).

Many women experience the change from paid worker to unpaid full-time mom as stressful. The changes from a 9-to-5 schedule to being on call 24 hours a day, from adult company to isolation with an infant, from feeling competent to feeling overwhelmed with new tasks, all require adjustments. Women who return to paid work have their own stresses, juggling many old and new demands. Mothers are encouraged to evaluate themselves against images of ideal mothers such as the radiant, serene Madonna and the superwoman who juggles the demands of house, children, husband, and job while providing her children with unfailing love and plenty of quality time. One new mom, asked by a researcher what she'd expected before becoming a mother, said that she'd thought the baby would eat and sleep and she could "get on and do lots of things . . . be sort of Supermum, Superwife and Supereverything." Unfortunately she'd discovered that "it's not like that at all" (Choi et al., 2005, p. 173). Women often are not prepared for negative and ambivalent feelings and may feel like failures when they occur:

> I couldn't seem to do anything right; I felt so tired, the baby kept crying, and I kept thinking that this was supposed to be the most fulfilling experience of my whole life. It felt like the most lonely, miserable experience. (A mother 3 weeks after the birth of her first child, cited in Ussher, 1989, p. 82)

The difficulties of being a first-time mother may be offset by the rewards of getting to know one's growing baby, the belief that caring for one's children is worthwhile and important, and the sense of mastery that comes from learning how to do it well. In one study of Australian women who were assessed while pregnant and 4 months after the birth of their baby, the majority of women said that their experience was largely positive and exceeded their expectations (Harwood et al., 2007).

When conflict occurs, it often is linked to a discrepancy between the woman's expectations of her partner's involvement and the partner's actual behavior once the child is born (Choi et al., 2005). As we saw in Chapter 8, housework is still disproportionately done by women. Studies of the transition to parenthood suggest that although most men are positive about the idea of becoming a father, some do not follow through with a fair share of the increased work. In one study, new mothers kept time-use diaries and were also interviewed twice. Their workdays ranged from 11 to 17 1/2 hours a day, and they spent an average of 6 hours a day alone with their babies. Although they said the babies' fathers were their main source of support, fathers actually contributed only 0 to 2 hours a day of primary care (Croghan, 1991).

These studies suggest that new mothers are stressed when there is inequality in marital roles. Women may enter motherhood with expectations of equality in parenting but these expectations sometimes collide with reality (Choi et al., 2005). It is difficult for women and men to change parenting relationships because cultural images and social structures constantly reinforce the idea that mothers, not fathers, should have day-to-day responsibility for children. Myths of motherhood still imply that women should be fulfilled through self-sacrifice and grateful for any small contribution their husbands might make.

Psychological Effects of Bodily Changes during Pregnancy

The hormonal changes of pregnancy are much greater than those of the menstrual cycle. The levels of progesterone and estrogen in pregnant women are many times higher than in nonpregnant women, and many of the physical experiences of early pregnancy may be related to rapid hormonal changes. These include breast tenderness, fatigue, and "morning sickness" (which can actually occur at any time of the day): nausea, revulsion at the sight or odor of food, and sometimes vomiting.

In addition, other physiological changes may alter the functioning of the central nervous system. The level of the neurotransmitter norepinephrine drops during pregnancy while the levels of stress-associated hormones rise (Treadway et al., 1969). Norepinephrine and progesterone have both been related to depression.

In a study of mood changes during pregnancy, women were interviewed both before and during their pregnancies and compared with a control group of women who did not become pregnant. For the pregnant group, changes in mood increased compared with both their prepregnancy baseline and compared to the control group, mainly during the first three months of the pregnancy (Striegel-Moore et al., 1996).

Pregnancy also has implications for women's sexuality. When women become pregnant, they are confronted with many of the contradictions about sexuality that characterize Western society. (See Figure 9.2.) Becoming pregnant and giving birth highlight a woman's sexuality. At the same time, society may downplay the sexuality of the pregnant woman or the mother, fostering a split between the woman's body and sense of self (Ussher, 1989). The Madonna ideal—pure and serene—exists at the cost of desire: the Madonna must be a virgin (Young, 1998). The idea of a mother who has sexual desires and acts on them conflicts with the ideal of maternal selflessness and purity.

One example of this split is the disconnection between desire and behavior during pregnancy. Many women experience increased sexual desire while pregnant, especially in the middle three months (Kitzinger, 1983). This may reflect physical changes such as an increased blood supply to the pelvic area, as well as psychological factors. (For one thing, the woman and her partner don't have to worry about contraception!) In a normal pregnancy, intercourse and orgasm are safe until 4 weeks before the due date; these activities do not harm the fetus or cause miscarriage (Masters & Johnson, 1966). Yet women may engage in sexual activities less often, out of fear of harming the fetus, feeling unattractive, or physical awkwardness.

FIGURE 9.2
This photo of model Jerry Hall by noted photographer Annie Leibovitz is disturbing to many viewers because Hall's sexuality and the maternal behavior of breastfeeding a baby are both on display. With it, Leibovitz asks the viewer to think about our sentimental images of mothers.

Pregnancy is a time of dramatic weight gain and changes in body shape. Many women feel extremely ambivalent about these changes (Ussher, 1989). Reactions include feeling temporarily free from cultural demands to be slim, feeling awe and wonder, feeling afraid and disgusted by their size, and feeling alienated and out of control (see Box 9.1). In a study of more than 200 women, changes in body image were among the most frequently reported stressors of pregnancy and early motherhood, second only to physical symptoms (Affonso & Mayberry, 1989). As young women's body image concerns increase due to the pervasive objectification of women in American culture, these stressors may increase as well.

Indeed, the pregnant woman does lose some control over her body. Changes will occur no matter what she does. She is helpless (short of terminating the pregnancy) to govern her own body. And yet society defines her mainly in terms of her body. Thus it should not be surprising if pregnant women feel unfeminine, moody, or insecure, even apart from hormonal causes.

BOX 9.1 ∽ A Brand New Body: One Woman's Account of Pregnancy

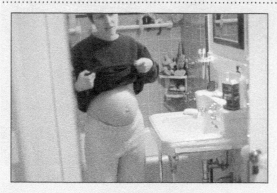

One woman's reactions to her changing body are captured in these entries from a journal she kept during her first pregnancy. Her pregnancy was planned and wanted, and she was in a stable relationship with a supportive male partner. How might the reactions of women to their changing bodies differ in differing social circumstances?

- I have the feeling that I brought a brand new body home from the doctor's office. I'm a new me. Nobody else would look at me and call me pregnant, but it's wonderful to know that I really am, and I look for every tiny sign to prove it's true. My developing breasts are encouraging, and my nipples have become much larger. My nipples stand erect at times, and they're at least three shades darker.
- I really do feel beautiful. In fact, I feel like I'm a pretty good place for a baby to stay and grow in. Nice, round, firm, with just enough fat all over to make it really soft and safe for the baby.

- I rub cocoa butter on my tummy and breasts every morning after showering. The skin has become pink and smooth and I can't help feeling it all the time. The other day we were in the bookstore, and I was absent-mindedly rubbing myself and staring into space. A young woman with a child called to me from across the store, "That's a lovely belly you have there!"
- I've begun to feel huge. I remember hearing other pregnant women hassle themselves about getting fat. I never could figure it out. To me they looked beautiful, round, and blooming. I assured myself that I would never feel that way, and I would love my tummy and all the extra pounds. Well, that's great in theory—but suddenly the day comes when I look in the mirror and my face is round and I really do look like an orange! even holding my stomach in. So yesterday I spent the whole day feeling fat, ugly, and unlovable. Despite every nice thing John has said, I knew he would soon see how unappealing I am.
- I never thought it would come to this. I can't reach over my stomach to get to my feet. John has to lace up my hiking boots!
- Sometimes it seems as though I've been pregnant all my life. I can't remember being unpregnant.

Source: Excerpt from Suzanne Arms (1993). *A Season to Be Born.* Reprinted by permission of Suzanne Arms.

How Do Others React to Pregnant Women?

Pregnant women are powerful stimuli for the behavior of others. A woman who is visibly pregnant has already begun to be defined as a mother in the eyes of society. Her body symbolizes the eternal power of women:

> The atmosphere of approval in which I was bathed—even by strangers on the street, it seemed—was like an aura I carried with me, in which doubts, fears, misgivings, met with absolute denial. This is what women have always done (Rich, 1976, p. 26).

Pregnant women may be genuinely cherished. One woman, who married into a Puerto Rican family, was delighted by her special status when she became pregnant:

> I'm treated like a precious, fragile person by my in-laws. I . . . get the best seat on the couch and am served dinner first. When my mother-in-law found out I was pregnant with my first child, she created a special ritual for me that involved a warm, scented candle-lit bath. She placed my husband's baby picture on the mirror and told me all about her experiences with pregnancy and birth (Johnston-Robledo, 2000, p. 132–133).

On the other hand, pregnancy may elicit sexist behavior. Benevolent sexism is primed because pregnant women are seen as fragile and in need of protection. Hostile sexism may occur if the pregnant woman seems not to accept her traditional role. A field study demonstrated both these kinds of sexism directed at pregnant women in a real-world setting (Hebl et al., 2007). Female experimenters (with the help of a little padding) posed as pregnant women who were job applicants or customers at retail stores in a large mall, and the researchers observed and recorded the behavior of store employees toward them.

The good news from the results was that employees did not overtly discriminate against pregnant women—they weren't ignored or refused job applications. However, observations of subtle sexism yielded some not-so-good news. The employees showed more patronizing and benevolent behavior (being overfriendly and overhelpful, touching) toward the supposedly pregnant women posing as customers (a traditional and nonthreatening female role), but more hostile behavior (rudeness, staring) to the pregnant women applying for jobs. The hostility was greater when the women were applying for gender-incongruent (masculine) jobs. The researchers pointed out that this combination—rewards for conventionally feminine women, and punishments for those who violate gender roles—is exactly the kind of subtle sexism that sustains social inequality. Pregnant women may get an extra dose of sexism because their visible condition primes sexist attitudes.

Motherhood and Women's Identity

Pregnancy and mothering affect women's sense of self. In a Canadian study, for example, the women experienced themselves as profoundly changed. Middle-class women described the changes in terms of personal growth and self-actualization; working-class women described a process of "settling down." For both groups, motherhood involved a moral transformation in which they became deeply connected to their babies. However, the flip side of such connectedness—feeling totally responsible for the child—was described as one of the hardest things about motherhood (McMahon, 1995).

In another study, women who were interviewed during pregnancy described several ways their identities were changing. They talked about creating themselves as mothers and beginning to develop a relationship with their unborn child. They also described changes in social identity—learning how to situate themselves with family and societal expectations about motherhood. They said they had to "add motherhood to the mix"—to integrate their new identities with the other parts of their lives (Messias & DeJoseph, 2007).

An intensive case study of one woman's pregnancy illustrates the experience of personal identity change (Smith, 1991). Clare's change during early pregnancy involved imagining the child-to-be. As she explained, "In one respect, it's—it's a person, a whole person that just happens to be in there, and in another way, it's something different" (p. 231). In the middle phase, Clare experienced a growing sense of psychological relatedness with others—partner, mother, and sister. Near the end of the pregnancy, Clare believed that she had changed in important ways, saying "I'm one of two and I'm one of three." Her identities as a partner to the baby's father and as a mother were now an integrated part of her self.

The transition to motherhood involves losses as well as gains. The woman ceases to be seen as an autonomous individual and is instead viewed as an "expectant mother" and then "mother." It is not surprising that feelings of loss are experienced. It is hard to change from being "Joy Williams, secretary/jogger/painter/daughter/spouse and more" to being "Timmy's mom." I remember my own feelings of sadness and loss shortly after the birth of my first child when the nurses in the hospital referred to all the women in the maternity unit as "Mother" ("Mother, are you ready for your lunch tray?") rather than by our names. It seemed as if everything that had gone before was now to be put aside for the all-encompassing identity and job of Mother.

Because feelings of loss conflict with the motherhood mystique, women may be ashamed of them, label themselves as ill or abnormal, or believe that "baby blues" are inevitable and biologically determined. One of the ways cultural constructions of motherhood may oppress women is that they are not allowed to mourn or grieve the old, lost self (Nicolson, 1993).

So far, we have been talking about the transition to motherhood mainly as it has been constructed for White, middle-class women exposed to the motherhood mystique. What does the identity of mother mean for poor women? An eloquent expression of class and color differences in ideals of womanhood and motherhood comes from a famous speech attributed to Sojourner Truth, a crusader for abolition and suffrage and an ex-slave, to the Akron Convention for Women's Rights in 1852:

> That man over there says that women need to be helped into carriages, and lifted over ditches and have the best place everywhere. Nobody ever helps me into carriages, or over mud puddles or gives me any best place, and ain't I a woman? Look at me! Look at my arm! I have ploughed, and planted, and gathered into barns, and no man could head me! And ain't I a woman? I could work as much and eat as much as a man—when I could get it—and bear the lash as well! And ain't I a woman? I have borne thirteen

children, and seen them most all sold off to slavery, and when I cried out with my mother's grief, none but Jesus heard me. And ain't I a woman? (Adapted from Ruth, 1990, pp. 463–464)

Attitudes toward pregnant women still vary by social class. Middle-class women in heterosexual marriages may be treated as delicate and special, but poor single women are labeled "welfare moms," undeserving of respect. Middle-class mothers are urged to stay home with their children, but poor mothers are forced to look for paid employment. Heterosexual women's connectedness with their children is seen as positive, but lesbians' connectedness with theirs is pathologized. Women's identity as mothers is a product of the social context of mothering.

The Event of Childbirth

If a woman were training to run a marathon, climb a cliff, or go on an Outward Bound trek, she would probably think of the upcoming event as a challenge. She would acknowledge that her body would be worked hard and stressed, her courage tested, and her life put at some risk. Yet she could feel in control and prepare for the challenge. She might undertake the experience as a way of knowing her own self or of developing her strengths and resources. Childbirth is a normal physical process with some of the same potential for empowerment, yet women are rarely encouraged to think of it in this way (Reiger & Dempsey, 2006). Instead, they are taught to think of it as an event in which they will be dependent, passive, subject to authority, and in need of expert medical intervention.

In virtually all cultures, birth is associated with fear, pain, awe, and wonder; it is viewed as both the worst pain anyone could suffer and as a peak experience. Yet there are surprisingly few literary accounts of childbirth *by women*, and women's experiences of childbirth are invisible in Western art. Images of war and death are innumerable but images of birth are virtually nonexistent (Chicago, 1990). (See Figure 9.3.)

Is Childbirth a Medical Crisis?

In some countries, birth is considered a natural phenomenon that needs no medical intervention in the majority of cases. For example, the Netherlands is well known for its high percentage of home births and low rate of medical procedures (Christiaens et al., 2008). The Dutch philosophy is that a healthy woman can best accomplish her task of birthing her baby if she is self-confident, in familiar surroundings—preferably her own home—and attended by a birth specialist such as a midwife.

In contrast, the United States has adopted a ***medical model of birth***. Over 99 percent of U.S. births take place in hospitals (NCHS, 2009). Nurse-midwives attend only about 8 percent of U.S. births, with the rest attended by physicians. Even the language of childbirth reflects the centrality of the physician: People routinely speak of babies being *delivered* by doctors instead of birthed by women.

Is the medical model of birth best for women? On the one hand, basic health care and education for pregnant women can save lives and improve maternal and

FIGURE 9.3
Judy Chicago's image "Crowning" represents the moment the baby's head first becomes visible at the vaginal opening.

infant health. On the other hand, the medical monopoly may lead to women being regarded as incompetent and passive patients, depriving them of control during one of life's most awesome experiences. Many of the customary procedures surrounding birth in the United States are virtually unknown in other societies and are not necessarily in the best interest of mother or baby. For example, in hospital births the woman lies on her back during delivery, whereas in most cultures women give birth in a squatting or semi-seated position. The supine position puts pressure on the spine, may slow labor, works against gravity, increases the risk of vaginal tearing, and makes it more difficult for the woman to push actively during the process. Why, then, do hospitals insist on this position? It is easier for the physician, who can view the birth more conveniently.

American women experience childbirth with feet in the air, drugged, shaved, purged with an enema, denied food and water, hooked up to machines and sensors, and psychologically isolated to a degree that is virtually unknown in other parts of the world (Nelson, 1996). Research shows that giving birth in an unfamiliar environment, being surrounded by strangers, and being moved from one room to another during labor affect the birth process adversely even in nonhuman animals, yet these practices are routine in medicalized childbirth (MacFarlane, 1977; Newton, 1970).

In the United States, women have also been routinely taught that they will need pain relief during normal birth. The use of tranquilizers, barbiturates, and anesthetics during childbirth has become routine, but it is also controversial. On the one hand, drugs can spare women unnecessary pain. On the other hand, there are well-documented negative effects on both mother and baby (Hyde & DeLamater,

2011). For example, anesthetics in the mother's bloodstream are passed to the infant, depressing its nervous system. Anesthetics may prolong labor by inhibiting contractions and making the mother unable to help push the baby through the birth canal. Psychologically, they reduce the woman's awareness and her ability to control one of the most meaningful events of her life.

The medical model of birth encourages physicians and pregnant women to focus on possible complications and emergencies and may cause them to react to even remote possibilities with drastic medical interventions. In the past 25 years, there has been a dramatic increase in the number of caesarean (surgical) births in the United States, from about 4 percent to over 30 percent of all births (NCHS, 2009). This rate is much higher than in other developed countries such as Great Britain (where it is about 10 percent) and is *not* associated with lower infant mortality. Other medical procedures such as artificial induction of labor are also rising dramatically in the United States (NCHS, 2009).

Why the epidemic of medical intervention? Some critics have rather cynically suggested that scheduled surgical births are more convenient and profitable for physicians. Others have attributed the increase to physicians' fear of malpractice suits. It has also been suggested that the high rate of surgical deliveries is an attempt by the medical profession to keep its dominant role in childbirth, despite women's increasing insistence on viewing birth as a normal process.

Many feminist activists and health specialists are concerned about the over-medicalization of birth. When birth is defined as a medical event, helping and supporting the laboring woman seems inadequate, and heroic medical measures seem appropriate. Because medical and surgical interventions are now so common, normal vaginal delivery is starting to be seen as difficult, even unattainable by the average woman. Young women, it seems, increasingly express fear of giving birth and lack of confidence in their bodies' ability to cope with pregnancy and childbirth (Reiger & Dempsey, 2006).

Family-Centered Childbirth

After undergoing medically-managed childbirth, many second-wave feminists began to write about their experiences and work toward more woman- and family-centered birthing practices. Women organizers founded the International Childbirth Education Association in 1960. Widely read books such as *Our Bodies, Ourselves; Immaculate Deception; Of Woman Born;* and *The Great American Birth Rite* helped change public attitudes in the 1970s.

At about the same time, methods of ***prepared*** or ***natural childbirth*** were introduced to the American public. The most popular type of prepared childbirth is the ***Lamaze method,*** named after a French obstetrician. Women who use this approach learn techniques of relaxation and controlled breathing. Relaxation helps to reduce tension, decrease the perception of pain, and conserve energy during labor. Controlled breathing helps the woman work with, not against, the strength of each uterine contraction. The Lamaze method does not rule out the use of pain-relieving drugs, but it emphasizes that with proper preparation they may not be needed, and it leaves the choice to the laboring woman.

Another part of the Lamaze technique is the help of a "coach," or trusted partner—usually the baby's father—during labor and birth. The coach helps the mother with relaxation and controlled breathing and provides emotional support and encouragement. Men had been banished from the delivery room at the heyday of the medical model, regarded as unhygienic and likely to get in the way (MacFarlane, 1977). Today, many men feel that participating in the birth of their child is an important part of becoming a father.

Studies comparing women who used Lamaze and other methods of prepared childbirth with women who had no special preparation have shown benefits associated with prepared childbirth. These include shorter labor, fewer complications, less use of anesthetics, less reported pain, and increased feelings of self-esteem and control (Hyde & DeLamater, 2011). These studies must be interpreted carefully. Perhaps women who sign up for Lamaze training are largely those who are motivated to experience childbirth positively under any circumstances. In other words, the studies do not rule out the sampling bias of self-selection.

One study of support during childbirth does rule out self-selection effects (Kennell et al., 1991). More than 600 pregnant women, mostly Hispanic, poor, and unmarried, were randomly assigned to one of three groups in an experimental design. One group received emotional support during labor from a specially trained female helper. The helpers, who were recruited from the local community, stayed with the laboring women to provide encouragement, explain the birth process, and offer soothing touch and handholding. A second group had a noninteractive female observer present, and the third group had standard hospital care.

Women in the emotional support group had a caesarean rate of 8 percent, compared with 13 percent in the observed group and 18 percent in the standard procedure group. They experienced less pain during labor: The standard group was almost seven times as likely to need anesthesia as the emotional support group. Moreover, for women in the supported group their labor time was shorter, and they and their babies spent less time in the hospital. Clearly, emotional support made a large difference. The study's director estimated that investing small amounts of money in providing this kind of support would save $2 billion a year in hospital costs.

Women's efforts to regain control of the event of birth have resulted in many changes from the extreme medical model of thirty years ago. Today, fathers are more likely to be with the birthing woman. More births are taking place in home-like birth centers, attended by nurse-midwives. Women and their partners are far more likely to be educated about the normal processes and events of pregnancy and birth. This knowledge reduces fear and helplessness, and thus reduces discomfort. Learning techniques to use during labor can replace passive suffering with active involvement and coping. However, new technology is continually being introduced, and each new intervention can readily be overused.

Women's struggle for choice and control in childbirth is part of women's larger struggle for self-determination, a social revolution that is not yet complete. The medical model of birth illustrates the way social institutions can decrease the power of women. When real control is lacking, women perceive themselves as helpless and passive, and this perception in turn contributes to powerlessness.

Treating birth as a normal, woman- and family-centered event, rather than a medical one, could prove very beneficial to women, their partners, and their children.

Depression Following Childbirth: Why?

The first weeks following childbirth (the **postnatal period**) are often characterized as a time of mood swings and depression. For the first few days after giving birth, most women feel elated: the waiting is over, the labor complete, and the baby has arrived. Soon, however, they experience depression and crying spells. Between 50 percent and 80 percent of women experience mood swings for a day or two. Longer-lasting depression (6 to 8 weeks) occurs in about 13 percent of women; it includes feelings of inadequacy and inability to cope, fatigue, tearfulness, and insomnia. The most severe form, a major clinical disorder, affects one-tenth of 1 percent of new mothers (Barr, 2008; Hyde & DeLamater, 2011).

Are postnatal mood disorders due to hormonal changes? Birth is followed by dramatic decreases in the high levels of estrogen and progesterone that characterize pregnancy. However, hormone changes have not been shown to *cause* depression; in fact, there is no direct link between postnatal hormone levels and mood (Johnston-Robledo, 2000; Treadway et al., 1969). The hormonal changes of pregnancy and the postnatal period are real. They give rise to bodily changes and sensations that must be interpreted by the woman who is experiencing them. But the social context of interpretation is crucial; postnatal depression may be more of a social construction than a medical condition. It is virtually unknown in many countries, including India, China, Mexico, and Kenya, suggesting that the causes are at least partly cultural (Mauthner, 1998).

Many physical, social, and interpersonal factors may contribute to depression and mood swings among new mothers. A large-scale study of over 1,200 women showed that caesarean births did not lead to more postnatal depression, but women who experienced severe pain following childbirth (regardless of type of delivery) had a three times greater risk of depression in the following weeks compared to those whose pain was mild (Eisenach et al., 2008). In a study of 42 Australian women with major clinical depression after childbirth, the psychosocial risk factors were being 16-years-old or younger, having a past history of psychiatric illness, experiencing stressful life events during the pregnancy, being in an unhappy marriage, having little social support, having a vulnerable personality, and having a baby of the nondesired sex (Boyce & Hickey, 2005). In an intensive study of a small sample of English women experiencing postnatal depression, a key factor was conflicts between their expectations of motherhood and their actual experiences. Different mothers resolved these conflicts in different ways, but in all cases a woman's recovery was a process of accepting herself and rejecting the impossible ideals of motherhood (Mauthner, 1998). This result was echoed in a larger study of 71 first-time mothers who completed questionnaires during pregnancy and at 4 months postpartum. Most of the women's expectations were fulfilled and their experiences as new parents were positive. However, when experiences were negative compared to expectations, there was greater depression following the birth (Harwood et al., 2007).

As a mother, I believe that sleep deprivation has been overlooked as a factor in postnatal mood disorders. During the last weeks of pregnancy, a woman may not sleep well due to the discomfort caused by the heavy, restless fetus. Next, the hard physical work and stress of birthing a child are followed by many consecutive nights of disturbed sleep. Babies rarely sleep for a 6- or 7-hour stretch before they are 6-weeks-old, and some take much longer to settle down. I know of no studies of postnatal depression that have examined sleep deprivation as a factor or compared moodiness in new mothers with moodiness in a sleep-deprived comparison group, though new moms readily talk about it in interview studies (Choi et al., 2005). Going without sleep for a few days can make anyone cranky and depressed. The lack of attention to this possibility is a striking example of how sociocultural influences are often overlooked in studying women's lives.

Countries in which postnatal depression is rare offer a period of rest and special care for the new mother, practical and emotional support from other women, and positive attention to the mother, not just the baby (Johnston-Robledo, 2000; Mauthner, 1998). For example, in Guatemala, a new mother gets an herbal bath and a massage. In Nigeria, she and her baby are secluded in a "fattening room" where her meals are prepared by others. Customs like these may help the new mother interpret her bodily changes and sensations more positively and ease her adjustment to motherhood. One U.S. psychologist who studied new mothers suggests, "Next time a friend or relative has a baby, in addition to a gift for the baby, bring her a meal and offer to help around the house" (Johnston-Robledo, 2000, p. 139). And maybe somebody else could get up with the baby so she can get a good night's sleep.

Experiences of Mothering

The realities of mothering are as different as the social circumstances of women who mother. In this section, let's look at what motherhood involves for diverse groups of women.

Teen Mothers

Each year in the United States three-quarters of a million young women under the age of 20 become pregnant—about 7 percent of all women in this age group. Most of these teens are unmarried. Over half of teen pregnancies result in the birth of a child; about 32 percent are terminated by abortion and the rest end in miscarriage. The rate of births to teen mothers is much higher for young women of color than for Whites (Guttmacher Institute, 2010c).

The rate of teen pregnancy dropped dramatically throughout the 1990s, probably because teens were using contraception more reliably, but has now risen again for all ethnic groups (Guttmacher Institute, 2010c). It's too soon to tell if this upward trend will continue. The teen pregnancy rate in the United States is much higher than in comparable countries (see Figure 9.4). U.S. teens are not more sexually active than their European counterparts but they are much less likely to use contraception reliably and effectively (Alan Guttmacher Institute, 2002).

What factors put girls at risk for early pregnancy? First and foremost, teen pregnancy and childbearing are related to social class disadvantages. Living in a

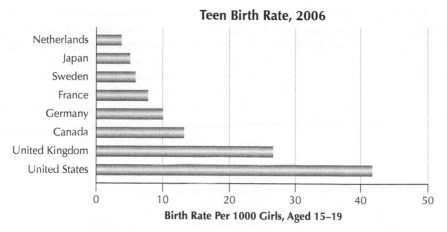

Teen Birth Rate, 2006

Birth Rate Per 1000 Girls, Aged 15–19

FIGURE 9.4 **U.S. teenagers have higher birthrates than adolescents in other developed countries.**

Sources: United Nations Statistics Division (2006). *Demographic Yearbook 2006.* New York: United Nations, The National Campaign to Prevent Teen and Unplanned Pregnancy http://www.thenationalcampaign.org/national-data/teen-pregnancy-birth-rates.aspx

poor or dangerous neighborhood, growing up in a poor family with a single parent, and being sexually abused are all linked to teen pregnancy. Parents who supervise and regulate their teens' activities and teach them to avoid unprotected sex may lower the risk to some extent (Miller et al., 2001).

Adolescent motherhood has serious consequences for the young women involved, their children, and society as a whole. These include interrupted education and lowered job opportunities for the mothers, health problems for the babies, and the costs of public assistance and interventions (Elise, 1995). In one longitudinal study, 281 teen mothers in Indiana were followed through pregnancy and when their children reached ages 3, 5, and 8. The average age of the mothers at the time of childbirth was 17; almost two-thirds were African American, one-third White, and 4 percent Hispanic. Although most of the children were of normal weight and health at birth, they suffered increasing physical, emotional, and behavioral problems. By the age of 8, more than 70 percent were having problems in school. The mothers were suffering disadvantages, too. They did not know very much about taking care of children and did not have the cognitive maturity to be effective parents. Five years after their child's birth, most remained undereducated, underemployed, and weighed down by depression, anxiety, and stress.

However, there was a great deal of variability in the group. About 18 percent of the mother–child pairs were thriving: The mothers were working, had continued their education, and showed high self-esteem and little depression or anxiety. Their children were developmentally normal. The women who had managed to overcome the disadvantages of early motherhood were those who started off with more advantages in the first place (for example, they had more education before they got pregnant), those who received emotional support from a partner, and those whose coping skills and cognitive readiness for parenthood were high (Whitman et al., 2001).

Another study focused on a group of disadvantaged inner-city teens from New York. Ranging in age from 14 to 19, most were African American or Puerto Rican; two-thirds came from families on welfare. The young mothers who were doing best at a 5-year follow-up had active lives that typically involved working, going to school, spending time with their partner and families, and taking care of their children. What contributed to their strengths? In-depth interviews revealed themes of having been raised in a strict home environment, receiving support from their family with the expectation that they would make something of themselves, having role models and support for education, and having confidence, a strong will, and a passion to succeed (Leadbeater & Way, 2001).

These research findings show that statistics alone do not convey the meaning of teen pregnancy. Teen pregnancy is often used as a symbol of moral and social decay, and teen mothers are accused of undermining family values. Research shows that adolescent mothers are a diverse group who are often struggling to overcome disadvantages that go far beyond just having a baby. Many teen mothers show resilience and courage in overcoming the obstacles they face. Surprisingly, early motherhood does not always result in permanent disadvantage. The majority of teen mothers eventually finish high school, get stable jobs, move into their own apartments or houses, and raise children who do not go on to become teen parents themselves (Leadbeater & Way, 2001).

I am not arguing that early childbearing is desirable. But its meaning and consequences depend on its cultural context. Though teen pregnancy is seen as a huge social problem today, rates were actually higher in the 1950s than now (Nettles & Scott-Jones, 1987). It was less of an issue then, because most teen mothers were married, or hastily got married on becoming pregnant.

Today, there are ethnic and cultural differences in the acceptance of teen pregnancy. Most African American teen mothers live with and receive support from their own mothers. Among Hispanic families, teen pregnancy may not be seen as problematic as long as it results in marriage. Some young women see any child as a gift from God, no matter how unfortunate the circumstances of its birth (Leadbetter & Way, 2001; Whitman et al., 2001). And some teen mothers become inspired to better their lives for the sake of their child (Leadbetter & Way, 2001).

Young mothers need access to programs to help them learn parenting skills, complete their education, and take control of their contraceptive use. Moreover, they need support from their families, their communities, and the educational system. There is also a great need for more research on teen fathers—it takes two to make a baby. A particular need is programs that help fathers take responsibility for birth control, family planning, and their children's economic and social support. With help, the negative effects of early childbearing can be overcome.

Single Mothers

The number of families headed by single women has increased dramatically over the past 30 years. Minority children are more likely to grow up in single-parent families; 23 percent of White, 25 percent of Hispanic, and 48 percent of African American children are in single-parent households (Grall, 2009). The great majority—83 percent—of these families are headed by women. For Whites, the primary reason for single parenthood is the high separation and divorce rate (see Chapter 8). For Hispanic and Black women, the primary reason is a rise in births to single women.

Single mothers, whether they are unmarried, separated, or divorced, are more likely to be holding down jobs than mothers with husbands present in the home. Over half of single mothers work full time, and another 28 percent work part time. Yet families headed by women are far more likely to be poor than other families; their poverty rate is twice that of the general population (Grall, 2009). Poverty among women-headed families is one of the most serious social problems in the United States today.

Why are women-headed households so likely to be poor? Some of the reasons for women's poverty are the same as men's: they may lack education or job skills, or live in a region with few jobs. But women are poor for gender-related reasons as well: women in general are underpaid and underemployed (see Chapter 10). In addition, the lack of publicly subsidized child care makes it nearly impossible for a single working mother to get ahead. If she works full time at minimum wage, child care will consume a large part of her income—if she can even find decent child care. Of all the Western industrialized nations, only the United States fails to provide family support benefits as a matter of public policy (Lorber, 1993). These are sociocultural-level problems, not ones that a single mom can easily solve by herself.

Another gender-related reason for single mothers' poverty is men's failure to provide financial support for their children. In Chapter 8, we looked at the problem of defaults in child support from absentee fathers after divorce. When all single mothers are considered as a group—those who never married as well as those who divorced—the most recent data show that only 54 percent are awarded child support through a court or legal agreement. Of those, 47 percent get the full amount; another 30 percent get some but not all. The average amount received by a mother-headed family is just $3,350 per year (Grall, 2009).

The primary response to the feminization of poverty in the United States seems to be to blame the victims. Women who accept public assistance are accused of causing the very problems they are trying to cope with. Since the 1980s, public aid programs to help people help themselves out of poverty have been repeatedly cut (Polakow, 1993; Sapiro, 1994). In 1996 welfare reform legislation mandated that mothers of young children who receive benefits find paid employment. Consider that many middle-class mothers, with safe homes, good child care, decent jobs, and employed husbands find it difficult or impossible to manage full-time employment when they have babies or toddlers—then think about doing it alone, poor, at a minimum-wage job, and in a dangerous neighborhood.

Many conservative policymakers assume that marriage is the answer to poverty among women and children. However, the majority of women who have children outside of marriage are poor before they become pregnant. Even if these women married the fathers of their babies, they would still be poor, because the fathers are likely to be unemployed and living in economically depressed areas (Dickerson, 1995). Many of the fathers are simply not available or have so many problems of their own that they cannot help support a family. For example, in a study of inner-city young mothers, by the time their first child was 6, 10 percent of the fathers were dead, 25 percent were in jail, and 24 percent were selling or using drugs. Only a few couples had managed to stay together (Leadbetter & Way, 2001). Even among middle-class divorced women, remarriage is not always an option for mothers of small children, and second marriages are more likely than first marriages to end in divorce (see Chapter 8).

But there is more to single-mother families than poverty and despair. Studies show that single mothers are proud that they are handling a difficult job well. They are just as satisfied with motherhood as married mothers are. Among White families, single-parent homes seem to be less gender-typed than two-parent homes. They encourage more gender-neutral play in children and create more flexible attitudes about gender roles (Smith, 1997). This result makes sense when we consider that fathers are more prone than mothers to treating children in gender-stereotypical ways (see Chapter 6), and that children of single mothers see their moms as both the provider and nurturer. Among African American single-parent families, strengths include role flexibility (many adults may "mother" a child), spirituality (relying on inner strength rather than material possessions for happiness), and a sense of community ("It takes a village to raise a child") (Randolph, 1995).

Black Mothers and the Matriarchal Myth

African women were brought to the United States to work as slaves and to produce more slaves, sometimes through rape and forced childbearing. If they were given a few days off from slave labor after childbirth, it was more to protect the owner's investment than to allow them to rest and recover. They were able to care for their own children only after all of their other work was done and, as Sojourner Truth eloquently testified, were likely to see their children sold away from them (Almquist, 1989).

African Americans, under slavery, experienced the systematic, widespread destruction of their families. In addition to this legacy of slavery, there has since been a scarcity of Black men to be providers and husbands. The causes for this scarcity include poor health care and other effects of poverty and discrimination, leading to drug use, imprisonment, and violent death. Thus, Black women have been (and still are) more likely than White women to be raising families without a resident father/husband. For African American women, motherhood is not equated with being dependent on a man (Collins, 1991; Dickerson, 1995).

Black women have coped with oppression in many ways. They often form extended households, with two or three generations living together and sharing resources. Grandmothers, sisters, cousins, and aunts care for the children of young mothers. Black families are less likely than White ones to give children up for adoption by strangers, and more likely to take in the children of friends and relatives. In the Black community, these informal adoptions are seen as better than stranger adoption, because children can stay in contact with their mothers and live with people they know and trust (Almquist, 1989). This collective, cooperative child rearing may reflect a West African heritage (Collins, 1991; George & Dickerson, 1995; Greene, 1990).

Unfortunately, Black women have long been judged against a White middle-class norm of female submission and traditional marriage arrangements (Collins, 1991). Sociologists and psychiatrists have accused them of castrating their husbands and sons by being unfeminine and domineering (Giddings, 1984). Blaming Black women for social problems avoids confronting the real problems of racism, classism, and sexism. Moreover, it obscures the unique contributions of African American family patterns. Black women's involvement in social activism often stems from their definition of motherhood: A good mother does not just take care of her own offspring, she works to meet the needs of her entire community (Collins, 1991; Naples, 1992).

Lesbian Mothers

Based on U.S. census data, it is estimated that about one-third of lesbian couples (and one-fifth of gay male couples) are bringing up children (Peplau & Fingerhut, 2007). Some women who marry or cohabit with men and have children within these relationships later identify as lesbian and bring up their children in lesbian households. Other lesbians have a child through adoption. A growing trend is medical methods such as donor insemination (one partner carries the pregnancy) or IVF (one partner contributes the egg and the other is the birth mother). Given the biological and social obstacles to lesbian and gay parenthood, it is safe to say that most children born to LG parents are the result of pregnancies that were wanted and planned (Renaud, 2007).

What are the special issues and stresses that confront lesbian mothers? One of the biggest potential problems is negotiating the marginalized identity of lesbian with the mainstream identity of mother (Ben-Ari & Livni, 2006). Lesbian mothers may feel little in common with the heterosexual families of their children's friends. Turning to the lesbian community for support, they may find that the lives of their child-free lesbian friends are very different from their own. As more lesbians decide to have children, support groups and networks of lesbian families are growing, and family counselors are more aware of their needs (Erwin, 2007).

Lesbian mothers also may confront problems of internalized homophobia:

> Lesbians should not be surprised or ashamed to find themselves grappling with questions such as: Is this natural? Is it okay for lesbians to have kids? Am I hurting my children . . . is it unfair to bring them into a homophobic world? Am I a woman who is able to mother like other women? These . . . are questions that have been answered in positive ways by many lesbian mothers over the years (Crawford, 1987, p. 197).

Do lesbians raise children differently than heterosexual mothers, and do their children turn out differently? Research suggests that the children of lesbian families are remarkably similar to those of heterosexual families.

One study of African American women compared the attitudes of 26 heterosexual and 26 lesbian mothers. The two groups were similar in the value they placed on independence and self-sufficiency for their children. The lesbian mothers, however, were more tolerant about rules, less restrictive of sex play, less concerned with modesty, and more open in providing sex education. They also viewed boys and girls as more similar to each other than the heterosexual mothers did and expected more traditionally masculine activities from their daughters (Hill, 1987). Another study of 33 heterosexual and 33 lesbian couples measured the gender development of their preschool children (Fulcher et al., 2006). The children's gender role attitudes were related to the parents' behavior, not their sexual orientation. In other words, parents who divided the chores and jobs equally, thereby setting an example of mutual respect, had kids with less traditional attitudes, regardless of whether the parents were gay or straight.

In the United Kingdom, children in a representative sample of lesbian families were compared with those in two-parent and single-mother heterosexual families. Parents, teachers, and a child psychiatrist assessed the children's adjustment. There were few differences in lesbian and heterosexual mothers' parenting styles except that the lesbian mothers hit their children less often and engaged in more imaginative play with them. Overall, the children of lesbian mothers were well-adjusted and had positive relationships with their parents and peers (Golombok et al., 2003). Another British study tracked 78 children, half raised by lesbian mothers and half by heterosexual single mothers, from middle childhood to young adulthood (Tasker & Golombok, 1997). As young adults, these participants were asked to look back on their family life. Children of lesbians were more positive about their family life than children of heterosexuals, especially if their mother was open about her sexual orientation and active in lesbian politics. Children of lesbians were no more likely to identify as gay or lesbian, but those who did were more likely to be involved in a relationship than were gay children of heterosexuals. Children raised by lesbians reported that their mothers had been more open and comfortable communicating with them about sexual development and sexuality as they were growing up. There was no difference in psychological adjustment in the two groups.

On the whole, it seems that lesbian family life produces children who are very much like children from heterosexual families. Research reviews (Fulcher et al., 2006; Tasker, 2005) have found no detrimental effects of lesbian or gay parenting on children's cognitive abilities, self-esteem, gender identity, peer relations, or overall psychological adjustment. This research has decreased discrimination against LG families and fostered changes in laws and public policy in some U.S. states and other countries (Short, 2007).

Commonalities

The experiences of women who mother are shaped by social class, sexual orientation, economic status, and many other factors. Are there any overall similarities? Many mothers have written of their feelings and thoughts about motherhood. Several themes emerge in these accounts. Here are examples of five such themes in the words of mothers who told their stories in *Balancing Acts*, a book edited by Katherine Gieve (1989).

1. Becoming a mother results in large, significant, and permanent changes in identity and life circumstances.

   Daniel is seven, Matthew, five, and when I think about the past seven years I feel like a person watching the dust begin to settle after an earthquake (p. 41).

   I did not imagine the force or the excitement—nor how I would willingly be taken over by my children. . . . I look at the world with different eyes and inward with a new vision. I feel riven, torn apart, and made again (p. 51).

I am not where I was before—not in a single detail. I have learned to pride myself on new abilities, some I had never considered of value. I was blown wide open by motherhood and by the emotions that came with it. . . . I had no idea that I could love that well. . . . Conversely, other abilities by which I had set great store, producing words on time, selling an idea, keeping myself fired up . . . seem useful but little more than that (pp. 127–128).

2. Motherhood can involve feelings of intense love, competence, and achievement.

The rewards of motherhood were immediate and lasting. I have established a relaxed physical intimacy with both my children which tolerates anger and laughter, built up over a decade of washing them, reading to them, and tumbling about with them (p. 114).

Pregnancy had suited me, I enjoyed giving birth, but nothing prepared me for the reality of the new baby. I was almost paralyzed by the joy that shot through me as I looked through the plastic (hospital crib) that morning . . . it's just impossible to put into words . . . I was transported (p. 124).

She's brought into a room. . . . Not much hair, toothless, a fat bald child in a scratchy pink dress. It is love at first sight. . . . I feel as if I've been waiting all my life for this moment, for this child. . . . The "I" who adopts this four-month-old baby is forced to recognize that, physically and symbolically, she is another being, formed by other bodies, in relationships I know nothing of. But in my imagination, she is the missing part of myself, at last returned. I am complete (pp. 138–139).

3. Motherhood is a constantly changing relationship, as both child and mother grow and develop. Mothers and children move from a relationship of profound inequality to one of (ideally) equality. Throughout the process, the mother moves from meeting physical needs to meeting intellectual ones; emotional demands remain a constant.

It was not the hard work of child care that I found so difficult (probably because I shared it with others) but the constantly changing relationship which continued in terms not chosen by me at an unpredictable and changeable pace. It required constant reassessment and with it pain, anger, and remorse, as well as excitement and pleasure. Daniel elicited from me both my greatest love and generosity and my darkest anger and frustration (p. 45).

As our children grow and change, and new pleasures, new battles, take the place of the early ones, I feel I live in a constant state of surprise and suspense. It is like reading the best of novels, combined with being in love; I want things to stand still yet can't wait to see what will happen next. And, above all, I don't want the story to end (p. 159).

4. Both child and mother must confront the limitations of love and care.

With all my love, I cannot be everything she wants and needs any more than I can shield her from pain . . . indeed I must add to her pain. . . . My fantasy, that if I love her enough nothing else matters, has to give way (p. 140).

"You are not my real mother," says my daughter to me. I did not feel either that my mother was my real mother, perhaps every daughter, every child, has this doubt. . . . The gap between the ideal Mother, and the mother we actually have, is perhaps always there. If the Mother is the fixed perfect image of the ideal, a mother (small m) is always what falls short of that image (pp. 143–144).

5. Mothers and children must adapt to a society that is structured as though children did not exist and does not provide necessary support for those who care for the young.

> The world suddenly became a much more dangerous place once I had a baby dependent on me for his very life. For the first time I was thrown into a world that did not recognize my physical, emotional, social, and political needs. This applied to design, architecture, roads, public transport, dangerous machinery; not to mention lack of community child care facilities. . . . it isn't the child that makes your life hard, it is the adult world and the powers that be. Usually, it is the very people who sentimentalize and idealize motherhood who stop listening (pp. 53–54).

> Motherhood . . . has made me aware of time in many different ways. In particular how women's time is taken for granted so that there is little concordance between the way time is structured in the so-called public world and the rhythm of time associated with caring for a young child (p. 77).

These five commonalities emerged from the writings of diverse women about their experiences of motherhood. Perhaps you can think of others.

Making a Difference

Bringing up children is a great joy and an awesome responsibility. Traditionally, in Western societies it has been divided into a nurturing role, assigned to women, and a provider role, assigned to men. This arrangement has many limitations. It does not allow for individual differences in personality and ability—some men might make better nurturers than providers, and some women better providers than nurturers. It keeps women and children economically dependent on men; when men default, families live in poverty. It overlooks the diversity of families. Single-parent families, gay and lesbian families, and families from different cultural traditions do not conform to the patriarchal ideal. Social change over the past several decades has been uneven. Although the majority of women now participate in the provider role, the majority of men have not correspondingly increased their participation in nurturing. How might our society support mothers and children and help fathers develop their parenting potential?

Transforming Social Policy: Redefining Family Values

Public policy on families in the United States lags behind policies in every other industrialized country in the world, and even behind some that are much poorer and less developed (Crittenden, 2001). For example, new mothers and fathers are guaranteed not a single day of paid leave from work in the United States. To those of us who live in the United States, this situation seems normal. But 177 countries guarantee paid leave for new mothers; more than 100 guarantee 14 weeks or more. New fathers are guaranteed paid leave in 74 countries, which can contribute significantly to their becoming involved in caring for their babies. (See Box 9.2.) In the United States, moms and dads are expected to depend on the good will of

BOX 9.2 ⟡ Redefining Fatherhood—and Masculinity

In the United States, it is common, and expected, that women will be the primary caretakers of the children, even though both women and men serve as breadwinners. Maternity and parental leave policies in the United States reflect these stereotypical expectations. Women often receive between 6 and 12 weeks parental leave, while men often get a week or less, and parental leave is likely to be without pay. Unfortunately, the United States lags significantly behind other countries when it comes to providing equal opportunity for both men and women to take care of their children.

In Sweden, laws are far more progressive. Although women still take more time off to take care of children, they expect their husbands to take time off, too. Laws in Sweden provide a 13-month paid parental leave to be shared by mothers and fathers, and at least two months of that leave is required to be taken by fathers. While in the United States many companies balk at the thought of a man asking for extended paternal leave, organizations in Sweden *expect* men to take leave when they have a child. Consequently, 85 percent of men in

Sweden take parental leave, and those who do not face criticism from their families and workplaces.

There are both economic and social benefits when fathers take time off to help raise their children. Divorce rates have gone down. Children get to spend time with both of their parents. Women are earning more money, and men are not penalized for taking leave when they come up for promotion. And most interestingly, conceptions of masculinity have begun to shift. Birgitta Ohlsson, Sweden's European Affairs Minister and an advocate for parental leave stated, "Machos with dinosaur values don't make the top-10 lists of attractive men in women's magazines anymore . . . Now men can have it all—a successful career and being a responsible daddy." She added. "It's a new kind of manly. It's more wholesome."

Contributed by Annie B. Fox

Source: Bennhold, S. (2010, June 15). Paternity leave law helps to redefine masculinity in Sweden. *The New York Times Online.* Retrieved August 3, 2010, from http://query.nytimes.com/gst/fullpage.html?res=9F0CE5DD1338F936A25755C0A9669D8B63&sec=&spon=&pagewanted=all

their employers for paid parental leave and other family-friendly policies. But only 12 percent of companies provide paid maternity leave and only 7 percent offer paid paternity leave (Heymann, 2010).

Parents in the United States need parental leave, subsidized child care, flexible working hours, and other policies that contribute to family well-being. One initiative in this direction is the organization MOTHERS (Mothers Ought to Have Equal Rights). Founded in 2002, MOTHERS seeks to recognize the vital contribution mothers and other caregivers make to society by working to provide them with economic and social recognition. Its agenda includes gaining Social Security credit for primary caregivers of children and establishing a national policy of 6 months paid family leave when parents give birth or adopt a child (Heitner, 2003). (See Box 9.3.)

Transforming Social Meanings: Redefining Parenthood

Our society has assigned mothers sole responsibility for their children's well-being to an extent that few other cultures around the world or throughout history have done. It has asked them to fulfill their responsibilities in relative isolation, often without the support they need. Moreover, it has created myths that disguise the

Box 9.3 ∽ Equal Rights for Mothers: An Agenda for Economic Empowerment

MOTHERS (Mothers Ought To Have Equal Rights) is committed to improving the economic status of caregivers. MOTHERS was founded in 2002 by a group of mothers, writers, and women's advocates around the country. The founders include Ann Crittenden, author of *The Price of Motherhood*, and the National Association of Mothers' Centers (http://www.motherscenter.org/). Its mission is to improve the economic well-being of mothers and other family caregivers.

As the organization's Web site points out, "America loves its moms and its kids. So why shouldn't American mothers and children have the same economic support that moms and kids do in Britain, Canada, France, Belgium, Holland, Scandinavia? The answer is—THEY SHOULD!" MOTHERS has drawn up an Economic Empowerment Agenda which includes the basic family friendly policies that American caregivers need and

deserve. The organization asserts that fairness to those who take care of children and other family members is "the unfinished work of the women's movement."

Because caregiving is unpaid and is not recognized as work under Social Security, unemployment insurance, and other government programs, it can impoverish the women who do it. "It is no coincidence that motherhood is the single greatest risk factor for poverty in old age in the United States . . . Millions of mothers remain economic dependents, despite the fact they produce the most important source of national wealth— our future citizens, taxpayers, and labor force."

The MOTHERS Web site helps caregivers engage in netroots mobilization, enabling them to quickly contact their state and national legislators on key issues.

Source: www.mothersoughttohaveequalrights.org

realities of parenting. Despite their enormous responsibilities and lack of resources, mothers get blamed for everything that goes wrong with children.

"Mother-blaming is like air pollution"—so pervasive that it often goes unnoticed (Caplan, 1989, p. 39). Psychology and psychiatry have a long tradition of viewing Mom as the source of all problems. A review of 125 articles published in major mental health journals between 1970 and 1982 found that mothers were blamed for 72 different kinds of problems in their offspring. The list included aggressiveness, agoraphobia, anorexia, anxiety, arson, bad dreams, bedwetting, chronic vomiting, delinquency, delusions, depression, frigidity, hyperactivity, incest, loneliness, marijuana use, minimal brain damage, moodiness, schizophrenia, sexual dysfunction, sibling jealousy, sleepwalking, tantrums, truancy, an inability to deal with color blindness, and self-induced television epilepsy (Caplan & Hall-McCorquodale, 1985)!

Where are the fathers when blame is handed out? They seem to be invisible. In the past, psychology contributed to the problem by omitting fathers from research on children's psychological adjustment. A review of 544 empirical research studies of children's psychological disorders published between 1984 and 1991 found that only 1 percent focused exclusively on fathers, while 48 percent focused exclusively on mothers. Another 25 percent included both parents but did not analyze for sex differences (Phares & Compas, 1993). It's easy to blame Mom when Dad is left out of the picture.

It is important to value fathers' contributions to their families and support their efforts to be good fathers. This would give men an equal opportunity for intimacy and emotional connection with their families. Fathering is being recognized as a feminist issue. Many feminists have called for redefining fatherhood and helping men become better fathers. There is more to being a father than providing a paycheck; good fathers are responsive and emotionally available to their children (Silverstein, 2002) (see Figure 9.5). At present, much of the poverty and dysfunction among women and children in the United States can be linked to men who father children and then fail to take care of them. Rather than condemn these men as "deadbeat dads," our society could consider them "dads in training" and provide social programs to help them be better fathers (Leadbetter & Way, 2001).

What are the payoffs for redefining parenthood? Research reviews have shown that a father's love is good for children, whose cognitive and emotional development is better when their fathers are involved in their lives (Rohner & Veneziano, 2001; Silverstein, 1996). Father involvement is good for couples, who report greater marital satisfaction, and for mothers, who report decreased stress. And it is good for fathers themselves, who report higher

FIGURE 9.5
A father who is emotionally involved with caring for his child fosters the child's healthy development.

self-esteem and satisfaction with their role as parent (Deutsch, 1999). In a study of 20 first-time fathers in Sweden (a country with generous paternity leave), the men described the experience as fun, amazing, exciting, and much more wonderful than they ever could have imagined (Fägerskiöld, 2008).

Redefining motherhood *and* fatherhood is a revolution that is past due. What is needed is a post-gender definition that allows for flexibility and diversity of family patterns (Silverstein & Auerbach, 1999).

Exploring Further

Crittenden, Ann (2001). *The price of motherhood: Why the most important job in the world is still the least valued.* New York: Henry Holt.

> An eye-opening analysis of how society exploits those who care for children. A strength of this book is its many specific ideas for changing U.S. society so we can "bring children up without putting women down."

Goldberg, Susan, & Chloe Brushwood Rose (2009). *And baby makes more: Known donors, queer parents, and our unexpected families.* Ontario, Canada: Insomniac Press.

An entertaining and thoughtful collection of memoirs by lesbian and gay couples about their experiences with various means of conception and diverse ways of parenting.

The Society for the Psychology of Women, Division 35 of APA, has countered misinformation about so-called post abortion syndrome by launching an informative section on the Pro-Choice Forum Web site (www.prochoiceforum.org).

To reach the psychology section directly, go to http://www.prochoiceforum.org.uk/psy_issues.php

Waldman, Ayelet (2010). *Bad mother: A chronicle of maternal crimes, minor calamities, and occasional moments of grace.* New York: Anchor Books.

She's not every mother, but Waldman, a middle-class mother of four, writes honestly about her conflicts over the motherhood mystique, her abortion, and her marriage.

CHAPTER 10

Work and Achievement

❦

- **If She Isn't Paid, Is It Still Work?**
  Housework: The Double Day
  Relational Work: Keeping Everybody Happy
  Status Work: The Two-Person Career
  What Are the Costs and Benefits of Invisible Work?

- **Working Hard for a Living: Women in the Paid Workforce**
  Sex Segregation
  Women's Work as Extension of Family Roles: "It's Only Natural"
  The Wage Gap

- **Doing Gender in the Workplace**
  Evaluating Women's Performance
  Discrimination in Hiring and Promotion
  Social Reactions to Token Women
  Role Models and Mentors
  Leadership: Do Women Do It Differently?

- **Sexual Harassment from Nine to Five**
  Defining Sexual Harassment
  The Prevalence of Harassment
  What Are the Causes of Harassment?
  The Consequences of Harassment

- **Women's Career Development**
  Do Women Have Different Values and Interests?
  Are Women Less Motivated to Achieve?
  High-Achieving Women

- **Putting It All Together: Work and Family**
  What Are the Costs of the Balancing Act?
  What Are the Benefits of the Balancing Act?

- **Making a Difference: Women, Work, and Social Policy**

- **Exploring Further**

*W*ork is a part of almost every woman's life, but the world of work is a gendered world. Often, women and men do different kinds of work, face different obstacles to satisfaction and achievement, and receive unequal rewards. This chapter examines the unpaid and paid work of women, women's values about work and achievement, the differing work patterns of women and men, and factors affecting women's achievement. We listen to the voices of women as they talk about their work: its problems, its satisfactions, and its place in their lives.

If She Isn't Paid, Is It Still Work?

Much of the work women do is unpaid and not formally defined as work. When women's work caring for their homes, children, and husbands is taken into account, virtually everywhere in the world, women work longer hours than men and have less leisure time (United Nations, 2000). Let's look first at this unpaid and often socially invisible work: women's contributions in housework, meeting others' emotional needs, and enhancing the status of their male partners.

Housework: The Double Day

Scrubbing floors and toilets, shopping for food and cooking meals, changing beds, washing clothes, doing household planning, and record keeping—all the chores required to keep a household functioning—are classified as housework. Fewer women today, than in the past, make housework their single full-time job, it is still a big part of life for most women around the world.

Women's work in the home demands more hours each day than many paid jobs. In developing countries, housework may include gathering firewood, carrying water, and grinding grain for cooking. In industrialized countries, technology (household electricity, running water, and appliances) has made the work less dirty and arduous than it used to be, and the smaller size of modern families means less work, but new tasks have taken the place of old ones. For example, driving children to sports and music lessons keeps many suburban moms busy. Having bigger houses and more possessions means that there is more "stuff" to take care of. And standards have risen, as icons of domesticity like Martha Stewart encourage women to cook gourmet meals, grow their own vegetables, and obsess over decorating details.

Is Housework Shared?

Chapters 8 and 9 documented that equality in the domestic realm is rare. Although men are more involved in it than they used to be, housework and child care remain largely the responsibility of women (see Figure 10.1). Chores tend to be assigned by gender: men do outside work, women do inside work, and women tend to do the chores that come up most often. In a random sample of married or cohabiting couples in which both partners worked for pay, women did more than twice as much housework (14.89 hours each week) as men (6.81 hours) (Stevens et al., 2001). Women's chores are not only more numerous but also more demanding

FIGURE 10.1 **Women's unpaid work of housework and child care often involves multitasking.**

because often they have to be done on a tighter schedule—you can put off washing the car until it's convenient, but it's not so easy to put off making dinner.

For most women, working outside the home is followed each day by another round of working at home, the second shift. The pattern—overworked women and resistant to moderately involved men—is quite consistent across cultures. U.N. studies of daily time use in developing countries shows that, compared with men, women are doing less paid work, more unpaid work, and working longer hours overall (United Nations, 2000).

Is Housework Trivial?

Within individual families the unpaid domestic work of women is often accorded very little value. As one stay-at-home mom said:

> The garbage could overflow and no one would dump it, or the dog may need to be fed . . . and everybody relies on mother to do it . . . some days I feel that they're taking me for granted. . . . every once in a while I hear one of my sons say, "Well, you don't do anything all day long." . . . If they didn't have clean clothes or their beds weren't changed or something like that they might realize that their mother does do something. But most of the time they don't. I don't think men feel that a woman does a day's work (Whitbourne, 1986, p. 165).

The devaluation of housework is also apparent at the societal level. The phrases *working woman* and *working mother* suggest that a woman is not really a worker unless she is in the paid workforce. Unpaid housework is not listed in the U.S. Department of Labor's Dictionary of Occupational Titles. Its monetary value is not computed into the gross national product—an "official denial that this work is socially necessary" (Ciancanelli & Berch, 1987).

Obviously, families could not thrive without the unpaid work of women. But exactly how much is her work worth? Its dollar value is difficult to compute. One way is to estimate the cost of replacing her services with paid workers—cook, driver, babysitter, dishwasher, janitor, and so forth. But many women feel that their services could not be replaced with paid workers because the work requires loving care and an intimate knowledge of the family. Who could calculate the appropriate pay for planning a small child's birthday party or the overtime involved when a woman takes charge of children, pets, house, bills, and yard work while her husband travels on business? Women's homemaking responsibilities involve not only skills but also personal involvement.

Another method is to calculate the wages the homemaker loses by working at home instead of at a paid job. If she could earn $500 a week as a bank clerk, for example, that is the value of 40 hours of housework. By this method, however, housework done by a woman who could earn $300 an hour as an attorney is worth 30 times as much as the identical chores done by a woman who could only earn $10 an hour as a food server.

Neither method of calculating the value of housework really captures the unique characteristics of homemaking, because homemaking does not fit androcentric definitions of work. Imagine how a "help wanted" ad for a stay-at-home mom might look:

> WANTED: Full-time employee for small family firm. DUTIES: Including but not limited to general cleaning, cooking, gardening, laundry, ironing and mending, purchasing, bookkeeping, and money management. Full-time child care also required. HOURS: Flexible, but standby duty required 24 hours/day, 7 days/wk. Extra workload on holidays. SALARY AND BENEFITS: No salary, but food, clothing, and shelter provided at employer's discretion; job security and benefits depend on continued goodwill of employer. No vacation. No retirement plan. No opportunities for advancement. REQUIREMENTS: No previous experience necessary, can learn on the job. Only women need apply.

The homemaker's job looks unattractive indeed in this description. Women do find it unsatisfying in many ways. They dislike the boring, repetitive, and unchallenging nature of much of the work. On the other hand, they enjoy the rewards that come from taking care of their children and husbands. In the rare cases in which men take primary responsibility for housework and child care, their feelings about the job are similar to women's—they like the emotional involvement with their families and dislike the housework (Deutsch, 1999).

Relational Work: Keeping Everybody Happy

Women are largely responsible for caring for others' emotional needs. Keeping harmony in the family has long been defined as women's work (Parsons & Bales, 1955). In a study of marital interaction in which more than 100 couples kept diaries about their communication patterns, wives did more relational work than husbands. They focused on their husbands, friends, and family; spent time talking and listening with them; talked about relationships more; and worked to keep harmony in the family (Ragsdale, 1996). In another study of dual-earner couples, both partners were asked about how much time they and their spouse spent confiding thoughts and feelings, trying to help the partner get out of a bad mood, trying to talk things over when there was a problem, and so on. Women reported doing more of this emotion work than men did and were less satisfied with the division of emotion work between the partners (Stevens et al., 2001).

Relational work goes beyond a woman's immediate family to a wider network of relatives. Women are more likely than men to be in charge of visits, e-mails, texting, and phone calls to distant family members. They buy the presents and remember to send the card for Aunt Anna's birthday. They organize weddings, family reunions, and holiday celebrations, negotiating conflicts and allocating tasks. Although the specifics of the family rituals vary according to social class and ethnic group, families' dependence on women's labor is similar, whether they are upper-class Mexican, working-class African American, middle-class Italian American, migrant Chicano farm workers, or immigrants to America from rural Japan (research reviewed in Di Leonardo, 1987).

Like housework, the relational work of women is largely ignored in traditional definitions of work. The time it takes may be considerable, as everyone relies on Mom to smooth emotional crises. After all, aren't women the relationship specialists? Relational work also has economic and social value. Exchanging outgrown children's clothes with a sister-in-law or sending potential customers to a cousin's business are ways of strengthening relationships that also help families maximize financial resources (Di Leonardo, 1987).

Perhaps most important, relational work fosters marital satisfaction and happiness. But women do not want to do it all. Couples who balance emotional work, with each partner doing about the same amount, are more satisfied with their marriages than couples in which one person is responsible for doing it all (Holm et al., 2001; Stevens et al., 2001).

Status Work: The Two-Person Career

Women's unpaid work benefits their husbands' careers. The terms **status-enhancing work** and **two-person career** describe situations in which wives serve as unofficial (and often unacknowledged) contributors to their husbands' work (Papanek, 1973; Stevens et al., 2001). The most studied example is the corporate wife (e.g., Kanter, 1977); the wives of clergymen and college presidents are other examples. So is the politician's wife, who must be able to "give the speech when he can't make it but to shut her mouth and listen adoringly when he is there" (Kanter, 1977, p. 122).

The role of helper to a prominent man may be rewarding, but it restricts a woman's freedom of action and ties her fate to her spouse's. Consider that Hillary Rodham Clinton, who did not take her husband's name when she married, was later pressured into doing so for political reasons (Marshall, 1997). When she took on the important task of health care reform, the press seemed more interested in her hairstyle than her health care plan. And as First Lady she was subjected to hostile jokes and public humiliation over her husband's sexual activities. Only when her husband left public office was Rodham Clinton able to build her own political career.

What kinds of work do women do in the service of their husbands' careers? The specific tasks vary, depending on the husband's job and career stage (Kanter, 1977). She may entertain clients in her home and make friends with people who can be useful in advancing her husband's career. She is expected to be available at any time for complete care of their children, so that he can travel or work evenings and weekends. She participates in volunteer work or community service related to his position. She may also contribute direct services in place of a paid employee—taking sales calls, keeping his books or tax records, or scheduling his travel. Finally, she provides emotional support. She is expected to listen to his problems, cheerfully accept his absences and work pressures, avoid burdening him with domestic trivia, and motivate him to achieve to his fullest potential. She is, indeed, "the woman behind the man."

What Are the Costs and Benefits of Invisible Work?

Obviously, housework, relational work, and the ladies' auxiliary do not provide a paycheck. Traditionally, women were supposed to be rewarded by a sense of ***vicarious achievement*** (Lipman-Blumen & Leavitt, 1976). In other words, a woman is supposed to identify with her husband and feel gratified by his successes. Many women do report this kind of gratification; others feel exploited. One corporate wife complained to an interviewer, "I am paid neither in job satisfaction nor in cash for my work. I did not choose the job of executive wife, and I am heartily sick of it" (Kanter, 1977, p. 111).

Women who achieve through their husbands are vulnerable. If the marriage ends through the husband's death or divorce or if he does not achieve fame and glory, she may have little to put on a résumé and few skills that prospective employers would regard as valuable. Increasingly, women are insisting that divorce courts recognize that their unpaid work is vital to their husband's success (see Box 10.1).

The availability of some women as unofficial employees for their husbands' companies also has implications for women who are employed and competing with men. There is no corporate husband position to match that of the corporate wife. Instead, the world of work assumes that workers are men and that these men have wives to take care of them (Wajcman, 1998).

A female employee may appear less talented and motivated than her male colleague because she lacks his invisible support staff. High-level female executives are much less likely to be married than high-level male executives. If she is married, her husband is unlikely to invest his future in vicarious achievement. A study of more than 1,600 U.S. corporate employees showed that men at the highest executive levels were significantly more likely to have spouses who were full-time homemakers than men at lower levels and women at all levels (Burke, 1997). Similar results were found in a U.K. study of high-level managers: 88 percent of the married women, and only 27 percent of the married men, had partners who were employed full-time. In other words, the career success of men is given an invisible boost by their at-home support staff. Corporations know this very well; men are seen as bringing two people to their jobs, and women, because of their family duties, as bringing less than one (Wajcman, 1998).

Box 10.1   ∽   It's Her Job Too

Once upon a time, a good corporate wife was to be seen and not heard. She was to make sure nothing, but nothing, came between her man and his work. She was to shield him from the tedious and distracting details of domestic life. She was to raise beautiful, well-mannered children and maintain a beautiful, well-appointed home, making it look effortless. She was to work the charity circuit—to be the belle of the charity ball and also its unpaid CEO. She was to smile through scores of business dinners. And she was never, ever, to make a stink. Even in the worst of times, even when things unraveled, she was expected to know her place and, if need be, to slip quietly offstage. Lorna Wendt did all of these things except the last. When her 32-year marriage to GE Capital CEO Gary Wendt came apart . . . she raised a big ruckus. "She wanted half of the $100 million she estimated he was worth. . . . She wanted respect. She wanted acknowledgment, just once and writ large, that society valued all those things she'd done on the home front . . ."

Lorna Wendt was awarded a $20 million divorce settlement, leaving many high-earning men astonished that a woman's work could be considered so valuable. But her case resonated with women:

Lorna Wendt is rich, privileged, hardly everywoman. But . . . she has come to stand for the many things that wives still mostly end up doing and that society seems mostly to take for granted . . . "I complemented him by keeping the home fires burning and by raising a family and by being the CEO of the Wendt corporation and by running the household and grounds and social and emotional ties so he could go out and work very hard at what he was good at," she says. "If marriage isn't a partnership between equals, then why get married? If you knew that some husband or judge down the road was going to say, 'You're a 30% part of this marriage, and he's a 70% part,' would you get married?"

Source: From Betsy Morris, "It's Her Job Too." From *Fortune* Magazine, February 2, 1998, pp. 65–67. © 1998 Time Inc. Used under license. *Fortune* Magazine and Time Inc. are not affiliated with, and do not endorse products or services of, Licensee.

Gay men and lesbians also are disadvantaged in the workplace by the expectation that everyone has a wife to help out. A gay friend of mine in graduate school shared the feelings of many career-oriented women, lesbian, and heterosexual, single and married, when, juggling school, laundry, errands and cleaning, he observed, "I need a wife!"

Working Hard for a Living:
Women in the Paid Workforce

More women are working outside the home than ever before, a worldwide social change (United Nations, 2000). Overall, about 60 percent of American women (and 73 percent of American men) are in the workforce. About 59 percent of White women, 61 percent of African American women, 56 percent of Hispanic women, and 59 percent of Asian American women are working for pay (U.S. Department of Labor, 2010).

Sex Segregation

Legally, U.S. women have equal opportunity for employment in virtually all jobs. In reality, the workplace in the United States and elsewhere is still characterized by *sex segregation.* The workforce separation of women and men "extends to all regions and countries irrespective of the level of economic development, the political system, or the religious, social or cultural environment" (United Nations, 2000, p. 128). We will look at two varieties: *horizontal sex segregation* (the tendency for women and men to hold different jobs) and *vertical sex segregation* (the tendency for women to be clustered at the bottom of the hierarchy within occupations).

Horizontal Segregation

There are not many occupations in which the proportion of women and men is about equal. Instead, there are women's jobs and men's jobs. Ninety-eight percent of all secretaries, 93 percent of all nurses, and 84 percent of all elementary schoolteachers are women. Ninety-nine percent of auto mechanics, more than 90 percent of engineers, and 70 percent of computer scientists are men (Gilbert & Rader, 2001). (See Box 10.2.) Some occupations have an overall equal ratio of women and men but remain segregated at the level of the individual workplace or task (Gutek, 2001). For example, in retail sales, men more often sell appliances, computers, and cars (the big-ticket items), while women more often sell clothing and cosmetics. Women are more likely to wait tables in diners; men are more likely to be waiters and chefs in upscale restaurants.

The fact that workplaces tend to be "his" or "hers" is a product of the gender system. The jobs where women are clustered tend to be relatively low in pay and status, with little job security and few opportunities for career advancement. Most are service-oriented and associated with stereotypical feminine characteristics such as caring (United Nations, 2000).

The good news is that horizontal sex segregation has declined considerably since the 1970s. Professional and management careers are much less gender-typed than they used to be. Still, gender ratios in lower-level jobs, such as those held by high-school graduates, have changed less. Overall, women made fewer gains in the 1990s relative to the 1970s and 1980s, and horizontal sex segregation is still substantial (Gutek, 2001).

Vertical Segregation

Vertical sex segregation is present when men tend to hold positions that have higher status and better pay than the jobs women hold within an organization or occupation (Gutek, 2001). For example, in the health care industry the nurses' aides, social workers, laboratory technicians, dental hygienists, medical receptionists, and nurses are more likely to be women; physicians, surgeons, dentists, and hospital administrators are more likely to be men. Women more often get stuck in dead-end jobs—even in Sweden, a country committed to gender equality. When researchers analyzed wage mobility for more than one million Swedish workers over a 4-year time period, they found that women were more likely to hold dead-end jobs with little chance of a raise or promotion (Bihagen & Ohls, 2007).

BOX 10.2 ∾ ### Where the Women Are . . . and Where the Money Is

Top Ten Occupations for Women

In 2008, for women who are full time, wage and salary workers, the 10 most prevalent occupations are:

1. Secretaries and administrative assistants
2. Registered nurses
3. Elementary and middle school teachers
4. Cashiers
5. Retail salespersons
6. Aides for nursing, psychiatric, and home health care
7. First-line supervisors/managers of retail sales workers
8. Waiters and waitresses
9. Receptionists and information clerks
10. Bookkeeping, accounting, and auditing clerks

But if you want to earn a high income, these jobs are not the place to go. Women who earn the most are in pharmacy, upper management, or computer science, or they are lawyers and physicians. Note that none of the top paying occupations appear in the list of the most prevalent occupations for women.

Top Ten Highest Paying Occupations for Women

Among women who are full time, wage and salary workers, the 10 occupations with highest median weekly earnings are:

1. Pharmacists, $1,647
2. Chief executives, $1,603
3. Lawyers, $1,509
4. Computer software engineers, $1,351
5. Computer and information systems managers, $1,260
6. Physicians and surgeons, $1,230
7. Management analysts, $1,139
8. Human resource managers, $1,137
9. Speech-language pathologists, $1,124
10. Computer scientists and systems analysts, $1,082

Source: U.S. Department of Labor. (2010). Employment status of women and men in 2008. Retrieved May 27, 2010, from http://www.dol.gov/wb/factsheets/Qf-ESWM08.htm

The closer to the top of the hierarchy, the fewer women there are. Although women are 51 percent of those employed in managerial and professional occupations, they are seldom near the top of the pay scale (Cheung & Halpern, 2010). In a study of more than 500 companies in the United Kingdom, only 8 percent of top executives were female; in the United States, only about 5 percent of senior executives are women (Gilbert & Rader, 2001; Wajcman, 1998). Women hold between 1 and 5 percent of top executive positions in Canada, Brazil, and Germany (United Nations, 2000). In fact, there is not a single field open to both women and men in which there are more women than men at the top, in any country in the world.

The pervasive phenomenon of women being blocked from advancement has been called the ***glass ceiling***: The woman can see her goal, but she bumps into a barrier that is both invisible and impenetrable (Cheung & Halpern, 2010). Women are not totally excluded from business and the professions, but they find it difficult to move past midlevel positions. Women on their way up perceive the glass ceiling as very real, but men in power do not agree. In one survey of women who were corporate vice presidents, 71 percent said there was a glass ceiling for women in their organization. However, 73 percent of the male chief executive officers in the same organizations said there was not (Federal Glass Ceiling Commission, 1998).

Women's Work as Extension of Family Roles: "It's Only Natural"

Looking at the top occupations for women in Box 10.2, you may have noticed that many of them involve service to others, similar to the unpaid work wives and mothers do. Administrative assistants take care of others' to-do lists and health care aides look after their physical needs. Nurses are expected to provide tender loving care to patients, manage the unit like good housekeepers, and serve as handmaidens to physicians (Cassell, 1997). Teachers provide emotional nurturance to young children.

Even when women and men are in equivalent jobs, such as corporate management, women are expected to be more caring and supportive than men. In a study of corporate senior managers and CEOs, both male and female respondents believed that women were more effective than men at caretaking leader behaviors like supporting others and giving praise, whereas men were more effective than women at take-charge leader behaviors like delegating and problem solving. (Prime et al., 2009). These expectations reflect the prescriptive nature of gender stereotypes discussed in Chapter 3—women *are* nurturing, and they *should* be. Though caring is expected from women, it is simultaneously devalued. For example, one psychologist who received excellent teaching evaluations was described by her department chair as being "mama-ish" and "charming" in the classroom—hardly the qualities valued by the tenure and promotion committee (Benokraitis, 1997). Another reported that her good teaching evaluations were derided as being due to her "touchy-feely" approach with students.

Because caring fits into a feminine stereotype, it is often seen as a natural by-product of being female rather than an aspect of job competence. This contributes to the devaluation of women's work: If women perform certain functions naturally, the reasoning goes, virtually any woman can do them, and the woman who does so deserves no special recognition. When *The New York Times* described new customer-service

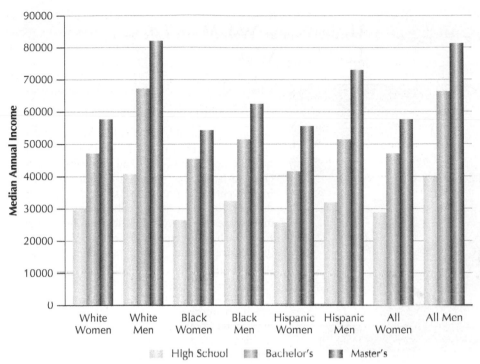

FIGURE 10.2   Median annual full-time earnings by race, gender, and education.
Source: Current Population Survey (CPS). Annual Social and Economic Supplement. Table PINC-03: Education Attainment—People 25 Years Old and over, by Total Money Earnings in 2008, Work Experience in 2008, Age, Race, Hispanic Origin, and Sex.

software that can detect an irate caller, the article suggested that the software could be used to route "an angry man on the line" to "a soothing female operator" ("Press '1' If You're Steamed," 2002). Reading this, I wondered if the female operators will get bonuses, promotions, or raises for their "soothing" skills. Somehow, I doubt it. After all, women just naturally know how to calm down angry men.

The Wage Gap

Women earn less money than men. Indeed, as you can see in Figure 10.2, no group of women has a median income that comes close to the median income of White men. Journalist Barbara Ehrenreich has documented just how hard it is to get by on the jobs available to ordinary working women (see Box 10.3). And the difference between men's and women's wages holds for every level of education. Although young people are urged to get a college education to increase lifetime earnings, the financial payoff of education is much greater for men. Economists have calculated that a female college graduate will earn, over a lifetime of work, $1.2 *million* less than a male college graduate.

The gender gap in wages has decreased somewhat over the past 40 years. As shown in Figure 10.3, this is partly because women are earning more, and partly

BOX 10.3 〜 Undercover at Wal-Mart: Life as a Low-Wage Worker

Can America's low-wage workers survive on their weekly paychecks? This is the question journalist Barbara Ehrenreich set out to answer when she went undercover as a minimally skilled laborer. Shedding the privileges of her education and social class, Ehrenreich took on the identity of a homemaker of modest education and job skills attempting to reenter the job market. Ehrenreich traveled to several states, spending approximately 1 month in each location and working at jobs such as housecleaner, waitress, and sales clerk. Using only the money she earned from her jobs, Ehrenreich attempted to pay for housing, food, transportation, and other living expenses.

Ehrenreich soon learned that minimum wage does not equate to a living wage. Although she was physically fit, a native English speaker, and had no dependents, she had difficulty financially sustaining her simple needs on her earnings. Even working two jobs, seven days a week did little to help. Additionally, being short of money created many unforeseen problems for Ehrenreich, who found it difficult to obtain safe inexpensive housing, pay for reliable transportation, and maintain a healthy diet. For example, because she could not afford security deposits for an apartment, Ehrenreich had to live in a motel, which was more expensive and less safe. Living in a motel room created additional hardships. Lacking a refrigerator or stove, Ehrenreich had to make do with fast food, an expense she had not anticipated.

Ehrenreich's experience makes it clear that those who fill the low-wage rung on America's economic ladder are greatly disadvantaged. This includes especially the millions of women forced into the workforce because of welfare reform. The American dream of attaining wealth through hard work does not take into account the reality of the working poor, whose hard labor is not even enough to pay the bills.

Sources: Barbara Ehrenreich, *Nickel and dimed: On (not) getting by in America.* Contributed by Roxanne Donovan.

because men are earning less. Women now earn about 77 cents for every dollar of men's annual earnings. Earning 23 cents less out of every dollar has huge costs to women workers. The National Committee on Pay Equity has (not so jokingly) proposed that all working women should get a Pay Equity Coupon offering 23 percent off on housing, food, clothing, transportation, and all the other expenses of life! Around the world, the wage gap is even greater, with women earning about 66 cents for every dollar earned by men (United Nations, 2000).

Why this large and persistent inequity in earnings? One traditional explanation is that women invest less in their work roles than men—they are less committed to their work, less likely to obtain extra training and education, more likely to

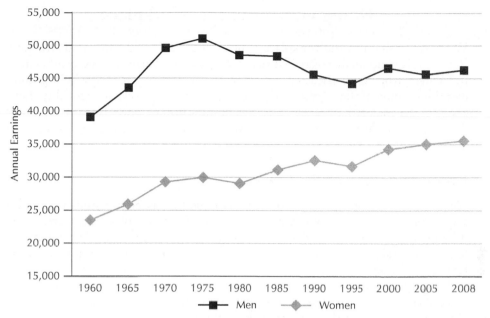

FIGURE 10.3   The wage gap over time: Median annual income by gender, 1960–2008.

Source: Institute for Women's Policy Research. (2010). The gender wage gap: 2009. Available at http:www.iwpr.org/pdf/C350.pdf

be absent or to quit a job. However, little evidence exists to support these claims. On the contrary, women are more likely than men to invest in higher education— currently, women are 57 percent of all college students (Cheung & Halpern, 2010). The gender gap in earnings remains substantial when variables such as education, absences, number of hours worked, and years on the job are controlled (Gutek, 2001; Tsui, 1998; Valian, 1998; Wajcman, 1998). The individual investment hypothesis also does not explain why women's jobs that require high levels of education and skill (like preschool teacher) pay less than men's jobs with lower requirements (like drywall installer).

Another explanation focuses on the jobs rather than the gender of the worker—secretaries and clerks are paid less than electricians and truck drivers, and since more women choose to be secretaries and clerks, they earn less on average. It is certainly true that women are clustered in a few low-paying job sectors, but is this entirely a matter of choice? Moreover, there are substantial wage differences when women and men do exactly the same jobs. Female truck drivers, for example, earn 76 percent of what their male counterparts earn (U.S. Department of Labor, 2002).

It is hard to escape the conclusion that men are paid more for whatever they do simply because they are men. The income discrepancy between women and men is part of a larger pattern of overvaluing whatever is male and undervaluing whatever is female.

Doing Gender in the Workplace

Women's position in the workplace is not just a static aspect of social structure. Rather, it is continually re-created as people make workplace decisions influenced by gender. Chapter 2 discussed how men and women do gender within groups, describing some of the cognitive and social processes that sustain inequality. Let's take a closer look at how sexism operates in the world of work. In particular, how does gender influence evaluations of work? How does it influence hiring and advancement?

Evaluating Women's Performance

"Are women prejudiced against women?" is a question asked in a study that set off a wave of research on how people judge the performance of women versus men (Goldberg, 1968). Female college students were asked to rate the quality and importance of several professional articles. Some of the articles were from stereotypically female professions, such as dietetics; others from stereotypically male professions, such as city planning; and others from relatively gender-neutral areas. Each article was prepared in two versions, as though written either by "John MacKay" or "Joan MacKay." Except for the authors' names, the two versions of each article were identical. The students rated the articles more highly when they thought the articles had been written by a man (including the articles from stereotypically feminine fields). Other researchers found that male raters showed similar prejudice (Paludi & Bauer, 1983; Paludi & Strayer, 1985).

Sometimes highly competent performance by a woman is actually evaluated more positively than comparable performance by a man—as though female competence has more value because it is unexpected (Abramson et al., 1977). In general, though, many experimental studies from the 1960s to the recent past made a convincing case that work attributed to a woman is often devalued. For example, a classic study used psychologists as the participants. Fictitious sets of credentials for psychologists were sent to psychology department chairpersons; the credentials were identical except for the gender of the applicant. The chairpersons were asked how likely they would be to hire the individual described and what level of job they might offer. When the chairpersons thought they were evaluating a female psychologist, "she" was rated less favorably and considered qualified for a lower-level position than when "he" was evaluated (Fidell, 1970).

Are these experimental studies of the past relevant to employees today? A meta-analysis of studies of actual supervisors' ratings of employees showed little overall bias: supervisors did *not* typically devalue female employees. However, pro-male biases did show up when the raters were all male and when the rating dimensions were masculine (e.g., leadership ability). Pro-female bias showed up when the rating dimensions were feminine (e.g., concern for others) (Bowen et al., 2000). These results suggest that biased judgments are not as common as they used to be. However, when the evaluators are men or the attributes being rated are gender stereotyped, ratings of job performance still may not be gender-neutral.

Women's own stories about their experiences at work suggest that evaluation bias affects how they are treated on a daily basis. "Women report that their comments and suggestions are ignored or ridiculed; that men making the identical comments receive praise whereas they do not, and that they are excluded from meetings, networks, lunches and other activities that are part of the 'old boy' network and of the road to career advancement" (Landrine & Klonoff, 1997, p. 11). For women of color, sexism may be compounded by racism. In a study of a matched sample of 200 African American and European American women in professional and managerial positions, the majority of both groups reported differential treatment at work due to their gender, and a majority of the African American women also perceived differential treatment due to their race (Weber & Higginbotham, 1997). All these studies are at least a decade old and times may be changing. There is a need for new research, both experimental and qualitative, on gender bias in evaluation.

Discrimination in Hiring and Promotion

Sex discrimination in employment has been illegal since 1964, when the Civil Rights Act was passed. Before that time, many employers discriminated as a matter of policy. For example, AT&T allowed women to only work up to certain pay levels and in a limited range of tasks (Gutek & Larwood, 1987). Many states had laws that "protected" women by excluding them from certain jobs. For example, women were banned from jobs that required working at night, working around chemicals, serving drinks, or lifting more than 30 pounds (McCormick, 2002). (And just how much does the average 3-year-old weigh?)

Although employers today cannot directly refuse to hire or promote applicants because of race or gender, a great deal of discrimination still occurs. One source of evidence comes from experimental studies of evaluation bias that used simulated job résumés or applications. A meta-analysis of 49 such studies showed a strong preference for men when the job was seen as masculine and a somewhat weaker preference for women when the job was seen as feminine (Davison & Burke, 2000). Unfortunately, leadership roles are still usually perceived as masculine (Eagly & Karau, 2002). In a real-world study of managers at a major corporation, the managers were less likely to promote women because they believed that the women weren't a good fit to their jobs and were likely to have work-family conflicts (Hoobler et al., 2009).

More direct evidence of discrimination comes from sex discrimination lawsuits. Companies that have been sued (and the costs of the settlements) include State Farm ($200 million), Home Depot ($104 million), Novartis ($250 million), Lucky Stores ($95 million), AT&T ($66 million), and Mitsubishi Motors ($34 million). As I write this book, a sex discrimination suit against Walmart, the largest employer in the United States, is about to go to trial, 9 years after it first was filed. According to the lawsuit, on behalf of 1.6 million women workers (past and present), Walmart has kept women in the lowest-paying jobs and favored male managers in hiring and promotion. Although 65 percent of Walmart's low-level employees are female, only 33 percent of its managers are (Abelson, 2004; Greenhouse & Hays, 2004).

Time will tell if the Walmart case, the largest of its type in U.S. history, stands up in court, but the pattern is one familiar to many women. In a U.S. sample of more than 1,200 women, over 40 percent said that at some time in their lives they had been denied a raise, a promotion, or some other deserved reward at work because they were women. One in five (and more women of color than White women) had experienced such discrimination within the past year (Landrine & Klonoff, 1997). Many other studies indicate that equally qualified women are less likely than men to be hired or are offered lower-paying, less desirable jobs (Eagly & Karau, 2002; Fassinger, 2002). Sexism is alive and well in the workplace.

Unfortunately, patterns of discrimination are often very hard to see. For example, if you are a woman with a bachelor's degree who has been with a company for 5 years and you are not promoted, you might compare yourself with a male coworker who was promoted. Suppose this man has been with the company for only 3 years but he has a master's degree: It's hard to decide whether or not you have been discriminated against. But suppose you look further in the company and find a man who was promoted with only a high school diploma and 10 years of service and a woman who was not promoted with 2 years of college and 8 years of service. A pattern begins to form. That pattern is apparent only when many cases are averaged and discrimination is usually examined one case at a time (Crosby et al., 1986). One important function of affirmative action programs is to keep records so that patterns of discrimination become evident over time. You can't fix a problem if nobody knows the problem exists (Crosby, 2003).

Social Reactions to Token Women

From the local fire department or welding shop to the U.S. Senate, the corporate boardroom, and everywhere in between, women in nontraditional careers are likely to work mostly with men. They are a minority in workplaces where the environment is highly masculine. Just by being there, a woman in a male-dominated field sticks out. This is true for other disadvantaged groups, too. The "odd person," whether Black, Hispanic, disabled, or female, becomes a *token.* Generally, researchers define a token as a member of a group that is less than 15 percent of the larger group. Female firefighters and male nurses, for example, are usually tokens in their workplaces.

Because of their visibility, tokens feel a lot of performance pressure. As one woman commented, "If it seems good to be noticed, wait until you make your first major mistake" (Kanter, 1977, p. 213). When a White male employee makes a mistake, it is interpreted as an individual error and no more; if the token woman or minority makes a similar mistake, it may be taken as evidence that "those people" should not have been hired and are bound to fail. Paradoxically, the token must also worry about being too successful. Because all eyes are on the token employee, a token who performs well enough to show up members of the dominant group may be criticized for being a workaholic or too aggressive.

Tokens are also socially isolated and stereotyped. They get pigeonholed into familiar roles such as mother, wife, or sex object. One female commercial pilot reported that her copilot questioned whether she was following the directions from air traffic control, saying "Oh well my wife gets lost when she goes to the supermarket" (Davey & Davidson, 2000, p. 213).

FIGURE 10.4

Source: DILBERT: © Scott Adams / Dist. by United Feature Syndicate, Inc.

When the token does not play along with stereotyped roles, she may be cast as the archetypal unfeminine iron maiden or bitch. (There is even a corporate training program, Bully Broads, aimed at women executives who are perceived as too aggressive. Its goal is to help them re-learn indirect and manipulative techniques such as crying, wearing more provocative clothing, and pretending to be incompetent. Personally, I don't think this is progress for women!)

Women and minorities are much more likely than White men to experience token status. However, when White men are the tokens, they suffer no disadvantages. Men in female-dominated occupations (nurse, librarian, elementary teacher, and social worker) fare better than women in the same occupations in several ways—they are more satisfied with their jobs, get better evaluations, and advance faster. This has been dubbed the *glass escalator* to contrast with the glass ceiling experienced by women (Budig, 2002; Williams, 1992).

Comparisons of male and female tokens show that the negative effects of being a token are not due just to numbers. Rather, they reflect differences in status and power. When women or ethnic minorities enter a group that was formerly all White and male, they are perceived as interlopers and deviants (see Figure 10.4).

The negative effects of tokenism for women and ethnic minorities decrease once they are about 35 percent of the larger group (Yoder, 2002). But increasing their numbers alone is not the answer, because tokens are still seen as lower in status.

How can people in the token slot become more respected and effective? Just getting the job and having the expertise to do it are not enough. In one experimental study, when women were appointed leaders of all-male task groups and supplied with task-relevant expertise to help them lead the groups, they still were not very successful or appreciated as leaders. However, when a male experimenter specifically told group members that the woman leader had special training and useful information for their task, she was able to be effective despite being in a token position (Yoder et al., 1998). While it is worrisome that women's leadership still needs to be given legitimacy by high-status men, this study suggests that fair-minded men can use their organizational power to support token women.

Role Models and Mentors

Role models are members of one's own reference group who are visibly successful (Yoder et al., 1985). Just knowing that other women have managed to overcome the obstacles to success may help the newcomer (Basow & Howe, 1980; O'Connell & Russo, 1980). For example, female graduate students who had female professors as role models described themselves as more career-oriented, confident, instrumental, and satisfied than those who had male role models (Gilbert et al., 1983). In a study of over 400 undergraduate psychology students, having a good relationship with a supportive role model was an important factor in helping the students decide their future career goals (Perrone et al., 2002).

Unlike White men, women and minority men have had few role models. Lack of role models probably contributes to loneliness and feelings of deviance. Adding a few token women to the workplace does not solve the role model problem. In fact, the pressure to be a role model adds to the existing pressures on the token.

Role models may be admired from afar; *mentors* are people who take a personal interest in the newcomer (Yoder et al., 1985). Knowing the formal rules in a workplace is rarely enough. Whether you are working in a corporation, factory, hospital, or office, there is inside knowledge that is not written down in the employee manual. Instead, workers rely on informal social networks to work the system to their advantage (Lorber, 1993). Successful older men frequently serve as mentors to young men on their way up, providing them with introductions to important people, special training, and hints about office politics. They may also stand up for the young man if he makes a controversial decision and they raise his status simply by associating with him.

Having a mentor increases job satisfaction and career advancement for both women and men. The beneficial effects of mentoring have been shown for many groups. A study of 231 female attorneys showed that those who had had mentors earned more money, were more successful, and were more satisfied in their careers than those who had not (Wallace, 2001). A study of women psychologists showed that those who had a research mentor were more likely to do research and also to become research mentors for others (Dohm & Cummings, 2002).

Why do women have more difficulty finding a mentor than men do? One reason is that women lack access to the ***old-boy network,*** with its "bands of brothers" who look out for each other's interests (Lorber, 1993). As one female corporate executive put it: "It's always been men at the top of this company and the top of the company I was in before. They all know each other. They've all come up the same route together, all boys together" (Wajcman, 1998, p. 97).

Often, high-status men are reluctant to mentor women. Quite simply, they feel more comfortable with people that they perceive as more similar to themselves. Also, young women may not always realize the importance of finding mentors. Or they may be reluctant to ask senior men for mentoring because they fear the relationship would be misinterpreted as sexual (Gutek, 2001).

Having a male mentor definitely has its benefits. In a study of female attorneys, women who had been mentored by men earned more (Wallace, 2001). Having a senior male mentor may be particularly beneficial for women in male-dominated and masculine-typed occupations. This was shown in a study of more than 3,000 U.S. college graduates that assessed their career status 15 years after graduation. In industries where there were few women—and/or an aggressive, engineering-intensive, competitive culture—women who had male mentors were earning more money and were happier with their career progress than women with female mentors or no mentors at all. In a tough corporate climate, senior male mentors gave them legitimacy and sponsorship (Ramaswami et al., 2010).

What about women mentoring other women? Women may be better mentors for women in creating a professional self-image, empowerment, and supportive personal counseling (Burke & McKeen, 1997; Gilbert & Rossman, 1992). Among a sample of female attorneys, those mentored by women reported less conflict between work and family and greater career satisfaction. They were also more likely to continue practicing law (Wallace, 2001). Female mentors also provide models of leadership that women can identify with. A human resources manager for an international telecommunications company, who was interviewed as part of a study of global managers, put it this way:

> Of the two women mentors that I had, one has children and it has been really refreshing for me to see that she is very senior, that she has kept a balance in her life, and she hasn't become macho. . . . it is refreshing to see that you can get there and not sacrifice yourself in getting more like men (Linehan & Scullion, 2008).

Women in professional fields often sponsor mentoring opportunities for other women. For example, APA's Division 35, the Society for the Psychology of Women, matches beginning researchers with accomplished ones for mentoring. And MentorNet, a national e-mail network, offers opportunities for women in engineering, math, and science majors to connect with supportive experts in their fields (www.mentornet.net). MentorNet reports that 95 percent of its mentored students complete their degrees. In 2010, MentorNet announced a partnership with AT&T to provide mentors for science and engineering students at historically Black colleges and universities. (See Figure 10.5.)

FIGURE 10.5   As the world of work becomes more diverse, problems of tokenism and lack of mentors for women and ethnic minorities will probably ease.

Leadership: Do Women Do It Differently?

Clearly, there are barriers that prevent many women from reaching the top of the career ladder. Despite such obstacles, more women are moving into positions of leadership. Once they are in leadership positions, do women lead differently from men? This question was not considered important throughout most of psychology's history. Most leadership research was done with men; women, and particularly women of color, were simply left out of the studies (Sanchez-Hucles & Davis, 2010). Fortunately, researchers are now paying more attention to women as leaders.

Contrary to stereotype, there are no dramatic gender differences in leadership style. In a meta-analysis of 370 studies, women were somewhat more democratic and participative leaders than men. However, the difference depended on the situation; for example, it was larger in laboratory studies than real-life settings (Eagly & Johnson, 1990). In laboratory studies, people are usually strangers to each other and the manager role is simulated; gender roles may be salient. In actual workplaces, where people have clear job responsibilities and long-term relationships, the demands of the manager role may be more important than gender roles (Eagly & Johannesen-Schmidt, 2001).

Are women more effective as leaders? Effectiveness is usually defined as how well the leader helps the group reach its stated goals. A meta-analysis of 76 studies of leadership effectiveness showed that there were no gender differences except in the military, where men were more effective (Eagly et al., 1995). Again, the effect of situation is apparent—military leadership takes place in an extremely masculine realm where women are a small minority in each work group.

In contrast to these findings of overall similarity, a study of managers from the United States and eight other countries found some significant gender differences. Women were rated higher on several positive attributes such as motivating others, showing optimism about goals, mentoring others, being considerate, and rewarding others for good performance. Men were more likely to be critical about others' mistakes, to be absent or uninvolved during a crisis, and to wait until problems were severe before trying to solve them. Overall, in this study the women were perceived as more effective managers (Eagly & Johannesen-Schmidt, 2001).

In summary, the evidence suggests that once women are seen as legitimate leaders, they behave similarly to men in the same kinds of positions and they are equally likely to succeed. However, where there are differences in leadership style, the styles that women are more likely to use may enhance the effectiveness of their organizations. But any advantage that women may have in leadership style may be offset by the resistance of men in power to accept women's leadership. As more women enter formerly masculine domains, gender will become less noticeable in leadership contexts, and we can hope that leaders will be evaluated as individuals.

Sexual Harassment from Nine to Five

Sexual harassment has been around for a long time, and it has been formally defined and studied for at least the past 30 years (Gutek & Done, 2001; Pina et al., 2009). Second-wave feminist activists and researchers first named it as a form of sex discrimination and violence against women, drawing public attention and stimulating research on the topic. What used to be considered just part of life for a working woman is now recognized as harmful and classified as illegal.

Defining Sexual Harassment

The legal definition of sexual harassment distinguishes two kinds. ***Quid pro quo*** harassment is unwanted sexual advances or behavior that is a condition of employment. In other words, the harasser makes it clear that the employee will be fired, given unpleasant tasks, receive a negative evaluation, or otherwise suffer bad consequences unless she complies with sexual demands. For example, one woman reported, "This man went after every girl in the office and he went after me . . . We got fired if we did not go out with him" (Gutek, 1985, p. 82).

The second kind of harassment is the creation of a ***hostile work environment***. This could include obscene remarks, demeaning jokes about women, or suggestive comments about the worker's sexuality or personal life, as well as threatening or aggressive sexually-toned materials in the workplace. In one case, a female shipyard worker was subjected to pornographic pictures and graffiti at work. Her male coworkers also put up a dartboard drawn like a woman's breast with the nipple as the bulls-eye (Fitzgerald, 1993).

There is room for confusion and disagreement even in legal definitions of sexual harassment. What seems like an unwanted advance or a hostile environment to one person may seem like a friendly invitation or innocent fun to another (Pina et al., 2009). Sometimes the victim herself is not sure whether she is being harassed. In a qualitative study of the sexual harassment experiences of women of color, this participant described the sexual remarks at work and her ambivalence about them:

> I think, just someone saying, "You have big beautiful breasts" or whatever. Or, "she's got that Black girl ass or that's that Jennifer Lopez booty." You know, but that's what you run up against and sometimes it's hard to deal seriously with people when people are telling a joke you don't know if they are meaning it or what all their words are meaning (Richardson & Taylor, 2009, p. 259).

The Supreme Court has changed and enlarged its definition of sexual harassment several times over the past decades to encompass changing social definitions, and will most likely continue to do so (Gutek & Done, 2001). Some researchers have created psychological definitions that differ from the legal ones, classifying a behavior as sexual harassment if the recipient perceives it as offensive and detrimental to her well-being (Fitzgerald et al., 1997). In the courts, both the victim's perspective and the outsider's perspective are taken into account. The victim must show that the behavior is severe or pervasive and detrimental to her well-being, and the behavior must be such that a reasonable person would call it harassment (Gutek & Done, 2001).

These legal and psychological definitions are important in distinguishing sexual attention from sexual harassment; the latter must be severe, pervasive, and unwanted. For example, if a supervisor asks an employee to go out on a date, it is not sexual harassment (although it may be unwise, divisive in the office, or contrary to company policy). However, if the supervisor repeatedly asks for a date despite the worker's evident dismay or disinterest, or suggests directly or indirectly that she might get that raise or that vacation time if they get together, the supervisor is violating the law and committing sexual harassment. In the case of hostile environment harassment, an occasional sexist joke or sexual remark does not qualify as a hostile climate, but a pattern of sexist behavior that interferes with work or creates an offensive tone in the office does.

The Prevalence of Harassment

Anyone can be subjected to sexual harassment. Like other forms of violence against women (see Chapter 12), harassment is likely to go unrecognized and under-reported, and only the most extreme cases go to court. A meta-analysis showed that when women are asked directly if they have been sexually harassed, the reported rate is much lower than when they are presented with a list of sexually harassing behaviors and asked to check any that have happened to them (Ilies et al., 2003). This indicates that victims may not label what happens to them as harassment, which means that they are unlikely to report it even though it fits into the legal definition.

Random-sample surveys indicate that 35 to 50 percent of women have experienced workplace sexual harassment (Gutek & Done, 2001). Some of the most consistent data come from periodic random sample surveys of federal employees (U.S. Merit Systems Protection Board, 1981, 1987, 1995). In these surveys, 42 to 44 percent of women workers reported that they had experienced harassment within the past 24 months, a proportion that remained steady over the 14 years covered by these studies. Men can be sexually harassed, too, although this happens much less often than male-to-female harassment. In these cases, the harasser may be either another man or a woman (Gutek & Done, 2001; Pina et al., 2009).

Anyone may be vulnerable to harassment, but there are some factors that may elevate a person's risk. For example, women in male-dominated occupations are particularly likely to experience harassment (Gutek & Done, 2001). Younger women and those who are unattached to men (unmarried, divorced, or lesbian women) are more likely to be harassed than older, married women. Women of color may be more likely to be harassed than White women, although too few studies have been done to reach a definite conclusion. Ethnic minority women may be particularly vulnerable because stereotypes portray them as sexually available (African Americans and Latinas) or docile and submissive (Asian Americans). Women of color, as a group, also hold less power and status in the workplace than White women, which may increase their risk. Sexual harassment often, but not always, goes downward in the power hierarchy. In about half the cases, the harasser is a supervisor, but may also be a coworker, a customer, or even a subordinate of the victim (Gutek & Done, 2001; Pina et al., 2009).

What Are the Causes of Harassment?

There are several theories about the causes of sexual harassment (Tangri & Hayes, 1997). The *sex-role spillover theory* suggests that harassment occurs when a woman's gender is more salient than her role as a worker, so that men see her first and foremost as a sex object. Gender is most salient when the woman is in a token position; thus this theory predicts that the more male-dominated the occupation, the more harassment will occur. Gender can also be salient when the job has objectification built in to it—as when waitresses are required to wear short skirts or tight T-shirts.

Another theory stresses that sexual harassment is an abuse of power. Men have more formal power in organizations and often have more informal influence as well. They can misuse their power to treat women as sex objects, then claim that the incidents never occurred or that the woman was trying to sleep her way to the top. This theory is consistent with evidence that sexual harassment is more prevalent in hierarchical organizations such as the military than in less hierarchical ones such as universities (Ilies et al., 2003).

A third theory points to the broader sociocultural context of male dominance. Men are still being socialized toward taking the sexual initiative, being sexually persistent, and feeling entitled to have what they want. Women are still being socialized toward being compliant, considerate, taking the role of sexual gatekeeper, and putting others' needs first. Thus, according to the sociocultural theory, sexual harassment at work is just part of a larger pattern of societal dominance by men (Tangri & Hayes, 1997). Each of these theories has been supported by some research, suggesting that sexual harassment may stem from all these causes, and differ from one setting (and perpetrator) to another. To date, there has been very little research on the characteristics of men who harass (Pina et al., 2009).

The Consequences of Harassment

The economic consequences of workplace sexual harassment are enormous. A U.S. government agency estimated that sexual harassment of federal employees cost $327 million in 2 years due to workers' being less productive, taking sick leave to cope with its effects, or changing jobs (U.S. Merit Systems Protection Board, 1995). In surveys, more than one woman in five reports that she has quit a job, gotten transferred, been fired, or stopped trying to get a job because of harassment (Gutek, 1985). Quitting may seem better than protesting, as one woman explained:

> I was the only woman and the only Black woman . . . but I didn't want to react to it like the way they thought I would. Like "she's Black and she's going to get all angry." I didn't even want to give them that satisfaction. That's another reason why I just quit (Richardson & Taylor, 2009, p. 263).

The psychological consequences of harassment can be devastating. Harassment interferes with women's commitment to their jobs and the satisfaction they get from doing them, as shown by studies done in many different occupations. In a large utility company, harassment was linked to being absent more often and wanting to leave the company (Fitzgerald et al., 1997); in a sample of office workers, it was linked to lower job satisfaction (Piortrkowski, 1998); in Navy personnel, it was linked to dissatisfaction with the Navy and plans to leave military service (Rosenfeld et al., 1998).

A woman's initial reactions to harassment may include self-doubt, confusion, and guilt, as she asks herself if she did anything to cause or encourage it (Richardson & Taylor, 2009). She may worry about losing her job or fear that the harassment will escalate into rape, and her anxiety may become chronic. Her self-confidence and self-esteem drop. Several studies have shown that the experience of sexual harassment can lead to depression, irritability, physical symptoms (extreme fatigue and headaches), and psychological distress (Gutek & Done, 2001). A national study of over 3,000 women found that prior harassment was linked with major depression and post-traumatic stress disorder (PTSD). The effects were large: only 9 percent of non-harassed women, and nearly 30 percent of those who had been harassed, suffered from PTSD (Dansky & Kilpatrick, 1997). The more severe the harassment, the more likely it is to cause psychological damage, and this occurs whether or not the woman labels her experience as harassment (Gutek & Done, 2001).

Sexual harassment is not inevitable. Organizations can reduce it by educating people about the problem, and many have developed policies and programs designed to do so. However, these programs may be designed primarily to protect the company from potential lawsuits. This kind of education is not enough in itself and may even be counterproductive. In one study, faculty and staff at a university were given a 30-minute program that included a video about the university's policies, an oral presentation, and discussion. When participants were then compared to a control group of nonparticipants, they had more knowledge about harassment—a positive result. However, men who had participated in the training were *less* likely than control-group men to recognize sexual harassment or say they would report it, and *more* likely to blame the victim (Bingham & Scherer, 2001). In this case, the educational effort seems to have backfired, making men more resistant to recognizing the problem.

Individuals can help solve the problem by confronting harassment. This woman told a researcher how she did just that:

> a lot of times I would have to . . . spend a lot of time with the engineer. And then he would always talk off to me you know. "Hey man give me a blow job. Blah blah blah blah." And he was a friend but he became serious about it and I didn't like it. I said, "Hey you know what you're saying here, I thought we were friends. I don't want to have nothing to do with you. You might think it's funny and all but I don't" (Richardson & Taylor, 2009, p. 264).

But relying on the victim to confront the harasser or file a report is not enough. Organizations must also have a strong policy in place, send clear messages to employees that harassment will not be tolerated, and punish those who violate standards (Gutek, 1985). Moreover, they should provide support systems for women who have been harassed and protect them from retaliation when they report it. There is also a need for more research on why some men harass women, whereas the majority of men do not (Pina et al., 2009). Preventing sexual harassment is more than just a matter of preventing lawsuits; it is a matter of creating an organizational climate that is healthy for all its workers.

Women's Career Development

So far our discussion of obstacles to women's job and career satisfaction has focused on forces in the social environment. We now turn to psychological factors—individual differences in beliefs, values, motives, and choices.

Do Women Have Different Values and Interests?

Do women workers want different rewards than men? Do they end up in feminized occupations because these occupations fit with their personal values? A great deal of research has attempted to answer these questions: a meta-analysis found 242 different samples totaling well over half a million people (Konrad et al., 2000), and has provided a clearer picture of what women and men value in their jobs.

In general, gender differences were small. Women tended to value intrinsic rewards more highly. These are rewards that come from actually doing the job, such as intellectual stimulation, a chance for creativity, a sense of accomplishment, and feeling that the work is meaningful. Men tended to value different intrinsic rewards, such as freedom, challenge, and power. They also valued extrinsic rewards more highly—those that come after the job is done or as a by-product of the job, such as pay and promotion, fringe benefits, and job security. Women placed higher value on a pleasant working environment—friendly coworkers, comfortable surroundings, commuting ease, and convenient hours. Perhaps women value comfort and convenience on the job more than men do because many women leave paid work at the end of the day for a second shift of housework and child care.

Women's and men's values seem to be converging, especially when they occupy similar positions. In the meta-analysis just described, job attributes like wanting responsibility became more important to women in the 1980s and 1990s, and many sex differences found in the 1970s disappeared. This suggests that women's aspirations have risen with their opportunities (Konrad et al., 2000). In a study of senior managers of multinational corporations, women and men agreed that a sense of achievement and enjoying the job were their most important motives. In fact, they agreed on every motive they were asked about—respect from colleagues, developing other people, meeting goals, and so on. The only gender differences were that women were slightly more likely than men to care about having power and slightly less likely to care about money (Wajcman, 1998). Thus, it is highly unlikely that the wage gap or the glass ceiling can be attributed to gender differences in values.

Although values may help determine one's occupational setting, the occupational setting may also affect one's values. When a person is given opportunities to advance, he or she is likely to develop a strong work commitment and aspirations for promotions and raises. A person placed in a job with little upward mobility tends to become indifferent, to complain, and to look for extrinsic satisfactions. Thus, the social structure of the workplace is a powerful force in shaping values and behavior. But its effects are often overlooked. When women in dead-end jobs develop poor attitudes, these attitudes are sometimes seen as characteristic of women as a group instead of a human response to blocked opportunities. As one pioneering organizational researcher put it, "What the clerical worker with low motivation to be promoted might need is a promotion; what the chronic complainer might need is a growthful challenge. But who would be likely to give it to them?" (Kanter, 1977, p. 158).

Are Women Less Motivated to Achieve?

For more than 50 years, psychologists have explored the question of why some people strive for success. **Achievement motivation** is the desire to accomplish something valuable and important and to meet high standards of excellence. Starting in the 1950s, researchers devised tests for measuring achievement motivation and predicting achievement oriented behavior (McClelland et al., 1953). Achievement behaviors of any sort—from running a marathon to winning a beauty contest—could theoretically be predicted by one's score on an achievement-motivation measure. For research purposes, however, scores were used to predict performance in academic settings and competitive games in the laboratory.

Early research showed that achievement-motivation scores predicted the achievement behavior of men but not women. Reflecting the strong gender bias of research at that time, the intriguing question of why women behaved less predictably than men was not explored. Instead, researchers just excluded women from their future studies, concluding that they must lack achievement motivation (Veroff et al., 1953).

Today, it is recognized that women and men have similar motivation to achieve, but that motivation may be channeled in different directions. As they are growing up, girls and boys continually make choices, both consciously and unconsciously, about how they will spend their time and efforts. This decision making is complex and multidimensional (Hyde & Kling, 2001). The most important current theory for understanding these choices and their relationship to achievement motivation is the **expectancy X value model** (Eccles, 1994).

The expectancy part of the theory involves the individual's *expectations of success*. Research shows that junior high and high school students have gender-linked expectations for success: boys are more confident in math, and girls in English. But even if a girl believes she can succeed at a task, she is unlikely to attempt it unless it is important to her—this is where the value part of the theory comes in. The *subjective value* of various options (Do I enjoy English more than math? Will I really need math for my chosen career?) strongly affects decision making; for example, girls typically view math as less useful and important to them than boys do.

Expectancies and values are shaped by parental attributions ("My daughter got an A in math because she works hard, my son because he's bright"), gender-role beliefs ("Scientists are nerdy guys"), and self-perceptions ("I can't do physics"). Because gender socialization affects values, definitions of success, and the kinds of activities seen as crucial to one's identity, it affects virtually every aspect of achievement-related decision making.

One example of differently socialized values is the importance placed on being a parent. Gender differences in the subjective value of having children, and its effects on career planning, were demonstrated in a study of college students (Stone & McKee, 2000). When they responded to surveys, both women and men were strongly career oriented. However, interviews with the same students gave a different picture. Men consistently planned to put their career first, whereas most of the women planned to cut back or stop their careers once they had children. As one said, "Once I'm a parent, my career is on hold." Perhaps because of these differences in the value attached to parenthood, women had much less knowledge than men did about the fields they planned to enter (the graduate training needed and how much they could earn) and were not gaining as much relevant work experience. Although they expected to work and to be successful, the women's values about family life were leading them to do less planning and preparation for their future career. Do you think that results would be similar or different on your campus?

High-Achieving Women

Today many women continue to enter the traditionally female-dominated professions of teaching, social work, and nursing. Meanwhile, others are entering formerly male-dominated professions—law, medicine, accounting, psychology, science, engineering, the military, and business management. For example, women went from 3 percent of all law school graduates in the 1970s to about 25 percent in the 1990s and nearly 50 percent in the past decade (Chapman, 2008; Valian, 1998). It is still the case that relatively few women achieve professional success. Yet despite the many obstacles, some women do. How are these women different? What factors in their personalities and backgrounds make the difference?

What Factors Affect Women's Career Development?

High-achieving women in the professions provide potential models for other women. Their backgrounds suggest ways to bring up girls without limiting their aspirations and development. Their achievements represent the possibility of breaking down sex segregation in the workplace. If a few women can make it, a world of equal power and status for all women and men becomes easier to imagine.

In general, high-achieving women come from backgrounds that provide them with a relatively unconstricted sense of self and an enriched view of women's capabilities (Lemkau, 1983). Their families and their upbringing are unusual in positive ways (see Table 10.1). As social learning theory would predict, girls who are exposed to less gender-stereotyped expectations are more likely to become high achievers. Attending all-girls' schools and women's colleges can provide role models and opportunities for leadership. Not surprisingly, parents play an important role. Employed mothers—especially when they enjoy their work and are successful at it—provide an important model for achievement. Because fathers usually encourage gender typing in their children more than mothers do, a father who supports and encourages his daughter's achievements may be especially influential

TABLE 10.1 Characteristics Associated with Achievement in Women

Individual variables	Background variables
High ability	Working mother
Liberated sex role values	Supportive father
Instrumentality	Highly educated parents
Androgynous personality	Female role models
High self-esteem	Work experience as adolescent
Strong academic self-concept	Androgynous upbringing
Educational variables	**Adult lifestyles variables**
Higher education	Late marriage or single
Continuation in mathematics	No or few children
Girls' schools and women's colleges	

Source: Betz, N., & Fitzgerald, L. F. (1987). *The Career Psychology of Women*, Table 9.1 (p. 143). Copyright © 1987 by Academic Press, Inc. Reprinted by permission of Elsevier.

(Weitzman, 1979). One Black woman who became a distinguished physician provided an eloquent description of her parents' belief in her:

> As a woman, I was told, I would be able to do whatever I wanted. I was taught that my skin had a beautiful color. This constant, implicit reinforcement of positive self-image was my parents' most valuable gift to me. I grew up loving my color and enjoying the fact that I was a woman. . . . In school, I performed well because my mother and father expected it of me. When I entered high school, I elected the college preparatory program as a matter of course (Hunter, 1974, pp. 58–59).

Setting high goals and being persistent despite setbacks are important factors in women's career development. In a survey of more than 200 African American women attorneys, 80 percent said that their families and teachers had encouraged them to work hard and set high goals. They also said they had benefited from having access to Black women role models and to equal opportunity programs (Simpson, 1996). In a longitudinal study, an ethnically diverse group of high school girls who expressed interest in math and science careers in 1980 were followed up to 13 years later. Those who had achieved their goals had taken more elective math and science in high school, set high standards for themselves, and stressed how important it is to "hang in there" when difficulties arise. Those who had experienced their parents' divorce were especially motivated to be financially independent because they had seen what happens to women who have to support their children on their own. Among the group that had not achieved their goals, some were stopped by family socialization (they were taught that the most important goal for a woman is marriage) or critical life events such as an unplanned pregnancy (Farmer et al., 1997).

Variations among Successful Women

The research summarized in Table 10.1 has been useful in helping psychologists understand the dynamics of achievement in women, but it does have limitations. Obviously, all these characteristics are not true of all high-achieving women. Some women who do not have any of the characteristics manage to succeed anyway, and some even report having been spurred on by a disapproving parent or an attempt to hold them back (Weitzman, 1979). In one study, Black and White women who came from poor families in which neither parent had finished high school were extensively interviewed. Despite their disadvantaged backgrounds, these women had achieved extraordinary success in business, academia, or government service. The odds-defying achievers had an unusually strong belief in their ability to control their lives. They believed that "You can do anything if you put your mind to it" (Boardman et al., 1987).

Research on high-achieving women has been done mostly with White women. More research is needed on diverse groups of women achievers to give a complete profile of successful women. Family background and socialization probably affect Hispanic, Asian American, and African American women differently. For example, Black women generally grow up expecting to support themselves; some Asian American groups stress academic achievement but also expect subservience to family. It is likely that racism and sexism interact in the career development of women of color (Sanchez-Hucles & Davis, 2010).

Models of career development based on heterosexuals may have limited applicability to lesbian and bisexual women. The process of coming out and accepting a lesbian identity is personally demanding (see Chapter 7) and, in some cases, may delay career development. However, coming out is a normal phase for lesbian and bisexual women, one that should be taken into account in career counseling (Boatwright et al., 1996).

Cause—Or Effect?

Studying the factors leading to success by looking at successful women is an example of *retrospective research* in which participants look back at factors influencing them at an earlier time. It can show us what characteristics successful women tend to share. However, it can also lead us to assume that we know the *causes* of success when we may be observing its *results*.

In other words, women who—for whatever reason—have the opportunity to test themselves in a demanding career may develop high self-esteem, assertiveness, independence, and achievement motivation as a consequence of their success. From this perspective, opportunity creates a "successful" personality, rather than vice versa (Kanter, 1977). Retrospective memory is not always accurate, either. Successful women may remember more achievement emphasis in their backgrounds and childhoods than less successful women simply because this dimension is relevant to them as adults (Nieva & Gutek, 1981).

Putting It All Together: Work and Family

Women's increasing involvement in paid work has been one of the strongest social trends of the past 40 years. It is interesting that women's work became a topic of psychological research only in the 1970s, when middle-class White women began entering the workforce in greater numbers. The fact that working-class women and women of color had always held paid jobs had not been considered worthy of psychological research. Unlike most research on work, which focuses on men, research on the problems of combining work and family has focused almost exclusively on women, especially on White, upper-middle-class heterosexual women who are pursuing high-status careers.

When psychologists first began studying working women, they emphasized the social and personal costs of multiple roles, rather than their rewards (Crawford, 1982; Gilbert & Rader, 2001). For example, researchers investigated whether women's work was detrimental to their mental health or their marriages. They were much less likely to ask whether family involvement or a happy marriage may make one a better and more productive worker. Researchers are now examining work and family from a broader perspective, looking at how activities at work and at home converge and affect each other.

Although people sometimes say that "You shouldn't bring your work home from the office" or "You shouldn't let personal problems affect your work," they do affect each other. Men and women's work, along with their family roles, function as a system. Each component affects the other (Gilbert & Rader, 2001; Lorber, 1993). Combining the multiple obligations of spouse, parent, and worker has often been described as a balancing act. Let's look at some costs and benefits of the balancing act for working women and their families.

What Are the Costs of the Balancing Act?

There is no doubt that combining work and family is hard for both women and men. The double day of paid and unpaid work done by many women is particularly demanding. *Role conflict* refers to the psychological effects of being faced with sets of incompatible expectations or demands; *role overload* describes the difficulties of meeting these expectations. Think of a secretary who is asked to work overtime on short notice and must scramble to find child care. She may experience both conflict (feeling torn between her two obligations) and overload (as she calls babysitters while formatting the overdue report). Here her mother and worker roles are incompatible with each other and there is no really satisfactory resolution of the conflict. Research has consistently shown that women workers experience role conflict (Crosby, 1991; Gilbert, 1993; Wajcman, 1998). In some studies, men also report role conflict. Chronic role conflict and overload are linked to guilt, anxiety, and depression, and contribute to fatigue, short temper, and lowered resistance to illness.

Both women and men make trade-offs to keep up with the balancing act, and their choices are shaped by sociocultural aspects of gender as well as by their own attitudes and beliefs. In U.S. studies, women are much more likely than men to adjust their jobs around their family responsibilities (Mennino & Brayfield, 2002). For example, women are more likely than men to arrange flextime schedules, work part-time, turn down opportunities for promotion or overtime, and use their own sick days to care for others. When more than 900 men and women in a national U.S. survey were asked about the trade-offs they made and their gender-role attitudes, individual attitudes had little effect. In other words, more traditionally oriented people did not make different choices than more egalitarian people. However, both women and men in male-dominated occupations made more trade-offs that put family needs second to work needs. For example, they were more likely to take on extra work and to miss a family event. These results suggest that "male-typed occupations, regardless of whether they are held by women or men, are less accommodating to job-family balance" (Mennino & Brayfield, 2002, p. 251).

On the other hand, a large scale survey of Dutch couples found that women had more favorable attitudes toward housework and child care than men did: Women said they enjoy it more, set higher standards for it, and feel more responsible for it. Women's positive and men's negative attitudes toward chores predicted women doing more household labor (Poortman & Van Der Lippe, 2009). Some couples work out mutual strategies such as sharing child care and housework or hiring someone else to do chores. But as long as women are still being socialized to be more responsible for home and family, the balancing act will continue to be more of a problem for them than for their spouses.

What Are the Benefits of the Balancing Act?

Side by side with research showing widespread problems with role conflict and overload is a great deal of research showing *benefits* associated with multiple roles. Indeed, study after study shows that involvement as a spouse, parent, and worker is beneficial for both women and men. The value of the balancing act is reflected in better mental health, physical health, and relationship quality as well as more satisfaction at work (Barnett & Hyde, 2001; King et al., 2009).

Why does involvement in many roles benefit well-being? One reason may be that a job or career is generally a source of self-esteem and social involvement (Steil, 1997). Another reason is that success in one domain may help people keep a sense of perspective about the other domains (Crosby, 1982, 1991). Being passed over for promotion might seem less of a disaster if one is happily involved in leading a Girl Scout troop; dealing with a difficult teenager at home may be made easier by being respected at the office.

Employment also increases women's power in the family (see Chapter 8). And it provides families with higher incomes, which benefits everyone and reduces the pressure on husbands (Barnett & Hyde, 2001). Men who get involved with the care of their children are often surprised to find how deeply rewarding this can be and say that they would never give it up (Deutsch, 1999).

There are some limitations to the research in this area. Research samples are self-selected—people have sorted themselves into employed and non-employed groups before being studied. It is possible that multiple roles and happiness go together simply because better-adjusted people are more likely to attempt multiple roles in the first place. Furthermore, most of the research on the benefits of multiple roles has been done on people with high incomes and status. Role conflict and overload may be overwhelming in dead-end jobs where women are the majority of workers (Greenglass & Burke, 1988; Statham et al., 1988).

What about the children? Do they suffer when both parents work outside the home? It's easy to find conservative commentators and experts who claim that working mothers (but never working fathers) contribute to juvenile delinquency, behavior problems, and poor adjustment in children. Day care scare articles tell parents that their children will be abused and neglected if they are not home with mom. And employed mothers are sometimes viewed as second-class mothers, with the stay-at-home mom still the ideal. These views echo the long tradition of mother-blaming discussed in Chapter 9.

However, research does not confirm the popular wisdom. A meta-analysis of 59 studies confirmed that children cared for by their mothers did not differ developmentally in any important way from those cared for by other adult caretakers (Erel et al., 2000). In general, children in day care do not suffer from disruption of their bond with their mothers; they may experience increased intellectual growth and development, especially if they come from low-income homes that cannot provide an enriched environment; and they are at least as socially skilled as other children (Scarr, 1998; Scarr et al., 1990). And as for juvenile delinquency, a study of over 700 adolescents showed that mothers' work status (both when the teens were preschoolers and currently) was unrelated to the teens' delinquency (Vander-Ven et al., 2001). For most families today, the issue is not whether mom and dad should both work, because they both do—but how to find high quality and affordable child care.

Researchers may have overlooked potential benefits associated with working mothers—an example of bias in the framing of research questions. For example, employed mothers can provide role models for their children. Several studies have shown that daughters of employed women are more independent and self-confident. Both daughters and sons of employed women hold more egalitarian attitudes about women and view women (including their own mothers) as more competent (Steil, 1997). The benefits of having a successful working mom may be especially great for girls. As adults, daughters of employed women are more likely to become high achievers (Betz & Fitzgerald, 1987).

Making A Difference:
Women, Work, and Social Policy

Clearly, the world of work presents women with many problems. Equity for women workers is not an impossible dream. How to go about achieving that dream is, however, an open ended question. Different ideas about the causes of inequity lead to different proposed solutions. Some researchers and policymakers focus on the individual level, others on the interpersonal or intergroup level, and still others on the structural level.

At the individual level, there has been an emphasis on problems within women themselves: Women may lack the skills or motivation to succeed. According to this model, the best way to change women's work situation is to provide self-improvement and training programs to help women overcome their deficiencies.

Examples are assertiveness training and time management courses for women (Crawford, 1995). Individual change may be helpful for some women, but, as we have seen, there is little evidence that women, as a group, lack ability or motivation. The individual-deficit model runs the risk of blaming the victim by ignoring social factors that are beyond the control of the individual (Fassinger, 2002). It leaves the work of change to women, without questioning the masculine values that underlie both corporate culture and the double day at home.

A better approach at the individual level is to focus on women who have achieved top-level career success while maintaining a satisfying family life. The good news is that these women manage not just to balance their roles as workers, wives, and mothers, but to integrate them. Their career success is *not* due to spending all their time at work. Instead, they find ways to bring work and family into harmony, making for a rich and satisfying life (Ford et al., 2007; Friedman & Greenhaus, 2000).

The research on these high-performing women shows that they set clear goals and priorities with both family and work in mind. They are good at time scheduling and multitasking. They do not feel guilty about not baking cookies or sewing little Blake's Halloween costume. Instead, they delegate and outsource at home just like they do at work. Far from being superwomen who try to do it all, these women have learned to define their roles as mothers, spouses, and workers in ways that suit their own abilities and let all the rest go (Cheung & Halpern, 2010).

A structural-level approach focuses on the impact of organizations on the people in them. It proposes that the situation a person is placed in shapes his or her behavior. From this perspective, women will advance if real opportunities for advancement become available to them. The system, not the individual, must change for equity to be achieved. Rather than viewing women as unique, it sees their problems as similar to the problems faced by other disadvantaged groups such as racial and ethnic minorities. Legislation for equal opportunity and affirmative action is one route to change (Crosby, 2003). (See Box 10.4.) Family leave policies and affordable, high-quality child care are important structural changes, too.

A final approach is based on intergroup power, which has been stressed throughout this book and is the focus of Chapter 2. From this perspective, when men have more social power, women are treated as an out-group. This model explains why women's work is devalued, why male career patterns and definitions of work and achievement are taken as the norm, and why occupations so frequently end up segregated by sex. Stereotypes about differences between women and men reinforce the in-group–out-group distinction.

The intergroup perspective views change in the workplace as dependent on societal change. Educating people about stereotyping might help in the short run, but fundamental change depends on altering the power structure. Power-oriented strategies include passing and enforcing equal-opportunity legislation, increasing women's political power, and forming women's organizations and networks to exert pressure for social change. Many women and men today are engaged in these strategies.

Box 10.4 ∾ The Lilly Ledbetter Equal Pay Act

. . . Equal pay is by no means just a women's issue—it's a family issue. . . . And in this economy, when so many folks are already working harder for less and struggling to get by, the last thing they can afford is losing part of each month's paycheck to simple and plain discrimination. . . . Ultimately, equal pay isn't just an economic issue for millions of Americans and their families, it's a question of who we are—and whether we're truly living up to our fundamental ideals; whether we'll do our part, as generations before us, to ensure those words put on paper some 200 years ago really mean something.

—*President Barack Obama, on signing the Lilly Ledbetter Fair Pay Act into law, January 29, 2009*

In 1998, Lilly Ledbetter, who had worked at Goodyear Tire and Rubber Company for almost 20 years and was one of very few female supervisors, decided to sue her employer for pay discrimination after she found out that male supervisors were making significantly more money than she was for the same work. A jury awarded her more than $3 million in back pay and punitive damages. However, the case was eventually overturned and made its way to the Supreme Court.

In 2007, the Supreme Court ruled that employees could not sue their employers for wage discrimination if the discriminatory event had taken place more than 180 days earlier. That meant that employees who'd been underpaid due to discrimination over a long time period could not sue if the pay decision had occurred in the past. Of course, an employee may not know about pay discrimination until some time has gone by, because he or she doesn't have access to pay data for others. Previous interpretations of the law treated each new paycheck as a new discriminatory act, allowing individuals to sue for pay discrimination even if the original event took place more than 180 days ago. The Supreme Court ruling essentially tied the hands of employees, making it extremely difficult to sue an employer for pay discrimination.

On January 29, 2009, President Barack Obama signed into law the Lilly Ledbetter Fair Pay Act, a law that overturned the Supreme Court's decision. Once again, in claims of pay discrimination, a "paycheck accrual rule" will be used, meaning that discriminatory paychecks an employee receives accrue over time, resetting the clock for when someone can file a discrimination claim. Since the bill was signed by President Obama, the courts have reinstated many of the pay discrimination claims that were overturned as a result of the Supreme Court's ruling in 2007. And Lilly Ledbetter got the money she rightfully earned.

Sources: http://www.nwlc.org/fairpay/ledbetterfactsheets.html
http://www.pay-equity.org/index.html
Contributed by Annie B. Fox.

By showing how discrimination works, psychological research can help point the way to change. How can gender bias in hiring and promotion be eliminated? Both individuals and organizations must change (Valian, 1998):

- Develop clear, specific criteria for performance evaluation, and make people responsible for meeting the criteria.
- Allow enough time and attention for performance evaluations. The quicker and more automatic the decision making, the more people rely on cognitive biases that disadvantage women.
- Increase the number of women in the pool, which reduces the salience of gender.
- Appoint leaders who are committed to gender equity.
- Develop clear institutional policies about gender equity and sexual harassment. Make sure they are communicated and implemented consistently.

Parallel changes are also needed to eliminate bias due to race, ethnic group, sexual orientation, age, disability, and other dimensions of disadvantage.

The information and analysis in Chapters 8 through 10 show that women's and men's experiences in relationships, families, and workplaces are interdependent. Women who cannot achieve economic parity at work are disadvantaged by having less power in their marriages. Much of the work women do is unpaid and undervalued. Sex discrimination at work affects productivity and quality of life. If women are to have the same career opportunities as men, they must be able to decide if and when they will bear children. Families suffer when social policy is based on myths of motherhood instead of the realities of contemporary life. These are just a few examples of the complex relationships among family roles and work-place issues. Models of change that focus on gendered social structures and power inequities are more useful than those that stress changing only women's attitudes and values.

Exploring Further

∽

Alice H. Eagly, & Linda L. Carli (2007). *Through the labyrinth: The truth about how women become leaders.* Boston: Harvard Business School Press.
   A readable analysis of the psychological and other social science research on how and why women have been excluded from leadership, how the situation is changing, and how to reach the feminist ideal of diversity in leadership.

Crosby, Faye (2003). *Affirmative action is dead: Long live affirmative action.* New Haven: Yale University Press.
   Affirmative action is probably the most misunderstood social policy of our times. Crosby's clear thinking and lively writing clear up misconceptions and show why affirmative action is still needed.

Hays, Sharon (2003). *Flat broke with children.* New York: Oxford University Press.
   The impact of welfare reform seen through the eyes of welfare recipients, most of whom are poor women forced onto the labor market in low-wage jobs with few benefits. Hays' study is based on interactions with welfare recipients and caseworkers.

Institute for Women's Policy Research. www.iwpr.org

> The Institute works with policymakers, scholars, and public interest groups around the country to design, execute, and disseminate research that clarifies social policy issues affecting women and families, and to build a network of individuals and organizations that conduct and use women-oriented policy research.

National Committee on Pay Equity. http://www.pay-equity.org/index.html

> NCPE is a coalition of women's and civil rights organizations, labor unions, religious, professional, legal, and educational associations, commissions on women, state and local pay equity coalitions and individuals, all working to eliminate sex- and race-based wage discrimination and to achieve pay equity. NCPE's purpose is to close the wage gap that disadvantages women, as well as people of color, compared to men.

CHAPTER 11

The Second Half:
Midlife and Aging

∾

- **Not Just a Number: The Social Meanings of Age**
  Is There a Double Standard of Aging?
  Ageism
  Cross-Cultural Differences
  Self Identity and Social Identity

- **Images of Older Women**
  Invisibility
  Grannies and Witches: Images and Stereotypes of Older Women
  The Effects of Age Stereotypes

- **In an Aging Woman's Body**
  Physical Health in Middle and Later Life
  Menopause and Hormone Replacement Therapy
  The Medicalization of Menopause
  Constructing the Object of Desire
  Exercise and Fitness
  Sexuality in Middle and Later Life

- **Relationships: Continuity and Change**
  Friends and Family
  Becoming a Grandmother
  Caregiving: Its Costs and Rewards
  Loss of a Life Partner

- **Work and Achievement**
  Women in Their Prime
  Retirement
  Poverty in Later Life

- **Making A Difference**
  Transforming Society: Elder Activism
  Transforming Social Interaction: Taking Charge of the Second Half
  Transforming Ourselves: Resisting Ageism

- **Exploring Further**

- Cynthia, who is White, was born in 1930. As a teenager, she felt attraction to other women but had no words for it and no idea anyone else might feel the same way. She was 41 when the gay rights movement began, 45 when homosexuality was removed from the DSM, and 70 when the TV character Ellen came out on TV. After years of secrecy and stress, Cynthia feels that she has a positive lesbian identity in her old age (Kimmel & Martin, 2001).

- Rebecca W. is White, upper-middle-class, 58-years-old, and has been married for 40 years. Her husband, age 67, is a retired executive. When their five children were still at home, she took care of her husband's elderly father, who lived with them for several years until his death. Now Mrs. W. takes care of her 84-year-old mother who is forgetful, resentful, and has physical disabilities. She always hoped that she would travel and take up new interests when her children left home, but that is not possible. Mrs. W. suffers from depression (Brody, 2004).

- Dorothy, who is African American, was born in a small southern town and grew up under racial segregation. She earned a high school diploma and wanted to be a secretary, but at that time, only White women could get clerical jobs. She worked all her life cleaning the houses of White families. A widow, she survives on $6,000 a year and has to ask her family to help out with necessities like food and medicine (Ralston, 1997).

- Mercedes is a Mexican American woman now in her late 60s. When she was growing up, her father did not see the point of sending a daughter to school. She married very young and remembers wanting to play jump rope with her friends but having to cook for her husband instead. She had six children, all of whom now live nearby. People call her *la abuela*, the grandmother, as a sign of respect. Mercedes is sought out by many people in her community as a *curandera*—a person who can heal mind and body (Facio, 1997).

- Annette is a Baby Boomer, one of the large group of Americans born between 1946 and 1964. Hers was the first generation to have the Pill and she was in no hurry to get married. She has worked outside the home ever since her only child started school. After some early struggles against sex discrimination at work, she had a satisfying career. Divorced, living alone, and with little money saved, she is looking forward to retirement with mixed feelings (Scott, 1997).

$\mathcal{I}$t is often said that age is the great leveler—it happens to everyone. As these real-life examples show, individuals experience aging differently depending on social class and ethnic background. Another important factor is an individual's **age cohort**—the group of people born in about the same decade. Different age cohorts have different experiences as a group. My mother's cohort, for example, grew up during the Great Depression and lived through World War II as young adults; these experiences shaped their values in many ways.

In this chapter we explore the lives of women at midlife and beyond. Midlife is usually defined as the period that begins at 45 and ends at 65 years of age, and old age as the period beyond age 65. Psychology traditionally has paid less attention to the second half of life than the first, particularly where women are concerned (Sugar, 2007). This is unfortunate because women and men experience aging somewhat differently, and the accumulated inequities of a lifetime can leave older women vulnerable to many problems. However, the second half of a woman's life can be as full of surprises, challenges, and rewards as the first. Let's start by looking at how age is socially defined.

Not Just a Number: The Social Meanings of Age

To a teenager, a 45-year-old may seem ancient; but my 85-year-old aunt says that *old* is anyone five years older than she is. How would you define *old?* Are you old once you reach a certain age? Does it happen when you become a grandparent? When you retire? Or are you only as old as you feel? Age is subjective. Its meaning is defined by social consensus and the criteria differ from one time and place to another (Sokolovsky, 1997). In our own society, we use chronological age as a marker. However, age in years is only loosely correlated with abilities or roles; at best, it is a convenient number that lumps together quite different people. One 70-year-old woman might be in a nursing home, whereas another is volunteering on an archaeological dig, teaching math at a university, or delivering meals to the elderly.

Is There a Double Standard of Aging?

Many people hold a ***double standard of aging***. They think women are old at an earlier age than men, and they see being old as more negative for women. Historically, women's value and status often depended on their sexual attractiveness and reproductive ability. Men's status, in contrast, was derived from their achievements. Therefore, a woman was considered old when she could no longer attract men or reproduce, whereas a man was not old until he became mentally or physically incapacitated. Many experimental studies show that the physical characteristics of age (such as wrinkles and gray hair) are rated more negatively for women than for men (Canetto, 2001).

The double standard of aging can often be seen in the portrayal of older women and men in the media. I'll discuss media images in more detail shortly, but for now here is one example. In a content analysis of a British magazine aimed at older people, all the females shown in ads were well under the age of 50, except for one gray-haired 60ish woman shown using a vacuum cleaner. In contrast, a gray-haired man was featured in an ad for a senior rail pass, which showed him in a wetsuit, carrying a large surfboard into the waves. The ad claimed, "60 isn't what it used to be. There are sights to see, friends to visit, waves to catch" (Blytheway, 2003, p. 46).

Although the double standard of aging is prevalent, it's not only women who lose status as they age. Women may be seen as less attractive as they grow older but men may be seen as less competent (Kite et al., 2005). The double standard doesn't show up in every study that looks for it. In one recent study, U.S. college students held generally favorable attitudes about older people, and rated older

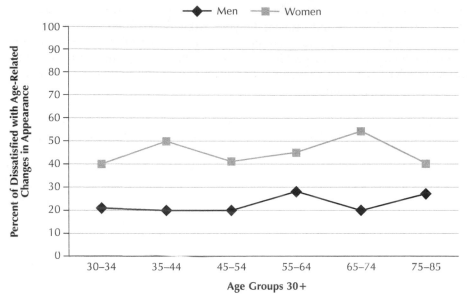

FIGURE 11.1   Gender and age related changes in appearance.
In a study of Swedish adults, women in every age group were more likely than men of the same age to be dissatisfied with the effects of age on their appearance. Do you think the results would be similar or different in the United States?

Source: Adapted from Öberg, P. (2003). Images versus experience of the aging body. In Christopher A. Faircloth, (Ed.), *Aging Bodies: Images and Everyday Experience* (New York: Alta Mira Press), Figure 4.4 (p. 118). Reprinted by permission.

women *higher* than older men on positive characteristics such as friendly, cooperative, patient, and generous (Narayan, 2008). In this case, it seems that the "women are nicer" stereotype trumped the double standard of aging.

Do people apply the double standard to themselves? A survey of a random national sample of people aged 20 to 85 years in Sweden examined perceptions of age (Öberg, 2003). Figure 11.1 shows the proportion of people over 30 who said they were disturbed by age related changes in their appearance. You can see that there is a gender gap; women expressed more body dissatisfaction than men did. However, the gap does not increase with age. In an interview study done in England, older women were more distressed about changes in *appearance*, and older men by changes in their bodies' *function* (loss of stamina, running speed, etc.). Men spoke of their aging bodies as a holistic entity, whereas women spoke of parts (legs, thighs, and neck) (Halliwell & Dittmar, 2003). Both these studies' results reflect the pervasive objectification of the female body.

Ageism

Prejudice and discrimination based on age is termed **ageism**. Like other forms of prejudice, ageism characterizes individuals on the basis of their membership in a group and can affect beliefs, attitudes, and behavior toward group members.

Psychological research shows that ageism is very real. When Mary Kite and her colleagues (2005) conducted a meta-analysis of 232 studies comparing attitudes and beliefs about younger/older people, they found an overall preference for the young. Younger adults were rated less stereotypically, seen as more attractive and competent, and evaluated more favorably than older adults. Surprisingly, it wasn't young people who had the strongest anti-age attitudes—it was middle-aged people.

As a form of oppression, ageism has the potential to touch everyone, even those who are most privileged. Aging happens to everyone who lives long enough, be they female or male, rich or poor, ethnic minority or White. In a survey of people over the age of 60, nearly 80 percent of respondents reported experiencing ageism. The most common form was being told jokes that made fun of older people. However, ageism was sometimes more personal. Respondents reported that others assumed they had memory problems, ignored them, or did not take them seriously because of their age (Palmore, 2001).

Most people, especially younger people, barely notice that age is being made into a form of stigma. But the message that being old is repulsive, embarrassing, or pitiable is visible everywhere in our society. Writing this chapter, I became more sensitized to small examples of ageism. In the space of a few days, I heard a tiny apartment described as a granny flat, came across several cartoons depicting old women as ugly (with drooping breasts, skinny legs, and wrinkled faces), and heard a memory lapse described as a "senior moment." (When a 20-year-old forgets the car keys, we don't call it a "young adult moment"!) Looking for a birthday card for a friend turning 60, I found way too many with jokes about wrinkles, flab, and forgetfulness or messages of the "Ha! Too bad you're another year older!" variety. Next, my copy of the *New Yorker* arrived in the mail. The cover art—intended to be funny—showed an old woman using a walker who was about to slip on a banana peel. I was not amused to read that the artist had titled this cover "Spring Break."

Cross-Cultural Differences

White American culture is individualistic and materialistic. These values work best for the young and strong. Those at midlife usually can cope fairly well but "the old are bound to fail" when judged on "rugged individualism" (Cruikshank, 2003, p. 10). The older one gets, the less possible it is to maintain total autonomy and independence. Aging brings the need for help from others and in U.S. culture this need is often seen as shameful. In cultures that value interdependence and connection, the willingness to rely on others may not be so different for older people than for younger ones. Thus, the meaning of old age depends on culture.

Furthermore, the knowledge held by the old may seem unimportant in post-industrial modern societies. In contrast, some cultures, past and present, have respected and venerated the old as keepers of knowledge. For example, Buddhist tradition honors old teachers, and Native American tribes relied on the old to pass on knowledge. The wise elder, most often personified as male, is an ancient archetype still with us (think Obi Wan Kenobi and Gandalf).

When old people have meaningful roles in a society, there is less emphasis on their bodies and more on their contributions. The old may have special status as peacekeepers, mediators, or keepers of tradition. In some Asian societies, spiritual power is thought to increase as the body becomes frailer. Old women are honored with the right to name children in some African and Native American groups.

In North American society, meaningful roles for the old are most evident in minority communities. For example, Native American women often become important leaders and artists in old age, and older African American women are an important source of influence in Black churches and civic groups. In contrast, mainstream American society views age largely as a process of decline, which tends to push old people to the margins.

Nevertheless, the idea that old people are always venerated elsewhere compared to our own society is oversimplified. In pre-industrial societies, just as in our own, how an old person is treated depends on his or her gender, status, and power, aside from age. In poor and developing countries, old people may have to do hard physical labor as long as they can, and retirement is an unknown concept. Women may be valued primarily as caregivers for others, a role that is increasingly difficult to fill as one gets older. Religious beliefs may stress respect for the old but this does not always happen in practice. Physical infirmities, illness, and disabilities seem to lower one's status almost everywhere. Still, most cross-cultural research suggests that the status of the old in the United States is lower than in many other cultures, past and present. As one ageism researcher put it, "age prejudice is one of the most condoned, institutionalized forms of prejudice in the world—especially in the United States—today" (Kite et al, 2005).

Self-Identity and Social Identity

Like other forms of bias, ageism can be internalized, affecting the individual's identity and self-esteem. "This is the heart of ageism: We deny that we are aging, and when we are forced to confront it, we treat it as ugly and tragic" (Calasanti & Slevin, 2001, p. 186). For example, a 65-year-old may refuse to go to a senior citizen center or retirement community because she does not want to be around "all those old people." A common research finding is that older people have a pessimistic view of the health of other people in their age group, but consider themselves the lucky exceptions (Cruikshank, 2003).

In one study, older adults in Finland were asked to look in a mirror and describe their reflection. One 79-year-old woman said, "It isn't a reflection of me. I know myself pretty well . . . Spiritually I don't feel old, like 'oh dear how old I am.' But I can see it in the appearance" (cited in Öberg, 2003, p. 107). This woman is making a distinction between her *self-identity* (her own subjective feeling of age) and her *social identity* (the way she looks to others).

The discrepancy between self- and social identities was explored in a Swedish study (Öberg, 2003), where participants aged 20 to 85 answered these questions:

In my inner self I feel as if I am _____ years old.

I would most like to be _____ years old.

I think that other people see me as _____ years old.

Figure 11.2 shows that every age group except the 20-year-olds reported a difference between their chronological age and their subjective age. The great majority

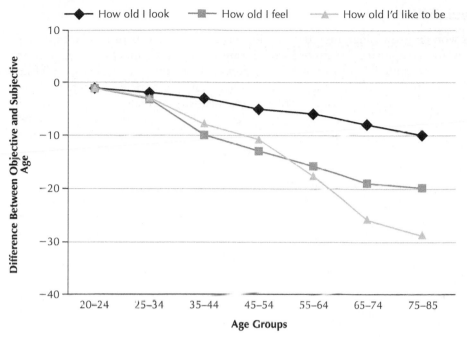

FIGURE 11.2

The discrepancy for respondents in different age groups between how old they think they look, how old they feel, and how old they would like to be.

Source: Öberg and Tomstam, 2001, as summarized in Öberg, 2003.

of people said they felt younger, wanted to be younger, and thought that others saw them as younger than they actually were. The gaps between self, ideal, and social identities increased with age. Respondents in their 80s wanted to be 50, felt like 60, and thought that they looked like 70 to others.

Distancing yourself from your age may be a form of resistance against the stigma of being old. "If I emphasize that I differ from the 'typical' old who are deteriorating, I try to dodge the scorn often heaped on them. . . . And the more I claim difference, the better I feel about myself" (Cruikshank, 2003, p. 11). However, when each old person thinks of himself or herself as the exception, it is unlikely that older people will bond with each other or act collectively to change the sociocultural forces that construct old age so negatively. Instead, each of us believes that getting old is something that only happens to other people.

Images of Older Women

Think about the last few TV dramas or sitcoms you watched. Were there any women over 40 in leading roles? If so, how were they portrayed? Older women in the media are few and far between, and those who do appear are often stereotyped as unattractive, useless, and boring (Markson & Taylor, 2000).

Invisibility

As women grow older, they become less visible in all forms of media, as though they are so repulsive that no one would want to look at them. Older men, too, are underrepresented, but to a much lesser degree. In an analysis of the top 100 films of 2002, major male characters outnumbered major female characters almost 3 to 1 (73 percent versus 27 percent); the majority of male characters were in their 30s and 40s, and the majority of female characters were a decade or two younger. Both women and men in their 60s and older were underrepresented compared to their proportion of the population—for example, 60ish women got only 8 percent of the roles although they are 22 percent of the population. It wasn't just the numbers that differed. Men in their 40s, 50s, and 60s had more roles involving leadership, power, and achievement than women in the same age groups (Lauzen & Dozier, 2005). It seems that, to some extent, men are allowed to mature in popular culture, but women are expected to remain 20-something babes, frozen in time.

The most invisible aspect of older women is their sexuality. Although young women's bodies are sexually objectified and exploited by the media, old women are almost never portrayed as sexual, unless their sexual desire is targeted for ridicule. The bodies of young women are used to sell everything from fishing tackle to vodka, but the bodies of old women are evaded. This invisibility "deprives women of all ages from knowing what old bodies look like . . . the ways beauty can be expressed through old female forms is yet to be known" (Cruikshank, 2003, p. 149). Older men's virility is displayed by showing them with much younger women, not women their own age. In movie romances, Jack Nicholson at age 60 was paired with Helen Hunt, 34; Michael Douglas, 53, with Gwyneth Paltrow, 25; and Jeff Bridges, 60, with 32-year-old Maggie Gyllenhaal.

A few exceptions prove the rule: nude scenes for young actresses are so commonplace that they are unremarkable, but when Diane Keaton (age 58) appeared in a split-second nude shot in the 2003 movie *Something's Gotta Give*, she was lauded as a brave, risk-taking pioneer. (One critic noted that the nudity was "part of the marketing schtick" for a movie whose target audience was "aging women who worry that they'll never find romance—or even basic human respect—in our youth-obsessed society" (Tally, 2006, p. 38)). A 2004 episode of *NYPD Blue* featured a 60ish woman who was happily sexual, but her character was played for laughs as inept Officer Medavoy managed to bed her. And, unlike the steamy nude sex scenes of the young characters in this series, their sex scene showed only a jiggling bed and two pairs of legs—from the knees down. It was left up to 88 ½-year-old Betty White to make muffin jokes on *SNL* in 2010—a refreshing transgression of the norm that old women are utterly asexual.

Older LGBTQ people are invisible not only in mainstream media but even in media aimed at the gay community. In an analysis of LGBTQ magazines such as *Out* and *The Advocate*, there were only 2 articles on older people in the 542 pages of text. There were no pictures at all of anyone who looked to be age 60 or older (Apuzzo, 2001).

Grannies and Witches: Images and Stereotypes of Older Women

One of the most pervasive images of old women is the kindly grandmother, a portrayal that is consistent with trait stereotypes of warmth and nurturance (Canetto, 2001). Granny images are reinforced by the clothes and props assigned to older women in their media representations. The granny figure wears a housedress, a shawl, or an apron. She sits in a rocking chair, knitting, or stirs a pot over the stove. Her gray hair, worn in a bun, and her outdated, unfashionable clothes signify that she has not kept up with the times. This grandmother figure abounds in films made over the past 6 decades. A comic variation is the outrageous granny (think Beverly Hillbillics) (Markson, 2003).

Other prototypes of older women in the media are the mother-in-law from hell (*Sex and the City*'s Bunny), the manipulative, selfish elderly mother (Livia in *The Sopranos*), and the comical but powerless "little old lady" (Cruickshank, 2003). An analysis of Disney movies concluded that old women were depicted as ugly, evil, greedy, power-hungry, and crazy (Perry, 1999). (See Figure 11.3.)

Everyday language reflects the stereotypes of old people and of old women in particular. The very word *old* is so unpleasant that it is avoided whenever possible

"It sounds like Osama bin Laden, but it could be your mother."

FIGURE 11.3

Source: © Frank Cotham/The New Yorker Collection/www.cartoonbank.com.

with euphemisms like *senior citizen* and *golden ager*. Some terms trivialize, derogate, or patronize the old—such as *geezer*, *little old lady*, and *dirty old man*. In Sweden, dances for older people are called *raisins disco* (Öberg, 2003); in England, violence against the elderly is called *granny bashing*. Terms for old women are particularly harsh. There are few terms for older men that rival *old hag*, *old biddy*, and *old bag* in negativity.

Age stereotypes aren't always hostile—they can be subtly condescending, as when old people are thought of as incompetent but cute or loveable—a "doddering but dear" stereotype (Cuddy & Fiske, 2002; Nelson, 2009). In one study, college students rated less competent elderly targets as warmer and nicer than more competent ones. This cute-but-incompetent stereotype of the elderly has been found in several cultures (Cuddy et al., 2005).

Age stereotyping is often triggered by appearance. In interview studies, older women repeatedly say that their aging bodies are the first cues that others use to classify them. When they are with friends and family, they are treated as individuals; but when they interact with strangers in public settings, all anyone seems to see is a generic old woman. A meta-analysis of age stereotype studies confirmed that older women were evaluated less positively overall than older men, but the difference, though significant, was not large (Kite et al., 2005).

The Effects of Age Stereotypes

Age stereotyping can have insidious effects on judgments about older people. In one study, college students listened to a taped lecture read by a gender-neutral and age-neutral voice and rated the "professor" on teaching skills. Some were told that the professor was under age 35, and others that he/she was over age 55. Although the lecture was identical for all participants, students rated the professor as more enthusiastic, vocally expressive, and showing more interest when they thought he was young and male than in any other condition (Arbuckle & Williams, 2003). This study shows the interaction of age and gender stereotypes: students' evaluations were filtered though their negative stereotypes about older professors as well as female professors.

Another effect of age stereotypes is often apparent in social interaction: When people talk to the elderly, they sometimes switch to *elderspeak* (Nelson, 2009). Elderspeak is like baby talk (speech by adults to young children) or the way people talk to their pets: it is grammatically simplified, repetitious, slowed down, and exaggerated in pitch. Only listeners who suffer from hearing loss or dementia are likely to find elderspeak helpful. For the majority of older people, it is patronizing, conveying the expectation that they are not competent to understand normal speech.

When people speak to elders as though they are incompetent, they may create a self-fulfilling prophecy. Because elderspeak is simplified, it conveys less information, thereby leading the old person to respond in a more simplistic way and reinforcing the belief in his or her incompetence (Ruscher, 2001). The end result is that older people may be *infantilized,* or treated like children: They are given overly simple information about complex issues, they are protected from information that others think may upset them, and their opinions are disregarded (Nelson, 2009).

Younger people may accept and internalize age stereotypes without thinking much about them because the stereotypes are not personally relevant. As people get older, however, belief in age stereotypes can have an effect on health. Recent research shows that holding negative stereotypes about the old earlier in life predicts heart attacks and strokes later in life. Researchers theorize that this occurs because, as people get older and the negative stereotypes start to become self-relevant, they trigger stress responses (Levy, 2009). What would happen if positive stereotypes of the elderly were substituted for negative ones? In one study, participants ranging in age from 63 to 82 played a video game that exposed them to either positive or negative stereotypes about the old. Before and after the game, their speed and style of walking were measured. Those who had been exposed to positive stereotypes walked faster and more energetically—suggesting that the slower gait of older people may be partly due to internalized stereotypes and not entirely to the physical changes of aging (Hausdorff et al., 1999). Other research shows that older people who have more positive stereotypes about aging are more likely to lead a generally healthy lifestyle (Levy, 2009). A positive belief can be a powerful thing!

In an Aging Woman's Body

> I was conversing with a middle-aged friend . . . the talk turned to personal matters, and she told me about using herbs to manage her hot flashes, while I shared some concerns about my arthritis and needing a cane to get around. We laughed when we realized that though we are past worrying about having periods and getting pregnant, we never really are free of concerns about our bodies (a woman in her 70s, quoted in Doress-Worters & Ditzion, 1998).

As bodies grow older, they change. Acknowledging and accepting this is an important part of aging. But the meaning of an aging body is not just a matter of its physical state; it depends on the social context. Track and field athletes are relegated to Masters status at age 35 (women) and 40 (men). In contrast, symphony conductors often lead major orchestras into their 80s, and some U.S. Senators have served into their 90s (Calasanti & Slevin, 2001). Because women, more than men, are evaluated throughout their lifetimes by their bodies, living in an aging body is a particular challenge for women.

Physical Health in Middle and Later Life

Measures of women's health in later life are somewhat contradictory. On the one hand, women as a group have a long life expectancy, outliving men on average. On the other hand, women are more likely than men to have chronic illnesses and disabilities as they age (Canetto, 2001). Here we look at some of the most common health problems of older women.

Heart Disease

What is your best guess about the three leading causes of death for U.S. women? Many people's list would include breast cancer. Although one woman in nine will be diagnosed with breast cancer during her lifetime, the top three causes of death for women in industrialized countries are the same as for men: heart disease, all types of cancer, and stroke (Canetto, 2001). Over the past 35 years, death from heart disease has actually decreased for men while increasing for women, and the death rate is higher for ethnic minority women than for other women. In fact, African American and Native American women have the highest mortality rates from heart disease of any group (Mather, 2008).

Because most research on heart disease was conducted with men, there has been a shortage of information about women's symptoms, which may differ from men's. There is also a serious gender gap in treatment. Analyzing a national U.S. database of over 10 million cases, psychologist Cheryl Travis (2005) found that men were twice as likely to have lifesaving bypass surgery as women with similar medical symptoms. No one knows for sure why physicians and others in the medical system are slow to recognize and treat heart disease in women, but one likely explanation is that their cognitive biases interfere. When thinking of a person with heart disease, most people's image is of an overweight, sedentary White male. Because women with heart disease don't fit the prototype, their lives are put at risk.

The effects of gender bias in the diagnosis and treatment of heart disease were evident in a survey of over 200 female cardiac patients (Marcuccio et al., 2003). Almost half of the sample had been unaware that they were at risk for heart disease before their diagnosis. Over half were dissatisfied with their treatment, citing physicians who were rude, condescending, abrupt, or inattentive. Over one in ten who were dissatisfied said that their condition was initially misdiagnosed as panic disorder, menopausal symptoms, or hypochondria, and resented being told in effect, "It's all in your head." Only 60 percent of the sample was referred to a cardiac care program. Despite knowing that their disease put their lives at risk, fewer than 15 percent adopted a healthier lifestyle, probably because they were given little support and information about how to do so. Other studies also have shown that women receive very little counseling about exercise, diet, and weight control, and much less than men do, after heart disease is diagnosed.

Chronic Illnesses

Midlife and older women are likely to live with chronic illnesses such as arthritis and diabetes. Conditions that limit activity (such as spinal degeneration, varicose veins, and joint problems) are two to three times more prevalent in women over the age of 75 than in men of the same age group. The probability of all these conditions increases with age. It is not uncommon for a woman in her 70s to have several chronic health concerns simultaneously, such as arthritis, heart disease, high blood pressure, back pain, and diabetes (Canetto, 2001).

Chronic illness has psychological effects on identity. After a short-term illness like the flu, a person stops focusing on the disruptive body and goes back to normal, once again taking the body for granted. Chronic illness forces a continued focus on the body: on good days, life goes on, but on bad days, the damaged body defines and limits the person (Gubrium & Holstein, 2003). The patient must face the fact that her disorder cannot be cured. Instead, she must cope with whatever physical pain and limitations it brings, along with changes in activities and roles. For example, a woman with diabetes may no longer be able to enjoy cooking favorite foods or taking her grandchildren out for ice cream. Illness and loss of the ability to do everyday activities decrease the quality of life for older people

(Bourque et al., 2005). It is not surprising that many people with chronic illnesses experience depression (Chrisler, 2001).

Chronic illness also increases dependency and the need for help. When an older woman can no longer take care of herself, she may not have anyone to turn to. Women with diseases such as multiple sclerosis and cancer are more likely to be abandoned by their partners than men with the same problems (Chrisler, 2001). Although only 5 percent of people over the age of 65 are in nursing homes at any given time, women make up 75 percent of that number.

Shortcomings of the U.S. health care system aggravate the problems of the chronically ill. Although large numbers of old people need help with daily living tasks, and their numbers are increasing, providing home help and services seems to be a very low priority for government spending. The U.S. medical system is better at spectacular one-time interventions (like heart transplants) than at managing long-term conditions and helping people maintain wellness as they age.

Ethnicity and Health

Women of Hispanic and African American heritage have poorer health than European American women, and they are more likely to die from diseases that could be treated and managed if they had access to good health care (Cox, 2005). For example, Black women are more likely to have high blood pressure, which can lead to strokes if untreated (Cruikshank, 2003). African American, Native American, and Hispanic women also have higher death rates from diabetes than European Americans (Canetto, 2001). In every ethnic group, women tend to live longer than men, but some groups are disadvantaged compared to others. People of color, both men and women, have shorter lives than White people. Black women have the lowest life expectancy of any group of women.

Socioeconomic status is the single most important predictor of health in old age and probably is the root cause of many ethnic differences in health status as well as the shorter lifespans of people of color. Poverty is linked to ill health and early death because it is connected to many physical and psychological stressors such as unemployment, crowding, poor diet, unsanitary living conditions, pollution, and violence (Chrisler, 2001). Poor people are unlikely to get consistent high-quality care for the chronic illnesses associated with poverty. The link between poverty and ill health is dramatically obvious in the health status of Native Americans, whose rates of serious chronic diseases are 600 percent higher than for the rest of the population, and whose disabilities at age 45 are similar to the disabilities of 65-year-olds in the rest of the population (Cox, 2005). The effects of low socioeconomic status accumulate over a lifetime, reducing quality of life and shortening the lifespan.

Menopause and Hormone Replacement Therapy

The U.S. medical and pharmaceutical system does seem eager to cure one huge problem affecting millions of women. Unfortunately, the "problem" is not a disease or disorder but a natural aspect of aging, and the "cure" may be unnecessary and even harmful.

Menopause refers to the end of the menstrual cycle and monthly periods. It is caused by a decrease in the production of estrogen and progesterone by the ovaries. It can occur any time between the mid-40s and the late 50s, but the average age is 51.

Physical Signs of Menopause

The menopausal transition takes place over several years, as periods become less and less regular. A woman can be sure that she has reached menopause when she has not had a period for a full year.

Other bodily changes may accompany menopause. In Western societies, about 50 to 85 percent of all women experience *hot flashes:* brief episodes of suddenly increasing heart rate, warmth, and sweating. Hot flashes may occur as infrequently as once a month or as often as several times an hour. They are caused by the decline in estrogen that triggers menopause. Over time, the body accommodates to the lower estrogen levels and the hot flashes disappear. However, there are cross-cultural differences that call into question whether hot flashes have a single biological cause. For example, women in Japan and Mayan women in Mexico very rarely experience hot flashes with menopause (Beyene, 1989; Boston Women's Health Book Collective, 1998). Is this because of dietary differences or is it because menopause is less stressful in cultures that value old women more than our own does? This question is still unanswered.

Many women also experience vaginal changes with menopause: the skin and membranes in this area become thinner and drier, which may make sexual penetration by a partner uncomfortable. However, this can be remedied with lubricating gels. In a community-based study, 20 percent of postmenopausal women reported this condition, and only 15 percent of those reported it as bothersome (Boston Women's Health Book Collective,1998).

Psychological Experiences of Menopause

There is a long history of attributing women's psychological distress to their reproductive systems. Starting in the 1860s, psychiatry developed diagnostic categories for the supposed craziness of postmenopausal women, including "old maid's insanity" and "involutional melancholia," a form of depression (Markson, 2003). Psychiatric diagnoses like involutional melancholia were part of the myth that women are mentally unstable because of their reproductive hormones: Raging "PMS" hormones make us crazy in our reproductive years and waning hormones do so later in life. The belief that women become depressed, moody, irritable, and hypersensitive at menopause is still prevalent among health care providers and women themselves (Avis, 2003).

Contrary to these beliefs, research shows no evidence that the onset of menopause leads to depression or that women suffer more depression after menopause than before (Avis, 2003). Instead, the evidence suggests that depression during the menopausal transition is predicted by a prior history of depression, health problems, and social factors. Depression is not a normal part of menopause.

Menopause may be linked with short-term moodiness and irritability in some women. This may be partly due to physical changes; when sleep is disturbed by hot flashes, irritability can result. It may also be due to expectations created by stereotypes. If everyone expects a menopausal woman to be moody, mood changes caused by stressful life events may be misattributed to her hormones.

An old expression for menopause is "change of life." Indeed, like menarche, it marks a major life change that is unique to females. In one study of 2,500 women, the majority experienced this change with neutral or positive feelings (Avis & McKinlay, 1991). In studies comparing African and European American women, the Black women had more positive attitudes than the White women, viewing menopause as a normal and unremarkable part of life (Sampselle et al., 2002; Sommer et al., 1999). A woman may be relieved that she no longer can become pregnant and can stop using birth control; she may be happy to say goodbye to pads, tampons, and cramps. Very few 50-year-olds want to have a baby. Contrary to the stereotype of crazy, moody menopausal women, most women cope with the signs of menopause with little fuss and the transition is not the biggest thing in their lives.

Exercise and fitness are important factors in keeping the menopausal transition smooth. A correlational study of 133 women whose average age was 51 showed that being physically active was linked to higher feelings of self-worth, fewer physical symptoms, and better quality of life (Elavsky & McAuley, 2005). Following up on these results, the same researchers conducted a 4-month randomized controlled exercise trial in which participants (164 relatively inactive women whose average age was 50) were assigned to a walking, yoga, or no-exercise control group. Both walking and yoga led to very positive outcomes, including better mood, better self-rated quality of life around menopausal issues, and, as physical fitness increased, fewer menopausal symptoms (Elavsky & McAuley, 2007). There were also fewer mental health problems in the exercise groups compared to the no-exercise control group. The researchers concluded that increasing cardio fitness is one good way to reduce the physical and psychological impact of menopausal symptoms on women.

The Medicalization of Menopause

Because menopause happens to over 50 percent of the adult population, there is a great deal of money to be made in treating it as a disease. Increasingly, U.S. society defines age as a sickness that can be treated and cured (Calasanti & Slevin, 2001). This trend was apparent in the use of reproductive hormones to relieve signs of menopause and prevent signs of aging, termed *estrogen replacement therapy* (ERT) or *hormone replacement therapy* (HRT) depending on whether estrogen alone or a combination of hormones is used. Proponents argued that ERT/HRT could prevent osteoporosis (bone density loss), heart disease, and some types of cancer. Some claimed that it also could prevent age-related changes in cognition (memory loss and dementia) and appearance (wrinkles and weight gain). Pharmaceutical companies, some scientists, and many physicians urged women to stay forever young by taking hormones to offset menopause.

However, these claims were made before there was sufficient research. Recently, a national study of 25,000 women aged 50 to 79 examined the effect of diet, exercise, and ERT/HRT on heart disease, cancer, and osteoporosis. The HRT part of the study was ended early when results showed that HRT was associated with a slightly *increased* risk of breast cancer, heart attack, and stroke (Mather, 2008). Soon after, the ERT results were analyzed and also showed that the risks outweighed the benefits. ERT was linked to an increased risk of stroke and had no effect on preventing heart disease (Women's Health Initiative Steering Committee, 2004). Moreover, both HRT and ERT were linked to increased cognitive impairment such as memory loss and dementia (Espeland et al., 2004; Shumaker, 2004). Women's health activists are outraged that this "therapy" was prescribed to so many women in the absence of scientific evidence for its benefits. In the process, many women have probably been harmed.

These results should give pause to those who think that aging can be stopped or reversed by medical interventions. The signs of menopause, such as hot flashes, usually can be controlled with simple measures such as wearing layers, exercising, and meditation (Boston Women's Health Book Collective, 1998). If hot flashes or vaginal dryness are severe, short-term, low dose ERT or an estrogen cream applied to the vaginal area may offer relief.

Women can have more control over their own lives by resisting the medicalization of menopause and aging. When menopause and midlife are defined as illnesses, every woman over a certain age becomes a perennial patient in a system that is not designed to respect and value women.

Constructing the Object of Desire

Increasingly, both women and men are expected to spare no effort to disguise or eliminate the bodily changes that come with age. For men, Viagra is aggressively marketed as a way to restore the sexual vigor of youth. For women, much more than a pill is required. As they grow older, many women view their bodies as the site of an ever-more laborious project in which the goal is to masquerade as a younger woman (Calasanti & Slevin, 2001).

Of course, attempts to avoid old age are ultimately futile. Nevertheless, attempts to avoid the *appearance* of old age are rapidly increasing in Western societies, aided by aggressive marketing of anti-aging products. Women are exhorted by advertisers to go to war with their own bodies, to "fight," "resist," "overcome," and "outwit" aging. These messages are directed most strongly to White middle-class and affluent women. Research suggests that the most privileged women are most concerned about their appearance and most invested in treating their body as an improvement project, while working class women regard their body more in terms of how well it functions (Calasanti & Slevin, 2001).

The number of cosmetic surgery procedures performed in the United States has increased greatly since the 1990s. Nonsurgical medical techniques such as Botox (injections of a neurotoxin that paralyzes facial muscles), dermabrasion, and chemical skin peels are becoming more popular, too, and women are encouraged to have them every few months to avoid the dreaded appearance of facial lines. TV programs like *Extreme Makeover* (which ran for five seasons) raised the bar, justifying even the most radical, gruesome, and painful surgical procedures in the quest for perfect (youthful) features. What the hype doesn't say is that cosmetic surgery and other medical procedures are expensive, not covered by health insurance, carry risks of disfigurement and death, and must be repeated periodically to maintain the effect.

Feminist theorists are divided about the meaning of the "beauty work" that so many middle-aged and older women do. Some have argued that it represents a kind of false consciousness, as women accept the sexist attitude that their youthful attractiveness is the only important thing about them, and give in to self-objectification. Others have argued that a focus on appearance is a rational choice for aging women, because there is ample evidence of ageism, and women face prejudice and discrimination based on looks more than men do. Therefore, working on her face and body is one way for a woman to hold on to social power as she ages (Clarke, 2007; Clarke & Griffin, 2008).

Women seem to be conflicted about beauty work. In an interview study of 44 women aged 50 to 70, many participants wished that they could look young without trying to; their ideal was to age "naturally" or "gracefully." However, their behavior was anything but natural, as they reported using a variety of methods to avoid the appearance of aging, ranging from makeup (84 percent) and hair dye (61 percent) to Botox injections (14 percent); smaller numbers of women had also used chemical peels, injections of fillers under the skin, microdermabrasion, liposuction, and cosmetic breast surgery (Clarke & Griffin, 2008). One reason they gave was age discrimination at work:

> I'm 52-years-of-age and sometimes it's been held against me. . . . It happened today to me—she's tall and blonde and long-legged and flirts with the bosses and has no computer skills and only has reception experience. I have 15 years' experience and a computer background. I get along awesomely with the staff. They kept her and they're letting me go. But she has the look. I'm devastated (p. 663).

Another reason for undertaking beauty work was the belief that it was necessary to catch or hold on to a man, as this 59 year-old single woman said:

> My face is sagging and I'm at a stage in my life when I'm looking for a new partner, hopefully to spend the rest of my life with. . . . So, my appearance is very important to me right now. It's difficult to find men in my age range who are not going out with younger women . . . I am seriously thinking about . . . major surgery on my face (p. 665).

A third reason was that they were painfully aware of the social invisibility of older women. One 55-year-old said,

> Men of all ages find youthful women attractive. What the fuck is that all about? . . . What a shame that the ideal is young as opposed to being old and wise. What a shame. What a reflection on our society that we don't see the beauty in ageing (p. 667).

Only two of the 44 women interviewed did not use any beauty work interventions, but even they were conflicted about their choice. One woman, 65, put it this way:

> As I grow older, it's very difficult to see the wrinkles appearing and the skin losing its elasticity. My radical feminism, on the one hand, is saying, "Don't be so absurd." The other side of me struggles. When I look through magazines and see all of these advertisements for wrinkle creams and . . . cosmetic surgeons . . . I am just absolutely appalled at what's going on . . . but I've considered getting rid of these wrinkles, and the facelifts and all that. Whether I'll ever do it or not, I don't know, but certainly I've considered it (p. 668).

Some women respond to the pressure to maintain a youthful appearance by opting out at midlife. If society is saying that they must do what they manifestly

FIGURE 11.4

Source: © Roz Chast/The New Yorker Collection/www.cartoonbank.com

cannot do (be slim, toned, smooth-skinned, and young), they choose not to participate in the game of objectification. Instead, they wear relaxed clothes and comfortable shoes, defining a feminine appearance in terms of ease and freedom of movement (see Figure 11.4). Author Carolyn Heilbrun quipped that she was glad when she reached 50 because she could stop wearing drag. And one

64-year-old woman said that she got all the attention she needed from husband and family:

> I don't mind being invisible. . . . Like when I go to the gym with all these gorgeous young things around me, I can just look any way I want and just be pedalling away and do whatever I want. No one is paying any attention to me and it's really nice; I really enjoy that (Clarke & Griffin, 2008, p. 667).

Exercise and Fitness

One of the most important factors in maintaining good health in the second half of life is regular exercise. I've already discussed the research showing that exercise and fitness reduces menopausal symptoms, but the value of fitness does not end after menopause. The benefits of exercise are both psychological (improved mood stability, energy levels, and body self-esteem) and physical (lowering the risk of life-threatening conditions such as diabetes, high blood pressure, obesity, and heart disease). Exercise relieves arthritis pain, maintains strength and posture, strengthens the immune system, benefits thinking and memory, and improves skin tone. In the elderly, exercise helps prevent the loss of muscle tone that causes falls, broken bones, and perma-

FIGURE 11.5   Exercise provides physical and psychological benefits at every stage of life.

nent disability. Scientific research has unequivocally shown the benefits of exercise for older people, not only those who are already fit but those who have been sedentary for years and even those in their 90s (Cruikshank, 2003).

In every age group, women exercise less than men. This gender difference may be related to socialization and to the fact that women have less leisure time than men. Many of today's older women did not have the opportunity for sports and outdoor recreation when they were younger. Women's lower incomes also contribute to the difference, as they are less likely to have money to purchase gym memberships and sports equipment. But when older women do get out and start moving, they often find that exercising and staying fit are fun (see Figure 11.5).

Fortunately, it is never too late to start exercising. Physicians in the past often responded to older people's reports of weakness and lack of energy by saying, "What do you expect at your age? Get used to it." However, strength training can not only delay but actually reverse the process of muscle loss. Pioneering studies at Tufts University showed that men in their 60s and 70s gained 100 to 175 percent in muscle strength after 12 weeks of a high-intensity strength-training program. The research program was then extended to nursing home residents ranging in age from 86 to 96. In 8 weeks, these frail elders increased their strength on average by 175 percent. Their walking speed and balance greatly improved. Later studies recruited healthy postmenopausal women, also with dramatic results: after a one-year program, the exercise group, compared to a no-treatment control group, gained bone density and muscle tone, improved their balance, and became more active, energetic, and physically flexible (Nelson, 2000).

Sexuality in Middle and Later Life

Visualize an old woman wearing a miniskirt. What is your first reaction to this image? What reaction do you think your friends would have?

A mini-skirted old woman is deviant because she dares to appear sexual past her reproductive years (Calasanti & Slevin, 2001). Sexuality and sexual activity in older people are widely considered disgusting or ridiculous, and this is conveyed in jokes and stories. However, even these are gender biased—there are plenty of approving jokes about Viagra, but an immense cultural negativity about the sexuality of older women.

One factor limiting sexual expression for older heterosexual women is that there aren't enough men to go around. Because women live longer than men, the gender ratio at age 65 is 149 women for every 100 men. By the age of 85, there are 259 women for every 100 men (Hatch, 1995). The gender ratio means that heterosexual women are likely to spend the last decades of their lives without a marital or sexual partner (Fields & Casper, 2001). African American women are twice as likely as White women to be divorced, separated, or widowed in later life because of early mortality among African American men (Ralston, 1997).

Opportunities for relationships are limited not just because of a man shortage, but because men usually choose younger partners. It is socially acceptable for older men to enter relationships with women many years younger than they are, with the result that fewer older women than older men have partners (Grambs, 1989; Öberg, 2003). Research has consistently shown that one of the biggest factors influencing the sexual desire and activity of middle-aged and older women is the lack of a partner (Calasanti & Slevin, 2001; DeLamater & Sill, 2005).

The lack of men and the unrelenting focus on youthful women can be a frustrating situation for midlife women. As one heterosexual woman pointed out:

> I'm no longer worried about pregnancy; the children are gone; my energy is released. I have a new surge of interest in sex. But at the same time the culture is saying, "You are not attractive as a woman; act your age. . . ." It's a terrible bind for a middle-aged woman (Boston Women's Health Book Collective, 1998, p. 563).

Sexual Desire and Satisfaction in Old Age

Older adults have been almost entirely neglected in sex research. However, medical and behavioral studies show that many people desire and are capable of enjoying sexual intimacy into old age (see Box 11.1). In a survey of a large representative sample of Americans over the age of 45, the surprising result was that even at age 75, about half the men and women still experienced sexual desire. Biomedical factors (age, illnesses, and medications) were important correlates of desire, but having a positive attitude about the importance of sex was even more important (DeLamater & Sill, 2005). In a study of over 400 married people recruited from centers for the elderly in Greece, more than 50 percent of participants aged 60 to 90 reported still being sexually active, enjoying intercourse once a week on average. Like the U.S. study, the Greek study found that socioeconomic and interpersonal factors were more important than biomedical ones. For example, couples who had married for love and said they were still in love were more sexually active (Papaharitou et al., 2008).

Box 11.1 ∾ Research Focus: Online Match Making among Older Adults

Online dating is a popular way for people to find that special someone. Although commercials for Internet dating sites would have you believe that it is only twentysomethings who are online looking for love, older adults are also using the Web to find romance. What are people looking for in a match?

A recent study compared adult men and women of all ages to see what people are seeking in a mate and how those characteristics might vary by age.

Researchers recruited 600 heterosexual men and women from Yahoo!Personals to complete a survey and write an essay about themselves and their desired partner. Participants were categorized into four age groups, 20 to 34 year olds, 40 to 54 year olds, 60 to 74 year olds, and 75+ year olds. The research team found that as men age, there is a larger discrepancy between the man's age and the age of his desired partner. In other words, while a 25-year-old man might prefer a woman who was no older than 24, a 60-year-old man preferred a woman who was no older than 52, and a 75-year-old man desired a woman no older than 65. The pattern for women was quite different. Generally, women sought a partner who was older than them. However, as women age, the difference between their age and their desired partner's age gradually decreased. For women in the 60 to 74 age group, the age difference approached zero, and by age 75+, women sought a younger man.

In addition to age, the researchers also examined differences in the importance of status and attractiveness. Women of all ages sought men of higher status, while men were more likely to desire someone who was attractive. Regardless of age, however, women were more selective than men.

Source: Alterovitz, S., & Mendelsohn, G.A. (2009). Partner preferences across the life span: Online dating by older adults. *Psychology and Aging, 24,* 513–517. Contributed by Annie B. Fox.

Older lesbians

> Now in my 50s, I am 18 years into what I hope will be a lifelong relationship with a woman. Sex for us is a steady friend. During our busy work week, we cuddle and that's good. On weekends and on vacations, we make time for lovemaking and cherish how it reconnects and refreshes us (Boston Women's Health Book Collective, 1998, pp. 563–564).

There has been very little research on sexuality among older lesbians and bisexual women. It seems that the idea that not all old people are heterosexual has not yet occurred to most researchers (Clarke et al., 2010). And it is not easy to do research with older cohorts of LGBTQ people. Among women who are now in old age, those who have had relationships with other women often were not out and did not use the word lesbian to describe themselves; therefore they may be overlooked in research.

In one survey that included 119 self-identified lesbians and bisexual women with an average age of 68, about half the women were currently living with a partner. Compared with those who lived alone, those living with a partner reported better mental health, higher self-esteem, and less loneliness (Grossman et al., 2001). A British study of more than 300 LGB people aged 50 to 70 found that 60 percent of the women were currently in a relationship, and almost half of these were living with their partners (Heaphy et al., 2004). Participants said that being in a relationship was very important and became even more so as they got older. Although these studies did not assess sexual activity directly, they demonstrate the importance of long-term intimate relationships in the lives of older LGB people.

Relationships: Continuity and Change

There is much more to the second half of life than changes in the physical self. Midlife is often a time of major changes in relationships with partners, friends, and family. Children grow up and leave home. Grandchildren are born. A husband may become dependent on his wife for daily help and care, or die unexpectedly. Here we look at some important relationships for women in middle and later life.

Friends and Family

Older women tend to be involved with rich networks of friends and family. Compared to men in the same age group they have more friends and feel closer to their friends (Canetto, 2001). Longtime women friends provide companionship and support for older women (Adams, 1997). Close friends may be particularly important for older lesbians; in studies of lesbian and bisexual women in their 60s and older, friends are named as a very important source of support by virtually all the participants (Grossman et al., 2001; Heaphy et al., 2004).

Consistent with their extended family patterns, African American women are more involved with family than European American women. Older Black women are closer to their adult children and have more frequent contact with them than do older White women. They are also more involved with their grandchildren and may develop a particularly close guiding relationship with a granddaughter (Ralston, 1997).

For older women of all ethnic groups, relationships with sisters can be a vital source of social support. Sibling relationships are unique because of their long duration, similar family history, shared memories, and same age cohort. This was brought home to me when my mother-in-law Mary's younger sister died at the age of 83. Mary said sadly, "I knew her for 83 years; we went through life together." In studies of sibling relationships, sister–sister dyads are the most consistently rated as the most positive and intimate, whereas brother–brother dyads are more often hostile or distant (Scott, 1997). The relative lack of closeness among older male siblings may be a late-life legacy of raising boys to be independent and competitive. The positive quality of relationships between sisters in later life has been documented not only in the United States but also in Canada, Europe, and Israel. Relationships with sisters may intensify in old age, after a woman is widowed. Having a sister nearby is related to life satisfaction and mental health in old age (Scott, 1997).

Involvement with friends and family has costs as well as rewards. Like the younger women discussed in Chapters 8 and 9, older women provide more care and more different kinds of care for other people than older men do, regardless of whether they also work outside the home (Canetto, 2001). We will return shortly to a discussion of the costs and benefits of care work in later life.

Becoming a Grandmother

The grandmother is one of the few positive images of older women. She is easy to visualize: white haired, kindly, and warm, she dishes out homemade cookies, babysits for free, and indulges her grandchildren. A Google search for grandma turns up dozens of sentimental quotes like this one: "Grandmas are moms with lots of frosting."

Adapting to a New Role

Grandparenting gives midlife and older women a meaningful and important place in their families. Grandmothers are often relied on for advice, babysitting, help in a crisis, emotional support, financial assistance, and maintaining family customs and rituals. All these provide an important cushion for young families. For the grandparents, it can be very satisfying to see the family line continue and to once again experience the love of a small child (Scott, 1997). (See Figure 11.6.) However, becoming a grandmother is an involuntary role change. Its meaning, and its effects on women's lives, is more complex than its image suggests.

A woman may become a grandmother at any time from her 30s to her 70s. The timing of grandparenthood is an important factor in how women adapt to this new role. Younger grandmothers may not be ready:

> When my daughter called me from Florida to tell me I was now a grandmother, I was not in the least elated. I had recently remarried and was seeing myself as a young, passionate lover. I didn't want to think of myself as a grandmother (Doress-Worters & Siegal, 1994, pp. 139–140).

FIGURE 11.6   The rewards of being a grandmother.

A grandmother who is still working full time may have little spare time to spend with babies and young children. Cohort effects are important too. Baby Boomer grandmothers may lead active lives that leave little time to be a traditional grandma (Scott, 1997).

Because the role expectations for grandmothers are so strong, some grandmothers feel the need to set limits. For example, in a study of middle-age Chicanas, one woman said about being a grandmother, "I love it, but I'm not the kind of grandma where I'm going to sit down and only knit little things." Another said that she would help out when needed, but not "stay home and take care of children so (the daughter) could have a good time . . . grandparents have the right to be free and enjoy themselves when they're old" (Facio, 1997, p. 343). These women recognized that a grandmother's caregiving may be taken for granted, and they chose to define grandparenthood for themselves.

Ethnicity, Social Class, and Grandmothers' Roles

A woman's ethnicity is a key determinant of how she will experience her grandmother role. Among Native American families, the grandmother is the center of the family and the one who holds it all together. Native American women often become grandmothers at a young age, and this transition is seen as even more important than becoming a mother because of the symbolic responsibilities it carries. Relationships between grandmother and grandchildren are characterized as warm and loving, and the grandmother is not just a caregiver but a storyteller and teacher who passes on tribal knowledge to the next generation. In Native American communities, it is not unusual for a child to ask to live with his or her grandparents, and the request is usually granted (John et al., 1997).

In African American communities, too, extended multi-generational families offer scope for grandparental involvement in grandchildren's daily lives. The greater contact and involvement of Black grandparents holds even when socioeconomic status is controlled, implying that it is a cultural difference rather than an economic one (Ralston, 1997).

Due to divorce, as well as HIV/AIDS and drug epidemics in poor and minority communities, increasing number of grandparents are taking primary responsibility for grandchildren. Some grandmothers provide full-time day care for working single moms; others take in their grandchildren and raise them, with or without legal custody. Women in ethnic minority groups are much more likely than European American women to have primary responsibility for one or more grandchildren. The number of grandparent-headed households increased by 87 percent between 1980 and 2000, and about 6 percent of all children now live in such households. More than 75 percent of all grandparents raising children are women; almost half do not have a spouse; and over half are above the age of 55 (Calasanti & Slevin, 2001; Pittman & Boswell, 2007). Many grandmothers who became full-time caregivers report that it seemed like a nondecision: faced with grandchildren whose parents were incapacitated by drug addiction, physical illness, or mental disability, the grandmother's attitude was "you do what you have to do" (Scott, 1997).

Over 57 percent of grandmother-alone households are poor (Calasanti & Slevin, 2001). Women in this situation have multiple stressors that detract from physical health, emotional well-being, and financial security (Scott, 1997). They report more depression and poorer physical health than other grandparents (Calasanti & Slevin, 2001). Grandmothers bringing up children often mourn their dreams of financial security and freedom in later life. These women are unsung heroes who give to the next generation, often at their own expense:

> My other children were all in high school when one of my daughters developed a drug problem, and I had to take her two little ones to raise. I was afraid I couldn't do it. I thought I was done raising kids, and they were babies! But I felt it was my responsibility because they were my blood. I didn't want them to go to foster care . . . I raised them both . . . and they still call me Ma . . , I am proud that both of my grandkids are doing well now, and that I was able to raise them (Boston Women's Health Book Collective, 1998, p. 553).

Caregiving: Its Costs and Rewards

Women's care work is not limited to their children and grandchildren. They also provide care to their aging parents and spouses.

Caring for Elderly Parents

There is more and more need for care work for the elderly because their numbers are increasing. According to national surveys, about 17 percent of people over the age of 65 have some form of disability that requires long-term help from others (Brody, 2004). Older people with physical or cognitive disabilities may need assistance with basic personal care, such as getting in and out of bed, bathing, dressing, eating, and toileting, as well as help with life tasks such as cooking, housework, shopping, transportation, and money management.

The great majority of caregivers to the old—about 75 percent—are women. This is true across all ethnic groups except Asian Americans, where men are almost as likely to be care providers for elderly parents as women are (Calasanti & Slevin, 2001).

Women who take responsibility for elderly parents, in-laws, and other relatives are often called "women in the middle" because they are most often in their middle years, they are the middle generation in their families, and they are caught in the middle between the requirements of being a wife, parent, worker, and caregiver (Brody, 2004). They are also in the middle of conflicting values, because they may have jobs, careers, or activities they want to do, yet traditional values still prescribe care work as their responsibility.

Women in the middle are a diverse group in ethnicity and social class as well as in other ways. Some have young children of their own; others are in their 70s. Their numbers and their problems have been virtually ignored by society until quite recently.

Caring for a Spouse

Because women marry men older than themselves, and men have shorter life expectancies, it is highly likely that the husband in a heterosexual couple, rather than the wife, will receive spousal care during his old age and final illness (Calasanti & Slevin, 2001; Cox, 2005). Our society assumes that old women will be responsible for their even older husbands. The older a married woman is, the more likely she will take on the physical and emotional work of elder care despite health problems of her own.

Lucy's case history is typical of a White, working-class caregiver:

> Her husband is bedridden and his entire care is left up to her. She feels tremendous pressure from this responsibility, and she attributes her heart problems to it. Inadequate finances, approximately $500 a month for the two of them, also contribute to her unhappiness. . . . At 74, Lucy wishes she were still working not just because she needs the money but also because she needs to get out of the house. She told an interviewer that her only trips outside the home were to the doctor, the pharmacy, and the grocery store. "Honey, I haven't been in a store downtown for years" (Calasanti & Slevin, 2001, p. 136).

Caring for an elderly spouse can be heartbreaking when it involves prolonged deterioration of physical or mental abilities. One woman, Sara, spoke of her concerns in a support group for Alzheimer's caregivers:

> Can I ever finally close him out of my life and say, "Well, it's done. It's over. He's gone"? How do I really know that the poor man isn't hidden somewhere, behind all that confusion, trying to reach out and say, "I love you Sara"? (Faircloth, 2003, pp. 217–218).

Lesbian couples have similar experiences of care work as heterosexual couples do, but they may also have to cope with heterosexist treatment that adds to their stress. Getting help for a partner may mean coming out about the relationship, and the partner's relatives may withhold help if they do not approve of the relationship (Hash, 2001).

The Costs of Care Work

Care work takes a toll on a woman's economic security, largely because it's impossible to combine it with full-time paid work. In a national study of elder care, 33 percent of women caregivers had cut back their hours at work, 29 percent had passed up an opportunity for job advancement, 22 percent had taken a leave, and 13 percent took early retirement (Cox, 2005). These decisions lead not only to an immediate loss of income for caregivers, but to lower Social Security and retirement benefits when they themselves get old. A national longitudinal study of women age 59 to 61 assessed how many hours a week they spent caring for elderly parents and, 9 years later, how well they were doing economically (Wakabayashi & Donato, 2006). Women who put in the most hours of caretaking (over 20 hours per week) were more likely to end up living below the poverty level and receiving public assistance such as food stamps. Their caretaking responsibilities had forced them into poverty.

The economic cost of caregiving falls most heavily on women who are poorer to begin with. Other negative effects fall on middle-class and poor alike, affecting the caregiver's psychological well-being, physical health, family relationships, and lifestyle. Symptoms of emotional strain are the most prevalent consequence of being a caregiver. In study after study, caregivers report depression, anger, anxiety, guilt, feelings of helplessness, and emotional exhaustion (Brody, 2004).

Women often try to enlist others in helping with care work, but with limited success. One husband rigged up buzzers so that his wife could respond immediately whenever his 95-year-old mother called from her upstairs room—but did not offer to respond himself. Another woman, desperately needing a respite, sent her mother to her sister's house for a visit, but reported that "after a couple of weeks, my brother-in-law put her in a taxi back to us" (Brody, 2004, p. 105). Although some family members do share care, it is most often left to a daughter who is perceived as suitable by others—or is the only one who offers. The huge sacrifice on the part of women who take care of the elderly and infirm is largely taken for granted by society.

Why Do Women Do More Care Work?

Given its psychological and economic costs, why do women continue to do care work, even into their old age? Some women who care for elderly relatives say they do the job willingly and that they derive many benefits from it: satisfaction from fulfilling a big responsibility, following religious teachings, expressing their love, and returning care received from the parent in the past. As these two daughters express:

> I never regret caring for her. She's the only mother I have (Brody, 2004, p. 118).

> He (her father) gave me so much and so caringly, and so completely. There's no way there's too much I could be doing. It's not an exchange. He just deserves it (Brody, 2004, p. 137).

Some psychologists and sociologists have argued that nurturing is central to a woman's identity. Others have said that women have less attachment to their paid work and therefore are freer to do unpaid work. However, research shows that personality makes little difference in who gets assigned care work, and over half of female caregivers keep on working despite their caregiving responsibilities (Martire & Stephens, 2003).

Care work is not just a free choice. Rather, responsibility for caring for others is structured by the gender-based division of labor in families, the devaluing of unpaid work, and the reluctance of society to provide social services for those in need. Paid care is too expensive for most families, and federal funding has been cut back over several decades. As one researcher said, women's lifelong devotion to taking care of others "may seem 'natural' and a 'choice,' but what are the alternatives?" In the words of female caregivers themselves, "Who else is going to do it?" (Calasanti & Slevin, 2001, p. 149).

Loss of a Life Partner

Nearly half of all U.S. women over the age of 65—and 83 percent of African American women in that age group—are widows (Whitbourne & Skultety, 2006). The average widow lives for more than 15 years after her partner's death (Canetto, 2001).

Losing a spouse to death is one of life's most difficult experiences. A Danish study of widowed women and men whose average age was 75 showed that, shortly after the spouse's death, 27 percent of the bereaved partners met the official criteria for post-traumatic stress syndrome (Elklit & O'Connor, 2005). Symptoms associated with depression—sadness, loneliness, anguish, and hopelessness—are common and a normal part of grieving (Dutton & Zisook, 2005). Although the symptoms of psychological distress decline over time, they may never disappear entirely. One woman in her late 70s said, "Once you have had your husband to fall asleep with for 53 years, it never gets any easier to be alone at night" (Covan, 2005, p. 11).

Women seem to cope with the loss of a spouse better than men do. Although they report high levels of emotional pain and distress, they have less severe depression and fewer serious physical health problems than men in similar circumstances. They are less likely to abuse alcohol, suffer a heart attack, or commit suicide following the death of a spouse (Canetto, 2001; Stroebe et al., 2001).

The gender difference in coping with spousal loss may be due to several factors. First, women have better support networks than men; widows typically rely on close friends, children, and grandchildren throughout the grieving process (Covan, 2005). Second, men who lose a wife lose a caregiver, whereas women who lose a husband usually have been providing work on his behalf. Finally, women may cope better because widowhood occurs at a younger age than for men and "women expect to spend part of their lives as widows" (Canetto, 2001, p. 187). It is sad but true that almost every woman over 60 knows others her age who have been widowed and to some degree she may mentally prepare for becoming a widow.

When older women are widowed, they are much less likely to remarry than widowed men in their age group. One result is that older women are increasingly likely to live alone. Loneliness and isolation are potential problems for widows; however, for many, living alone is a positive choice, bringing independence and freedom from care work (Canetto, 2001).

Ethnicity and social class shape different experiences of widowhood. Among Latina women, for example, a widow is expected to respect the memory of her marriage by refraining from sexual activity for the rest of her life and devoting herself to taking care of others. *La abuela* is asexual; to be otherwise is shameful (Facio,

1997). However, some Latinas resist this form of social control. Maria G. has been widowed for 10 years and has a "friend" despite her daughter's disapproval:

> Your kids think that once you're old, you're dead or something. They get very jealous. And the first thing they say is, "What about my father?" Well, what about their father, he's dead, may he rest in peace, but I'm not! (Facio, 1997, p. 346).

Little is known about partner loss in lesbian couples. Although lesbians have an advantage in that their partner is likely to live longer, coping with the loss of a lesbian life partner is made more difficult by heterosexism (Cruikshank, 2003). If the couple has not been out to friends and family, the grief may have to be borne alone. Others do not recognize that the "friend who died" was more than just a friend. This deprives the surviving partner of the support network that helps heterosexual women cope with bereavement.

With time, most people who have lost a life partner report that they experience life positively again. In a study of resilience following bereavement (Dutton & Zisook, 2005), many participants, like these, spoke of how they had coped and what they had learned:

> My experience in losing my precious husband has made me more aware of the beauty in everyday life, the need to share the hurts and joys of others. . . . It sustains me and I look forward to the challenge of each day with an appreciation much keener than before (a 54-year-old woman, p. 884).

> This is the first Christmas I will be a widow. It is certainly not easy, but not nearly as difficult as I thought it would be. I've gotten involved in the community and helping others who are homeless or otherwise worse off than myself (a 68-year-old woman, p. 885).

> I have found and am convinced that the following have strengthened me: faith in God and in his direction in my life each day, and love of other people and being sensitive to their needs. A great help is to simply itemize in two columns your blessings and your hurts. The list of blessings is so much longer and richer (a 61-year-old man, p. 886).

Work and Achievement

For women who are socioeconomically privileged, midlife can be a very positive and fulfilling time. Moreover, women in recent age cohorts are likely to be invested in multiple roles as partner, mother, and paid worker, which is associated with better psychological adjustment. Is midlife the prime of life for (some) women?

Women in Their Prime

Several studies have shown that for college educated women midlife typically is a time of self-confidence, achievement, and happiness. A sample of Canadian women between the ages of 45 and 65 described themselves as satisfied with themselves and their accomplishments and optimistic about growing older (Quirouette & Pushkar, 1999). Samples of U.S. women show similar results. For example, in a longitudinal study, women's positive identity and self-confidence in their personal

FIGURE 11.7   For some women, midlife is a time to achieve long-postponed goals.

power increased from their 20s to their 60s. A woman's belief that she was contributing to the world and caring for the next generation increased up to midlife and then leveled off (Zucker et al., 2002).

In another study of college graduates between the ages of 26 and 80, women in their early 50s had the highest life satisfaction. Compared with other age groups, both older and younger, these midlife women had fewer childcare responsibilities, better health, and higher income. They were self-confident and involved in the world (Mitchell & Helson, 1990). The researchers suggested that women's prime time of life is their 50s.

For some women, midlife is a chance to explore new career directions or return to school. Psychological theories of personality development have overlooked this developmental pathway because they have largely been based on a White middle-class male norm (finish school, get a job, work until you retire or die, whichever comes first). For women, the stimulus for making a change varies. For some, the death or serious illness of a friend or family member who is near their own age prompts the realization that time is limited and it is important to make the most of it. For other women, divorce is the catalyst for forging a new path. Still others, relieved of childcare responsibilities for the first time, decide to follow a long-postponed dream:

> All my life I had wanted to be a nurse but instead was a secretary. Finally, at age 57, when the youngest of our children graduated from college, I took a year from the workaday world to attend school and become a licensed practical nurse. I made the highest grade in our class on the state board exam (Boston Women's Health Book Collective, 1998, p. 552).

Midlife patterns of change vary by socioeconomic class. Women from poor or working-class backgrounds often experience health problems sooner than more advantaged women do, because they do more physically demanding and hazardous work and have poorer health care. For these women, slowing down, not speeding up, may be a major midlife goal (Boston Women's Health Book Collective, 1998). However, for others, education becomes an important means of redefining the self. Some of the most hard-working and dedicated college students are older working class women who are making up for the education they could not afford at 18 (Cruickshank, 2003). Education can be a lifelong process (see Figure 11.7).

Retirement

Psychological theories of men's retirement conceptualize it as a major life change. The retiree's social status, power, and income drop. His daily activities and interpersonal interactions change drastically as he gains large amounts of free time but loses daily contact with coworkers.

This model of retirement is a poor fit for women (Calasanti & Slevin, 2001; Canetto, 2001; Sugar, 2007). Until quite recently, very few women had the kinds of jobs that provide high status, power, and income. Retirement for women more often meant leaving low-status work and subordinate positions. Furthermore, women, more often than men, make the decision to retire because of events unrelated to work itself: a husband retires and pressures his wife to do so, or someone in the family needs care. And many low-income workers must keep working as long as possible to make ends meet. Often, low-income women work "off the books" into their old age, without accumulating pensions or benefits (Cruikshank, 2003).

When women, especially working class women, retire from paid work, their total workload may not change a great deal because of all the unpaid work they do. For a woman who is caring for her elderly parent, cooking and cleaning for her husband, and babysitting for active grandchildren, retiring from her job may make little difference. In fact, her unpaid work may expand. As one woman said in an interview, she liked being retired because "Now I got time to do my work" (Calasanti & Slevin, 2001, p. 130).

When a man retires, he rarely does more housework unless his wife becomes disabled. When men speak of the freedom of retirement, they mean not having to go to the office or report to a supervisor. Women, in contrast, describe the "freedom" to do the laundry at any time of day. However, this may be most true for White couples; African American families appear to be more flexible than White families in midlife gender roles (Calasanti & Slevin, 2001).

Divorced or never-married women tend to work longer than married women, because they cannot afford to retire as early. There has been very little research on retirement among gay and lesbian individuals or couples. In one recent study, lesbian couples had a lower average income before retirement than gay male, heterosexual married, or heterosexual cohabiting couples (Mock, 2001). Lesbians are more likely to have been continuously employed through their adult years than heterosexual women, but their long years of work may not lead to a financially secure retirement (Kitzinger, 2001).

In media images, retirees are eager consumers of travel and leisure products—healthy, smiling seniors cycling country roads, going on cruises, and sipping wine in outdoor cafes. The reality may differ. Retirement is part of wider sociocultural patterns of economic advantage and disadvantage. "Retirement is not simply leisure, the early bird special, and senior discounts on Tuesday; it is a mechanism for income reduction" (Cruikshank, 2003, p. 130).

Poverty in Later Life

Women's poverty in old age reflects the accumulation of a lifetime of gender-linked inequities. Women now in old age have earned less than men for their work, and are far less likely to have held the kinds of jobs that provide pensions. They have probably taken time out from paid work to take care of their children (Sugar, 2007). For every year a woman works taking care of her children, her spouse, or her elderly family members, a zero is entered into her Social Security account, unless she has done over 35 years of paid work. "Defining an older woman's caregiving years as 'zero years' is blatant gender discrimination. Women are penalized for doing the work society expects of them" (Cruikshank, 2003, p. 128).

About two-thirds of all poor older adults in the United States are women, and the majority of these are ethnic minority women (Canetto, 2001). Poverty among old women is a problem in less-developed nations due to sex discrimination in education, employment, and access to wealth such as land. However, the United States is alone among industrialized nations in having large numbers of old women living in poverty. In Sweden, France, and the Netherlands, the poverty rate of old women living alone is less than 2 percent; in the United States, it is 18 percent (Cruikshank, 2003; Wakabayashi & Donato, 2006).

Older married women are better off than single or widowed women of the same age because of their partner's economic resources. However, a middle-class woman who is relying on her husband's retirement plan may slip into poverty as she ages. Often, savings are depleted during his final illness. His pension may end with his death, and her Social Security benefits drop. Older women living alone have a poverty rate five times higher than older men living alone (Canetto, 2001).

A woman's social class during her earning years makes a huge difference in the odds that she will be poor in her old age:

> A middle-class professional woman in her twenties can afford to buy an IRA (retirement saving fund) each year, but the woman who cleans her office cannot. Forty-five years later, the former may have accumulated several hundred thousand dollars, the latter nothing. To acquire this wealth, all the first woman has to do is keep breathing. . . . Her husband has a secure job that will provide a pension. . . . The working-class woman's parents will probably need her caregiving help sooner. . . . In late life, home ownership is often the key to financial security, but when working-class people of color own a home, it may have declining value in an inner-city neighborhood (Cruikshank, 2003, pp. 116–117).

The plight of old women who are poor is not what anyone would look forward to in the last years of life:

> I try to buy the cheapest things. I always make my own milk from powder. . . . If I need clothes I go across the street to the thrift shop. I watch for yard sales. . . . If I have 80 cents I can go to the Council on Aging for a hot lunch. But the last two weeks of the month are always hard. . . . I'm down to my last $10, and I've got more than two weeks to go (a woman in her 70s, quoted in Doress-Worters & Siegal, 1994, p. 192).

Will future cohorts of women escape poverty in old age? Economists calculate that even today's working women face a steep climb to save enough money to cover basic living expenses in retirement. According to their computations, women now at the lowest income levels could not save enough no matter how soon they started or how hard they tried. More than one-third of Baby Boomer women will be single when they retire over the next few decades. In 2001, the median net worth of households headed by single women was $27,850, compared to $140,000 for households of married couples. Only 35 percent of single women had retirement accounts. The gender gap in retirement resources reflects the fact that women's lifetime earnings are still much lower than men's (Duenwald & Stamler, 2004).

Making a Difference

Age is a dimension of life that is both biological and cultural. Physical, psychological, and social factors all interact to define a person's age and its meaning. Although aging and death are inevitable, poor quality of life in later years is not.

Transforming Society: Elder Activism

Because older people are an increasingly large proportion of the population, their political clout is growing. At the beginning of the twentieth century, older people made up about 4 percent of the U.S. population; by the year 2030, they will be 20 percent—some 70 million people. One researcher joked, "It will be Florida all over the country" (Dobrof, 2001). The oldest old are the most rapidly growing population of all. There will be 19 million people over the age of 85 in the population by the year 2050 (Brody, 2004).

There are many organizations dedicated to political activism on behalf of people over 60. However, these organizations have sometimes treated the old as a gender-neutral group, ignoring issues of particular concern to women. Women's organizations have often focused on issues crucial to younger women, such as reproductive rights. Moreover, organizations dedicated to women's issues and those dedicated to older people's issues have sometimes failed to connect with each other. Thus, the problems of aging *women* in our society are only beginning to be recognized and addressed.

Maggie Kuhn is one example of a woman who has made a difference for older people. When she was forced to retire at the age of 70, Kuhn founded the multigenerational activist group now known as the Gray Panthers and became one of its most visible spokespersons. Kuhn was proud to be what she called "an elder of the tribe." When she died in 1995 at the age of 89, she left a thriving organization and a legacy of successful activism on issues such as forced retirement, pension rights, and nursing home reform (Kuhn, 1991).

Activism on behalf of older women and men is likely to increase now that the large Baby Boomer cohort has reached midlife. This cohort grew up with the civil rights movement, the women's movement, and the peace and environmental movements. They are better educated than previous cohorts, they expect a higher standard of living, and they know that "the squeaky wheel gets the grease" when it comes to changing social policy. Moreover, thanks to pioneers like Maggie Kuhn, they have a well-established network of organizations already in place to educate and advocate for older people (see Box 11.2).

Transforming Social Interaction: Taking Charge of the Second Half

Among the current cohort of midlife women are some who are envisioning new paths for their later years. Women are more likely to be single, widowed, or divorced at midlife now than in previous cohorts, and such women are realizing that they cannot look forward to a spouse's companionship—or retirement pension—in old age. Some women are choosing to live collectively with other women for companionship, mutual support, and economic benefits. This option builds on one of women's strengths, their lifelong bonds with women friends (Adams, 1997).

A *New York Times* article (Gross, 2004) profiled some women who are teaming up for old age. Christine P., a contractor in her 60s, built a house for herself and three friends to share, complete with exercise room and hot tub. Two other women

---

BOX 11.2   ∞   Resources for Activism

There are many ways for you to become an activist on behalf of older women. Below are some national organizations committed to the social advancement of women, particularly issues of women's health and well-being later in life.

www.blackwomenshealth.org
Black Women's Health Imperative: An African American health education, research, advocacy, and leadership development institution. This organization is the leading force for health for African American women, promoting optimum health for Black women across the lifespan—physically, mentally, and spiritually.

www.graypanthers.org
Gray Panthers: A national organization of intergenerational activists dedicated to changing social policy on issues such as peace, employment, housing, antidiscrimination (ageism, sexism, and racism), and family security. Over the years, the Gray Panthers have stopped forced retirement at age 65, exposed nursing-home abuse, and worked towards universal health care.

www.latinahealth.org
National Latina Health Organization: Works toward the goal of bilingual access to quality health care and self-empowerment of Latinas through culturally respectful educational programs, health advocacy, outreach, research, and public policy.

www.nsclc.org
National Senior Citizens Law Center: Provides legal services support for poor senior citizens. Advocates to promote the independence and well-being of low-income elderly and those with disabilities.

www.womenshealth.gov
National Women's Health Information Center: A service of the Office on Women's Health in the Department of Health and Human Services, this Web site provides an array of women's health information and resources, including minority women's health.

www.nwhn.org
National Women's Health Network: Develops and promotes a critical analysis of health issues in order to affect policy and support consumer decision making.

www.sageusa.org
Senior Action in a Gay Environment (SAGE): World's oldest and largest organization devoted to meeting the needs of aging gay, lesbian, bisexual, and transgender elders.

www.nawho.org
National Asian Women's Health Organization (NAWHO): A national nonprofit health organization dedicated to achieving health equity for Asian women and their families. The Web site provides information about a number of health topics including osteoporosis.

www.owl-national.org
Older Women's League (OWL): A grassroots organization focused exclusively on issues related to women in midlife and later. OWL has more than 60 chapters nationwide and its members conduct research and advocate for economic, social, and health equality for women 40 and older.

Contributed by Michelle R. Kaufman and Annie B. Fox.

in their mid-60s bought adjoining apartments in a city high-rise, planning to help each other enjoy life as long as they are able. I know one collective-living group that consists of one heterosexual married couple, one lesbian couple, and two single women. This group pooled their resources to buy a house; they designated private living space for each individual or couple, as well as shared space. In the future, they plan to share the cost of caregivers for help with daily living. Like other pioneers of the new collective living, this group consulted attorneys and drew up an agreement that protects individual financial assets. They also purchased long-term care insurance so they would not become burdens to each other.

There are no official statistics on how many older women are creating family-of-choice living arrangements, but interest in this option is growing rapidly. Baby Boomer women often have previous experience of communal living and are used to controlling their own lives. Laura Young, executive director of the Older Women's League, commented, "We lived together in dorms and sororities. We shared apartments after graduation. We traveled together. We helped each other through divorce and the death of our parents. Why not take it to the next level?" (Gross, 2004).

At present, the new collective living seems to be largely a middle-class trend. However, activists for the elderly have long pointed out that publicly subsidized housing usually is designed on the assumption that tenant will be either a married couple or a woman living alone. Why not have units for two women, designed with both private and shared space? (Cruikshank, 2003). Because friendship is so important to women, the quality of older women's lives may depend on being able to choose how and with whom they would like to live. The stakes are high, as women (and some men) seek to avoid isolation and poverty in old age.

Transforming Ourselves: Resisting Ageism

As members of an ageist society, none of us can claim to be completely free of ageism. However, we can try to analyze and resist it. How often do we stereotype old women? When we compliment someone by saying "you don't look your age" the implicit message is that if she did look her age it would be a misfortune. When we praise an older woman for being active or busy all the time, we are forgetting that young people do not have to stay frantically busy in order to be seen as worthwhile people. When you meet a person who says she is retired, do you think she has nothing much to talk about? Do you stay silent when someone uses the word *old* as a putdown?

Even stereotypes that seem positive can be harmful, because they treat all members of the category as if they are alike and set standards for behavior. The media tend to pay attention only to seniors who run marathons or go bungee jumping, implying that older people who are not superbly healthy or incredibly active are somehow not aging successfully or productively. Another positive but perhaps insidious image is the wise elder stereotype. Not everyone who is old is wise! The old, like the young, are individuals. What they want is to define themselves and to have the social support they need in order to thrive. Two older women who write about women and aging (Doress-Worters & Siegal, 1994) put it this way:

We proudly claim our age and experience as demonstrating our right to define who we are and what we need to live lives of dignity, activity, and involvement in our communities; decent health care and housing; an income sufficient to enjoy, rather than simply to endure, our later years; and the recognition that we are important members of society with much to contribute (p. 439).

As a society, we owe no less to our elders.

Exploring Further

Cruikshank, Margaret (2003). *Learning to be old: Gender, culture, and aging.* Westport, CT: Greenwood Press.
   As its title says, this book puts gender first in its analysis of aging. Its feminist perspective leads to many new insights about women's aging and many concrete suggestions for social change.

Delaney, Sarah Louise, Delaney, A. Elizabeth, et al. (1993). *Having our say: The Delaney sisters' first 100 years.* New York: Kodansha International.
   At the ages of 101 and 103, two African American sisters talk about their lives as pioneering Black professionals (a teacher and a dentist respectively). They are wise and funny, and their story recounts their triumphs over racial and gender inequities.

Friedan, Betty (1993). *The fountain of age.* New York: Simon & Schuster.
   Friedan, an influential second-wave feminist activist, was in her 70s when she wrote this insightful analysis of women's aging. Her passion for social change did not diminish with age.

Positive Aging. www.positiveaging.net
   This e-newsletter is coordinated by psychologists Mary Gergen and Kenneth Gergen. It offers summaries of new research on aging and a variety of resources for making the most of the second half of life.

PART 5

Gender and Well-Being

CHAPTER 12

Violence against Women

Mary Crawford and Annie B. Fox

$\mathcal{P}$erhaps the clearest demonstration of the worldwide harm done by patriarchal social systems is violence against girls and women. Gender-based violence shares some common features. First, even though it is pervasive, it is very often hidden. Second, it tends to be underreported; statistics on crimes against girls and women are often unreliable and they typically err in the direction of underestimating the problem. In previous chapters we have described gender-linked harassment of girls by peers and teachers (Chapter 6), forced genital surgery or mutilation (Chapter 7), and sexual harassment in the workplace (Chapter 10). In this chapter, we examine other forms of gender-linked violence and we describe how violence against women involves all levels of the gender system: cultural, interpersonal, and individual. Let's look at an example of patriarchal violence against women in our own society to see how these levels are linked.

In 2003, a major scandal erupted at the U.S. Air Force Academy. Over 50 female cadets and former cadets alleged that they had been sexually assaulted or raped while attending the Academy. When the women tried to report the assaults they were shunned, pressured to keep quiet, or disciplined. None of the perpetrators had been punished. At the broadest level, the men who held the social and political power at the Academy tolerated a climate that was hostile and dangerous for women. At the interpersonal level, the male cadets who harassed and assaulted their classmates abused the status and power they held as upperclassmen, and *as men*. For example, two women testified in a military hearing that an upperclassman lured them to his room and forced one to fondle him. The women reported that they were afraid to disobey because they are taught that upperclassmen may order first-year students to do anything they want. At the individual level, the assaults were traumatizing to the women; being disbelieved or socially shunned for reporting an assault added to the trauma.

How can this kind of violence be stopped? Interventions must encompass all the levels of the gender system. If you were in charge of solving this problem, which level would be your starting point? At the end of this chapter, we will return to the question of how to end violence against girls and women by intervening at all three levels of the gender system.

Violence against Girls and Women: A Global Perspective

According to the United Nations (García-Moreno et al., 2005; UNIFEM, 2007) violence against women is one of most widespread human rights violations across the globe. As many as 60 percent of women worldwide will experience some form of violence in their lifetime (UNIFEM, 2007). Often, when thinking about violence against women, people focus on the perpetrators or the victims as individuals. However, the pervasiveness of violence against women suggests that its origins and mechanisms lie at the sociocultural level of the gender system.

The Gender System and Violence

Gender-linked violence is often justified, condoned, or overlooked. In virtually every culture, some kinds of violence against girls and women are taken for granted. Some forms of violence, such as stoning women (but not men) for adultery, may be officially permitted by the state; others represent a kind of semiofficial or unofficial terrorism. Although they are not technically legal, everyone knows they happen, and the government rarely intervenes (Sidanius & Pratto, 1999). For example, in Turkey, India, Nigeria, and other developing countries, young girls from rural areas may be sold into sexual slavery in brothels. The sex trade involves many people: villagers who lie to the girls and their families about jobs in the city; families who may close their eyes to their daughter's fate; brokers who take the girls from the village to the city or across national borders; brothel owners and pimps who keep them in bondage; men who buy the use of their bodies. In many countries, organized crime syndicates run the sex trade (McCabe & Manian, 2010). Until recently, the governments of the countries involved did little to intervene.

Research has documented many examples of the prevalence of gendered violence:

- In studies conducted around the world, one-third of women have been physically assaulted, subjected to coerced sexual activity, and victimized by severe emotional abuse (Heise et al., 1999).
- Rape and other violent acts against women are widespread in war zones and refugee camps throughout the world (Kristoff & WuDunn, 2009).
- In some countries, over half of all female murder victims are killed by a current or former partner (Neft & Levine, 1997).

Not every woman will experience violence directly but the threat of it is an important part of the fabric of life for all women. Such violence can be seen as a culturally useful way of controlling girls and women. The danger attached to simply being a woman can be seen in the profound negative effects of gender-based violence on women's physical health and psychological well-being. For those who experience it directly, it can lead to not only physical injury, but also chronic pain, disability, unwanted pregnancy, sexually transmitted diseases, depression, anxiety, elevated suicide risk, substance abuse, and post-traumatic stress syndrome. The inequalities and oppression suffered by women led one expert in public health to state, "Being born female is dangerous for your health" (Murphy, 2003, p. 205). Some estimate that as a result of gender-based violence and discrimination, the world is missing more than 100 million women and girls, and each year, two million more girls disappear (Kristoff & WuDunn, 2009; Sen, 1990).

According to the World Health Organization (WHO), gender-linked forms of violence share an underlying cause: "The lower social status of women and the belief that women are the property of men" (as cited in Murphy, 2003, p. 208). Violence against women is inextricably bound to the social context of male domination and control. The patriarchal view of society gives men a higher value than women. It is taken for granted that men should dominate in politics, economics, and the social world, including family life and interpersonal relationships. This is seen as normal and natural. Violence against women is an assertion of the power and control men have over women (White et al., 2000).

Rape-Prone Societies

The status of women is strongly correlated with rates of violence against women across cultures (Archer, 2006; Vandello & Cohen, 2006). In societies in which women have access to power and resources, there are fewer incidences of violence against women like wife abuse (Rudman & Glick, 2008). In fact, self-reported rates of violence within relationships are strongly and negatively correlated with the U.N.'s measure of gender empowerment (Archer, 2006). In other words, women are mostly vulnerable to abuse when they have the least power in their societies.

Peggy Sanday (1981, 1990, 1996, 2007) further argues for the relationship between women's power within a society and rates of violence against women. Sanday distinguishes between rape-prone and rape-free societies. Rape-prone societies are those in which the occurrence of rape is high, rape is connected to expressions of masculinity, and where rape is viewed as an acceptable tool for punishing and controlling women. In contrast, in rape-free societies, rape and sexual aggression are rare because these societies value and respect women and there is relative balance in power between men and women. As one might predict, there are many more rape-prone societies than there are rape-free societies. Let's look at one rape-prone society as an example.

In South Africa, where women have limited access to power and resources, rape and sexual violence are commonplace. One study found that 40 percent of women reported being sexually assaulted (Kalichman et al., 2005). Additionally, survey studies suggest that nearly one-third of adolescent girls' first sexual experiences involve coerced sex (Jewkes & Abrahams, 2002). Cultural views and social norms connect masculinity to the sexual domination and control of women. Both South African men and women endorse the view that women are expected to be passive and submissive and a significant percentage endorse rape myths that place the blame for sexual violence on women (Kalichman et al., 2005). Because women are expected to be subordinate and men are expected to control relationships, women are unable to refuse sex, ask their partners to use condoms, or to prevent their partners from engaging in multiple sexual relationships, placing them at greater risk for sexual violence and acquiring a sexually transmitted infection like HIV/AIDS. A 2002 study estimates that 13 percent of women in South Africa are HIV positive and the women who have HIV are more likely to experience sexual violence (Shisana & Simbayi, 2002).

Honor Killings and Honor Rapes

Another example of violence against women stemming from sociocultural factors is honor killings. In some cultures, men's honor is tied to the sexual purity and fidelity of the women in their families. Honor killings occur when a woman's actions are thought to bring shame to her male relatives; honor can only be restored by killing the woman. Dishonor can occur for any number of reasons. The woman may have refused an arranged marriage, may have married outside her religion or caste, or may have been accused of an extramarital affair. Or, she may have been sexually assaulted or raped. The U.N. estimates that 5,000 women are murdered each year in honor killings (UNFPA, 2000), a number that likely underestimates the prevalence of honor killings since many go unreported (Solberg, 2009). Honor killings occur in countries all over the world, including Afghanistan, Pakistan, Iran, Egypt, Israel, Lebanon, and the United Kingdom. In Pakistan, there were nearly 2,000 honor killings from 2004 to 2007, accounting for nearly one-fifth of all homicides during that time period (Nasrullah et al., 2009).

In many countries where honor killings occur, laws reduce or eliminate punishment for men who kill their wives; other countries have laws that are designed to protect women from violence, but these law are ignored (Parrot & Cummings, 2006). In Brazil, men who kill their wives, daughters, or sisters can argue for the "legitimate defence of honour" to avoid punishment. Although such a defense cannot be found in any Brazilian penal code, it is nevertheless used and sometimes successful (Pimental et al., 2006). That honor killings are condoned, ignored, or legally sanctioned by the law enforcement and governments of countries in which they occur demonstrates how embedded the devaluation of women is in many societies.

In countries engaged in armed conflict and war, such as Sierra Leone, Liberia, Sudan, Uganda, and the Congo, mass rape has become a tool of war. *Honor rapes* are designed not only to shame the victim, but to shame her tribe, clan, or ethnic group. Often, the women who are raped have no recourse. If they seek treatment at a hospital or tell the police, they can be thrown in jail for having sex outside of marriage (Kristoff & WuDunn, 2009). A U.N. report estimated that during the Liberian civil war, 90 percent of girls and women over the age of 3 were sexually assaulted (cited in Kristoff & WuDunn, 2009). A former U.N. commander commented that, "It has probably become more dangerous to be a woman than a soldier in an armed conflict" (cited in Kristoff & WuDunn, 2009).

Sex Trafficking

There is a global sex trade in children. In Southeast Asia alone, UNICEF estimates that 1 million children are trafficked into commercial sex work each year (Meier, 2000). (See Box 12.1.) This sex trafficking takes many forms. In Thailand, children in urban slums near resort areas may be prostituted to Western tourists who are pedophiles (Montgomery, 2001). In Nepal, rural girls may be lured or sold to traffickers who take them to India to work in brothels where they are held as prisoners (Crawford, 2010). The United Nations has recognized human trafficking, including trafficking for sexual exploitation, as a global problem (United Nations, 2000). But sex trafficking is still a huge and successful industry. Millions of women and children have been trafficked into the sex trade. According to Kristoff and WuDunn (2009),

> . . . there are 3 million women and girls worldwide . . . enslaved in the sex trade. That is a conservative estimate that does not include many others who are manipulated and intimidated into prostitution. Nor does it include millions more who are under

eighteen and cannot meaningfully consent to work in brothels. We are talking about 3 million people who in effect are the property of another person and in many cases could be killed by their owner with impunity (pg. 10).

Patterns of trafficking are shaped by gender-related inequities in material resources (Farr, 2005). In general, countries that are less developed, less wealthy, and less politically stable serve as *source countries*, from which girls and women are trafficked. Underdeveloped countries such as Nepal and Cambodia as well as industrialized ones with high unemployment, such as the newly independent states of the former Soviet Union, are where trafficking most often originates. More affluent countries serve as destination sites, where trafficked girls and women are enslaved in brothels or otherwise constrained to participate in prostitution. Some countries are hubs, with venues where women can be bought and sold by multinational traffickers. Hub countries typically have highly developed sex industries (Thailand, the Philippines) and/or powerful organized crime sectors (Albania, Turkey, and Nigeria).

Trafficking of women and children takes place in contexts of extreme poverty, gender inequality, and limited choices that make families vulnerable. In Thailand, for example, some parents allow their children to be sexually abused because the only survival alternative is for the child to work 12-hour days picking through garbage and trash in dumps (Montgomery, 2001). In Nepal, rural poverty, civil war, and lack of educational opportunities make many girls want to head to India despite

---

BOX 12.1 ∾ Lek: The Story of a Child Prostitute

Lek grew up in a slum near a tourist resort area in Thailand. Her story, documented in an ethnographic study by anthropologist Heather Montgomery, is one of exploitation from a very early age:

> Lek was introduced to commercial sex at the age of three by Ta, her eight-year-old neighbour . . . She was taken by Ta to meet James, a British businessman . . . Lek . . . remembers watching as Ta was paid to masturbate him. A few weeks later Lek did the same and continued to do so until she began, at the age of six, to have intercourse with him. In return for this, James gave money to Lek's family . . . She has been a prostitute ever since, averaging around twenty men a year, although her most regular source of income is still James. She refuses to call him a client or a customer, referring to him instead as a boyfriend. She also refuses to see him as an exploiter; she says "he is so good to me, how can you say he's bad?"

When I met her, Lek was twelve and pregnant by another of her foreign customers. She gave birth prematurely . . . to a daughter . . . Lek debated putting the child into an orphanage, but eventually decided against it, returning to prostitution as a means of supporting the child. There was no money in the family for the medical expenses of the birth, and so she turned to her cousin Nuk's client, a sixty year-old Australian called Paul, for help. Paul paid all her medical expenses, and in return she traded sex after she gave birth. Six weeks after the birth, she was back at work as a prostitute . . .

Source: From Heather Montgomery, *Modern Babylon? Prostituting children in Thailand* (New York: Berghahn Books, 2001), p. 80. Reprinted by permission of the publisher. All rights reserved.

the risk of ending up in a brothel (Crawford, 2010). Moreover, the HIV/AIDS epidemic has increased the market value of very young girls in many parts of the world, as men seek virginal sex partners to avoid acquiring HIV.

It is not only young girls who are trafficked. Adult women who are suffering from poverty and lack of opportunity, whether in Africa, South America, or eastern Europe, are also vulnerable to being trafficked. Here is one woman's story:

Marika was desperate. She needed to earn money to help support her mother and two younger sisters, and there were no jobs in her Ukrainian hometown. The recruiter swore on the names of Jesus, Joseph, and Mary he could get her a legitimate job as a waitress in Tel Aviv. They would save money on airfares by flying through Cairo. But after being met in Cairo by a Russian man and forced to travel overland to Israel by jeep and on foot through the Sinai desert, Marika was imprisoned in a deserted house, sold to the man in charge and told that she would be his property until she paid off a $20,000 debt:

> That night, I felt for the first time what it was to be a whore. I had to service eight men. I felt so terrible and ashamed. . . . Over the next four months, I don't know how many hundreds of Israeli men I was forced to have sex with . . . I had to work or I would be punished (Malarek, 2005, p. xv).

Trafficking is a grave violation of the fundamental human rights of women and girls. There are many testimonies from survivors and their advocates about the misery, pain, and degradation of forced prostitution (Crawford, 2010; Kristoff & WuDunn, 2009; McCabe & Manian, 2010). Even when girls and women are rescued, returning home is difficult, because they may be severely traumatized, and because they are stigmatized for having been in the sex trade.

In countries where child prostitution is rampant, governments are beginning to take measures against it. In addition, a large number of nongovernmental organizations have responded to the trafficking problem with innovative programs aimed at preventing future trafficking and helping survivors. Efforts so far include anti-trafficking legislation, educational programs for those at risk and their communities, rescue, shelter, and medical/psychological care for survivors, and prosecution of traffickers. International organizations dedicated to ending the sex trade in children, and the poverty that fuels it, include Oxfam (www.oxfam.org.uk) and the Asia Foundation (www.asiafoundation.org). For example, the Asia Foundation has initiated village task forces in rural Nepal to plan local ways to reduce trafficking to India, and has sponsored job training for girls at risk for trafficking and girls rescued from the sex trade. But it is not just poverty that causes sex trafficking; it is also the devaluation of women and the belief that they are property, not people.

Violence and the Media

We have noted that violence against girls and women is often normalized or even condoned. Often, media coverage of violence participates in this process by de-emphasizing the perpetrator, the violence, or its consequences.

Language about Violence

In Chapter 3, we learned that, linguistically, men are most often treated as though they stand for all of humanity. However, there is one place where men are rendered linguistically invisible: when they have committed violence against women. Consider the following sentences:

1. In the United States, a man rapes a woman every 6 minutes.
2. In the United States, a woman is raped by a man every 6 minutes.
3. In the United States, a woman is raped every 6 minutes.

Do the meanings of these sentences differ? Feminist theorists have claimed that in talking and writing about rape and other kinds of violence against women, people often use the passive voice, as in Sentences 2 and 3. Further, they argue that relying on passive verbs, especially with the actor deleted, as in Sentence 3, deflects attention from the perpetrator of violence.

The tendency to deflect attention from the perpetrator is particularly striking in the mass media. In one analysis of real-life talk, the researcher examined how participants in a public radio educational program on acquaintance rape talked about male rapists and the women they raped (Crawford, 1995). Here are some of the phrases they used:

> Alcohol . . . can permit men to do things they ordinarily wouldn't do.
> It definitely is rape season . . . it happens to the young freshmen because they are very unaware.
> (The young woman) in this sort of drinking fraternity house sort of situation that gets raped . . .

In these phrases, rape is just something that happens, not a behavior chosen and enacted by a man against a woman's will. Even when men are "doing things," it's really alcohol that deserves the blame; men's choices to drink do not enter into the picture.

Other researchers have tested the hypothesis that news reports using the passive voice in the reporting of violence against women leads readers to be more accepting of such violence. When they classified over 1,500 examples of verb use in print media, Nancy Henley and her colleagues found that for both rape and murder, reporters used the passive voice more often than they did for stories about nonviolent crime or non-crime topics. To determine whether verb use matters, they asked college students to read news reports of rape, robbery, and murder and rate how much harm was done to the victim, how responsible the victim and perpetrator were for the crime, and how acceptable such crimes are. The news reports were identical except for the use of active or passive verb forms. Both male and female participants thought that violence against women was more acceptable after reading the passive-voice stories. Men, but not women, also thought the victim had suffered less harm and the perpetrator was less responsible (Henley et al., 1995).

Other researchers have extended Henley's work by comparing the use of active and passive voice in the description of male and female domestic violence. When college students were given basic information about a domestic violence scenario (e.g., name and gender of perpetrator, date of incident, and weapon used) and asked to create a story describing the event, participants were more likely to use the passive voice to describe crimes in which the perpetrator was male (Frazer & Miller, 2009). In other words, the students' verb choice subtly deflected attention from the male (but not female) perpetrators.

The tendency to focus on the victims rather than the perpetrators of violence against women is widespread. Taking the emphasis away from the perpetrator's acts makes it harder to perceive him as responsible for his behavior. Instead the focus is on the woman, and the reader may think, "What did she do to bring on this attack?" (Ruscher, 2001). Passive and indirect language about violence against women may be used without sexist intentions but it can still have sexist effects.

Gender Violence as Entertainment

Both children and adults see gender violence every day on television and at the movies. The Parents Television Council (2009) examined the incidence of violence against women on the four major television networks during prime time in 2004 and again in 2009. They found that from 2004 to 2009, general violence on television increased only 2 percent; however, the number of storylines featuring a female victim increased 120 percent. Beatings were the most common type of violence against women shown, comprising 29 percent of the total number of incidents. In 19 percent of the incidents recorded, women were killed. In 92 percent of the cases, the violence against women was actually depicted on the screen, not merely described or implied.

Children's exposure to violence in the media is a particular cause for concern. The majority of TV programs and video games contain violence, and the violent acts are usually portrayed as trivial, justified, or funny. By the time a U.S. child finishes elementary school, he or she has seen more than 100,000 acts of violence on TV, including 8,000 murders. Thirty years of research have definitively shown that exposure to media violence is related to an increase in aggressive emotions, thoughts, and behavior in children and adolescents (Anderson et al., 2003; Anderson & Carnagey, 2009). Media violence desensitizes people to real violence, and at the same time builds schemas of the world as a dangerous, scary place where a person must be aggressive in order to survive (Fanti et al., 2009; Larson, 2003).

Video games are the newest technology for teaching children to be aggressive. Over 85 percent of popular video games in the United States and Japan contain some violent content. Many psychologists are concerned that video games have an even greater potential for fostering violence than other forms of media because the child actively participates in the game's violence. Meta-analyses have shown that exposure to violent video games is related to increases in aggressive thoughts, beliefs, attitudes, emotions, and behavior, and decreases in socially positive behavior such as helping others (Anderson et al., 2003). Recent research with high school students shows that preferences for violent TV shows, movies, and video games predict violent and aggressive behavior (Boxer et al., 2009). Additionally, a longitudinal study of American and Japanese children found that habitual playing of violent video games is associated with increases in physical aggression 3 and 6 months later (Anderson et al., 2008).

Female characters in video games are rare, but when they do appear, they are often portrayed as promiscuous sex objects or targets of aggression (Burgess et al., 2007; Dill & Thill, 2007). A Japanese game, RapeLay, released in 2006, has date rapes of female avatars as its entire purpose—including avatars dressed as school-girls. In the top-selling video game series *Grand Theft Auto*, a player can hire a prostitute, engage in explicit and demeaning sex talk, have sex, and then kill the prostitute to get his money back. What effect does engaging in such behavior in video gaming have on attitudes and behaviors towards women? Karen Dill and her colleagues (2008) asked college students to view either sex-stereotypical images of men and women from video games (including *Grand Theft Auto)* or neutral images. They were then asked to read a real-life story involving a complex and ambiguous sexual harassment incident and were asked whether the incident constituted sexual harassment. They found that men who viewed the stereotypical images of women from video games were more tolerant of the sexual harassment incident compared to those who viewed neutral images. They also found that in the long-term, violent video game use was positively associated with rape supportive attitudes (Dill et al., 2008).

When violence against women is treated as a form of entertainment, people may view it as more acceptable and less harmful. It also reinforces the view that women are weak and that it is acceptable to use force to control them. The technological advances in television graphics and viewing equipment (e.g., high definition and 3D television) means that the violence against women shown on television is increasingly graphic and vivid. High-tech graphics are meant to enhance the viewing experience, but what effect do they have on people's attitudes toward violence against women, and how do they affect the already established relationship between media violence and aggressive behaviors? These are questions that still need to be addressed.

Pornography

Probably the most controversial of all the depictions of women are those found in pornography. What to do about pornography is a subject of debate among feminist researchers and activists. Some maintain that pornography is a form of violence against women and should be prohibited. Others believe that whether an image is pornographic depends upon the perspective of the beholder: what some consider pornographic, others consider artistic; what some consider morally objectionable or sexist, others defend as free speech. Here, we consider pornography from multiple perspectives.

What Is "Pornography?"

It may seem difficult to pin down exactly what is pornography and what isn't, but sexual images can be distinguished in terms of their potential psychological impacts and social consequences. Social psychological experiments demonstrate that the sexual explicitness of the material does not matter nearly so much as whether the sex is presented in a violent or degrading context. Several scholars therefore suggest that the term *pornography* should be reserved for material that combines sexual themes with violence, dehumanization, degradation, or abuse, whereas material that is merely sexually arousing without these other themes might best be called *erotica* (e.g., Longino, 1980; Russell, 1993; Scott, 2008; Steinem, 1980). In most pornography, *women* are the ones subject to the degradation and abuse. When researchers content analyzed a random sample of 122 scenes from 44 of the most-rented adult videos for 2004 and 2005, they found a total of nearly 1,500 acts of physical or verbal aggression, 87 percent of which were directed toward women (Sun et al., 2008).

Pornography Is Pervasive

In the past 2 decades, pornographic images of women have become *much* more available to all citizens in the United States, male and female, adults and children. The porn industry grew dramatically starting in the 1990s, due primarily to the popularity of adult videos, the availability of subscription cable TV, and the proliferation of porn sites on the Internet. Although it is difficult to determine the exact size of the pornography industry, some estimate that more than 13,000 adult videos are produced annually, and that 957 million adult movies are sold or rented per year (Ropelato, 2006). Estimates of the number of pornography pages currently on the Internet range upwards of 420 million. The production and distribution of pornography in the United States is now a 12-billion-dollar-a-year industry (AVN, 2006 as cited in Sun et al., 2008), making it a bigger business than the NFL, the NBA, and Major League Baseball combined. Much of the distribution of adult content is done by large companies such as AOL Time Warner, DirecTV, and Comcast (ABC News, 2003; CBS News 60 minutes, 2003).

As the pornography industry has flourished, it has had a tangible influence on U.S. popular culture. Pornography has been mainstreamed in unprecedented ways. Advertisers use themes from porn to sell mundane objects such as wristwatches and jeans, and porn stars are recruited to hawk products such as athletic shoes. References to porn and appearances by porn stars are increasingly common on prime time TV and in Hollywood films (Farrell, 2003). The PornStar line of clothing and accessories does a multimillion dollar international business. Adult in-room movies are available in many U.S. hotel chains including Hilton, Marriott, Hyatt, Sheraton, and Holiday Inn, accounting for almost 70 percent of in-room profits (CBS News 60 Minutes, 2003). Evidence of the mainstreaming of pornography is abundant.

Is Pornography a Form of Violence against Women?

Pornographic violence against women can be found in many forms of entertainment, and often there is a mocking or boastful tone to the material. For example, one amateur videographer filmed nude women being hunted in the desert by camouflage-clad men wielding paintball guns. He made the video series, called "Hunting for Bambi," available on his Web site, which featured several pages touting sexual violence against women. The front page of the Web site describes the video as, "Men hunting naked women. It's about f**k'n time! That's right bitch . . . it's hunting season!" The description of the video continues,

Let's face it. For those of you that have a wife, girlfriend, significant other, even an ex-wife, or ex-girlfriend (you get the point) or some other **Bambi Bitch** that has done you wrong in the past, nagged you to death over the stupidest things, complained and whined that you didn't spend enough time with her, didn't take out the garbage, yada, yada, yada. . . . This would be a great way to "Domesticate" your Bambi.

Those feminists who believe that porn should be restricted argue that pornographic images are of particular concern not just because they portray sexual violence but also because of the ways that the creation and use of pornography are intimately linked to actual violence against women. Many of the blatantly violent pornographic images of women from recent years are not merely "images" but are *documentation* of actual sexual violence or humiliation. Women in these pictures may have volunteered for such treatment in exchange for money or other rewards, but according to first-hand accounts, some may have been coerced. Linda Lovelace, the star of the classic porn movie *Deep Throat*, reported in her autobiography that she was forced by her husband at gunpoint to make the film and that the bruises visible on her body in the film were the result of beatings (Lovelace & McGrady, 1981). Lovelace's claims have been widely disputed by porn industry insiders, but it is difficult to believe that images of women being burned by cigarettes, slashed with knives, forcibly penetrated by objects such as vacuum cleaner hoses, covered in excrement, etc., were produced with their eager consent (Russell, 1993).

Women involved in the making of porn are not the only ones hurt by it. We know from experimental research that pornography, more so than erotica, has at least temporary negative effects on men's attitudes and behaviors toward women. Sexually violent or degrading images, explicit or not, desensitize male viewers to violence against women, increase men's belief in rape myths, lower men's support for sexual equality, and increase men's dominant behaviors toward women (e.g., Linz et al., 1987; Mulac et al., 2002). For practical and ethical reasons, experimental research cannot be used to test the relationship between pornography and violence against women in the real world; however, correlational studies support the link. A meta-analysis of non-experimental studies found a significant positive association between men's use of pornography and their attitudes supporting violence against women (Hald et al., 2010). In interviews with battered women, researchers have found that 40 to 60 percent of the abusers used pornography and tried to force their victims to act out violent scenes from it (Cole, 1987; Cramer & McFarlane, 1994; Sommers & Check, 1987).

We cannot conclude from this research that pornography *causes* male violence against women, but it is clear that pornography is associated with sexual violence and that it can provide sexually arousing behavioral scripts for men with aggressive impulses. Pornography is used for masturbation; men who masturbate to pornography may be conditioning their bodies to respond pleasurably to violence against women (e.g., Reed, 1994; Seto et al., 2001).

Among all the popular media images of women in our culture, some feminists believe that pornographic ones are potentially the most damaging. Jensen (2007) argues that pornography reflects and perpetuates how our society views women: as objects for men to sexually dominate. On the other hand, there are feminists who want to keep a clear distinction between words or images and actions. The organization *Feminists for Free Expression* (FFE) argues that censoring pornography could lead to the censorship of women in general (ffeusa.org). Historically, women were denied information related to their own sexuality in the name of "protecting" them. Treating pornography as obscenity and therefore censoring it is a slippery slope that could lead to the censorship of any material that anyone finds offensive, such as lesbian erotica or woman-focused sex education.

Not all pornography is consumed by male heterosexuals. Heterosexual women, lesbians, and gay men also purchase and use pornography. Some fear that because of disagreements about where to draw the line, attempts to censor porn could lead to denying people access to material that they find interesting, enjoyable, and related to their normal, healthy sexual expression. FFE argues that women rent or purchase 50 percent of adult videos and that pornography can help women interested in sexual experimentation. Moreover, some couples use pornography to stimulate consensual sexual activity.

The feminist debate over the porn problem is unlikely to be resolved any time soon. There are convincing arguments on both sides. However, the debate is productive if it keeps people on both sides engaged in thinking critically about the depiction of women in erotic and pornographic media.

Violence against Children

Violence against girls and women can occur at any phase of life and in virtually any setting. Here we examine violence against children that takes place largely within family relationships.

Child Sexual Abuse

Childhood is not always a time of toys and books, safety and security, and a loving Mom and Dad. Because they are small and dependent on others, children are vulnerable to victimization and exploitation by adults. It is unfortunately true that some children learn far too young "the major lesson of patriarchy: The more powerful control the less powerful" (White et al., 2001).

A significant minority of children experience ***childhood sexual abuse***, defined as coercive sexual interaction between a child and an adult. Girls are more likely to be abused than boys, according to phone surveys of randomized national samples (White et al., 2001). In one such sample of adults, 27 percent of women and 16 percent of men reported that they had experienced sexual abuse as children; in another sample of young people aged 10 to 16, 15 percent of girls and 6 percent of boys reported a history of abuse. It is likely that over one-quarter of U.S. women have experienced sexual abuse during childhood (Gazmarian et al., 2000). Tragically, children, and particularly girls, are most often abused by someone they know and trust. For example, family members and acquaintances are responsible for almost 90 percent of child rapes. Older relatives, brothers, and the child's own father or stepfather are the leading abusers of girls within the family (Laumann et al., 1994).

Who is most at risk for child sexual abuse? Any child can be abused, and there seem to be few differences in rates of abuse among various ethnic and racial groups. Rather, there are particular kinds of families that provide a context in which abuse is likely. Abusive families are most often emotionally distant and unaffectionate. They tend to be strongly patriarchal: Father is the head of the household, Mother is subservient, and children are taught to obey without question. Finally, they are families with a lot of conflict among family members (White et al., 2001).

Before the abuse starts, the perpetrator may gradually earn the child's love and trust by treating her as special. The perpetrator may buy her toys, tuck her in at night, or take her out for treats. He may increase his inappropriate contact gradually, for example proceeding from tucking in, to touching and patting the child's back, to sexual touching. By the time the child realizes that the behavior is sexual and wrong, it is already part of an established pattern. After each abusive episode, he may apologize and promise it will never happen again. However, the loving, apologetic behavior gives way to another period of building the child's trust, and then to more sexual transgressions, in a cycle of abuse. Because the abuser has power and authority over the child, and may even live in the same home, the child may feel overwhelmed, with nowhere to turn to for help. Living in a patriarchal, authoritarian family, the victim of childhood sexual abuse may be emotionally neglected and afraid to question the power and authority of adults. Under these conditions, the perpetrator may succeed in convincing the child that their relationship is a special, loving secret, rather than the crime and betrayal of trust it is (White et al., 2001).

Sexual abuse may negatively affect many aspects of a child's emotional, cognitive, and social development (Kendall-Tackett, 2001). For example, the child may show seemingly irrational emotions like fear of the dark, of going to bed at night, or of being alone. Later, the child may experience depression and withdrawal. Behavioral responses include problems in school, bedwetting, nightmares, and, later, running away from home or becoming sexually active at an early age. Survivors of abuse are at increased risk for suicide. In adulthood, abuse survivors may have impaired relationships with intimate partners, be at increased risk for intimate partner violence, and experience lower relationship satisfaction (Daigneault et al., 2009; Walker et al., 2009). A recent review of the literature on outcomes associated with childhood sexual abuse found that survivors are more at risk for a variety of psychological disorders including depression, anxiety, eating disorders, sexual dysfunction, personality disorders, suicidal and self-injurious behavior, and substance abuse (Mangiolio, 2009).

In a study of adult survivors' recovery narratives, some survivors noted that while they felt recovery was possible, actual healing was not. Take the following quotation from one survivor:

> I don't think you can ever be healed. If you were in an accident and your right arm was cut off, you're never going to get that arm back, but you will learn to go on and manage. It doesn't mean that you can't have a good life. It's just that it's always going to be there (Anderson & Hiersteiner, 2008: p. 418).

Healing was associated with being cured or made whole again—something these survivors did not think was possible. Instead, their recovery was advanced through disclosure, supportive relationships, and trying to make meaning of their experiences (Anderson & Hiersteiner, 2008). A study of survivors who managed to function well as adults showed that these women had developed coping strategies that kept them from giving in psychologically to the abuse. They dreamed about the future and immersed themselves in school achievements or creative activities such as writing in order to cope with their pain (DiPalma, 1994). Despite attempts to develop coping strategies, the majority of adult women who have survived childhood abuse say that it has significantly affected their entire lives (Laumann et al., 1994).

How Can Abuse of Children Be Ended?

In the United States, many schools now sponsor programs to teach children that they have the right not to be touched inappropriately and encourage them to tell an adult if someone acts in a sexual way toward them (Wurtele, 2002). However, these programs have limitations because they place the responsibility for prevention largely on the child. Other programs designed to end child abuse focus on educating parents and families, as well as the community at large. The Child Abuse Prevention Association (www.childabuseprevention.org) operates a national child abuse/neglect hotline and promotes a variety of family support and counseling services. For example, they offer a program for families that teaches effective communication skills, and they also provide an in-home assessment and intervention for families that are at high risk for violence. As children progress through the school system, teachers and school officials need to be attuned to signs and symptoms of potential abuse. Identifying and ending abuse early in childhood may improve outcomes for victims as they get older. As we have seen, abusers play on the cognitive limitations and emotional vulnerability of their child victims, whose minds may become even more traumatized than their bodies. Childhood sexual abuse is a form of exploitation that no child should have to endure.

Violence in Intimate Relationships

Overall, men are more likely to be victims of violence from the hands of strangers, and women are much more likely to be victims of violence at the hands of friends, lovers, acquaintances, and family members.

Here we look at verbal, physical, and sexual aggression in relationships. When physical aggression and violence occur in a relationship, it is often referred to as *intimate partner violence* (IPV). IPV occurs in all types of intimate relationships, including those in which the partners are dating or married.

Dating Violence

Dating and romantic relationships can provide a host of valuable experiences such as intimacy, companionship, sexual experimentation, and learning how to negotiate conflicts and differences (White et al., 2001). However, there is another, less positive side to many dating relationships. Relationship problems can lead to anger, frustration, and confusion. Unfortunately, violence is an all-too-common means of exerting control in sexual encounters and romantic relationships.

Violence between intimate partners is so common that virtually everyone has witnessed a couple screaming, arguing, or yelling ugly names at each other, or one partner sulking resentfully or stomping off in a huff. In national U.S. surveys, over 80 percent of college students say they have been on the sending or receiving end of this kind of verbal aggression within the past year. Moreover, over one-third reported having engaged in physical aggression during the same time period: grabbing, shoving, throwing something, or hitting. The rates are similar for women and men, across different ethnic groups, regions of the country, and types of colleges and universities. In sum, dating violence is a pervasive problem (White et al., 2001).

Some studies have shown that women are more likely to initiate aggression against their partners than vice versa (Archer, 2000). However, qualitative research on women's initiation of partner violence found that although women said they initiated violence more than their partners, there was a lot of variability in how women defined "initiation." For some, it was getting angry or upset, bringing up a conflict, or trying to get their partner to talk about something repeatedly (Olson & Lloyd, 2005). Gender stereotypes define women as the caretakers of relationships. Therefore, women may feel responsible when violence or aggression occurs in their relationships and thus respond affirmatively when asked if they initiated the violence. However, when delving deeper into how women conceptualize initiation, it is clear that women's so-called initiation of violence may be anything but violent.

Although women and men report similar rates of aggression, their motives tend to be different. For men, staying in control is often an important relationship goal (Lloyd, 1991). Men are more likely to say that they aggress in order to intimidate and frighten the partner and control the relationship, while women say that they do so in self-defense or because they lost control of themselves (Campbell, 1992). Another motive for women's aggression is sensitization to the possibility of harm. Women who have experienced aggression in the past—for example, those who witnessed parental violence or were in a prior abusive relationship—may be primed to respond to aggression with more aggression, and even to initiate violence (White et al., 2001).

Is it possible to predict whether a partner is likely to be violent? Studies show a consistent pattern of characteristics in violence-prone men and women. For men, the characteristics are related to a need for dominance and control. Violent men are quick to anger and have used violence to get their way in the past. They believe that violence helps win arguments and that violence against a partner is justifiable. They do not hold benevolent and protective beliefs about women. They are likelier than other men to use drugs, have divorced parents, and to be undergoing life stress. For women, the predictors are somewhat different: a history of child abuse, as well as anxiety, depression, and drug use, all increase the likelihood of being aggressive (Sullivan et al., 2005; White et al., 2001). However, there are some gender similarities: for both women and men, the single biggest predictor of aggressive behavior is having an aggressive partner. Truly, violence begets more violence.

The consequences of dating violence are more severe for women than for men. Women report more fear in violent situations, and they are three to four times as likely to sustain major emotional trauma and serious physical injuries due to dating violence than are men (Makepeace, 1986; Sugarman & Hotaling, 1989). The psychological effects can spread to virtually every area of life, affecting emotional states (hyperarousal and depression), cognitive functioning (lack of ability to concentrate and poor performance in school or at work), and identity (low self-esteem). Dating violence also is associated with risk of unwanted pregnancy, substance abuse, suicide, eating disorders, and high-risk sexual behaviors (Hanson, 2002; Silverman et al., 2001). In sum, being on the receiving end of dating violence can disrupt a young woman's healthy development in many serious ways.

Unfortunately, the ideology of romance (discussed in Chapter 7) encourages women to believe that they must stay in a relationship even if this means accepting violence and abuse (Carey & Mongeau, 1996). Studies of women who are in ongoing abusive relationships, compared to those who are not, show that they have more traditional attitudes toward women's roles and more romantic attitudes about love. They say they are committed to their partner and in love with him. They allow their partner to control them and often offer excuses for his abuse (Follingstad et al., 1992). For these women, a romantic relationship has become a self-destructive trap (Carey & Mongeau, 1996). Belief in a fairy-tale ending can be harmful if it allows a woman to tolerate an abusive relationship (Jackson, 2001).

Sexual Coercion and Acquaintance Rape

Rape is defined as sexual penetration without the person's consent, obtained through force or threat of harm, or when the person is incapable of giving consent (Bachar & Koss, 2001). The more general terms *sexual assault* and *sexual coercion* include other kinds of unwanted sexual contact (such as groping and fondling) (White et al., 2004). Here, we examine sexual coercion within relationships.

In national samples of adult women (Tjaden & Thoennes, 1998) and college students (Koss et al., 1987) in the United States, more than half of respondents report experiencing some form of sexual coercion. For example, in one survey, 54 percent of college women reported a history of sexual victimization. About 12 percent reported being verbally pressured into sexual intercourse and an additional 14 percent reported unwanted contact (such as forced sexual touching or kissing). Over 15 percent had experienced sexual penetration without their consent (in other words, they had experienced acts that meet the legal definition of rape) and another 12 percent had experienced attempted rape (Koss et al., 1987). However, 73 percent of the women who had experienced acts legally defined as rape did not label their experience as rape.

Most unacknowledged rapes are committed by someone known to the victim.

Lenore stopped by her boyfriend's apartment to hang out, but her boyfriend wasn't there. His roommate, a foreign exchange student, invited her in to wait for her boyfriend and then suggested that they watch a sex video. Lenore felt uncomfortable but thought that maybe he did not know how to act around American girls and did not want to embarrass him. She said no to the sex video by changing the subject. Then he proceeded to kiss and fondle her, although she said that her boyfriend might come back and that she wasn't interested in him in that way. He forced her to have sex on the couch and then held the door open for her to get up and leave. Lenore did not think she had been raped but she knew that she felt terrible because she had not wanted to have sex. (From an account told to me by an anonymous student, with her permission).

Sexual assault by a dating partner or someone known to the victim is termed *acquaintance rape.* Most of the public thinks of rape in terms of a stranger jumping out of a dark alley but acquaintance rape occurs far more often than stranger rape. Like other forms of violence against women, it has largely been a hidden crime (Parrot & Bechhofer, 1991). Acquaintance rape is fostered by sexual scripts that encourage women to be passive and offer token resistance. This encourages men to take the initiative physically and ignore a woman's refusals.

In a recent study of college students about 20 percent of the sample reported experiences of sexual coercion. These included forced but nonpenetrative sex acts (i.e., a woman's date held her head down to force her to perform oral sex on him) and intercourse in situations where the woman was too impaired by alcohol or drugs to give consent:

> We were drunk. I didn't have control over myself & I didn't have the cognitive ability to say NO. I can't remember everything, but I know we had sex and if I were sober it would not have happened. I just could not control myself at all (Kahn et al., 2003, p. 241).

Women also commonly reported giving in to unwanted sex because a partner would not stop begging, whining, and pleading: "If he was really in the mood and I wasn't, he couldn't take no for an answer. We would just argue and argue about it until I gave in . . ." (Kahn et al., 2003, p. 240). Even though some of the women's experiences qualified as rape, a woman was likely to use that term only if the man had used a high degree of force and intimidation or if she woke up to find him sexually penetrating her. If the assailant was a boyfriend, or the woman was too drunk to consent, she was less likely to call the incident rape. Some feminists argue that using the label rape is important; without it, the incident is not recognized as a crime, and goes unreported and unpunished. Moreover, the woman is unlikely to get the help and support she needs. Others point out that a woman's choice of label may be part of how she copes with sexual assault, and she has the right to define her own experience (Kahn et al., 2003). The difficulty of defining and labeling rape may partly be due to the way our society defines normal heterosex to include some degree of male aggression and subtle coercion (Gavey, 2005).

Whatever the label, such an experience has consequences for the survivor. Many studies have shown that victims of sexual coercion, like victims of other kinds of violence, suffer psychological consequences in such areas as emotional functioning (anxiety, phobias, and depression), social relations (loss of trust and sexual dysfunction), and identity (lowered self-esteem). The physical aftereffects include injuries sustained during the rape, unwanted pregnancy, and infection with an STD. The victim may also suffer from physical effects of trauma and anxiety, such as nightmares and inability to sleep. The psychological effects of rape are more severe when the assailant is an acquaintance or boyfriend than when he is a stranger, because the acquaintance rape violates not only the woman's body but also her trust. When the woman knows her rapist, she is also more likely to blame herself for what happened (Katz, 1991). The physical, emotional, and psychological aftereffects of rape interact with each other to impair the woman's ability to function, sometimes very severely (Koss & Kilpatrick, 2001).

Who is likely to inflict coercive sex? Unfortunately, there is no easy way to spot a potential rapist in advance, because most men who commit acquaintance rape look and act much like other men. However, certain factors in a man's background, personality, and social setting have been associated with sexual aggression toward women. Background factors include coming from a violent or abusive family, getting into trouble with the authorities as a teen, and being exceptionally sexually active at a young age. Personality factors include impulsivity, a need to dominate women, and low self-esteem. Factors in the social environment include involvement in a sports team or fraternity, alcohol use, exposure to pornography, and having friends who encourage sexual conquests and objectification of women (Frintner & Rubinson, 1993; Koss & Gaines, 1993; Seto et al., 2001; White & Koss, 1993).

Rape myths also play an important role in coercive sex. **Rape myths** are widely held, stereotypical, false beliefs about rape, rape victims, and rapists that perpetuate and normalize male sexual violence against women (Brownmiller, 1975; Burt, 1980; Lonsway & Fitzgerald, 1994). They provide powerful cultural messages about victims and perpetrators of sexual assault. The idea that all women secretly desire to be raped, that women "ask for it," and that women are responsible for rape if they were drunk or dressed provocatively, are all examples of rape myths (see Box 12.2). Rape myths justify male sexual aggression as natural, minimize sexual assault, and encourage victim blaming (Lonsway & Fitzgerald, 1995).

Men tend to endorse rape myths more than women (Aosved & Long, 2006; Lonsway & Fitzgerald, 1994) and men who endorse rape myths are more likely to endorse a proclivity to rape (Ben-David & Schneider, 2005; Osland et al., 1996). Additionally, rape myth endorsement is associated with higher levels of oppressive and intolerant attitudes, including hostile sexism, racism, homophobia, ageism, classism, conservatism, and right-wing authoritarianism (Aosved & Long, 2006; Chapleau et al., 2007; Hockett et al., 2009). Rape myths also serve a purpose for women. They may provide a sense of control because they suggest that there are actions that women can take to avoid being raped. For example, one common rape myth is that women who dress provocatively are asking to be raped. Because what a woman wears is up to her, she presumably has the power to choose more conservative clothing, and hypothetically reduce her risk of being raped. Unfortunately, although women's endorsement of rape myths might provide a sense of control, there is no evidence that it would reduce their risk, and rape myth acceptance makes it easier to blame women who are raped.

The widespread belief in rape myths is supported by their prevalence in the media. In a content analysis of headlines following the Kobe Bryant rape case, researchers found that about 10 percent of the headlines contained statements related to rape myths. The myth that "she's lying" was the most common. Additionally, they found that headlines were more likely to use the phrase "accuser" instead of "alleged victim" (Franiuk et al., 2008). In another study, college students were asked to read an article containing multiple rape myth endorsing or

BOX 12.2 ∽ Research Focus
Measuring Attitudes about Rape

Researchers have designed a number of scales to measure the extent to which people endorse rape myths. One of the more popular scales is the *Illinois Rape Myth Acceptance Scale*, which contains either 45 items (long form) or 20 items (short form). Items in the scale represent seven broader rape myths. Below are a few items from the scale and the broader rape myth they represent (in italics).

1. If a woman is raped while she is drunk, she is at least somewhat responsible for letting things get out of control. *She asked for it.*
2. Although most women wouldn't admit it, they generally find being physically forced into sex a real "turn-on." *She wanted it.*

3. If a woman is willing to "make out" with a guy, then it's no big deal if he goes a little further and has sex. *Rape is a trivial event.*
4. If a woman doesn't physically fight back, you can't really say that it was rape. *It wasn't really rape.*
5. Men from nice middle-class homes almost never rape. *Rape is a deviant event.*
6. Rape accusations are often used as a way of getting back at men. *She lied.*
7. Men don't usually intend to force sex on a woman, but sometimes they get too sexually carried away. *He didn't mean to.*

Source: Payne, D. L., Lonsway, K. A., & Fitzgerald, L. F. (1999). Rape myth acceptance: Exploration of its structure and its measurement using the *Illinois Rape Myth Acceptance Scale. Journal of Research in Personality, 33,* 27–68.
Contributed by Annie B. Fox.

contradicting statements. Those participants who read the article containing rape myths rated Kobe Bryant less guilty after reading the article than they had rated him beforehand (Franiuk et al., 2008).

Rape myths also have implications for how victims feel about themselves and what happened to them. An analysis of victim narratives from a national crime survey found that 20 percent of the narratives contained at least one rape myth (Weiss, 2009). For example, women blamed themselves for the incident or justified it by saying that male sexual aggression is natural. Rape myths are so much a part of our cultural understanding of sex that even victims themselves use them to understand their experiences. Unfortunately, rape myths perpetuate the acceptability of sexual coercion by removing blame from the perpetrators, encouraging women to blame themselves, and preventing women from reporting the crime (Weiss, 2009).

Violence in Long-Term Relationships

Millions of women around the world have been subjected to violence from their male partners—husbands, boyfriends, cohabiting partners, and ex-partners. A recent multi-country study of violence against women found that the number of women who had ever been physically or sexually assaulted by a partner ranged from 9 percent (Hong Kong) to 40 percent (Mozambique) (Johnson et al., 2008). A generic term for this abuse, used by sociologists as well as law enforcement personnel, is "domestic violence." However, this seemingly gender-neutral term obscures the fact that by far the most serious "domestic" violence is perpetrated by men against women.

Abuse by a partner is one of the most frequent causes of physical injury for women across cultures (United Nations Children's Fund, 2000). In the United States, researchers estimate that between 21 percent to 34 percent of women will be physically assaulted by a husband or boyfriend at least once in their lifetimes, and that partners are responsible for the beatings of 2 to 4 million women every year (Smith et al., 1999). Rates in Europe are similar to the United States (Neft & Levine, 1997), and rates in Africa, Asia, and Latin America are even higher (Pickup, 2001). Statistics probably underestimate the actual incidence of wife abuse, which tends to be underreported due to shame, fear, and the belief that nothing will be done about it (Ellsberg et al., 2001). Additionally, women with physical or mental disabilities may be more susceptible to violence in relationships (Brownridge, 2009). A recent study found that 68 percent of the disabled women who were sampled reported at least one instance of abuse (physical, emotional, or sexual) in the past year (Curry et. al., 2009). Using self-reported data, a recent study by the World Health Organization found that worldwide, women who reported experiences of partner violence also reported overall poorer health (Ellsberg et al., 2008). In the United States, between one-third and one-half of all women seen in hospital emergency rooms have been injured by their husband or boyfriend (Warshaw, 2001). Clearly, the impact of violence against women by intimate partners is a worldwide public health problem.

Physical violence against a partner is almost always accompanied by psychological abuse—the woman may be threatened, publicly humiliated, criticized, and belittled. The abuser may be extremely jealous, using accusations of infidelity to keep her from seeing friends or going out. Psychological abuse may be equally as traumatic as physical abuse (Walker, 2000), and the combination of the two can be devastating, as a woman's life becomes governed by the threat of harm:

> But each day I lived in fear. I was afraid he was gonna come in while I was taking . . . I would wait to take a shower. I would hurry up and wash up. I mean, I know I wasn't getting clean enough, under my arms, between my legs but that was it, because I had to make it a minute and a half . . . because I was afraid he was gonna come in and just, you know, go off (Smith et al., 1999, p. 184).

Recognizing a Hidden Problem

For many years, domestic violence was a hidden problem, because it takes place within the privacy of the home. Moreover, traditional attitudes condone a man's right to dominate and control his wife or partner. Wife beating was considered a normal, if regrettable, part of life. Even today, in countries where patriarchal ideology is strong, wife-beating may be viewed as a morally acceptable means of control (Crawford, 2010; Haj-Yahia, 1998). For example, in Mozambique, patriarchal values make it acceptable for men to beat their wives. Divorce is unacceptable and there are few options available to women trying to leave abusive relationships (Johnson et al., 2008). In the United States, the scope and impact of partner violence has been made visible through two important kinds of research: random-sample surveys and studies of women in hospitals, courts, and battered women's shelters. Surveys of the general population and studies of abuse survivors reveal different kinds and amounts of violence (Johnson, 1995).

In surveys, women and men both report inflicting violence on their partners about equally often (Straus, 1999). This kind of relatively gender-neutral violence has been called ***common couples violence*** (Johnson, 1995). It does not occur often in a relationship, it rarely escalates over time, and it is sparked when the couple's coping skills are not sufficient for dealing with a particular conflict. In other words, common couples violence results from a breakdown in the couple's ability to handle a conflict constructively. It probably is as likely to occur in gay and lesbian as in heterosexual relationships. However, common couples violence in heterosexual couples is not entirely gender-neutral. Although it involves a degree of mutuality, that does not mean the violence is symmetrical. When mutual violence occurs in relationships, men are more likely to be the primary perpetrators. Surveys reveal that women's violence against their partners was not as frequent or severe as the violence they experienced (Weston et al., 2005). Women are also much more likely to sustain physical injury than to inflict it and their aggressive acts are often done in self-defense.

Studies of battered women show a pattern of severe, escalating male violence in which women rarely fight back and almost never initiate aggression. This kind of violence, termed ***patriarchal terrorism*** or ***intimate terrorism,*** has been the main focus of feminist research and activism (Johnson, 1995; Johnson & Ferraro, 2000). (See Figure 12.1.) It is much more frequent in a relationship than common couples violence, pervading the whole context of the couple's interaction. Its motives are rooted in patriarchal tradition: the male perpetrator feels that he owns his woman and is entitled to control her by any means necessary. Both women who have been victims (Eisikovits & Buchbinder, 1999) and men who have been perpetrators (Anderson & Umberson, 2001; Reitz, 1999) report that without this

FIGURE 12.1

Some researchers make a distinction between common couples violence (left), which occurs when couples fail to deal constructively with conflicts, and patriarchal terrorism (right), a severe and escalating pattern of abuse aimed at controlling a woman.

control the batterer does not feel like a real man. To exercise and display his control, the abuser uses a variety of psychological techniques (see Figure 12.2). The ongoing psychological abuse is punctuated by episodes of physical violence, which escalate in intensity and frequency as time goes on. Thus, patriarchal terrorism is a continuous process for its victims, one that exposes them to prolonged and severe stress and fear (Frieze, 2005) (see Figure 12.3). The following items, from a scale designed to measure women's experiences of battering (Smith et al., 1999, p. 189), were developed from battered women's own accounts:

He makes me feel unsafe even in my own home.

I feel ashamed of the things he does to me.

I try not to rock the boat because I am afraid of what he might do.

FIGURE 12.2   The power and control wheel.

Source: "The Power and Control Wheel," from R. J. Gelles & D. R. Loseke (Eds.), *Current Controversies on Family Violence*, pp. 47–62. Minnesota Program Development, Inc. Reprinted by permission.

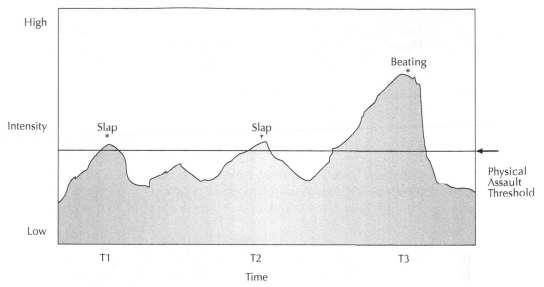

FIGURE 12.3   Battering as a chronic and continous process.

Source: Smith, P. H., Smith, J. B., & Earp, J. A. (1999). Beyond the measurement trap: A reconstructed conceptualization and measurement of woman battering. *Psychology of Women Quarterly, 23,* 177–193, from Figure 1 (p. 182). Copyright © 1999 by John Wiley & Sons. Reprinted by permission.

I feel like he keeps me prisoner.

He can scare me without laying a hand on me.

He has a look that goes straight through me and terrifies me.

"Why Doesn't She Leave?"

Attitudes about the abuse of women in marital and cohabiting relationships are changing. In U.S. studies, the majority of respondents believe that partner abuse is wrong (Drout, 1997; Locke & Richman, 1999). As a result of feminist activism, it is no longer a hidden problem; more people now acknowledge that abuse happens all too often and that any woman—rich, poor, middle-class, married, cohabiting, of any ethnic or racial group—is vulnerable. However, some myths about abuse remain. The most prevalent is the idea that there is a quick and easy solution for abuse: "Why doesn't she just leave?" Let's look at the evidence about ending an abusive relationship.

Women face many obstacles to leaving an abusive partner. Some of these are practical: She may have no money, no job, and no safe place to go. She may not have a car to leave in. If she takes the children out of school, she will upset them and draw the attention of authorities; if she leaves them behind, the abuser may harm them or she may lose custody.

One very important practical consideration is that attempting to leave may increase the violence. Research shows that a woman is more likely to be seriously injured or killed by her partner *after* she leaves him than when they are living together (Jacobson & Gottman, 1998). It is chillingly common to open the newspaper and see a headline like, "Man, Woman Die After Apparent Murder-Suicide In West Haven" (Becker, 2010). The article explained that the 25-year-old murdered woman had received a protective order against her husband two days prior, and that her husband had been arrested for assault a few months earlier. Their case was pending in a family violence program. The day of the murder, police went to the home twice after receiving 911 calls. On their second visit, they found the woman shot to death and her husband dead of a self-inflicted gunshot wound. According to the U.S. Department of Justice (2007), 30 percent of all female murder victims—and only 3 percent of male murder victims—are killed by current or former partners. Violent men often make it clear that there is no escape. One survivor reported, "He'd always threaten me saying that if I decided to ever leave that he'd hunt me down like a dog and shoot me and the girls" (Smith et al., 1999, p. 185).

In addition to the practical problems and risks, there are psychological issues involved in the decision to leave an abuser. Much (though not all) abuse is **cyclical:** the perpetrator goes through a period of increasing tension, a violent episode, and then a loving phase (Frieze, 2005; Walker, 2000). A cyclical abuser is apologetic and repentant after an episode of violence, and the woman may believe his promises to change. She may feel tied by love for him and their children, and she may accept the belief, based in romantic ideology, that it is a woman's job to stand by her man and transform him with her love.

After prolonged abuse, a woman may be so disempowered that she cannot conceive of making an escape. She feels stupid, worthless, and responsible for the violence. More than half of abused women become clinically depressed (Warshaw, 2001). As one said, "He programmed me over a long, long period of time" (Smith et al., 1999, p. 186). She may develop **battered women's syndrome,** a type of post-traumatic stress disorder (Stein & Kennedy, 2001; Walker, 2000). She may become incapable of taking action on her own behalf.

Nevertheless, women in abusive relationships do try to cope with the violence and get help. Women may withdraw emotionally, or minimize the abuse in an attempt to deal with the stress they are experiencing (Frieze, 2005). Another coping strategy is "managing," in which a women tries to keep the peace by anticipating and avoiding anything that might make her partner angry. She takes on more and more responsibility and spends increasing energy on this task, becoming hyper-alert to signs of impending violence. However, ultimately, the effort fails because it is the man who gets to decide whether he has a good reason to be angry. One battered woman concluded, "There was no way to tell what was going to happen because most of our arguments were not about anything serious . . . it was like, 'you got the wrong kind of bread' or 'I don't like that kinda candy bar'" (Smith et al., 1999, pp. 184–185).

When coping strategies fail, women often seek help from clergy, family members, police, counselors, and helping agencies. When women turn to their families for help, they may be told that marriage is sacred, that they should go home, apologize, and try harder, or simply, "You made your bed, now lie in it." Often, they are disbelieved or blamed for the abuse, even by those trained to help

(Dutton, 1996). Feminist therapy is a useful approach to helping women in abusive relationships because feminist therapists are likely to understand the patriarchal basis of wife abuse. However, not everyone can afford therapy or has access to a feminist therapist. And some groups of women, for example, immigrant and African American women, tend to be distrustful of social services and do not want to take their troubles to a stranger (Joseph, 1997).

The limited research on long-term outcomes suggests that the great majority of women in abusive relationships do manage to end them. However, leaving is a long process, and some women go back to the abuser more than once before they are able to make a final break (Bell et al., 2009). Perhaps this is partly due to the mixed messages they receive from the abusive spouse as well as from others.

In a longitudinal study, Margret Bell and colleagues (2009) found that consistency of relationship status was associated with a decrease in the violence women experienced over the course of a year. In other words, women who consistently stayed away or who consistently remained with their partners experienced less violence (although they still experienced some violence) than those women who exited and re-entered the relationship multiple times over the course of the year. Bell and colleagues (2009) suggest that when women are thinking of leaving a relationship, they may be better off waiting until they have the emotional and financial resources to do so, so that they are in a better position to stay away.

How Can Relationship Violence Be Ended?

Patriarchal ideology is a root cause of violence against women. To the extent that a society accepts men's right to dominate women and women's second-class status, violence in heterosexual relationships is inevitable (Bograd, 1988). The ideology of patriarchy contributes to material inequalities that make women vulnerable to violence. Husbands usually earn more money, have higher status jobs, and have more decision-making power than their wives (see Chapter 8). When women reach out for help, they may encounter patriarchal attitudes from social services, law enforcement, and the court system. In order to truly end relationship violence, it is necessary to change not just individuals, but social structures as well.

The *battered women's movement* is an international movement to educate the public about domestic violence, reform the legal system, and provide direct help to women whose partners are violent. In three decades of activism, this movement has made huge changes in society's view of partner abuse. For example, all 50 U.S. states have passed laws designed to protect battered women and criminalize marital rape (Roberts, 1996). Police in many areas are now better trained to recognize domestic abuse and intervene to protect the woman. Physicians increasingly are being taught to screen for domestic abuse when interviewing female patients (Eisenstat & Bancroft, 1999). These changes make it easier for women to report abuse and get help, despite the powerlessness, shame, and fear they may feel.

Unfortunately, change is uneven. In most developing countries, abused women still have little legal protection (Levesque, 2001). In countries such as South Africa, the physical and sexual subordination of women, along with high rates of violence generally, are linked to high rates of HIV infection, injury, and death. In Asian countries, many people still defend a man's right to beat his wife (Crawford, 2010; Pickup, 2001).

Battered women's shelters are refuges where a woman can find temporary safety, emotional support, information about their legal rights, and sometimes counseling. The first shelter for battered women opened in London in 1964, followed by the first U.S. shelter in 1974. Currently, there are about 2,000 shelters in the United States. Unfortunately, this is not nearly enough; thousands of women each year are turned away from shelters that have no space for them (Walker, 2001). Shelters are often underfunded, which means that they must rely on volunteers, and staff have to spend time fund-raising rather than offering services to women. Few shelters exist outside the United States, Canada, and Great Britain, although this is slowly changing. A study of battered women in South Africa showed that access to a shelter was crucial to their safety and their ability to change their situation (Angless et al., 1998).

In fostering the development of shelters, the battered women's movement created safe havens for women and saved many thousands of women and children from further harm. When asked what helped them the most in dealing with abuse, women most often said that it was access to a shelter (Gordon, 1996). However, the shelter initiative may be more useful in individualistic societies like the United States than in collectivist societies, where women are part of a much larger family structure. In India or Pakistan, for example, a woman who left her family home would lose a web of vital social connections and her identity as a member of her society. In collectivist societies, and in working with more collectivist groups within our own society, such as African American and Native American women, other approaches need to be developed (Haaken & Yragui, 2003).

Another feminist initiative is to focus on the perpetrators. In the case of dating violence and acquaintance rape, studies suggest that programs run *by* men *for* men are most effective in changing men's behavior. Some of these programs are organized through men's fraternities or athletic teams. For example, West Chester University of Pennsylvania has a peer education program for fraternity members (Mahlstedt, 1999), and Northeastern University sponsors a MVP program (Mentors in Violence Prevention) for athletes, educating them to become involved in preventing violence against women (www.sportinsociety.org). Men can make an important contribution to feminism and to women's lives by working to end violence against women. This goal has spurred an international movement by men, the White Ribbon Campaign (www.whiteribbon.ca/).

In the case of domestic abuse, a focus on the perpetrators includes doing research to understand the attitudes, personality characteristics, and family histories of violent men. This research is difficult because most abusive men deny and minimize their violence and blame their wives or girlfriends for it. In one innovative study, men who were domestic violence offenders in court-ordered programs participated in interviews where they described their own perceptions of violent incidents they had perpetrated. One man had broken his wife's neck; another had held a knife in his wife's face and threatened her with death. These men framed relationships with other people as win/lose situations in which they either felt good, up, and strong, or bad, down, and weak. From their perspective, the world was a threatening place where they could easily be rendered powerless, and their response was to try to subjugate their partners (Reitz, 1999). Such research has implications for counseling violent men. For example, cognitive therapy that helps men restructure their oppositional view of relationships may be useful, along with behavioral therapy that helps them manage anger.

To date, there have been few studies on the effectiveness of treatment programs for men. Few violent men volunteer to participate in programs aimed at changing them, and of those who do, many drop out. When court-ordered to attend, men who manage to complete a treatment program are less likely to be charged with abuse in the future, suggesting that such programs do help change attitudes and behavior (Shepard et al., 2002). It is also important that the criminal justice system take a firm stand against violence by arresting and prosecuting offenders. Research suggests that arrest and conviction effectively deter a man from perpetrating future abuse (Garner & Maxwell, 2000; Wooldredge & Thistlewaite, 2002). Clearly, the psychological and physical abuse of women in relationships is a complex problem demanding intervention on many fronts: Changing patriarchal social structures, helping the victims, and stopping the perpetrators.

Violence in Later Life

Even in old age, women are not free from the threat of violence. Unfortunately, the abuse that older women experience is often a hidden problem with devastating consequences. Across the globe, older women experience physical, emotional, and sexual abuse, often from those who are their caretakers. Here we examine some of the types of violence that women may experience in later life.

Elder Abuse

Violence against the elderly, termed *elder abuse,* may involve physical injury, emotional stress, sexual violence, neglect, and misappropriating the victim's possessions or money (Carp, 1997). Most of the harm caused by elder abuse is borne by women, and most elder abuse occurs when the older person lives with family members. Old people are reluctant to complain about abuse when complaining could mean losing their homes, and family members are reluctant to report each other (Carp, 1997).

Elder abuse has much in common with other forms of intimate violence. It reflects patriarchal power imbalances, it takes place in private settings, and it is fostered by secrecy and the isolation of its victims (White et al., 2001). Like other forms of domestic violence, elder abuse can be chronic yet still remain a family secret.

Too few studies have been done to fully assess the prevalence of elder abuse, but one random-sample study in a northeastern city found that 2 percent of people over the age of 65 had been physically abused by a caregiver (Pillemer & Finkelhor, 1988). In other studies, estimates of abuse range from .5 percent to 32 percent. The higher estimates come from surveys of physicians, nurses, and social workers, who report seeing cases of elder abuse among their patients (Carp, 1997). A study conducted by the National Center on Elder Abuse (NCEA) found that more than half a million reports of elder abuse were made to adult protective services in 2003, and almost 200,000 of those reports were substantiated (NCEA, 2006). This represents almost a 20 percent increase in the number of reported incidents since 2000. The incidence of elder abuse is likely to continue to increase as the percentage of people over age 65 in the population increases; by the year 2030, more than 2 million elder adults may be victims of abuse (Baker, 2007).

Older women are not immune from violence at the hands of husbands and boyfriends. Unfortunately, they are not likely to report the abuse. In a qualitative study of older women who had experienced domestic violence, women identified a number of barriers to seeking help. They felt powerless and blamed themselves. They wanted to protect their family members or spouses from going to jail. In cases where the abuser was also elderly, the oldest women in the sample reported wanting to take care of their spouses rather than report the abuse. Some women reported that they felt there was nothing to be done to end abuse in a long-term marriage. Generational values prohibited divorce as an option and encouraged secrecy with respect to family matters. Many women also reported they felt that domestic violence services were targeted at younger adults and that they would not be comfortable with the help they would get from those services (Beaulaurier et al., 2008).

Sexual abuse of old people is still largely a taboo topic, although it is beginning to receive attention. One study in the United Kingdom reported that the victims were female by a 6:1 ratio, and the perpetrators were usually family members, more often sons than husbands. Elderly women in nursing homes may be raped and sexually abused. Memory impairment and physical frailty in nursing home residents make their victimization easy and prosecution unlikely (White et al., 2001). Rape myths contribute to the under-acknowledgement of elder sexual abuse. Older women are not usually seen as physically or sexually attractive and do not fit the stereotypical image of someone who could be raped. Because today's elder generation grew up when sexist beliefs dominated, they may blame themselves and feel guilty if they are assaulted (Vierthaler, 2008).

Like other types of violence against women, elder abuse is associated with a number of negative physical and psychological outcomes. Victims of elder abuse may experience depression, PTSD, chronic stress, or other psychological distress. The stress associated with experiencing abuse may exacerbate existing physical or mental conditions, contributing to early mortality (Baker, 2007).

Widow Abuse

The loss of a spouse or partner can be a difficult time, as a woman adjusts emotionally and financially to living without her husband. Unfortunately, in many countries across the world, the loss of a husband is compounded by experiences of ostracism, homelessness, poverty, neglect, and physical or sexual abuse. Widow abuse is largely an unacknowledged problem. Widows are often left out of reports of development, health, and poverty in the developing world. According to the

United Nations Division for the Advancement of Women (2001), "there is no one group more affected by the sin of omission" (p. 2). This omitted group is not just a small number of women. Widows are numerous in developing countries because of the practice of marrying younger women to much older men. For example, India has one of the highest rates of widowhood, with 54 percent of women over age 60 being widowed.

In Africa and Asia, widows are thought to be evil, and may be referred to as whores or beggars. In countries such as Nepal and India, some widows are subjected to shunning, torture, and even murder because they are thought to be witches (Crawford, 2010). In higher castes, women are not permitted to remarry. Often, they are seen as a burden for their families and may be cast out of their homes. Unless a son volunteers to support the widow, she has little recourse, and being forced to live with the family of a reluctant son is a source of stress and deprivation. Inheritance laws and practices in many countries prohibit a widow from inheriting money or property, leaving her destitute and homeless. Widows may be physically abused or even murdered so that their husband's family may keep the widow's dowry.

How Can Elder Abuse Be Ended?

Elder abuse is a hidden problem with devastating consequences. As the proportion of older adults increases over the next few decades, more than a million women may experience abuse in later adulthood, making the issue a timely one. More systematic research is needed in order to understand the nature and extent of elder abuse. In order to reduce and eliminate elder abuse, health care professionals who attend to older adults on either a regular or emergency basis must be educated on the risk factors associated with abuse (Baker, 2007). Because a great deal of elder abuse goes unreported, accurate assessments are needed to determine if someone is being victimized. Many elderly women who are abused are unable to advocate for themselves.

Collaboration between community providers appears to be one way of increasing the quantity and quality of services for those experiencing sexual abuse, at least in developed countries such as the United States. For example, a 3-year project, The Pennsylvania Elder Sexual Abuse Project, was conducted to encourage the collaboration of rape crisis centers and adult protective services to better address the issue of elder sexual abuse (Vierthaler, 2008). Initial interviews with workers from both sectors found that these service providers had very little contact with victims and did not know the signs and symptoms of elder sexual abuse. Workers from both sectors were cross-trained on elder sexual abuse, and the project funded an elder sexual abuse awareness campaign. Rape crisis advocates were invited to serve on elder sexual abuse task forces, and in some cases, adult protective services workers were invited to serve on sexual assault response teams. The overall reaction to the project was positive—awareness of the issue was increased and community service providers were successfully collaborating (Vierthaler, 2008). The Pennsylvania Elder Sexual Abuse Project demonstrates the lack of knowledge people have about elder sexual abuse and the value of education and collaboration.

Making a Difference

At the beginning of this chapter, we highlighted how the prevalence of sexual assault and abuse at the U.S. Air Force Academy reflected the links between the three levels of the gender system. Thinking in terms of the gender system can also be useful in designing interventions to prevent, reduce, and eliminate violence against women. Let's return to the case of the U.S. service academies to see how the gender system is involved in ending violence against women.

Since the scandal at the Air Force Academy in 2003, the U.S. Department of Defense and the U.S. military academies have taken action to prevent sexual harassment and assault and provide appropriate resources for women who have been victimized. At the sociocultural level, sexual assault prevention education has been integrated into the academies' curricula. Sexual assault response teams and victim advocates are now in place at all of the military academies. At the interpersonal level, midshipmen at the U.S. Naval Academy can serve as peer educators in a sexual harassment and assault prevention program. At the Air Force Academy, a Red Flag Campaign takes place during Sexual Assault Awareness month, which brings widespread attention to sexual assault, and also serves as an outreach program for those who have been assaulted. At the individual level, women are now able to make restricted reports of sexual assault. Restricted reports allow women to report the assault and receive services (both physical and psychological) before the authorities become involved. Women have access to a variety of support services both inside and outside the academy as they proceed through the military justice process (DoD, 2009).

Despite the changes that have been made at the service academies, sexual harassment and assault are still occurring. Each year, servicemen and women at the academies are surveyed about experiences of sexual harassment and violence. These surveys reveal that sexual harassment and assault are still underreported. For example, in 2008, there were only eight reported incidents of sexual assault at the Air Force Academy. However, the annual survey found that 10 percent of women surveyed experienced unwanted sexual contact in 2008 (DMDC, 2008). When the victims were asked why they didn't report the incidents, some of the most common responses were that they felt shame or embarrassment, that they took care of the issue themselves, or that they felt uncomfortable making a report (DMDC, 2008). Clearly, there is still quite a lot of work that needs to be done to address sexual assault and harassment at the service academies.

A Multifaceted Approach to Interventions

Many interventions designed to prevent, reduce, or eliminate violence against women occur at the individual level of the gender system. In schools and colleges throughout the United States, girls and women are educated on ways in which they can avoid being assaulted. For example, women are often told never to walk alone at night and to avoid drinking excessively. Children are also taught to tell an adult if anyone ever touches them inappropriately. Although such self-protective strategies can be useful, they can be problematic. First, they place the responsibility for prevention on the individual. However, some women and children may be unable to speak for themselves due to their age, physical or mental disability, or because speaking out may jeopardize their safety. Second, by addressing potential victims rather than potential perpetrators, the likelihood of victim blaming may be increased. If a woman wears suggestive clothing and walks alone at night, people might be more inclined to blame her if she is assaulted because she failed to act in ways that would protect her. Consequently, while it is good to teach women and children ways in which they may be able to protect themselves, interventions that address both the perpetrators and cultural norms that perpetuate violence against women must be developed.

As mentioned previously, interventions run *by* men and *for* men are effective in changing men's behaviors and reducing sexual assault. More of these types of interventions are needed in order to begin to change attitudes towards the acceptability of violence against women on a larger scale. Colleges and universities across the United States are beginning to implement rape prevention programs that are primarily directed at men and women separately. *One in Four* is a national organization that promotes "The Men's Program." The program is run by and for men and is designed to teach participants how to help women who have been raped with the hope that it will also decrease men's likelihood of raping. Currently, 40 colleges and universities across the United States have a *One in Four* chapter. Other types of rape prevention programs can also be effective in ending violence against women. Some advocate for focusing on the role of social norms in rape prevention (e.g., Fabiano et al., 2003), while others focus on empowering bystanders (e.g., McMahon & Farmer, 2009).

At the sociocultural level, movements such as the battered women's movement help address the structural barriers to ending violence against women. Women who experience violence often encounter resistance when they seek help or report abuse. Although strict laws protecting women from violence are in place throughout the United States, these laws need to be enforced by the police and court system. Police officers, as well as legal and medical professionals, need to be educated on the signs and consequences of abuse, and be vigilant in enforcing the law and protecting women. Other local and national campaigns that bring attention to the prevalence of violence against women are also beneficial. For example, Eve Ensler's V-Day (see Box 12.3), Sexual Assault Awareness Month, and *Take Back the Night* (www.takebackthenight.org) are all ways of educating people on preventing violence against women.

Women's Rights Are Human Rights

Violence against women occurs in every country and is one of the most widespread human rights violations across the world (see Box 12.4). Women of all ages are vulnerable to abuse because of the patriarchal power imbalance that exists in most societies. In many countries, women are denied basic rights. They are treated as property, to be bought, sold, used, and abused. Women are denied access to education, employment, and the right to own property. The widespread gender inequality that exists across the globe makes women more susceptible to violence.

BOX 12.3 ∾ V-Day

"I think that women have had it. They've had it with being abused, they've had it with being quiet, they've had it with bad sex, they've had it. I think they've reached a point where things have to change."* And Eve Ensler sought to make that change. It all began when she performed her award winning play, *The Vagina Monologues*, in 1998 to a 20,000-seat audience in New York City. Ensler had gathered the material for her play through interviews with women across the country. Her monologues deal with topics ranging from rape to first sexual encounters to childbirth. Ensler

then recognized that her play had the power to bring women's issues and sexuality to the public and be a catalyst for change through the founding of V-Day, a movement and organization to end violence against women. V-Day activism entails raising funds to promote awareness and support existing anti-violence organizations. The V-Day College Initiative brings awareness to college campuses through student productions of *The Vagina Monologues* in which the proceeds go to benefit local anti-violence charities. V-Day also created The Afghan Women's Summit, The Stop Rape Contest, and Indian Country Project to further raise awareness about violence against girls and women that occurs internationally. In 2010, V-Day, UNICEF, and the Panzi Foundation opened the *City of Joy* in the Democratic Republic of Congo. The *City of Joy* provides resources and opportunities for sexual assault survivors, including economic empowerment, group therapy, and sexuality education.

V-Day is now celebrated each February 14 as a celebration of women's sexuality and a site of social change. What started out as one woman's play has become a movement. In 2001, V-Day was named one of 100 Best Charities by *Worth Magazine*, and in 2010, was named one of the top organizations by GreatNonprofits. Ensler and the V-Day movement have raised more than 75 million dollars in the past 12 years and continue to campaign for ending violence against women across the globe.

For more information about Eve Ensler and the V-Day movement, go to http://www.vday.org

*Eve Ensler (2001) in "Virginia Braun in conversation with Eve Ensler: Public talk about 'private parts.'" in M. Crawford & R. Unger (Eds.) *In our own words: Writings from Women's Lives* (pp. 288–293). Boston: McGraw Hill.

Source: http://www.vday.org/about/more-about/eveensler

One of the most important ways in which gender-based violence can be ended is by encouraging women's economic empowerment. For example, some banks in developing countries are offering poor women microcredit, or small loans, to start a small business to employ themselves. Microcredit allows for women to work and begin to independently increase their wealth. Such programs have been successful in decreasing the number of women living in poverty. Some microcredit

BOX 12.4   ∽   Nicole Kidman and UNIFEM

Nicole Kidman, UNIFEM, and the Global Fight to End Violence Against Women

Nicole Kidman is not only an Academy Award winning actress, she also serves as a Goodwill Ambassador for the United Nations Development Fund for Women (UNIFEM). Kidman's primary focus is to bring international attention to ending violence against women across the globe. In addition to her duties as a Goodwill Ambassador, Kidman is also the international spokesperson for UNIFEM's *Say NO—UNiTE to End Violence Against Women Initiative*. The *Say NO* campaign (www.saynotoviolence.org) began in November 2009 and their goal is to encourage individuals, organizations, and governments to take action to stop violence against women. The *Say NO* Web site keeps track of the number of people who have pledged to take action.

Actions range from volunteering at a women's shelter to advocating for legislation.

The U.S. government is starting to take action in the global fight to end violence against women. In 2009, the International Violence Against Women Act (I-VAWA) was re-introduced into both houses of Congress (it was previously introduced in 2007 but never debated). The bill would improve practices in the United States designed to prevent violence against women, would prioritize violence against women as an issue in U.S. diplomatic dealings, and would save the lives of thousands, if not millions, of girls and women, particularly those who live in countries with widespread and systematic gender-based violence.

In October 2009 and in support of I-VAWA, Kidman testified before Congress about her work with UNIFEM, telling the stories of the women she has encountered who have survived extreme violence. In her testimony, she stated,

These champions need and deserve our support. Not with a box of band-aids, but with a comprehensive, well-funded approach that acknowledges that women's rights are human rights. It is time for policies that intentionally involve society's key communities—from health and education departments to the police and judiciary—to deliver on that commitment. To succeed, it requires political will at the highest levels.

Sources: UNIFEM. (2009). UNIFEM Goodwill Ambassador Nicole Kidman and U.N. Trust Fund Grantee testify at U.S. House Committee on Foreign Affairs—Press release. Available at http://www.unifem.org/news_events/story_detail.php?StoryID=959

Say NO—UniTE to End Violence Against Women Web site. Available at:http://www.saynotoviolence.org
Contributed By Annie B. Fox.

programs, such as the *Hand in Hand* program in India, go beyond just providing a small amount of money. Hand in Hand also provides extensive business and financial training that is designed to increase the likelihood of the business succeeding. Hand in Hand was so successful it has expanded to Afghanistan, South Africa, and China (Colvin, 2009).

In Pakistan, women can get microfinance from the Kashf Foundation. Kashf lends money to groups of women who meet every other week to make their payments and discuss important social issues. Once women pay off their initial loans, they can return for larger loans. Although Pakistani women are not permitted to leave their homes without their husbands' permission, their husbands allow them to participate because they benefit from the success of their wives' businesses. According to one woman, "Now women earn money and so their husbands respect them more. . . . If my husband starts to hit me, I tell him to lay off or next year I won't get a new loan. And then he sits down and is quiet" (Kristoff & WuDunn, 2009).

Empowering women economically is one way in which women may achieve greater equality with men and decrease their vulnerability to violence. According to Kristoff and WuDunn, "Microfinance has done more to bolster the status of women, and to protect them from abuse, than any laws could accomplish. Capitalism, it turns out, can achieve what charity and good intentions sometimes cannot" (p. 187). But we also need to challenge existing views of gender, power, and inequality. Advocates, lobbyists, and international organizations such as the U.N., UNIFEM, and Amnesty International continue to try to bring attention to this important human rights issue, but until governments take action and work together, violence against women throughout the world will continue.

Exploring Further

∽

Crawford, M. (2010). *Sex trafficking in South Asia: Telling Maya's story.* New York: Routledge.
   The author lived in Nepal and worked with a women's organization that offered shelter, counseling, and rehabilitation to girls and women who had been rescued from Indian brothels. Her book is a personal memoir of this work as well as a feminist analysis of how to end sex trafficking.

Frieze, I. H. (2005). *Hurting the one you love: Violence in relationships.* Belmont, CA: Wadsworth/Thomson Learning.
   Written by a feminist psychologist, this book draws on the most recent and definitive empirical research on IPV. It is both authoritative and readable.

Gavey, N. (2005). *Just sex? The cultural scaffolding of rape.* New York: Routledge.
   This important book uses a social constructionist perspective to analyze how normative scripts for heterosexual relationships endorse a degree of coercion that fosters cultural acceptance of rape.

The National Organization of Women Media Hall of Shame. http://www.now.org/issues/media/hall-of-shame/index.php
   This blog and Web site brings attention to misogynistic representations of women from the national press, prime time television, movies, music, advertising, the Internet, and much more. Each post features a detailed analysis and encourages readers to take action by providing a link where readers can express their outrage to the offending source.

CHAPTER 13

Psychological Disorders, Therapy, and Women's Well-Being

∽

$\mathcal{R}$ead the title of this chapter. What do you think it means? Does it imply that women's disorders are cured by therapy, thereby enhancing their well-being? Not exactly. Does it suggest a simple list of topics that will be addressed in turn: first women's psychological problems, then how to treat them, and then something about women's psychological health? Not quite. Replace "and" with "versus" and you'll get a better sense of the gist of much of this chapter. Before discussing how feminist therapy contributes to women's well-being, and how you can make differences in society and in yourself that do the same, I will first address the ways that traditional psychiatry and psychological practice have sometimes done the opposite. Topics include sexist bias in the diagnosis of disorders, the ways in which gender roles and stereotypes interact with our understanding of disordered behaviors, and some history of how psychiatrists have responded to women's nonconformist behavior by incarcerating or sedating them. After describing ways that traditional approaches to mental health have been less than woman-friendly, I will turn to feminist alternatives.

Sexist Bias in Defining Disorders

In her autobiographical memoir, *Girl, Interrupted*, Susanna Kaysen (1993) contemplates the etiology or causes of mental illness. She invites the reader to select from a list of explanations for atypical behavior, including that the person in question is "possessed," "a witch," "bad," "ill," "a victim of society's low tolerance for deviant behavior," and "sane in an insane world." Most of us living in the United States today would be unlikely to invoke demon possession or witchcraft as explanations for unusual behavior. We are much more comfortable with the idea of mental illness, which we now attribute to biological and social causes, rather than spiritual ones. We consider mental distress and disorders treatable and individuals suffering from them deserving of treatment. But how do we decide who is mentally ill and who is normal? As the last two explanations on Kaysen's list suggest, sometimes the decision depends not on the behavior itself, but on society's perception of that behavior.

The Social Construction of Abnormality

"Normal" is a relative term. We can define something as normal based on statistical probability. We could say, for example, that if it falls within a certain range around the population mean, then it is normal. This may seem like an objective way to define normality, but in everyday life we rarely know the statistical probability of a characteristic or behavior before we label it. And even when we do have a sense of the numbers, we are not necessarily guided by them. To use a non-behavioral example, the average height of women in the United States is five feet, 3.7 inches (National Center for Health Statistics, 2004); yet "petite" sizes begin at five-foot-four. Why are sizes for average women labeled with a special designation? Social factors (in this case, fashion industry standards) affect whether something that is statistically probable is considered "normal."

Social factors also influence whether a behavior is statistically probable in the first place. Behaviors vary with culture and historical period. For example, piercing body parts other than ears, which has been common in many indigenous cultures for thousands of years, has become commonplace in the industrialized West only recently. Just 25 years ago, a college student with a nose ring would have been considered abnormal by conventional standards, whereas today she may be seen as a bit alternative, but not far outside the norm.

The norm itself is also determined by social factors such as the status and relative power of the persons making the judgment and the persons being judged. Those of dominant status in the population are in a position to designate what is normal, and will likely define the norm in relation to themselves. In patriarchal societies such as the United States, there is a pervasive tendency to consider males the norm, and females a special category (Tavris, 1992). This can have negative consequences for women.

Women's Behavior as Abnormal

In general, women have been labeled the unreasonable and crazy ones in androcentric cultures. Feminine "madness" has been contrasted with masculine "rationality" in science, religion, literature, art, and humor (Showalter, 1986; Ehrenreich & English, 1973). Women have been called mad for challenging the limitations of a traditional feminine gender role, and they have experienced genuine psychological distress as a result of how this devalued role has limited their access to education, economic independence, sexual self-expression, and political power.

In psychology, the male as norm perspective has influenced researchers' and clinicians' views of women's behavior. In one of the first studies of gender stereotypes, practicing clinical psychologists were asked to choose the traits that characterized a healthy adult male and a healthy adult female (Broverman et al., 1970). Their profiles of a healthy adult and healthy adult male matched each other and were discrepant from the healthy adult female. Until feminist scholarship gained a solid foothold in the discipline of psychology in the late 1970s, psychiatrists and psychologists routinely labeled women's behavior as disordered or deficient when compared to a male standard, and attributed the disorder to reproductive pathology and natural feminine frailty (e.g., Chesler, 2005; Ussher, 1992; Showalter, 1986).

A male-as-norm bias has permeated not only academic psychology, but pop psychology as well. Most advice columns and self-help books are aimed at women. Women are told they have low self-esteem, are too emotional, and too dependent—compared to whom? If *women* were the standard of comparison, would there be more self-help books for men guiding them to temper their inflated self-esteem, develop sensitivity skills, and become less overly independent? Instead of women reading books about *Men Who Can't Love* and *Women Who Love Too Much*, might men read books about how to love as much as women do? Perhaps men would be the target audience for self-help books in general, instead of women constantly getting the message that they are the ones who need to change.

Blaming Women for Distress and Disorders

In 1909, Sigmund Freud was invited by former American Psychological Association president G. Stanley Hall to make his first and only trip to the United States. Freud delivered a series of lectures on psychoanalysis at Clark University, stirring up enthusiasm among progressive listeners who were excited about his candid acknowledgment of human sexuality. Feminists thought his early ideas about female sexuality held promise and encouraged him to write more about women; however, when he did, many women were dismayed at his formulation of femininity. Freud defined female sexuality and the feminine personality in terms of their difference from a male norm. According to Freud, in the process of resigning themselves to their inferior genitalia, females develop specific feminine personality characteristics, including masochism (Freud, 1933). Masochism is defined as deriving pleasure from one's own pain.

The idea that women are masochistic caught on, perhaps because it provided a rationalization for women's subordinate status and the pain they experienced at the hands of abusive men; if women *like* to suffer, then there is no need to critically examine the circumstances that promote their suffering. Like-minded psychoanalysts embraced Freud's proposition, and so did many other psychiatrists and psychotherapists. The assumption that women are naturally masochistic leads logically to the conclusion that they bring their problems on themselves by seeking out unhealthy relationships and damaging situations. Paula Caplan (1985) relates a vivid example in her book *The Myth of Women's Masochism*,

> [A graduate student] had been doing an internship at a local hospital, seeing patients for psychotherapy. One of her patients was Sylvia, a woman whose first husband, after they married, had refused to have any sexual relationship with her at all and had also begun to beat her. They were soon divorced and, some time later, Sylvia married another man. While married to her second husband, she became bulimic, going on massive eating binges and then forcing herself to vomit until her throat began to bleed. [The supervising psychiatrist explained] that Sylvia was a masochist. "You see how beautifully her masochism works," he said. "When her first husband isn't there to beat her anymore, she *becomes* her first husband and forces herself to vomit until she bleeds. He's not there to hurt her, so she hurts herself." (p. 192)

Take a moment to engage in some critical thinking. What other explanations might there be for Sylvia's bulimia besides "she is a masochist"?

Women have been blamed for their own distress and disorders, and they have also been blamed for the distress and disorders of others around them. In particular, mothers have been blamed for the psychological problems of their children. The mother-blaming described in Chapter 9 has a long history. An early example appears in the book *The Borderland of Insanity*, published in 1875 in London. The author claimed that insanity is inherited from the mother twice as often as it is inherited from the father; however, he had no scientific evidence to support this assertion (Russell, 1995). In the United States, mother-blaming became fashionable within psychiatry and psychology, and among the general public, during and after World War II.

Mothers were considered responsible not only for the well-being of their own children, but for the health of society in general. One of the more popular authors to point the finger at mothers for society's problematic behavior was Phillip Wylie, who, in his 1942 book, *A Generation of Vipers*, put it this way,

> Mom got herself out of the nursery and the kitchen . . . she also got herself the vote and, although politics never interested her (unless she was exceptionally naïve, a hairy foghorn, or a size forty scorpion), the damage she forthwith did to society was so enormous and so rapid that even the best men lost track of things. Mom's gracious presence at the ballot box was roughly concomitant with the start toward a new all-time low in political scurviness, hoodlumism, gangsterism, labor strife, thuggery, moral degeneration, civic corruption, smuggling, bribery, theft, murder, . . . financial depression, chaos, and war (pp. 188–189).

Of course, it wasn't mothers who were mugging people and starting wars, but Wylie (and others) held them responsible. Wylie's hostile tirade continues with a description of the typical middle-aged, middle-class mother as a useless, repulsive, smothering, and manipulative drain on society whose demand for devotion from her son saps him of his masculine autonomy. The American man was a coddled, simpering, emasculated mother-worshiper, according to Wylie and his contemporaries.

This epidemic flight from manhood that mothers were supposedly causing was deemed especially severe among African Americans because of the so-called Black matriarchy (Buhle, 1998). African American men were criticized for being childlike, impulsive, manipulative, and irrational—and these characteristics were attributed to the fact that most African American families were headed by relatively economically independent working mothers. The role of systemic racism in shaping the behaviors of African American men—and in distorting perceptions of them—was overlooked by the mother-blamers.

During the post-World War II baby boom, mothering was elevated to the status of patriotic public service. Women had been called to the paid workforce while men were away fighting during both World Wars, and had often been the primary breadwinners while men were unemployed during the Great Depression between the wars. After World War II, women were encouraged (even pressured) to resume their place in the domestic sphere. The country as a whole was counting on population growth and scientific technology to restore the prosperity and progress that had been disrupted by the wars and the Depression. In the home, science was applied not only through innovations in gadgetry, but also through expertise-based approaches to childrearing. Mothering was in the limelight and mothers faced unprecedented scrutiny of their efforts. Women's magazines regularly featured authoritative warnings about the dangers of improper parenting, from sources such as the now legendary Dr. Benjamin Spock (Ehrenreich & English, 2005; Walker, 1998). More than ever before, physicians and psychologists emphasized the primary influence of mothers to raise psychologically healthy—or unhealthy—children.

Within the discipline of psychiatry, Wylie's smothering mother became the schizophrenogenic mother. Though not all theorists took an environmental stance on the etiology of schizophrenia, among those who did were several who pointed specifically to overprotective and domineering mothering (Hartwell, 1996). Mothers have been blamed for many other disorders as well by psychiatrists, psychologists, and social workers (Caplan & Hall-McCorquodale, 1985; Caplan, 2000).

Dr. Edward Strecker, author of the mother-blaming book *Their Mothers' Sons: The Psychiatrist Examines an American Problem*, gave a lecture to 700 medical students at Bellevue Hospital in 1946 in which he identified various types of (unfit) mothers who were responsible for the nearly two million men found psychologically unfit to serve in World War II and for the 600,000 psychiatric discharges (Hartwell, 1996). Apparently, the Depression and the horrors of a World War II were not as compelling an explanation for these men's psychopathology.

The Diagnostic and Statistical Manual (DSM)

The *Diagnostic and Statistical Manual of Mental Disorders* (DSM) is produced by the American Psychiatric Association for use by clinicians. It catalogs recognized disorders, listing them with background information and diagnostic criteria. Including the first *DSM*, published in 1952, there have been six versions (I, II, III, III-Revised, IV, IV-Text Revision) and the seventh (*DSM-V*) is due to be published in spring of 2013. Revisions have been necessary in some cases because of research findings that have clarified known disorders or suggested new ones. Revisions have also occurred because of subjective factors that influence judgments of normality. For example, until 1973, homosexuality was included in the *DSM* as a mental illness. Whether due to advances in research on sexual orientation, political pressure, or both, the American Psychiatric Association opted to exclude it from *DSM-III*. Activists for gay and lesbian rights interpreted this to mean that homosexuality had officially been declared "normal" (Caplan, 1995).

A "mental disorder," according to the *DSM-IV-TR* is,

> . . . a clinically significant behavioral or psychological syndrome or pattern that occurs in an individual and that is associated with present distress (e.g., a painful symptom) or disability (i.e., impairment in one or more important areas of functioning) or with a significantly increased risk of suffering death, pain, disability, or an important loss of freedom. In addition, this syndrome or pattern must not be merely an expectable and culturally sanctioned response to a particular event, for example, the death of a loved one. Whatever its original cause, it must currently be considered a manifestation of a behavioral, psychological, or biological dysfunction in the individual. Neither deviant behavior (e.g., political, religious, or sexual) nor conflicts that are primarily between the individual and society are mental disorders unless the deviance or conflict is a symptom of a dysfunction in the individual, as described above (p. xxxi).[1]

Several of the terms in this definition are open to subjective interpretation. Who decides whether something is "clinically significant," a "syndrome," "an expectable and culturally sanctioned response," or a "symptom of dysfunction in the individual"?

Some feminist critics of the *DSM* have suggested that gender, race/ethnicity, and class all affect whether a behavior is tolerated from particular individuals within a given cultural context. They object to the sharp lines delineating normal

---

[1]Reprinted with permission from the *Diagnostic and Statistical Manual of Mental Disorders, Fourth Edition, Text Revision* (Copyright 2000). American Psychiatric Association.

from abnormal, and distinguishing one disorder from another, claiming that such pigeonholing obscures the complex variability of behavior and its causes in a given social environment (e.g., Caplan, 1995). For example, at what point should a clinician conclude that a woman's unhealthy pattern of desperate dieting and depriving herself of adequate nutrition is an eating disorder? If a college student lives in a dorm where binging and purging are accepted and even encouraged as a reasonable way to respond to social pressure to be thin, is she suffering from bulimia nervosa if she joins in?

Another concern raised by critics of the *DSM* approach is that the manual has the potential to legitimize labels that have far-reaching implications, even when sound scientific support for the labels is lacking. For example, one of the appendices in the *DSM* lists provisional categories needing further study. Even though diagnostic labels in this appendix are pending, they may be applied by clinicians. One category that appears in the *DSM-IV* appendix is ***premenstrual dysphoric disorder*** (PMDD). It did not appear as an official category because of insufficient support; however, it is used by psychiatrists (and other doctors) as a diagnosis. Controversy continues to rage regarding the inclusion of PMDD in the *DSM*. Supporters claim it is an identifiable clinical syndrome and its inclusion in the *DSM* is important to legitimize some women's cyclical suffering (e.g., Pearlstein, 2010). Some critics agree that the validation of women's experience is important, but assert that women should not require a mental illness diagnosis to receive attention for physical and emotional symptoms commonly associated with menstruation (Caplan, 2004). Also, the existence of this diagnostic category may reinforce the stereotype of premenstrual women as emotionally unstable (Nash & Chrisler, 1997). See Box 13.1 for more on PMDD.

With *DSM-V* on the horizon, numerous authors have advocated that gender be carefully considered during the revision (Narrow et al., 2007; Riecher-Rössler, 2010). They argue that gender may play an important role in how mental illness develops and is expressed. A particular concern raised by these authors is the presence of gender bias in diagnostic criteria. For example, in a study on the criteria currently used to diagnose personality disorders, researchers interviewed nearly 600 participants and found that women and men with similar levels of pathology responded differently on six specific criteria; men were more likely to endorse some items, and women were more likely to endorse others. It seems these items are not gender-neutral (Jane et al., 2007). The question remains whether gender bias should be remedied by the inclusion of gender-specific criteria, or by the creation of more gender-neutral criteria (Riecher-Rössler, 2010). What do you think?

Gender-Linked Psychological Disorders

Among the diagnostic labels used today, several are applied at different rates to women and men. The primary categories in which women are overrepresented relative to men are eating disorders, mood and anxiety disorders, and some personality disorders. On the other hand, women are underrepresented relative to men in diagnostic frequency for substance abuse disorders, some antisocial conduct

BOX 13.1   ∾   Premenstrual Dysphoric Disorder in the *DSM*

Since PMDD was included in the appendix of *DSM-IV*, debate has raged about whether it belongs there. The committee that decided to include it did so despite having concluded from a review of more than 500 studies that "no high-quality research supported the existence of PMDD" (Caplan, 2008, p. 63). Since that time, numerous researchers have been inspired to generate additional empirical evidence that may inform decisions about PMDD's inclusion in *DSM-V*.

One recent study measured the prevalence of PMDD by collecting 2 months' worth of daily symptom data from more than 1,200 women between the ages of 13 and 55 in urban and rural areas of the United States (Gehlert et al., 2009). The researchers found that only 1.3 percent of the sample met the criteria for PMDD and concluded that the actual prevalence is lower than the 5 to 8 percent estimates reported in the *DSM-IV* and previous studies. Importantly, the finding that some women do suffer from severe enough premenstrual distress to meet the diagnostic criteria for PMDD does not answer the question of whether this cluster of symptoms belongs in the *DSM*.

Much of the controversy regarding the inclusion of PMDD in the *DSM* stems from the fact that the specific criteria listed for diagnosis include not only emotional disturbance, but also physical symptoms such as fatigue, changes in appetite, sleep problems, breast tenderness, headaches, and bloating. Keep in mind that the diagnostic criteria are intended to describe a *mental* illness. What are the implications for women of labeling premenstrual distress in this way?

A few studies have investigated—and have failed to find support for—the effectiveness of non-medical treatments for PMDD, such as cognitive-behavioral therapy (Lustyk et al., 2009). Researchers who studied the diagnosis and treatment of PMDD in five countries (United States, Canada, United Kingdom, France, and Germany) concluded that the diagnosis is relatively rare, but when it is diagnosed, it is usually treated with medication rather than psychotherapy (Weisz & Knaapen, 2009).

---

disorders, and all of the sexual disorders. First we will consider some general reasons why these sex-related differences in diagnostic rates may exist, and then we will take a closer look at explanations for why specific disorders appear more often in women.

Why Are There Sex-Related Differences in the Rates of Some Disorders?

Before answering the question about why sex-related differences in rates exist, we must first consider the possibility that the reported sex ratios are inaccurate. Clinical samples are not random and may not represent the sex ratios in the general population (Hartung & Widiger, 1998). The samples employed in research studies on disorders also are typically non-random and non-representative. This bias in sampling can lead to bias in the understanding of the disorder, which can then lead to bias in diagnostic criteria, which may lead to differences in application of the criteria . . . it is a vicious cycle. For example, what is now diagnosed as **somatization disorder**, characterized by the presence of physical symptoms with no known physical cause, was originally diagnosed as ***hysteria,*** which literally translated, means "wandering womb" (Hartung & Widiger, 1998). The name of the disorder was changed, but the diagnostic criteria continued to include reproduction-related symptoms that applied only to women (e.g., irregular menstruation). In an effort to prevent diagnostic sex bias, the authors of the *DSM-IV* added what they considered a parallel set of symptoms for men (e.g., erectile dysfunction), but this was not based on any research with men. The current diagnostic criteria are based entirely on research with samples of all women and, therefore, may lead to more frequent diagnosis in women, whether or not the disorder actually occurs more often in women.

Assuming that at least some of the reported sex ratios in disorders are fairly accurate, it may be tempting to name biology as the source of the differences. It would be convenient to conclude, for example, that women get depressed because of their hormones and men develop sexual fetishes because of theirs. Certainly, biological factors predispose some individuals to particular psychological disorders, but for the most part these factors are found in both women and men; for example, both women and men can have a genetic predisposition for depression. There is some evidence that the genetic and hormonal differences between the sexes may contribute to a few specific sex-related differences in disorders, such as the tendency for women with bipolar disorder to cycle more rapidly between bouts of depression and mania than men do (Leibenluft, 1996). Still, most sex-related differences in psychological disorders have thus far not been adequately accounted for by biological factors.

Some disorders may be diagnosed more frequently in women because women may be more likely to report their distress and seek help; help-seeking is more consistent with a feminine gender role than with a masculine one in our culture (e.g., Addis & Mahalik, 2003). Some studies comparing women's and men's relative likelihood to seek psychological help have found that women report greater willingness (e.g., Oliver et al., 2005); however, the fact that some disorders are diagnosed more frequently in men suggests that even if women are typically more willing than men to seek psychological or psychiatric care, this is an inadequate explanation for all the observed sex-related differences in diagnosis frequency.

A careful examination of which disorders are diagnosed at significantly different rates in the sexes reveals a pattern consistent with traditional gender roles and gender stereotypes. For example, Rosenfield (2000) suggests that women's higher rates of ***internalizing disorders,*** where negative affect is turned inward, and men's higher rates of ***externalizing disorders,*** where negative behavior is expressed outwardly, are tied to gender socialization. Moodiness and fear are more characteristic of stereotypical femininity, whereas heavy drinking, aggression, and sexual expression are seen as more masculine behaviors.

Gender stereotypes may influence not only the contrasting behaviors that women and men exhibit, but how the same behaviors are perceived and labeled differently when exhibited by a woman versus by a man. Therapists' own preconceptions about gender may color their interpretations of female and male clients differently, causing them to overdiagnose certain conditions in women and underdiagnose others. For example, given the same set of symptoms, clinicians may be more inclined to diagnose depression in women than in men (Potts et al., 1991), or to diagnose women with "borderline" or "histrionic" personality disorders and men with "antisocial" personality disorder (Becker & Lamb, 1994; Samuel & Widiger, 2009). Stereotypes about women may lead to paradoxical diagnostic biases: sometimes they contribute to overdiagnosis of psychopathology in women—because women are the crazy ones—and sometimes they cause clinicians to overlook women's actual problems—because, after all, emotional distress is common in women, right? (Lopez, 1989; Robinson & Worell, 2002).

Finally, some disorders may be diagnosed more frequently in women because they actually occur more frequently in women—not just because of biology, but because of gender roles and gender prejudice. For example, women may be more likely to develop eating disorders because of the strong link between femininity and appearance pressure (Martz et al., 1995). They may be more prone to other disorders including depression and anxiety because of gender-specific stressors such as sex discrimination. Support for this idea was found by Klonoff and colleagues (2000) when they compared women and men on psychiatric symptoms after assessing how frequently the women had experienced sexist events, such as being called a sexist name (bitch and chick) or hearing sexist jokes. Only the women who had frequently experienced sexist stressors reported more symptoms than the men. As described in Chapter 12, the worldwide prevalence of violence against girls and women also takes a huge toll on women's psychological well-being.

Which Disorders Are Diagnosed More Frequently in Women?

The disorders discussed below all are diagnosed at higher rates in women than in men. Although they are discussed separately, keep in mind that they commonly occur together; women who suffer from depression often exhibit anxiety disorders, eating disorders, and borderline and dependent personality disorders (Sprock & Yoder, 1997; Widiger & Anderson, 2003).

Depression

Women are twice as likely as men to suffer from *major depressive disorder* and two to three times as likely to experience the more long-lasting variant, *dysthymic disorder* (*DSM-IV-TR*). Both of these disorders are characterized by chronically low mood and disabling symptoms such as marked loss of interest in activities, appetite changes, sleep disruption, fatigue, inability to concentrate, and excessive negative thinking. The higher incidence of depression in females emerges in adolescence (Hilt & Nolen-Hoeksema, 2009) and has been found cross-culturally (Grant & Weissman, 2007). Explanations for higher rates of depression in girls and women have focused on internal factors, such as genetics, hormones, and cognitive style, and on external influences such as sexism, poverty, and violence. The most recent theoretical models propose that these factors interact in complex ways to cause the observed gender difference in depression (e.g., Hyde et al., 2008).

Depression and other mood-related disorders have a genetic component. For example, individuals who inherit the tendency to have low levels of the neurotransmitter serotonin are more likely to suffer from depression than individuals with average levels of serotonin. Depression runs in families, but it is equally inherited by males and females (Agrawal et al., 2004), so genes alone don't explain the gender difference. Some research suggests that sex hormones may interact with stress hormones to make women more vulnerable to depression and anxiety (Solomon & Herman, 2009), but, in general, hormonal explanations are insufficient to fully account for the sex-related difference in depression (Kessler, 2003).

Cognitive explanations for the sex-related difference in depression suggest that girls and women may respond to negative life events with thinking patterns that contribute to low mood. For example, women engage more than men in ***rumination,*** passively dwelling on distress, its causes and consequences, instead of actively distracting themselves or seeking social support (see Figure 13.1). Rumination predicts the onset of depression and makes it worse (Nolen-Hoeksema et al., 2009). Women's subordinate social status may cause them to feel less control than men do over their life circumstances and emotions and yet more responsible for maintaining positive relationships with others; therefore, they worry rather than act (Nolen-Hoeksema et al., 1999; Nolen-Hoeksema & Jackson, 2001). The attributions people make to explain negative life events may also make them vulnerable to depression. Women, more so than men, tend to exhibit a "hopeless" style, attributing negative events to stable, global, internal causes instead of thinking, "Well, it's a one-time event, it's just one aspect of my life, and it wasn't my fault!" (Abramson & Alloy, 2006; Hankin & Abrahmson, 2001).

Biological and cognitive vulnerability alone won't necessarily lead to depression. Most times depression is triggered by negative or stressful life circumstances

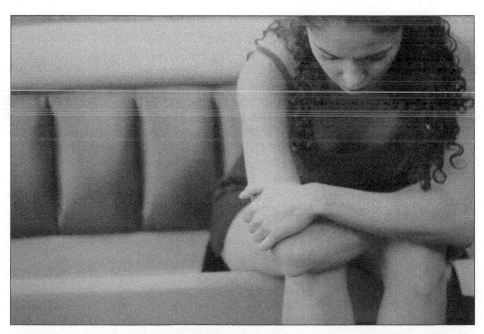

FIGURE 13.1   **Women's lower social status relative to men may predispose them to rumination, which is predictive of depression.**

or events. An example of a stressful life circumstance is poverty, which disproportionately affects more women. Poverty and its associated hardships are correlated with depression, especially among mothers with small children (Belle & Doucet, 2003; Heflin & Iceland, 2009). Another external factor that predicts women's depression is interpersonal violence (Golding, 1999). Childhood sexual abuse, rape, and battering are all associated with elevated levels of depression in women (Koss et al., 2003). Most research on depression has been done with White women in the United States, but research suggests violence also predicts depression in women from varied cultural backgrounds including African American women (Banyard et al., 2002), Latina women (Hazen et al., 2008), Native American women (Bohn, 2003), Chinese American women (Hicks & Li, 2003), and women in Norway (Nerøien & Schei, 2008), Northern Ireland (Dorahy et al., 2007), Brazil (Ludermir, 2008), and sub-Saharan Africa (Gelaye et al, 2009).

Anxiety Disorders

Generalized anxiety disorder is somewhat more common in females than in males, but a more pronounced sex-related difference is found for panic disorder. *Panic disorder* is diagnosed when an individual has experienced repeated, unexpected periods of sudden intense fear or discomfort (accompanied by physical symptoms such as heart palpitations, dizziness, trembling, and a feeling of choking) followed by at least a month of worry about having another panic attack. Because these attacks can occur in public, it is not surprising that panic disorder is associated with *agoraphobia,* which is intense fear of being in places from which it might be difficult or embarrassing to escape (e.g., outside the home alone, in a crowd, or traveling on an airplane). Panic disorder without agoraphobia is diagnosed twice as often in women as in men, and panic disorder with agoraphobia is diagnosed three times as often in women (*DSM-IV-TR*).

Some explanations for the sex-related difference in agoraphobia focus on gender, suggesting, for example, that feminine socialization may contribute to women's greater fear of being in public spaces. Traditionally, girls and women have been encouraged to reside in the domestic, private sphere and discouraged from asserting themselves in the public sphere. Also, public places can be aversive for women due to the sex discrimination, sexual objectification, sexual harassment, and sexual violence that they may encounter. Other explanations for the sex-related diagnostic difference also focus on gender, but suggest that the difference may be an artifact: Perhaps men also fear public spaces, but, because of masculine gender role expectations that they boldly enter the arena of the public sphere, men may be unwilling to admit their fear and instead choose to mask it with coping behaviors such as drinking alcohol (e.g., Bekker, 1996).

In addition to agoraphobia, most other phobias are about twice as common in women as in men, but the sex ratios vary across phobia type. For example, 75 to 90 percent of individuals with natural environment and animal phobias are women (*DSM-IV-TR*). This is particularly interesting given the long tradition in many cultures and religions of associating women more closely than men with nature as nurturers and creators of life (Merchant, 1995). Earth-based spiritual traditions honor earth goddesses and Mother Nature, yet women in the United States today are much more likely than men to exhibit an intense fear of nature. Perhaps the roots of women's phobias about the natural environment and animals lie in gender socialization that discourages girls from exploring wild places and accepting their natural physical selves.

Eating Disorders

Ninety percent or more of individuals diagnosed with *anorexia nervosa* and *bulimia nervosa* are female (*DSM-IV*). The word anorexia refers to a loss of appetite, but individuals with anorexia nervosa do not usually lose their appetites; instead, they exert rigorous control over their food intake and physical activity level so as to achieve a lower than minimally normal body weight. Distorted perception of body shape and size is typical. Although widespread concern about the prevalence of anorexia nervosa among girls and women is relatively recent among medical professionals and the general public, self-starvation behaviors among women have been documented as far back as the Middle Ages (Bemporad, 1996; Brumberg, 2000; Liles & Woods, 1999). Like anorexia, bulimia is related to extreme concern about weight gain, but individuals exhibiting bulimia are very often of normal weight or above normal weight. They do not tend to restrict their food intake, instead engaging in food binges followed by purging through vomiting or use of laxatives. Many girls and women engage in unhealthy eating habits and suffer from distressing body preoccupation but do not meet the specific diagnostic criteria for these disorders.

Both depression and anxiety in women often co-occur with eating disorders (e.g., Godart et al., 2007; Swinbourne & Touyz, 2007), though the precise nature of the relationship is unclear. It is possible that depression and anxiety predispose women to eating disorders (Keel et al., 2001; Strober et al., 2007). Or it may be that other factors, such as negative social comparison, low self-esteem, and body dissatisfaction affect both mood and eating disorders (Green et al., 2009). All of the research on the associations between these factors is correlational, so it is difficult to determine causal links between them.

What we do know is that the associations between depression, anxiety, body dissatisfaction, and eating disorders vary in different populations of women. For example, a study of Mexican American women found that endorsement of U.S. societal values (which include the emphasis on thinness for women) was significantly correlated with bulimic symptoms, while a study of African American women conducted by the same researchers found no association between these factors, nor between depressive symptoms and bulimic symptoms (Lester & Petrie, 1995; 1998). One study with postpartum women found that weight gained during pregnancy is associated with depression for White women, but not for African American women (Cameron et al., 1996), perhaps because African American women are less likely than Caucasian women to perceive body changes related to pregnancy negatively (Walker et al., 2002).

Research suggests that the prevalence of eating disorders in general also varies among different populations of women, although the discrepancies may be shrinking. Some populations of women may be less prone to eating disorders because of their greater social distance from the mainstream beauty ideal, which is not only thin, but also young, White, heterosexual, and middle-class; it may be easier for women who do not fit into these categories to reject the dominant standard (e.g., Gilbert, 2003). Some researchers have found that increased identification with mainstream culture, known as **acculturation,** is related to increased rates of eating disorders in girls and women of color in the United States (e.g., Gowen et al., 1999; Cachelin et al., 2000). Others suggest that the increased rate is due not only to acculturation itself, but also to the stress associated with trying to fit into a culture that is different from one's culture of origin (Gordon et al., 2010).

Borderline and Dependent Personality Disorders

Several personality disorders show sex-related discrepancies in prevalence rates, including antisocial and narcissistic disorders (diagnosed more in men) and dependent and borderline disorders (diagnosed more in women). There is a large amount of literature debating whether these differences are real, or are artifacts of imprecise sampling, the result of bias in diagnostic constructs or criteria, or due to assessment bias by clinicians or self-report instruments.

Borderline personality disorder (BPD), the diagnosis applied to the author of *Girl, Interrupted,* is characterized by a pattern of instability in relationships, self-concept, and emotions accompanied by impulsivity and a severe fear of abandonment (*DSM-IV-TR*). Seventy-five percent of the individuals diagnosed with BPD in clinical settings are female; however, some studies of BPD prevalence in the general population find no gender difference, so there may be a sampling bias (Skodol & Bender, 2003). Taking the clinical rates as representative, several researchers have explored the possibility that the diagnostic criteria for BPD are sexist. In one study, undergraduate students sorted the diagnostic criteria for the personality disorders on the basis of how characteristic they were of women versus of men (Sprock et al., 1990). All of the BPD criteria were rated as more characteristic of women, with the exception of the criterion describing intense, inappropriate anger.

Dependent personality disorder (DPD) is characterized by an excessive need to be cared for that leads to submissive and clingy behavior (*DSM-IV-TR*). Individuals with dependent personality traits experience intense longings to be loved, nurtured, and protected. They have extreme trouble making independent decisions, even minor daily ones, and they require a lot of reassurance and advice. They have difficulty expressing disagreement with others because they fear it will lead to a loss of support or approval. They have trouble initiating projects because of low self-confidence in their abilities. Importantly, these dependent behaviors are to be considered signs of the personality disorder only when they exceed age-appropriate or culturally-appropriate norms. What about gender-appropriate norms? How about differences in gender socialization and gender roles? And what about factors confounded with gender, such as economic dependence and being the victim of domestic abuse? The *DSM-IV-TR* doesn't offer any guidance to clinicians on these points except to say that " . . . societies may differentially foster and discourage dependent behaviors in males and females" (p. 723).

Some Other Disorders Diagnosed More Frequently in Women

A few other disorders are diagnosed more frequently in women than in men according to the *DSM-IV-TR*. One of these is *factitious disorder,* which involves intentionally producing or feigning psychological or physical symptoms so as to meet a psychological need to assume the sick role; only the most serious variant is diagnosed more frequently in men. (Keep factitious disorder in mind when you read in the next section about the "Cult of Invalidism" among privileged American and Western European women in the late nineteenth century.) Another disorder worth mentioning here is *depersonalization disorder,* feeling an extreme sense of detachment or estrangement from oneself as if one is an observer of one's own mental processes or body; this disorder is diagnosed at least twice as often in women as in men in clinical samples (*DSM-IV-TR*). Chapter 3 discussed self-objectification among women; might depersonalization represent a more extreme form of women's common out-of-body state? Some bulimic women report feelings of dissociation following eating binges (*DSM-IV-TR*).

The *DSM-IV* includes an appendix of *culture-bound syndromes* that are not officially recognized by the American Psychiatric Association, but are well-known in other cultures. Listed among these are two that are more reportedly observed more often in women than in men. *Latah* is a Malaysian term to describe hypersensitivity to sudden fright that leads to dissociative or trancelike behavior. The syndrome goes by different names in the many regions of the world where it is recognized, including Thailand, Japan, and the Philippines. In Malaysia, Latah is most common in middle-aged women. *Mal de ojo*, literally "evil eye" in Spanish, is widely found in Mediterranean cultures. Sufferers exhibit fitful sleep, crying for no apparent reason, and intestinal distress. Though it is most frequently reported in children, mal de ojo tends to strike women more often than men when it occurs in adults.

Sexist Bias in the Treatment of Psychological Disorders

Broadly speaking, treatment for psychological disorders can be defined in terms of two general approaches: a psychiatric model that utilizes medical therapies including drugs and hospitalization, and a non-medical psychotherapeutic approach. Psychoanalysis, the therapy originally developed by Freud, falls into both categories in that it is a nonmedical "talk" therapy but is practiced by a (relatively small) subset of psychiatrists. Both the psychiatric and psychotherapeutic approaches have suffered from gender bias. This section will first address the sexism that has pervaded psychiatric institutionalization and drug therapies, and then will describe criticisms of traditional psychotherapy.

Institutionalizing Women

Residential facilities for severely mentally ill or developmentally disabled people serve important caretaking and rehabilitative functions in our society today. Sometimes, however, people are wrongfully incarcerated in these institutions (e.g., Szasz, 1973). A look at the history of women's institutionalization in the United States and Europe reveals a pattern of unwarranted involuntary commitment as punishment for socially deviant behavior and unwillingness to conform to the limits of a socially-prescribed feminine gender role (Appignanesi, 2008; Showalter, 1986; Ripa, 1990; Chesler, 2005; Ussher, 1992).

Charcot, Freud, and the Salpêtrière

From the seventeenth to the nineteenth centuries, the Salpêtrière in Paris was an infamous institution housing primarily women. Initially built as a gunpowder factory, it was remodeled and expanded under the reign of Louis XIV into an alms-house to shelter some of the 40,000 homeless Parisians, 10 percent of the city's population (Vallois, 1998). Many of the women forcibly housed in the Salpêtrière were prostitutes who were later shipped to Louisiana and Canada to help populate France's new territories. Women considered (in the parlance of the time) "feeble-minded" or "deranged" were routinely chained to the walls. Things changed, however, under the direction of Phillipe Pinel, who, perhaps inspired by the humanitarian themes of the French Revolution, unchained the "insane" at the Salpêtrière in the last years of the eighteenth century.

Women who were homeless, suspected or known prostitutes, or merely deviant in their behavior (e.g., were loud or aggressive) were likely candidates for involuntary commitment in the Salpêtrière during the nineteenth century. Jean-Martin Charcot, the founder of modern neurology, opened a clinic in the Salpêtrière to study individuals who displayed *hysterical symptoms,* physical problems with no apparent organic cause. Charcot disagreed with predecessors who thought hysteria was caused by a wandering womb (he saw hysteria in men as well), but he did attribute hysteria to sexual dysfunction. The majority of Charcot's patients were women. The most famous and favored of these was Blanche Wittmann, nicknamed the "Queen of Hysterics," whose dramatic displays of hysteria on demand served Charcot well in his theatrical lectures to colleagues, as depicted in André Brouillet's painting, *Une leçon clinique à la Salpêtrière* (see Figure 13.2).

Charcot's work on hysteria was highly influential to a certain young physician who came to work with him for a few months in 1885. That physician's name was Sigmund Freud. Freud was impressed with Charcot's ability to use hypnosis to produce and relieve hysterical symptoms. Here was the first hint that the unconscious mind might be connected to some forms of physical distress. Freud was also impacted when he overheard Charcot assert quietly to a colleague that the cause of hysteria "*c'est toujours la chose genitale . . . toujours . . . toujours . . . toujours*" (translation: "it is always something genital . . . always . . . always . . . always") (Freud, 1914, p.14).

It was while in residence at the Salpêtrière that Freud first developed his own ideas about hysteria and its origins in childhood sexual trauma. Later, Freud retracted his claim that the hysteria he observed in his women patients at his clinic in Vienna was due to actual childhood sexual trauma and developed the alternative explanation that the symptoms stemmed from unconscious conflict regarding wishful sexual fantasies. This about-face in Freud's thinking may have been due to the negative reaction his theory elicited from his peers in the medical community; after all, he was essentially claiming that childhood sexual abuse was commonplace in their high-status households (Masson, 1984). Undoubtedly, this shift had a significant impact on the treatment received by women who actually had been abused.

FIGURE 13.2   Reproduction of painting (*Une leçon clinique à la Salpêtrière* by Andrè Brouillet).

True Women and Madwomen in the Victorian Era

In the mid-to-late-nineteenth century United States, involuntary commitment of "madwomen" by their husbands or other family members who found their attitudes or behaviors inconvenient, unacceptable, or uncontrollable was not unheard of among the middle and upper classes. At the time, economically privileged women were expected to aspire to "True Womanhood," to be passive, pious, domestic, and morally pure (Welter, 1966). According to medical wisdom of the time, intellectual activity—such as that required when pursuing higher education or engaging in social reform activism—was contraindicated for women. The only recommended activity was childbearing; however, this was somewhat of a double bind due to the fact that pregnancy and lactation were also seen as causes of women's mental illness (Geller & Harris, 1994).

A cult of invalidism flourished among affluent women in the United States and Europe during the latter nineteenth century and into the beginning of the twentieth (Ehrenreich & English, 1973). With their physical and intellectual exercise severely limited by corsets and conventions, fashionable women manifested chronic sickness in the form of vague "nervous" ailments. Frailty, weakness, and acute sensitivity came to be romanticized as a variation on the True Woman ideal (Geller & Harris, 1994). Like the True Woman, the so-called neurasthenic woman was no threat to a patriarchal household or society.

Because women's reproductive organs were believed to be the primary source of their mental distress, physicians used woman-specific therapies including the surgical removal of ovaries, electrical shocks to the uterus, hot water injections into the vagina, and clitoral cauterization (Geller & Harris, 1994; Russell, 1995). An influential doctor named Silas Weir Mitchell popularized the "rest cure," months of confinement in bed with no activity, not even a book to read. Weir Mitchell's idea was that women enjoyed being ill, and that making the conditions of illness extremely aversive would hasten their recovery. His approach treated women as unruly children in need of paternal discipline. In her short story, *The Yellow Wallpaper*, suffragist and feminist foremother Charlotte Perkins Gilman (1892) relates a first-person account of a woman's descent into madness *caused* by her physician husband's implementation of the rest cure,

> If a physician of high standing, and one's own husband, assures friends and relatives that there is really nothing the matter with one but temporary nervous depression—a slight hysterical tendency—what is one to do? . . . I am absolutely forbidden to "work" until I am well again . . . Personally, I believe that congenial work, with excitement and change, would do me good (p. 1).

The woman in the story proceeds to develop delusions about a female prisoner lurking behind the garish designs on the peeling wallpaper in her room. Perkins Gillman, herself, was institutionalized and put on the rest cure by Weir Mitchell

FIGURE 13.3   Charlotte Perkins Gilman

for a month in 1887. She suffered from "nervous prostration" following the birth of her daughter (today she would probably be diagnosed with postpartum depression). When she was sent home she was instructed to "live as domestic a life as possible," to limit her intellectual activity to 2 hours per day, and to never write another word. After complying with this protocol for several months, Gilman "came perilously near to losing [her] mind." She recovered after her divorce. (See Figure 13.3.) Stories from other women confined to asylums during the latter nineteenth century are in Box 13.2.

Institutionalization of girls and women who defied socially-imposed limits on their behavior is not a horror of only the distant past. The Miramax film, *The Magdalene Sisters* (2003) is a fictionalized account of real abuses suffered by many of the 30,000 girls in Ireland who were sent against their will to live and work as laundresses in the Magdalene asylums between the 1880s and the 1990s (Gordon, 2003).

BOX 13.2   ∽   Women's Voices from the Nineteeth-Century Asylum

My youngest brother I loved with all the tender love of a sister, and I wanted him to have an education, and I worked in the factory to get money to help educate him; and is it possible that a brother, or a human being, could be so hardened or cruel, on account of difference of religion, to put a sister in prison and hire men to try experiments, and to commit rape on a sister, and to delight in her sufferings! . . . Is this the state of our country, that the rights of a female are trampled upon . . .

— *Elizabeth T. Stone (1840–1842)*

It is now twenty-one years since people found out that I was crazy, and all because I could not fall in with every vulgar belief that was fashionable . . . I find that active nervous temperaments that are full of thought and intellect want full scope to dispose of their energy, for if not they will become extremely excitable. Such a mind cannot bear a tight place, and that is one great reason why women are much more excitable than men, for their minds are more active; but they must be kept in a nut-shell because they are women.

— *Phebe R. Davis (1850–1853)*

It was in a Bible-class . . . that I defended some religious opinions . . . which brought upon me the charge of insanity. . . . Early on the morning of the 18th of June, 1860, as I arose from my bed, preparing to take my morning bath, I saw my husband approaching my door with two physicians, both members of his church and of our Bible class . . . Fearing exposure I hastily locked my door . . . [but] my husband forced an entrance into my room through the window with an axe! . . . And I, for shelter and protection against exposure in a state of almost entire nudity, sprang into bed . . . The trio approached my bed, and each doctor felt my pulse, and without asking a single question both pronounced me insane.

— *Elizabeth Parsons Ware Packard (1860–1863)*

Here, women of intelligence, of spirit, of refinement, with homes, with families, and possessing the power to comfort, cherish, and adorn these, are left to stagnate . . . they are prisoners. It is very generally believed . . . that an asylum confines only the violent, dangerous, or utterly imbecile . . . This is a remarkably wide-spread error.

— *Adeline T. P. Lunt (Date unknown)*

Source. All excerpts from Geller, J. L., & Harris, M. (1994). *Women of the asylum. Voices from behind the walls, 1840–1945.* New York: Anchor Books.

These institutions were built by the Sisters of Mercy as spiritual refuges for morally shamed girls—girls who were seen as too promiscuous, girls who were considered too attractive, girls whose reputations had suffered as a result of rape, girls who had become pregnant before marriage. Instead, as portrayed in the film, girls were subject to severe psychological and physical cruelty inflicted by the nuns and priests staffing the institutions. Although these asylums may not seem to have much to do with mental illness from a contemporary perspective, it is important to keep in mind that during the nineteenth century, when the Magdalene asylums first opened, "hypersexuality" in females was considered by European and American doctors to be a form of psychopathology (Lunbeck, 1994).

Women and Deinstitutionalization

In the 1960s and '70s, a number of writers in the United States and Europe penned anti-psychiatry critiques that focused on the social construction of madness and the authoritarian abuses perpetrated by psychiatric institutions (e.g., Goffman, 1961;

Laing, 1970; Szasz, 1970). The claim that the so-called mentally ill were yet another marginalized group, labeled and punished for their nonconformist behavior, had a particular appeal against the backdrop of the civil rights movement and counter-culture activism. There followed a trend promoting the deinstitutionalization of mental patients and reliance on community-based care facilities. Unfortunately, these facilities were underfunded and limited in number. The result was that many psychologically distressed individuals ended up homeless (Isaac & Armat, 1990).

Deinstitutionalization has had particular implications for women. When family and community care take the place of institutional care, who are the primary care-givers? Most of the time, it is women (Ascher-Svanum & Sobel, 1989; Bachrach, 1984; Thurer, 1983). In Chapter 11, we discussed women as caregivers for elderly parents and spouses who have dementia. Many other women provide care for family members with serious psychological disorders. Consider, for example, the real case of one 63-year old woman who is the only family member available to care for her 67-year-old brother, who has suffered from schizophrenia for most of his adult life and is now experiencing increased confusion and dementia. He is in a subsidized apartment, but left to himself, cannot cope with daily life tasks such as shopping and preparing food, so his caregiver drives to his home daily to take care of his needs. She is experiencing depression as she realizes that the situation is likely only to get worse for the forseeable future.

Deinstitutionalization is related to women's role as the primary caregivers in their families in other ways as well: women with serious mental disorders are more likely to be at home raising their children than they were when community-based outpatient services were unavailable (Oyserman et al., 2000). And, deinstitutionalized women may be more likely to become mothers than women living within a facility that provides family planning services (Bachrach, 1984).

Medicating Women

Like institutional care, when properly applied, psychotropic drugs can serve as an effective component in treatment programs for many forms of psychological distress such as depression and generalized anxiety. As in the case of institutionalization, however, an historical look at the use of psychiatric medications suggests that women have been disproportionately targeted as candidates for this form of therapy, especially when they experienced distress related to their traditional feminine roles as mothers and homemakers.

Sedatives for Stepford Wives

Since tranquilizers and sedatives were first introduced for widespread use in the 1950s, they have been prescribed more often for women than for men (Herzberg, 2009; Metzl, 2003). This difference may be due, in part, to women's higher rates of disorders appropriately treated with these types of drugs but it can also be attributed to a sexist bias stemming from the perception of certain behaviors in women as disruptive to the social order. Concurrent with the mid-century mother-blaming described earlier in this chapter, tranquilizers were promoted in magazines such as the *Ladies Home Journal* and *Cosmopolitan* as the cure for women's frigidity, infidelity, single status, career-mindedness, and rejection of motherhood (Herzberg, 2009; Metzl, 2003).

Miltown, a muscle relaxant, was introduced to the American public in 1955. Demand for it soon exceeded that for any previous prescription drug. By the end of 1956, 1 in 20 Americans, the majority women, were taking tranquilizers (Metzl, 2003). In 1969, Valium became the most widely prescribed medication in the United States with 1 in 10 Americans taking it, three-quarters of whom were women (Chambers, 1972). Tranquilizers were so commonly prescribed to married, middle-class women in North America and Europe that they earned the nickname "mother's little helper," popularized in a 1966 Rolling Stones song by the same name and satirized by Artist Judy Olausen (see Figure 13.4). In the 1950s, '60s, and '70s, tranquilizers were recommended for women not only to relieve their own distress, but also to relieve the distress men experienced living with troublesome women (Metzl, 2003).

FIGURE 13.4 **"Mother's Little Helpers" by Judy Olausen.**

Advertising Drugs to Psychiatrists

Long before it was legal to advertise prescription drugs directly to consumers, pharmaceutical companies targeted physicians through ads in medical journals. Still today more than 80 percent of promotional funds are spent on advertising to physicians (U.S. General Accounting Accountability Office, 2002). Researchers have found gendered patterns in the content of these ads that contradict reality.

A study of more than 200 ads for a variety of prescription drugs from American medical journals found that when both women and men were pictured, women were twice as likely to be portrayed as consumers of the drugs, though national health statistics at the time suggested that women made fewer office visits and spent fewer days in hospitals than men did (Hawkins & Aber, 1993). Consistent with the face-ism in advertising described in Chapter 3, just parts of women's bodies were pictured significantly more often than just parts of men's, and women appeared naked four times as often as men. An analysis of portrayals of women in United States and Canadian medical journals found that drug advertisements reinforced negative stereotypes of women (Ford, 1986). For example, one ad pictured a male bus driver on one page, with the copy, "He is suffering from estrogen deficiency,"; on the next page was a picture of an older woman passenger who appeared to be talking loudly, and the rest of the copy, "She is the reason why." Other ads portrayed women as childlike, complaining, and unable to cope.

In a study of psychotropic drug advertisements in primary psychiatry journals from North America and Great Britain, women were overrepresented compared to psychiatric epidemiological data, especially in the U.S. journal (Munce et al., 2004). An analysis of all the psychotropic drug advertisements appearing in a family physician journal for a period of four years revealed that 77 percent of them depicted women patients (Hansen & Osborne, 1995). In this family practice journal, and a psychiatry journal the researchers also analyzed, nearly all of the ads for antidepressant medications portrayed women consumers—100 percent and 80 percent, respectively. These percentages are distinctly inconsistent with the typical 2:1 sex ratio of depression diagnosis.

Ads for antidepressants distort reality in that they tend to portray stereotypically idealized life circumstances, subtly discouraging physicians from exploring the social causes of women's depression such as sexism, poverty, and intimate partner violence (Nikelly, 1995). Ads for psychiatric medications also neglect racism as a source of psychological distress. An ad that appeared in the *Archives of General Psychiatry* in 1974 pictured an African American woman, dressed in professional clothing, looking menacing and raising a fist, with the heading, "Assaultive and belligerent? Cooperation often begins with HALDOL" (Metzl, 2003). This ad, which ran during the heyday of the civil rights movement and the feminist second wave, implied that the remedy for African American women's outrage was medication rather than social change.

Ads for antidepressants are misleading also in that they imply that these medications are a generally effective treatment. A meta-analysis of 35 drug trials submitted to the U.S. Food and Drug Administration (FDA) in support of four new generation antidepressants found that the benefits of antidepressants depended on how severely depressed patients were initially. Antidepressants were significantly effective for treating the most severely depressed patients, but for those with initially low levels of depression, drugs like Paxil and Prozac worked no better than a placebo (Kirsch et al., 2008). Given that clinicians have been led to believe that antidepressants work for most every depressed individual, these drugs are likely overprescribed.

Selling Drugs Directly to Women

In 1985, the FDA lifted its moratorium on direct-to-consumer advertising for prescription drugs. The annual number of direct-to-consumer appeals submitted to the FDA for approval has quadrupled since 1999 (U.S. General Accountability Office, 2008). According to FDA guidelines, drug manufacturers may solicit consumers with three types of advertisements: *product claim ads*, which describe the drug, what it does, and must include information about risks and side effects; *reminder ads*, which mention the drug by name but do not make any claims about what it does, and so do not have to include risk information; and *help-seeking ads*, which describe a disorder or condition without mention of a specific drug, and are not regulated by the FDA (U.S. General Accountability Office, 2002).

A content analysis of 10 leading U.S. magazines, researchers found that prescription drug advertisements appeared more often in the publications aimed at women than in those geared toward men or general readership (Woloshin et al., 2001). What are women readers to conclude when they routinely encounter antidepressant ads in magazines like *Self* and *Marie Claire* alongside articles about how to be more attractive and how to find love (Metzl, 2003)? Print ads for the antidepressant Paxil have appeared since 1993 and have overwhelmingly featured women—who happen to be young, White, conventionally attractive, thin, well-dressed, and heterosexual (Hanganu-Bresch, 2008). In one of these ads, a woman is standing separated from her helpless looking husband and son, and the text reads, "What's standing between you and your life?" In the "after" picture, she is crouched next to her son, hugging him and gazing happily upward (at her husband?). Her normal life as a mother and wife has been restored.

Consider another example: this time it is a brochure spotted in a women's health clinic in 2003. On the cover is a smiling woman, her hair and clothes blowing in the wind. Above her are the words "mood swing," with "mood" crossed out. Underneath, in smaller text, it says, "Think it's PMS? Think again. It could be PMDD." Inside the brochure are more pictures of smiley women and the words "Irritability," with "Irrit" crossed out, and "low energy," with "low" crossed out. There are also three pages of text asking the reader whether she has mood swings, bloating, breast tenderness, and other symptoms in conjunction with her menstrual cycle—and then encouraging her to ask her doctor whether medication for PMDD might be right for her. Nowhere in this brochure does Eli Lilly, the pharmaceutical company who produced it, identify the drug, "Sarafem," or disclose that this drug is the antidepressant Prozac, rebranded to boost sales. Neither does the brochure identify PMDD as a psychiatric diagnosis. FDA approval of the use of this drug to treat menstrual distress was contingent on expert opinion that PMDD was a distinct mental disorder. Of course, a so-called mental disorder that can affect half the population under 50 every month is a lucrative one for drug companies. Interestingly, five of the six psychiatrists who made the decision to include PMDD in the *DSM-IV* had financial ties to Eli Lilly (Cosgrove et al., 2006).

Because of the gender biases that exist in the use of psychotropic drugs, some psychiatrists and psychologists advocate "feminist psychopharmacology" (e.g., Hamilton & Jensvold, 1995; Marsh, 1995). They argue that a feminist perspective will help counter sexism in psychiatric diagnosis and prescription patterns. In addition, they suggest that a feminist perspective would add social and cultural context to biologically-focused research on sex-related differences in responses to psychotropic drugs and their effectiveness. Especially lacking from outcome research is a consideration of ethnic and racial factors; psychopharmacological treatment for women of color has been studied very little although psychiatrists seem particularly inclined to favor drugs over other forms of therapy for people of color (Jacobsen, 1994). A contemporary feminist approach would consider ethnic and racial factors along with gender.

Traditional Psychotherapy

Critics of traditional psychotherapy are referring not only to psychological treatment before the rise of feminist practice in the 1970s, but also to the work of contemporary clinicians who fail to adopt a non-sexist or feminist approach. The primary criticisms that have been leveled at traditional psychotherapy include the following:

1. The theoretical orientation and/or personal perspective that informs the therapist's appraisal of the client's distress and guides the treatment may be based on gender stereotypes and sexist attitudes.
2. Traditional psychotherapeutic orientations focus on the individual as the source of the psychological distress with little or no consideration of social contextual factors that may contribute to the client's problems, such as sexism and racism.
3. The relationship between the therapist and client is an unequal one in which the therapist is the more powerful expert and the client is in a subordinate and vulnerable position.

The second of the two criticisms listed apply to pre-feminist psychotherapy in general, whereas the first one applies to individual therapists or primarily to psychoanalysis and its offshoots.

Sexism in Therapy

The influence of Freudian thinking on American and European psychiatry and psychology should not be underestimated. Although most therapists today are not psychoanalytically oriented per se, Freud's notions about things such as women's masochism may still exert an influence on their thinking (Caplan, 1985). Women who undergo Freudian psychoanalytic therapy will likely come to understand that they are maladjusted if they are ambitious (this is a sign of "penis envy," according to Freud), immature if they have not transferred the focus of their sexuality from the clitoris to the vagina, and have unresolved unconscious conflicts if they report memories of childhood sexual abuse (which are most likely fantasies, according to Freud). For these reasons and more, most feminists in the United States have rejected psychoanalysis as a beneficial therapeutic approach for women; however, French feminism and post-feminism draws heavily on psychoanalysis (relying more on the work of French psychoanalyst Jacques Lacan than on Freud). And, as will be discussed in the section on feminist therapy, there are feminist psychoanalytic clinics in the United States and England.

Most therapists today are *eclectic* in their orientations—they borrow from classic behavioral therapy, cognitive therapy, Freudian and post-Freudian psychodynamic thought, tailoring their approach to the client and the problem. The most popular single approach is *cognitive-behavioral therapy,* in which the therapist and client work on changing not only maladaptive behavioral patterns, but also destructive thought patterns. This approach is not in itself sexist; however, it may be biased if the therapist thinks in sex stereotypical ways. For example, a traditional cognitive-behavioral therapist might respond to a woman client's continual fears about her mothering with the suggestion that she take a parenting class to bolster her skills, instead of critically examining the unrealistic and idealized version of mothering that pervades our popular culture. The cognitive-behavioral approach may be less than optimal for women unless the therapist infuses it with a distinctly feminist orientation (e.g., Cohen, 2008; Hurst & Genest, 1995; Srebnik & Saltzberg, 1994).

Whether a therapist is eclectic, cognitive-behavioral, psychoanalytic, or otherwise, if that therapist is traditionally schooled and does not employ a feminist approach, he or she will tend to ignore how the client's gender, sexual orientation, race, ethnicity, disability, or other social categories may affect her experience. By focusing only on intrapsychic factors, such as personality and counterproductive thought patterns, a traditional therapist will overlook factors outside the individual that may be contributing to her distress. Instead of challenging those factors, perhaps working with the client to change the ones that are under her control and find new ways to deal with those that are not, a traditional therapist would more likely focus on the client's maladaptive response to her situation. The goal of traditional therapy is to adapt the client to the social context, not critically examine the social context itself.

Sexual Misconduct by Therapists

When people seek psychotherapy, they are in a needy position, which automatically makes them less powerful relative to the therapist from whom they desire treatment. They are psychologically distressed and eager to feel better, so they are probably more open and trusting than they might normally be in a new relationship with a stranger. Add to this the therapist's impressive title and academic credentials, and the relationship ends up very unbalanced, indeed. This power differential need not necessarily be a problem—after all there are many circumstances under which people need to make themselves vulnerable to others; however, some therapists have abused their higher status. The most egregious form of abuse is sexual misconduct between the therapist and client, which in the vast majority of cases involves male therapists and female clients.

In national studies about 7 percent of male therapists report having had sexual relationships with their clients, compared to 1.5 percent of female therapists (Pope, 2001). The therapist-client relationship is an intimate one, and sexual attraction between therapists and clients is not uncommon; however, professional ethical guidelines for both psychologists and psychiatrists in the United States prohibit sexual interaction with clients. Every state in the United States prohibits therapist–client sexual relationships through licensing regulations; offenders may be sued for malpractice in civil court, and in some states may be charged with criminal conduct (Pope, 2001). Sexual interaction between therapists and their clients is considered unethical precisely because of the power imbalance between them.

Sexual relationships between therapists and clients are potentially psychologically damaging to the clients, and may, of course, have repercussions for the therapist and his family as well. Women who have had sexual relationships with their therapists later report a variety of negative feelings including shame, guilt, anger, helplessness, and powerlessness (Nachmani & Somer, 2007; Somer & Saadon, 1999; Pope, 2001). In a survey of 958 patients who had been sexually involved with their therapists, 90 percent reported having been harmed by the experience, 14 percent attributed suicide attempts to their experience, and 11 percent required hospitalization during their recovery from it (Pope & Vetter, 1991). Sometimes the negative feelings are mixed with an illusory sense of achievement for having been chosen as a sexual partner and having supposedly gained control over the therapist (Nachmani & Somer, 2007) or with a sense of romance that may temporarily shield women against the ultimate negative effects of the abusive relationship (Somer & Nachmani, 2005).

Feminist Therapy

The characteristics that define feminist therapy read like a list of remedies to the problems of traditional therapy described above. The general principles of feminist therapy have been outlined by numerous authors (e.g., Ballou & Brown, 2002; Brown, 2010; Ballou et al., 2008; Enns, 2004; Hill & Ballou, 2005; Worell & Remer, 2003). From a feminist therapy perspective,

1. Women's subjective experiences are valid and important to attend to, given the androcentrism that has pervaded psychological theory;
2. Not all problems originate in the individual and "personal" problems are not merely personal but are sometimes social and political.
3. Therapy should be an egalitarian collaboration between therapist and client rather than a hierarchical relationship.
4. The goals of therapy are to help women feel positive about themselves and empowered to make social change, not to educate them about what is wrong with them.
5. The therapist must be aware of the fact that women are diverse and their experiences are affected by social factors such as their age, race, ethnicity, sexual orientation, class, disability, etc.

Feminist therapy is not a theoretical orientation in the same way as cognitive-behaviorism or psychoanalysis; rather, it is a set of values that may be applied in a variety of therapeutic contexts.

Conducting Feminist Therapy

In a survey study of feminist therapists, Hill & Ballou (1998) asked whether the therapists had "adapted a specific therapeutic strategy so that it is feminist." Their respondents explained how they had taken traditional tools, such as cognitive techniques and dream analysis, and revised them so as to incorporate feminist principles. For example, one therapist challenges women to question whether their negative thinking may be a learned response to gender expectations; another teaches self-hypnosis as a skill under the control of the client, instead of using standard hypnosis which can lead to feelings that the therapist is controlling the client. See Box 13.3 for an example of psychoanalytic practice informed by feminist principles.

Studies comparing the practices of therapists who identify as feminist and those who do not suggest that, even when traditional tools are used, feminist therapy is

BOX 13.3 ∾ Feminist Psychoanalytic Therapy

Luise Eichenbaum

In 1976, inspired by the second wave of feminism in the United States and England, psychotherapists Luise Eichenbaum and Susie Orbach founded the Women's Therapy Centre (WTC) in London. The orientation of the Centre's therapists is psychoanalytic, but fundamental to their approach is an understanding of how social issues affect women's lives at the individual and institutional level. These social issues include not only gender, but race, class, disability, and sexuality. The WTC makes a concerted effort to provide services to women who do not usually have access to therapy; thus, they reserve half of their slots for women from Black and minority ethnic communities, young women, disabled women, and low-income women. The staff is culturally diverse and they offer therapy in several languages other than English.

When students and I visited the WTC as part of our study-abroad Psychoanalysis and Feminism course, we met in small groups with the analysts. A burning question we had was how they resolved the inconsistencies between Freudianism and feminism. We wondered what it meant to them to practice psychoanalytic therapy within a woman-centered context. One analyst responded by highlighting their diverse training; not all of them were grounded in Freudian psychoanalysis but used the work of other analysts, such as object-relations theorist Melanie Klein, to guide their work. Another offered an example

Continued on next page

distinctly different than non-feminist therapy. Feminist and non-feminist therapists respond differently to items such as, "I consider my clients' problems through a gender-role perspective" (Worell & Johnson, 2001). In one study, clients who had worked with feminist therapists reported that they felt more respected, validated, and empowered than did those who worked with non-feminist therapists (Piran, 1999). In another study, clients reported feeling that sessions with feminist therapists were more egalitarian than sessions with traditional therapists (Rader & Gilbert, 2005).

Though feminist therapists use mostly traditional techniques that they have adapted to be consistent with the principles of feminist therapy, some are employing novel techniques that may not be well-established in traditional psychotherapy but seem particularly suited to the goals of feminist therapy. One such example is exercise therapy. Only since the 1980s has there been much research on the use of exercise in treating mental illness (Rejeski & Thompson, 1993). Some of this research has shown exercise to be effective in treating anxiety and depression (for a review, see Salmon, 2001), both of which are more common in women than in

BOX 13.3 ∽ Feminist Psychoanalytic Therapy *(Concluded)*

Susie Orbach

of how a psychodynamic understanding was often helpful in highlighting unproductive patterns in group therapy: She found that when working with groups of women, men often came to represent the "bad object" and, as a result, the group spent all their time blaming men for their distress instead of focusing on constructive change—both personal and political. In general, these analysts found no contradiction between thinking psychoanalytically about women's internal worlds and thinking as feminists (though they may not label themselves as such) about women's external circumstances.

Five years after founding the WTC, Eichenbaum and Orbach, with Carol Bloom, cofounded the Women's Therapy Centre Institute (WTCI) in New York City. The WTCI offers some group therapy for eating and body-image problems, but focuses primarily on training therapists in the integration of contemporary psychoanalysis and feminism.

For more information about the work of the psychodynamic therapists at the WTC, see Marilyn Lawrence and Marie Maguire's (1999) edited volume, *Psychotherapy with women: Feminist perspectives* (Florence, KY: Taylor & Francis/Routledge).

men. But, it is not merely the antidepressant and anxiety-reducing effects of exercise that make it appealing to some feminist therapists. Women's engagement in exercise can contribute to the goals of feminist therapy because of its empowering effects, and because it can be considered a form of resistance to the oppressive idea that strength and activity are unfeminine (Chrisler & Lamont, 2002).

Although exercise therapy has the potential to benefit women especially, therapists who use it should be aware of cultural factors that may affect individual women's attitudes toward exercise. For example, exercise may be viewed differently by African American women than by Caucasian American women (e.g., Hall, 1998), or by veiled Muslim women than by women who are accustomed to presenting themselves less modestly. Many other things may also affect a woman's receptivity to exercise therapy and what form it might take for her; such factors might include her socioeconomic status (does she have leisure time and access to recreational facilities?), her family situation (if she is a stay-at-home mother of small children, does she have childcare while she exercises?), and her physical condition. Fortunately, because exercise can take so many different forms (walking, swimming, dancing, yoga, or weight-lifting), it can potentially be adapted as a positive form of feminist therapy for almost any woman.

Feminist Therapy for a Diversity of Women

One of the unifying principles of feminist therapy is sensitivity on the part of the therapist to characteristics of the individual such as age, race, ethnicity, sexual orientation, class, and disability (see Figure 13.5). Certainly this is not a complete list of the social contextual factors that influence women's experience, but they are the primary ones addressed in the feminist therapy literature. This section will briefly address just a few of the issues that arise in feminist therapy with three particular populations of women: older women, women of color, and lesbian and bisexual women.

Aging Women

It may seem peculiar to refer to age as a diversity characteristic. Most women (if they are fortunate) will eventually fall into the category of older or elderly. Yet, older women are relatively invisible within the clinical context just as they are in our broader social context. For example, when researchers study body image and eating disorders, they typically focus on young women, even though the physical appearance changes that come with aging are a source of concern for many women (Chrisler & Ghiz, 1993; Hurd, 2000; Midlarsky & Nitzburg, 2008) and eating disorders may be increasing in this group (Gura, 2007). As women in our youth-oriented society reach their 50s and 60s, they may experience what Pearlman (1993) refers to as "late midlife astonishment," a sudden awareness that they in the eyes of the culture they have become stigmatized as unimportant and undesirable, especially because of their perceived loss of physical attractiveness and sexual appeal.

Changes in physical appearance are by no means the only, or most important, potential sources of psychological distress for women as they grow older. As women mature into the middle and latter stages of their lives, they may have to deal with issues that were not as immediate, or perhaps not even relevant, when they were younger. Thinking back to Chapter 11, can

FIGURE 13.5

Feminist therapists are sensitive to personal characteristics of the client such as age, ethnicity, sexual orientation, and social class.

you recall some of these issues? They include retirement, economic stress, loss of a life partner (and diminishing prospects for new partners), loss of peers, physical limitations, caretaking of elderly parents (and perhaps children at the same time), health concerns, living alone, poverty in old age, ageism . . . the list could go on.

Therapists need to be mindful of cohort factors when working with older women. For example, women who are in their eighties today were in their forties during the women's movement of the 1970s; they are likely to have lived a more gender-traditional life than a young therapist and may be somewhat resistant to some feminist ideas. This may present a particular challenge for feminist therapists who encourage women to question traditional gender roles. On the other hand, it would be a mistake to assume that older women will have less-than-positive attitudes toward feminism—just as it is a mistake to assume anything else about them.

Feminist therapists are already well aware of the ways in which gender stereotypes can color perceptions and behaviors; when treating older women they must be equally attuned to effects of age stereotypes. Therapists seeking to understand the sources of an older woman's psychological distress may not think to explore certain possibilities if they rely on age stereotypes. For example, just because a woman is older, and is in a relationship with an older partner, does not mean that she is not being physically or emotionally abused (Bonomi et al., 2007). Just because she is someone's grandmother does not mean she isn't struggling with an addiction to alcohol or other drugs (Katz, 2002). She may be well past menopause and living in a nursing home but that does not mean that her sexual functioning is unimportant to her (Aizenberg et al., 2002). The narrow thinking and patronizing attitude sometimes displayed by traditional health care providers working with older women (Feldman, 1999) are potentially minimized when the provider adopts an age-aware, feminist perspective.

Women of Color

Feminist therapists working with women of color must first understand one basic fact: women "of color" often have common experiences, such as being the target of racial or ethnic prejudice, but the experiences of women identified by this label also vary tremendously (Comas-Díaz & Greene, 1994). Issues of central importance to Native American women will likely be different than the concerns of recent Somali immigrant women. African American women come from a very different cultural background than Asian American women. Latina women living in Texas are worlds apart from Hmong women living in Minnesota. And yet, all of these women—and many more—are typically considered "women of color" in the United States.

Some women of color are more reluctant than White women to seek mental health care. This is sometimes due to cultural norms against seeking help. For example, Asian American women who enter therapy may feel that they are admitting personal failure and bringing shame to their families (Bradshaw, 1994). Women of color may also be hesitant to seek therapy because it is very probable that their only option will be to work with a White therapist of European descent. This therapist probably will have little personal experience with racism, will not likely be fluent in any language other than English, will be highly educated and financially comfortable, and will have only limited knowledge of ethnic or religious cultures other than her own. The therapist is likely to have learned stereotypes about the client's nationality, race, culture, and religion, etc.

Of particular relevance in feminist therapy is the potential gap between feminist ideals—originally formulated by mostly White, middle-class women within a Western European tradition—and the ideas about gender that women of color may bring with them from their cultures of origin. Women from Asian and South Asian origins may subscribe to very rigid gender roles in which girls are considered property from birth and are prepared throughout childhood for an eventual arranged marriage (Jayakar, 1994), whereas Native American women may be accustomed to a variety of flexible gender roles such as the bold and assertive "manly-hearted" role for post-menopausal women among the Canadian Blackfeet and the *two-spirit* role for gender-benders in many North American Indian cultures that was described in Chapter 5 (LaFramboise et al., 1994). Also relevant are the preconceived notions that the therapist may have regarding gender roles in the client's culture of origin. For example, what is your stereotype of gender relations within Latina/o cultures? Do you think of dominant *macho* men and submissive, second-class women? Many scholars have characterized Latina/o cultures in this way, yet some studies have suggested that this stereotype is an exaggeration and overgeneralization (Vasquez, 1994). Feminist therapists must be careful not to assume that they know how a woman of color feels about gender. At the same time, a feminist therapist will be more prepared than a non-feminist therapist to deal with the intersections between gender, race, and ethnicity for women of color.

Lesbian and Bisexual Women

Throughout traditional psychological theory and practice, "healthy" sexuality has been very narrowly defined. Assumptions of heterosexuality and homosexuality permeate the literature (Worell & Remer, 2003; Garnets & Peplau, 2001; Peplau & Garnets, 2000). Heterosexuality has been viewed as normal, while homosexuality and bisexuality have been pathologized. Sexual orientation has been presumed stable across the lifetime, casting a suspicious light on deviations later in life. Gender and sexual orientation have been confounded (much as they are in common stereotypes) such that lesbian women all have been presumed masculine. Sexual orientation has been conceptualized as an attribute of the individual, rather than a variable pattern of erotic and romantic attractions influenced by the social and cultural context of women's lives (Garnets & Peplau, 2001).

Garnets and Peplau (2001) recommend that therapists abandon these outdated models of women's sexual orientation in favor of a model where women's sexual orientation cannot be categorized, nor attributed to a single cause. They suggest that much of the theorizing about sexual orientation has been based on a male norm. As discussed in Chapter 7, women's sexual orientation may be more variable across the lifespan than men's; therefore, therapists should not be surprised if a woman client who felt her sexual identity was well-established ends up confused and distressed when she experiences changes in her sexual attractions. And when a woman does experience such changes, according to Garnets and Peplau, the therapist should not assume that the client's new sexual orientation is her "true" identity.

A Word about Feminist Therapy for Men

Can men benefit from feminist therapy? Several feminist therapists think so, some of whom are men themselves (Remer & Rostosky, 2001a; 2001b). For example, Carlton Parks and his colleagues have described the use of feminist therapy with gay and bisexual adult male sexual assault survivors (Parks et al., 2000–2001). As an approach that is sensitive to sexual orientation, feminist therapy may have more to offer gay and bisexual men than a traditional approach would. Other feminist therapists have suggested that heterosexual men may benefit from a relationship with a female feminist therapist because it can help illuminate some aspects of their relationships with women that a more traditional therapist might miss (Remer & Rostosky, 2001b). Finally, feminist therapists may be able to help increase male clients' awareness of the costs of rigidly conforming to a traditional masculine gender role (Remer & Rostotsky, 2001a).

Evaluating Feminist Therapy

In principle, feminist therapists strive to remedy the shortcomings of traditional therapy, but are they successful? At this point we have very little formal data on the effectiveness of the feminist therapeutic approach (Worell & Johnson, 2001). Anecdotally, feminist clinicians have been very successful at identifying and treating psychological distress specific to women, such as trauma experienced by survivors of sexual assault, incest, and battering—all things that were unnamed and untreated by pre-feminist therapists (Chesler, 2005; Marecek, 1999). Several feminist therapists have published accounts of successful treatment of other kinds of distress as well (Brown, 2006). And, if the international growth of feminist therapy since the 1970s is any indication, there is a substantial demand for woman-friendly, gender-aware, and diversity-sensitive therapy (Chesler, 2005).

It will be increasingly important, however, to generate support for feminist therapy effectiveness that goes beyond mere anecdote. Psychotherapies are typically evaluated by **outcome studies** that measure reductions in personal distress. Judith Worell (2001), a pioneer of feminist therapy, suggests that its assessment should also measure empowerment; that is, she considers feminist therapy successful if it not only makes a woman feel better, but also inspires her to work for social change in her community. In any case, the lack of outcome data regarding feminist therapy raises questions about its viability given that the current trend in healthcare and health insurance is in the direction of evidence-based practice—that is, only providing treatments that have been empirically supported with scientific research (Brown, 2006). If a practitioner provides an empirically supported treatment, such as cognitive-behavioral therapy, and infuses it with a feminist perspective, this is not a problem; however, if a therapist wants to formally and exclusively identify her (or his) treatment as "feminist therapy," there may be problems with the insurance company (Brown, 2006).

Feminist therapy is not without its critics. Even supporters of the approach have highlighted its limitations. Ussher (1992) points out that as highly educated, professionally credentialed individuals, feminist therapists, like traditional therapists, still represent a privileged group. She warns that feminist theory generated by elite academics and activists may not be applicable or accessible to all women. The academics and clinicians who write about and practice feminist therapy constitute a less diverse group than women in general.

Speaking of women in general, some have warned against the tendency of some feminist therapists to think of all women as sharing characteristics unique to their sex (e.g., Cosgrove, 2003). For example, when researchers interviewed a sample of feminist therapists about their practice, many of the implied a belief in a fundamental feminine or womanly nature—referring to "the essence of being a woman" and "the feminine character" (Maracek & Kravetz, 1998, p. 18). Assuming that all women share a uniquely feminine perspective as women ignores the diversity among women. It can contribute to biased attitudes favoring women as a group with special qualities—a kind of benevolent sexism that has costs as well as benefits for women.

Making a Difference

By now you have a better sense of why this chapter began with the idea that traditional clinical practice may be at odds with women's well-being. Feminist therapy is a step in the right direction toward improving the mental health context for women. Equally important is social change that will challenge the perception of women's madness relative to a male norm, and will lead to a reduction in the external factors that contribute to women's real psychological distress.

Transforming Ourselves: Finding (or Becoming) a Feminist Therapist

Not all feminist therapists are alike. In fact, not all therapists who call themselves feminist are necessarily feminist. Why would a therapist adopt the feminist label if his or her work is not truly informed by feminist therapy principles? Hypothetically, an unscrupulous clinician might do so in order to attract business (Caplan, 1992). But it's also possible that a self-named feminist therapist might *seem* not feminist because of different ideas about what feminism means.

There are many flavors of feminism and potentially as many different varieties of feminist therapy. So, how does one find the right feminist therapist? Besides referrals from family, friends, or other clinicians, an individual in search of a feminist therapist could consult some of the several therapist search engine sites on the Internet, most of which list feminist therapy as a specialty option. Some larger metropolitan areas have woman-centered social services that can direct people to feminist clinicians, such as the Feminist Therapy Referral Project (FTRP) in Berkley, CA.

If you are a student of psychology who aspires to become a therapist, consider whether the feminist label may be right for your future practice. At this point in time, there is no centralized institute that trains feminist therapists; when such training is available, it tends to be in the form of sporadic opportunities, such as continuing education courses or conference workshops (Brown, 2010). Still, given that nearly all of the founders of feminist therapy practice are still alive today (and are still writing and teaching about feminist therapy), future feminist therapists may yet have the opportunity to learn directly from first generation predecessors (Brown, 2010).

Transforming Social Relations: Challenging the "Crazy Woman" Stereotype

How many times have you heard someone make a wisecrack about women being "nuts" when they are "on the rag"? Have you ever had a guy (or his new girlfriend) tell you with a shudder that all of his ex-girlfriends were "psycho"? Do you and your friends agree that your mothers are all "crazy"? The idea that women as a group are mentally ill permeates our culture. From now on, pay attention to the examples you encounter in everyday conversation, movies and television, crime reports, advice columns, and stand-up comedy routines etc. Take note when women's behavior is pathologized relative to a male standard of rationality and wellness. And then: Challenge it! Challenge yourself and your acquaintances to steer clear of the loony women comments and jokes. Treat women's perspectives and experiences with the respect that they deserve (including your own, if you are a woman). Question the "experts" who would have us believe that women are irrational, illogical, too dependent, and emotionally overwrought.

Another way to challenge the crazy woman stereotype is to become an informed advocate for women who *are* mentally ill. One place to start is the National Alliance on Mental Illness (NAMI), a grassroots organization that has provided more than 30 years of support, education, advocacy, and research to help mentally ill individuals. NAMI's Web site (www.nami.org) offers numerous ways to get involved, such as becoming one of their "stigma-busters," currently more than 20,000 individuals across the world who speak out against inaccurate and harmful representations of mental illness in media in an effort to reduce the prejudice and discrimination commonly faced by mentally ill individuals and their families.

Transforming Society: Promoting Women's Psychological Well-Being

Clearly, women's well-being is intimately tied to their social circumstances. Sexism, racism, poverty, violence—all of these are significant contributors to women's psychological distress. Women have long been told that the remedy for their distress is individual change (or medication or hospitalization), but no amount of therapy for an individual woman is going to alleviate her symptoms if the source of the problem is economic inequality, sexual harassment, or domestic abuse. Feminist therapists encourage their clients to seek relief through social change. By engaging in activism to address the social problems that women face, you, too, can work to promote women's mental health.

Exploring Further

∾

Ballou, M. (2008) (Ed). *Feminist therapy theory and practice: A contemporary perspective*. New York: Springer.

Diverse contributors discuss key issues in feminist therapy and how they are played out in the actual practice of therapy.

Chesler, P. (2005). *Women and madness* (Revised and updated for the first time in 30 years). New York: Palgrave Macmillan.

First published in 1972, this groundbreaking book challenges traditional definitions of madness and critiques the use of psychiatry as a form of social control over women.

Girl, Interrupted

Showalter, E. (1986). *The female malady: Women, madness, and English culture, 1830–1980*. New York: Pantheon Books.

This book explores sexism embedded in psychiatric practices from the nineteenth and twentieth centuries including institutionalization, medication, and psychosurgery.

The Magdalene Sisters

Worell, J., & Remer, P. (2003). *Feminist perspectives in therapy: Empowering diverse women*. Hoboken, NJ: Wiley.

Two pioneering feminist therapists show how feminist therapy is not just about adjustment, it's about empowerment.

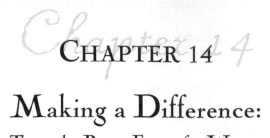

CHAPTER 14

Making a Difference:
Toward a Better Future for Women

- **Contemporary Feminism**
- **Imagery and Attitudes**
    Negative Images and Stereotypes of Feminists
    Is Feminism for Women Only?
    Women's Attitudes toward Feminism

- **Feminist Psychology and Social Change**
    The Changing Face of Psychology
    Imagine a World . . .
    What Can One Student Do?

*T*hroughout history, women have struggled to have their voices heard and their contributions to society accepted. For over 150 years, the women's movement has provided a powerful force for change.

The first wave of feminist activists included the suffragists who achieved the vote for women in the early 1900s. The second wave, whose activism began in the 1960s, worked on issues such as reproductive rights, workplace equality, sexism in the media, nonsexist child raising, the integration of women into science and politics, and an end to violence against women. Today, third-wave feminists continue the tradition, working on some of the same inequities that second-wave feminism tackled, and adding new ones: the continued objectification of women, reproductive rights in a high-tech era, global trafficking in girls and women, LGBTQ rights, and many more.

Contemporary Feminism

Feminists are a diverse group on dimensions such as nationality, ethnicity, social class, and religion. This diversity is a strength because it encourages people to work for social change in many areas and to use a variety of strategies. Throughout this book, we have seen that the problems faced by working-class women are quite different from those faced by professional women. Older women experience different forms of sexism than younger women. Women who mother run into a different kind of stereotyping and inequality than those who do not. Anyone whose sexual orientation is different from the heterosexual norm may encounter prejudice and discrimination on that basis. People whose bodies are marked by difference are beginning to claim a right to their own dimensions of diversity, as shown by activism for the rights of intersex and transgender people. And women of color have taken their rightful place in feminist leadership and activism. One Asian American third-wave feminist, Jee Yeun Lee, eloquently stated the importance of women-of-color perspectives:

> Women of color do not struggle in feminist movements simply to add cultural diversity, to add the viewpoints of different kinds of women. Women of color feminist theories challenge the fundamental premises of feminism, such as the very definition of "women," and call for recognition of the constructed racial nature of all experiences of gender. . . . These days, whenever someone says the word "women" to me, my mind goes blank. What "women"? What is this "women" thing you're talking about? Does that mean me? Does that mean my mother, my roommates, the white woman next door, the checkout clerk at the supermarket, my aunts in Korea, half the world's population? . . . This thing called "feminism" takes a great deal of hard work, and I think this is one of the primary hallmarks of young feminists' activism today: We realize that coming together and working together are by no means natural and easy (Lee, 1995).

Respect for differences is a cornerstone of feminist philosophy and activism. Feminists also have other shared values and goals. At the most basic level, a feminist is one who believes in the worth and value of women. As a 1970s bumper sticker proclaimed, "Feminism is the radical notion that women are people." Moreover, feminists recognize that social change is necessary and that no one can create social justice by herself. They believe that people should work together to change society so that women can lead more secure, satisfying, and fulfilling lives. This belief in **collective action,** or group solidarity toward social change, differentiates feminism from just individual women achieving success.

Increasingly, feminism is a global social movement. International conferences like the landmark Beijing Conference of 1995 and Beijing + 15, a 2010 forum, have brought women together to learn from each other about the particular forms that patriarchy takes in each society and to share effective strategies for change. And international activism is growing, based on the recognition that the unfulfilled promise of human rights for women is one of the biggest issues of the twenty-first century (see Box 14.1).

Box 14.1 ∾ Half the Sky: Turning Oppression into Opportunity for Women Worldwide

Half the Sky is a call to arms, a call for help, a call for contributions, but also a call for volunteers. It asks us to open our eyes to this enormous humanitarian issue . . . I really do think this is one of the most important books I have ever reviewed.

—*Carolyn See, Washington Post*

Nicholas Kristof and Sheryl WuDunn are journalists, Pulitzer Prize winners, and most importantly, strong advocates for women's rights across the globe. In 2009, they published *Half the Sky: Turning Oppression into Opportunity for Women Worldwide*. The phrase "half the sky" comes from a Chinese proverb, "Women hold up half the sky."

In the book, Kristof and WuDunn tell the stories of courageous women in the developing world. These women have experienced some of the most egregious forms of violence and oppression, from trafficking and forced prostitution to genital cutting and rape. Their book also brings attention to the issue of maternal mortality, as thousands of women die needlessly each year from inadequate access to medical care. Although the stories are anecdotal, they serve as a powerful reminder of the kinds of experiences that women are subjected to on a daily basis in countries hampered by violence and poverty.

Probably the most important contribution that Kristof and WuDunn have made to improving the lives of women is their advocacy for "outsiders" (us!) to get involved in the education and economic empowerment of women. For only a few dollars, someone could sponsor the education of a young girl or provide microcredit to a woman to start her own business. Such small actions can dramatically improve the lives of women across the globe.

In addition to encouraging activism through the book, Kristof and WuDunn also maintain a Web site, www.halftheskymovement.org, which serves as a hub of information for people who are looking to get involved in activism to end poverty and violence against women. The Web site provides links to more than 40 organizations that deal with violence against women, economic empowerment, education, maternal mortality, sex trafficking, and humanitarian relief. They also encourage people to use social media such as Facebook and Twitter to get the message out.

In September 2009, Kristof and WuDunn spoke to government representatives and the media in Washington DC about their book and stressed the need to make improving the lives of women across the globe a top priority. Kristof stated, "There is a tipping point on this issue . . . now, increasingly, the role of women is seen, not only as a good thing to do but as a security issue as well as an economic issue, and all these things are coming together and I think, making it the time to address this truly as the cause of our time."

Sources: Half the Sky Movement. www.halftheskymovement.org "Nick Kristof and Sheryl WuDunn bring their Half the Sky global women's movement to Washington." *White House Correspondents: Insider.* Available at: http://www.whitehouse correspondentsweekendinsider.com/2009/09/12/nick-kristof-and-sheryl-wudunn-bring-their-half-the-sky-global-women%E2%80%99s-movement-to-washington/ Contributed by Annie B. Fox.

Imagery and Attitudes

Like other progressive movements for social justice, feminism has met with resistance from those who benefit from inequality. Each time that feminist perspectives have gained power, there has been a ***backlash***—attempts to put women, and particularly feminists, back in their place (Faludi, 1991). The backlash has taken different forms at different times in history, but some characteristic patterns emerge repeatedly. One form of backlash is to label feminists and their ideas as crazy. As noted in Chapter 13, women until recently risked being labeled mad if they wanted to think or act independently. Another form of backlash is to claim that feminism is a mere quarrel among women, of no importance to men or society in general. Let's look more closely at each of these forms of resistance to feminism.

Negative Images and Stereotypes of Feminists

When first-wave feminists began organizing to win the right to vote, political cartoonists depicted them in ways that seem very familiar today. Figure 14.1 shows suffragists as ugly, cigar-smoking, angry women who foist their babies off on men. Their exposed legs represent their dangerously out-of-control sexuality. They are labeled as brassy, sharp-tongued man-tamers.

In the 1970s, these images and stereotypes resurfaced. The media image of second-wave feminists was negative:

> News reports and opinion columnists created a new stereotype, of fanatics, "braless bubbleheads," Amazons, "the angries," and "a band of wild lesbians." The result is

FIGURE 14.1   Backlash against first-wave feminists.

that we all know what feminists are. They are shrill, overly aggressive, man-hating, ball-busting, selfish, hairy, extremist, deliberately unattractive women with absolutely no sense of humor who see sexism at every turn. They make men's testicles shrivel up to the size of peas, they detest the family and think all children should be deported or drowned. Feminists are relentless, unforgiving, and unwilling to bend or compromise; they are single-handedly responsible for the high divorce rate, the shortage of decent men and the unfortunate proliferation of Birkenstocks in America (Douglas, 1994, p. 7).

By the 1980s, the media began to declare feminism outdated, claiming that equal rights had been fully achieved, society was now in a "post feminist" era, and women were abandoning feminism because it had terrible costs. In the 1980s version of backlash, everything from infertility to the breakdown of society was blamed on feminism, and its time was declared long past (Faludi, 1991).

Today, the public image of feminists has both positive and negative aspects. Feminists are viewed positively as women working together to achieve goals and negatively as man-hating extremists. Even when people do not hold negative beliefs themselves, they think that others do. In one study, 171 women completed measures of attitudes toward feminism for themselves and also were asked to complete the measures as they thought other people would. Both feminists and non-feminists believed that others have negative views of feminists and consider them more likely to be lesbian than straight (Ramsey et al., 2007). Men's attitudes are mixed, too. Interviews with British male high-school students and adult men revealed that they had "Jekyll and Hyde" views: Feminists are reasonable women who just want equality *and* ugly, man-hating lesbians who go around "banging and shouting" and just want men to "jump in the river." Surprisingly, many men held *both* these contradictory views (Edley & Wetherell, 2001).

A recurring theme in these stereotypes is that feminists are man-haters. Psychologist Kristin Anderson and her colleagues decided to get some empirical evidence on this claim (Anderson et al., 2009). In an ethnically diverse sample of nearly 500 college students, they found that feminists had significantly *less* hostility toward men than non-feminists.

Conservatives with influence in the media play to all the negative stereotypes. For example, the Catholic Archbishop of Boston denounced feminism as a threat to the Church and society (McNamara, 2004). Two days after the 9/11 tragedy, televangelists Jerry Falwell and Pat Robertson famously concurred that "pagans, and the abortionists, and the feminists, and the gays and the lesbians," had contributed to the attacks by undermining moral standards and causing God to stop protecting America. In the news media, conservative commentators try to scare men and turn women away from working together for equality by referring to "feminazis" and characterizing any criticism of the status quo as "male-bashing." A favorite right-wing term is "militant feminist," though what it means is unclear. Personally, I have never met a feminist with an assault weapon or heard of any feminist armies about to march on Congress or the guys' locker room. Feminism, of course, is not about "bashing" or making war on men; it is about working to change the social structural, interactional, and individual levels of the gender system that disadvantage girls and women.

Is Feminism for Women Only?

One of the ways that feminists and their ideas are trivialized is to treat equality as an issue that only women need to care about. I remember when sexual harassment on college campuses was first defined and specified as a violation of academic integrity. Across the country, universities began to develop sexual harassment policies and procedures and disseminate them to faculty. Each time my university mailed an informational brochure to faculty, I would find a dozen or more copies of the brochure stuffed in my mailbox. What happened was that my male colleagues would glance at it in the mailroom, think "women" and immediately pass it on to me! After all, I was the "woman person" and the token feminist on the faculty.

If it weren't so annoying this might have been funny. I certainly wasn't harassing anyone, and was already familiar with the guidelines. The professors who really needed the information—those who might have to counsel a student who'd been harassed or whose own behavior might step over the line at some point—were dismissing the need to inform themselves by classifying the problem as a "woman's issue."

If feminism is only for women, the next step in dismissing it is to portray women as fighting with each other over it (Douglas, 1994). Any woman who attacks the ideals and practices of feminism is almost guaranteed a hearing in the news media. It is even better if she claims to be a feminist, and it doesn't seem to matter if her expertise on the issues is minimal. This prevents male social theorists and political analysts from having to study and consider feminist ideas themselves and allows them to claim that sensible women see through feminism and reject it.

In the 1970s, the media ignored the many groups of women working collectively for women's rights. Instead, they focused on Gloria Steinem, a feminist journalist and activist, versus Phyllis Schlafly, a conservative activist who called feminists a "bunch of bitter women seeking a constitutional cure for their personal problems." The effect was to make feminism seem like a catfight between two fanatical women rather than a widespread social movement. National media such as *Time* and *Newsweek* referred to the debate over the Equal Rights Amendment to the U.S. Constitution as "women versus women" and "the war between the women." The amendment was never passed. Today, the catfight is still used as a way for the news media to trivialize women's struggles for equality and power. For example, conservative media celebrities such as Dr. Laura get attention by pitting stay-at-home and working mothers against each other.

Women's Attitudes toward Feminism

The societal images of feminism and feminists clearly influence women. On the one hand, studies during the 1980s and 1990s show that college women describe feminists as strong, caring, capable, open-minded, knowledgeable, and intelligent (Berryman-Fink & Verderber, 1985; Buhl, 1989). On the other hand, being labeled a feminist brings a certain stigma. When college women were asked to report their own beliefs and those of a "typical feminist," even those who identified themselves as feminists felt that the typical feminist was more extreme in beliefs than they themselves were (Liss et al., 2000). Many women are reluctant to label themselves feminists. In one survey, 78 percent of college women said they were not feminists, although the majority agreed with some or most of the goals of the women's movement (Liss et al., 2001). And even the feminists reported that they didn't always admit to being feminists in public!

Despite the negative stereotypes, some women do identify themselves as feminists and support collective action for social change on behalf of women. Psychologists Miriam Liss and Mindy Erchull and their colleagues have explored feminist identity and its correlates. For example, they conducted several studies of the factors that predict whether a woman will choose to identify as a feminist. Exposure to feminist ideas, having a generally positive view of feminists, and recognizing that discrimination exists are important (Liss et al., 2001). In a study of 282 women college students, they found that life experiences such as having a feminist mother, taking a women's studies course, and having personal experience with sexism predicted liberal beliefs. In turn, these beliefs led to identifying oneself as a feminist and believing in collective action (Nelson et al., 2008).

I invite you to think critically about the ways that feminists and feminism are portrayed in our society. Contrary to stereotype, feminists are not monsters. In a study of over 650 women who filled in an online questionnaire about their feminist beliefs and identity, those who called themselves feminists acknowledged the existence of sexism, perceived the current gender system as unjust, and believed that women should work together to change it (Liss & Erchull, 2010). In addition, those who call themselves feminists support the goals of the women's movement and tend not to hold conservative beliefs (Liss et al., 2001). They neither hate men nor idealize them (Anderson et al., 2009). Feminists are more likely than non-feminists to see through and reject unrealistic ideals for women—such as the overemphasis on extreme thinness, appearance, and romantic relationships (Hurt et al., 2007). Personally, I am proud to call myself a feminist, and I find it disturbing that the media so often trivialize and distort feminism and its goals. Consider this question: Whose interests does it serve if a movement to end sexism is made to seem irrational, destructive, and futile?

Despite the attacks, feminism is a vital arena of theory and research. Women's rights are human rights. They are so important that, far from holding to an inflexible party line, feminists have always encouraged debate and a plurality of viewpoints. In writing this book, I have tried to present a variety of feminist perspectives with the goal of encouraging you to think critically about them.

Feminist Psychology and Social Change

The second wave of the women's movement had important effects on psychology. One of the most basic changes was the number of women in psychology and their status within the field. Even more important than numbers is the influence of feminist theory and research.

The Changing Face of Psychology

Only a few short years ago, psychologists who happened to be women could not get hired by high-status universities and were rarely taken seriously as scientists (Marecek et al., 2002). Ethnic minority psychologists, too, were marginalized (Jenkins et al., 2002). Today, women earn the majority of higher degrees in psychology. Psychologists who are women and ethnic minorities lead well-established professional organizations, produce many books and journals, and participate in every aspect of psychological research, education, and practice.

I saw a small example of the changing gender norms within psychology recently. At my university, there are regular lunchtime research talks for faculty and graduate students. At one, the speakers were a married couple (with different last names) who do their research jointly. With them were their two children, a 4-year-old son and a 1-month-old infant. The man started their research presentation, while Mom took the children to play outside. Sexist? Not exactly. Halfway through the talk, she returned, Dad took the kids outside, and she concluded the presentation and discussion of their research. A lunchtime psychology program became an example of collaborative research, shared parenting, and the balancing act of multiple roles for both women and men.

Progress is uneven, however. It will probably be a while before such a scene occurs regularly enough that it is taken for granted.

Imagine a World . . .

Imagine a world that is free of gender-based violence against girls and women. Imagine a world where husbands do half the housework, every child is protected from sexual abuse, and no old woman is forced to end her life in poverty. Imagine a world where half of the CEOs, judges, generals, and members of parliament or congress are women—in every country. What would the world be like if all pregnancies were chosen and all children wanted? If the human capacity for emotion and empathy were considered manly as well as womanly? If all body shapes and sizes were accepted, and no woman felt she had to starve herself to look good?

It's true that none of these visions is close to becoming reality. But nobody expected it would be easy to remedy the patriarchal power imbalances that shape women's lives. The psychology of women and gender has made a huge contribution toward a more just society. Its contribution began with naming androcentrism and sexism in psychological theories and research. It continued with the development of many new research topics and theories. Think back for a moment to the hundreds of research articles described in this book. These are just a sample of the scientific research that forms the basis of feminist psychology. Feminist psychologists also founded organizations (such as Division 35 and AWP), started new research journals, and developed feminist approaches to counseling and therapy.

However, there are signs that women and feminist perspectives have not yet been fully integrated into psychology. Publishing one's research in a psychology of women journal still may have less impact than if it were published in a more mainstream journal. Despite the wealth of feminist books and journals, college textbooks and course syllabi too often still exclude gender, women, ethnicity, and diversity (Bronstein & Quina, 2003). The continued lack of integration of feminist scholarship is a serious problem, because throughout history, women's contributions have often been curtailed by their exclusion from powerful positions and erased by their omission from the historical record.

What Can One Student Do?

> Never doubt that a small group of thoughtful, committed people could change the world. Indeed, it's the only thing that ever has.
>
> — *Margaret Mead*

Over the years, I have encountered some students who seem disconnected from their courses in psychology. Although they are psychology majors, they don't seem to feel a part of their major or department, and they don't see themselves as active shapers of their own educational experience. I believe that this is partly a legacy of psychology's past as a science defined and controlled by a dominant social group. Today, the entire field of psychology is becoming more diverse, and you can participate in creating a psychology of all people.

You can make a difference as a student by contributing to research and by using your knowledge of the psychology of women and gender to work for change. When you have a choice of topic, you can write term papers on women or gender in your psychology, history, and literature courses. You can do an independent study or thesis on women and gender. You can ask questions in class when women are excluded or trivialized in readings and lectures. These strategies can help raise awareness for yourself and others.

You can connect with the women's center on your campus. If your campus has no women's center or women's studies program, start asking why. By taking courses that focus on women and gender, and recommending them to others, you can show the administration that there is a demand for this knowledge.

You can join an organization for women's equality, such as the National Organization for Women (www.NOW.org), or the Feminist Majority Foundation (www.feminist.org). Your dues will support activism on behalf of all women, and you will be kept updated on issues of gender equity. You can also volunteer your time. Many feminist organizations have internship opportunities for college students—just check their Web sites for information. Become a Big Sister or Big Brother to a girl or boy in need of guidance (www.bbbs.org). Or do an internship or volunteer work at a rape crisis hotline or domestic violence shelter in your community, or help out an elderly woman or single mom who needs assistance.

Your knowledge of the psychology of women and gender can help in your career planning. If you are planning to apply to graduate schools in psychology (or any other area), look carefully at the number of women faculty in the programs you consider, and how many have tenure. Look for courses on women and gender in the catalog, and find out whether there are women's studies and ethnic studies programs and a women's center. When visiting, ask about the level of support for feminist scholarship on campus. Psychology students (both male and female) can find information and support on a variety of gender issues by joining the Association for Women in Psychology (www.awpsych.org) or Division 35 of APA (www.apa.org/about/division/div35.html) as student affiliates. These organizations allow students to become part of networks of people with similar concerns. Through organizations like these, you can develop friendships with others who share your values and work together for social change.

If you are seeking employment after graduation, look carefully at the gender-related policies and family sensitivity of the companies you consider. Do they have flex-time, on-site day care, parental leave, and benefits for same-sex partners? Does the health care plan cover women's reproductive needs? What proportion of management are women? How often do women get promoted from inside the company? Is there ethnic and racial diversity? What is the company's record on sexual harassment complaints? Ask questions based on your knowledge of the psychology of women and gender.

One of the most important things you can do is to continue to educate yourself on the issues facing girls and women. Even though you have completed this book and your current course, continue to challenge the androcentrism in your education and the sexism in the world around you. This will help you think critically about what you read and hear in other textbooks, classes, and the media. It also will help you become an equal partner in relationships, an effective employee, and a responsible citizen after graduation.

Psychological research and theory have provided a wealth of evidence and reason on why women want and deserve full human rights. I offer the research and theory in this book as a resource and a gift. This gift can be made meaningful only by the one who receives it. How will you use your knowledge of psychology to make a difference?

References

2009 College Bound Seniors Average SAT Scores. (2010). Retrieved February 17, 2010, from www.fairtest.org/files/2009%20SAT%20Scores.pdf

Aarons, S. J., & Jenkins, R. (2002). Sex, pregnancy, and contraception-related motivators and barriers among Latino and African-American youth in Washington D.C. *Sex Education, 2,* 5–30.

ABC News. (2003). American porn: Corporate America is profiting from porn—quietly. Retrieved January 28, 2005, from http://abcnews.go.com

Abelson, R. (2004, June 23). Bias suit a hope to move up at Wal-Mart. *The New York Times,* pp. C1, C8.

Abortion foes win a round in health overhaul. (2010). Retrieved July 19, 2010, from http://news.yahoo.com/s/ap/20100719/ap_on_bi_ge/us_health_overhaul_abortion

Abramson, L. Y., & Alloy, L. B. (2006). Cognitive vulnerability to depression: Current status and developmental origins. In T. E. Joiner, J. S. Brown, & J. Kistner (Eds.), *The interpersonal, cognitive, and social nature of depression* (pp. 83–100). Mahwah, NJ: Erlbaum.

Abramson, P. E., Goldberg, P. A., Greenberg, J. H., & Abramson, L. M. (1977). The talking platypus phenomenon: Competency ratings as a function of sex and professional status. *Psychology of Women Quarterly, 2,* 114–124.

Abusharaf, R. M. (1998, March/April). Unmasking tradition. *The Sciences,* 22–27.

Adamczyk, A. (2008). The effects of religious contextual norms, structural constraints, and personal religiosity on abortion decisions. *Social Science Research, 37*(2), 657–672.

Adams, R. C. (1997). Friendship patterns among older women. In J. M. Coyle (Ed.), *Handbook on women and aging* (pp. 400–417). Westport, CT: Greenwood Press.

Addis, M. E., & Mahalik, J. R. (2003). Men, masculinity, and the contexts of help seeking. *American Psychologist, 58,* 5–14.

Ader, D. N., & Johnson, S. B. (1994). Sample description, reporting and analysis of sex in psychological research: A look at APA and APA division journals in 1990. *American Psychologist, 49,* 216–218.

Affonso, D. D., & Mayberry, L. J. (1989). Common stressors reported by a group of childbearing American women. In P. N. Stern (Ed.), *Pregnancy and parenting* (pp. 41–55). New York: Hemisphere.

AFP. (2010, June 4). Cosmetics flood Iran's markets. *The Express Tribune.* Retrieved January 27, 2011, from http://tribune.com.pk/story/18445/cosmetics-flood-irans-markets/

Agrawal, A., Jacobson, K. C., Gardner, C. O., Prescott, C. A., & Kendler, K. S. (2004). Population-based twin study of sex differences in depressive symptoms. *Twin Research, 7,* 176–181.

Aizenberg, D., Weizman, A., & Barak, Y. (2002). Attitudes toward sexuality among nursing home residents. *Sexuality and Disability, 20,* 185–189.

Alan Guttmacher Institute. (2002). *Facts in brief: Teenagers' sexual and reproductive health.* New York: Author.

Aldrich, N., & Tenenbaum, H. (2006). Sadness, anger, and frustration: Gendered patterns in early adolescents' and their parents' emotion talk. *Sex Roles, 55*(11–12), 775–785. doi:10.1007/s11199-006-9131-y.

Algoe, S. B., Buswell, B. N., & DeLamater, J. D. (2000). Gender and job status as contextual cues for the interpretation of facial expression of emotion. *Sex Roles, 42,* 183–208.

Alindogan-Medina, N. (2006). Women's studies: A struggle for a better life. In M. Crawford & R. Unger (Eds.), *In our own words: Writings from women's lives* (2nd ed., pp. 45–57). Long Grove, IL: Waveland Press.

Almquist, E. M. (1989). The experiences of minority women in the United States: Intersections of race, gender, and class. In J. Freeman (Ed.), *Women: A feminist perspective* (4th ed., pp. 414–445). Mountain View, CA: Mayfield Publishing.

Altman, M. (1984). Everything they always wanted you to know. In C. S. Vance (Ed.), *Pleasure and danger: Exploring female sexuality* (pp. 115–130). Boston: Routledge & Kegan Paul.

Alvarez, M. J., & Garcia-Marques, L. (2009). Condom inclusion in cognitive representations of sexual encounters. *Journal of Sex Research, 45,* 358–370.

Amaro, H., Raj, A., & Reed, E. (2001). Women's sexual health: The need for feminist analyses in public health in the decade of behavior. *Psychology of Women Quarterly, 25*, 324–334.

Amato, P. R., Booth, A., Johnson, D. R., & Rogers, S. J. (2007). *Alone together: How marriage in America is changing.* Cambridge, MA: Harvard University Press.

Amato, P. R., & Previti, D. (2003). People's reasons for divorcing: Gender, social class, the life course, and adjustment. *Journal of Family Issues, 24*, 602–626.

American Association of University Women Educational Foundation. (2001). *Hostile hallways: Bullying, teasing and sexual harassment in school.* Washington, DC: Author.

American Psychiatric Association. (1994). *Diagnostic and statistical manual of mental disorders* (3rd ed.). Washington, DC: Author.

American Psychiatric Association. (2000). *Diagnostic and statistical manual of mental disorders: DSM-IV-TR* (4th ed.).Washington, DC: Author.

American Psychiatric Association. (2000). *Diagnostic and statistical manual of psychological disorders* (4th edition, text revision). Washington, DC: Author.

American Psychological Association. (2007). Task force on the sexualization of girls. Washington, DC: Author.

American Psychological Association. (2010). Race/ethnicity of doctorate recipients in psychology in the past ten years: 2010. Retrieved from http://www.apa.org/workforce/publications/10-race/index.aspx

Amp up before you score. (2009, October 12). *The Huffington Post.* Retrieved October 15, 2009, from http://www.huffingtonpost.com/2009/10/12/amp-up-before-you-score-p_n_317716.html

Anderson, C. A., Berkowitz, L., Donnerstein, E., Huesmann, L. R., Johnson, J. D., Linz, D., et al. (2003). The influence of media violence on youth. *Psychological Science in the Public Interest, 4*, 81–110.

Anderson, C. A., & Carnagey, N. L. (2009). Causal effects of violent sports video games on aggression: Is it competitiveness or violent content? *Journal of Experimental Social Psychology, 45*, 731–739.

Anderson, C. A., Sakamoto, A., Gentile, D. A., Ihori, N., Shibuya, A., Yukawa, S., et al. (2008). Longitudinal effects of violent video games on aggression in Japan and the United States. *Pediatrics, 122*, 1067–1072.

Anderson, K. A., & Hiersteiner, C. (2008). Recovering from childhood sexual abuse: Is a "storybook ending" possible? *The American Journal of Family Therapy, 36*, 413–424.

Anderson, K. J., Kanner, M., & Elsayegh, N. (2009). Are feminists man haters? Feminists' and nonfeminists' attitudes toward men. *Psychology of Women Quarterly, 33*, 216–224.

Anderson, K. J., & Leaper, C. (1998). Meta-analysis of gender effects on conversational interruptions: Who, what, when, where, and how. *Sex Roles, 39*, 225–252.

Anderson, K. L., & Umberson, D. (2001). Gendering violence: Masculinity and power in men's accounts of domestic violence. *Gender & Society, 15*, 358–380.

Anderssen, N. (2002). Does contact with lesbians and gays lead to friendlier attitudes? A two year longitudinal study. *Journal of Community and Applied Social Psychology, 12*, 124–136.

Angless, T., Maconachie, M., & Van Zyl, M. (1998). Battered women seeking solutions: A South African study. *Violence Against Women, 4*, 637–658.

Aosved, A. C., & Long, P. J. (2006). Co-occurrence of rape myth acceptance, sexism, racism, homophobia, ageism, classism, and religious intolerance. *Sex Roles, 55*, 481–492.

Appignanesi, L. (2008). *Mad, bad, and sad: A history of women and the mind doctors from 1800 to the present.* London, UK: Virago.

Apuzzo, V. M. (2001). A call to action. In D. C. Kimmel & D. L. Martin (Eds.), *Midlife and aging in gay America: Proceedings of the SAGE conference 2000* (pp. 1–11). New York: Harrington Park Press.

Arbuckle, J., & Williams, B. D. (2003). Students' perceptions of expressiveness: Age and gender effects on teacher evaluations. *Sex Roles, 49*, 507–516.

Archer, D., Iritani, B., Kimes, D. D., & Barrios, M. (1983). Faceism: Five studies of sex differences in facial prominence. *Journal of Personality and Social Psychology, 45*, 725–735.

Archer, J. (2000). Sex differences in physical aggression to partners: A meta-analytic review. *Psychological Bulletin, 126*, 651–680.

Archer, J. (2006). Cross-cultural differences in physical aggression between partners: A social role analysis. *Personality and Social Psychology Review, 10*, 133–153.

Arendell, T. (1997). A social constructionist approach to parenting. In R. Arendell (Ed.), *Contemporary parenting: Challenges and issues* (pp. 1–44). Thousand Oaks, CA: Sage.

Arima, A. N. (2003). Gender stereotypes in Japanese television advertisements. *Sex Roles, 49*, 81–90.

Armenta, B. E. (2010). Stereotype boost and stereotype threat effects: The moderating role of ethnic identification. *Cultural Diversity and Ethnic Minority Psychology, 16*, 94–99.

Arnold, D. H., & Doctoroff, G. L. (2003). The early education of socioeconomically disadvantaged children. In S. T. Fiske, D. L. Schacter, & C. Zahn-Waxler (Eds.), *Annual review of psychology: Vol. 54* (pp. 517–545). Palo Alto, CA: Annual Reviews.

Arnold, S. C. (1994). Transforming body image through women's wilderness experiences. In Cole, E. Erdman, & E. Rothblum (Eds.), *Wilderness therapy for women: The power of adventure* (pp. 43–54). New York: Hayworth Press.

Aronson, J., Lustina, M. J., Good, C., Keough, K., Steele, C. M., & Brown, J. (1999). When White men can't do math: Necessary and sufficient factors in stereotype threat. *Journal of Experimental Social Psychology, 35,* 29–46.

Ascher-Svanum, H. & Sobel, T. S. (1989). Caregivers of mentally ill adults: A woman's agenda. *Hospital and Community Psychiatry, 40,* 843–845.

Ashcraft, C. (2008). So much more than "Sex Ed": Teen sexuality as vehicle for improving academic success and democratic education for diverse youth. *American Education Research Journal, 45,* 631–667.

Ault, A. (1996). Ambiguous identity in an unambiguous sex/gender structure: The case of bisexual women. *The Sociological Quarterly, 37,* 449–463.

Avis, N. (2003). Depression during the menopausal transition. *Psychology of Women Quarterly, 27,* 91–100.

Avis, N. E., & McKinlay, S. M. (1991). A longitudinal analysis of women's attitudes toward the menopause: Results from the Massachusetts women's health study. *Maturitas, 13,* 65–79.

Baber, K. M., & Allen, K. R. (1992). *Women and families: Feminist reconstructions.* New York: Guilford.

Bachar, K., & Koss, M. (2001). Rape. In J. Worell (Ed.), *Encyclopedia of women and gender* (pp. 893–903). San Diego, CA: Academic Press.

Bachrach, L. L. (1984). Deinstitutionalization and women: Assessing the consequences of public policy. *American Psychologist, 39,* 1171–1177.

Baculinao, E. (2004, September 14). *China grapples with legacy of its "missing girls": Disturbing demographic imbalance spurs drive to change age-old practices.* Retrieved September 21, 2004, from http://www.msnbc.com/id/5953508/print/1/displaymode/1098/

Bailey, D., & Jackson, J. (2005). The occupation of household financial management among lesbian couples. *Journal of Occupational Science, 12,* 57–68.

Bailey, M. J. (2009). What is sexual orientation and do women have one? *Sexual and Relationship Therapy, 4,* 377–390.

Baker, M. W. (2007). Elder mistreatment: Risk, vulnerability, and early mortality. *Journal of the American Psychiatric Nurses Association, 12,* 313–321.

Baker, R., Kiger, G., & Riley, P. J. (1996). Time, dirt, and money: The effects of gender, gender ideology, and type of earner marriage on time, household-task, and economic satisfaction among couples with children. *Journal of Social Behavior and Personality, 11,* 161–177.

Ballou, M., & Brown, L. S. (Eds.). (2002). *Rethinking mental health and disorder: Feminist perspectives.* New York: Guildford.

Ballou, M., Hill, M., & West, C. (Eds.) (2008). *Feminist therapy theory and practice.* New York: Springer.

Bandura, A. (1965). Influence of model's reinforcement contingencies on the acquisition of imitative responses. *Journal of Personality and Social Psychology, 1,* 589–595.

Bandura, A., & Walters, R. H. (1963). *Social learning and personality development.* New York: Holt, Rinehart & Winston.

Banner, L. (2006). *American beauty: A social history . . . through two centuries of the American idea, ideal, and image of the beautiful woman.* Los Angeles: Figueroa Press.

Bannon, L. (2000, March). More kids' marketers pitch number of single-sex products. *The Wall Street Journal,* pp. B1, 4.

Banyard, V. L., Williams, L. M., Siegel, J. A., & West, C. M. (2002). Childhood sexual abuse in the lives of Black women: Risk and resilience in a longitudinal study. *Women & Therapy, 25,* 45–58.

Barak, A., Feldman, S., & Noy, A. (1991). Traditionality of children's interests as related to their parents' gender stereotypes and traditionality of occupations. *Sex Roles, 24,* 511–524.

Baretto, M., & Ellmers, N. (2005). The burden of benevolent sexism: How it contributes to the maintenance of gender inequalities. *European Journal of Social Psychology, 35,* 633–642.

Bargad, A., & Hyde, J. S. (1991). Women's studies: A study of feminist identity development in women. *Psychology of Women Quarterly, 15,* 181–201.

Barnett, R. C., & Hyde, J. S. (2001). Women, men, work, and family: An expansionist theory. *American Psychologist, 56,* 78–96.

Barr, J. (2008). Postpartum depression, delayed maternal adaptation, and mechanical infant caring: A phenomenological hermeneutic study. *International Journal of Nursing Studies, 45*(3), 362–369.

Barrett, L. F., Lane, R. D., Sechrest, L., & Schwartz, G. E. (2000). Sex differences in emotional awareness. *Personality and Social Psychology Bulletin, 26,* 1027–1035.

Bart, P. B. (1971). Sexism and social science: From the gilded cage to the iron cage, or, the perils of Pauline. *Journal of Marriage and the Family, 33,* 734–735.

Bartsch, R. A., Burnett, T., Diller, T. R., & Rankin-Williams, E. (2000). Gender representation in television commercials: Updating an update. *Sex Roles, 43,* 735–743.

Baruch, G. K., Barnett, R. C., & Rivers, C. (1983). *Lifeprints: New patterns of love and work for today's women.* New York: New American Library.

Basow, S. A., & Howe, K. G. (1980). Role model influence: Effects of sex and sex-role attitude in college students. *Psychology of Women Quarterly, 4,* 558–572.

Basu, J., & Ray, B. (2001). Friends and lovers: A study of human mate selection in India. *Psychologia: An International Journal of Psychology in the Orient, 44,* 281–291.

Baumgardner, J., & Richards, A. (2000). *Manifesta: Young women, feminism, and the future.* New York: Farrar, Straus and Giroux.

Baumgardner, J., & Richards, A. (2005). *Grassroots: A Field Guide for Feminist Activism.* New York: Farrar, Straus, and Giroux.

Bay-Cheng, L. Y., & Zucker, A. N. (2007). Feminism between the sheets: Sexual attitudes among feminists, nonfeminists, and egalitarians. *Psychology of Women Quarterly, 31,* 157–163.

Beals, K. P., & Peplau, L. A. (2001). Social involvement, disclosure of sexual orientation, and the quality of lesbian relationships. *Psychology of Women Quarterly, 25,* 10–19.

Beaman, R., Wheldall, K., & Kemp, C. (2006). Differential teacher attention to boys and girls in the classroom. *Educational Review, 58,* 339–366.

Beaulaurier, R. L., Seff, L. R., & Newman, F. L. (2008). Barriers to help seeking for older women who experience intimate partner violence: A descriptive model. *Journal of Women and Aging, 20*(3/4), 231–248.

Beauvoir, S. (1953). *The second sex* (H. M. Parshley, Trans.). New York: Knopf.

Becker, A. L. (2010, January 18). Man, woman die after apparent murder-suicide in West Haven. *Hartford Courant Online.* Retrieved January 18, 2010, from http://www.courant.com/news/domestic-violence/hc-murder-suicide-0118.artjan18,0,1640867.story

Becker, D., & Lamb, S. (1994). Sex bias in the diagnosis of borderline personality disorder and post traumatic stress disorder. *Professional Psychology: Research and Practice, 25,* 55–61.

Becker, D., Kenrick, D., Neuberg, S., Blackwell, K., & Smith, D. (2007). The confounded nature of angry men and happy women. *Journal of Personality and Social Psychology, 92*(2), 179–190. doi:10.1037/0022-3514.92.2.179.

Beggs, J. M., & Doolittle, D. C. (1993). Perceptions now and then of occupational sex typing: A replication of Shinar's 1975 study. *Journal of Applied Social Psychology, 23,* 1435–1453.

Bekker, M. (1996). Agoraphobia and gender: A review. *Clinical Psychology Review, 16,* 129–146.

Bell, M. E., Goodman, L. A., & Dutton, M. A., (2009). Variations in help-seeking, battered women's relationship course, emotional well-being, and experiences of abuse over time. *Psychology of Women Quarterly, 33,* 149–162.

Belle, D. (2008). Poor women in a wealthy nation. In J. C. Chrisler, C. Golden, & P. D. Rozee (Eds.), *Lectures on the psychology of women* (4th ed., pp. 26–41). New York: McGraw-Hill.

Belle, D., & Doucet, J. (2003). Poverty, inequality, and discrimination as sources of depression among U.S. women. *Psychology of Women Quarterly, 27,* 101–103.

Bem, S. L. (1981). Gender schema theory: A cognitive account of sex typing. *Psychological Review, 88,* 354–364.

Bem, S. L. (1983). Gender schema theory and its implications for child development: Raising gender-aschematic children in a gender-schematic society. *Signs, 8,* 598–616.

Bem, S. L. (1993). *The lenses of gender.* New Haven, CT: Yale University Press.

Bem, S. L. (1998). *An unconventional family.* New Haven, CT: Yale University Press.

Bemporad, J. R. (1996). Self-starvation through the ages: Reflections on the pre-history of anorexia nervosa. *International Journal of Eating Disorders, 19,* 217–237.

Ben-Ari, A., & Livni, T. (2006). Motherhood is not a given thing: Experiences and constructed meanings of biological and nonbiological lesbian mothers. *Sex Roles, 54*(7–8), 521–531.

Ben-David, S., & Schneider, O. (2005). Rape perceptions, gender role attitudes, and victim-perpetrator acquaintance. *Sex Roles, 53,* 385–399.

Benokraitis, N. V. (Ed.). (1997). *Subtle sexism: Current practice and prospects for change.* Thousand Oaks, CA: Sage.

Ben-Zeev, T., Duncan, S., & Forbes, C. (2005). Stereotypes and math performance. In J. I. D. Campbell (Ed.), *Handbook of mathematical cognition* (pp. 235–249). New York: Psychology Press.

Ben Ze'ev, A., & Goussinsky, R. (2008). *In the name of love: Romantic ideology and its victims.* New York: Oxford University Press.

Berger, J. (1972). *Ways of seeing.* London: Penguin Books.

Berger, R. M. (1990). Passing: Impact of the quality of same-sex couple relationships. *Social Work, 35,* 328–332.

Bernard, J. (1974). *The future of motherhood.* New York: Penguin.

Berryman-Fink, C., & Verderber, K. S. (1985). Attributions of the term feminist: A factor analytic development of a measuring instrument. *Psychology of Women Quarterly, 9,* 51–64.

Best, D. L. (2001). Cross-cultural gender roles. In J. Worell (Ed.), *Encyclopedia of women and gender* (pp. 279–290). San Diego, CA: Academic Press.

Betz, N. E., & Fitzgerald, L. E. (1987). *The career psychology of women.* New York: Academic Press.

Beyene, Y. (1989). *From menarche to menopause: Reproductive lives of peasant women in two cultures.* Albany, NY: State University of New York Press.

Biernat, M., & Kobrynowicz, D. (1999). A shifting standards perspective on the complexity of gender stereotypes and gender stereotyping. In W. B. Swann, Jr., J. H. Langlois, & L. A. Gilbert (Eds.), *Sexism and stereotypes: The gender science of Janet Taylor Spence* (pp. 75–106). Washington, DC: American Psychological Association.

Bigler, R. S. (1999). Psychological interventions designed to counter sexism in children: Empirical limitations and theoretical foundations. In W. B. Swann Jr., J. H. Langlois, & L. A. Gilbert (Eds.), *Sexism and stereotypes in modern society: The gender science of Janet Taylor Spence* (pp. 129–151). Washington, DC: American Psychological Association.

Bihagen, E., & Ohls, M. (2007). Are women over-represented in dead-end jobs? A Swedish study using empirically derived measures of dead-end jobs. *Social Indicators Research, 84,* 159–177.

Bing, V. M., & Reid, P. T. (1996). Unknown women and unknowing research: Consequences of color and class in feminist psychology. In N. R. Goldberger & J. M. Tarule (Eds.), *Knowledge, difference, and power: Essays inspired by "women's ways of knowing"* (pp. 175–202). New York: Basic Books.

Bingham, S. G., & Scherer, L. L. (2001). The unexpected effects of a sexual harassment educational program. *The Journal of Applied Behavioral Science, 37*, 125–153.

Bishop, N. (1989). Abortion: The controversial choice. In J. Freeman (Ed.), *Women: A feminist perspective* (4th ed., pp. 45–56). Mountain View, CA: Mayfield.

Black, K. A., Marola, J. A., Littleman, A. I., Chrisler, J. C., & Neace, W. P. (2009). Gender and form of cereal box characters: Different medium, same disparity. *Sex Roles, 60*, 882–889.

Blair, I. V. (2002). The malleability of automatic stereotypes and prejudice. *Personality and Social Psychology Review, 6*, 242–261.

Blakemore, J. E., & Centers, R. E. (2005). Characteristics of boys' and girls' toys. *Sex Roles, 53*, 619–633.

Blashill, A. J., & Powlishta, K. K. (2009). Gay stereotypes: The use of sexual orientation as a cue for gender-related attributes. *Sex Roles, 61*, 783–793.

Bleier, R. (Ed.). (1986). *Feminist approaches to science.* Elmsford, NY: Pergamon Press.

Blood, R. O., & Wolfe, D. M. (1960). *Husbands and wives.* New York: Free Press.

Blumstein, P., & Schwartz, P. (1983). *American couples.* New York: William Morrow.

Blytheway, B. (2003). Visual representations of late life. In C. A. Faircloth, (Ed.), *Aging bodies: Images and everyday experiences* (pp. 11–49). New York: AltaMira Press.

Boardman, S. K., Harrington, C. C., & Horowitz, S. V. (1987). Successful women: A psychological investigation of family class and education origins. In B. A. Gutek & L. Larwood (Eds.), *Women's career development* (pp. 66–85). Newbury Park, CA: Sage.

Boatwright, K. J., Gilbert, M. S., Forrest, L., & Ketzenberger, K. (1996). Impact of identity development upon career trajectory: Listening to the voices of lesbian women. *Journal of Vocational Behavior, 48*, 210–228.

Bograd, M. (1988). Feminist perspectives on wife abuse: An introduction. In K. Yllo & M. Bograd (Eds.), *Feminist perspectives on wife abuse* (pp. 11–26). Berkeley, CA: Sage.

Bohan, J. S. (1996). *Psychology and sexual orientation: Coming to terms.* New York: Routledge.

Bohn, D. K. (2003). Lifetime physical and sexual abuse, substance abuse, depression, and suicide attempts among Native American women. *Issues in Mental Health Nursing, 24*, 333–352.

Bolin, A. (1996). Transcending and transgendering: Male-to-female transsexuals, dichotomy, and diversity. In G. Herdt (Ed.), *Third sex, third gender: Beyond sexual dimorphism in culture and history* (pp. 447–485). New York: Zone Books.

Bonomi, A. E., Anderson, M. L., Reid, R. J., Carrell, D., Fishman, P. A., Rivara, F. P., & Thompson, R. S. (2007). Intimate partner violence in older women. *The Gerontologist, 47*, 34–41.

Borland, S. (2008). *Glossy magazines face airbrush ban.* Retreived August 9, 2010, from http://www.telegraph.co.uk/news/uknews/1583638/Glossy-magazines-face-airbrush-ban.html

Bornstein, K. (1994). *Gender outlaw: On men, women, and the rest of us.* New York: Routledge.

Boston Women's Health Book Collective. (1998). *Our bodies, ourselves for the new century.* New York: Simon & Schuster.

Boswell, S. L. (1979). *Nice girls don't study mathematics: The perspective from elementary school.* Paper presented at the meeting of the American Educational Research Association, San Francisco, CA.

Boswell, S. L. (1985). The influence of sex-role stereotyping on women's attitudes and achievement in mathematics. In S. F. Chipman, L. R. Brush, & D. M. Wilson (Eds.), *Women and mathematics: Balancing the equation* (pp. 175–198). Hillsdale, NJ: Erlbaum.

Bourque, P., Pushkar, D., Bonneville, L., & Beland, F. (2005). Contextual effects on life satisfaction of older men and women. *Canadian Journal of Aging, 24*, 31–44.

Boxer, A. M., Cook, J. A., & Herdt, G. (1999). Experiences of coming out among gay and lesbian youth: Adolescents alone. In J. Blustein, C. Levine, & N. N. Dubler (Eds.), *The adolescent alone: Decision making in health care in the United States* (pp. 121–136). Cambridge, England: Cambridge University Press.

Boxer, P., Huesmann, L. R., Bushman, B. J., O'Brien, M., & Moceri, D. (2009). The role of violent media preference in cumulative developmental risk for violence and general aggression. *Journal of Youth and Adolescence, 38*, 417–428.

Boyce, P., & Hickey, A. (2005). Psychosocial risk factors to major depression after childbirth. *Social Psychiatry and Psychiatric Epidemiology, 40*(8), 605–612.

Bradshaw, C. K. (1994). Asian and Asian American women: Historical and political considerations in psychotherapy. In L. Comas-Díaz & B. Greene (Eds.), *Women of color: Integrating ethnic and gender identities in psychotherapy* (pp. 72–113). New York: Guilford Press.

Bramlet, M. D., & Mosher, W. D. (2001). *First marriage dissolution, divorce, and remarriage: United States.* Hyattsville, MD: National Center for Health Statistics.

Bridges, J. S. (1993). Pink or blue: Gender-stereotypic perceptions of infants as conveyed by birth congratulations cards. *Psychology of Women Quarterly, 17*(2), 193–205. doi:10.1111/j.1471-6402.1993.tb00444.x

Brimhall, A., Wampler, K., & Kimball, T. (2008). Learning from the past, altering the future: A tentative theory of the effect of past relationships on couples who remarry. *Family Process, 47*, 373–387.

Bringaze, T. B., & White, L. J. (2001). Living out proud: Factors contributing to healthy identity development in lesbian leaders. *Journal of Mental Health Counseling, 23*, 162–173.

Brinkman, L. (2007). Gender assignment and medical history of individuals with different forms of intersexuality: Evaluation of medical records and the patients' perspective. *The Journal of Sexual Medicine, 4,* 964–980.

Brodsky, A. (1973). The consciousness-raising group as a model for therapy with women. *Psychotherapy: Theory, Research, and Practice, 10,* 24–29.

Brodsky, A. E. (2003). *With all our strength: The revolutionary association of the women of Afghanistan.* New York: Routledge.

Brody, E. M. (2004). *Women in the middle: Their parent care years* (2nd ed.). New York: Springer.

Brody, L. R., & Hall, J. A. (2000). Gender, emotion, and expression. In M. Lewis & J. Haviland-Jones (Eds.), *Handbook of emotions* (pp. 338–349). New York: Guilford.

Bronstein, P. (2006). The family environment: When gender role socialization begins. In J. Worrell & C. Goodheart (Eds.), *Handbook of girls' and women's psychological health.* New York: Oxford University Press.

Bronstein, P., & Quina, K. (Eds.). (2003). *Teaching gender and multicultural awareness: Resources for the psychology classroom.* Washington, DC: American Psychological Association.

Brooks-Gunn, J. (1988). Antecedents and consequences of variations in girls' maturational timing. *Journal of Adolescent Health Care, 9,* 365–373.

Broverman, I. K., Broverman, D. M., Clarkson, F. E., Rosenkrantz, P. S., & Vogel, S. R. (1970). Sex-role stereotypes and clinical judgments of mental health. *Journal of Consulting and Clinical Psychology, 34,* 1–7.

Broverman, I. K., Vogel, S. R., Broverman, D. M., Clarkson, F. E., & Rosenkrantz, P. S. (1972). Sex-role stereotypes: A current appraisal. *Journal of Social Issues, 28,* 59–78.

Brown, L. M. (1998). *Raising their voices: The politics of girls' anger.* Cambridge, MA: Harvard University Press.

Brown, L. M., & Gilligan, C. (1992). *Meeting at the crossroads: Women's psychology and girls' development.* Cambridge, MA: Harvard University Press.

Brown, L. S. (2006). Still subversive after all these years: The relevance of feminist therapy in the age of evidence-based practice. *Psychology of Women Quarterly, 30,* 15–24.

Brown, L. S. (2010). *Feminist therapy.* Washington, DC: American Psychological Association.

Browne, K. (2004). An unhealthy idea of beauty: Big business tells women whiter is better. *Ms., 13,* 60–62.

Brownmiller, S. (1975). *Against our will: Men, women and rape.* Newark: Simon & Schuster.

Brownridge, D. A. (2009). *Violence against women: Vulnerable populations.* New York: Routledge/Taylor & Francis Group.

Brumberg, J. J. (2000). *Fasting girls: The history of anorexia nervosa.* New York: Vintage Books.

Buchholz, A., Henderson, K. A., Hounsell, A., Wagner, A., Norris, M., & Spettigue, W. (2007). Self-silencing in a clinical sample of female adolescents with eating disorders. *Journal of the Canadian Academy of Child and Adolescent Psychiatry/Journal de l'Académie canadienne de psychiatrie de l'enfant et de l'adolescent, 16*(4), 158–163.

Budig, M. J. (2002). Male advantage and the gender composition of jobs: Who rides the glass elevator? *Social Problems, 49,* 258–277.

Buhl, M. (1989, September/October). The feminist mystique. *View,* 16.

Buhle, M. J. (1998). *Feminism and its discontents: A century of struggle with psychoanalysis.* Cambridge, MA: Harvard University Press.

Bullock, H. E., Wyche, K. F., & Williams, W. R. (2001). Media images of the poor. *Journal of Social Issues, 57,* 229–246.

Burgess, M. C. R., Stermer, S. P., & Burgess, S. R. (2007). Sex, lies, and videogames: The portrayal of male and female characters on videogame covers. *Sex Roles, 57,* 419–433.

Burke, R. J. (1997). Alternate family structures: A career advantage? *Psychological Reports, 81,* 812–814.

Burke, R. J., & McKeen, C. A. (1997). Gender effects in mentoring relationships. In R. Crandall (Ed.), *Handbook of gender research* (pp. 91–104). Corte Madera, CA: Select Press.

Burt, M. (1980). Cultural myths and supports for rape. *Journal of Personality and Social Psychology, 38,* 217–230.

Buss, D. M., Abbott, M., Angleitner, A., & Asherian, A. (1990). International preferences in selecting mates: A study of 37 cultures. *Journal of Cross-Cultural Psychology, 21*(1), 5–47, doi:10.1177/0022022190211001.

Bussey, K., & Bandura, A. (2004). Social cognitive theory of gender development and functioning. In A. H. Eagly, A. E. Beall, & R. J. Sternberg (Eds.), *The psychology of gender* (pp. 92–119). New York: Guilford Press.

Cabaj, R. P., & Purcell, D. W. (Eds.). (1998). *On the road to same-sex marriage: A supportive guide to psychological, political, and legal issues.* San Francisco: Jossey-Bass.

Cachelin, F. M., Veisel, C., Barzegarnazari, E., & Striegel-Moore, R. H. (2000). Disordered eating, acculturation, and treatment-seeking in a community sample of Hispanic, Asian, Black, and White women. *Psychology of Women Quarterly, 24,* 244–253.

Cai, C. (2008). Women's participation as leaders in the transformation of the Chinese media: A case study of Guanghzhou City. Unpublished Dissertation.

Calasanti, T. M., & Slevin, K. F. (2001). *Gender, social inequalities, and aging.* New York: AltaMira Press.

Callister, L. C. (2007). Improving literacy in women and girls globally. *The American Journal of Maternal Child Nursing, 32,* 194.

Cameron, D. (1996). The language-gender interface: Challenging co-optation. In V. L. Bergvall, J. M. Bing, & A. F. Freed (Eds.), *Rethinking language and gender research: Theory and Practice* (pp. 31–53). New York: Addison-Wesley.

Cameron, D. (1997). Performing gender identity: Young men's talk and the construction of heterosexual masculinity. In S. Johnson & U. H. Meinof (Eds.), *Language and masculinity* (pp. 47–64). Cambridge, MA: Blackwell.

Cameron, R. P., Grabill, C. M., Hobfoll, S. E., & Crowther, J. H. (1996). Weight, self-esteem, ethnicity, and depressive symptomatology during pregnancy among inner-city women. *Health Psychology, 15,* 293-297.

Campbell, A. (1992). *Men, women, and aggression.* New York: Basic Books.

Canetto, S. S. (2001). Older adult women: Issues, resources, and challenges. In R. K. Unger (Ed.), *Handbook of the psychology of women and gender* (pp. 183–197). New York: Wiley.

Caplan, P. J. (1985). *The myth of women's masochism.* New York: E.P. Dutton

Caplan, P. J. (1989). *Don't blame mother.* New York: Harper & Row.

Caplan, P. J. (1992). Driving us crazy: How oppression damages women's mental health and what we can do about it. *Women & Therapy, 12,* 5–28.

Caplan, P. J. (1995). *They say you're crazy: How the world's most powerful psychiatrists decide who's normal.* Reading, MA: Perseus Books.

Caplan, P. J. (2000). *The new don't blame mother: Mending the mother-daughter relationship.* New York: Routledge.

Caplan, P. J. (2004). The debate about PMDD and Sarafem: Suggestions for therapists. In J. C. Chrisler (Ed.), *From menarche to menopause: The female body in feminist therapy* (pp. 55–67). New York: Haworth Press.

Caplan, P. J. (2008, Summer). Pathologizing your period. *Ms.,* 63–64.

Caplan, P. J., & Hall-McCorquodale, I. (1985). Mother-blaming in major clinical journals. *American Journal of Orthopsychiatry, 55,* 345–353.

Carey, C. M., & Mongeau, P. A. (1996). Communication and violence in courtship relationships. In D. D. Cahn & S. A. Lloyd (Eds.), *Family violence from a communication perspective* (pp. 127–150). Thousand Oaks, CA: Sage.

Carli, L. L. (2001). Gender and social influence. *Journal of Social Issues, 57,* 735–741.

Carp, F. M. (1997). Retirement and women. In J. M. Coyle (Ed.), *Handbook on women and aging* (pp. 112–128). Westport, CT: Greenwood Press.

Carpenter, L. M. (2005). *Virginity lost: An intimate portrait of first sexual experiences.* New York: New York University Press.

Carter, G. (2010, February 19–21). Mo'Nique talks. *USA Weekend,* p. 9.

Cassell, J. (1997). Doing gender, doing surgery: Women surgeons in a man's profession. *Human Organization, 56,* 47–52.

Cassidy, T., & Sintrovani, P. (2008). Motives for parenthood, psychosocial factors and health in women undergoing IVF. *Journal of Reproductive and Infant Psychology, 26,* 4–17.

Castañeda, D. (2008). Gender issues among Latinas. In J.C. Chrisler, C. Golden, & P. Rozee (Eds.), *Lectures on the psychology of women* (4th ed., pp. 250–267). New York: McGraw Hill.

CBS News 60 Minutes. (2003, November 23). *Porn in the USA: Adult entertainment industry becoming mainstream.*

Chambers, C. (1972). An assessment of drug use in the general population. In J. Sussman (Ed.), *Drug use and social policy,* 50–61.

Ceci, S. J., Williams, W. M., & Barnett, S. M. (2009). Women's underrepresentation in science: Sociocultural and biological considerations. *Psychological Bulletin, 135*(2), 218–261. doi:10.1037/a0014412

Chan, C. S. (2008). Asian American women and adolescent girls: Sexuality and sexual expression. In J. C. Chrisler, C. Golden, & P. Rozee (Eds.), *Lectures on the psychology of women* (4th ed., pp. 220–231). New York: McGraw Hill.

Chandani, A. T., McKenna, K. T., & Maas, F. (1989). Attitudes of university students towards the sexuality of physically disabled people. *British Journal of Occupational Therapy, 52,* 233–236.

Chapleau, K. M., Oswald, D. L., & Russell, B. L. (2007). How ambivalent sexism toward women and men support rape myth acceptance. *Sex Roles, 57,* 131–136.

Chapman, H. (2008). *Women lawyers still struggling to the top.* Retrieved June 1, 2010, from http://www.theglasshammer.com/news/2008/11/11/women-lawyers-still-struggling-to-the-top/

Charlesworth, W. R., & LaFreniere, P. (1983). Dominance, friendship utilization and resource utilization in preschool children's groups. *Ethology and Sociobiology, 4,* 175–186.

Chen, M., & Bargh, J. A. (1997). Nonconscious behavioral confirmation processes: The self-fulfilling nature of automatically-activated stereotypes. *Journal of Experimental Social Psychology, 33,* 541–560.

Chesler, P. (1972). *Women and madness.* New York: Doubleday.

Chesler, P. (1997). *Women and madness* (25th anniversary ed.). New York: Four Walls Eight Windows.

Chesler, P. (2005). *Women and madness* (Revised and updated for the first time in thirty years). New York: Palgrave Macmillan.

Cheung, F. M., & Halpern, D. F. (2010). Women at the top: Powerful leaders define success at work + family in a culture of gender. *American Psychologist, 65,* 182–193.

Chicago, J. (1990, March). *The birth project.* Women's History Month Lecture, Trenton State College, Trenton, NJ.

Choi, P., Henshaw, C., Baker, S., & Tree, J. (2005). Supermom, superwife, supereverything: Performing femininity in the transition to motherhood. *Journal of Reproductive and Infant Psychology, 23*(2), 167–180.

Choo, P., Levine, T., & Hatfield, E. (1997). Gender, love, schemas, and reactions to romantic break-ups. In R. Crandall (Ed.), *Handbook of gender research* (pp. 143–160). Corte Madera, CA: Select Press.

Chrisler, J. C. (2001). Gendered bodies and physical health. In R. K. Unger (Editor), *Handbook of the psychology of women and gender* (pp. 289–302). New York: Wiley.

Chrisler, J. C., & Ghiz, L. (1993). Body image issues of older women. *Women & Therapy, 14,* 67–75.

Chrisler, J. C., & Lamont, J. M. (2002). Can exercise contribute to the goals of feminist therapy? In R. L. Hall & C. A. Oglesby (Eds.), *Exercise and sport in feminist therapy: Constructing modalities and assessing outcomes* (pp. 9–22). New York: Haworth Press.

Christiaens, W., Verhaeghe, M., & Bracke, P. (2008). Childbirth expectation and experiences in Belgian and Dutch models of maternity care. *Journal of Reproductive and Infant Psychology, 26*(4), 309–322.

Christian-Smith, L. K. (1994). Young women and their dream lovers: Sexuality in adolescent fiction. In J. M. Irvine (Ed.), *Sexual cultures and the construction of adolescent identities* (pp. 206–227). Philadelphia: Temple University Press.

Christopher, A. N., & Mull, M. S. (2006). Conservative ideology and ambivalent sexism. *Psychology of Women Quarterly, 30,* 223–230.

Chun, H., & Gupta, M. (2009). Gender discrimination in sex selective abortions and its transition in South Korea. *Women's Studies International Forum, 32*(2), 89–97. doi:10.1016/j.wsif.2009.03.008

Ciancanelli, P., & Berch, B. (1987). Gender and the GNP. In B. B. Hess & M. M. Ferree (Eds.), *Analyzing gender: A handbook of social science research* (pp. 244–266). Newbury Park, CA: Sage.

Clarke, L. H. (2007). The body natural and body unnatural: beauty work and aging. *Journal of Aging Studies, 21,* 187–201.

Clarke, L. H., & Griffin, M. (2008). Visible and invisible aging: beauty work as a response to ageism. *Aging & Society, 28,* 653–674.

Clarke, V., Burns, M., & Burgoyne, C. (2008). "Who would take whose name?" Accounts of naming practices in same-sex relationships. *Journal of Community & Applied Social Psychology, 18,* 420–439.

Clarke, V., Ellis, S. J., Peel, E., & Riggs, D. W. (2010). *Lesbian, gay, bisexual, trans and queer psychology: An introduction.* Cambridge: Cambridge University Press.

Cohen, B. P., Berger, J., & Zelditch, M. (1972). Status conceptions and interactions: A case study of developing cumulative knowledge. In C. McClintock (Ed.), *Experimental social psychology* (pp. 408–411). New York: Holt, Rinehart, & Winston.

Cohen, J. N. (2008). Using feminist, emotion-focused, and developmental approaches to enhance cognitive-behavioral therapies for posttraumatic stress disorder related to childhood sexual abuse. *Psychotherapy: Theory, Research, Practice, Training, 45,* 227–246.

Cohen, S. A. (2007). New data on abortion incidence, safety illuminate key aspects of worldwide abortion debate.

Guttmacher Policy Review, 10. Retrieved March 10, 2010, from http://www.guttmacher.org/pubs/gpr/10/4/gpr100402.html

Cole, E. R., Zucker, A. N., & Duncan, L. E. (2001). Changing society, changing women (and men). In R. K. Unger (Ed.), *Handbook of the psychology of women and gender* (pp. 410–423). New York: Wiley.

Cole, S. G. (1987). *Pornography and harm.* Toronto: Metro Action Committee on Public Violence Against Women and Children.

Coley, R. J. (2001). *Differences in the gender gap: Comparisons across racial/ethnic groups in education and work.* Princeton: Educational Testing Service.

Collaer, M. L., Brook, C. G. D., Conway, G. S., Hindmarsh, P. C., & Hines, M. (2009). Motor development in individuals with congenital adrenal hyperplasia: Strength, targeting and fine motor skills. *Psychoneuroendocrinology, 34,* 249–258.

Collaer, M. L., & Hines, M. (1995). Human behavioral sex differences: A role for gonadal hormones during early development? *Psychological Bulletin, 118,* 55–107.

Collins, L. (2010, January 11). Number nine: Sonia Sotomayor's high-profile debut. *The New Yorker,* pp. 42–55.

Collins, P. H. (1991). The meaning of motherhood in Black culture and Black mother-daughter relationships. In P. Bell-Scott, B. Guy-Sheftall, J. J. Royster, J. Sims-Wood, M. DiCosta-Willis, & L. P. Fultz (Eds.), *Double stitch: Black women write about mothers and daughters* (pp. 42–60). New York: HarperCollins.

Collins, R. L., Ellickson, P. L., & Klein, D. J. (2006). The role of substance use in young adult divorce. *Addiction, 102,* 786–794.

Coltrane, S., & Adams, M. (1997). Work-family imagery and gender stereotypes: Television and the reproduction of difference. *Journal of Vocational Behavior, 50,* 323–347.

Coltrane, S., & Messineo, M. (2000). The perpetuation of subtle prejudice: Race and gender imagery in 1990s television advertising. *Sex Roles, 42,* 363–389.

Colvin, G. (2009). A CEO masters micro-credit. *Fortune Magazine Online.* Retrieved April 1, 2010, from http://money.cnn.com/2009/01/09/magazines/fortune/colvin_barnevik.fortune/index.htm

Comas-Díaz, L., & Greene, B. (1994). *Women of color: Integrating ethnic and gender identities in psychotherapy.* New York: Guilford Press.

Commuri, S., & Gentry, J. (2005). Resource allocation in households with women as chief wage earners. *Journal of Consumer Research, 32*(2), 185–195.

Condit, C. M. (1996). Media bias for reproductive technologies. In R. L. Parrott & C. M. Condit (Eds.), *Evaluating women's health messages* (pp. 341–355). Thousand Oaks, CA: Sage.

Cosgrove, L. (2003). Resisting essentialism in feminist therapy theory: Some epistemological considerations. *Women & Therapy, 25,* 89–112.

Cosgrove, L., Krimsky, S., Vijayaraghavan, M., & Schneider, L. (2006). Financial ties between DSM-IV panel members and the pharmaceutical industry. *Psychotherapy and Psychosomatics, 75*(3), 154–160.

Costos, D., Ackerman, R., & Paradis, L. (2002). Recollections of menarche: Communication between mothers and daughters regarding menstruation. *Sex Roles, 46,* 49–59.

Covan, E. K. (2005). Meaning of aging in women's lives. *Journal of Women & Aging, 17*(3), 3–22.

Covert, J. J., & Dixon, T. L. (2008). A changing view: Representation and effects of the portrayal of women of color in mainstream women's magazines. *Communication Research, 35,* 232–258.

Cox, C. B. (2005). *Community care for an aging society: Issues, policies, and services.* New York: Springer.

Cozzarelli, C., & Major, B. (1998). The impact of anti-abortion activities on women seeking abortions. In L. J. Beckman & S. M. Harvey (Eds.), *The new civil war: The psychology, culture, and politics of abortion* (pp. 81–104). Washington, DC: American Psychological Association.

Cramer, E., & MacFarlane, J. (1994). Pornography and abuse of women. *Public Health Nursing, 11,* 268–272.

Crawford, M. (1982). In pursuit of the well-rounded life: Women scholars and the family. In M. Kehoe (Ed.), *Handbook for women scholars* (pp. 89–96). San Francisco: Americas Behavioral Research.

Crawford, M. (1988). Gender, age, and the social evaluation of assertion. *Behavior Modification, 12,* 549–564.

Crawford, M. (1995). *Talking difference: On gender and language.* London: Sage.

Crawford, M. (2000). Editor's introduction: How to make sex and do gender. *Feminism & Psychology, 10,* 7–10.

Crawford, M. (2001). Gender and language. In R. K. Unger (Ed.), *Handbook of the psychology of women and gender* (pp. 228–244). New York: Wiley

Crawford, M. (2010). *Sex trafficking in South Asia: Telling Maya's story.* London: Routledge.

Crawford, M., & English, L. (1984). Generic versus specific inclusion of women in language: Effects on recall. *Journal of Psycholinguistic Research, 13,* 373–381.

Crawford, M., Kerwin, G., Gurung, A., Khati, D., Jha, P., & Regmi, A. C. (2008). Globalizing beauty: Attitudes toward beauty pageants among Nepali women. *Feminism & Psychology, 18,* 62–86.

Crawford, M., Lee, I., Portnoy, G., Gurung, A., Khati, D., Jha, P., & Regmi, A. C. (2009). Objectified body consciousness in a developing country: A comparison of mothers and daughters in the US and Nepal. *Sex Roles, 60,* 174–185.

Crawford, M., & Marecek, J. (1989). Psychology reconstructs the female. *Psychology of Women Quarterly, 13,* 147–166.

Crawford, M., & Popp, D. (2003). Sexual double standards: A review and methodological critique of two decades of research. *The Journal of Sex Research, 40,* 13–26.

Crawford, M., Stark, A., & Renner, C. (1998). The meaning of *Ms.:* Social assimilation of a gender concept. *Psychology of Women Quarterly, 22,* 197–208.

Crawford, M., & Unger, R. (Eds.). (2006). *In our own words: Writings from women's lives* (2nd ed.). Long Grove, IL: Waveland Press.

Crawford, S. (1987). Lesbian families: Psychosocial stress and the family-building process. In Boston Lesbian Psychologies Collective, *Lesbian psychologies* (pp. 195–214). Urbana, IL: University of Illinois Press.

Crick, N. R., & Rose, A. J. (2000). Toward a gender-balanced approach to the study of social-emotional development: A look at relational aggression. In P. H. Miller & E. K. Scholnick (Eds.), *Toward a feminist developmental psychology* (pp. 153–168). New York: Routledge.

Crittenden, A. (2001). *The price of motherhood.* New York: Metropolitan Books.

Croghan, R. (1991). First-time mothers' accounts of inequality in the division of labour. *Feminism & Psychology, 1,* 221–246.

Crolley, L., & Teso, E. (2007). Gendered narratives in Spain: The representation of female athletes in *Marca* and *El Pais. International Review for the Sociology of Sport, 42,* 149–166.

Crosby, F. J. (1982). *Relative deprivation and working women.* New York: Oxford University Press.

Crosby, F. J. (1991). *Juggling: The unexpected advantages of balancing career and home for women and their families.* New York: Free Press.

Crosby, F. J. (2004). *Affirmative action is dead: Long live affirmative action.* New Haven, CT: Yale University Press.

Crosby, F. J., Clayton, S., Alksnis, O., & Hemker, K. (1986). Cognitive biases in the perception of discrimination: The importance of format. *Sex Roles, 14,* 637–646.

Crosby, F. J., Iyer, A., Clayton, S., & Downing, R. A. (2003). Affirmative action: Psychological data and the policy debates. *American Psychologist, 58,* 93–115.

Cruikshank, M. (2003). *Learning to be old: Gender, culture, and aging.* Lanham, MD: Rowman & Littlefield.

Cuddy, A. J. C., & Fiske, S. T. (2002). Doddering but dear: Process, content, and function in stereotyping of older persons. In T. D. Nelson (Ed.), *Ageism: Stereotyping and prejudice against older persons* (pp. 3–26). Cambridge, MA: MIT Press.

Cuddy, A., Norton, M., & Fiske, S., (2005). This old stereotype: The pervasiveness and persistence of the elderly stereotype. *Journal of Social Issues, 61,* 267–285.

Curry, M. A., Renker, P., Hughes, R. B., Robinson-Whelen, S., Oschwald, M. M., Swank, P., & Powers, L. E. (2009). Development of measures of abuse among women with disabilities and the characteristics of their perpetrators. *Violence Against Women, 15,* 1001–1025.

Daigneault, I., Hebert, M., & McDuff, P. (2009). Men's and women's childhood sexual abuse and victimization in adult partner relationships: A study of risk factors. *Child Abuse & Neglect, 33,* 638–647.

Dallos, S., & Dallos, R. (1997). *Couples, sex, and power: The politics of desire*. Philadelphia: Open University Press.

Daniel, S., & Bridges, S. K. (2010). The drive for muscularity in men: Media influences and objectification theory. *Body Image, 7*, 32–38.

Daniluk, J. C. (1996). When treatment fails: The transition to biological childlessness for infertile women. *Women & Therapy, 19*, 81–98.

Dansky, B. S., & Kilpatrick, D. G. (1997). Effects of sexual harassment. In W. O'Donohue (Ed.), *Sexual harassment: Theory, research and treatment* (pp. 152–174). Boston: Allyn & Bacon.

Dardenne, B., Dumont, M., & Bollier, T. (2007). Insidious dangers of benevolent sexism: Consequences for women's performance. *Journal of Personality and Social Psychology, 93*, 764–779.

Darwin, C. (1872/1998). *The expression of emotions in man and animals*. New York: Oxford University Press.

Das, A. (2007). Masturbation in the United States. *Journal of Sex & Marital Therapy, 33*, 301–317.

Davey, C. L., & Davidson, M. J. (2000). The right of passage? The experiences of female pilots in aviation. *Feminism and Psychology, 10*, 195–225.

Davidson, M. (2007). Seeking refuge under the umbrella: Inclusion, exclusion, and organizing within the category transgender. *Sexuality Research and Social Policy, 4*, 60–120.

Davis, S., Crawford, M., & Sebrechts, J. (Eds.). (1999). *Coming into her own: Encouraging educational success in girls and women*. San Francisco: Jossey-Bass.

Davis, T. L. (1995). Gender differences in masking negative emotions: Ability or motivation? *Developmental Psychology, 31*, 650–667.

Davison, H. K., & Burke, M. J. (2000). Sex discrimination in simulated employment contexts: A meta-analytic investigation. *Journal of Vocational Behavior, 56*, 225–248.

Deaux, K., & Lewis, L. L. (1984). The structure of gender stereotypes: Interrelationships among components and gender labels. *Journal of Personality and Social Psychology, 46*, 991–1004.

Deaux, K., & Major, B. (1987). Putting gender into context: An interactive model of gender-related behavior. *Psychological Review, 94*, 369–389.

Deaux, K., Winton, W., Crowley, M., & Lewis, L. L. (1985). Level of categorization and content of gender stereotypes. *Social Cognition, 3*, 145–167.

De Cuypere, G., T'Sjoen, G., Beerten, R., Selvaggi, G., De Sutter, P., Hoebeke, P., et al. (2005). Sexual and physical health after sex reassignment surgery. *Archives of Sexual Behavior, 34*(6), 679–690. doi:10.1007/s10508-005-7926-5

Defense Manpower Data Center (DMDC). (2008). *2008 Service academy gender relations survey*. Retrieved February 10, 2010, from http://www.sapr.mil/media/pdf/research/DMDC2008ServiceAcademyGenderRelationsSurvey.pdf

DeLamater, J. D., & Sill, M. (2005). Sexual desire in later life. *The Journal of Sex Research, 42*, 138–149.

Denmark, F. L., Russo, N. F., Frieze, I. H., & Sechzer, J. A. (1988). Guidelines for avoiding sexism in psychological research: A report of the ad hoc committee on nonsexist research. *American Psychologist, 43*, 582–585.

Department of Defense (DoD). (2009). *Annual report on sexual harassment and violence at the U.S. military service academies: Academic program year 2008-2009*. Retrieved February 10, 2010, from http://www.sapr.mil/media/pdf/reports/2009_msa_report.pdf

Dermer, M., & Theil, D. L. (1975). When beauty may fail. *Journal of Personality and Social Psychology, 31*, 1168–1176.

Desmarais, S., & Curtis, J. (1997). Gender differences in pay histories and view on payment entitlement among university students. *Sex Roles, 37*, 623–642.

Dessens, A. B., Slijper, F. M. E., & Drop, S. L. S. (2005). Gender dysphoria and gender change in chromosomal females with congenital adrenal hyperplasia. *Archives of Sexual Behavior, 34*, 389–397.

Deutsch, F. (1999). *Halving it all: How equally shared parenting works*. Cambridge, MA: Harvard University Press.

Devine, P. G., & Sharp, L. B. (2009). Automaticity and control in stereotyping and prejudice. In T. D. Nelson (Ed.), *Handbook of prejudice, stereotyping, and discrimination* (pp. 61–87). New York: Psychology Press.

Devor, H. (1997). *FTM: Female-to-male transsexuals in society*. Bloomington, IN: University of Indiana Press.

Diamond, L. M. (2000). Sexual identity, attractions, and behavior among young sexual-minority women over a 2-year period. *Developmental Psychology, 36*, 241–250.

Diamond, M., & Watson, L. A. (2004). Androgen insensitivity syndrome and Klinefelter's syndrome: Sex and gender considerations. *Child and Adolescent Psychiatric Clinics of North America*, 623–640.

Diamond-Smith N., Luke, N., & McGarvey, S. (2008). "Too many girls, too much dowry": Son preference and daughter aversion in rural Tamil Nadu, India. *Culture, Health and Sexuality, 10*(7), 697–708.

Dickerson, B. J. (Ed.). (1995). *African-American single mothers*. Thousand Oaks, CA: Sage.

Dickhäuser, O., & Meyer, W. (2006). Gender differences in young children's math ability attributions. *Psychology Science, 48*, 3–16.

Didi-Huberman, G. (2003). *The invention of hysteria: Charcot and the photographic iconography at the Salpêtrière* (Alisa Hartz, Trans.). Cambridge, MA: MIT Press.

Diekman, A. B., & Eagly, A. H. (2000). Stereotypes as dynamic constructs: Women and men of the past, present, and future. *Personality and Social Psychology Bulletin, 26*, 1171–1188.

Diekman, A. B., McDonald, M., & Gardner, W. L. (2000). Love means never having to be careful: The relationship between reading romance novels and safe sex behavior. *Psychology of Women Quarterly, 24*, 179–188.

Di Leonardo, M. (1987). The female world of cards and holidays: Women, families, and the work of kinship. *Signs, 12*, 440–453.

Dill, K. E., & Thill, K. P. (2007). Video game characters and the socialization of gender roles: Young people's perceptions mirror sexist media depictions. *Sex Roles, 57*, 851–865.

Dill, K. E., Brown, B. P., & Collins, M. A. (2008). Effects of exposure to sex-stereotyped video game characters on tolerance of sexual harassment. *Journal of Experimental Social Psychology, 44*, 1402–1408.

Dion, K. L. (1987). What's in a title? The Ms stereotype and images of women's titles of address. *Psychology of Women Quarterly, 11*, 21–36.

DiPalma, L. M. (1994). Patterns of coping and characteristics of high-functioning incest survivors. *Archives of Psychiatric Nursing, 8*, 82–90.

Dittmar, H., Halliwell, E., & Ive, S. (2006). Does Barbie make girls want to be thin? The effect of experimental exposure to images of dolls on the body image of 5- to 8-year old girls. *Developmental Psychology, 42*, 283–292.

Dixon, D. A., Antoni, M., Peters, M., & Saul, J. (2001). Employment, social support, and HIV sexual-risk behavior in Puerto Rican women. *AIDS and Behavior, 5*, 331–342.

Dobrof, R. (2001). Aging in the United States today. In D. C. Kimmel & D. L. Martin (Eds.), *Midlife and aging in gay America: Proceedings of the SAGE conference 2000* (pp. 15–17). New York: Harrington Park Press.

Dodson, B. (1987). *Sex for one: The joy of self-loving.* New York: Crown.

Dohm, F. A., & Cummings, W. (2002). Research mentoring and women in clinical psychology. *Psychology of Women Quarterly, 26*, 163–167.

Dorahy, M. J., Lewis, C. A., & Wolfe, F. A. M. (2007). Psychological distress associated with domestic violence in Northern Ireland. *Current Psychology, 25*, 295–305.

Doress-Worters, P. B., & Siegal, D. L. (1994). *The new ourselves growing older.* New York: Simon & Schuster.

Doress-Worters, P., & Ditzion, P. (1998). Women growing older. In The Boston Women's Health Book Collective, *Our bodies, ourselves for the new century* (pp. 547–589). New York: Simon & Schuster.

Dorian, L., & Garfinkel, P. E. (2002). Culture and body image in Western society. *Eating and Weight Disorders, 7*, 1–19.

Douglas, S. J. (1994). *Where the girls are: Growing up female with the mass media.* New York: Times Books/Random House.

Dovidio, J. F., Ellyson, S. L., Keating, C. F., Heltman, K., & Brown, C. E. (1988). The relationship of social power to visual displays of dominance between men and women. *Journal of Personality and Social Psychology, 54*, 233–242.

Drout, C. E. (1997). Professionals' and students' perceptions of abuse among married and unmarried cohabiting couples. *Journal of Social Behavior and Personality, 12*, 965–978.

Dryden, C. (1999). *Being married, doing gender.* New York: Routledge.

Duenwald, M., & Stamler, B. (2004, April 13). On their own, in the same boat. *The New York Times*, p. B13.

Dugger, C. W. (2001, April 22). Abortions in India spurred by sex test skew the ratio against girls. *The New York Times*, p. 12.

Duncan, M. C. (1990). Sports photographs and sexual difference: Images of women and men in the 1984 and 1988 Olympic games. *Sociology of Sport Journal, 7*, 22–43.

Durik, A., Hyde, J., Marks, A., Roy, A., Anaya, D., & Schultz, G. (2006). Ethnicity and gender stereotypes of emotion. *Sex Roles, 54*(7–8), 429–445. doi:10.1007/s11199-006-9020-4.

Dutton, D. G. (1996). Patriarchy and wife assault: The ecological fallacy. In L. K. Hamberger & C. Renzetti (Eds.), *Domestic partner abuse* (pp. 125–151). New York: Springer.

Dutton, Y. C., & Zisook, S. (2005). Adaptation to bereavement. *Death Studies, 29*, 877–903.

Duval, L. L., & Ruscher, J. B. (1994, July). *Men use more detail to explain a gender-neutral task to women.* Poster presented at the annual meeting of the American Psychological Society, Washington, DC.

Dworkin, S. L., & O'Sullivan, L. (2007). "It's less work for us and it shows us she has good taste:" Masculinity, sexual initiation, and contemporary sexual scripts. In M. Kimmell (Ed.), *The sexual self: The construction of sexual scripts* (pp. 105–121). Nashville, TN: University of Vanderbilt Press.

Eagly, A. H., & Johannesen-Schmidt, M. C. (2001). The leadership styles of women and men. *Journal of Social Issues, 57*, 781–797.

Eagly, A. H., & Johnson, B. T. (1990). Gender and leadership style: A meta-analysis. *Psychological Bulletin, 108*, 233–256.

Eagly, A. H., & Karau, S. J. (2002). Role congruity theory of prejudice toward female leaders. *Psychological Review, 109*, 573–598.

Eagly, A. H., Karau, S. J., & Makhijani, M. (1995). Gender and the effectiveness of leaders: A meta-analysis. *Psychological Bulletin, 117*, 125–145.

Eagly, A. H., & Mladinic, A. (1993). Are people prejudiced against women? Some answers from research on attitudes, gender stereotypes, and judgments of competence. In W. Strobe & M. Hewstone (Eds.), *European review of social psychology* (pp. 1–35). New York: Wiley.

Eagly, A. H., & Wood, W. (1999). The origins of sex differences in human behavior: Evolved dispositions versus social roles. *American Psychologist, 54*, 408–423.

East, P. L. (1998). Racial and ethnic differences in girls' sexual, marital, and birth expectations. *Journal of Marriage and the Family, 60*, 150–162.

Eastwick, P. W., & Finkel, E. J. (2008). Sex differences in mate preference revisited: Do people know what they initially desire in a romantic partner? *Journal of Personality and Social Psychology, 94*, 245–264.

Eccles, J. S. (1989). Bringing young women to math and science. In M. Crawford & M. Gentry (Eds.), *Gender and thought: Psychological perspectives* (pp. 36–58). New York: Springer Verlag.

Eccles, J. S. (1994). Understanding women's educational and occupational choices: Applying the Eccles et al. model of achievement-related choices. *Psychology of Women Quarterly, 18*, 585–610.

Eccles, J. S., Barber, B., Jozefowicz, D., Malenchuk, D., & Vida, M. (2000). Self-evaluations of competence, task values, and self-esteem. In N. G. Johnson, M. C. Roberts, & J. Worell (Eds.), *Beyond appearances: A new look at adolescent girls* (pp. 53–83). Washington DC: American Psychological Association.

Eckes, T. (1994). Features of men, features of women: Assessing stereotypic beliefs about gender subtypes. *British Journal of Social Psychology, 33*, 107–123.

Eder, D., Evans, C., & Parker, S. (1995). *School talk: Gender and adolescent culture.* New Brunswick, NJ: Rutgers University Press.

Edley, N., & Wetherell, M. (2001). Men's construction of feminism and feminists. *Feminism & Psychology, 11*, 439–458.

Edwards, C. P., Knoche, L., & Kumru, A. (2001). Play patterns and gender. In J. Worell (Ed.), *Encyclopedia of women and gender* (pp. 809–815). San Diego, CA: Academic Press.

Ehrenreich, B., & English, D. (1973). *Complaints and disorders: The sexual politics of sickness.* New York: The Feminist Press.

Ehrenreich, B., & English, D. (2005). *For her own good: Two centuries of the experts' advice to women.* New York: Anchor Books.

Eichler, M. (1988). *Nonsexist research methods.* Boston: Allen & Unwin.

Einstein, G. (2007). *Sex and the brain.* Boston: MIT Press.

Eisenach, J. C., Pan, P. H., Smiley, R., Lavand'homme, P., Landau, R., & Houle, T. T. (2008). Severity of acute pain after childbirth, but not type of delivery, predicts persistent pain and postpartum depression. *Pain, 140*(1), 87–94. doi:10.1016/j.pain.2008.07.011

Eisenstat, S. A., & Bancroft, L. (1999). Domestic violence. *New England Journal of Medicine, 341*, 886–892.

Eisikovits, Z., & Buchbinder, E. (1999). Talking control: Metaphors used by battered women. *Violence Against Women, 5*, 845–868.

Elavsky, S., & McAuley, E. (2005). Physical activity, symptoms, esteem, and life satisfaction during menopause. *Maturitas, 52*, 374–285.

Elfenbein, H. A., & Ambady, N. (2003). Universals and cultural differences in recognizing emotions. *Current Directions in Psychological Science, 12*, 159–164.

Elise, S. (1995). Teenaged mothers: A sense of self. In B. J. Dickerson (Ed.), *African American single mothers* (pp. 53–79). Thousand Oaks, CA: Sage.

Elkind, S. N. (1991, Winter). Letter to the editor. *Psychology of Women, 18*, 3.

Elklit, A., & O'Connor, M. (2005). Post-traumatic stress disorder in a Danish population of elderly bereaved. *Scandinavian Journal of Psychology, 46*, 439–445.

Elliot, P. (2009). Engaging trans debates on gender variance: a feminist analysis. *Sexualities, 12*, 5.

Elliot, R. (1989). *Song of love.* New York: Harlequin.

Ellsberg, M., Heise, L., Pena, R., Agurto, S., & Winkvist, A. (2001). Researching domestic violence against women: Methodological and ethical considerations. *Studies in Family Planning, 32*, 1–16.

Enns, C. Z. (2004). *Feminist theories and feminist psychotherapies: Origins, themes and variations.* Binghampton, NY: Haworth Press.

Erel, O., Oberman, Y., & Yirmiya, N. (2000). Maternal versus nonmaternal care and seven domains of children's development. *Psychological Bulletin, 126*, 727–747.

Erkut, S., Fields, J. P., Sing, R., & Marks, F. (1997). Diversity in girls' experiences: Feeling good about who you are. In B. J. R. Leadbeater & N. Way (Eds.), *Urban girls: Resisting stereotypes, creating identities* (pp. 53–64). New York: New York University Press.

Erwin, T. (2007). Two moms and a baby: Counseling lesbian couples choosing motherhood. *Women & Therapy, 30*(1–2), 99–149.

Espeland, M. A., Rapp, S. R., Shumaker, S. A., Brunner, R., Manson, J. E., & Sherwin, B. (2004). Conjugated equine estrogens and global cognitive function in postmenopausal women: Women's health initiative memory study. *Journal of the American Medical Association, 291*, 2959–2968.

Espin, O. M. (1986). Cultural and historical influences on sexuality in Hispanic/Latin women. In J. Cole (Ed.), *All American women: Lines that divide, ties that bind* (pp. 272–284). New York: Free Press.

Espin, O. M. (1987). Issues of identity in the psychology of Latina lesbians. In Boston Lesbian Psychologies Collective (Ed.), *Lesbian psychologies: Explorations and challenges* (pp. 35–55). Urbana: University of Illinois Press.

Etaugh, C., & Liss, M. B. (1992). Home, school, and playroom: Training grounds for adult gender roles. *Sex Roles, 26*, 129–147.

Etcoff, N. (1999). *Survival of the prettiest: The science of beauty.* New York: Anchor Books/Doubleday.

Evans, G. W. (2004). The environment of childhood poverty. *American Psychologist, 59*, 77–92.

Evans, L., & Davies, K. (2000). No sissy boys here: A content analysis of the representation of masculinity in elementary school reading textbooks. *Sex Roles, 42*, 255–270.

Fabiano, P., Perkins, W., Berkowitz, A., Linken-bach, J., & Stark, C. (2003). Engaging men as social justice allies in ending violence against women: Evidence for a social norms approach. *Journal of American College Health, 52,* 105–112.

Facio, E. (1997). Chicanas and aging: Toward definitions of womanhood. In J. M. Coyle (Ed.), *Handbook on women and aging* (pp. 335–350). Westport, CT: Greenwood Press.

Faderman, L. (1981). *Surpassing the love of men: Romantic friendship and love between women from the Renaissance to the present.* New York: William Morrow.

Fägerskiöld, A. (2008). A change in life as experienced by first time fathers. *Scandinavian Journal of Caring Science, 22,* 64–71.

Fagot, B. I., & Leinbach, M. D. (1995). Gender knowledge in egalitarian and traditional families. *Sex Roles, 32,* 513–526.

Faircloth, C. A. (Ed.). (2003). *Aging bodies: Images and everyday experiences.* New York: AltaMira Press.

Faludi, S. (1991). *Backlash: The undeclared war against American women.* New York: Doubleday.

Fanti, K. A., Vanman, E., Henrich, C., & Avramides, M. N. (2009). Desensitization to media violence over a short period of time. *Aggressive Behavior, 35,* 179–187.

Farmer, H. S. (Ed.). (1997). *Diversity & women's career development: From adolescence to adulthood.* Thousand Oaks, CA: Sage.

Farr, K. (2005). *Sex trafficking: The global market in women and children.* New York: Worth.

Farrell, B. (2003, August 17). American TV raises the stars and strips: The major US networks are doing the unthinkable—putting porn in their schedules. *The Observer,* p. 8.

Fassinger, R. E. (2002). Hitting the ceiling: Gendered barriers to occupational entry, advancements, and achievement. In L. Diamant & J. A. Lee (Eds.), *The psychology of sex, gender, and jobs: Issues and resolutions* (pp. 21–46). Westport, CT: Praeger.

Fasula, A. M., Miller, K. S., & Wiener, J. (2007). The sexual double standard in African American adolescent women's sexual risk reduction. *Women & Health, 46,* 3–21.

Fausto-Sterling, A. (2000). *Sexing the body: Gender politics and the construction of sexuality.* New York: Basic Books.

Favreau, O. E. (1997). Sex and gender comparisons: Does null hypothesis testing create a false dichotomy? *Feminism and Psychology, 7,* 63–81.

Federal Glass Ceiling Commission. (1998). Working women face barriers to advancement. In M. E. Williams (Ed.), *Working women: Opposing viewpoints* (pp. 64–72). San Diego, CA: Greenhaven Press.

Feinberg, L. (1996). *Transgender warriors: Making history from Joan of Arc to Dennis Rodman.* Boston: Beacon.

Feldman, S. (1999). Please don't call me "dear": Older women's narratives of health care. *Nursing Inquiry, 6,* 269–276.

Feminists for Free Expression (FFE). *The free speech pamphlet series: Pornography.* Retrieved from http://www.ffeusa. org/html/statements/statements_pornography.php

Fidell, L. S. (1970). Empirical verification of sex discrimination in hiring practices in psychology. *American Psychologist, 25,* 1094–1098.

Fields, J., & Casper, L. (2001, June). America's families and living arrangements 2000: Population characteristics. *U.S. Department of Commerce: Economics and Statistics Administration.* Retrieved July 8, 2004, from http://www. census.gov/prod/2001pubs/p20-537.pdf

Filardo, E. K. (1996). Gender patterns in African American and White adolescents' social interactions in same-race, mixed-gender groups. *Journal of Personality and Social Psychology, 71,* 71–82.

Fine, M. (1988). Sexuality, schooling, and adolescent females: The missing discourse of desire. *Harvard Educational Review, 58,* 29–53.

Fine, M., & Asch, A. (1988). *Women with disabilities: Essays in psychology, culture, and politics.* Philadelphia: Temple University Press.

Fink, J. S., & Kensicki, L. J. (2002). An imperceptible difference: Visual and textual constructions of femininity in *Sports Illustrated* and *Sports Illustrated for Women. Mass Communication and Society, 5,* 317–339.

Firestein, B. A. (1998, March 7). Bisexuality: A feminist vision of choice and change. Paper presented at the annual meeting of the Association for Women in Psychology, Baltimore, MD.

Fischer, A. H., & Manstead, A. S. R. (2000). The relation between gender and emotion in different cultures. In A. H. Fischer (Ed.), *Gender and emotion: Social psychological perspectives* (pp. 71–94). Cambridge, England: Cambridge University Press.

Fisher, J. D., & Fisher, W. A. (2000). Theoretical approaches to individual-level change in HIV risk behavior. In J. L. Peterson & R. J. DiClemente (Eds.), *Handbook of HIV prevention, AIDS prevention and mental health* (pp. 3–55). New York: Kluwer Academic/Plenum.

Fisher, J. D., Fisher, W. A., Misovich, S. J., Kimble, D. L., & Malloy, T. E. (1996). Changing AIDS risk behavior: Effects of an intervention emphasizing AIDS risk reduction information, motivation, and behavioral skills in a college student population. *Health Psychology, 15,* 114–123.

Fisher, W. A., Williams, S. S., Fisher, J. D., & Malloy, T. E. (1999). Understanding AIDS risk behavior among sexually active urban adolescents: An empirical test of the information-motivation-behavioral skills model. *AIDS and Behavior, 3,* 13–23.

Fiske, A. P., Haslam, N., & Fiske, S. T. (1991). Confusing one person with another: What errors reveal about the elementary forms of social relations. *Journal of Personality and Social Psychology, 60,* 656–674.

Fiske, S. T., Bersoff, D. N., Borgida, E., Deaux, K., & Heilman, M. E. (1991). Social science research on trial: Use of sex stereotyping research in Price Waterhouse v. Hopkins. *American Psychologist, 46,* 1049–1060.

Fiske, S. T., Xu, J., Cuddy, A. C., & Glick, P. (1999). (Dis) respecting versus (dis)liking: Status and interdependence predict ambivalent stereotypes of competence and warmth. *Journal of Social Issues, 55*, 473–489.

Fitch, R. H., & Denenberg, V. H. (1998). A role for ovarian hormones in sexual differentiation of the brain. *Behavior and Brain Science, 21*, 311–352.

Fitzgerald, L. F. (1993). Sexual harassment: Violence against women in the workplace. *American Psychologist, 48*, 1070–1076.

Fitzgerald, L. F., Drasgow, F., Hulin, C. L., Gelfland, M. J., & Magley, V. J. (1997). Antecedents and consequences of sexual harassment in organizations: A test of an integrated model. *Journal of Applied Psychology, 82*, 578–589.

Fitzgerald, L. F., Swan, S., & Magley, V. J. (1997). But was it really sexual harassment? Legal, behavioral, and psychological definitions of the workplace victimization of women. In W. O'Donohue (Ed.), *Sexual harassment: Theory, research, and treatment* (pp. 5–28). Boston: Allyn & Bacon.

Fivush, R. (1989). Exploring sex differences in the emotional content of mother-child conversations about the past. *Sex Roles, 20*, 675–692.

Fivush, R., Brotman, M. A., Buckner, J. P., & Goodman, S. H. (2000). Gender differences in parent-child emotion narratives. *Sex Roles, 42*, 233–253.

Fivush, R., & Buckner, J. P. (2000). Gender, sadness, and depression: The development of emotional focus through gendered discourse. In A. H. Fischer (Ed.), *Gender and emotion: Social psychological perspectives* (pp. 232–254). Cambridge, England: Cambridge University Press.

Flanders, L. (1997). Real majority, media minority: The costs of sidelining women in reporting. Monroe, ME: Common Courage Press.

Follingstad, D. R., Rutledge, L. L., McNeill-Hawkins, K., & Polek, D. S. (1992). Factors related to physical violence in dating relationships. In E. C. Viano (Ed.), *Intimate violence: Interdisciplinary perspectives* (pp. 121–135). New York: Hemisphere.

Forbes, G. B., Adams-Curtis, L. E., Holmgren, K. M., & White, K. B. (2004). Perceptions of the social and personal characteristics of hypermuscular women and of the men who love them. *Journal of Social Psychology, 144*, 487–506.

Ford, A. R. (1986). When women outlive their ovaries. *New Internationalist, 165*.

Ford, M. T., Heinen, B. A., & Langkamer, K. L. (2007). Work and family satisfaction and conflict: A meta-analysis of cross-domain relations. *Journal of Applied Psychology, 92*, 57–80.

Foreit, K. G., Agor, A. T., Byers, J., Larue, J., Lokey, H., Palazzini, M., et al. (1980). Sex bias in the newspaper treatment of male-centered and female-centered news stories. *Sex Roles, 6*, 475–480.

Forste, R., & Tanfer, K. (1996). Sexual exclusivity among dating, cohabiting, and married women. *Journal of Marriage and Family, 58*, 33–47.

Foucault, M. (1972). *The archaeology of knowledge.* New York: Pantheon.

Fouts, G., & Burggraf, K. (2000). Television situation comedies, female weight, male negative comments, and audience reactions. *Sex Roles, 42*, 925–932.

Franiuk, R., Seefelt, J. L., & Vandello, J. A. (2008). Prevalence and effects of rape myths in print journalism: The Kobe Bryant case. *Violence Against Women, 14*, 287–309.

Fraser, L. (2002, December 1). The islands where boys grow up to be girls: In the South Pacific, the fa'fafine men who spend their lives as women—turn gender roles upside down. *Marie Claire, 9*, 72–78.

Frazer, A. K., & Miller, M. D. (2009). Double standards in sentence structure: Passive voice in narratives describing domestic violence. *Journal of Language and Social Psychology, 28*, 62–71.

Frederickson, B. L., & Roberts, T. (1997). Objectification theory: Toward understanding women's lived experiences and mental health risks. *Psychology of Women Quarterly, 21*, 173–206.

Frederickson, B. L., Roberts, T., Noll, S. M., Quinn, D. M., & Twenge, J. M. (1998). That swimsuit becomes you: Sex differences in self-objectification, restrained eating, and math performance. *Journal of Personality and Social Psychology, 75*, 269–284.

Freedman, R. (1986). *Beauty bound.* Lexington, MA: Lexington Books.

French, H. W. (2003, June 29). Victims say Japan ignores sex crimes committed by teachers. *The New York Times*, p. A4.

Frenzel, A. C., Pekrun, R., & Goetz, T. (2007). Girls and mathematics—A "hopeless" issue? A control-value approach to gender differences in emotions towards mathematics. *European Journal of Psychology of Education, 22*(4), 497–514.

Freud, S. (1914). On the history of the Psycho-Analytic movement. New York: W. W. Norton, Inc., 1966

Freud, S. (1933). Femininity. In J. Strachey (Ed. & Trans.), *New introductory lectures on psycho-analysis* (pp. 112–135). New York: Norton, 1965.

Friedman, S. D., & Greenhaus, J. H. (2000). *Work and family—Allies or enemies?* New York: Oxford University Press.

Frieze, I. H. (2005). *Hurting the one you love: Violence in relationships.* Belmont, CA: Wadsworth/Thomson Learning.

Frintner, M. P., & Rubinson, L. (1993). Acquaintance rape: The influence of alcohol, fraternity membership, and sports team membership. *Journal of Sex Education and Therapy, 19*, 272–284.

Frisch, R. E. (1983). Fatness, menarche, and fertility. In S. Golub (Ed.), *Menarche: The transition from girl to woman* (pp. 5–20). Lexington, MA: Lexington Books.

Fugere, M. A., Excoto, C., Cousins, A. J., Riggs, M. L., & Haerich, P. (2008). Sexual attitudes and double standards: A literature review focusing on participant gender and ethnic background. *Sexuality & Culture, 12*, 169–182.

Fulcher, M., Sutfin, E. L., Chan, R. W., Scheib, J. E., & Patterson, C. J. (2006). Lesbian mothers and their children. In A. M. Omoto & H. S. Kurtzman (Eds.), *Sexual orientation and mental health: Examining identity and development in lesbian, gay, and bisexual people* (pp. 281–99). Washington, DC: American Psychological Association.

Furdyna, H., Tucker, M., & James, A. (2008). Relative spousal earnings and marital happiness among African American and white women. *Journal of Marriage and Family, 70*, 332–344.

Furnham, A., & Mak, T. (1999). Sex-role stereotyping in television commercials: A review and compendium of fourteen studies done on five continents over twenty-five years. *Sex Roles, 41*, 413–437.

Gagnon, J. H., & Simon, W. (1973). *Sexual conduct: The social sources of human sexuality.* Chicago: Aldine.

Gabriel, U., & Gygax, P. (2008). Can societal language amendments change gender representation? The case of Norway. *Scandianavian Journal of Psychology, 49*, 451–457.

Galliano, G. (2003). *Gender: Crossing boundaries.* Belmont, CA: Wadsworth/Thomson Learning.

Ganahl, D. J., Prinsen, T. J., & Netzley, S. B. (2003). A content analysis of prime time commercials: A contextual framework of gender representation. *Sex Roles, 49*, 545–551.

Gannon, L. R., Luchetta, T., Rhodes, K., Pardie, L., & Segrist, D. (1992). Sex bias in psychological research: Progress or complacency? *American Psychologist, 47*, 389–396.

Ganong, L. H., & Coleman, M. (2000). Remarried families. In C. Hendrick & S. S. Hendrick (Eds.), *Close relationships: A sourcebook* (pp. 155–170). Thousand Oaks, CA: Sage.

Ganong, L., Coleman, M., & Hans, J. (2006). Divorce as a prelude to stepfamily living and the consequences of redivorce. In M. A. Fine & J. H. Harvey (Eds.), *Handbook of divorce and relationship dissolution* (pp. 409–434). Mahwah, NJ: Lawrence Erlbaum Associates.

García-Moreno, J. (2005). *WHO Multi-country study on women's health and domestic violence against women.* Initial results on prevalence, health outcomes and women's responses, Geneva: WHO.

Garner, D. M., Garfinkel, P. E., Schwartz, D., & Thompson, M. (1980). Cultural expectations of thinness in women. *Psychological Reports, 47*, 483–491.

Garner, J. H., & Maxwell, C. D. (2000). What are the lessons of the police arrest studies? *Journal of Aggression, Maltreatment & Trauma, 4*, 83–114.

Garnets, L. D. (2008). Life as a lesbian: What does gender have to do with it? In J. Chrisler, C. Golden, & P. Rozee (Eds.), *Lectures on the psychology of women* (4th ed., pp. 233–249). New York: McGraw-Hill.

Garnets, L. D., & Peplau, L. A. (2001). A new paradigm for women's sexual orientation: Implications for therapy. *Women & Therapy, 24*, 111–121.

Garofoli, J. (2007, May 13). White men get the lion's share. *San Francisco Chronicle.* Retrieved February 2, 2011, from http://www.sfgate.com/cgi-bin/article.cgi?f=/c/a/2007/05/13/GUESTS.TMP

Garu, S. L., Roselli, G., & Taylor, C. R. (2007). Where's Tamika Catchings? A content analysis of female athlete endorsers in magazine advertisements. *Journal of Current Issues and Research in Advertising, 29*, 55–66.

Gavey, N. (2005). *Just sex: The cultural scaffolding of rape.* New York: Routledge.

Gazmarian, J., Petersen, P., Spitz, A., Goodwin, M., Saltzman, L., & Marks, J. (2000). Violence and reproductive health: Current knowledge and future research directions. *Maternal and Child Health Journal, 4*, 79–84.

Ge, X., Conger, R. D., & Elder, G. H., Jr. (2001). Pubertal transition, stressful life events, and the emergence of gender differences in adolescent depressive symptoms. *Developmental Psychology, 37*, 404–417.

Ge, X., & Natsuaki, M. N. (2009). In search of explanations for early pubertal timing effects on developmental psychopathology. *Current Directions in Psychological Science, 18*, 327–331.

Gehlert, S., Song, I. H., Chang, C. H., & Hartlage, S. A. (2009). The prevalence of premenstrual dysphoric disorder in a randomly selected group of urban and rural women. *Psychological Medicine: A Journal of Research in Psychiatry and the Allied Sciences, 39*, 129–136.

Gelaye, B., Arnold, D., Williams, M. A., Goshu, M., & Berhane, Y. (2009). Depressive symptoms among female college students experiencing gender-based violence in Awassa, Ethiopia. *Journal of Interpersonal Violence, 24*, 464–481.

Geller, J. L., & Harris, M. (1994). *Women of the asylum: Voices from behind the walls, 1840–1945.* New York: Anchor Books.

Gender bias in college admissions tests. (2007). Retrieved February 17, 2010, from www.fairtest.org/gender-bias-college-admissions-tests

Gender verification suspended on trial basis at Sydney Olympics. Retrieved April 10, 2000, from http://www.isna.org

George, S. M., & Dickerson, B. J. (1995). The role of the grandmother in poor single-mother families and households. In B. J. Dickerson (Ed.), *African American single mothers* (pp. 146–163). Thousand Oaks, CA: Sage.

Gerstel, N. (1988). Divorce, gender, and social integration. *Gender & Society, 2*, 343–367.

Giddings, P. (1984). *When and where I enter: The impact of black women on race and sex in America.* New York: Morrow.

Gieve, K. (1989). *Balancing acts: On being a mother.* London: Virago.

Gilbert, L. A. (1993). *Two careers/One family: The promise of gender equality.* London: Sage.

Gilbert, L. A., & Rader, J. (2001). Current perspectives on women's adult roles: Work, family, and life. In R. Unger (Ed.), *Handbook of the psychology of women and gender* (pp. 156–170). New York: Wiley.

Gilbert, L. A., Galessich, J. M., & Evans, S. L. (1983). Sex of faculty role model and students' self-perceptions of competency. *Sex Roles, 9,* 597–607.

Gilbert, L. A., & Rossman, K. M. (1992). Gender and the mentoring process for women: Implications for professional development. *Professional Psychology: Research and Practice, 23,* 233–238.

Gilbert, L., & Kearney, L. (2006). Sex, gender, and dual-earner families: Implications and applications for career counseling for women. In W. B. Walsh & M. J. Heppner (Eds.), *Handbook of career counseling for women* (2nd ed., pp. 193–217). Mahwah, NJ: Erlbaum.

Gilbert, S. C. (2003). Eating disorders in women of color. *Clinical Psychology: Science and Practice, 10,* 444–455.

Gilman, C. P. (1892). The yellow wallpaper. Reprinted in *The Yellow Wallpaper and Other Stories.* Mineola, NY: Dover Publications Incorporated, 1997.

Glick, P., Diebold, J., Bailey-Werner, B., & Zhu, L. (1997). The two faces of Adam: Ambivalent sexism and polarized attitudes toward women. *Personality and Social Psychology Bulletin, 23,* 1323–1334.

Glick, P., & Fiske, S. T. (1996). The ambivalent sexism inventory: Differentiating hostile and benevolent sexism. *Journal of Personality and Social Psychology, 70,* 491–512.

Glick, P., & Fiske, S. T. (2001). An ambivalent alliance: Hostile and benevolent sexism as complementary justifications for gender inequality. *American Psychologist, 56,* 109–118.

Glick, P., Fiske, S. T., Mladinic, A., Saiz, J. L., Abrams, D., Masser, B., et al. (2000). Beyond prejudice as simple antipathy: Hostile and benevolent sexism across cultures. *Journal of Personality and Social Psychology, 79,* 763–775. doi:10.1037/0022-3514.79.5.763

Glick, P., Larsen, S., Johnson, C., & Branstiter, H. (2005). Evaluations of sexy women in low- and high-status jobs. *Psychology of Women Quarterly, 29,* 389–395.

Godart, N. T., Perdereau, F., Rein, Z., Berthoz, S., Wallier, J., Jeammet, P., et al. (2007). Comorbidity studies of eating disorders and mood disorders. Critical review of the literature. *Journal of Affective Disorders, 97,* 37–49.

Goffman, E. (1961). *Asylums: Essays on the social situation of mental patients and other inmates.* New York: Doubleday.

Goldberg, P. A. (1968). Are women prejudiced against women? *Transaction, 5,* 28–30.

Golden, C. (1987). Diversity and variability in women's sexual identities. In Boston Lesbian Psychologies Collective (Eds.), *Lesbian psychologies* (pp. 18–34). Urbana: University of Illinois Press.

Golden, C. (2008). The intersexed and the transgendered: Rethinking sex/gender. In J. C. Christler, C. Golden, & P. D. Rozee (Eds.), *Lectures on the psychology of women* (4th ed., pp. 136–153). New York: McGraw-Hill.

Golding, J. M. (1999). Intimate partner violence as a risk factor for mental disorders: A meta-analysis. *Journal of Family Violence, 14,* 99–132.

Golombok, S., Perry, B., Burston, A., Murray, C., Mooney-Somers, J., Stevens, M., & Golding, J. (2003). Children with lesbian parents: A community study. *Developmental Psychology, 39,* 20–33.

Gomez, C. A., & Vanoss-Marin, B. (1996). Gender, culture, and power: Barriers to HIV prevention strategies for women. *Journal of Sex Research, 33,* 355–362.

Gonzales, P. M., Blanton, H., & Williams, K. J. (2002). The effects of stereotype threat and double-minority status on the test performance of Latino women. *Personality & Social Psychology Bulletin, 28,* 659–670.

Gooden, A. M., & Gooden, M. A. (2001). Gender representations in notable children's picture books: 1995–1999. *Sex Roles, 45,* 89–101.

Goodwin, R., & Pillay, U. (2006). Relationships, culture, and social change. In A. L. Vangelsiti & D. Perlman (Eds.), *The Cambridge handbook of personal relationships* (pp. 695–707). New York: Cambridge University Press.

Gooren, L. (2006). The biology of human psychosexual differentiation. *Hormones and Behavior, 50,* 589–601.

Gordon, J. S. (1996). Community services of abused women: A review of perceived usefulness and efficacy. *Journal of Family Violence, 11,* 315–329.

Gordon, K. H., Castro, Y., Sitnikov, L., & Holm-Denoma, J. M. (2010). Cultural body shape ideals and eating disorder symptoms among White, Latina, and Black college women. *Cultural Diversity and Ethnic Minority Psychology, 16,* 135–143.

Gordon, M. (2003, August 3). How Ireland hid its own dirty laundry. *The New York Times,* section 2, p.1.

Gordon, M. K. (2008). Media contributions to African American girls' focus on beauty and appearance: Exploring the consequences of sexual objectification. *Psychology of Women Quarterly, 32,* 245–256.

Gould, S. J. (1980). *The panda's thumb.* New York: Norton.

Gould, S. J. (1981). *The mismeasure of man.* New York: Norton.

Gove, W. R., & Shin, H. C. (1989). The psychological well-being of divorced and widowed men and women: An empirical analysis. *Journal of Family Issues, 10,* 122–144.

Gowen, L. K., Hayward, C., Killen, J. D., Robinson, T. N., & Taylor, C. B. (1999). Acculturation and eating disorder symptoms in adolescent girls. *Journal of Research on Adolescence, 9,* 67–83.

Grabe, S., & Hyde, J. S. (2006). Ethnicity and body dissatisfaction among women in the United States: A meta-analysis. *Psychological Bulletin, 132,* 622–640.

Grabe, S., Ward, L. M., & Hyde, J. S. (2008). The role of the media in body image concerns among women: A meta-analysis of experimental and correlational studies. *Psychological Bulletin, 134,* 460–476.

Grady, K. E. (1977, April). *The belief in sex differences.* Paper presented at the meeting of the Eastern Psychological Association, Boston.

Grall, T. S. (2009). *Custodial mothers and fathers and their child support: 2007.* Retrieved May 22, 2010, from http://singleparents.about.com/gi/o.htm?zi=1/XJ&zTi=1&sdn=singleparents&cdn=parenting&tm=101&gps=311_67_1259_626&f=00&su=p284.9.336.ip_p504.3.336.ip_&tt=11&bt=0&bts=0&zu=http%3A//www.census.gov/prod/2009pubs/p60-237.pdf

Grambs, J. D. (1989). *Women over forty: Visions and realities.* New York: Springer.

Grana, S. J. (2002). *Women and (in)justice: The criminal and civil effects of the common law on women's lives.* Boston: Allyn & Bacon.

Grant, B. F., & Weissman, M. M. (2007). Gender and the prevalence of psychiatric disorders. In W. E. Narrow, M. B. First, P. J. Sirovatka, & D. A. Regier (Eds.), *Age and gender considerations in psychiatric diagnosis: A research agenda for DSM-V.* Arlington, VA, US: American Psychiatric Publishing, Inc.

Gray, H. M., & Phillips, S. (1998). *Real girl real world: Tools for finding your true self.* Seattle, WA: Seal Press.

Greeff, A. P., & Du Toit, C. (2009). Resilience in remarried families. *The American Journal of Family Therapy, 37,* 114–126.

Green, S. E., Liao, K. Y.-H., Hollengren, J. J., Davids, C. M., Carter, L. P., Kugler, D. W., et al. (2009). Eating disorder behaviors and depression: A minimal relationship beyond social comparison, self-esteem, and body dissatisfaction. *Journal of Clinical Psychology, 65,* 989–999.

Greenberg, B. S., & Worrell, T. R. (2007). New faces on television: A 12-season replication. *The Howard Journal of Communications, 18,* 277–290.

Greene, B. (2000). African American lesbian and bisexual women. *Journal of Social Issues, 56,* 239–250.

Greene, B. A. (1990). Sturdy bridges: The role of African-American mothers in the socialization of African-American children. In J. P. Knowles & E. Cole (Eds.), *Motherhood: A feminist perspective* (pp. 205–225). New York: Haworth.

Greene, K., & Faulkner, S. L. (2005). Gender, belief in the sexual double standard, and sexual talk in heterosexual dating relationships. *Sex Roles, 53,* 239–251.

Greenglass, E. R., & Burke, R. J. (1988). Work and family precursors of burnout in teachers: Sex differences. *Sex Roles, 18,* 215–229.

Greenhouse, S., & Hays, C. L. (2004, June 23). Wal-Mart sex-bias suit given class-action status. *The New York Times,* pp. A1, C8.

Greenwell, A., & Hough, S. (2008). Culture and disability in sexuality studies: A methodological and content review of the literature. *Sexuality & Disability, 26,* 189–196.

Greenwood, D. (2009). Idealized TV friends and young women's body concerns. *Body Image, 6,* 97–104.

Gremaux, R. (1996). Woman becoming man in the Balkans. In G. Herdt (Ed.), *Third sex, third gender: Beyond sexual dimorphism in culture and history* (pp. 241–281). New York: Zone Books.

Gresky, D., Ten Eyck, L., Lord, C., & McIntyre, R. (2005). Effects of salient multiple identities on women's performance under mathematics stereotype threat. *Sex Roles, 53*(9–10), 703–716. doi:10.1007/s11199-005-7735-2.

Groesz, L. M., Levine, M. P., & Murnen, S. K. (2002). The effect of experimental presentation of thin media images on body satisfaction: A meta-analytic review. *International Journal of Eating Disorders, 31,* 1–16.

Gross, J. (2004, February 27). Older women team up to face future together. *The New York Times,* p. A1.

Grossman, A. H., D'Augelli, A. R., & O'Connell, T. S. (2001). Being lesbian, gay, bisexual, and 60 or older in North America. In D. C. Kimmel & D. L. Martin (Eds.), *Midlife and aging in gay America: Proceedings of the SAGE conference, New York City, 2000* (pp. 23–40). New York: Harrington Park Press.

Grossman, A. L., & Tucker, J. S. (1997). Gender differences and sexism in the knowledge and use of slang. *Sex Roles, 37,* 101–110.

Grossman, F. K., Gilbert, L. A., Genero, N. P., Hawes, S. E., Hyde, J. S., & Marecek, J. (1997). Feminist research: Practice and problems. In J. Worell & N. G. Johnson (Eds.), *Shaping the future of feminist psychology: Education, research, and practice* (pp. 73–91). Washington, DC: American Psychological Association.

Grossman, J. B., & Tierney, J. P. (1998). Does mentoring work? An impact study of the Big Brothers Big Sisters program. *Evaluation Review, 22,* 403–426.

Grossman, M., & Wood, W. (1993). Sex differences in intensity of emotional experience: A social role interpretation. *Journal of Personality and Social Psychology, 65,* 1010–1022.

Gubrium, J. F., & Holstein, J. A. (2003). The everyday visibility of the aging body. In C.A. Faircloth (Ed.), *Aging bodies: Images and everyday experiences* (pp. 205–227). New York: AltaMira Press.

Guillet, E., Sarrazin, P., & Fontayne, P. (2000). If it contradicts my gender role, I'll stop: Introducing survival analysis to study the effects of gender typing on the time of withdrawal from sport practice: A 3-year study. *European Review of Applied Psychology, 50,* 417–421.

Gura, T. (2007). *Lying in weight: The hidden epidemic of eating disorders in adult women.* New York: Harper Collins.

Gutek, B. A. (1985). *Sex and the workplace.* San Francisco: Jossey-Bass.

Gutek, B. A. (2001). Women and paid work. *Psychology of Women Quarterly, 25,* 379–393.

Gutek, B. A., & Done, R. S. (2001). Sexual harassment. In R. K. Unger (Ed.), *Handbook of the psychology of women and gender* (pp. 367–387). New York: Wiley.

Gutek, B. A., & Larwood, L. (Eds.). (1987). *Women's career development*. Newbury Park, CA: Sage.

Guthrie, R. V. (1976). *Even the rat was white: A historical view of psychology*. New York: Harper & Row.

Guttmacher Institute. (2010a). *Facts on induced abortion in the United States*. Retrieved on May 15, 2010, from http://www.guttmacher.org/pubs/fb_induced_abortion.html

Guttmacher Institute. (2010b). *State policies in brief: an overview of minors' consent laws*. Retrieved on May 17, 2010, from http://www.guttmacher.org/statecenter/spibs/spib_omcl.pdf

Guttmacher Institute. (2010c). *U.S. teenage pregnancies, births and abortions: National and state trends and trends by race and ethnicity*. Retrieved May 21, 2010, from http://www.guttmacher.org/pubs/ustptrends.pdf

Gygax, P., Gabriel, U., Sarrasin, O., Oakhill, J., & Garnham, A. (2008). Generically intended, but specifically interpreted: When beauticians, musicians and mechanics are all men. *Language and Cognitive Processes, 23*, 464–485.

Haaken, J., & Yragui, N. (2003). Going underground: Conflicting perspectives on domestic violence shelter practices. *Feminism & Psychology, 13*, 49–71.

Hahn, C. S. (2001). Review: Psychosocial well-being of parents and their children born after assisted reproduction. *Journal of Pediatric Psychology, 26*, 525–538.

Haj-Yahia, M. M. (1998). Beliefs about wife beating among Palestinian women: The influence of their patriarchal ideology. *Violence Against Women, 4*, 533–558.

Hald, G. M., Malamuth, N. M., & Yuen, C. (2010). Pornography and attitudes supporting violence against women: Revisiting the relationship in nonexperimental studies. *Aggressive Behavior, 36*, 14–20.

Hall, J. A. (1996). Touch, status, and gender at professional meetings. *Journal of Nonverbal Behavior, 20*, 23–44.

Hall, J. A. (2006). How big are nonverbal sex differences? The case of smiling and nonverbal sensitivity. In K. Dindia & D. J. Canary (Eds.), *Sex differences and similarities in communication* (2nd ed., pp. 59–81). Mahwah, NJ: Lawrence Erlbaum Associates Publishers.

Hall, J. A., Carter, J. D., & Horgan, T. G. (2000). Gender differences in nonverbal communication of emotion. In A. H. Fischer (Ed.), *Gender and emotion: Social psychological perspectives* (pp. 97–117). New York: Cambridge University Press.

Hall, K. (1995). Lip service on the fantasy lines. In K. Hall & M. Bucholtz (Eds.), *Gender articulated* (pp. 183–216). New York: Routledge.

Hall, R. L. (1998). Softly strong: African American women's use of exercise in therapy. In K. F. Hays (Ed.), *Integrating exercise, sports, movement and mind: Therapeutic unity* (pp. 81–100). Binghamton, NY: The Haworth Press.

Hall, R. L. (2008). Sweating it out: The good news and the bad news about women and sport. In J. C. Chrisler, C. Golden, & P. D. Rozee (Eds.), *Lectures on the psychology of women* (4th ed., pp. 97–115). New York: McGraw-Hill.

Halliwell, E., & Dittmar, H. (2003). A qualitative investigation of women's and men's body image concerns and their attitudes toward aging. *Sex Roles, 49*, 675–684.

Halpern, D. F. (1992). *Sex differences in cognitive abilities* (2nd ed.). Hillsdale, NJ: Erlbaum.

Hamilton, J. A., & Jensvold, M. F. (1995). Sex and gender as critical variables in feminist psychopharmacology research and pharmacotherapy. *Women & Therapy, 16*, 9–30.

Hamilton, M. C. (1991). Masculine bias in the attribution of personhood: People = male, male = people. *Psychology of Women Quarterly, 15*, 393–402

Hamilton, M. C., Anderson, D., Broaddus, M., & Young, K. (2006). Gender stereotyping and under-representation of female characters in 200 popular children's picture books: A twenty-first century update. *Sex Roles, 55*, 757–765.

Hammer, J. C., Fisher, J. D., Fitzgerald, P., & Fisher, W. A. (1996). When two heads aren't better than one: AIDS risk behavior in college-age couples. *Journal of Applied Social Psychology, 26*, 375–397.

Hanganu-Bresch, C. (2008). *Faces of depression: A study of antidepressant advertisements in the American and British journals of psychiatry, 1960–2004*. Unpublished dissertation: University of Minnesota.

Hankin, B. L., & Abramson, L. Y. (2001). Development of gender differences in depression: An elaborated cognitive vulnerability-transactional stress theory. *Psychological Bulletin, 127*, 773–796.

Hansen, F. J., & Osborne, D. (1995). Portrayal of women and elderly patients in psychotropic drug advertisements. *Women & Therapy, 16*, 129–141.

Hanson, R. (2002). Adolescent dating violence: Prevalence and psychological outcomes. *Child Abuse and Neglect, 26*, 449–453.

Harasty, A. S. (1997). The interpersonal nature of social stereotypes: Differential discussion patterns about ingroups and out-groups. *Personality and Social Psychology Bulletin, 23*, 270–284.

Hardin, M., & Greer, J. D. (2009). The influence of gender-role socialization, media use and sports participation on perceptions of gender-appropriate sports. *Journal of Sport Behavior, 32*, 207–226.

Harding, R., & Peel E. (2006). "We do"? International perspectives on equality, legality and same sex relationships. *Lesbian & Gay Psychology Review, 7*(2), 123–140.

Harding, S. (1986). *The science question in feminism*. Ithaca, NY: Cornell University Press.

Hare-Mustin, R. T., & Marecek, J. (Eds.). (1990). *Making a difference: Psychology and the construction of gender*. New Haven, CT: Yale University Press.

Harris, G. (2004, May 8). Morning-after-pill ruling defies norm. *The New York Times*, p. A13.

Harris, B. J. (1984). The power of the past: History and the psychology of women. In M. Lewin (Ed.), *In the shadow of the past* (pp. 1–5). New York: Columbia University Press.

Harris, S. (1994). Racial differences in predictors of college women's body image attitudes. *Women and Health, 21,* 89–104.

Harrison, K. (2003). Television viewers' ideal body proportions: The case of the curvaceously thin woman. *Sex Roles, 48,* 255–265.

Hartung, C. M., & Widiger, T. A. (1998). Gender differences in the diagnosis of mental disorders: Conclusions and controversies of the DSM-IV. *Psychological Bulletin, 123,* 260–278.

Hartwell, C. E. (1996). The schizophrenogenic mother concept in American psychiatry. *Psychiatry: Interpersonal and Biological Processes, 59,* 274–297.

Harville, M. L., & Rienzi, B. M. (2000). Equal worth and gracious submission: Judeo-Christian attitudes toward employed women. *Psychology of Women Quarterly, 24,* 145–147.

Harwood, K., McLean, N., & Durkin, K. (2007). First-time mothers' expectations of parenthood: What happens when optimistic expectations are not matched by later experiences? *Developmental Psychology, 43,* 1–12.

Hash, K. (2001). Preliminary study of caregiving and post-caregiving experiences of older gay men and lesbians. In D. C. Kimmel & D. L. Martin (Eds.), *Midlife and aging in gay America: Proceedings of the SAGE conference, New York City, 2000* (pp. 87–94). New York: Harrington Park Press.

Hatch, L. R. (1995). Gray clouds and silver linings: Women's resources in later life. In J. Freeman (Ed.), *Women: A feminist perspective* (5th ed., pp. 182–196). Mountain View, CA: Mayfield.

Hatton, B. J. (1994, March). *The experiences of African American lesbians: Family, community, and intimate relationships.* Poster presented at the Southeastern Psychological Association Convention. New Orleans, LA.

Hausdorff, J., Levy, B. R., & Wei, J. Y. (1999). The power of ageism on physical function in older persons: Reversibility of age-related gait changes. *Journal of the American Geriatric Society, 47,* 1346–1349.

Hawkins, J. W., & Aber, C. S. (1993). Women in advertisements in medical journals. *Sex Roles, 28,* 233–242.

Hazen, A. L., Connelly, C. D., Soriano, F. I., & Landsverk, J. A. (2008). Intimate partner violence and psychological functioning in Latina women. *Health Care for Women International, 29,* 282–299.

Heaphy, B., Yip, A. K. T., & Thompson, D. (2004). Ageing in a non-heterosexual context. *Ageing and Society, 24,* 881–902.

Hebl, M., King, E., Glick, P., Singletary, S., & Kazama, S. (2007). Hostile and benevolent reactions towards pregnant women: Complementary interpersonal punishments and rewards that maintain traditional roles. *Journal of Applied Psychology, 92,* 1499–1511.

Hecht, M. A., & LaFrance, M. (1998). License or obligation to smile: The effect of power and sex on amount and type of smiling. *Personality and Social Psychology Bulletin, 24,* 1332–1342.

Hedges, L. V., & Becker, B. J. (1986). Statistical methods in the meta-analysis of research on gender differences. In J. G. Hyde & M. C. Linn (Eds.), *The psychology of gender: Advances through meta-analysis* (pp. 14–50). Baltimore: Johns Hopkins University Press.

Heflin, C. M., & Iceland, J. (2009). Poverty, material hardship, and depression. *Social Science Quarterly, 90,* 1051–1071.

Heilman, M. E., & Saruwatari, L. R. (1979). When beauty is beastly: The effects of appearance and sex on evaluations of job applicants for managerial and non-managerial jobs. *Organizational Behavior and Human Performance, 23,* 363–372.

Heise, L., Ellsberg, M., & Gottemoeller, M. (1999). Ending violence against women (Population Reports, Series L. 11). Baltimore: Johns Hopkins University School of Public Health.

Heitner, K. (2003). MOVIExperience: A tool to empower girls. *The Feminist Psychologist, 30,* 18.

Helwig, A. A. (1998). Gender-role stereotyping: Testing theory with a longitudinal sample. *Sex Roles, 38,* 403–424.

Henderson, K., & Roberts, N. (1998). An integrative review of the literature on women in the outdoors. In K. M. Fox, L. H. McAvoy, & M. D. Bialeschki (Eds.), *Coalition for education in the outdoors fourth research symposium proceedings* (pp. 9–21). Bradford Woods, IN: Coalition for Education in the Outdoors.

Henley, N. M. (1973). Status and sex: Some touching observations. *Bulletin of the Psychonomic Society, 2,* 91–93.

Henley, N. M. (1977). *Body politics: Power, sex, and nonverbal communication.* Englewood Cliffs, NJ: Prentice-Hall.

Henley, N. M. (1989). Molehill or mountain? What we do know and don't know about sex bias in language. In M. Crawford & M. Gentry (Eds.), *Gender and thought* (pp. 59–78). New York: Springer-Verlag.

Henley, N. M., Meng, K., O'Brien, D., McCarthy, W. J., & Sockloskie, R. (1998). Developing a scale to measure the diversity of feminist attitudes. *Psychology of Women Quarterly, 22,* 317–348.

Henley, N. M., Miller, M., & Beazley, J. (1995). Syntax, semantics, and sexual violence: Agency and the passive voice. *Journal of Language and Social Psychology, 14,* 60–84.

Hequembourg, A. (2007). *Lesbian motherhood: Stories of becoming.* Binghamton, NY: Harrington Park Press.

Herdt, G. (1997). *Same sex, different cultures.* Boulder, CO: Westview.

Herek, G. M. (2002). Gender gaps in public opinion about lesbians and gay men. *Public Opinion Quarterly, 66,* 40–66.

Herrett-Skjellum, J., & Allen, M. (1996). Television programming and sex stereotyping: A meta-analysis. In B. Burleson (Ed.), *Communication yearbook 19* (pp. 157–185). Thousand Oaks, CA: Sage.

Herzberg, D. (2009). *Happy pills in America: From Miltown to Prozac.* Baltimore: Johns Hopkins University Press.

Hess, U., & Bourgeois, P. (2010). You smile—I smile: Emotion expression in social interaction. *Biological Psychology, 84,* 514–520.

Heuer, C. A., McClure, K. J., & Puhl, R. M. (in press). Obesity stigma in online news: A visual content analysis. *Journal of Health Communication.*

Hewlett, S. A., & West, C. (1998). *The war against parents: What we can do for America's beleaguered moms and dads.* Boston: Houghton Mifflin.

Heymann, J. (2010). *If companies really mean business on work and family issues.* Retrieved May 23, 2010, from http://www.huffingtonpost.com/dr-jody-heymann

Hicks, M. H. R., & Li, Z. (2003). Partner violence and major depression in women: A community study of Chinese Americans. *Journal of Nervous and Mental Disease, 191,* 722–729.

Hill, C., Corbett, C., & St. Rose, A. (2010). *Why so few? Women in science, technology, engineering, and mathematics.* Washington, DC: AAUW.

Hill, M. (1987). Child-rearing attitudes of black lesbian mothers. In Boston Lesbian Psychologies Collective (Eds.), *Lesbian psychologies* (pp. 215–225). Urbana: University of Illinois Press.

Hill, M., & Ballou, M. (1998). Making therapy feminist: A practice survey. *Women & Therapy, 21,* 1–16.

Hill, M., & Ballou, M. (Eds.). (2005). *The foundation and future of feminist therapy.* New York: Haworth Press.

Hill, S. A. (2002). Teaching and doing gender in African American families. *Sex Roles, 47,* 493–506.

Hilt, L. M., & Nolen-Hoeksema, S. (2009). The emergence of gender differences in depression in adolescence. In S. Nolen-Hoeksema & L. M. Hilt (Eds.), *Handbook of depression in adolescents* (pp. 111–135). New York: Routledge/Taylor & Francis Group.

Hines, M. (2004). *Brain gender.* Oxford, England: Oxford University Press.

Hines, M. (2009). Sex hormones and human destiny. *Journal of Neuroendocrinology: Briefing 32,* 437–38.

Hite, S. (1976). *The Hite report.* New York: Macmillan.

Hoburg, R., Konik, J., Williams, M., & Crawford, M. (2004). Bisexuality among self-identified heterosexual college students. *Journal of Bisexuality, 4,* 25–36.

Hochschild, A. R. (1989). *The second shift: Working parents and the revolution at home.* New York: Viking.

Hockett, J.M., Saucier, D. A., Hoffman, B. H., Smith, S. J., & Craig, A. W. (2009). Oppression through acceptance? Predicting rape myth acceptance and attitudes toward rape victims. *Violence Against Women, 15,* 877–897.

Hoffnung, M. (1989). Motherhood: Contemporary conflict for women. In J. Freeman (Ed.), *Women: A feminist perspective* (4th ed., pp. 157–175). Mountain View, CA: Mayfield.

Hogue, M., & Yoder, J. D. (2003). The role of status in producing depressed entitlement in women's and men's pay allocations. *Psychology of Women Quarterly, 27,* 330–337.

Holewa, L. (2010). Wisconsin DA threatens arrest for local sex-ed teachers. *AOL News Online.* Retrieved August 2, 2010, from http://www.aolnews.com/nation/article/wis-da-threatens-arrest-for-local-sex-ed-teachers/19430578

Holm, K. E., Werner-Wilson, R. J., Cook, A. S., & Berger, P. S. (2001). The association between emotion work balance and relationship satisfaction of couples seeking therapy. *American Journal of Family Therapy, 29,* 193–205.

Hoobler, J. M., Wayne, S. J., & Lemmon, G. (2009). Bosses' perceptions of family-work conflict and women's promotability: Glass ceiling effects. *Academy of Management Journal, 52,* 939–957.

hooks, b. (1984). *Feminist theory: From margin to center.* Boston: South End Press.

hooks, b. (1989). *Talking back: Thinking feminist, thinking black.* Boston: South End Press.

hooks, b. (2000). *Feminism is for everybody: Passionate politics.* Cambridge, MA: South End Press.

Horne, S., & Biss, W. (2009). Equality discrepancy between women in same-sex relationships: The mediating role of attachment in relationship satisfaction. *Sex Roles, 60,* 721–730.

Hrdy, S. B. (1988, April). Daughters or sons. *Natural History,* 64–82.

Hunter, G. T. (1974). Pediatrician. In R. B. Kundsin (Ed.), *Women and success: The anatomy of achievement* (pp. 58–61). New York: Morrow.

Hunter, J., & Mallon, G. P. (2000). Lesbian, gay, and bisexual adolescent development: Dancing with your feet tied together. In B. Greene & G. L. Croom (Eds.), *Education, research, and practice in lesbian, gay, bisexual, and transgendered psychology* (pp. 226–243). Thousand Oaks, CA: Sage.

Hurd, L. C. (2000). Older women's body image and embodied experience: An exploration. *Journal of Women and Aging, 12,* 77–97.

Hurlbert, D. F., & Whittaker, K. E. (1991). The role of masturbation in marital and sexual satisfaction: A comparative study of female masturbators and nonmasturbators. *Journal of Sex Education and Therapy, 17,* 272–282.

Hurst, S. A., & Genest, M. (1995). Cognitive-behavioural therapy with a feminist orientation: A perspective for therapy with depressed women. *Canadian Psychology, 36,* 236–257.

Hurt, M. M., Nelson, J. A., Turner, D. L., Haines, M. E., Ramsey, L. R., Erchull, M. J., et al. (2007). Feminism: What is it good for? Feminine norms and objectification as the link between feminist identity and clinically relevant outcomes. *Sex Roles, 57,* 355–363.

Huston, T. L., Caughlin, J. P., Houts, R. M., Smith, S. E., & George, L. J. (2001). The connubial crucible: Newly-wed years as predictors of marital delight, distress, and divorce. *Journal of Personality and Social Psychology, 80,* 237–252.

Hyde, J. S., & DeLamater, J. (1997). *Understanding human sexuality* (6th ed.). New York: McGraw-Hill.

Hyde, J. S., & DeLamater, J. D. (2003). *Understanding human sexuality* (8th ed.). New York: McGraw Hill.

Hyde, J. S., & DeLamater, J. D. (2011). *Understanding human sexuality* (11th ed.). New York: McGraw Hill.

Hyde, J. S., Fennema, E., Ryan, M., Frost, L., & Hopp, C. (1990). Gender comparisons of mathematics attitudes and affects: A meta-analysis. *Psychology of Women Quarterly, 14,* 299–324.

Hyde, J. S., & Jaffe, S. R. (2000). Becoming a heterosexual adult: The experiences of young women. *Journal of Social Issues, 56,* 283–296.

Hyde, J. S., & Kling, K. C. (2001). Women, motivation, and achievement. *Psychology of Women Quarterly, 25,* 364–378.

Hyde, J. S., & Linn, M. C. (Eds.). (1986). *The psychology of gender: Advances through meta-analysis.* Baltimore: Johns Hopkins University Press.

Hyde, J. S., Mezulis, A. H., & Abramson, L. Y. (2008). The ABCs of depression: Integrating affective, biological, and cognitive models to explain the emergence of the gender difference in depression. *Psychological Review, 115,* 291–313.

Hyde, J. S., Rosenberg, B. G., & Behrman, J. (1977). "Tomboyism." *Psychology of Women Quarterly, 2,* 73–75.

Ihinger-Tallman, M., & Pasley, K. (1987). *Remarriage.* Beverly Hills, CA: Sage.

Ilies, R., Hauserman, N., Schwochau, S., & Stibal, J. (2003). Reported incidence rates of work-related sexual harassment in the United States: Using meta-analysis to explain reported rate disparities. *Personnel Psychology, 56,* 607–631.

Impett, E. A., Sorsoli, L., Schooler, D., Henson, J. M., & Tolman, D. L. (2008). Girls' relationship authenticity and self-esteem across adolescence. *Developmental Psychology, 44,* 722–733.

India's religious leaders condemn sex selection practices. Retrieved July 14, 2001, from http://womenshealth.medscape.com

Inzlicht, M., & Ben-Zeev, T. (2000). A threatening intellectual environment: Why females are susceptible to experiencing problem-solving deficits in the presence of males. *Psychological Science, 11,* 365–371.

Irmen, L. (2006). Automatic activation and use of gender subgroups. *Sex Roles, 55,* 435–444.

Isaac, R. J., & Armat, V. C. (1990). *Madness in the streets: How psychiatry and the law abandoned the mentally ill.* New York: Simon & Schuster.

Jackson, S. (2001). Happily never after: Young women's stories of abuse in heterosexual love relationships. *Feminism and Psychology, 11,* 305–321.

Jacobs, A. (1998, September 13). His debut as a woman. *The New York Times Magazine,* 48–51.

Jacobsen, F. M. (1994). Psychopharmacology. In L. Comas-Diaz & B. Green (Eds.), *Women of color: Integrating ethnic and gender identities in psychotherapy.* New York: The Guilford Press.

Jacobson, N. S., & Gottman, J. M. (1998). *When men batter women.* New York: Simon & Schuster.

James, D., & Drakich, J. (1993). Understanding gender differences in amount of talk: A critical review of research. In D. Tannen (Ed.), *Gender and conversational interaction* (pp. 281–312). New York: Oxford University Press.

James, J. (1999). The contribution of women's studies programs. In S. Davis, M. Crawford, & J. Sebrechts (Eds.), *Coming into her own: Encouraging educational success in girls and women* (pp. 23–36). San Francisco: Jossey-Bass.

Jane, J. S., Oltmanns, T. F., South, S. C., & Turkheimer, E. (2007). Gender bias in diagnostic criteria for personality disorders: An item response theory analysis. *Journal of Abnormal Psychology, 116,* 166–175.

Jayakar, K. (1994). Women of the Indian subcontinent. In L. Comas-Díaz & B. Greene (Eds.), *Women of color: Integrating ethnic and gender identities in psychotherapy* (pp. 161–181). New York: Guilford Press.

Jenkins, A. M., Albee, G. W., Paster, V. S., Sue, S., Baker, D. B., Comas-Diaz, L., et al. (2002). Ethnic minorities. In I. B. Weiner (Series Ed.) & D. K. Freedheim (Vol. Ed.), *Comprehensive handbook of psychology: Vol. 1. The history of psychology* (pp. 483–506). New York: Wiley and Sons.

Jensen, R. (2007). *Getting off: Pornography and the end of masculinity.* Cambridge, MA: South End Press.

Jewkes, R., & Abrahams, N. (2002). The epidemiology of rape and sexual coercion in South Africa: An overview. *Social Science and Medicine, 55,* 1,231–1,244.

Joffe, H. (1997). Intimacy and love in late modern conditions: Implications for unsafe sexual practices. In J. M. Ussher (Ed.), *Body talk: The material and discursive regulation of sexuality, madness and reproduction* (pp. 159–175). New York: Routledge.

Johansson, P. (2001). Selling the "modern woman": Consumer culture and Chinese gender politics. In S. Munshi (Ed.), *Images of the modern woman in Asia: Global media local meanings* (pp. 94–122). Richmond, Surrey, UK: Curzon Press.

John, R., Blanchard, P. H., & Hennessy, C. H. (1997). Hidden lives: Aging and contemporary American Indian women. In J. M. Coyle (Ed.), *Handbook on women and aging* (pp. 290–315). Westport, CT: Greenwood Press.

John, B. A., & Sussman, L. E. (1989). Initiative taking as a determinant of role-reciprocal organization. In R. K. Unger (Ed.), *Representations: Social constructions of gender* (pp. 259–272). Amityville, NY: Baywood.

Johns, M., Schmader, T., & Martens, A. (2005). Knowing is half the battle: Teaching stereotype threat as a means of improving women's math performance. *Psychological Science, 16,* 175–179.

Johnson, H., Ollus, N., & Nevala, S. (2008). *Violence against women: An international perspective*. New York: Springer.

Johnson, K. (2007). Transsexualism; Diagnostic dilemmas, transgender politics and the future of transgender care. In V. Clarke & E. Peel (Eds.), *Out in psychology; lesbian, gay, bisexual, trans and queer perspectives* (pp. 445–464). New York: Wiley.

Johnson, M. P. (1995). Patriarchal terrorism and common couple violence: Two forms of violence against women. *Journal of Marriage and the Family, 57*, 283–294.

Johnson, M. P., & Ferraro, K. J. (2000). Research on domestic violence in the 1990's: Making distinctions. *Journal of Marriage and the Family, 62*, 948–963.

Johnston-Robledo, I. (2000). From postpartum depression to the empty nest syndrome: The motherhood mystique revisited. In J. C. Chrisler, C. Golden, & P. D. Rozee (Eds.), *Lectures on the psychology of women* (pp. 129–148). Boston: McGraw-Hill.

Johnston-Robledo, I., Barnack, J., & Wares, S. (2006). "Kiss your period good-bye": Menstrual suppression in the popular press. *Sex Roles, 54*, 353–360.

Jonason, P. K., & Marks, M. J. (2009). Common vs. uncommon sexual acts: Evidence for the sexual double standard. *Sex Roles, 60*, 357–365.

Jones, R., Zolina M., Henshaw, S., & Finer, L. (2008). Abortion in the United States: Incidence and Access to Services, 2005. *Perspectives on Sexual and Reproductive Health, 40*(1), 6–16.

Jordan, J. V., Kaplan, A. G., Miller, J. B., Stiver, I. P., & Surrey, J. L. (1991). *Women's growth in connection*. New York: Guilford.

Jordan, K. M., & Deluty, R. H. (2000). Social support, coming out, and relationship satisfaction in lesbian couples. *Journal of Lesbian Studies, 4*, 145–164.

Jorge, J. C., Echeverri, C., Medina, Y., & Acevedo, P. (2008). Male gender identity in an XX individual with congenital adrenal hyperplasia. *Journal of Sexual Medicine, 5*, 122–131.

Joseph, D., & Newman, D. (2010). Emotional intelligence: An integrative meta-analysis and cascading model. *Journal of Applied Psychology, 95*(1), 54–78. doi:10.1037/a0017286.

Joseph, G. I., & Lewis, J. (1981). *Common differences: Conflicts in black and white feminist perspectives*. Boston: South End Press.

Joseph, J. (1997). Woman battering: A comparative analysis of black and white women. In G. Kaufman Kantor & J. L. Jasinski (Eds.), *Out of darkness: Contemporary perspectives on family violence* (pp. 161–169). Thousand Oaks, CA: Sage.

Jost, J. T. (1997). An experimental replication of the depressed entitlement effect among women. *Psychology of Women Quarterly, 21*, 387–393.

Jussim, L., Cain, T. R., Crawford, J. T., Harber, K., & Cohen, F. (2009). The unbearable accuracy of stereotypes. In T. D. Nelson (Ed.), *Handbook of prejudice, stereotyping, and discrimination* (pp. 199–227). New York: Psychology Press.

Kahn, A. S., Jackson, J., Kully, C., Badger, K., & Halvorsen, J. (2003). Calling it rape: Differences in experiences of women who do or do not label their sexual assault as rape. *Psychology of Women Quarterly, 27*, 233–242.

Kahn, A. S., & Yoder, J. D. (1989). The psychology of women and conservatism: Rediscovering social change. *Psychology of Women Quarterly, 13*, 417–432.

Kalichman, S. C., Simbay, L. C., Kaufman, M., Cain, D., Cherry, C., Jooste, S., et al. (2005). Gender attitudes, sexual violence, and HIV/AIDS risks among men and women in Cape Town, South Africa. *Journal of Sex Research, 42*, 299–305.

Kane, M. J. (1996). Media coverage of the post Title IX female athlete: A feminist analysis of sport, gender, and power. *Duke Journal of Gender Law & Policy, 3*, 95–127.

Kane, M. J., & Parks, J. B. (1990). Mass media images as a reflector of historical social change: The portrayal of female athletes before, during and after Title IX. In L. Vander Velden & J. H. Humphrey (Eds.), *Psychology and Sociology of Sport: Current Selected Research, 133*, 146–147.

Kanter, R. M. (1977). *Men and women of the corporation*. New York: Basic Books.

Karraker, K. H., Vogel, D. A., & Lake, M. A. (1995). Parents' gender stereotyped perceptions of newborns: The eye of the beholder revisited. *Sex Roles, 33*, 687–701.

Katz, B. L. (1991). The psychological impact of stranger versus nonstranger rape on victims' recovery. In A. Parrot & L. Bechhofer, (Eds.), *Acquaintance rape: The hidden crime* (pp. 251–269). New York: Wiley.

Katz, P. A. (1996). Raising feminists. *Psychology of Women Quarterly, 20*, 323–340.

Katz, R. S. (2002). Older women and addictions. In S. L. A. Straussner & S. Brown (Eds.), *The handbook of addiction treatment for women* (pp. 272–297). San Francisco: Jossey-Bass.

Kaufman, M. R. (2010). Testing of the healthy "little" lives project: A training program for big sister mentors. *American Journal of Sexuality Education, 5*(4), 305–327.

Kaysen, S. (1993). *Girl, interrupted*. New York: Turtle Bay Books, a Division of Random House.

Keel, P. K., Mitchell, J. E., Davis, T. L., & Crow, S. J. (2001). Relationship between depression and body dissatisfaction in women diagnosed with bulimia nervosa. *International Journal of Eating Disorders, 30*, 48 56.

Kelle, H. (2000). Gender and territoriality in games played by nine-to-twelve-year-old schoolchildren. *Journal of Contemporary Ethnology, 29*, 164–197.

Keller, J. (2003, September). The H-Bomb. *Boston Magazine*, pp. 70–78.

Keller J. (2007). Stereotype threat in classroom settings: The interactive effect of domain identification, task difficulty and stereotype threat on female students' maths performance. *British Journal of Educational Psychology, 77,* 323–338.

Keltner, D., Capps, L., Kring, A. M., Young, R. C., & Heerey, E. A. (2001). Just teasing: A conceptual analysis and empirical review. *Psychological Bulletin, 127,* 229–248.

Keltner, D., Gruenfeld, D., & Anderson, C. (2003). Power, approach, and inhibition. *Psychological Review, 110,* 265–284.

Kendall-Tackett, K. A. (2001). Victimization of female children. In C. M. Renzetti, J. L. Edelson, & R. K. Bergen (Eds.), *Sourcebook on violence against women* (pp. 101–116). Thousand Oaks, CA: Sage.

Kennell, J., Klaus, M., McGrath, S., Robertson, S., & Hinkley, C. (1991). Continuous emotional support during labor in a US hospital. *Journal of the American Medical Association, 265,* 2197–2201.

Kenney-Benson, G., Pomerantz, E., Ryan, A., & Patrick, H. (2006). Sex differences in math performance: The role of children's approach to schoolwork. *Developmental Psychology, 42,* 11–26.

Kessler, E.-M., Rakoczy, K., & Staudinger, U. R. (2004). The portrayal of older people in prime time television series: The match with gerontological evidence. *Aging & Society, 24,* 531–552.

Kessler, R. C. (2003). Epidemiology of women and depression. *Journal of Affective Disorders, 74,* 5–13

Kessler, S. J. (1990). The medical construction of gender: Case management of intersexed infants. *Signs, 16,* 3–26.

Kessler, S. J. (1998). *Lessons from the intersexed.* New Brunswick, NJ: Rutgers University Press.

Kessler, S. J. (2002, October). *Intersexuality in the 21st century: Medical emergency or medical invention?* Colloquium presented to the Social Psychology Division, University of Connecticut, Storrs.

Kessler, S. J., & McKenna, W. (1978). *Gender: An ethnomethodological approach.* New York: John Wiley.

Khazan, I., McHale, J., & Decourcey, W. (2008). Violated wishes about division of childcare labor predict early coparenting process during stressful and nonstressful family evaluations. *Infant Mental Health Journal, 29,* 343–361.

Kilbourne, J. (2002). *Killing us softly 3: Advertising's image of women* (Videotape). Northampton, MA: Media Education

Kim, J. L., Sorsoli, C., Collins, K., Zylbergold, B. A., Schooler, D., & Tolman, D. L. (2007). From sex to sexuality: Exposing the heterosexist script on primetime network television. *Journal of Sex Research, 44,* 145–157.

Kimball, M. M. (1995). *Feminist visions of gender similarities and differences.* New York: Harrington Park Press.

Kimball, M. M. (2001). Gender similarities and differences as feminist contradictions. In R .K. Unger (Ed.), *Handbook of the psychology of women and gender* (pp. 66–83). New York: Wiley.

Kimmel, D. C., & Martin, D. L. (Eds.). (2001). *Midlife and aging in gay America: Proceedings of the SAGE conference, New York City, 2000.* New York: Harrington Park Press.

Kimmel, E., & Crawford, M. (Eds.). (2000). *Innovations in feminist psychological research.* Cambridge: Cambridge University Press.

Kimmell, M. (Ed.). (2007). *The sexual self: The construction of sexual scripts.* Nashville: University of Vanderbilt Press.

King, E. B., Botsford, W. E., & Huffman, A. H. (2009). Work, family, and organizational advancement: Does balance support the perceived advancement of mothers? *Sex Roles, 61,* 879–891.

Kinsey, A. C., Pomeroy, W. B., & Martin, C. E. (1948). *Sexual behavior in the human male.* Philadelphia: Saunders.

Kinsey, A. C., Pomeroy, W. B., Martin, C. E., & Gebhard, P. H. (1953). *Sexual behavior in the human female.* Philadelphia: Saunders.

Kirsch, I., Deacon, B. J., Huedo-Medina, T. B., Scoboria, A., Moore, T. J., & Johnson, B. T. (2008). Initial severity and antidepressant benefits: A meta-analysis of data submitted to the food and drug administration. *PLoS Medicine, 5*(2). Retrieved January 24, 2011, from http://www.plosmedicine.org/article/info%3Adoi%2F10.1371%2Fjournal.pmed.0050045_

Kitayama, S., Markus, H. R., & Kurokawa, M. (2000). Culture, emotion, and well-being: Good feelings in Japan and the United States. *Cognition and Emotion, 14,* 93–124.

Kite, M. E., Stockdale, G. D., Whitley, B. E., Jr, & Johnson, B. T. (2005). Attitudes toward younger and older adults: An updated meta-analytic review. *Journal of Social Issues, 61*(2), 241–266.

Kitzinger, C. (1987). *The social construction of lesbianism.* London: Sage.

Kitzinger, C. (2001). Sexualities. In R. K. Unger (Ed.), *Handbook of the psychology of women and gender* (pp. 272–285). New York: Wiley.

Kitzinger, S. (1983). *Women's experience of sex.* London: Dorling Kindersley.

Kling, K. C., Hyde, J. S., Showers, C., & Buswell, B. (1999). Gender differences in self-esteem: A meta-analysis. *Psychological Bulletin, 125,* 470–500.

Klonoff, E. A., & Landrine, H. (1995). The schedule of sexist events: A measure of lifetime and recent sexist discrimination in women's lives. *Psychology of Women Quarterly, 19,* 439–472.

Klonoff, E. A., Landrine, H., & Campbell, R. (2000). Sexist discrimination may account for well-known differences in psychiatric symptoms. *Psychology of Women Quarterly, 24,* 93–99.

Knight, J. L., & Giuliano, T. A. (2001). He's a Laker; she's a "Looker": The consequences of gender-stereotypical portrayals of male and female athletes by the print media. *Sex Roles, 45,* 217–229.

Knight, J. L., & Guiliano, T. A. (2003). Blood, sweat, and jeers: The impact of the media's heterosexist portrayals on perceptions of male and female athletes. *Journal of Sport Behavior, 26,* 272–284.

Knudson-Martin, C., & Mahoney, A. (1996). Gender dilemmas and myth in the construction of marital bargains: Issues for marital therapy. *Family Process, 35,* 137–153.

Knudson-Martin, C., & Mahoney, A. (2005). Moving beyond gender: Processes that create relationship equality. *Journal of Marital and Family Therapy, 31*(2), 235–246.

Kohlberg, L. (1966). A cognitive-developmental analysis of children's sex role concepts and attitudes. In E. E. Maccoby (Ed.), *The development of sex differences* (pp. 82–173). Stanford, CA: Stanford University Press.

Koivula, N. (1999). Gender stereotyping in television media news coverage. *Sex Roles, 41,* 589–604.

Koivula, N. (2001). Perceived characteristics of sports categorized as gender-neutral, feminine and masculine. *Journal of Sport Behavior, 24,* 377–393.

Konrad, A. M., Ritchie, J. E., Lieb, P., & Corrigall, E. (2000). Sex differences and similarities in job attribute preferences: A meta-analysis. *Psychological Bulletin, 26,* 593–641.

Konrath, S. H., & Schwarz, N. (2007). Do male politicians have big heads? Face-ism in online self-representation of politicians. *Media Psychology, 10,* 436–448.

Koropeckyj-Cox, T., & Call, V. A. (2007). Characteristics of older childless persons and parents: Cross-national comparisons. *Journal of Family Issues, 28*(10), 1362–1414. doi:10.1177/0192513X07303837

Koropeckyj-Cox, T., Romano, V., & Moras, A. (2007). Through the lenses of gender, race, and class: Student's perceptions of childless/childfree individuals and couples. *Sex Roles, 56*(7–8), 415–428.

Koss, M. P., Bailey, J. A., Yuan, N. P., Herrera, V. M., & Lichter, E. L. (2003). Depression and PTSD in survivors of male violence: Research and training initiatives to facilitate recovery. *Psychology of Women Quarterly, 27,* 130–142.

Koss, M. P., & Gaines, J. A. (1993). The prediction of sexual aggression by alcohol use, athletic participation, and fraternity affiliation. *Journal of Interpersonal Violence, 8,* 94–108.

Koss, M. P., Gidycz, C. A., & Wisniewski, N. (1987). The scope of rape: Incidence and prevalence of sexual aggression and victimization in a national sample of higher education students. *Journal of Consulting and Clinical Psychology, 55,* 162–170.

Koss, M. P., & Kilpatrick, D. G. (2001). Rape and sexual assault. In E. Gerrity, T. M. Keane, & T. Garis (Eds.), *The mental health consequences of torture* (pp. 177–193). New York: Plenum.

Koyama, E. (2002, January 7). Intersex activists respond to the Vagina Monologues. E-mail posted to Women's Studies Listserv.

Krahé, B., Bieneck, S., & Scheinberger-Olwig, R. (2007). Adolescents' sexual scripts: Schematic representations of consensual and nonconsensual heterosexual interactions. *Journal of Sex Research, 44,* 316–327.

Kramarae, C., & Treichler, P. A. (1985). A feminist dictionary. Boston: Pandora.

Krassas, N. R., Blauwkamp, J. M., & Wesselink, P. (2003). "Master your johnson": Sexual rhetoric in *Maxim* and *Stuff* magazines. *Sexuality & Culture, 7*(3), 98–119.

Kravetz, D. (1980). Consciousness-raising and self-help. In M. Brodsky & R. Hare-Mustin (Eds.), *Women and psychotherapy* (pp. 267–283). New York: Guilford.

Kregear, D. A., & Staff, J. (2009). The sexual double standard and adolescent peer acceptance. *Social Psychology Quarterly, 72,* 143–164.

Kristoff, N. D., & WuDunn, S. (2009). *Half the sky: Turning oppression into opportunity for women worldwide.* New York: Knopf.

Krumrei, E., Coit, C., Martin, S., Fogo, W., & Mahoney, A. (2007). Post-divorce adjustment and social relationships: A meta-analytic review. *Journal of Divorce & Remarriage, 46,* 145–166.

Kuhn, M. (1991). *No stone unturned: The life and times of Maggie Kuhn.* New York: Ballantine.

Kurdek, L. A. (1988). Perceived social support in gays and lesbians in cohabitating couples. *Journal of Personality and Social Psychology, 54,* 504–509.

Kurdek, L. A. (1997). Adjustment to relationship dissolution in gay, lesbian, and heterosexual partners. *Personal Relationships, 4,* 145–161.

Kurdek, L. A. (2007). The allocation of household labor by partners in gay and lesbian couples. *Journal of Family Issues, 28,* 132–148.

LaFramboise, T. D., Berman, J. S., & Sohi, B. K. (1994). American Indian women. In L. Comas-Díaz & B. Greene (Eds), *Women of color: Integrating ethnic and gender identities in psychotherapy* (pp. 30–71). New York: Guilford Press.

LaFrance, M. (1992). Gender and interruptions: Individual infraction or violation of the social order? *Psychology of Women Quarterly, 16,* 497–512.

LaFrance, M. (2001). Gender and social interaction. In R. K. Unger (Ed.), *Handbook of the psychology of women and gender* (pp. 245–255). New York: Wiley.

LaFrance, M., Hetcht, M. A., & Paluck, E. (2003). The contingent smile: A meta-analysis of sex differences in smiling. *Psychological Bulletin, 129,* 305–334.

Laing, R. D. (1970). *The divided self.* New York: Random House.

Lambdin, J. R., Greer, K. M., Jibotian, K. S., Wood, K. R., & Hamilton, M. C. (2003). The animal = male hypothesis: Children's and adult's beliefs about the sex of non-sex specific stuffed animals. *Sex Roles, 48,* 471–483.

Landa, A. (1990). No accident: The voices of voluntarily childless women–An essay on the social construction of fertility choices. In J. P. Knowles & E. Cole (Eds.), *Motherhood: A feminist perspective* (pp. 139–158). New York: Haworth.

Landrine, H. (1985). Race x class stereotypes of women. *Sex Roles, 13*, 65–75.

Landrine, H., & Klonoff, E. A. (1997). *Discrimination against women: Prevalence, consequences, remedies.* Thousand Oaks, CA: Sage.

Landrine, H., Klonoff, E. A., Gibbs, J., Manning, V., & Lund, M. (1995). Physical and psychiatric correlates of gender discrimination: An application of the schedule of sexist events. *Psychology of Women Quarterly, 19*, 473–492.

LaRossa, R., Jaret, C., Gadgil, M., & Wynn, G. R. (2001). Gender disparities in Mother's Day and Father's Day comic strips: A fifty-four year history. *Sex Roles, 44*, 693–718.

Larson, M. S. (2003). Gender, race, and aggression in television commercials that feature children. *Sex Roles, 48*, 67–76.

Laumann, E. O., Gagnon, J. H., Michael, R. T., & Michaels, S. (1994). *The social organization of sexuality: Sexual practices in the United States.* Chicago: University of Chicago Press.

Laumann, E. O., & Michael, R. T. (Eds.). (2000). *Sex, love, and health in America: Private choices and public policies.* Chicago: University of Chicago Press.

Laumann, E. O., Paik, A., & Rosen, R. C. (1999). Sexual dysfunction in the United States: Prevalence and predictors. *JAMA, 281*, 537–544.

Laurance, J. (2001, August 22). Doctors must refuse to collude in this abusive practice: "Genital mutilation is one of many harmful practices affecting women in traditional societies." *The Independent*, p. 5.

Lauzen, M. M., & Dozier, D. M. (2005). Maintaining the double standard: portrayals of age and gender in popular films. *Sex Roles, 52*, 437–446.

Lauzen, M. M., Dozier, D. M., & Horan, N. (2008, June). Constructing gender stereotypes through social roles in prime time television. *Journal of Broadcasting & Electronic Media*, 200–221.

Leadbeater, B. J. R., & Way, N. (2001). *Growing up fast: Transitions to early adulthood of inner-city adolescent mothers.* Mahwah, NJ: Erlbaum.

Leaper, C. (2000). The social construction and socialization of gender during development. In P. H. Miller & E. K. Scholnick (Eds.), *Toward a feminist developmental psychology* (pp. 127–152). New York: Routledge.

Leaper, C., Anderson, K., & Sanders, P. (1998). Moderators of gender effects on parents' talk to their children: A meta-analysis. *Developmental Psychology, 34*, 3–27.

Lee, E. (2009). The relationship of aggression and bullying to social preference: Differences in gender and types of aggression. *International Journal of Behavioral Development, 33*, 323–330.

Lee, G. R. (1988). Marital intimacy among older persons: The spouse as confidant. *Journal of Family Issues, 9*, 273–284.

Lee, I., & Crawford, M. (2007). Lesbians and bisexual women in the eyes of scientific psychology. *Feminism & Psychology, 17*, 109–127.

Lee, I., & Crawford, M. (in press). Lesbians in empirical psychological research: A new perspective for the 21st century? *Journal of Lesbian Studies.*

Lee, J. (1995). Beyond bean counting. In B. Findlen (Ed.), *Listen up! Voices from the next feminist generation* (pp. 205–211). Seattle, WA: Seal Press.

Lee, J. (2003). Menarche and the (hetero)sexualization of the female body. In R. Weitz (Ed.), *The politics of women's bodies* (2nd ed., pp. 82–99). Oxford, England: Oxford University Press.

Leibenluft, E. (1996). Women with bipolar illness: Clinical and research issues. *American Journal of Psychiatry, 153*, 163–173.

Leit, R. A., Gray, J., & Pope Jr., H. G. (2002). The media's representation of the ideal male body: A cause for muscle dysmorphia. *International Journal of Eating Disorders, 31*, 334–338.

Lemkau, J. P. (1983). Women in male-dominated professions: Distinguishing personality and background characteristics. *Psychology of Women Quarterly, 8*, 144–165.

Lenton, A. P., Bruder, M., & Sedekides, C. (2009). A meta-analysis on the malleability of automatic gender stereotypes. *Psychology of Women Quarterly, 33*, 183–196.

Leonhardt, D. (2003, November 16). Sugar and spice, and sour dads. *The New York Times*, p. BU 4.

Lester, R., & Petrie, T. A. (1995). Personality and physical correlates of bulimic symptomatology among Mexican American female college students. *Journal of Counseling Psychology, 42*, 199–203.

Lester, R., & Petrie, T. A. (1998). Physical, psychological, and societal correlates of bulimic symptomatology among African American college women. *Journal of Counseling Psychology, 45*, 315–321.

Lev, A. I. (2006). Disordering gender identity. *Journal of Psychology & Human Sexuality, 17*, 35–69.

Levesque, R. J. R. (2001). *Culture and family violence.* Washington, DC: American Psychological Association.

Levine, R., Sato, S., Hashimoto, T., & Verma, J. (1995). Love and marriage in eleven cultures. *Journal of Cross-Cultural Psychology, 26*, 554–571.

Levy, B. (2009). Stereotype embodiment: A psychosocial approach to aging. *Current Directions in Psychological Science, 18*, 332–336.

Lewis, J. (2002). *Playing the human part: Lupe Ontiveros on how not to be a diva.* Retrieved August 25, 2002, from http://www.laweekly.com/ink/02/16/cover-lewis2.php

Lewis, M. A., Lee, C. M., Patrick, M. E., & Fossos, N. (2007). Gender-specific normative misperceptions of risky sexual behavior and alcohol-related risky sexual behavior. *Sex Roles, 57*, 81–90.

Lewis, S. (1979). *Sunday's women: Lesbian life today*. Boston: Beacon.

Li, N. P., Bailey, J. M., Kenrick, D. T., & Linsenmeier, J. A. W. (2002). The necessities and luxuries of mate preferences: Testing the tradeoffs. *Journal of Personality and Social Psychology, 82*, 947–955.

Liles, E. G., & Woods, S. C. (1999). Anorexia nervosa as viable behaviour: Extreme self-deprivation in historical context. *History of Psychiatry, 10*, 205–225.

Lindberg, S. M., Grabe, S., & Hyde, J. S. (2007). Gender, pubertal development, and peer sexual harassment predict objectified body consciousness in early adolescence. *Journal of Research on Adolescence, 17*, 723–742.

Lindsey, E. W., & Mize, J. (2001). Contextual differences in parent-child play: Implications for children's gender role development. *Sex Roles, 44*, 155–176.

Lindsey, E. W., Mize, J., & Pettit, G. (1997). Differential play patterns of mothers and fathers of sons and daughters: Implications for children's gender role development. *Sex Roles, 37*, 643–662.

Lineham, M., & Scullion, H. (2008). The development of female global managers: The role of mentoring and networking. *Journal of Business Ethics, 83*, 29–40.

Linz, D., Donnerstein, E., & Penrod, S. (1987). Sexual violence in the mass media: Social psychological implications. In P. Shaver & C. Hendrick (Eds.), *Review of personality and social psychology: Vol. 7. Sex and gender* (pp. 95–123). Newbury Park, CA: Sage.

Lipman-Blumen, J., & Leavitt, H. J. (1976). Vicarious and direct achievement patterns in adulthood. *The Counseling Psychologist, 6*, 26–31.

Lirgg, C. D. (1991). Gender differences in self-confidence in physical activity: A meta-analysis of recent studies. *Journal of Sport and Exercise Psychology, 13*, 294–310.

Liss, M., & Erchull, M.J. (2010). Everyone feels empowered: Understanding feminist self-labeling. *Psychology of Women Quarterly, 34*, 85–96.

Liss, M., Hoffner, C., & Crawford, M. (2000). What do feminists believe? *Psychology of Women Quarterly, 24*, 279–284.

Liss, M., O'Connor, C., Morosky, E., & Crawford, M. (2001). What makes a feminist? Predictors and correlates of feminist social identity in college women. *Psychology of Women Quarterly, 25*(2), 124–133. doi:10.1111/1471-6402.00014

Lloyd, S. A. (1991). The dark side of courtship. *Family Relations, 40*, 14–20.

Locher, P., Unger, R. K., Sociedade, P., & Wahl, J. (1993). At first glance: Accessibility of the physical attractiveness stereotype. *Sex Roles, 28*, 729–743.

Locke, L. M., & Richman, C. L. (1999). Attitudes toward domestic violence: Race and gender issues. *Sex Roles, 40*, 227–247.

Logel, C., Walton, G. M., Spencer, S. J., Iserman, E. C., von Hippel, W., & Bell, A. E. (2009). Interacting with sexist men triggers social identity threat among female engineers. *Journal of Personality and Social Psychology, 96*(6), 1089–1103. doi:10.1037/a0015703

Loiacano, D. K. (1993). Gay identity issues among Black Americans: Racism, homophobia, and the need for validation. In L. D. Garnets & D. C. Kimmel (Eds.), *Psychological perspectives on lesbian and gay male experiences* (pp. 364–375). New York: Columbia University Press.

Longino, H. (1980). What is pornography. In L. Lederere (Ed.), *Take back the night* (p. 44). New York: William Morrow.

Longmore, M. A., Eng., A. L., Giordano, P. C., & Manning, W. D. (2009). Parenting and adolescents' sexual initiation. *Journal of Marriage and Family, 71*, 969–982.

Lonsway, K. A., & Fitzgerald, L. F. (1994). Rape myths: In review. *Psychology of Women Quarterly, 18*, 133–164.

Lonsway, K. A., & Fitzgerald, L. F. (1995). Attitudinal antecedents of rape myth acceptance: A theoretical and empirical reexamination. *Journal of Personality and Social Psychology, 68*, 704–711.

Lopez, S. R. (1989). Patient variable biases in clinical judgment: Conceptual overview and methodological considerations. *Psychological Bulletin, 106*, 184–203.

LoPiccolo, J., & Stock, W. E. (1986). Treatment of sexual dysfunction. *Journal of Consulting and Clinical Psychology, 54*, 158–167.

Lorber, J. (1993). *Paradoxes of gender*. New Haven, CT: Yale University Press.

Lott, B. (1987). Sexist discrimination as distancing behavior: I. A laboratory demonstration. *Psychology of Women Quarterly, 11*, 47–58.

Lovelace, L., & McGrady, M. (1981). *Ordeal*. New York: Berkley Books.

Ludermir, A. B., Schraiber, L., D'Oliveira, A. F. P. L., Franca-Junior, I., & Jansen, H. A. (2008). Violence against women by their intimate partner and common mental disorders. *Social Science & Medicine, 66*, 1008–1018.

Lueptow, L. B., Garovich, L., & Lueptow, M. B. (1995). The persistence of gender stereotypes in the face of changing sex roles: Evidence contrary to the sociocultural model. *Ethology & Sociobiology, 16*, 509–530.

Lunbeck, E. (1994). *The psychiatric persuasion: Knowledge, gender, and power in modern America*. Princeton, NJ: Princeton University Press.

Lustyk, M. K. B., Gerrish, W. G., Shaver, S., & Keys, S. L. (2009). Cognitive-behavioral therapy for premenstrual syndrome and premenstrual dysphoric disorder: A systematic review. *Archives of Women's Mental Health, 12*, 85–96.

Lytton, H., & Romney, D. M. (1991). Parents' differential socialization of boys and girls: A meta-analysis. *Psychological Bulletin, 109*, 267–296.

Maccoby, E. E. (1980). *Social development: Psychological growth and the parent-child relationship*. New York: Harcourt Brace Jovanovich.

Maccoby, E. E. (1998). *The two sexes: Growing up apart, coming together.* Cambridge, MA: Belknap Press of Harvard University Press.

Maccoby, E. E., & Jacklin, C. (1974). *The psychology of sex differences.* Stanford, CA: Stanford University Press.

MacFarlane, A. (1977). *The psychology of childbirth.* Cambridge, MA: Harvard University Press.

MacKenzie, D., Huntington, A., & Gilmour, J. A. (2009). The experiences of people with an intersex condition: A journey from silence to voice. *Journal of Clinical Nursing, 18,* 1775–1783.

MacKinnon, C. A. (1994). Sexuality. In A. C. Herrmann & A. J. Stewart (Eds.), *Theorizing feminism: Parallel trends in the humanities and social sciences* (pp. 257–287). Boulder, CO: Westview Press.

MacNeil, S., & Byers, E.S. (2009). Role of sexual self-disclosure in the sexual satisfaction of long-term heterosexual couples. *Journal of Sex Research, 16,* 3–14.

Mahalingam, R. (2003). Essentialism, culture, and beliefs about gender among the Aravanis of Tamil Nadu, India. *Sex Roles, 49,* 489–496.

Mahalingam, R., Haritatos, J., & Jackson, B. (2007). Essentialism and the cultural psychology of gender in extreme son preference communities in India. *American Journal of Orthopsychiatry, 77*(4), 598–609.

Mahay, J. W., Laumann, E. O., & Michaels, S. (2001). Race, gender, and class in sexual scripts. In E. O. Laumann & R. T. Michael (Eds.), *Sex, love, and health: Private choices and public policies* (pp. 197–238). Chicago: University of Chicago Press.

Mahlstedt, D. (1999). *Men's work: Fraternity brothers stopping violence against women.* New York: Insight Media.

Major, B. (1994). From social inequality to personal entitlement: The role of social comparisons, legitimacy appraisals, and group membership. In M. P. Zanna (Ed.), *Advances in experimental social psychology, Vol. 26* (pp. 293–355). New York: Academic Press.

Major, B., Appelbaum, M., Beckman, L., Dutton, M., Russo, N., & West, C. (2009). Abortion and Mental Health: Evaluating the Evidence. *American Psychologist, 64*(9), 863–890.

Major, B., Barr, L., Zubek, J., & Babey, S. H. (1999). Gender and self-esteem: A meta-analysis. In W. B. Swann Jr., J. H. Langlois, & L. A. Gilbert (Eds.), *Sexism and stereotypes in modern society: The gender science of Janet Taylor Spence* (pp. 223–253). Washington, DC: American Psychological Association.

Major, B., Gramzow, R. H., McCoy, S. K., Levin, S., Schmader, T., & Sidanius, J. (2002). Perceiving personal discrimination: The role of group status and legitimizing ideology. *Journal of Personality & Social Psychology, 82,* 269–282.

Major, B., Schmidlin, A. M., & Williams, L. (1990). Gender patterns in social touch: The impact of setting and age. *Journal of Personality and Social Psychology, 58,* 634–643.

Makepeace, J. M. (1986). Gender differences in courtship violence victimization. *Family Relations: Journal of Applied Family and Child Studies, 35,* 383–388.

Malarek, V. (2005). *The Natashas: Inside the global sex trade.* New York: Arcade Publishing.

Malcolmson, K. A., & Sinclair, L. (2007). The Ms. Stereotype revisited: Implicit and explicit facets. *Psychology of Women Quarterly, 31,* 305–310.

Malloy, T. E., Fisher, W. A., Albright, L., Misovich, S. J., & Fisher, J. D. (1997). Interpersonal perception of the AIDS risk potential of persons of the opposite sex. *Health Psychology, 16,* 480–486.

Mangiolio, R. (2009). The impact of child sexual abuse on health: A systematic review of reviews. *Clinical Psychology Review, 29,* 647–657.

Manlove, J., Ikramullah, E., Mincielli, L., Holcombe, E., & Danish, S. (2009). Trends in sexual experience, contraceptive use, and teenage childbirthing: 1992–2002. *Journal of Adolescent Health, 44,* 413–423.

Manning, W. D., & Landale, N. S. (1996). Racial and ethnic differences in the role of cohabitation in premarital childbearing. *Journal of Marriage and the Family, 58,* 63–77.

Mannino, C., & Deutsch, F. (2007). Changing the division of household labor: A negotiated process between partners. *Sex Roles, 56*(5–6), 309–324.

Maranto, C. L., & Stenoien, A. F. (2000). Weight discrimination: A multidisciplinary analysis. *Employee Responsibilities and Rights Journal, 12,* 9–24.

Marcuccio, E., Loving, N., Bennett, S. K., & Hayes, S. N. (2003). A survey of attitudes and experiences of women with heart disease. *Women's Health Issues, 13,* 23–31.

Marecek, J. (1999). Trauma talk in feminist clinical practice. In S. Lamb (Ed.), *New versions of victims: Feminists struggle with the concept* (pp. 158–182). New York: New York University Press.

Marecek, J., Crawford, M., & Popp, D. (2004). On the construction of gender, sex, and sexualities. In A. H. Eagly, A. E. Beall, & R. J. Sternberg (Eds.), *The psychology of gender* (2nd ed., pp. 192–216). New York: Guilford.

Marecek, J., Kimmel, E. B., Crawford, M., & Hare-Mustin, R. T. (2002). Psychology of women and gender. In I. B. Weiner (Series Ed.) & D. K. Freedheim (Vol Ed.), *Comprehensive handbook of psychology: Vol 1. The history of psychology* (pp. 249–268). New York: Wiley and Sons.

Marecek, J., & Kravetz, D. (1998). Power and agency in feminist therapy. In I. B. Seu & M. C. Heenan (Eds.), *Feminism and psychotherapy: Reflections on contemporary theories and practices* (pp. 13–29). Thousand Oaks, CA: Sage Publications.

Marks, M. J., & Fraley, R. C. (2005). The sexual double standard: Fact or fiction? *Sex Roles, 52,* 175–186.

Markson, E. W. (2003). The female aging body through film. In C. A. Faircloth (Ed.), *Aging bodies: Images and everyday experiences* (pp. 77–102). New York: AltaMira Press.

Markson, E. W., & Taylor, C. A. (2000). The mirror has two faces. *Aging and Society, 20,* 137–160.

Markus, H. R., & Kitayama, S. (1991). Culture and the self: Implications for cognition, emotion, and motivation. *Psychological Review, 98,* 224–253.

Marsh, M. (1995). Feminist psychopharmacology: An aspect of feminist psychiatry. *Women & Therapy, 16,* 73–84.

Marshall, A. (1997). Who's laughing? Hillary Rodham Clinton in political humor. In N. V. Benokraitis (Ed.), *Subtle sexism: Current practice and prospects for change* (pp. 72–90). Thousand Oaks, CA: Sage.

Martens, A., Johns, M., Greenberg, J., & Schimel, J. (2006). Combating stereotype threat: The effect of self-affirmation on women's intellectual performance. *Journal of Experimental Social Psychology, 42*(2), 236–243. doi:10.1016/j.jesp.2005.04.010.

Martin, C. L., & Fabes, R. A. (2001). The stability and consequences of young children's same sex peer interactions. *Developmental Psychology, 37,* 431–446.

Martin, C. L., & Halverson, C. F. (1983). The effects of sex-typing schemas on young children's memory. *Child Development, 54,* 563–574.

Martin, C. L., & Ruble, D. (2004). Children's search for gender cues. *Current Directions in Psychological Science, 13,* 67–70.

Martire, L. M., & Stephens, M. A. P. (2003). Juggling parent care and employment responsibilities: The dilemmas of adult daughter caregivers in the workforce. *Sex Roles, 48,* 167–173.

Martz, D. M., Handley, K. B., & Eisler, R. M. (1995). The relationship between feminine gender role stress, body image, and eating disorders. *Psychology of Women Quarterly, 19,* 493–508.

Marvan, M. L., Ramirez-Esparza, D., Cortes-Iniestra, S., & Chrisler, J. C., (2006). Development of a new scale to measure beliefs about and attitudes toward menstruation (BATM): Data from Mexico and the United States. *Health Care for Women International, 27,* 453–473.

Masser, B., Viki, G. T., & Power, C. (2006). Hostile sexism and rape procilivity amongst men. *Sex Roles, 54,* 565–574.

Masson, J. M. (1984). *The assault on truth: Freud's suppression of the seduction theory.* New York: Harper Perennial.

Masters, W. H., & Johnson, V. (1966). *Human sexual response.* Boston: Little, Brown.

Masters, W. H., & Johnson, V. (1979). *Homosexuality in perspective.* Boston: Little, Brown.

Mather, S. (2008). Women and coronary heart disease. In A. L. Clouse & K. Sherif (Eds.), *Women's health in clinical practice: A handbook for primary care* (pp. 71–96). New York: Humana Press.

Matthews, A. P. (1996). How evangelical women cope with prescription and description. In C. C. Kroeger, J. R. Beck, et al. (Eds.), *Women, abuse, and the Bible: How scripture can be used to hurt or to heal* (pp. 86–105). Grand Rapids, MI: Baker Books.

Matthews, G. A., Fane, B. A., Conway, G. S., Brook, C. G. D., & Hines, M. (2009). Personality and congenital adrenal hyperplasia: Possible effects of prenatal androgen exposure. *Hormones and Behavior, 55,* 285–291.

Matthews, J. L. (2007). Hidden sexism: Facial prominence and its connections to gender and occupational status in popular print media. *Sex Roles, 57,* 515–525.

Mauthner, N. S. (1998). "It's a woman's cry for help": A relational perspective on postnatal depression. *Feminism & Psychology, 8,* 325–355.

Mazur, T. (2005). Gender dysphoria and gender change in androgen insensitivity or micropenis. *Archives of Sexual Behavior, 34* (4), 411–421.

Mazzocco, M. M. M. (2009). Mathematical learning disability in girls with Turner Syndrome: A challenge to defining mild and its subtypes. *Developmental Disabilities Research Reviews, 15,* 35–44.

McCabe, K. A., & Manian, S. (2010). *Sex trafficking: A global perspective.* Lanham, MD: Lexington Books.

McClelland, D. C., Atkinson, J. W., Clark, R. A., & Lowell, E. L. (1953). *The achievement motive.* Englewood Cliffs, NJ: Prentice Hall.

McClure, K. J., Puhl, R. M., & Heuer, C. A. (in press). Obesity in the news: Do photographic images of obese persons influence anti-fat attitudes? *Journal of Health Communication.*

McCormick, M. J. (2002). The search for the ideal heterosexual role play. In L. Diamant & J. A. Lee (Eds.), *The psychology of sex, gender, and jobs: Issues and resolutions* (pp. 155–170). Westport, CT: Praeger.

McCreary, D. R., & Rhodes, N. D. (2001). On the gender typed nature of dominant and submissive acts. *Sex Roles, 44,* 339–350.

McGlone, M., & Aronson, J. (2007). Forewarning and forearming stereotype-threatened students. *Communication Education, 56*(2), 119–133. doi:10.1080/03634520601158681.

McGuffey, C. S., & Rich, B. L. (1999). Playing in the gender transgression zone: Race, class, and hegemonic masculinity in middle childhood. *Gender & Society, 13,* 608–627.

McHugh, M. D., Koeske, R. D., & Frieze, I. H. (1986). Issues to consider in conducting nonsexist psychological research: A guide for researchers. *American Psychologist, 41,* 879–890.

McKelvey, M. W., & McKenry, P. C. (2000). The psychosocial well-being of Black and White mothers following marital dissolution. *Psychology of Women Quarterly, 24,* 4–14.

McKinley, N. M., & Hyde, J. S. (1996). The objectified body consciousness scale: Development and validation. *Psychology of Women Quarterly, 20,* 181–215.

McMahon, M. (1995). *Engendering motherhood.* New York: Guilford.

McMahon, S., & Farmer, G. L. (2009). The bystander approach: Strengths-based sexual assault prevention with at-risk groups. *Journal of Human Behavior in the Social Environment, 19,* 1042–1065.

McNamara, E. (2004, April 11). Linking evil to feminism. *The Boston Globe,* p. B1.

McQuillan, J., Greil, A., Shreffler, K., & Tichenor, V. (2008). The importance of motherhood among Women in the contemporary United States. *Gender & Society, 22*(4), 477–496.

Meier, E. (2000). Legislative efforts to combat sexual trafficking and slavery of women and children. *Pediatric Nursing, 26,* 216–211.

Ménard, A. D., & Kleinplatz, P. J. (2008). Twenty-one moves guaranteed to make his thighs go up in flames: Depictions of "great sex" in popular magazines. *Sexuality & Culture, 12,* 1–20.

Mennino, S. F., & Brayfield, A. (2002). Job-family trade-offs: The multidimensional effects of gender. *Work and Occupations, 29,* 226–256.

Merchant, C. (1995). *Earthcare: Women and the environment.* New York: Routledge.

Merritt, R. D., & Kok, C. J. (1995). Attribution of gender to a gender-unspecified individual: An evaluation of the people – male hypothesis. *Sex Roles, 33,* 145–157.

Merskin, D. (1999). Adolescence, advertising, and the ideology of menstruation. *Sex Roles, 40,* 941–957.

Messias, D., & DeJoseph, J. (2007). The personal work of a first pregnancy: Transforming identities, relationships, and women's work. *Women and Health, 45*(4), 41–64.

Messner, M. A., Duncan, M. C., & Cooky, C. (2003). Silence, sports bras, and wrestling porn: Women in televised sports news and highlights shows. *Journal of Sport & Social Issues, 27,* 38–51.

Messner, M. A., Duncan, M. C., & Jensen, K. (1993). Separating the men from the girls: The gendered language of televised sports. *Gender & Society, 7,* 121–137.

Meston, C. M., Trapnell, P. D., & Gorzalka, B. B. (1996). Ethnic and gender differences in sexuality: Variations in sexual behavior between Asian and non-Asian university students. *Archives of Sexual Behavior, 25,* 33–72.

Metzl, J. (2003). *Prozac on the couch: Prescribing gender in the era of wonder drugs.* Durham: Duke University Press.

Meyer-Bahlburg, H. F. L., Dolezal, C, Baker, S. W., & New, M. I. (2008). Sexual orientation in women with classical or non-classical congenital adrenal hyperplasia as a function of degree of prenatal androgen excess. *Archives of Sexual Behavior, 37,* 85–99.

Michael, R. T., Gagnon, J. H., Laumann, E. O., & Kolata, G. (1994). *Sex in America: A definitive survey.* Boston: Little Brown.

Midlarsky, E., & Nitzburg, G. (2008). Eating disorders in middle-aged women. *Journal of General Psychology, 135,* 393–407.

Miller, B. C., Benson, B., & Galbraith, K. A. (2001). Family relationships and adolescent pregnancy risk: A research synthesis. *Developmental Review, 21,* 1–38.

Miller, B. C., Norton, M. C., Curtis, T., Hill, E. J., Schvaneveldt, P., & Young, M. H. (1997). The timing of sexual intercourse among adolescents. *Youth & Society, 29,* 54–83.

Miller, B. D. (2001). Female-selective abortion in Asia: Patterns, policies, and debates. *American Anthropologist, 103,* 1083–1095.

Miller, D. H. (1996). Medical and psychological consequences of legal abortion in the United States. In R. L. Parrott & C. M. Condit (Eds.), *Evaluating women's health messages* (pp. 17–32). Thousand Oaks, CA: Sage.

Miller, J. B. (1986). *Toward a new psychology of women* (2nd ed.). Boston: Beacon.

Miller, M. K., & Summers, A. (2007). Gender differences in video game characters' roles, appearances, and attire as portrayed in video game magazines. *Sex Roles, 57,* 733–742.

Mintz, S. B. (2003). In a word, *Baywatch.* In R. Dicker & A. Piepmeier (Eds.), *Catching a wave: Reclaiming feminism for the 21st century* (pp. 57–81). Boston: Northeastern University Press.

Mischel, W. (1966). A social learning view of sex differences in behavior. In E. Maccoby (Ed.), *The development of sex differences* (pp. 56–81). Stanford, CA: Stanford University Press.

Mischel, W. (1970). Sex-typing and socialization. In P. H. Mussen (Ed.), *Carmichael's manual of child psychology* (pp. 3–72). New York: Wiley.

Misovich, S. J , Fisher, J. D., & Fisher, W. A. (1997). Close relationships and elevated HIV risk behavior: Evidence and possible underlying psychological processes. *Review of General Psychology, 1,* 72–107.

Mitchell, V., & Helson, R. (1990). Women's prime in life: Is it the 50's? *Psychology of Women Quarterly, 14,* 451–470.

Mitten, D. (1996). A philosophical basis for a women's outdoor adventure program. In K Warren (Ed.), *Women's voices in experiential education* (pp. 78–84). Dubuque, IA: Kendall Hunt.

Moayedi, R. (1999). Mentoring a diverse population. In S. Davis, M. Crawford, & J. Sebrechts (Eds.), *Coming into her own: Educational success in girls and women* (pp. 229–243). San Francisco: Jossey-Bass.

Mock, S. E. (2001). Retirement intentions of same-sex couples. *Journal of Gay & Lesbian Social Services, 13,* 81–86.

Moffat, M. (1989). *Coming of age in New Jersey.* New Brunswick, NJ: Rutgers University Press.

Moller, L. C., & Serbin, L. A. (1996). Antecedents of toddler gender segregation: Cognitive consonance, gender-typed toy preferences, and behavioral compatibility. *Sex Roles, 35,* 445–460.

Monteith, M. J., & Czopp, A. M. (2003, October). *Confronting prejudice: Making social and personal norms against prejudice salient by meeting prejudice head-on.* Symposium conducted at the conference of the Society of Experimental Social Psychology, Boston.

Montgomery, H. (2001). *Modern Babylon: Prostituting children in Thailand*. New York: Berghahn.

Moradi, B., & Huang, Y.-P. (2008). Objectification theory and psychology of women: A decade of advances and future directions. *Psychology of Women Quarterly, 32*, 377–398.

Morell, C. (2000). Saying no: Women's experiences with reproductive refusal. *Feminism and Psychology, 10*, 313–322.

Morgan, B. L. (1998). A three generational study of tomboy behavior. *Sex Roles, 39*, 787–800.

Morgan, K. P. (1996). Describing the emperor's new clothes: Three myths of educational (in)equity. In A. Diller, B. Houston, K. P. Morgan, & M. Ayim (Eds.), *The gender questions in education: Theory, pedagogy, and politics* (pp. 105–122). Boulder, CO: Westview.

Morgan, S. W., & Stevens, P. E. (2008). Transgender identity development as represented by a group of female-to-male transgendered adults. *Issues in Mental Health Nursing, 29*, 585–599.

Morier, D., & Seroy, C. (1994). The effect of interpersonal expectancies on men's self-presentation of gender role attitudes to women. *Sex Roles, 31*, 493–504.

Morris, C. G. (2010). Changes in psychological science: Perspectives from textbook authors. *APS Observer, 23*, 18–24.

Morris, J. (1974). *Conundrum*. New York: Harcourt Brace Jovanovich.

Morris, J. F., Waldo, C. R., & Rothblum, E. D. (2001). A model of predictors and outcomes of outness among lesbian and bisexual women. *American Journal of Orthopsychiatry, 71*, 61–71.

Moya, M., Glick, P., Expósito, F., De Lemus, S. & Hart, J. (2007). It's for your own good: Benevolent sexism and women's reactions to protectively justified restrictions. *Personality and Social Psychology Bulletin, 33*, 1421–1434.

Muehlenhard, C. L., & Hollabough, L. C. (1988). Do women sometimes say no when they mean yes? The prevalence and correlates of women's token resistance to sex. *Journal of Personality and Social Psychology, 54*, 872–879.

Muehlenhard, C. L., & Rodgers, C. S. (1998). Token resistance to sex: New perspectives on an old stereotype. *Psychology of Women Quarterly, 22*, 443–463.

Muehlenkamp, J. J., & Saris-Baglama, R. (2002). Self-objectification and its psychological outcomes for college women. *Psychology of Women Quarterly, 26*, 371–379.

Mueller, K. A., & Yoder, J. D. (1997). Gendered norms for family size, employment, and occupation: Are there personal costs for violating them? *Sex Roles, 36*, 207–220.

Mulac, A., Jansma, L. L., & Linz, D. G. (2002). Men's behavior toward women after viewing sexually-explicit films: Degradation makes a difference. *Communication Monographs, 69*, 311–329.

Munce, S. E., Robertson, E. K., Sansom, S. N., & Stewart, D. E. (2004). Who is portrayed in psychotropic drug advertisements? *Journal of Nervous & Mental Disease, 192*, 284–288.

Murdoch, M., Pryor, J. B., Polusny, M., & Gackstetter, G. G. (2007). Functioning and psychiatric symptoms among military men and women exposed to sexual stressors. *Military Medicine, 172*, 718–725.

Murnen, S. K. (2000). Gender and the use of sexually degrading language. *Psychology of Women Quarterly, 24*, 319–327.

Murnen, S. K., Smolak, L., Mills, J. A., & Good, L. (2003). Thin, sexy women and strong, muscular men: Grade-school children's responses to objectified images of women and men. *Sex Roles, 49*, 427–437.

Murphy, E. M. (2003). Being born female is dangerous for your health. *American Psychologist, 58*, 205–210.

Murray, G., Judd, F., Jackson, H., Fraser, C., Komiti, A., Pattison, P., et al. (2008). Big boys don't cry: An investigation of stoicism and its mental health outcomes. *Personality and Individual Differences, 44*(6), 1369–1381. doi:10.1016/j.paid.2007.12.005.

Murray-Johnson, L., Witte, K., Liu, W. Y., Hubbell, A. P., Sampson, J., & Morrison, K. (2001). Addressing cultural orientation in fear appeals: Promoting AIDS-protective behaviors among Mexican immigrant and African American adolescents and American and Taiwanese college students. *Journal of Health Communication, 6*, 335–358.

Murry-McBride, V. (1996). An ecological analysis of coital timing among middle-class African American adolescent females. *Journal of Adolescent Research, 11*, 261–279.

Muzzatti, B., & Agnoli, F. (2007). Gender and mathematics: Attitudes and stereotype threat susceptibility in Italian children. *Developmental Psychology, 43*(3), 747–759. doi:10.1037/0012-1649.43.3.747.

Mwangi, M. W. (1996). Gender roles portrayed in Kenyan television commercials. *Sex Roles, 34*, 205–214.

Nachmani, I., & Somer, E. (2007). Women sexually victimized in psychotherapy speak out: The dynamics and outcome of therapist-client sex. *Women & Therapy, 30*, 1–17.

Nanda, S. (1990). *Neither man nor woman: The hijras of India*. Belmont, CA: Wadsworth.

Naples, N. A. (1992). Activist mothering: Cross-generational continuity in the community work of women from low-income urban neighborhoods. Special issue: Race, class, and gender. *Gender & Society, 6*, 441–463.

Narayan, C. (2008). Is there a double standard of aging? Older men and women and ageism. *Educational Gerontology, 34*, 782–787.

Narrow, W. E., First, M. B., Sirovatka, P. J., & Regier, D. A. (Eds.). (2007). *Age and gender considerations in psychiatric diagnosis: A research agenda for DSM-V*. Arlington, VA, US: American Psychiatric Publishing, Inc.

Nash, H. C., & Chrisler, J. (1997). Is a little (psychiatric) knowledge a dangerous thing? The impact of premenstrual dysphoric disorder on perceptions of premenstrual women. *Psychology of Women Quarterly, 21,* 315–322.

Nasrullah, M., Haqqi, S., & Cummings, K. J. (2009). Epidemiological patterns of honour killing of women in Pakistan. *European Journal of Public Health, 19,* 193–197.

Nassif, A., & Gunter, B. (2008). Gender representation in television advertisements in Britain and Saudi Arabia. *Sex Roles, 58,* 752–760.

National Center for Health Statistics (NCHS). (2009). *National vital statistics reports: Births final data for 2006. Volume 57, Number 7, January 7, 2009.* Retrieved May 22, 2010, from http://www.cdc.gov/nchs/data/nvsr/nvsr57/nvsr57_07.pdf

National Center for Health Statistics. (2004). *Unpublished data from the National Health and Nutrition Examination Survey.* Retrieved May, 2004, from http://www.cdc.gov/nchs/fastats/bodymeas.htm

National Center on Elder Abuse (NCEA). (2006). *The 2004 survey of state adult protective services: Abuse of adults 60 years of and older.* Retrieved February 3, 2011, from http://www.ncea.aoa.gov/ncearoot/main_site/pdf/2-14-06%20final%2060+report.pdf

National Merit Scholarship Corp. (2010). *National merit scholarship corp. bullies school to remove scores from web.* Retrieved February 17, 2010, from fairtest.org/national-merit-scholarship-corp-bullies-school-rem

National Public Radio. (2005, November 5). "Curling calendar" segment on *Only a Game.*

Neft, N., & Levine, A. D. (1997). *Where women stand: An international report on the status of women in 140 countries.* New York: Random House.

Nelson, A. (2000). The pink dragon is female: Halloween costumes and gender markers. *Psychology of Women Quarterly, 24,* 137–144.

Nelson, A. (2005). Children's toy collections in Sweden— A less gender-typed country? *Sex Roles, 52,* 93–102.

Nelson, E. J. (1996). The American experience of childbirth. In R. L. Parrott & C. M. Condit (Eds.), *Evaluating women's health messages* (pp. 109–123). Thousand Oaks, CA: Sage.

Nelson, H. L. (1992). Scrutinizing surrogacy. In H. B. Holmes (Ed.), *Issues in reproductive technology* (pp. 297–302). New York: Garland.

Nelson, J. A., Liss, M., Erchull, M. J., Hurt, M. M., Ramsey, L. R., Turner, D. L., et al. (2008). Identity in action: Predictors of feminist self-identification and collective action. *Sex Roles, 58,* 721–728.

Nelson, M. R. & Paek, H.-J. (2005). Predicting cross-cultural differences in sexual advertising content in a transnational women's magazine. *Sex Roles, 53,* 371–383.

Nelson, M. R., & Paek, H.-J. (2008). Nudity of female and male models in primetime TV advertising across seven countries. *International Journal of Advertising, 27,* 715–744.

Nelson, T. D. (2009). Ageism. In T. D. Nelson (Ed.), *Handbook of prejudice, stereotyping, and discrimination* (pp. 431–440). New York: Taylor & Francis.

Nerøien, A. I., & Schei, B. (2008). Partner violence and health: Results from the first national study on violence against women in Norway. *Scandinavian Journal of Public Health, 36,* 161–168.

Neto, F., & Pinto, I. (1998). Gender stereotypes in Portuguese television advertisements. *Sex Roles, 39,* 153–164.

Nettles, S. M., & Scott-Jones, D. (1987). The role of sexuality and sex equity in the education of minority adolescents. *Peabody Journal of Education, 64,* 183–197.

Neuville, E., & Croizet, J. (2007). Can salience of gender identity impair math performance among 7-8 year old girls? The moderating role of task difficulty. *European Journal of Psychology of Education, 22*(3), 307–316. doi:10.1007/BF03173428.

Nevid, J. S. (1984). Sex differences in factors of romantic attraction. *Sex Roles, 11,* 401–411.

Newton, N. (1970). The effect of psychological environment on childbirth: Combined crosscultural and experimental approach. *Journal of Cross-Cultural Psychology, 1,* 85–90.

Nguyen, H., & Ryan, A. (2008). Does stereotype threat affect test performance of minorities and women? A meta-analysis of experimental evidence. *Journal of Applied Psychology, 93*(6), 1314–1334. doi:10.1037/a0012702.

Nicolson, P. (1993). Motherhood and women's lives. In D. Richardson & V. Robinson (Eds.), *Thinking feminist: Key concepts in women's studies* (pp. 201–224). New York: Guilford.

Niemann, Y. F., Jennings, L., Leilani, R., Richard, M., Baxter, J. C., & Sullivan, E. (1994). Use of free responses and cluster analysis to determine stereotypes of eight groups. *Personality and Social Psychology Bulletin, 20,* 379–390.

Nieva, V. F., & Gutek, B. A. (1981). *Women and work: A psychological perspective.* New York: Praeger.

Nigro, G. N., Hill, D. E., Gelbein, M. E., & Clark, C. L. (1988). Changes in the facial prominence of women and men over the last decade. *Psychology of Women Quarterly, 12,* 225–235.

Nikelly, A. G. (1995). Drug advertisements and the medicalization of unipolar depression in women. *Health Care for Women International, 16,* 229–242.

Nolen-Hoeksema, S., & Jackson, B. (2001). Mediators of the gender difference in rumination. *Psychology of Women Quarterly, 25,* 37–47.

Nolen-Hoeksema, S., Larson, J., & Grayson, C. (1999). Explaining the gender difference in depressive symptoms. *Journal of Personality and Social Psychology, 77,* 1061–1072.

Nolen-Hoeksema, S., Wisco, B. E., & Lyubomirsky, S. (2009). Rethinking rumination. *Perspectives on Psychological Science, 3,* 400–424.

Noll, S. M., & Fredrickson, B. L. (1998). A mediational model linking self-objectification, body shame, and disordered eating. *Psychology of Women Quarterly, 22,* 623–636.

Noller, P. (2006). Marital relationships. In P. Noller & J. A. Feeney (Eds.), *Close relationships: Functions, forms and processes* (pp. 67–88). Hove England: Psychology Press/Taylor & Francis (UK).

Norton, K. I., Olds, T. S., Olive, S., & Dank, S. (1996). Ken and Barbie at life size. *Sex Roles, 34,* 287–294.

O'Connell, A. N., & Russo, N. F. (Eds.). (1980). Models for achievement: Eminent women in psychology. *Psychology of Women Quarterly, 5,* 6–10.

O'Sullivan, L. F., Graber, J. A., & Brooks-Gunn, J. (2001). Adolescent gender development. In J. Worell (Ed.). *Encyclopedia of women and gender* (pp. 55–67). San Diego, CA: Academic Press.

Oakhill, J., Garnham, A., & Reynolds, D. (2005). Immediate activation of stereotypical gender information. *Memory & Cognition, 33,* 972–983.

Öberg, P. (2003). Images versus experience of the aging body. In C. A. Faircloth (Ed.), *Aging bodies: Images and everyday experiences* (pp. 103–139). New York: AltaMira Press.

Odeku, K., Rembe, S., & Anwo, J. (2009). Female genital mutiliation: A human rights perspective. *Journal of psychology in Africa, 19,* 55–62.

Oliver, M. B., & Hyde, J. S. (1993). Gender differences in sexuality: A meta-analysis. *Psychological Bulletin, 114,* 29–51.

Oliver, M. I., Pearson, N., Coe, N., & Gunnell, D. (2005). Help-seeking behaviour in men and women with common mental health problems: Cross-sectional study. *British Journal of Psychiatry, 186,* 297–301.

Olson, L., & Lloyd, S. A. (2005). It depends on what you mean by starting: An exploration of women's initiation of aggression. *Sex Roles, 53,* 603–617.

Oransky, M., & Marecek, J. (2002). *Doing boy.* Unpublished manuscript, Swarthmore College.

Orbuch, T. L., & Brown, E. (2006). Divorce in the context of being African American. In M. A. Fine & J. H. Harvey (Eds.), *Handbook of divorce and relationship dissolution* (pp. 481–496). Mahwah, NJ: Erlbaum.

Osland, J. A., Fitch, M., & Willis, E. E. (1996). Likelihood to rape in college males. *Sex Roles, 35,* 171–183.

Ottati, V., & Lee, Y. (1995). Accuracy: A neglected component of stereotype research. In Y. Lee, L. J. Jussim, & C. R. McCauley (Eds.), *Stereotype accuracy: Toward appreciating group differences* (pp. 29–63). Washington DC: American Psychological Association.

Owen, P. R., & Laurel-Seller, E. (2000). Weight and shape ideals: Thin is dangerously in. *Journal of Applied Social Psychology, 30,* 979–990.

Owen, S. A., & Caudill, S. A. (1996). Contraception and clinical science. In R. L. Parrott & C. M. Condit (Eds.), *Evaluating women's health messages* (pp. 81–94). Thousand Oaks, CA: Sage.

Oyserman, D., Mowbray, C. T., Mears, P. A., & Firminger, K. B. (2000). Parenting among mothers with serious mental illness. *American Journal of Orthopsychiatry, 70,* 296–315.

Palmore, E. (2001). The ageism survey: First findings. *Gerontologist, 41,* 572–575.

Palomares, N. A. (2009). Women are sort of more tentative than men, aren't they? How men and women use tentative language differently, similarly, and counterstereotypically as a function of gender salience. *Communication Research, 36,* 538–560.

Paludi, M. A., & Bauer, W. D. (1983). Goldberg revisited: What's in an author's name? *Sex Roles, 9,* 387–390.

Paludi, M. A., & Strayer, L. A. (1985). What's in an author's name? Differential evaluations of performance as a function of author's name. *Sex Roles, 10,* 353–361.

Papaharitou, S., Nakopoulou, E., Kirana, P., Giaglis, G., Moraitou, M., & Hatzichristou, D. (2008). Factors associated with sexuality in later life: an exploratory study in a group of Greek married older adults. *Archives of Gerontology and Geriatrics, 46,* 191–201.

Papanek, H. (1973). Men, women, and work: Reflections on the two-person career. *American Journal of Sociology, 78,* 852–870.

Papp, L., Cummings, E., & Goeke-Morey, M. (2009). For richer, for poorer: Money as a topic of marital conflict in the home. *Family Relations, 58,* 91–103.

Parents Television Council. (2009). *Women in peril: A look at TV's disturbing new storyline trend.* Retrieved June 10, 2010, from http://www.parentstv.org/PTC/publications/reports/womeninperil/study.pdf

Park, K. (2005). Choosing childlessness: Weber's typology of action and motives of the voluntary childless. *Sociological Inquiry, 75*(3), 372–402.

Parlee, M. B. (1981). Appropriate control groups in feminist research. *Psychology of Women Quarterly, 5,* 637–644.

Parlee, M. B. (1985). Psychology of women in the 80s: Promising problems. *International Journal of Women's Studies, 8,* 193–204.

Parrot, A., & Bechhofer, L. (Eds.). (1991). *Acquaintance rape: The hidden crime.* New York: Wiley.

Parrot A., & Cummings, N. (2006). *Forsaken females: The Global brutalization of women.* New York: Rowman & Littlefield.

Parsons, T., & Bales, R. F. (1955). *Family, socialization, and interaction process.* Glencoe, IL: Free Press.

Pauwels, A. (1998). *Women changing language.* New York: Addison-Wesley Longman.

Pearlman, S. F. (1993). Late mid-life astonishment: Disruptions to identity and self-esteeem. *Women and Therapy, 14,* 1–12.

Pearlstein, T. (2010). Premenstrual dysphoric disorder: Out of the appendix. *Archives of Women's Mental Health, 13,* 21–23.

Pelak, C. F. (2008). The relationship between sexist naming practices and athletic opportunities at colleges and universities in the southern United States. *Sociology of Education, 81,* 189–210.

Peplau, L. A., & Conrad, E. (1989). Beyond nonsexist research: The perils of feminist methods in psychology. *Psychology of Women Quarterly, 13*(4), 379–400. doi:10.1111/j.1471-6402.1989.tb01009.x

Peplau, L. A., & Fingerhut, A. (2007). The close relationships of lesbian and gay men. *Annual Review of Psychology, 58,* 405–424.

Peplau, L. A., & Garnets, P. D. (2000). A new paradigm for understanding women's sexuality and sexual orientation. *Journal of Social Issues, 56,* 329–350.

Peplau, L. A., & Gordon, S. L. (1985). Women and men in love: Gender differences in close heterosexual relationships. In V. E. O'Leary, R. K. Unger, & B. S. Wallston (Eds.), *Women, gender, and social psychology* (pp. 257–292). Hillsdale, NJ: Erlbaum

Peplau, L. A., & Spalding, L. R. (2000). The close relationships of lesbians, gay men, and bisexuals. In C. Hendrick & S. S. Hendrick (Eds.), *Close relationships: A sourcebook* (pp. 111–124). Thousand Oaks, CA: Sage.

Perrone, K. M., Zanardelli, G., Worthington, E. L., & Chartrand, J. M. (2002). Role model influences on the career decidedness of college students. *College Student Journal, 36,* 109–112.

Perry, M. G. (1999). Animated gerontophobia: Ageism, sexism, and the Disney villainess. In S. M. Deats & L. T. Lenker (Eds.), *Aging and identity: A humanities perspective* (pp. 201–212). Westport, CT: Praeger.

Petersen, J. L., & Hyde, J. S. (2009). A longitudinal investigation of peer sexual harassment victimization in adolescence. *Journal of Adolescence, 32,* 1173–1188.

Phares, V., & Compas, B. E. (1993). Fathers and developmental psychotherapy. *Current Directions in Psychological Science, 2,* 162.

Phillips, J., & Sweeney, M. (2005). Premarital cohabitation and marital disruption among White, Black, and Mexican American women. *Journal of Marriage and Family, 67,* 296–314.

Phillips, L. (1998). *The girls report: What we know and need to know about growing up female.* New York: National Council for Research on Women.

Phoenix, A., Woollett, A., & Lloyd, E. (Eds.). (1991). *Motherhood: Meanings, practices, and ideologies.* London: Sage.

Pickup, E. (2001). *Ending violence against women: A challenge for development and humanitarian work.* Oxford, England: Oxfam.

Pierce, R. L., & Kite, M. E. (1999). Creating expectations in adolescent girls. In S. N. Davis, M. Crawford, & J. Sebrechts (Eds.), *Coming into her own: Educational success in girls and women* (pp. 175–192). San Francisco: Jossey-Bass.

Pillemer, K., & Finkelhor, D. (1988). The prevalence of elder abuse: A random sample survey. *The Gerontologist, 23,* 33–56.

Pimental, S., Pandjiarjian, V., & Belloque, J. (2006). The "legitimate defence of honour", or murder with impunity? A critical study of legislation and case law in Latin America. In L. Welchman & S. Hossain (Eds.), *"Honour": Crimes, paradigms, and violence against women* (pp. 245–262). New York: Zed Books Ltd.

Pina, A., Gannon, T. A., & Saunders, B. (2009). An overview of the literature on sexual harassment: Perpetrator, theory, and treatment issues. *Aggression and Violent Behavior, 14,* 126–138.

Pingitore, R., Dugoni, B. L., Tindale, R. S., & Spring, B. (1994). Bias against overweight job applicants in a simulated employment interview. *Journal of Applied Psychology, 79,* 909–917.

Piotrkowski, C. S. (1998). Gender harassment, job satisfaction, and distress among employed white and minority women. *Journal of Occupational Health Psychology, 3,* 33–43.

Pipher, M. (1994). *Reviving Ophelia: Saving the selves of adolescent girls.* New York: Putnam.

Piran, N. (1999). *The feminist frame scale.* Paper presented at the annual meeting of the American Psychological Association as part of a symposium entitled: Measuring process and outcomes in short- and long-term feminist therapy. J. Worell (Chair), Boston.

Pittman, L. D., & Boswell, M. K. (2007). The role of grandmothers in the lives of preschoolers growing up in urban poverty. *Applied Developmental Science, 11,* 20–42.

Plant, E. A., Baylor, A. L., Doerr, C. E., & Rosenberg-Kima, R. B. (2009). Changing middle-school students' attitudes and performance regarding engineering with computer-based social models. *Computers & Education, 53*(2), 209–215.

Plant, E. A., Hyde, J. S., Keltner, D., & Devine, P. G. (2000). The gender stereotyping of emotions. *Psychology of Women Quarterly, 24,* 81–92.

Polakow, V. (1993). *Lives on the edge: Single mothers and their children in the other America.* Chicago: University of Chicago Press.

Pomerleau, A., Bloduc, D., Malcuit, G., & Cossette, L. (1990). Pink or blue: Environmental gender stereotypes in the first two years of life. *Sex Roles, 22,* 359–367.

Ponse, B. (1978). *Identities in the lesbian world.* Westport, CT: Greenwood Press.

Poortman, A. R., & Van Der Lippe, T. (2009). Attitudes toward housework and child care and the gendered division of labor. *Journal of Marriage and Family, 71,* 526–541.

Pope, K. (2001). Sex between therapist and client. In J. Worell (Ed.), *Encyclopedia of women and gender* (pp. 955–962). New York: Academic Press.

Pope, K., & Vetter, V. (1991). Prior therapist-patient sexual involvement among patients seen by psychologists. *Psychotherapy, 28,* 429–438.

Popp, D., Donovan, R. A., Crawford, M., Marsh, K. L., & Peele, M. (2003). Gender, race, and speech style stereotypes. *Sex Roles, 48,* 317–325.

Potts, M. K., Burnam, M. A., & Wells, K. B. (1991). Gender differences in depression detection: A comparison of clinician diagnosis and standardized assessment. *Psychological Assessment, 3,* 609–615.

Powlishta, K. K., Sen, M. G., Serbin, L. A., Poulin-Dubois, D., & Eichstedt, J. A. (2001). From infancy through middle childhood: The role of cognitive and social factors in becoming gendered. In R. K. Unger (Ed.), *Handbook of the psychology of women and gender* (pp. 116–132). New York: Wiley.

Press "1" if you're steamed. (2002, July 7). *The New York Times,* p. 8.

Price, S. J., & McKenry, P. C. (1988). *Divorce.* Beverly Hills, CA: Sage.

Priess, H. A., Lindberg, S. M., & Hyde, J. S. (2009). Adolescent gender-role identity and mental health: Gender intensification revisited. *Child Development, 80,* 1531–1544.

Prime, J. L., Carter, N., & Welbourne, T. M. (2009). Women "take care," men "take charge": Managers' stereotypic perceptions of women and men leaders. *The Psychologist-Manager Journal, 12,* 25–49.

Purdy, L. M. (1992). Another look at contract pregnancy. In H. B. Holmes (Ed.), *Issues in reproductive technology* (pp. 303–320). New York: Garland.

Puri, J. (1997). Reading romance novels in postcolonial India. *Gender & Society, 11,* 434–452.

Quek, K., & Knudson-Martin, C. (2006). A push toward equality: Processes among dual-career newlywed couples in collectivist culture. *Journal of Marriage and Family, 68*(1), 56–69.

Quinn, D. M., & Spencer, S. J. (2001). The interference of stereotype threat with women's generation of math problem-solving strategies. *Journal of Social Issues, 57,* 55–72.

Quirouette, C. C., & Pushkar, D. (1999). Views of future aging among middle-aged, university-educated women. *Canadian Journal of Aging, 18,* 236–258.

Raag, T., & Rackliff, C. L. (1998). Preschoolers' awareness of social expectations of gender relationships to toy choices. *Sex Roles, 38,* 685–700.

Rader, J., & Gilbert, L. A. (2005). The egalitarian relationship in feminist therapy. *Psychology of Women Quarterly, 29,* 427–435.

Radlove, S. (1983). Sexual response and gender roles. In E. R. Allgeier & N. B. McCormick (Eds.), *Changing boundaries: Gender roles and sexual behavior* (pp. 87–105). Palo Alto, CA: Mayfield.

Radway, J. A. (1984). *Reading the romance: Women, patriarchy, and popular literature.* Chapel Hill, NC: University of North Carolina Press.

Raffaelli, M., & Ontai, L. L. (2001). "She's 16 years old and there's boys calling over to the house": An exploratory study of sexual socialization in Latino families. *Culture, Health and Sexuality, 3,* 295–310.

Raffaelli, M., & Ontai, L. L. (2004). Gender socialization in Latino/a families: Results from two retrospective studies. *Sex Roles, 50,* 287–299.

Ragsdale, J. D. (1996). Gender, satisfaction level and the use of relational maintenance strategies in marriage. *Communication Monographs, 63,* 354–369.

Ralston, P. A. (1997). Midlife and older black women. In J. M. Coyle (Ed.), *Handbook on women and aging* (pp. 273–289). Westport, CT: Greenwood Press.

Ramaswami, A., Dreher, G. F., Bretz, R., & Wiethoff, C. (2010). Gender, mentoring, and career success: The importance of organizational context. *Personnel Psychology, 63*(2), 385–405. doi:10.1111/j.1744-6570.2010.01174.x

Ramirez-Valles, J., Zimmerman, M. A., & Juarez, L. (2002). Gender differences of neighborhood and social control processes: A study of the timing of first intercourse among low-achieving, urban, African American youth. *Youth and Society, 33,* 418–441.

Ramsey, L. R., Haines, M. E., Hurt, M. M., Nelson, J. A., Turner, D. L., Liss, M., & Erchull, M. (2007). Thinking of others: Feminist identification and the perceptions of others' beliefs. *Sex Roles, 56,* 611–616.

Randolph, S. M. (1995). African American children in single-mother families. In B. J. Dickerson (Ed.), *African American single mothers* (pp. 117–145). Thousand Oaks, CA: Sage.

Raymond, J. G. (1993). *Women as wombs: Reproductive technologies and the battle over women's freedom.* New York: HarperCollins.

Rashotte, L. S., & Webster, M. (2005). Gender status beliefs. *Social science research, 34,* 618–633.

Reame, N. K. (2001). Menstruation. In J. Worell (Ed.). *Encyclopedia of women and gender* (pp. 739–742). San Diego, CA: Academic Press.

Reddy, G. (2005). *With respect to sex: Negotiating hijra identity in south India.* Chicago: Chicago University Press.

Reed, J. (2006). Not crossing the "extra line": How cohabitors with children view their unions. *Journal of Marriage and Family, 68,* 1117–1131.

Reed, M. D. (1994). Pornography addiction and compulsive sexual behavior. In D. Zillmann & J. Bryant (Eds.), *Media, children, and the family: Social scientific, psychodynamic, and clinical perspectives* (pp. 249–269). Hillsdale, NJ: Erlbaum.

Regan, P. C., Levin, L., Sprecher, S., Christopher, F. S., & Cate, R. (2000). Partner preferences: What characteristics do men and women desire in their short-term sexual and long-term romantic partners? *Journal of Psychology and Human Sexuality, 12,* 1–21.

Regan, P. C., Medina, R., & Joshi, A. (2001). Partner preferences among homosexual men and women: What is desirable in a sex partner is not necessarily desirable in a romantic partner. *Social Behavior and Personality, 29,* 625–633.

Reid, P. T. (1993). Poor women in psychological research: Shut up and shut out. *Psychology of Women Quarterly, 17,* 133–150.

Reid, P. T., & Kelly, E. (1994). Research on women of color: From ignorance to awareness. *Psychology of Women Quarterly, 18,* 477–486.

Reid, P. T., & Trotter, K. H. (1993). Children's self-presentations with infants: Gender and ethnic comparisons. *Sex Roles, 29,* 171–181.

Reiger, K., & Dempsey, R. (2006). Performing birth in a culture of fear: An embedded crisis of late modernity. *Health Sociology Review, 15*(4), 364–373.

Reitz, R. R. (1999). Batterers' experiences of being violent: A phenomenological study. *Psychology of Women Quarterly, 23,* 143–166.

Rejeski, W. J., & Thompson, A. (1993). Historical and conceptual roots of exercise psychology. In P. Seraganian (Ed.), *Exercise psychology: The influence of physical exercise on psychological processes* (pp. 3–35). New York: Wiley.

Remer, P., & Rostosky, S. (2001a). Gender role consciousness raising for male clients. *The Feminist Psychologist, Spring, 29*–30.

Remer, P., & Rostosky, S. (2001b). Building feminist therapeutic relationships with male clients. *The Feminist Psychologist, Summer, 22,* 25.

Renaud, M. (2007). We are mothers too: Childbearing experiences of lesbian families. *Journal of Obstetric, Gynecologic, & Neonatal Nursing: Clinical Scholarship for the Care of Women, Childbearing Families, & Newborns, 36*(2), 190–199.

Rheingold, H. L., & Cook, K. V. (1975). The contents of boys' and girls' rooms as an index of parents' behavior. *Child Development, 46,* 459–463.

Rhoades, G., Stanley, S., & Markman, H. (2006). Pre-engagement cohabitation and gender asymmetry in marital commitment. *Journal of Family Psychology, 20*(4), 553–560.

Rice, J. (1994). Reconsidering research on divorce, family life cycle, and the meaning of family. *Psychology of Women Quarterly, 18,* 559–584.

Rich, A. (1976). *Of woman born: Motherhood as experience and institution.* New York: Norton.

Richardson, B. K., & Taylor, J. (2009). Sexual harassment at the intersection of race and gender: A theoretical model of the sexual harassment experiences of women of color. *Western Journal of Communication, 73,* 248–272.

Richman, E. L., & Shaffer, D. R. (2000). "If you let me play sports": How might sports participation influence the self-esteem of adolescent females? *Psychology of Women Quarterly, 24,* 189–199.

Rideout, V., Foehr, U., Roberts, D., & Brodie, M. (1999). *Kids & media @ the new millennium.* Menlo Park, CA: Kaiser Family Foundation Report.

Ridgeway, C. (1992). *Gender, interaction, and inequality.* New York: Spring-Verlag.

Riecher-Rössler, A. (2010). Prospects for the classification of mental disorders in women. *European Psychiatry, 25,* 189–196.

Rintala, D. H., Howland, C. A., Nosek, M. A., Bennett, J. L., Young, M. E., Foley, C. C., et al. (1997). Dating issues for women with physical disabilities. *Sexuality and Disability, 15,* 219–242.

Ripa, Y. (1990). *Women and madness: The incarceration of women in nineteenth-century France.* Minneapolis, MN: University of Minnesota Press.

Risman, B. J. (1998). *Gender vertigo.* New Haven, CT: Yale University Press.

Risman, B. J., & Johnson-Sumerford, D. (1998). Doing it fairly: A study of postgender marriages. *Journal of Marriage and the Family, 60,* 23–40.

Roberts, A. R. (1996). Police responses to battered women: Past, present, and future. In A. R. Roberts (Ed.), *Helping battered women* (pp. 85–95). New York: Oxford University Press.

Roberts, D. E. (1998). The future of reproductive choice for poor women and women of color. In R. Weitz (Ed.), *The politics of women's bodies: Sexuality, appearance, and behavior* (pp. 270–277). New York: Oxford University Press.

Roberts, T. A., Goldenberg, J. L., Power, C., & Pyszczynski, T. (2002). "Feminine protection": The effects of menstruation on attitudes toward women. *Psychology of Women Quarterly, 26,* 131–139.

Robinson, D. A., & Worell, J. (2002). Issues in clinical assessment with women. In J. Butcher (Ed.), *Clinical personality assessment: Practical approaches* (2nd ed., pp. 190–207). New York: Oxford University Press.

Rohner, R. P., & Veneziano, R. A. (2001). The importance of father love: History and contemporary evidence. *Review of General Psychology, 5,* 382–405.

Ropelato, J. (2006). *Internet pornography statistics.* Internet Filter Review. Retrieved from http://internet-filter-review.toptenreviews.com/internet-pornography-statistics-pg8.html

Rosario, M., Meyer-Bahlburg, H. F. L., Hunter, J., & Exner, T. M. (1996). The psychosexual development of urban lesbian, gay, and bisexual youths. *The Journal of Sex Research, 33,* 113–126.

Roscoe, W. (1996). How to become a berdache: Toward a unified analysis of gender diversity. In G. Herdt (Ed.), *Third sex, third gender: Beyond sexual dimorphism in culture and history* (pp. 329–372). New York: Zone Books.

Rose, J. G., Chrisler, J. C., & Couture, S. (2008). Young women's attitudes toward continuous use of oral contraceptives: The effect of priming position attitudes toward menstruation on women's willingness to suppress menstruation. *Health Care for Women International, 29,* 688–701.

Rose, S., & Frieze, I. H. (1989). Young singles' scripts for a first date. *Gender & Society, 3,* 258–268.

Rosell, M. C., & Hartman, S. L. (2001). Self-presentation of beliefs about gender discrimination and feminism. *Sex Roles, 44*, 647–659.

Rosenberg, R. (1982). *Beyond separate spheres: Intellectual roots of modern feminism.* New Haven, CT: Yale University Press.

Rosenblum, K. E., & Travis, T. M. C. (1996). *The meaning of difference: American constructions of race, sex and gender, social class, and sexual orientation.* New York: McGraw-Hill.

Rosenbluth, S. C., Steil, J. M., & Whitcomb, J. H. (1998). Marital equality: What does it mean? *Journal of Family Issues, 19*, 227–244.

Rosenbluth, S. C., & Steil, J. M. (1995). Predictors of intimacy for women in heterosexual and homosexual couples. *Journal of Social and Personal Relationships, 12*, 163–175.

Rosenfeld, P., Newell, C. E., & Le, S. (1998). Equal opportunity climate of women and minorities in the Navy: Results from the Navy equal opportunity/sexual harassment (NEOSH) survey. *Military Psychology, 10*, 69–85.

Rosenfield, S. (2000). Gender and dimensions of the self: Implications for internalizing and externalizing behavior. In E. Frank (Ed.), *Gender and its effects on psychopathology* (pp, 23–36). Washington, DC: American Psychiatric Publishing, Inc.

Rosenthal, N. B. (1984). Consciousness raising: From revolution to reevaluation. *Psychology of Women Quarterly, 8*, 309–326.

Rosenthal, R., & Jacobson, L. (1968). *Pygmalion in the classroom.* New York: Holt, Rinehart, and Winston.

Ross, S. R., Ridinger, L. L., & Cuneen, J. (2009). Drivers to divas: Advertising images of women in motorsport. *International Journal of Sports Marketing & Sponsorship, 10*, 204–214.

Rothblum, E. D. (2000). Sexual orientation and sex in women's lives: Conceptual and methodological issues. *Journal of Social Issues, 56*, 193–204.

Rothblum, E., Brand, P. A., Miller, C. T., & Oetjen, H. J. A. (1990). The relationship between obesity, employment discrimination, and employment-related victimization. *Journal of Vocational Behavior, 37*, 251–266.

Rouselle, R. (2001). "If it is a girl, cast it out": Infanticide/exposure in ancient Greece. *Journal of Psychohistory, 28*, 303–333.

Rousso, H. (1988). Daughters with disabilities: Defective women or minority women? In M. Fine & A. Asch (Eds.), *Women with disabilities: Essays in psychology, culture, and politics* (pp. 139–171). Philadelphia: Temple University Press.

Roy, A. (1998). Images of domesticity and motherhood in Indian television commercials: A critical study. *Journal of Popular Culture, 32*, 117–134.

Ruble, D. N., Fleming, A. S., Hackel, L. S., & Stangor, C. (1988). Changes in the marital relationship during the transition to first time motherhood: Effects of violated expectations concerning division of household labor. *Journal of Personality and Social Psychology, 85*, 78–87.

Rudman, L. A., & Borgida, E. (1995). The afterglow of construct accessibility: The behavioral consequences of priming men to view women as sexual objects. *Journal of Experimental Social Psychology, 31*, 493–517.

Rudman, L. A., & Glick, P. (1999). Feminized management and backlash against agentic women: The hidden costs to women of a kinder, gentler image of middle managers. *Journal of Personality and Social Psychology, 77*, 1004–1010.

Rudman, L. A., & Glick, P. (2008). *The social psychology of gender: How power and intimacy shape gender relations.* New York: Guilford.

Ruscher, J. B. (2001). *Prejudiced communication: A social psychological perspective.* New York: Guilford.

Ruscher, J. B., & Duval, L. L. (1998). Multiple communicators with unique target information transmit less stereotypical impressions. *Journal of Personality and Social Psychology, 74*, 329–344.

Russell, D. (1995). *Women, madness, & medicine.* Cambridge, UK: Polity Press.

Russell, D. E. H. (1993). *Against pornography: The evidence of harm.* Berkeley, CA: Russell Publications.

Russett, C. E. (1989). *Sexual science: The Victorian construction of womanhood.* Cambridge, MA: Harvard University Press.

Russo, N. F. (1979). Overview: Sex roles, fertility, and the motherhood mandate. *Psychology of Women Quarterly, 4*, 7–15.

Russo, N. F. (2008). Understanding emotional responses after abortion. In J. C. Chrisler, C. Golden, & P. D. Rozee (Eds.), *Lectures on the psychology of women* (4th ed., pp. 172–189). New York: McGraw-Hill.

Russo, N. F., & Dumont, B. A. (1997). A history of division 35 (psychology of women): Origins, issues, activities, future. In D. A. Dewsbury (Ed.), *Unification through division: Histories of the divisions of the american psychological association, Vol. 2.* Washington, DC: American Psychological Association.

Rust, P. C. (1993). Neutralizing the political threat of the marginal woman: Lesbians' beliefs about bisexual women. *Journal of Sex Research, 30*, 214–228.

Rust, P. C. (2000). Bisexuality: A contemporary paradox for women. *Journal of Social Issues, 56*, 205–222.

Ruth, S. (1990). *Issues in feminism.* Mountain View, CA: Mayfield.

Ryan, C., Huebner, D., Diaz, R.M., & Sanchez, J. (2009). Family rejection as a predictor of negative health outcomes in White and Latino lesbian, gay, and bisexual young adults. *Pediatrics, 123*, 346–352. Retrieved May 10, 2010, from http://pediatrics.aappublications.org/cgi/content/full/123/1/346

Rydell, R., McConnvll, A., & Beilock, S. (2009). Multiple social identities and stereotype threat: Imbalance, accessibility, and working memory. *Journal of Personality and Social Psychology, 96*(5), 949–966. doi:10.1037/a0014846.

Sadker, M., & Sadker, D. (1994). *Failing at fairness: How America's schools cheat girls.* New York: Scribner.

Safdar, S., Friedlmeier, W., Matsumoto, D., Yoo, S., Kwantes, C., Kakai, H., et al. (2009). Variations of emotional display rules within and across cultures: A comparison between Canada, USA, and Japan. *Canadian Journal of Behavioural Science/Revue canadienne des sciences du comportement, 41*(1), 1–10. doi:10.1037/a0014387.

Safir, M. P., Rosenmann, A., & Kloner, O. (2003). Tomboyism, sexual orientation, and adult gender roles among Israeli women. *Sex Roles, 48,* 401–410.

Sakalli, N. (2002). Application of the attribution-value model of prejudice to homosexuality. *Journal of Social Psychology, 142,* 264–271.

Sakraida, T. (2005). Divorce transition differences of midlife women. *Issues in Mental Health Nursing, 26,* 225–249.

Salgado de Snyder, V. N., Acevedo, A., Diaz-Perez, M., & Saldivar-Garduno, A. (2000). Understanding the sexuality of Mexican-born women and their risk for HIV/AIDS. *Psychology of Women Quarterly, 24,* 100–109.

Salmon, P. (2001). Effects of physical exercise on anxiety, depression, and sensitivity to stress. A unifying theory. *Clinical Psychology Review, 21,* 33–61.

Sampselle, C. M., Harris, V., Harlow, S. D., & Sowers, M. (2002). Midlife development and menopause in African American and Caucasian women. *Health Care for Women International, 23,* 351–363.

Samuel, D. B., & Widiger, T. A. (2009). Comparative gender biases in models of personality disorder. *Personality and Mental Health 3,* 12–25.

Sanchez, D. T., Crocker, J., & Bolke, K. R. (2005). Doing gender in the bedroom: Investing in gender norms and the sexual experience. *Personality and Social Psychology Bulletin, 31,* 1445–1455.

Sanchez, F., & Vilain, E. (2009). Collective self-esteem as a coping resource for male-to-female transsexuals. *Journal of Counseling Psychology, 56,* 202–209.

Sanchez, L., & Thomson, E. (1997). Becoming mothers and fathers: Parenthood, gender, and the division of labor. *Gender & Society, 11,* 747–772.

Sanchez-Hucles, J. V., & Davis, D. D. (2010). Women and women of color in leadership: Complexity, identity, and intersectionality. *American Psychologist, 65,* 171–181.

Sanday, P. (1981). *Female power and male dominance: On the origins of sexual inequality.* Cambridge: Cambridge University Press.

Sanday, P. (1990). *Fraternity gang rape: Sex, brotherhood, and privilege on campus.* New York City: New York University Press.

Sanday, P. (1996). Rape-prone versus rape-free campus cultures. *Violence Against Women, 2,* 191–208.

Sanday, P. (2007). *Fraternity gang rape: Sex, brotherhood, and privilege on campus* (2nd ed.). New York City: New York University Press.

Sapiro, V. (1994). Women *in American society: An introduction to women's studies* (3rd ed.). Mountain View, CA: Mayfield.

Sassler, S., Miller, A., & Favinger, S. (2009). Planned parenthood? Fertility intentions and experiences among cohabiting couples. *Journal of Family Issues, 30,* 206–232.

Sayer, L. C. (2006). Economic aspects of divorce and relationship dissolution. M. A. Fine & J. H. Harvey (Eds.), *Handbook of divorce and relationship dissolution* (pp. 385–406). Mahwah, NJ: Erlbaum.

Scarborough, E., & Furumoto, L. (1987). *Untold lives: The first generation of American women psychologists.* New York: Columbia University Press.

Scarr, S., Phillips, D., & McCartney, K. (1990). Facts, fantasies and the future of child care in the United States. *Psychological Science, 1,* 26–35.

Scarr, S. (1998). American child care today. *American Psychologist, 53,* 95–108.

Schafer, A. T., & Gray, M. W. (1981). Sex and mathematics. *Science, 211,* 231.

Scheuble, L. K., & Johnson, D. R. (2005). Married women's situational use of last names: An empirical study. *Sex Roles, 53,* 143–151.

Schick, V. R., Zucker, A. N., & Bay-Cheng, L. Y. (2008). Safer, better sex through feminism: The role of feminist ideology in women's sexual well-being. *Psychology of Women Quarterly, 32,* 225–232.

Schmader, T., Johns, M., & Forbes, C. (2008). An integrated process model of stereotype threat effects on performance. *Psychological Review, 115*(2), 336–356. doi:10.1037/0033-295X.115.2.336.

Schultz, M. R. (1975). The semantic derogation of women. In B. Thorne & N. Henley (Eds.), *Language and sex: Difference and dominance* (pp. 64–73). Rowley, MA: Newbury House.

Schulz, S. (2007). Psychological theories of disability and sexuality: A literature review. *Journal of Human Behavior in the Social Environment, 19,* 58–69.

Schwartz, P. (1994). *Peer marriage.* New York: Free Press.

Scott, B. A. (2008). Women and pornography: What we don't know can hurt us. In J. Chrisler, , C. Golden, & P. D. Rozee (Eds.), *Lectures on the psychology of women* (4th ed., pp. 339–355). New York: McGraw-Hill.

Scott, J. P. (1997). Family relationships of midlife and older women. In J. M. Coyle (Ed.), *Handbook on women and aging* (pp. 367–384). Westport, CT: Greenwood Press.

Seal, D. W., Smith, M., Coley, B., Perry, J., & Gamez, M. (2008). Urban heterosexual couples' sexual scripts for three shared sexual experiences. *Sex Roles, 58,* 626–638.

Sears, D. O. (1986). College sophomores in the laboratory: Influences of a narrow data base on social psychology's view of human nature. *Journal of Personality and Social Psychology, 51,* 515–530.

Seepersad, S., Choi, M., & Shin, N. (2008). How does culture influence the degree of romantic loneliness and closeness? *The Journal of Psychology, 142*, 209–216.

Segal, J. (2005). *Values and the rhetoric of pleasure.* Presentation for women and the new sexual politics: Profits vs. pleasures, presented at the 2005 New View Conference, Montreal, Quebec. Retrieved from http://www.fsd-alert.org/connewviewconf2005.html

Seidah, A., & Bouffard, T. (2007). Being proud of oneself as a person or being proud of one's physical appearance: What matters for feeling well in adolescence? *Social Behavior and Personality, 35*, 255–268.

Sen, A. (1990, December). More than 100 million women are missing. *New York Review of Books, 37.* Retrieved November 15, 2010, from http://houstonhs.scsk12.org/~robinsonm/mr._robinsons_web_site_at_houston_high_school/APHG_Units_files/6.%20More%20Than%20100%20Million%20Women%20Missing.pdf

Seto, M. C., Maric, A., & Barbaree, H. E. (2001). The role of pornography in the etiology of sexual aggression. *Aggression and Violence Behavior, 6*, 35–53.

Shapiro, A. F., Gottman, J. M., & Carrere, S. (2000). The baby and the marriage: Identifying factors that buffer against decline in marital satisfaction after the first baby arrives. *Journal of Family Psychology, 14*, 59–70.

Shepard, M. F., Falk, D. R., & Elliott, B. A. (2002). Enhancing coordinated community responses to reduce recidivism in cases of domestic violence. *Journal of Interpersonal Violence, 17*, 551–569.

Sherif, C. W. (1979). Bias in psychology. In J. A. Sherman & E. T. Beck (Eds.), *The prisms of sex: Essays in the sociology of knowledge* (pp. 93–133). Madison: University of Wisconsin Press.

Sherif, C. W. (1983). Carolyn Wood Sherif (autobiography). In A. O'Connell & N. F. Russo (Eds.), *Models of achievement* (pp. 279–293). New York: Columbia University Press.

Sherman, J. A., & Fennema, E. (1978). Distribution of spatial visualization and mathematical problem solving scores: A test of Stafford's X-linked hypothesis. *Psychology of Women Quarterly, 3*, 157–167.

Shields, S. A. (1975). Functionalism, Darwinism, and the psychology of women: A study in social myth. *American Psychologist, 30*, 739–754.

Shields, S. A. (1982). The variability hypothesis: The history of a biological model of sex difference in intelligence. *Signs, 7*, 769–797.

Shields, S. A., (2002). *Speaking from the heart: Gender and the social meaning of emotion.* Cambridge, MA: Cambridge University Press.

Shih, M., Pittinsky, T. L., & Ambady, N. (1999). Stereotype susceptibility: Identity salience and shifts in quantitative performance. *Psychological Science, 10*, 80–83.

Shisana, O., & Simbayi, L. (2002). Nelson Mandela/HSRC study of HIV/AIDS: South African national HIV prevalence, behavioral risks and mass media, household survey 2002. Cape Town, South Africa: Human Sciences Research Council.

Short, L. (2007). Lesbian mothers living well in the context of heterosexism and discrimination: resources, strategies, and legislative change. *Feminism & Psychology, 17*(1), 57–74.

Showalter, E. (1986). *The female malady: Women, madness, and English culture, 1830–1980.* New York: Pantheon Books.

Shulman, J. L., & Horne, S. G. (2003). The use of self-pleasure: Masturbation and body image among African American and European American women. *Psychology of Women Quarterly, 27*, 262–269.

Shumaker, S. A. (2004). Conjugated equine estrogens and incidence of probable dementia and mild cognitive impairment in postmenopausal women: Women's health initiative memory study. *Journal of the American Medical Association, 291*, 2947–2958.

Shute, R., Owens, L., & Slee, P. (2008). Everyday victimization of adolescent girls by boys: Sexual harassment, bullying, or aggression? *Sex Roles, 58*, 477–489.

Sibley, C. G., Overall, N. C., Duckitt, J., Perry, R., Milfont, T. L., Khan, S. S., et al. (2009). Your sexism predicts my sexism: Perceptions of men's (but not women's) sexism affects one's own sexism over time. *Sex Roles, 60*(9–10), 682–693. doi:10.1007/s11199-008-9554-8

Sidanius, J., & Pratto, F. (1999). *Social dominance: An intergroup theory of social hierarchy and oppression.* New York: Cambridge University Press.

Sieg, E. (2000). "So tell me what you want, what you really want . . .": New women on old footings? *Feminism & Psychology, 10*, 498–503.

Sigelman, C. K., Thomas, D. B., Sigelman, L., & Ribich, F. D. (1986). Gender, physical attractiveness, and electibility: An experimental investigation of voter biases. *Journal of Applied Social Psychology, 16*, 229–248.

Signorella, M. L., & Frieze, I. R. (2008). Interrelations of gender schemas in children and adolescents: Attitudes, preferences, and self-perceptions. *Social Behavior and Personality, 36*, 941–954.

Silveira, J. (1980). Generic masculine words and thinking. In C. Kramarae (Ed.), *The voices and words of women and men* (pp. 165–178). Oxford, England: Pergamon.

Silverman, J. G., Raj, A., Mucci, L. A., & Hathaway, J. E. (2001). Dating violence against adolescent girls and associated substance use, unhealthy weight control, sexual risk behavior, pregnancy, and suicidality. *Journal of the American Medical Association, 286*, 572–579.

Silverstein, L. B. (1996). Fathering is a feminist issue. *Psychology of Women Quarterly, 20*, 3–37.

Silverstein, L. B. (2002). Fathers and families. In J. P. McHale & W. S. Grolnick (Eds.), *Retrospect and prospect in the psychological study of families* (pp. 35–64). Mahwah, NJ: Erlbaum.

Silverstein, L. B., & Auerbach, C. F. (1999). Deconstructing the essential father. *American Psychologist, 54*, 397–407.

Simes, M. R., & Berg, D. H. (2001). Surreptitious learning: Menarche and menstrual product advertising. *Health Care for Women International, 22*, 455–469.

Simpson, G. (1996). Factors influencing the choice of law as a career by black women. *Journal of Career Development, 22*, 197–209.

Sinclair, A. H., Berta, P., Palmer, M. S., Hawkins, J. R., Griffiths, B. L., Smith, M. J., et al. (1990). A gene from the human sex-determining region encodes a protein with homology to a conserved DNA binding motif. *Nature, 346*, 240–244.

Skinner, S. R., Smith, J., Fenwick, J., Fyfe, S., & Hendrik, J. (2008). Perceptions and experiences of first sexual intercourse in Australian adolescent females. *Journal of Adolescent Health, 43(6)*, 593–599. doi:10.1016/j.jadohealth.2008.04.017

Skodol, A. E., & Bender, D. S. (2003). Why are women diagnosed borderline more than men? *Psychiatric Quarterly, 74*, 349–360.

Smith, E. A. (1989). A biosocial model of adolescent sexual behavior. In G. R. Adams, R. Montemayor, & T. P. Gullotta (Eds.), *Advances in adolescent development* (pp. 143–167). Newbury Park, CA: Sage.

Smith, G., Mysak, K., & Michael, S. (2008). Sexual double standards and sexually transmitted Illnesses: Social rejection and stigmatization of women. *Sex Roles, 58*, 391–401.

Smith, J. (1991). Conceiving selves: A case study of changing identities during the transition to motherhood. *Journal of Language and Social Psychology, 10*, 225–243.

Smith, M. (1997). Psychology's undervaluation of single motherhood. *Feminism & Psychology, 7*, 529–532.

Smith, P. H., Smith, J. B., & Earp, J. A. (1999). Beyond the measurement trap: A reconstructed conceptualization and measurement of woman battering. *Psychology of Women Quarterly, 23*, 177–193.

Smith, T., Berg, C., Florsheim, P., Uchino, B., Pearce, G., Hawkins, M, et al. (2009). Conflict and collaboration in middle-aged and older couples: I. Age differences in agency and communion during marital interaction. *Psychology and Aging, 24*, 259–273.

Smith-Rosenberg, C. (1975). The female world of love and ritual: Relations between women in nineteenth-century America. *Signs, 1*, 1–30.

Smolak, L., & Striegel-Moore, R. (2001). Body image concerns. In J. Worell (Ed.), *Encyclopedia of sex and gender* (pp. 201–210). New York: Academic Press.

Snyder, M., & Klein, O. (2005). Construing and constructing others: On the reality and the generality of the behavioral confirmation scenario. *Interaction Studies: Social Behaviour and Communication in Biological and Artificial Systems, 6*, 53–67.

Snyder, M., Tanke, E. D., & Berscheid, E. (1977). Social perception and interpersonal behavior: On the self-fulfilling nature of social stereotypes. *Journal of Personality and Social Psychology, 35*, 656–666.

Sokolovsky, J. (1997). Culture, aging and context. In J. Sokolovsky (Ed.), *The cultural context of aging: Worldwide perspectives* (2nd ed., pp. 1–15). Westport, CT: Bergin & Garvey.

Solberg, K. E. (2009). Killed in the name of honour. *The Lancet, 373*, 1933–1934.

Solinger, R. (2005). *Pregnancy and power: A short history of reproductive politics in America.* New York: NYU Press.

Solomon, M. B., & Herman, J. P. (2009). Sex differences in psychopathology: Of gonads, adrenals and mental illness. *Physiology & Behavior. 97*, 250–258.

Somer, E., & Nachmani, I. (2005). Constructions of therapist-client sex: A comparative analysis of retrospective victim reports. *Sexual Abuse: Journal of Research and Treatment, 17*, 47–62.

Somer, E., & Saadon, M. (1999). Therapist-client sex: Clients' retrospective reports. *Professional Psychology: Research and Practice, 30*, 504–509.

Sommer, B., Avis, N., Meyer, P., Ory, M., Madden, T., Kagawa-Singer, M., et al. (1999). Attitudes toward menopause and aging across ethnic/racial groups. *Psychosomatic Medicine, 61*, 868–875.

Sommers, E. K., & Check, J. V. (1987). An empirical investigation of the role of pornography in the verbal and physical abuse of women. *Violence and Victims, 2*, 189–209.

Southworth, S. (2010, March 24). 2009 Wisconsin Act 134—Sex Education Mandates. [Letter from Scott Southworth to School Board Members and District Administrators, Juneau County].

Spence, J. T., & Buckner, C. E. (2000). Instrumental and expressive traits, trait stereotypes, and sexist attitudes. *Psychology of Women Quarterly, 24*, 44–62.

Spencer, S. J., Steele, C. M., & Quinn, D. M. (1999). Stereotype threat and women's math performance. *Journal of Experimental Social Psychology, 35*, 4–28.

Spitzer, B. L., Henderson, K. A., & Zivian, M. T. (1999). Gender differences in population versus media body sizes: A comparison over four decades. *Sex Roles, 40*, 545–565.

Sprecher, S., Barbee, A., & Schwartz, P. (1995). "Was it good for you, too?": Gender differences in first sexual intercourse experiences. *The Journal of Sex Research, 32*, 3–15.

Sprecher, S., & Regan, P. C. (2000). Sexuality in relational context. In C. Hendrick & S. S. Hendrick (Eds.), *Close relationships: A sourcebook* (pp. 217–228). Thousand Oaks, CA: Sage Publications, Inc.

Sprock, J., Blashfield, R. K., & Smith, B. (1990). Gender weighting of *DSM-III-R* personality disorder criteria. *American Journal of Psychiatry, 147*, 586–590.

Sprock, J., & Yoder, C. Y. (1997). Women and depression: An update on the report of the APA task force. *Sex Roles, 36*, 269–303.

Srebnik, D. S., & Saltzberg, E. A. (1994). Feminist cognitive-behavioral therapy for negative body image. *Women & Therapy, 15*, 117–133.

Stangor, C. (1995). Content and application inaccuracy in social stereotyping. In Y. Lee, L. J. Jussim, & C. R. McCauley (Eds.), *Stereotype accuracy: Toward appreciating group differences* (pp. 275–293). Washington, DC: American Psychological Association.

Stapleton, K. (2001). Constructing a feminist identity: Discourse and the community of practice. *Feminism and Psychology, 11,* 459–491.

Statham, A., Miller, E. M., & Mauksch, H. O. (Eds.). (1988). *The worth of women's work: A qualitative synthesis.* Albany, NY: State University of New York Press.

Steele, J., James, J. B., & Barnett, R. C. (2002). Learning in a man's world: Examining the perceptions of undergraduate women in male-dominated academic areas. *Psychology of Women Quarterly, 26,* 46–50.

Steiger, J. (1981). The influence of the feminist subculture in changing sex-role attitudes. *Sex Roles, 7,* 627–634.

Steil, J. M. (1997). *Marital equality: Its relationship to the well-being of husbands and wives.* Thousand Oaks, CA: Sage.

Steil, J. M. (2001). Family forms and member well-being: A research agenda for the decade of behavior. *Psychology of Women Quarterly, 25,* 344–363.

Steil, J. M., & Hoffman, L. (2006). Gender conflict and the family. In M. Deutsch, P. Coleman, & E. Marcus, (Eds.), *Handbook of conflict resolution: Theory and practice* (2nd ed., pp. 223–241). San Francisco: Jossey-Bass.

Steil, J. M., McGann, V. L., & Kahn, A. S. (2001). Entitlement. In J. Worell (Ed.), *Encyclopedia of women and gender* (pp. 403–410). San Diego, CA: Academic Press.

Steil, J. M., & Turetsky, B. A. (1987a). Marital influence levels and symptomatology among wives. In F. Crosby (Ed.), *Spouse, parent, worker: On gender and multiple roles* (pp. 74–90). New Haven, CT: Yale University Press.

Steil, J. M., & Turetsky, B. A. (1987b). Is equal better? The relationship between marital equality and psychological symptomatology. In S. Oskamp (Ed.), *Family processes and problems: Social psychological aspects* (pp. 73–97). Beverly Hills, CA: Sage.

Steil, J. M., & Weltman, K. (1991). Marital inequality: The importance of resources, personal attributes, and social norms on career valuing and the allocation of domestic responsibilities. *Sex Roles, 24,* 161–179.

Stein, M. B., & Kennedy, C. (2001). Major depressive and post-traumatic stress disorder comorbidity in female victims of intimate partner violence. *Journal of Affective Disorders, 66,* 133–138.

Steinem, G. (1980). Erotica and pornography: A clear and present difference. In L. Lederer (Ed.), *Take back the night* (pp. 35–39). New York: William Morrow.

Steinem, G. (1983). *Outrageous acts and everyday rebellions.* New York: New American Library.

Stevens, D., Kiger, G., & Riley, P. J. (2001). Working hard and hardly working: Domestic labor and marital satisfaction among dual-earner couples. *Journal of Marriage and Family, 63,* 514–526.

Stewart, A. J., Copeland, A. P., Chester, N. L., Malley, J. E., & Barenbaum, N. B. (1997). *Separating together: How divorce transforms families.* New York: Guilford.

Stewart, S., Stinnett, H., & Rosenfeld, L. B. (2000). Sex differences in desired characteristics of short-term and long-term relationship partners. *Journal of Social and Personal Relationships, 17,* 843–853.

Stice, E., Presnell, K., & Bearman, S. K. (2001). Relation of early menarche to depression, eating disorders, substance abuse, and comorbid psychopathology among adolescent girls. *Developmental Psychology, 37,* 608–619.

Stice, E., & Whitenton, K. (2002). Risk factors for body dissatisfaction in adolescent girls: A longitudinal investigation. *Developmental Psychology, 38,* 669–678.

Stone, L., & McKee, N. P. (2000). Gendered futures: Student visions of career and family on a college campus. *Anthropology and Education Quarterly, 31,* 67–89.

Storrs, D., & Kleinke, C. L. (1990). Evaluation of high and equal status male touchers. *Journal of Nonverbal Behavior, 14,* 87–95.

Straus, M. A. (1999). The controversy over domestic violence by women: A methodological, theoretical, and sociology of science analysis. In X. B. Arriaga & S. Oskamp (Eds.), *Violence in intimate relationships* (pp. 12–44). Thousand Oaks, CA: Sage.

Striegel-Moore, R. H., Goldman, S. L., Garvin, V., & Rodin, J. (1996). Within-subjects design: Pregnancy changes both body and mind. In F. E. Donelson (Ed.), *Women's experiences: A psychological perspective* (pp. 430–437). Mountain View, CA: Mayfield.

Stroebe, M., Stroebe, W., & Schut, H. (2001). Gender differences in adjustment to bereavement: An empirical and theoretical review. *Review of General Psychology, 5,* 62–83.

Strober, M., Freeman, R., Lampert, C., & Diamond, J. (2007). The association of anxiety disorders and obsessive compulsive personality disorder with anorexia nervosa: Evidence from a family study with discussion of nosological and neurodevelopmental implications. *International Journal of Eating Disorders, 40* (Supl), S46–S51.

Stryker, S. (1998). The transgender issue. *GLQ—A Journal of Lesbian and Gay Studies, 4,* 145–158.

Sugar, J. A. (2007). Work and retirement: challenges and opportunities for women over 50. In V. Muhlbauer J. C. Chrisler (Eds.), *Women over 50: Psychological perspectives* (pp. 164–181). New York: Springer.

Sugarman, D. B., & Hotaling, G. T. (1989). Dating violence: Prevalence, context, and risk markers. In M. A. Pirog-Good & J. E. Stets (Eds.), *Violence in dating relationships* (pp. 3–32). New York: Praeger.

Sullivan, T. P., Meese, K. J., & Swan, S. C. (2005). Precursors and correlates of women's violence: Child abuse, traumatization, victimization of women, avoidance coping, and psychological symptoms. *Psychology of Women Quarterly, 29,* 290–301.

Sun, C., Bridges, A., Wosnitzer, R., Scharrer, E., & Liberman, R. (2008). A comparison of male and female directors in popular pornography: What happens when women are at the helm?. *Psychology of Women Quarterly, 32*(3), 312–325. doi:10.1111/j.1471-6402.2008.00439.x

Sutfin, E. L., Fulcher, M., Bowles, R., & Patterson, C. J. (2008). How lesbian and heterosexual parents convey attitudes about gender to their children: The role of gendered environments. *Sex Roles, 58*, 501–513.

Suzuki, M. F. (1995). Women and television: Portrayal of women in the mass media. In K. Fujimura-Fanselow & A. Kameda (Eds.), *Japanese women: New feminist perspectives on the past, present and future* (pp. 75–90). New York: Feminist Press.

Swaab, D. (2009). Sexual differentiation of the human brain in relation to gender identity and sexual orientation. *Functional Neurology, 24*, 17–28.

Swim, J. K., Hyers, L. L., Cohen, L. L., & Ferguson, M. J. (2001). Everyday sexism: Evidence for its incidence, nature and psychological impact from three daily diary studies. *Journal of Social Issues, 57*, 31–54.

Swim, J. K., Johnston K., Pearson, N. (2009). Daily experiences with heterosexism. Relations between hetersexist hassles and psychological well-being. *Journal of Social and Clinical Psychology, 28*, 597–629.

Swinbourne, J. M., & Touyz, S. W. (2007). The co-morbidity of eating disorders and anxiety disorders: A review. *European Eating Disorders Review, 15*, 253–274.

Szasz, T. (1970). *The manufacture of madness: A comparative study of the inquisition and the mental health movement.* New York: Harper & Row.

Szasz, T. (Ed.). (1973). *The age of madness: The history of involuntary mental hospitalization, presented in selected texts.* Garden City, NY: Anchor Books.

Tally, M. (2006). "She doesn't let age define her": Sexuality and motherhood in recent "middle-aged chick flicks." *Sexuality & Culture, 10*, 33–55.

Tang, S., & Zuo, J. (2000). Dating attitudes and behaviors of American and Chinese students. *Social Science Journal, 37*, 67–78.

Tangri, S., & Hayes, S. (1997). Theories of sexual harassment. In W. O'Donohue (Ed.), *Sexual harassment: Theory, research, and treatment* (pp. 112–128). Boston: Allyn & Bacon.

Tashiro, T., Frazier, P., & Berman, M. (2006). Stress-related growth following divorce and relationship dissolution. M. A. Fine & J. H. Harvey (Eds.), *Handbook of divorce and relationship dissolution* (pp. 361–384). Mahwah, NJ: Lawrence Erlbaum Associates.

Tasker, F. (2005). Lesbian mothers, gay fathers, and their children: A review. *Journal of Developmental & Behavioral Pediatrics, 26*(3), 224–240.

Tasker, F. L., & Golombok, S. (1997). *Growing up in a lesbian family.* New York: Guilford.

Tavris, C. (1992). *The mismeasure of woman: Why women are not the better sex, the inferior sex, or the opposite sex.* New York: Simon & Schuster.

Taylor, J. (2007). Transgender identities and public policy in the United States: The relevance for public administration. *Administration & Society, 39*, 833.

Taylor, J., Gilligan, C., & Sullivan, A. (1995). *Between voice and silence: Women and girls, race and relationship.* Cambridge, MA: Harvard University Press.

Teachman, J., Tedrow, L., & Hall, M. (2006). The demographic future of divorce and dissolution. In M. A. Fine & J. H. Harvey (Eds.), *Handbook of divorce and relationship dissolution* (pp. 59–82). Mahwah, NJ: Lawrence Erlbaum Associates.

Teitelbaum, P. (1989). Feminist theory and standardized testing. In A. M. Jaggar & S. Bordo (Eds.), *Gender/body/knowledge* (pp. 324–335). New Brunswick, NJ: Rutgers University Press.

Tenenbaum, H. R., & Leaper, C. (2002). Are parents' gender schema related to their children's gender-related cognitions? A meta-analysis. *Developmental Psychology, 38*, 615–630.

Tevlin, H. E., & Leiblum, S. R. (1983). Sex-role stereotypes and female sexual dysfunction. In V. Franks & E. D. Rothblum (Eds.), *Stereotyping of women: Its effects on mental health* (pp. 129–148). New York: Springer.

The White House Project. (2005). *Who's talking now: A followup analysis of guest appearances by women on the Sunday morning talk shows.* New York: The White House Project.

Thibault, J. W., & Kelley, H. H. (1959). *The social psychology of groups.* New York: Wiley.

Thoits, P. A. (1987). Negotiating roles. In F. J. Crosby (Ed.), *Spouse, parent, worker: On gender and multiple roles* (pp. 11–22). New Haven: Yale University Press.

Turk, J. L., & Bell, N. W. (1972). Measuring power in families. *Journal of Marriage and the Family, 34*, 215–223.

Thompson, T. L., & Zerbinos, E. (1995). Gender roles in animated cartoons: Has the picture changed in twenty years? *Sex Roles, 32*, 651–673.

Thorne, B. (1993). *Gender play: Girls and boys in school.* New Brunswick, NJ: Rutgers University Press.

Thorne, B., & Luria, Z. (1986). Sexuality and gender in children's daily worlds. *Social Problems, 33*, 176–190.

Thurer, S. L. (1983). Deinstitutionalization and women: Where the buck stops. *Hospital and Community Psychiatry, 34*, 1162–1163.

Tiedemann, J. (2000). Parents' gender stereotypes and teachers' beliefs as predictors of children's concept of their mathematical ability in elementary school. *Journal of Educational Psychology, 92*, 144–151.

Tiedens, L. Z., Ellsworth, P. C., & Mesquita, B. (2000). Stereotypes about sentiments and status: Expectations about high- and low-status group members. *Personality & Social Psychology Bulletin, 26*, 560–574.

Tiefer, L. (1989, August). Feminist transformations of sexology. In M. Crawford (Chair), *Feminist psychological science: Frameworks, strengths, visions, and a few examples.* Symposium conducted at the meeting of the American Psychological Association, New Orleans, LA.

Tiefer, L. (1995). *Sex is not a natural act & other essays.* San Francisco: Westview.

Tiefer, L. (2000). Agreeing to disagree: Multiple views on gender laws and transsex. *Feminism & Psychology, 10,* 36–40.

Tiefer, L. (2007). Sexuopharmacology: A fateful new element in sexual scripts. In M. Kimmell (Ed.), *The sexual self: The construction of sexual scripts* (pp. 239–248). Nashville, TN: University of Vanderbilt Press.

Tiggemann, M., & Kuring, J. K. (2004). The role of body objectification in disordered eating and depressed mood. *British Journal of Clinical Psychology, 43,* 299–311.

Tighe, C. A. (2001). "Working at disability": A qualitative study of the meaning of health and disability for women with physical impairments. *Disability and Society, 16,* 511–529.

Timmerman, G. (2003). Sexual harassment of adolescents perpetrated by teachers and by peers: An exploration of the dynamics of power, culture, and gender in secondary schools. *Sex Roles, 48,* 231–244.

Tjaden, P., & Thoennes, N. (1998). *Stalking in American: Findings from the national violence against women survey.* Denver, CO: Center for Policy Research.

Tolman, D. L., & Brown, L. M. (2001). Adolescent girls' voices: Resonating resistance in body and soul. In R. K. Unger (Ed.), *Handbook of the psychology of women and gender* (pp. 133–155). New York: Wiley.

Totman, R. (2003). *The third sex: Kathoey: Thailand's ladyboys.* London: Souvenir Press.

Travaglia, L. K., Overall, N. C., & Sibley, C. G. (2009). Benevolent and hostile sexism and preferences for romantic partners. *Personality and Individual Differences, 47,* 599–604.

Travis, C. B. (2005). 2004 Carolyn Sherif award address: Heart disease and gender inequity. *Psychology of Women Quarterly, 29,* 15–23.

Travis, C. B., & Compton, J. D. (2001). Feminism and health in the decade of behavior. *Psychology of Women Quarterly, 25,* 312–323.

Treadway, C. R., Kane, F. J., Jarrahi-Zadeh, A., & Lipton, M. A. (1969). A psycho-endocrine study of pregnancy and puerperium. *American Journal of Psychiatry, 125,* 1380–1386.

Tsui, L. (1998). The effects of gender, education, and personal skills self-confidence on income in business management. *Sex Roles, 38,* 363–373.

Turk, J. L., & Bell, N. W. (1972). Measuring power in families. *Journal of Marriage and the Family, 34,* 215–223.

Tyler, M. (2009). No means yes: Perpetuating myths in the sexological construction of women's desires. *Women & Therapy, 32,* 40–50.

Tylka, T. L., & Hill, M. S. (2004). Objectification theory as it relates to disordered eating among college women. *Sex Roles, 51,* 719–730.

Udeze, B. B., Abdelmawla, N. N., Khoosal, D. D., & Terry, T. T. (2008). Psychological functions in male-to-female transsexual people before and after surgery. *Sexual and Relationship Therapy, 23*(2), 141–145. doi:10.1080/14681990701882077

Udry, J. R., Talbert, L., & Morris, N. M. (1986). Biosocial foundations for adolescent female sexuality. *Demography, 23,* 217–230.

Ujike, H., Otani, K., Nakatsuka, M., Ishii, K., Sasaki, A., Oishi, T., et al. (2009). Association study of gender identity disorder and sex hormone-related genes. *Progress in Neuro-Psychopharmacology & Biological Psychiatry, 33,* 1241–1244.

Ulrich, M., & Weatherall, A. (2000). Motherhood and infertility: Viewing motherhood through the lens of infertility. *Feminism and Psychology, 10,* 323–336.

UNESCO. (2000). *EFA 2000—literacy assessment: Progress in literacy.* Retrieved September 29, 2004, from http://www.accu.or.jp/litdbase/efa/progress/htm

Unger, R. K. (1979). Toward a redefinition of sex and gender. *American Psychologist, 34,* 1085–1094.

Unger, R. K. (1990). Imperfect reflections of reality: Psychology and the construction of gender. In R. Hare-Mustin & J. Marecek (Eds.), *Making a difference: Representations of gender in psychology* (pp. 102–149). New Haven, CT: Yale University Press.

UNIFEM. (2007). *Violence against women–facts and figures.* Retrieved May 10, 2010, from http://www.unifem.org/attachments/gender_issues/violence_against_women/facts_figures_violence_against_women_2007.pdf

United Nations. (1995). *The Beijing declaration and platform for action.* Retrieved February 3, 2011, from http://www.un.org/womenwatch/daw/beijing/pdf/BDPfA%20E.pdf

United Nations. (2000). *The world's women 2000: Trends and statistics.* New York: Author.

United Nations Children's Fund. (2000, May). Domestic violence against women and girls. *Innocenti Digest* (No. 6.) Florence, Italy: Innocenti Research Centre.

United Nations Division for the Advancement of Women. (2001). *Women 2000: Widowhood: Invisible women, secluded, or excluded.* Retrieved from http://www.un.org/womenwatch/daw/public/wom_Dec%2001%20single%20pg.pdf

United Nations Population Fund (UNFPA). (2000). *The state of the world population.* Retrieved from http://www.unfpa.org/swp/2000/english/

U.S. Department of Defense. (2009). *Annual report on sexual harassment and violence at U.S. Military service academies: Academic program year 2008–2009.* Retrieved May 10, 2010, from http://www.sapr.mil/media/pdf/reports/2009_msa_report.pdf

U.S. Department of Justice (2007). Intimate partner violence in the U.S. Report prepared by the Bureau of Justice Statistics. Retrieved on January 17, 2010 from bjs.ojp. usdoj.gov/content/pub/pdf/ipvus.pdf

U.S. Department of Labor. (2002). *Highlights of women's earnings in 2001* (Report 960) Washington, DC: U.S. Department of Labor, Bureau of Labor Statistics.

U.S. Department of Labor. (2010). *Employment status of women and men in 2008*. Retrieved May 27, 2010, from http://www.dol.gov/wb/factsheets/Qf-ESWM08. htm

U.S. General Accountability Office. (2002). *Prescription drugs: FDA oversight of direct-to-consumer advertising has limitations*. Retrieved May, 2004, from http://www.gao. gov/new.items/d03177.pdf

U.S. General Accountability Office. (2008). *Prescription drugs: Trends in FDA's oversight of direct-to-consumer advertising*. Retrieved June, 2010, from http://www.gao. gov/new.items/d08758t.pdf

U.S. Merit Systems Protection Board. (1981). *Sexual harassment in the federal workplace: Is it a problem?* Washington, DC: Office of Merit Systems Review and Studies/ Government Printing Office.

U.S. Merit Systems Protection Board. (1987). *Sexual harassment in the federal workplace: An update*. Washington, DC: Office of Merit Systems Review and Studies/Government Printing Office.

U.S. Merit Systems Protection Board. (1995). *Sexual harassment in the federal workplace: Trends, progress, continuing challenges*. Washington, DC: U.S. Government Printing Office.

U.S. v. Commonwealth of Virginia, U.S. 1941 (1994).

Ussher, J. (1992). *Women's madness: Misogyny or mental illness?* Amherst, MA: University of Massachusetts Press.

Ussher, J. M. (1989). *The psychology of the female body*. London: Routledge.

Valentine, J. C., Blankenship, V., Cooper, H., & Sullins, E. S. (2001). Interpersonal expectancy effects and the preference for consistency. *Representative Research in Social Psychology, 25*, 26–33.

Valian, V. (1998). *Why so slow? The advancement of women*. Cambridge, MA: MIT Press.

Vallois, T. (1998). La Salpêtrière. *Paris Kiosque, 5*. Retrieved December, 2003, from www.paris.org/Kiosque/

Vance, C. S. (1984). Pleasure and danger: Toward a politics of sexuality. In C. S. Vance (Ed.), *Pleasure and danger: Exploring female sexuality* (pp. 1–27). Boston: Routledge and Kegan Paul.

Vance, E. B., & Wagner, N. N. (1976). Written descriptions of orgasm: A study of sex differences. *Archives of Sexual Behavior, 5*, 87–98.

Vandello, J. A., & Cohen, D. (2006). Male honor and female fidelity: Implicit cultural scripts that perpetuate cultural violence. *Journal of Personality and Social Psychology, 84*, 997–1010.

Vander-Ven, T. M., Cullen, F. T., Carrozza, M. A., & Wright, J. P. (2001). Home alone: The impact of maternal employment on delinquency. *Social Problems, 48*, 236–257.

Vanity Fair's Hollywood Issue. (2010). *Huffington Post Online*. Retrieved April 10, 2010, from http://www. huffingtonpost.com/2010/02/01/vanity-fairs-hollywood-is_n_444763.html

Vartanian, L. R., Giant, C. L., & Passino, R. M. (2001). "Ally McBeal vs. Arnold Schwarzenegger": Comparing mass media, interpersonal feedback and gender as predictors of satisfaction with body thinness and muscularity. *Social Behavior and Personality, 29*, 711–723.

Vasey, P. & Bartlett, N. (2007). What can the Samoan "Fa'afafine" teach us about the western concept of gender identity disorder in childhood? *Perspectives in Biology and Medicine, 50*, 481–490.

Vasey, P. & VanderLaan, D. (2009). Materteral and avuncular tendencies in Samoa: A comparative study of women, men, and fa'afafine. *Humam Nature, 20*, 369–281.

Vasquez, M. J. T. (1994). Latinas. In L. Comas-Díaz & B. Greene (Eds), *Women of color: Integrating ethnic and gender identities in psychotherapy* (pp. 114–138). New York: Guilford Press.

Vatican angers many with "grave crimes" list. (2010). Retrieved July 17, 2010, from http://www.aolnews.com/world/article/vatican-puts-ordaining-women-priests-on-par-with-child-sex-abuse/19556837

Veroff, J., Wilcox, S., & Atkinson, J. W. (1953). The achievement motive in high school and college age women. *Journal of Abnormal and Social Psychology, 43*, 108–119.

Vicedo-Castello, M. M. (2005). The Maternal instinct: Mother love and the search for human nature. *Dissertation Abstracts International Section A: Humanities and Social Sciences, 66*(11-A), 4163.

Vierthaler, K. (2008). Best practices for working with rape crisis centers to address elder sexual abuse. *Journal of Elder Abuse & Neglect, 20*, 306–322.

Vigorito, A. J., & Curry, T. J. (1998). Marketing masculinity: Gender identity and popular magazines. *Sex Roles, 38*, 135–152.

Vilain, E. (2006). Genetics of intersexuality. *Journal of Gay & Lesbian Psychotherapy, 10*, 9–26.

Vobejda, B. (1994, June 16). Abortion rate slowing in U.S., study concludes. *The Washington Post*, p. A13.

von Baeyer, C. L., Sherk, D. L., & Zanna, M. P. (1981). Impression management in the job interview: When the female applicant meets the male (chauvinist) interviewer. *Personality and Social Psychology Bulletin, 7*, 45–51.

von Hippel, W., Sekaquaptewa, D., & Vargas, P. (1995). On the role of encoding processes in stereotype maintenance. In M. P. Zanna (Ed.), *Advances in experimental social psychology: Vol. 27* (pp. 177–254). New York: Academic Press.

von Pfetten, V. (2010). Sultry Katie Couric dishes on dating a younger man. Retrieved February 2, 2011, from http://tv.yahoo.com/blog/sultry-katie-couric-dishes-on-dating-a-younger-man--969

Waite, L. J., & Joyner, K. (2001). Emotional satisfaction and physical pleasure in sexual unions: Time horizon, sexual behavior, and sexual exclusivity. *Journal of Marriage and the Family, 63,* 247–264.

Wajcman, J. (1998). *Managing like a man: Women and men in corporate management.* Cambridge, England: Polity Press.

Wakabayashi, C., & Donato, K. M. (2006). Does caregiving increase poverty among women in later life? Evidence from the health and retirement survey. *Journal of Health and Social Behavior, 47,* 258–274.

Walker, E. C., Holman, T. B., & Busby, D. M. (2009). Childhood sexual abuse, other childhood factors, and pathways to survivor's adult relationship quality. *Journal of Family Violence, 24*(6), 397–407.

Walker, L. E. A. (2000). *The battered woman syndrome* (2nd ed.). New York: Springer.

Walker, L., Timmerman, G. M., Kim, M., & Sterling, B. (2002). Relationships between body image and depressive symptoms during postpartum in ethnically diverse, low income women. *Women and Health, 36,* 101–121.

Walker, N. A. (Ed.). (1998). *Women's magazines 1940–1960: Gender roles and the popular press.* Boston: Bedford/St. Martin's.

Wallace, J. E. (2001). The benefits of mentoring for female lawyers. *Journal of Vocational Behavior, 58,* 366–391.

Wallston, B. S., & Grady, K. E. (1985). Integrating the feminist critique and the crisis in social psychology: Another look at research methods. In V. E. O'Leary, R. K. Unger, & B. S. Wallston (Eds.), *Women, gender and social psychology* (pp. 7–34). Hillsdale, NJ: Erlbaum.

Walter, J. L., & LaFreniere, P. J. (2000). A naturalistic study of affective expression, gender competence, and sociometric status in preschoolers. *Early Education & Development, 1,* 109–122.

Walzer, S. (1998). *Thinking about the baby.* Philadelphia: Temple University Press.

Want, S. C. (2009). Meta-analytic moderators of experimental exposure to media portrayals of women on female appearance satisfaction: Social comparisons as automatic processes. *Body Image, 6,* 257–269.

Warren, M. P. (1983). Physical and biological aspects of puberty. In J. Brooks-Gunn & A. C. Petersen (Eds.), *Girls at puberty* (pp. 3–28). New York: Plenum.

Warshaw, C. (2001). Women and violence. In N. L. Stotland & D. E. Stewart (Eds.), *Psychological aspects of women's health care* (2nd ed., pp. 477–548). Washington, DC: American Psychiatric Press.

Wassersug, R., Gray, R. E., Barbara, A., Trosztmer, C., Raj, R., & Sinding, C. (2007). Experiences of transwomen with hormone therapy. *Sexualities, 10,* 101–122.

Waszak, C., Severy, L. J., Kafafi, L., & Badawi, I. (2001). Fertility behavior and psychological stress: The mediating influence of gender norm beliefs among Egyptian women. *Psychology of Women Quarterly, 25,* 197–208.

Watts, B. (1996). Legal issues. In M. A. Paludi (Ed.), *Sexual harassment on college campuses: Abusing the ivory power* (pp. 9–24). Albany, NY: State University of New York Press.

Weatherall, A., & Walton, M. (1999). The metaphorical construction of sexual experience in a speech community of New Zealand university students. *British Journal of Social Psychology, 38,* 479–498.

Weber, J. C. (1996). Social class as a correlate of gender identity among lesbian women. *Sex Roles, 35,* 271–280.

Weber, L. (1998). A conceptual framework for understanding race, class, gender, and sexuality. *Psychology of Women Quarterly, 22,* 13–32.

Weber, L., & Higginbotham, E. (1997). Black and white professional-managerial women's perceptions of racism and sexism in the workplace. In E. Higginbotham & M. Romero (Eds.), *Women and work: Exploring race, ethnicity, and class: Vol 6* (pp. 153–175). Thousand Oaks, CA: Sage.

Weiss, K. G. (2009). "Boys will be boys" and other gendered accounts: An exploration of victims' excuses and justifications for unwanted sexual contact and coercion. *Violence Against Women, 15,* 810–834.

Weisstein, N. (1968). *Kinder, Kirche, Kuche as scientific law: Psychology constructs the female.* Boston: New England Free Press.

Weisz, G., & Knaapen, L. (2009). Diagnosing and treating premenstrual syndrome in five western nations. *Social Science & Medicine, 68,* 1498–1505.

Weitz, R., & Gordon, L. (1993). Images of black women among Anglo students. *Sex Roles, 28,* 19–34.

Weitzman, L. J. (1979). *Sex role socialization.* Palo Alto, CA: Mayfield.

Welter, B. (1966). The cult of True Womanhood: 1820–1860. *American Quarterly, 18,* 151–174.

Werner, P. D., & LaRussa, G. W. (1985). Persistence and change in sex-role stereotypes. *Sex Roles, 12,* 1089–1100.

West, C. M. (2008). Mammy, Jezebel, and Sapphire: Developing an "oppositional gaze" toward the images of black women. In J. C. Chrisler, C. Golden, & P. D. Rozee (Eds.), *Lectures on the psychology of women* (4th ed., pp. 236–252). Boston: McGraw-Hill.

West, C., & Zimmerman, D. H. (1987). Doing gender. *Gender & Society, 1,* 125–151.

Weston, R., Temple, J. R., & Marshall, L. L. (2005). Gender symmetry and asymmetry in violent relationships: Patterns of mutuality among racially diverse women. *Sex Roles, 52,* 553–571.

Weyers, S., Elaut, E., De Sutter, P., Gerris, J., T'Sjoen, G., Heylens, G., et al. (2009). Long-term assessment of the physical, mental, and sexual health among transsexual women. *Journal of Sexual Medicine, 6*(3), 752–760.

Whitam, F. L., Daskalos, C., Sobolewski, C. G., & Padilla, P. (1998). The emergence of lesbian sexuality and identity cross-culturally: Brazil, Peru, the Philippines, and the United States. *Archives of Sexual Behavior, 27*, 31–56.

Whitam, F., Diamond, M., & Martin, J. (1993). Homosexual orientation in twins: A report on 61 pairs and three triplet sets. *Archives of Sexual Behavior, 22*, 187–206.

Whitbourne, S. (1986). *The me I know: A study of adult identity*. New York: Springer-Verlag.

Whitbourne, S. K., & Skultety, K. M. (2006). Aging and identity: How women face later life transitions. In J. Worell & C. D. Goodheart (Eds.), *Handbook of girls' and women's psychological health* (pp. 370–378). New York: Oxford University Press.

White, J. W., & Koss, M. P. (1993). Adolescent sexual aggression within heterosexual relationships. Prevalence, characteristics, and causes. In H. E. Barbabee, W. L. Marshall, & D. R. Laws (Eds.), *The juvenile sexual offender* (pp. 182–202). New York: Guilford.

White, J. W., Bondurant, B., & Donat, P. L. N. (2004). Violence against women. In M. Crawford & R. Unger (Eds.), *Women and gender: A feminist psychology* (pp. 439–475). New York: McGraw-Hill.

White, J. W., Bondurant, B., & Travis, C. B. (2000). Social constructions of sexuality. In C. B. Travis & J. W. White (Eds.), *Sexuality, society and feminism: Psychological perspectives on women* (pp. 11–33). Washington, DC: American Psychological Association.

White, J. W., Donat, P. L. N., & Bondurant, B. (2001). A developmental examination of violence against girls and women. In R. K. Unger (Ed.), *Handbook of the psychology of women and gender* (pp. 343–357). New York: Wiley.

Whitman, T. L., Borkowski, J. G., Keogh, D. A., & Weed, K. (2001). *Interwoven lives: Adolescent mothers and their children*. Mahwah, NJ: Erlbaum.

Widiger, T. A. (1998). Invited essay: Sex biases in the diagnosis of personality disorders. *Journal of Personality Disorders, 12*, 95–118.

Widiger, T. A., & Anderson, K. G. (2003). Personality and depression in women. *Journal of Affective Disorders, 74*, 59–66.

Wiederman, M. W. (2002). Women's body image self-consciousness during physical intimacy with a partner. *The Journal of Sex Research, 37*, 60–68.

Wiest, W. M. (1977). Semantic differential profiles of orgasm and other experiences among men and women. *Sex Roles, 3*, 399–403.

Wilkinson, S. (1997a). Feminist psychology. In D. Fox & I. Prilleltensky (Eds.), *Critical psychology: An introduction* (pp. 247–264). London: Sage.

Wilkinson, S. (1997b). Still seeking transformation: Feminist challenges to psychology. In L. Stanley (Ed.), *Knowing feminisms: On academic borders, territories and tribes* (pp. 97–108). Thousand Oaks, CA: Sage.

Williams, C. L. (1992). The glass escalator: Hidden advantages for men in the "female" professions. *Social Problems, 39, 253–267*.

Williams, J. E., & Best, D. L. (1990). *Measuring sex stereotypes: A multination study*. Newbury Park, CA: Sage.

Williams, L. S. (1992). Biology or society? Parenthood motivation in a sample of Canadian women seeking in vitro fertilization. In H. B. Holmes (Ed.), *Issues in reproductive technology* (pp. 261–274). New York: Garland.

Williams, P. J. (1997). My best white friend: Cinderella revisited. In M. Crawford & R. Unger (Eds.), *In our own words: Readings on the psychology of women and gender* (pp. 291–295). New York: McGraw-Hill.

Williams, S. S., Kimble, D. L., Covell, N. H., Weiss, L. H., Newton, K. J., Fisher, J. D., et al. (1992). College students use implicit personality theory instead of safer sex. *Journal of Applied Social Psychology, 22*, 921–933.

Williams, W. L. (1987). Women, men, and others: Beyond ethnocentrism in gender theory. *American Behavioral Scientist, 31*, 135–141.

Wilson, A. (1996). How we find ourselves: Identity development and two-spirit people. *Harvard Educational Review, 66*, 303–317.

Winston, A. (Ed.). (2003). *Defining difference: Race and racism in the history of psychology*. Washington, DC: American Psychological Association.

Wintero, K. (2006). Gender dissonance. *Journal of Psychology & Human Sexuality, 17*, 71–80.

Witkin, H. A., Mednick, S. A., Schulsinger, F., Bakke-Strom, E., Christiansen, K. O., Goodenough, D. R., et al. (1976). Criminality in XXY and XYY men. *Science, 193*, 547–555.

Wizemann, T. M., & Pardue, M. (Eds.). (2001). *Exploring the biological contribution to human health: Does sex matter?* Washington, DC: National Academy Press.

Woloshin, S., Schwartz, L. M., Tremmel, J., & Welch, H. G. (2001). Direct-to-consumer advertisements for prescription drugs: What are Americans being sold? *The Lancet, 358*, 1141–1146.

Women's Health Initiative Steering Committee. (2004). Effects of conjugated equine estrogen in postmenopausal women with hysterectomy: The women's health initiative randomized controlled trial. *Journal of the American Medical Association, 291*, 1701–1712.

Wooldredge, J., & Thistlewaite, A. (2002). Reconsidering domestic violence recidivism: Conditioned effects of legal controls by individual and aggregate levels of stake in conformity. *Journal of Quantitative Criminology, 18*, 45–70.

Wooley, H. T. (1910). Psychological literature: A review of the recent literature on the psychology of sex. *Psychological Bulletin, 7*, 335–342.

Worell, J., & Johnson, D. (2001). Therapy with women: Feminist frameworks. In R. K. Unger (Ed.), *Handbook of the psychology of women and gender* (pp. 317–329). New York: John Wiley & Sons.

Worell, J., & Remer, P. (2003). *Feminist perspectives in therapy: Empowering diverse women* (2nd ed.). New York: John Wiley & Sons.

Wylie, P. (1942). *A generation of vipers*. New York: Farrar & Rinehart.

Worell, J. (2001). Feminist interventions: Accountability beyond symptom reduction. *Psychology of Women Quarterly, 25*, 335–343.

Wu, P. (2010). From "iron girl" to "sexy goddess": An analysis of the Chinese media. In P. Markula (Ed.), *Olympic women and the media*. New York: Palgrave Macmillan.

Wurtele, S. K. (2002). School-based child sexual abuse prevention. In P. A. Schewe (Ed.), *Preventing violence in relationships: Interventions across the life span* (pp. 9–25). Washington, DC: American Psychological Association.

Xu, X., & Lai, S. C. (2002). Resources, gender ideologies, and marital power: The case of Taiwan. *Journal of Family Issues, 23*, 209–245.

Yoder, J. D. (2002). Context matters: Understanding tokenism processes and their impact on women's work. *Psychology of Women Quarterly, 26*, 1–8.

Yoder, J. D., Adams, J., Grove, S., & Priest, R. F. (1985). To teach is to learn: Overcoming tokenism with mentors. *Psychology of Women Quarterly, 9*, 119–132.

Yoder, J. D., Schleicher, T. L., & McDonald, T. W. (1998). Empowering token women leaders: The importance of organizationally legitimated credibility. *Psychology of Women Quarterly, 22*, 209–222.

Young, I. M. (1998). Breasted experience: The look and the feeling. In R. Weitz (Ed.), *The politics of women's bodies: Sexuality, appearance, and behavior* (pp. 125–136). New York: Oxford University Press.

Youngquist, J. (2008). The effect of gender and interruptions on perceptions of interpersonal dominance. *Dissertation abstracts international section A: Humanities and social sciences, Vol 68*(8-A), 3217.

Zanna, M. P., & Pack, S. J. (1975). On the self-fulfilling nature of apparent sex differences in behavior. *Journal of Experimental Social Psychology, 11*, 583–591.

Zeedyk, M. S., & Raitt, F. E. (1997). Psychological theory in law: Legitimating the male norm. *Feminism & Psychology, 7*, 539–546.

Zelnik, M., Kanter, J. F., & Ford, K. (1981). *Sex and pregnancy in adolescence*. Beverly Hills, CA: Sage.

Zernike, K. (1999, March 21). MIT women win a fight against bias. *The Boston Globe*, pp. F1, F4.

Zheng, Y. (2004). Hair-coloring product use and risk of non-Hodgkin's lymphoma: A population-based case-control study in Connecticut. *American Journal of Epidemiology, 159*, 148–154.

Zimmerman, D. H., & West, C. (1975). Sex roles, interruptions, and silences in conversation. In B. Thorne & N. Henley (Eds.), *Language and sex: Difference and dominance* (pp. 105–129). Rowley, MA: Newbury House.

Zosuls, K. M., Ruble, D. N., Tamis-LeMonda, C. S., Shrout, P. E., Bornstein, M. H., & Greulich, F. K. (2009). The acquisition of gender labels in infancy: Implications for gender-typed play. *Developmental Psychology, 45*(3), 688–701. doi:10.1037/a0014053

Zucker, A. N., Ostrove, J. M., & Stewart, A. J. (2002). College-educated women's personality development in adulthood: Perceptions and age differences. *Psychology and Aging, 17*, 236–244.

Zucker, K. (2001). Biological influences on psychosexual differentiation. In R. K. Unger (Ed.), *Handbook of the psychology of women and gender* (pp. 101–115), New York: Wiley.

Zucker, K. J. (2008). Gender identity disorder in children and adolescents. *Handbook of Sexual and Gender Identity Disorders*, 376–422.

Zuckerman, M., & Kieffer, S. C. (1994). Race differences in faceism: Does facial prominence imply dominance? *Journal of Personality and Social Psychology, 66*, 86–92.

Zurbriggen, E. L., & Morgan, E. M. (2006). Who wants to marry a millionaire? Reality dating television programs, attitudes toward sex, and sexual behaviors. *Sex Roles, 54*, 1–17.

Photo Credits

∾

Chapter 2   Figure 2.1: © PhotoAlto/PictureQuest RF; 2.2: © Annie Leibovitz/Contact Press; 2.3: © Fancy Photography/Veer RF; 2.4: © Photodisc/Getty RF

Chapter 3   Figure 3.1a: © Time Life Pictures/Getty; 3.1b: © Bettmann/Corbis; 3.2a: © Stockbyte/Getty RF; 3.2b: © Stockbyte/Punchstock RF; 3.3a: © Lars A. Niki; 3.3b: © Ingram Publishing/SuperStock RF; 3.4: © M. Caulfield/WireImage/Getty; p. 90: © Jean Kilbourne, photographer Anel Van Der Merwe

Chapter 4   Page 108: © Jupiter Images/Brand X/Alamy RF; 4.5a: © Corbis RF; 4.5b: © Glow Images/SuperStock RF

Chapter 5   Page 132: © Stu Forster/Getty; p. 137: Courtesy of Jessica Lord; 5.3a & b: © Matt Kailey www.mattkailey.com; 5.4: © FOX Searchlight/The Kobal Collection/Bill Matlock/The Picture Desk

Chapter 6   Figure 6.1 (left): © ELC/Alamy RF; 6.1 (right): © Jose Luis Pelaez/Blend Images/Corbis RF; 6.2: © 2009 JupiterImages Corporation RF; 6.3: © Digital Vision/PunchStock RF; 6.4: © Mary Crawford; p. 176: © Digital Vision RF; 6.5: Courtesy Michelle Kaufmann; p. 185: © BananaStock/age fotostock RF; p. 191: © Alamy RF

Chapter 7   Figure 7.1: © Steve Mason/Getty RF; 7.2: © The McGraw-Hill Companies, Inc./John Flournoy, photographer; p. 229: © Fred R. Conrad/The New York Times/Redux

Chapter 8   Figure 8.1: © Creatas/JupiterImages RF; 8.3: © BananaStock/Alamy RF; 8.6: © Digital Vision/PunchStock RF; 8.7: © The McGraw-Hill Companies, Inc./John Flournoy, photographer

Chapter 9   Figure 9.2: © Annie Leibovitz/Contact Press; p. 276: © Ingram Publishing/SuperStock RF; 9.3: *The Crowning*, from the Birth Project, © Judy Chicago 1984, Needlework and painting on 80-mesh canvas, 40 1/2" × 61". Needlework by Frannie Yablonsky. Collection of The Albuquerque Museum, Albuquerque, NM. Photo: © TTF Archives; 9.5: © Bananastock/PictureQuest RF

Chapter 10   Figure 10.1: © Big Cheese Photo/PunchStock RF; p. 303: © AP Photo/Richard Freeda; p. 308: © Sigrid Estrada; 10.5: © Digital Vision RF; p. 329: © Mark Wilson/Getty

Chapter 11   Figure 11.5: © ImageState/age fotostock RF; p. 353: © Brand X/JupiterImages/Getty RF; 11.6: © BananaStock/Alamy RF; 11.7: © Comstock Images/JupiterImages RF

Chapter 12   Figure 12.1 (left): © BananaStock/PunchStock RF; 12.1 (right): © Purestock/Getty RF; p. 402: © Robbie Jack/Corbis; p. 404: © George Pimentel/WireImage/Getty

Chapter 13   Figure 13.1: © Purestock/PunchStock RF; 13.2: © Erich Lessing/Art Resource, NY; 13.3: © Library of Congress; 13.4: © Judy Olausen; p. 431: © Luise Eichenbaum; p. 432: Reprinted by permission of Susie Orbach, photographer Charlie Hopkinson; 13.5: © Andrea Morini/Getty RF

Chapter 14   Figure 14.1: Library of Congress, Prints & Photographs Division (LC-USZC2-1921)

Text Credits

Chapter 2

pp. 29–30: John, B. A., & Sussman, L. E. (1989). Initiative taking as a determinant of role reciprocal organization. In Rhoda K. Unger, (Ed.), *Representations: Social Constructions of Gender*. Adapted from Figure 1 (p. 264). Copyright 1989 by Baywood Publishing Company, Inc. Reproduced with permission of Baywood Publishing Company, Inc. in the format Textbook via Copyright Clearance Center.

Chapter 7

p. 205: From Rachel Elliot, *Song of Love*, pp. 116–118. Copyright © 1988 Rachel Elliott. Used by permission of the publisher, Harlequin Enterprises Limited.

Chapter 9

pp. 290, 291: Excerpts from essay by Katherine Gieve, in *Balancing Acts: On Being a Mother*, ed. Katherine Gieve. Virago, 1989, pp. 41, 45, 51. Reprinted by permission of Katherine Gieve. **p. 291:** Excerpts from essay by Gillian Darley, in *Balancing Acts: On Being a Mother*, ed. Katherine Gieve. Virago, 1989, pp. 124, 127–128. © Gillian Darley by permission of United Agents Ltd. (www.unitedagents.co.uk) on behalf of the author. **p. 291:** Excerpt from essay by Elizabeth Peretz, in *Balancing Acts: On Being a Mother*, ed. Katherine Gieve. Virago, 1989, p. 114. **p. 291:** Excerpts from essay by Jean Radford, in *Balancing Acts: On Being a Mother*, ed. Katherine Gieve. Virago, 1989, pp. 138–139, 140, 143–144. Reprinted by permission of Jean Radford. **p. 291:** Excerpt from essay by Jennifer Uglow, in *Balancing Acts: On Being a Mother*, ed. Katherine Gieve. Virago, 1989, p. 159. **p. 292:** Excerpts from essay by Victoria Hardie, in *Balancing Acts: On Being a Mother*, ed. Katherine Gieve. Virago, 1989, pp. 53–54. **p. 292:** Excerpts from essay by Hillary Land, in *Balancing Acts: On Being a Mother*, ed. Katherine Gieve. Virago, 1989, p. 77.

Chapter 12

pp. 392–393: Smith, P. H., Smith, J. B., & Earp, J. A. (1999). Beyond the measurement trap: A reconstructed conceptualization and measurement of woman battering. *Psychology of Women Quarterly*, *23*, 177–193, from Table 3 (p. 189). Copyright © 1999 by John Wiley & Sons. Reprinted by permission.

Name Index

Subject Index